THE POLITICS OF
DIPLOMACY

THE

POLITICS OF

G. P. PUTNAM'S SONS

NEW YORK

DIPLOMACY

REVOLUTION, WAR AND PEACE

1989–1992

James A. Baker, III

WITH THOMAS M. DEFRANK

G. P. Putnam's Sons
Publishers Since 1838
200 Madison Avenue
New York, NY 10016

Library of Congress Cataloging-in-Publication Data

Baker, James Addison, date.
    The politics of diplomacy : revolution, war and peace, 1989–1992
    by James A. Baker, III with Thomas M. DeFrank.
        p.   cm.
    ISBN 0-399-14087-5
    1. United States—Foreign relations—1989–1993.
    2. Baker, James Addison, date.
    3. Statesmen—United States—Biography.
    I. DeFrank, Thomas M. II. Title.
    E881.B35   1995   95-12465   CIP
    327.73'009'048—dc20

Book design by Ann Gold

Printed in the United States of America
10 9 8 7 6 5 4 3 2 1

This book is printed on acid-free paper. ∞

*To my son, Paul,
with love, Mom
12/25/1995*

To my great-grandfather, my grandfather,
and my father, the three generations of James
Addison Bakers whose belief in God, integrity,
and hard work gave me a remarkable heritage
that inspired me.

And to my wonderful mother, whose love
and support gave me wings to fly.

ACKNOWLEDGMENTS

This book has been made possible by the generosity of many people. But, as in all of my endeavors, I have been particularly blessed by the encouragement and sage judgment of my wife, Susan Garrett Baker. I salute not only her loving familial support, but also her tireless efforts as an unofficial ambassador. Alone and with me, she represented her country with grace and dignity at hundreds of diplomatic and departmental events at home and abroad, and the diplomatic service was as lucky to have her as I am. I'd also like to thank my eight children—Jamie, Mike, John, Doug, Elizabeth, Bo, Will, and Mary Bonner—who for twelve years didn't see a lot of their father at important times in their lives, and saw even less of him during the State Department years.

Throughout my public service, I have benefited from the help and counsel of many friends, colleagues, and associates. But three men above all are responsible for my government career: the Presidents I have been privileged to serve. To Gerald Ford, Ronald Reagan, and George Bush, I owe a special debt of gratitude.

A small group of individuals who had served me in previous positions came with me to State as a core group of senior policy and personal advisers. Listed in order of length of service, they are Margaret Tutwiler, Bob Kimmitt, Bob Zoellick, and Dennis Ross. They were joined by some other outstanding political appointees and career public servants. Throughout the pages that follow, I've recorded some of the more meaningful of the many contributions that all of them made to me and to our country. But their value to me extended far beyond what you will read about them. Their dedication, loyalty, unvarnished judgments, and personal sacrifice were a constant source of sustenance. Their individual and collective performance reflect the highest traditions of service to the nation, and I'm fortunate indeed for their extraordinary efforts.

An exceptionally talented and hardworking team helped me research and write this book.

Tom DeFrank, my collaborator, has done a superb job in helping create the record that follows from literally thousands of documents, notes, and memoranda, official and unofficial, as well as hundreds of interviews with me and others. He has been faithful to my direction that I wanted to write an account that was serious and substantive, but at the same time one that would be interesting and readable. An accomplished wordsmith, he was able to achieve this difficult task by capturing not only events but the emotions behind them. He was my teammate in this endeavor and he has my gratitude, as does his wife, Melanie, who transcribed the many interviews that Tom conducted.

Andrew Carpendale, in my Washington, D.C., office, served very ably in Policy Planning while I was Secretary of State, and was thus particularly well equipped to help me with the many aspects of the planning and production of this book. His assistance was invaluable, and included help in conceptualizing various chapters, directing researchers, working with the State Department regarding retrieval of documents and clearances of the text, handling numerous procedural matters with Putnam's and others, and, most important, assisting in writing and editing segments of the book involving the Soviet Union and German unification.

Joe Barnes, a research fellow at the Baker Institute for Public Policy at Rice University who has assisted me at the State Department and during my return to private life, was immensely helpful in reviewing portions of the manuscript with a keen eye. Derek Chollet was invaluable as a resourceful and indefatigable research assistant, ably assisted by Chanel O'Neil and a host of youthful interns. My personal assistants, Caron Jackson, Bridget Montagne, Anne Johnston, Liz Rotan, and Ernie Caldwell, constantly juggled their regular duties with the demands of the book and were indispensable to this project, as were Robert Barnett, my attorney for this endeavor, and Linda Michaels, my agent for foreign rights. Neil Nyren at Putnam's edited the manuscript with a deft scalpel and wise hand. Baker & Botts was unfailingly generous in providing support services for an endeavor having nothing to do with the practice of law.

From the outset of this project, a small band of close associates graciously lent their time and counsel. What came to be known informally as the "Book Group" not only read the manuscript with a critical eye, but also offered valuable advice throughout that helped me shape and refine the book. I'm particularly grateful to Dick Darman, Bob Kimmitt, Dennis Ross, Margaret Tutwiler, and Bob Zoellick for their generosity.

My senior colleagues and friends in the Bush administration were especially helpful with their recollections and advice, and I thank Dick Cheney, Colin Powell, Brent Scowcroft, and my deputy and successor, Larry Eagleburger.

I'm also indebted to a large group of former associates and officials who agreed to be interviewed, read particular chapters, or contributed in various ways to this project: Peter Afanasenko, Bernie Aronson, His Royal Highness Bandar bin Sultan, Eitan Bentsur, Richard Boucher, George Bush, Bill Brownfield, Bill Burns, Dick Cheney, Jim Cicconi, Hank Cohen, Jim Collins, Lynne Davidson, Chris Dawson, Ed Djerejian, Ken Duberstein, Larry Eagleburger, Bob Fauver, Marlin Fitzwater, Steve Flanagan, Bob Gates, Roger George, Bob Gelbard, Claire Gilbert, Jim Goldgeier, Howard Graves, Steve Grummon, Richard Haass, Steve Hadley, John Hannah, Kenneth Juster, Walter Kansteiner, Arnie Kanter, Lonnie Keene, John Kelly, Mike Kozak, Dan Kurtzer, David Lewis, Ron Mazer, Eugene McAllister, Richard McCormack, Aaron Miller, Janet Mullins, Roman Popadiuk, Colin Powell, John Reichart, John F. W. Rogers, Harvey Sicherman, Brent Scowcroft, Dick Solomon, John Stremlau, Bill Swing, John Sylvester, Phil Zelikow, and Warren Zimmerman.

Secretary of State Warren Christopher graciously made the services of the Department available to assist in this effort. Pat Kennedy, Lynn Dent, Elijah Kelly, Jim Thessin, Frank Machak, Danielle Woerz-Koban, and Joyce Mabray arranged the necessary clearances and facilitated access to literally thousands of pages of official documents that were invaluable in the course of my research. As is customary, the State Department has reviewed the manuscript of this book to ensure that its contents do not compromise the national security. This review should not be construed as concurrence with the text. Opinions and characterizations are those of the author and do not necessarily represent official positions of the United States government.

One of my regrets is not being able to name the hundreds of men and women who literally made a demanding job doable and who seldom receive the acknowledgment so richly deserved: the air crews who flew me more than 700,000 miles to ninety nations, the advance teams, logisticians, administrators, security officers, telecommunications officials, encryption specialists, watch officers, drivers, note takers, baggage handlers, and many others whose yeoman efforts are essential to the effective conduct of the nation's foreign policy. The self-effacing professionalism and dedication of all these individuals—and of their spouses and families—is truly remarkable. These are the unsung heroes of this volume.

—J.A.B. III

C O N T E N T S

Acknowledgments   vii

Preface   xiii

1. The Day the Cold War Ended   1

2. Three Decades of Friendship   17

3. The World on the Eve of a Revolution   37

4. Rebuilding Bipartisanship: Lancing the Central American Boil   47

5. The Soviet Union: Gorbachev, Shevardnadze,
    and the "New Thinking"   61

6. A "Europe Whole and Free"   84

7. China: A Great Leap Backward   97

8. The Middle East: First Encounters with the Quagmire   115

9. The Spirit of Jackson Hole   133

10. The Fall of the Wall   153

11. Panama: The Day of the Dictator Is Over   177

12. The Arithmetic of Unification   195

13. Africa: The End of Apartheid   217

14. Spring of Tumult: German Unification, Lithuanian
    Independence, and Soviet Upheaval   230

15. Prelude to an Invasion   260

16. Building the Coalition   275

17. All Necessary Means   300

18. Forging Consensus at Home   329

19. The Last, Best Chance for Peace   345

20. The Shield Becomes a Sword   366

21. Passing the Brink   382

22. Gorbachev's Gambit   396

23. A Postwar Vision for the Mideast   411

24. Saddam Stays in Power   430

25. Prelude to a Mideast Conference:
     The Dead Cat on the Doorstep   443

26. From Berlin to the Balkans   470

27. Breakthrough for Peace   487

28. The Empire Shaken   514

29. Settlements, Loan Guarantees, and the Politics of Peace   540

30. Into the Dustbin—With a Whimper, Not a Bang   558

31. Entering a New Era   587

32. Supporting Freedom in the New Independent States   614

33. "Humanitarian Nightmare" in Bosnia   634

34. From Cold War to Democratic Peace   652

     Index   673

PREFACE

In the winter of 1980, hundreds of public-spirited men and women assembled in Washington to serve in a new administration. A dozen years later, only two remained at the most senior levels of government—George Bush and I. From start to finish, those twelve years were momentous ones for all of us in government service and, I believe, for our country as well. The record of those times is worthy of far more examination. Indeed, my reminiscences of the first eight of those years—the Reagan-Bush years—as well as the political campaigns related to them, may become the subject of another book in due course. This work, however, purposely chronicles only the final third of that period—the forty-three months I was privileged to serve as the sixty-first Secretary of State of the United States.

I've always known that I was more a man of action than of reflection. I certainly know that I'm not naturally disposed to the daunting task of writing history. As a young Texas lawyer, I never intended to become involved in either politics or diplomacy—much less write about them. It was only through the combination of fortuitous events, such as meeting George Bush, and a personal tragedy (the death of my first wife, Mary Stuart) that I became involved in politics at all.

Nevertheless, I feel a special sense of obligation to share with a broader audience my experiences, insights, and recollections of my years as Secretary of State. Make no mistake, those years were truly historic. Put simply, the world as we had come to see it for a half-century changed profoundly and irrevocably on my watch at State. This is my account of how we in the Bush administration sought to harness, shape, and manage those seismic geopolitical changes in the strategic interests of our country.

What follows is by design more personal narrative than classic memoir. I've attempted to reach beyond the conventional wisdom, which is as often wrong in diplomacy as in politics, and offer my observations about what I saw, felt, and thought at the time. I've tried to be as accurate as possible in recounting my experiences, and have drawn upon thousands of pages of official documents as well as the recollections of dozens of my colleagues to refresh my own reflections. Any errors are mine alone.

All such works of this sort, of course, are highly subjective—not only in terms of the author's own perspectives as a participant, but also in subject matter. By its very nature, this narrative is only a slice of near-history, and an incomplete one at that. Consequently, while the scope of this book encompasses my entire tenure as Secretary of State and touches on the various crises and diplomatic issues that crossed my desk, I have concentrated in the pages that follow on those stories and events where I feel I can offer a unique glimpse into the conduct of diplomacy during what has been described as a hinge of history.

I've tried to convey a sense of how our policies were formulated and how, once formulated, these issues of statecraft were managed day to day and negotiated face-to-face. My purpose here is to illuminate not only *how* various decisions were made, but the philosophic, strategic, and tactical calculations on which they were based, and the political realities involved as well. While I believe the Bush years will fare well by history's measure, I leave to scholars a more comprehensive assessment of our administration's stewardship.

From the outset, I was determined not to write the sort of kiss-and-tell account that seems so distressingly in vogue these days, and yet I have not hesitated in the interest of factual accuracy and completeness to take note of differences where they existed. To the extent that I deal with the personalities of my colleagues and interlocutors, I have done so only when I thought it was necessary to make larger points. I do not consider it necessary to tell tales out of school for the sake of evening scores.

In reflecting on these events and my participation in them with the benefit of some distance, I was reminded of something I learned in both the political and the governmental service I was privileged to render to President Ford, President Reagan, and President Bush: Politics (in its larger sense—as opposed to specific electoral campaigns) and policy are inextricably linked. It's only through politics that we can transform philosophy into policy. This is particularly true in geopolitics, where the difference between success and failure is often measured by the ability (or lack thereof) to understand how political constraints inevitably shape the outcome of any negotiation. Indeed, I would argue, with a nod to Clausewitz, that diplomacy *is* the continuation of politics—whether in revolution, war, or peace.

We sometimes overlook the fact that most foreign leaders are themselves politicians, frequently elected or members of some ruling party. These senior foreign officials view their problems, and opportunities, through political eyes. To persuade them, it is often helpful to put oneself in their shoes—to determine how to help them explain, justify, or even rationalize positions to their colleagues and publics. Not surprisingly, foreign political leaders also respect counterparts who can work domestically in order to deliver internationally.

The political skill extends beyond one-on-one relations to the task of building coalitions. Effective U.S. leadership often depends on the ability to persuade others to join with us so we can extend our influence; to build a coalition, a diplomat needs to appreciate what objectives, arguments, and trade-offs are important to would-be partners. To be successful over time, the politician-diplomat also needs to win the confidence of others. That means words must be matched by deeds and promises must be kept.

As in the political world at home, coalitions abroad tend to endure if they are based on shared ideas and purposes. Part of the political diplomat's job is to tend to these alliances, or partnerships, because the time will certainly come when their support will be critical. Differences are inevitable, but they need not overwhelm larger common causes.

In my experience, the most successful political leaders with whom I worked were adept at more than persuasion, negotiation, relationships, building coalitions, and forging longer-term partnerships, as important as these skills are. While solving present-day problems, they tended to consider how the results might fit into a larger whole and how to plant the seeds of future opportunities.

Ultimately, good politicians, like successful diplomats, appreciate power—its uses and limits. An effective leader recognizes how success can enhance power, and he or she also knows how to husband that precious asset until the timing is right. Power comes in many forms—economic and military might, group expectations and pressure, and most lastingly, through ideas. And an American political diplomat should always remember that power divorced from the purposes valued by our democracy will ultimately prove empty.

Indeed, as Secretary of State, I constantly had to juggle the opportunities and imperatives created by personal politics, the constraints of domestic politics, and the perpetually changing realities of global politics. In all those instances, I trust and believe that my political experience made me a more effective advocate, negotiator, and diplomat, which is why I call this book *The Politics of Diplomacy*. In any event, I'm fortunate and grateful to have had the opportunity to bring that experience to a larger arena in the service of this wonderful country of ours.

James A. Baker, III
Houston, Texas
May 5, 1995

CHAPTER 1

THE DAY THE COLD WAR ENDED

When the two of us meet, there should be results. We can't be silent in the face of such events.   —*Eduard Shevardnadze, August 3, 1990*

O n January 29, 1981, I walked with Ronald Reagan from the White House across West Executive Avenue to the Old Executive Office Building, a marvelous, massive gray battleship of a structure on the corner of Pennsylvania Avenue and Seventeenth Street. It was the new President's first press conference, and I was his Chief of Staff.

President Reagan had been in office only ten days, but he took that opportunity to lay down a marker—one that came to epitomize his cold-eyed view of the Soviet Union, which he and most Americans had correctly viewed with suspicion for most of their lives.

The Soviets, he said, "have openly and publicly declared that the only morality they recognize is what will further their cause, meaning they re-serve unto themselves the right to commit any crime, to lie, to cheat, in order to attain that. . . . When you do business with them, even as a detente, you keep that in mind."

They were hard-edged words, like the shock of cold water, but right on the mark, and almost a decade later, on August 3, 1990, and now as Secretary of State, I couldn't help remembering those words with a sense of irony. For on that day, I stood side by side with Soviet Foreign Minister Eduard Shevardnadze in the lobby of Vnukovo II Airport outside Moscow, and listened as he explained to reporters why his country had agreed to the unprecedented act of joining *with* the United States to condemn Iraq's invasion of Kuwait.

"Let me tell you that it was a rather difficult decision for us . . . because of the long-standing relations that we have with Iraq," he said. "But despite all this . . . we are being forced to take these steps . . . because . . . this aggression is inconsistent with the principles of new political thinking and, in fact, with the civilized relations between nations."

The implications of Shevardnadze's soliloquy were breathtaking. The Soviets had gone along with the dismantlement of their empire in Eastern Europe, and the Kremlin had acquiesced in the collapse of the Honecker government in East Germany, which had made the fall of the Berlin Wall inevitable. But these had been essentially passive reactions to an inexorable tide of events. Now, for the first time, the Soviet Union was actively engaged in joining the United States in condemning one of its staunchest allies.

Nine days earlier, on July 25, I had left Andrews Air Force Base, Maryland, to begin a trip to Asia and the Soviet Union, little realizing that by the time I returned home, the world as I had known it for my entire adult life would no longer exist. As the British had discovered at Yorktown two centuries before, the world had just turned upside down—and our new world was laden with hope and opportunity, as well as peril and uncertainty, for American diplomacy.

Saddam Hussein is a man of many defects, and fortunately for America and the rest of the civilized world, an atrocious sense of timing is one of them.

A more prudent despot would surely have chosen a moment other than August 2, 1990, to launch his invasion of a helpless neighbor. On that very day, the President of the United States was preparing to meet with the Prime Minister of Great Britain, an iron lady not known for counseling half measures in time of challenge. The American Secretary of State was in Siberia for talks with his Soviet counterpart. Senior diplomats from both countries were finalizing preparations for two days of long-scheduled joint policy-planning talks in Moscow.

Confronting tyrants is never easy work, but this fundamental tactical miscalculation by Saddam had enormous strategic ramifications. It gave us a critical running start in shaping our response to the crisis. Without this fortuitous advantage, we might never have been able to mobilize the will, both international and domestic, to counter his blatant aggression. If Saddam had been clever enough to have waited three weeks, until most governments and their leaders were scattered around the globe on vacation, the course of events could well have been otherwise.

As the world now knows, it was a disaster for Saddam, a triumph for American diplomacy and military might, and a centerpiece of George

Bush's legacy. Saddam's megalomaniacal fantasies sent tens of thousands of Iraqi soldiers to their death, cost the lives of close to four hundred brave Americans, and inflicted horrible and needless suffering on the innocent citizens of his own country, misery which endures to this day.

But in one critical respect, the entire planet is in this madman's debt. His brutal invasion of Kuwait provided the unexpected opportunity to write an end to fifty years of Cold War conflict with resounding finality.

That was the last thing on my mind, however, as I flew from Singapore via Hong Kong on July 31 to meet with Eduard Shevardnadze in Irkutsk, a Siberian city of 500,000 people. Our agenda would include issues such as nuclear arms control, conventional force reductions in Europe, and the conflicts in Afghanistan and Cambodia, as well as preparations for an upcoming summit between President Bush and President Mikhail Gorbachev. Shevardnadze had planned this meeting to reciprocate for our discussions amid the Grand Tetons the previous September in Wyoming. I had believed that moving our talks from the bureaucratic environment of Washington to the rugged grandeur of the American West might help forge a new spirit of cooperation, openness, and mutual trust between us and our staffs. That had proved to be the case, and the result was several important breakthroughs on nuclear arms control and chemical weapons. Shevardnadze was anxious to build on the spirit of Jackson Hole by hosting similar discussions in the scenic Lake Baikal region of Siberia. Afterward I was scheduled to fly to Mongolia for talks to encourage the fledgling reform government that was breaking away from seventy years of Communist rule. I was also still feeling the effects of the worst case of intestinal flu of my life, contracted during the annual Asia-Pacific Economic Cooperation (APEC) meeting in Singapore.

At the time, Saddam's newly bellicose rhetoric was a source of concern, but not alarm. Most U.S. government officials considered it a bully's premeditated attempt to intimidate Kuwait into buying off aggression and helping to pay down Iraq's huge foreign debt. Some thought Saddam was seeking concessions over his protracted border dispute with Kuwait—a dispute that included the lucrative Rumaila oil field. Our friends in the region—President Mubarak of Egypt, King Hussein of Jordan, King Fahd of Saudi Arabia, even the Israelis—told us Saddam was maneuvering for diplomatic advantage, not preparing for war. Take it easy, don't worry, they all said. We know him; he won't do anything crazy. The worst-case scenario assumed that Saddam might grab the disputed oil field in northern Kuwait, but anything more dramatic was considered illogical—even for Saddam.

When I arrived in Irkutsk at 2:20 A.M. on August 1, U.S. intelligence had detected more troubling omens: several Iraqi divisions had moved out of their bases and were deployed near the Kuwaiti border. Their classical offensive formation led our military analysts to an inescapable conclusion: Saddam was poised to attack.

Later that morning, Shevardnadze and I began a full day of activities with a two-hour meeting. That was followed by lunch and a hydrofoil cruise of Lake Baikal, the largest body of fresh water in the world, fed by more than 100 rivers. As with everything else in Siberia, Lake Baikal is larger than life. We had another meeting in a beautiful old fisherman's lodge we were told had been built for a visit by President Eisenhower which had been canceled after the collapse of his 1960 Paris summit with Soviet Premier Nikita Khrushchev. Then we broke for ninety minutes of fishing on the Angara River, where Shevardnadze and I each caught one fish. When we returned to the dock, Shevardnadze reached over and graciously grabbed my smaller fish just before the ritual picture-taking for photographers. We then returned to the lodge for another bilateral meeting, which lasted two and a half hours longer than scheduled, forcing an elaborate eight-course dinner to be served in one hour. In more than eight hours of formal meetings, we discussed Iraq, but not at length. While the situation appeared more ominous, the consensus—in Moscow, Washington, and the capitals in the Middle East—was still that Saddam was just playing a game of intimidation.

It wasn't until midnight that I returned to my Intourist hotel room in Irkutsk. Just before going to bed, I got a call from Bob Kimmitt, the Under Secretary for Political Affairs at State, who was monitoring the Iraq situation back in Washington. It was noontime in Washington, thirteen hours behind Irkutsk. Kimmitt reported that the situation appeared to be worsening; at a meeting of the Deputies' Committee (DC), the interagency crisis-management group, the Central Intelligence Agency had concluded that the odds were shifting toward an invasion. Kimmitt also said that the DC had recommended that President Bush consider telephoning Saddam Hussein directly in hopes of averting an attack. The President was literally discussing that option with aides when he received word of the Iraqi invasion.

At 7:45 the next morning, Kimmitt called back with another update. Taking no chances, he spoke elliptically, even though we were talking on a secure satellite communications link. (Although our security services routinely swept for bugs, we always assumed someone was listening in on our conversations when we traveled.) "Do you recall the subject we talked about before?" Kimmitt asked. "Yes," I replied. "Well, Dick Kerr's people now think it's more likely than not the country we spoke about is going to move." (Dick Kerr was the deputy director of the CIA.) I told him, "That's important to know, because I'm just heading off to see my friend here."

It was my hope that the agency's assessment was too apocalyptic. In the intelligence business, it's bureaucratically safer to be wrong predicting the worst than to underreact and miss the call. I wanted to know what the Soviets knew; they had close ties to Saddam, and far better intelligence assets on the ground. A little more than an hour later, at the start of our first meeting, I told Shevardnadze we had evidence the Iraqis were massing forces at the border and asked him to check with his own intelligence sources. "It looks bad," I told him. "We hope you can restrain them." I also told him that I was troubled by reports the Soviets were considering major new arms sales to Iraq. "That's about the last thing Iraq or the region needs right now," I suggested.

He completely dismissed the notion that Saddam was preparing to move; it would be irrational for Saddam to do anything of the sort, he said several times. "I can't believe that. What could he possibly gain?" It made no sense to him. Besides, he chided me, if something this momentous were in the works, he would know about it. But he ordered Sergei Tarasenko, his chief policy aide, to check with Soviet intelligence. By the end of the meeting, Tarasenko had reported back that "we don't have any reports of anything." Shevardnadze was satisfied. "Don't worry," he remarked. "Nothing's going to happen." I later learned that he had nevertheless cabled the Foreign Ministry with instructions to lean on the Iraqis to stand down in case the American rumors proved correct.

At nine-thirty, we broke to make brief statements about our talks and take questions from the press. There was no mention of the looming crisis. We were to have spent another hour together while the press filed their stories. Just as we resumed our meeting, my chief spokesman Margaret Tutwiler handed me a one-page note: "AMBASSADOR HOWELL [our ambassador in Kuwait] reported to the Ops Center that Iraqi troops crossed into Kuwait and have taken some border crossing points. They are apparently moving toward the city of Um Qasr. He said there had been some shooting.

"The Kuwaiti ambassador to the U.S. called Asst. Sec. Kelly with similar information. The ambassador had the same information and described it as a limited penetration. He said they had gone into Kuwait 2 or 3 kilometers. He did not request U.S. assistance at this time."

"Gentlemen," I said, "the State Department communications center has received a report that Iraq has crossed the border of Kuwait.

"I don't know if it's a partial grab. I don't know if they're going for the entire country, or if they plan to go beyond Kuwait. But this is a very solid report that they have invaded."

Shevardnadze was thunderstruck, embarrassed for being misled by his own intelligence services and enraged by the lunacy of the deed itself. "This is just totally irrational," Shevardnadze repeated several times. "I know he's a thug, but I never thought he was irrational. It would be more like him to go in and then withdraw."

Kimmitt's heads-up call had enabled me to leverage Shevardnadze's Georgian passion to the maximum advantage. Had I not been able to tell him we thought an invasion was likely, he might never have bothered to check it with his system. When they assured him I didn't know what I was talking about, his subsequent rage at being embarrassed made it easier for me to persuade him to take what was a profoundly difficult step. If you want someone to break with a client, it doesn't hurt to have him lied to by the client—or by the client's Arabist sympathizers in the Soviet Foreign Ministry. Shevardnadze's fury at being misled by Saddam worked to the advantage of American diplomacy throughout the entire crisis.

I pressed Shevardnadze to halt Soviet arms shipments to Iraq and to join with the United States in condemning the invasion and demanding an immediate withdrawal. Tarasenko had checked with Moscow and confirmed that my information was correct. Shevardnadze agreed that a strong response of some sort was required but said he could make no assurances until after he had spoken with Gorbachev.

"I think you should get a message to Saddam right away," I suggested.

It was apparent that my trip to Ulan Bator would have to be truncated, but it was important not to cancel altogether. Mongolia was a small, ethnically homogeneous country of two million with an uncomplicated economy, that had been dominated for decades by its giant Communist neighbors, the Soviet Union and China. Yet it was newly independent and democratic, the first Communist nation in Asia to commit itself to reform. Only days before, Mongolia had completed its first multiparty elections in nearly seventy years, with a voter turnout of more than 90 percent. The revolution in Eastern Europe was slow in spreading across the Urals, but Mongolian democracy had a real chance to flourish, and I wanted to lend the moral encouragement of the United States to their efforts at self-determination.

By fortuitous circumstance, Dennis Ross and Bob Zoellick, my top policy advisers, had arranged to bypass the Mongolia trip and fly directly to Moscow for joint policy-planning sessions with Tarasenko. It was a worthy impulse, but Zoellick and Ross also harbored a secret agenda: by skipping Mongolia, they'd get back home to their families two days before the rest of us. I suppose history is filled with such examples of commonplace decisions that later prove critical to the course of great events. For their side trip facilitated what I believe was a sine qua non in successfully managing the Gulf crisis—it helped produce the active cooperation of the Soviets against their erstwhile ally Saddam.

They hitched a ride to Moscow on Shevardnadze's aircraft. I later learned that on the Soviet plane, they were treated to a marvelous feast of caviar, cheeses, and rich black bread. It was a small but telling sign of misplaced Soviet priorities; the average Soviet had to wait for hours in bread lines, while their diplomats lunched on caviar. During the flight, there was still very little talk about Kuwait. My aides and Tarasenko agreed that too much was still unknown about Saddam's intentions; at that point, the smart money still thought he would occupy the disputed territories for leverage in shaking down the Kuwaitis and Saudis for financial concessions.

Instead of adjourning to a dacha outside Moscow for three days of cerebral discussions with Tarasenko, Zoellick and Ross drove directly to the American embassy, where they were joined by Peter Hauslohner, an aide to Ross, who came up with the idea of pushing the Soviets for a joint statement condemning the Iraqis. "But Baker has to come here," Zoellick insisted. "They've got to stand up together and issue a statement, or it won't be effective."

The calculation was obvious. For the two superpowers to demonstrate their solidarity would isolate Iraq and influence others to join us in reversing Saddam's aggression. Such common ground was essential to avoiding a split in the Arab world; if Saddam's primary patron stayed on the sidelines, he'd be able to hide behind the Soviets' silence, and many of the rest of the Arabs would do likewise. But if the Soviets could be persuaded to break with their client, it would be far more difficult for others in the region to remain on the fence. A joint statement would constitute an important step toward building a coalition to reverse Saddam's aggression.

However, when Ross first surfaced the idea with me, I really did not believe that we could get a joint statement. The Soviets would be cautious; they'd want to talk to Baghdad, then wait and see. The Arabists in the Foreign Ministry would oppose a joint statement, citing the risk to 8,000 Soviet citizens living in Iraq. But I thought the rewards were worth the risk of possible failure, and authorized Ross to broach the idea with Tarasenko.

Shortly before leaving Siberia for Mongolia, I talked with Brent Scowcroft, the President's National Security Adviser, who was in Colorado for the President's meeting with British Prime Minister Margaret Thatcher. Brent reported there was nothing new to be known; U.S. intelligence assets on the ground were virtually nonexistent, and it would take twelve hours for our spy satellite covering the region to make another pass. "We can't be sure he'll stop at Kuwait," Brent said, "and we won't know for several hours." It was an agonizing prospect; even if the Saudis allowed us to move U.S. troops and aircraft into the kingdom, the men and materiel couldn't arrive in sufficient time or numbers to block an Iraqi thrust down the Arabian peninsula. If Saddam had decided to move into Saudi Arabia, we were powerless to stop him.

Shortly after takeoff from Irkutsk, I reached Kimmitt, who told me it was now clear the Iraqis were moving on Kuwait City and had designs on occupying the entire country. Then the telephone lines to the aircraft inexplicably went down. The crew couldn't explain how their secure satellite lines had been lost. I later discovered that the communications satellite linking the plane to Washington had been diverted to provide more intelligence coverage of troop movements in Iraq and Kuwait.

Upon arriving in Ulan Bator, I was met by Ambassador Joe Lake, and we drove immediately to the Ikh-Tenghear compound, an austere, shopworn government guest complex nestled in a valley surrounded by mountains. Once the residence of the Prime Minister, it had been converted into a game preserve where elk and deer roamed freely throughout the grounds. On my ranch in Wyoming, I've slogged through waist-deep snow for an entire day hunting for elk; here I was surrounded by dozens of them, tantalizingly off limits.

In rapid order, I had meetings with several Mongolian leaders, and afterward, the entire party drove several miles out of town to watch an abbreviated version of a *nadam*, a traditional demonstration of Mongol skills. There were wrestling matches, an archery competition, and a three-mile children's horse race, won by a five-year-old girl over more than a hundred other contestants. At the request of my hosts, I tried my hand at archery and presented awards to the winners, who like all the participants and spectators wore brightly colored native costumes. It was a spectacular event.

Toward the end of this Mongolian combination rodeo and wrestling match, Army Lt. Gen. Howard Graves, the Joint Chiefs of Staff representative on the trip, told me he had some updated information for me. After we had landed in Ulan Bator, Graves had broken off from the motorcade and gone to the American embassy, which consisted of three rooms on a stairwell in an apartment building. He'd commandeered the embassy's only secure line and reached the Operations Center at State, where he'd been updated on the situation by Dick Clarke, the Assistant Secretary for Political-Military Affairs. Back in my car, Graves told me the aircraft carrier U.S.S. *Independence* and its battle group were in Diego Garcia and would probably be moved to the northern Arabian Sea, and a cruiser and frigate from the U.S. Middle East force were available to go to the Persian Gulf. An attack "package" of F-15 and F-16 jets was on alert in Europe, and we were beginning discussions with the Saudis to see if they would allow us to move those planes to their desert bases. The Deputies' Committee was meeting through the night to propose options. The President would convene the

National Security Council in four hours to consider those options, just before leaving for his meeting with Thatcher.

Before dinner I made the decision to cancel the balance of the visit to Mongolia, including a trip to the Gobi Desert. I then called the President and broached the idea of trying for a joint statement with the Soviets. I told him that I didn't know if we could get a statement, but he agreed with me that it was worth the effort to try. For the moment, we left open the decision on whether I would return to Washington or fly to Moscow, until we had a better sense of the Soviets' interest. I also told him that I was dispatching Dick Solomon, the Assistant Secretary of State for East Asian and Pacific Affairs who was with me in Ulan Bator, to Beijing. As one of the permanent five members of the United Nations Security Council, China's support for a resolution of condemnation and possible sanctions would be critical, and far from certain. At that moment, the Chinese were very unhappy because I had flown over their airspace from Siberia to Mongolia without adding at least a brief stop in China to my itinerary. (As it turned out, the easiest way for Solomon to travel to Beijing was via Moscow; in that part of the world, a straight line is oftentimes not the quickest route.)

Dinner was even more of a spectacle than the *nadam*. There were nine prodigious courses, including ground goat, mutton and noodles, beef tongue, mare's milk, and the traditional Mongolian hot pot. This was followed by wave upon wave of regional musicians, including a "throat singer," who made unusual guttural sounds while playing an instrument of horsehair strings. During the dinner I confided to the Foreign Minister that our trip would have to end the next day, and I announced the unhappy news in my toast.

The dinner went on for more than three hours, finally ending after midnight. Just before it concluded, I received an urgent message that Shevardnadze wanted me to meet with the Soviet ambassador to Mongolia immediately after dinner. Peter Afanasenko, our Russian interpreter, who had taken a sleeping pill, had to be roused from a deep sleep. The ambassador gave me a copy of the public statement the Soviets had released condemning Saddam's invasion, but his message was less heartening than the official reaction: Shevardnadze wanted me to know that it might be difficult to reach agreement on a joint statement.

The Mongolians couldn't have been more hospitable, but communications from there were a nightmare. In the entire country, there were only nine international phone lines, one of which they had made available for the exclusive use of me and my entourage. As a result, by the time I went to bed, shortly after 1:00 A.M., we still didn't know much more than we had upon our arrival twelve hours earlier. Coincidentally, Ross reached Tutwiler in Ulan Bator at about the same time and told her that Shevardnadze was willing to meet me at the airport in Moscow to talk about the joint statement. She woke me up, gave me a quick briefing, and added firmly, "If you want this to happen, you've got to call the President."

When I reached him at 1:45 A.M. Mongolian time, the President had already spoken with President Mubarak, King Hussein, and President Saleh of Yemen, and had calls pending with several other world leaders. With Shevardnadze willing to meet, he agreed it made sense to exploit our geographical advantage by having me fly to Moscow and work to negotiate the unprecedented joint statement with the Soviets. As a former United Nations ambassador, George Bush understood the value of diplomatic consensus in times of crisis.

I knew that flying to Moscow was a risky proposition. Shevardnadze had just warned me that a meaningful joint statement would be a tougher sell than he had realized. The danger was that I would show up in Moscow and not be able to reach an agreement, which would be disastrous to hopes of assembling a strong coalition against Saddam. Yet by going there, I could lay American prestige on the line—and given my relationship with Shevardnadze and Gorbachev, and the esteem in which they held President Bush, it might be possible to pull it off. I knew this much: if I *didn't* go to Moscow, there was no chance of getting a statement.

The President and I agreed that work should be started immediately on a U.N. draft resolution that could ultimately become the basis for economic sanctions against Iraq. He also mentioned that we should think about the possibility of organizing a naval blockade to enforce those sanctions.

Meanwhile, Tarasenko had picked up his American counterparts and chauffeured them to the Foreign Ministry for consultations. "Let's find out the latest information," he suggested. Ross assumed he would summon a subordinate for an intelligence briefing. Instead, he turned on CNN. For all their massive presence in Iraq, the Soviets were more in the dark than we were. Ross pushed Tarasenko hard for a joint statement. "It's time to demonstrate that we can be partners," he argued. "We've talked about an evolution from competitors to cooperation. Now we have to talk about partnership. If we've really entered a new era, nothing is going to demonstrate it more than our being together, and nothing is going to demonstrate more clearly that we *haven't* entered a new era if we can't be together.

"Saddam will take advantage of any distance between us and advantage of your silence. It won't do for you to be silent publicly and critical privately."

"I agree with you," Tarasenko said without hesitation. He telephoned Shevardnadze, who concurred and said he would contact Gorbachev. Andrew Carpendale, a Ross aide, set out in search of a typewriter and found an English-language model somewhere in the bowels of the building.

The first draft of the proposed statement was 135 words. It called the invasion "brutal and illegal . . . senseless, vicious." It demanded an immediate withdrawal from Kuwait, and urged all nations to join in an embargo on all arms shipments to Iraq. "Governments that engage in blatant aggression must know that the international community cannot and will not acquiesce in nor facilitate that aggression," it concluded.

Back at Spaso House, the U.S. Ambassador's residence, Ross telephoned me at 4:00 A.M. in Mongolia to read me the statement. It was pithy and unequivocal, precisely what we needed. I directed Ross to run it past Scowcroft, who was airborne with the President returning from Colorado.

When I awoke in Ulan Bator, Graves told me the Iraqis had more than 100,000 troops in Kuwait and were consolidating their occupation. However, the President's personal diplomacy had already paid off; Britain and France had joined us in freezing Kuwaiti assets to keep them away from the puppet government being set up by the invaders, and we had frozen Iraqi assets in the United States.

I felt that building and maintaining a broad international coalition against Iraq was critical and would be a monumental task, so I began the process immediately by asking the Mongolian Foreign Minister to join with us in condemning the invasion. "Our position is that being a small country ourselves, one should not use force," he said. "We really condemn this." His big fish–little fish analogy was a rationale I would use over and over in the next three months as we sought to enlist the help of smaller nations in our coalition.

Meanwhile, in Moscow, a sheepish Tarasenko turned up at Spaso House at 10:00 A.M. with a radically different version of the proposed joint statement. "I had a tough time with the ministry," he said. It was an understatement. Our language had been emasculated by the bureaucrats.

Their text eliminated our references to joint action and additional steps to deal with the crisis. Even worse, the call for an arms embargo had disappeared, replaced by a weasel-worded reference to "Iraq's needs." Saddam might as well have drafted it himself.

"Sergei," Ross complained, "this is not a counterdraft. This is a counterrevolution! It's absolutely unacceptable. This becomes an argument not to do a statement at all. If this is all you can do, I'm going to call Baker and recommend that he not come."

It was leverage Ross didn't have. In Mongolia, Tutwiler had already awakened the reporters traveling with us in the middle of the night to alert them I would be shortening the Mongolian visit and flying to Moscow. I knew that my going to Moscow would increase expectations and put more pressure on Shevardnadze and Gorbachev to do the right thing. But Tarasenko didn't know that my spokesman had publicly committed me to flying to Moscow. In fact, Ross didn't know it, either. Luckily the brinkmanship seemed to work.

"Relax," Tarasenko suggested. "Write it the way you want it, and we'll keep working." Ross retrieved the tougher language of the original draft. Tarasenko agreed to everything except a sentence saying both countries "are prepared to consider further actions" if Iraq refused to withdraw. Ross deleted the language; Tarasenko promised to stare down the ministry and said he'd be in touch shortly.

Four hours later, Ross hadn't heard back. Worried that Tarasenko wouldn't be able to deliver on the bargain, he actually tried to wave me off from leaving for Moscow, but I was already airborne. After hours of trying to get a call through, he finally reached me as my plane was about to land for a refueling stop back in Irkutsk. There was no time to talk, and since the Irkutsk airport was nestled in a valley, we wouldn't be able to link up with a communications satellite from the ground. I said I'd call him once we were airborne.

On landing, however, the plane blew a tire. Changing it proved to be a Rube Goldberg operation. First, the belly of the plane was completely off-loaded to retrieve the spare. Then it turned out the Soviets' antiquated jack wasn't strong enough to handle our Air Force jet, so a series of makeshift shims had to be improvised to budge the plane off the ground. The local governor saw an opening, and opportunistically laid on an impromptu driving tour of Irkutsk to pass the time.

Back in Moscow, Tarasenko finally produced a draft statement, much improved from his original but still unacceptable. The bureaucrats were insisting that a sterner statement would endanger the lives of the 8,000 Soviet citizens in Iraq.

"Look, I'm being told we're going to be responsible for Russian blood on our hands," he protested. "We can't do this; it goes too far. We have too many people there. We're singing to the American tune, and we can't do this. It's taken a major effort to get them [the bureaucracy] to come this far."

"Sergei, if I can reach Baker, I'm going to tell him to turn around," Ross threatened. "This is worse than not putting out a statement at all."

"All right," Tarasenko wearily capitulated, "tell me what you have in mind and let's go through this again line by line."

Ross and Tarasenko collaborated on one final compromise. Tarasenko left for the ministry, promising to be back in ten minutes; three hours later there was still no answer.

Unable to reach me by telephone, and with Tarasenko incommunicado as well, a frustrated Ross and his colleagues could do nothing, so they decided to take advantage of an uncharacteristically beautiful summer day in Moscow. To pass the time, they sat outside in the backyard of Spaso House, fearing the worst. "I think we're screwed," Ross admitted at one point.

Finally, Tarasenko reported back. The Arabists had been bludgeoned into submission, with a critical exception. "The statement is accepted," Tarasenko said, "except for the arms embargo." In the time-honored tradition of negotiations, the disputed language had been set in brackets. "We've got to have that," Ross protested. "Otherwise, there's no meat to the statement, no action."

When I landed at Vnukovo II Airport at 7:30 P.M., Ross and Zoellick came onto the plane to brief me while Shevardnadze waited nearby in a holding room. Despite Tarasenko's latest round of assurances, Ross was still plenty worried the Soviets would find yet another reason to walk back from the statement. Tarasenko's credibility was now suspect; his optimism had repeatedly been overruled by the hard-liners. "I'm not sure we can get this done," he said anxiously. "I don't know if Sergei can deliver."

"Well, we're here," I said. "It doesn't do any good to worry. We have got to go through with it."

"I think there's a chance," he said, "but you're really going to have to hit him hard, because it's for his audience. He's going to use your reaction to explain why he's taking out the brackets."

Shevardnadze met me on the steps of the terminal, and as reporters shouted questions at us, we went directly to an austere second-floor conference room. The meeting lasted ninety minutes. We sat side by side on a sofa in the corner of the room.

Shevardnadze began by conceding that he had been wrong about the Iraqis. "Of course, we were shocked by what has happened," he said. "I remember your question in Irkutsk, and I answered we did not expect this kind of development. To say nothing of the fact that this action by its nature should be condemned. I see no logic in this; they've just ended ten years of warfare." He added that Gorbachev had sent Saddam a tough letter urging an immediate withdrawal; no formal response had arrived yet, but Iraqi diplomats were passing word not to expect a long stay in Kuwait. I suspected Shevardnadze was as skeptical of such reports as I.

A joint statement was "right and correct," Shevardnadze said, and Gorbachev agreed. But two aspects worried him: a statement might put the 8,000 Soviet citizens in Iraq and an additional 900 in Kuwait at risk, and might also anger other Soviet clients in the Arab world. It wasn't easy to turn one's back on a relationship of such cooperation and friendship over the last decade, he mused. However, on balance, he had concluded it was necessary. The invasion "is just simply not civilized behavior, and we can't remain aloof from this, even if they have been our friends."

I began my response by saying that we too had citizens at risk in Iraq but that the joint statement needed to be substantive, not cosmetic, which was why the disputed language about an arms embargo was so critical. "I've come here because I thought it important to demonstrate that we can and will act as partners in facing new challenges to international security," I said. "While it is easy to talk about partnership, taking the unusual step of issuing a joint call for an international cutoff of arms would send a signal to the world and to the Iraqis that U.S.-Soviet partnership is real. It would also send a signal that together we have entered a new era and would demonstrate that when a crisis develops, we're prepared to act swiftly and affirmatively in a meaningful way.

"If we can't do this, what the press and the international community are going to say is, well, the United States and the Soviets got together and issued a statement that reaffirmed what each has already done. What's the point?"

His concerns about Soviet nationals in Iraq were understandable; more than 4,000 American citizens were also living in Kuwait and Iraq. "Nevertheless, it's important we not be deterred. It won't undo any of the courageous unilateral actions you have already taken. And with a dictator like Saddam, the appetite comes with the eating; we should not embolden him by backing off from an appropriate statement." Publicly calling for an arms cutoff would reinforce our seriousness of purpose; without it, I said, we would be left with "an empty declaration," thus raising questions about whether our countries could engage in a real partnership.

"The test comes down to this—can we act together in real partnership and ask others to do what we've already done, or only repeat jointly what each of us has said unilaterally?" I was consciously playing to genetic Soviet insecurities by offering Shevardnadze the opportunity to join us center stage in an appeal to the world.

"Well, what of the French?" Shevardnadze asked. France was Baghdad's biggest trading partner. An arms embargo would be pointless if Paris refused to join. I assured Shevardnadze that I would be talking soon with Roland Dumas, the French Foreign Minister. But if the two of us called for an embargo, I predicted, the French would be hard-pressed not to join us. "It would put them in a very difficult position."

If Shevardnadze resisted, I was prepared to say that our failure to agree on a worthwhile statement would be a painful reminder that the relationship between our nations wasn't what I had thought, and that I would have no choice but to relay that sobering conclusion to the President. It wasn't necessary. *"Horasho,"* Shevardnadze said. "Okay, I can see it's important to you. We'll take out the brackets on the one sentence. I believe this is an impressive statement."

I was relieved; I knew this had been difficult for Shevardnadze. Eduard was a courageous man, but he had been under enormous pressure from his Arabists, and I could tell he was still uneasy about being too exposed if other nations rejected our joint call for the arms embargo.* Seeking to reassure him, I told him that I was sending an envoy to Beijing to urge China, a major supplier of missile technology to the Iraqis, to join us.

Shevardnadze still wasn't sure how the Arabs would react. The attitude of Syria was critical, as well as that of Egypt, which he described as the key to forging Arab solidarity. I knew that Hosni Mubarak would be with us, and that we would need Israel's full cooperation. If the Israelis took too high a profile, Saddam might then be able to split the other Arabs by framing the issue as an Arab-Israeli dispute. I said the United States would try to persuade Israel to remain silent "so they don't become an issue in place of what really should be the focus of this concern."

"The less noise coming out of Israel, the better." Shevardnadze said. "That can only irritate the Arabs and make the issue more ambiguous." I assured Shevardnadze we'd already made that point to the Israelis.

In the space of a few minutes of dialogue, Shevardnadze and I had essentially sketched out the parameters of the diplomatic coalition that would have to be assembled against Saddam in the weeks ahead to persuade him to withdraw from his ill-gotten conquest.

Toward the end of the conversation, Shevardnadze voiced another concern that he would repeat with me constantly, often with great passion, over the next six months. "There are rumors," he said, "the U.S. intends to make military strikes against Baghdad." I assured him that it wasn't true. "I know that; otherwise, this meeting wouldn't be taking place," he said. But he wanted a commitment that "the U.S. is not going to take immediate military action and we're not going to be faced with something that is unexpected." Shevardnadze was shrewdly playing to the skeptics in his bureaucracy.

"I can tell you we're not," I said. "But I can also tell you this, and you need to know it in good faith. If they do anything to our citizens, all bets are off, and I would assume the same would be true for you. I'm not going to tie our hands."

"Well, that's understandable," he agreed.

---

*Much later, after he became President of Georgia, I learned from him that he had not had Gorbachev's okay on the arms-embargo language, and just did it on his own because he thought it right.

As we finished, I wanted to remind Shevardnadze of just how far we had come. "You know, Eduard, if this was five years ago, maybe even three years ago, this whole crisis would have been put in the context of an East-West competition and confrontation. Then this would have been far more dangerous. That's a measure of what we've accomplished."

Shevardnadze agreed, but suggested that as this crisis played out, the future might well hold challenges just as daunting as those we had maneuvered through in the past. "Let's focus on the results," he said. "It's important to make this thing work."

We then came downstairs to address a huge throng of reporters in the main area of the building. Before each of us read the joint statement, Shevardnadze began with his remarkable preamble, which would have been unthinkable from a Soviet Foreign Minister a year earlier. There was no mistaking the fact that we had just journeyed light-years from that wintry day in January of 1981, at President Reagan's first press conference. Ten year later, what he had termed the Evil Empire had joined with its most implacable adversary in a remarkable alliance against what Shevardnadze and I jointly denounced as "this blatant transgression of basic norms of civilized conduct" by a Soviet client state. After decades of Soviet mischief in places such as Central America, Afghanistan, and Angola, it was a historic demonstration of superpower solidarity.

I bade Shevardnadze farewell and left Vnukovo II for Andrews Air Force Base, arriving home at 2:21 A.M. Five hours later, I would be on a helicopter to Camp David for a meeting of the National Security Council. I knew that months of uncertainty lay ahead, but en route back to the States, we were all too exhausted to reflect much on the magnitude of the challenge confronting American diplomacy. Nevertheless, my whole team and I were certainly aware that something monumentally important had just occurred at Vnukovo.

Somewhere over the Atlantic, Ross introduced Peter Hauslohner to me as the originator of the joint-statement proposal. I congratulated him for a damn good idea.

"Mr. Secretary," he said, "this is a dramatic day. It's the end of the Cold War. You really closed a chapter today and started writing a new one." In fact, he was right. That August night, a half-century after it began in mutual suspicion and ideological fervor, the Cold War breathed its last at an airport terminal on the outskirts of Moscow.

CHAPTER 2

THREE DECADES OF FRIENDSHIP

Where would we be without friends?

—*George Bush*

Two days before the 1988 election, George Bush and I were having a drink at the Vice President's residence at the Naval Observatory. We'd come to the end of yet another hard, occasionally unpleasant campaign, and though we weren't taking anything for granted, the polls said he was about to become President of the United States. Out of the blue, he told me, "I want you to be Secretary of State if I win." I accepted on the spot; after more than thirty years of friendship, a whole lot more didn't need to be said. We quickly moved on to other matters, involving the campaign and his preliminary ideas on other possible Cabinet and White House staff positions in a Bush administration. In the cynical world of Washington power politics, where little is ever taken at face value, such an uncomplicated explanation for my appointment will surely be difficult to swallow. But it was just that simple.

It would be dishonest to suggest it wasn't on my mind. It was hardly a secret that I was interested in the job, and had been for a while. I'd been Chief of Staff at the White House for more than four years. I'd been Secretary of the Treasury for almost four more. I wasn't ready to go back to the practice of law in Houston, Texas. But the truth is that we had never discussed the appointment until the moment it was offered. Contrary to some published reports, my future wasn't raised when the Vice President asked me to leave Treasury to run his campaign. It would have been inappropriate to have offered me the job, and it certainly would have been the height of arrogance for me to have asked. But as it turned out, it didn't have to be

17

discussed; like many things between the two of us, we were on the same wavelength.

It doesn't take a rocket scientist to recognize that State, as the senior Cabinet position, is by definition a more important job than the others. More comes at you, and the stakes are higher for your country than with any other Cabinet portfolio.

I had reason to suspect that the circumstances might be right for me to succeed in the job. I felt I had the necessary political and negotiating skills to perform credibly. I was fortunate to be joined in the foreign-policy cluster by three men—the Secretary of Defense, National Security Adviser, and Chairman of the Joint Chiefs of Staff—who were friends and longtime colleagues. I had had almost eight years of experience in foreign-policy matters while at Treasury and as White House Chief of Staff. And there was one luxury none of my modern-day predecessors had ever enjoyed—an unprecedented personal relationship with the President of the United States.

George Bush and I have been very close friends for more than thirty-five years, dating from the time my first wife, Mary Stuart, and I were invited over to the Bushes' house for hamburgers, and someone suggested that we become tennis partners at the Houston Country Club. We went on to win two club championships, his strong volley and net play complementing my steady baseline game and ability to lob. We distinctly did not complement each other, however, in service. Our serves were so glacial that we liked to joke that we were the only two players we knew who could hit a serve and sprint across to the other side of the court in time to return it.

He and Barbara were there for me during Mary Stuart's illness from cancer. Other than her family, they were the last friends to visit with her early in 1970, before she slipped into a coma from which she never recovered. He's a man I looked up to, and someone to whom I turned when in need. I had admired his success in everything he'd undertaken in his life, and that, together with my great respect and affection for him, was why I asked him to be godfather to my daughter Mary Bonner.

In politics and government service, our careers have been inextricably linked and, to a large degree, mutually reinforcing since 1970. When George Bush ran for the Senate against Lloyd Bentsen that year, he tried to suggest that I should be the candidate for the congressional seat he was vacating. I felt that my responsibilities to my four young sons took precedence over launching a political career. Three days after I lost my race for Texas attorney general in 1978, he was on the phone to me in Florida, where I was trying to rest and unwind. "Let's get cracking," he said, asking me to immediately start putting together his 1980 presidential campaign. So I reduced my interest in my law firm, Andrews & Kurth, thereby walking away from what would have been a much greater share of the firm's financial interest in the Howard Hughes estate. I've never looked back. Who would have? In all honesty, I was ready for a change from the grueling and, at that point in my life, less challenging practice of law. Since then, I've had the opportunity to serve my country at the highest levels for almost twelve years, and that's due in very large part to George Bush.

He's responsible not only for getting me interested in politics, but also for getting me my first government job. To this day he's never admitted to being instrumental in my appointment as Under Secretary of Commerce in the Ford administration, but I know for a fact that he lobbied then-Secretary Rogers Morton hard on my behalf—even after leaving for Beijing to be the U.S. government's second liaison officer to the People's Republic of China.

Neither of us has ever been very comfortable stretching out on the couch and talking about our personal ties, but he's characterized it as a big brother–little brother relationship. I think that's a fairly accurate description, and one that I consider quite a compliment. Like most siblings, we've been known to argue and holler at one another in private, and there's a healthy measure of friendly competition between us. Neither of us is known for passing up an opportunity to needle the other good-naturedly. After the *New York Times Magazine* did a cover story on our relationship in May of 1990, for example, Dallas investment banker Ted Strauss wrote me a puckish letter suggesting that I should be entered in the *Guinness Book of World Records* for wearing a tie while pitching horseshoes with the President at the White House. Predictably, Ted's brother Bob, the former Democratic Party chairman and an old friend of the President's and mine, sent a copy to the President "because I seriously doubt that the Secretary of State has sufficient sense of humor to appreciate this letter." The President couldn't resist. "Your outrageous brother sent me your not so kind and not so gentle attack on my Hermès-tied Sec. State," he wrote back. "The boy has class— real sartorial elegance even at the 'pit. Anyway, I don't care what the Strauss boys say, I'll defend JAB III (most of the time)."

In truth, however, George Bush has always defended me—even when he may have preferred strangling me. As Secretary of State, he gave me an extraordinary degree of latitude. I had a license to operate, and occasionally I went too far. But he never cut my legs out from under me—even at times when he would have been justified. There were a couple of times he was understandably furious with me—most notably after my infamous joint statement with Soviet Foreign Minister Alexander Bessmertnykh, the press coverage of which interfered with the State of the Union speech in January of 1991. But he never said so publicly.

Now and then, the "little brother" has been able to return the favor. As Ronald Reagan's Chief of Staff, I made it clear to colleagues that my loyalty was to the President. But I also tried to make sure that Vice President Bush was always in the loop. His office was next to mine in the West Wing, and we'd frequently drop in on each other to compare notes and exchange information.

And throughout our association, I've always given him my unvarnished advice; in fact, I think he has said that I'm the one person who always told him exactly what I think—even when I knew he didn't want to hear it. More than once over the years, I've been on the receiving end of one of his favorite retorts: "If you're so smart, why am I Vice President [or President] and you're not?" That he felt comfortable saying this, even whimsically, was a good indication of the strength of our relationship. Of course, it was usually also his way of letting me know that our dialogue was over.

In 1975, President Ford wanted to appoint him director of the Central Intelligence Agency. Senate Democrats sent word they would confirm him—but only if Ford pledged publicly to bar him as a running mate in the 1976 election. It was an outrageous demand, but Ford left it up to George. I told my friend it was a serious mistake to let the opposition party in the Senate dictate the terms of his career path. "You really shouldn't do this," I argued. "You shouldn't negate your political future just to be confirmed." George disagreed with me. "This is something the President wants me to do," he said. "It's something that interests me, and I'm going to do it."

Until my tenure as Secretary of State, I believe my greatest service to George Bush was as his campaign manager in 1980. The credit, of course, belongs to him; it took a lot of courage to get out there as a virtual unknown and do what he did. "Do you think I'm crazy to do this?" he'd ask as we flew around the country in steerage, short of support, money, and name recognition in those early days of 1979. While I had strongly encouraged his candidacy, there were days I thought we were indeed certifiably nuts, but his doggedness and good cheer in the face of long odds enhanced my admiration for him. At the time, I was the only Republican who had run a general-election presidential campaign except for John Mitchell, and as a result of that experience, I believe I was able to contribute in a meaningful way to a campaign that began as an asterisk in the public-opinion polls and ended with my friend as Ronald Reagan's running mate.

The most difficult part was persuading him that it was time to throw in the towel. As President Ford's chief delegate hunter in 1976, I'd become reasonably proficient at counting votes, and despite impressive victories in Pennsylvania and Michigan, I knew the battle was lost. But George Bush has never been a quitter. I really had to wrestle with him to do the right thing for himself politically. "George, it's over," I told him. "We're out of money, it's mathematically impossible to win the nomination, and to continue on through the last primaries would destroy any chance whatsoever you may be picked as Vice President." He didn't like what he was hearing, believing that to withdraw would let down his supporters in upcoming primaries, particularly in Ohio and New Jersey. He spent the weekend in Houston agonizing over the decision with family and other close friends before reluctantly concluding that he should fold his tent.

It's very hard to be the campaign manager for a friend. I should know; I was George Bush's campaign manager in 1980 and 1988, and his Chief of Staff during the 1992 election. Invariably, you're the bearer of bad news, as well as the enforcer. When the candidate is exhausted, it falls to the campaign manager to encourage him to stay on the road one more day, to deliver one more speech, or spend an hour at the end of a brutal campaign day soliciting contributions on the telephone. It's easy to lose friendships in situations like this. We didn't.

Friendships mean a lot to George Bush. Indeed, his loyalty to friends is one of his defining personal strengths. Some have suggested it ended up being one of his greatest political weaknesses, as he stayed loyal for too long to people who hurt his presidency, out of concern for their friendship. But as he likes to say, "Where would we be without friends?" His political career would have happened without my help, although I'm certainly glad to have contributed in that regard. As far as I'm concerned, I know that without his support and friendship I would never have had the opportunities for public service I've experienced.

All in all, our partnership hasn't worked out so badly, given the dog-eat-dog atmosphere of politics. In May of 1990, he called my plane to thank me for my efforts to sell the "Two-plus-Four" formula for German unification to the Soviets and others in Bonn. Later in the flight, I wrote him a note. "We're not doing too bad for a couple of emotionless guys who have no vision whatsoever and operate only on instinct!" I said. "I still say—'Gee Whiz, who'd a thunk it!' " I still do.

George Shultz once told me, "The Secretary of State is the greatest job in government, but one thing you need to understand is that there aren't any well-defined parameters where foreign policy stops and other policy begins. Which means that everybody is out after your turf." But I was incredibly fortunate that I simply never had to worry about that. Being close to the President made doing the job a thousand times easier. I never worried about being undercut. I could operate without ever having to look over my shoulder or worry about my backside.

I had the additional good fortune to be part of a Bush national security team that consisted of a group of experienced, collegial peers who had worked together before in one capacity or another and who liked and respected one another. We not only enjoyed one another's company, we trusted one another. That's not to suggest we didn't disagree. We often argued like crazy—and loudly. It's also no secret that both Dick Cheney and Brent Scowcroft were more generically cautious about changing some policy approaches than I, which led to some major disagreements on arms control, Soviet-American relations, and the Middle East. But our differences never took the form of the backbiting of the Kissinger-Rogers, Vance-Brzezinski eras, or the slugfests of our national security teams during the Reagan years. There was no trashing of colleagues at the upper levels, and very little leaking to the press. Of course, we would all anonymously background reporters to send diplomatic signals, either to foreign governments or Capitol Hill. But we didn't do it to undercut one another. As a result, I firmly believe that one of the foremost accomplishments of the Bush presidency was that we made the national security apparatus work the way it is supposed to. This was fundamental in enabling us to manage properly the historic changes that occurred around the world from 1989 to 1992.

I met Dick Cheney for the first time in 1975, just a few days after I'd been sworn in as Rogers Morton's deputy at the Department of Commerce. Rog wanted me to meet President Ford, so I tagged along with him to the White House one afternoon. Rog walked into the Oval Office, asking me to wait in the office of Nell Yates, President Ford's personal secretary. After fifteen minutes, I was ushered into the Oval Office. The President had been meeting with several top aides, including Cheney, who had recently succeeded Don Rumsfeld as Chief of Staff. I was introduced to Dick—who very graciously offered me a chair. I said to myself that this was certainly a far cry from some of the horror stories I'd heard about the way things were in some hard-eyed Chief of Staff regimes in previous administrations. That same human decency and down-to-earth style characterize Dick to this day. It's hard to keep your sense of equilibrium in Washington, but the power game has never gone to his head.

During the 1976 Republican primary campaign, Dick bailed me out from my first embarrassing moment in government service, after I inadvertently announced Henry Kissinger's resignation from the government for him. As Under Secretary of Commerce, I was assigned political chores of extraordinarily modest importance. One of them was to meet with some Ford financial supporters in Oklahoma City, where Ronald Reagan was particularly strong. At one point, I was asked what role Kissinger would have in a second Ford term. I knew Kissinger was anathema to many Republicans in the South and West, and the event was closed to the press, so I blithely said I couldn't conceive of him being in the administration if Ford were elected. Unbeknownst to me, the audience included a reporter for the University of Oklahoma student newspaper.

A couple of days later, I was at the White House for a Rose Garden ceremony. Nell Yates asked me to "stick your head in Mr. Cheney's office before you leave." I walked into Cheney's elegant West Wing corner office, having absolutely no idea that it would be my own office five years later and again sixteen years later—for two different Republican Presidents. "I want to show you something," he said somberly, handing me some news clips of my Oklahoma comments. My Kissinger barb had been picked up by the wire services from the college paper and had caused quite a stir, particularly at the State Department, where Kissinger was furious. I had no idea I'd caused such trouble, and stammered my regrets. "Don't worry about it," Cheney said, laughing. "Just make it right with Henry." So in the time-honored ritual of Washington, I called Kissinger and groveled my apologies. Another Chief of Staff might have reamed me out on the spot—and would have been justified in doing so—but I remember thinking that Dick had taught me a lesson about being cautious in a very graceful fashion.

There was a later incident involving Cheney and Kissinger, this time on the issue of textiles. Anxious to expand President Nixon's historic opening to the People's Republic of China, the State Department in 1976 was encouraging the unlimited import of Chinese textiles into the United States. Not surprisingly, the idea was bitterly opposed by domestic textile manufacturers—many of whom had plants in southern states that were important to President Ford in his bitter primary fight against Ronald Reagan for the Republican presidential nomination. Politics aside, the Commerce Department believed that U.S. economic interests dictated a more balanced approach than State was pushing. In the draft of a March speech President Ford would be delivering to the American Textile Manufacturers Institute in San Francisco, there was a sentence committing the President "to ensure that our domestic market is not seriously disrupted." The language was vague but sympathetic, designed to assuage the concerns of his audience about Chinese textiles' flooding their markets. We knew that Kissinger wanted the sentence deleted, but as the event approached, State still hadn't weighed in with any comments on the speech draft. Henry was a superb bureaucratic infighter, and his style in these situations was often to lie in the weeds until the last instant, then persuade the President to do his bidding, leaving no time for a counterattack. As acting Secretary of Commerce, I asked the White House to let me know if Kissinger tried an end run on this occasion. Sure enough, after a meeting of the Economic Policy Board, I was alerted by Bob Hormats, then a young international economics specialist on the National Security Council staff, that Kissinger was going to wait until President Ford was en route to California, then telephone Air Force One and persuade him to delete the sentence on the grounds of the importance of the emerging relationship with the People's Republic of China. By the time I reached Cheney on Air Force One, Kissinger had already called, and a tentative decision had been made to remove the sentence. I argued that the language represented sound policy as well as good politics. Cheney agreed, and talked the President into keeping the original language. Not long afterward, I met the Secretary of State for the first time at a State Department reception. "Ah," he muttered, "so you're Textile Baker."

After we narrowly survived the Reagan challenge in the Republican primaries, Cheney and I worked even more closely together in the fall campaign against Jimmy Carter. He went out of his way to make sure that I got everything I needed as campaign chairman, and as a result the coordination between the campaign and the White House was very good—a model I looked to in the presidential elections of 1984 and 1992.

After the 1976 election, we stayed in touch and kept each other posted on our future political plans. In 1978, Cheney was elected to Congress in Wyoming, and proved to be a critical ally when I became White House Chief of Staff three years later. He would frequently call me with a heads-up on some important development on Capitol Hill that often beat my own legislative channels. It wasn't all sweetness and light, however. We engaged in some fairly major policy battles from time to time—particularly on the 1986 tax reform bill, which I was pushing as President Reagan's Secretary of the Treasury, and which he bitterly opposed. I remember Dick coming to see me one day, with Congressman Trent Lott of Mississippi, and vowing, "We're going to oppose you on this, and we're going to beat you." We prevailed over Dick's best efforts, but the conflict never became personal or affected our friendship. In the last decade, we've spent a fair amount of time together in the Wyoming wilderness on fishing expeditions—Dick is a native, I'm a newcomer. On a couple of these pack trips, we've even bunked in the same tent. Dick washes dishes, I dry.

Dick was more of a cold warrior than I was, and we sometimes disagreed about Soviet policy and arms control, but this, too, never got in the way of a strong friendship, mutual respect, and close working relationship.

After John Tower's nomination as Secretary of Defense fell apart in early 1989, I enthusiastically supported Brent Scowcroft's idea to replace Tower with Cheney. I was in the residence with the President when he picked up the telephone to offer Dick the job. I called Dick later, lobbied him hard, and was delighted that he gave up a distinguished congressional career to accept.

John Tower and I had been friends for a long time. I still remember a sweltering July day in San Antonio in 1978, after I had been bitten by the political bug, come home to Texas after the 1976 Ford campaign, and decided to run for attorney general. Tower and I were passing out leaflets in a Hispanic part of town, and we ran into each other. "Let's go get a drink," he suggested. So we adjourned to the historic Menger Hotel, where Teddy

Roosevelt had mustered in the Rough Riders to fight in the Spanish-American War. As we nursed our vodka martinis, Tower looked at me and said, "You know something, Baker? This is a squalid business we're in." And I said, "Speak for yourself, Senator, I'm new to all this." I thought about that many a time when he was being pilloried by his former colleagues during his ill-fated confirmation hearing.

I had supported John Tower's nomination, and felt sorry for him when it was defeated. But I had worried privately that he might tread upon foreign policy once confirmed. I've never known many mandarins of the Senate who didn't have sharp elbows, and while Tower was an old friend and political ally, he was no slouch at the power game. During the transition, Tower had come to me for help in landing the appointment. "Look, I know what it is to be Secretary of Defense and what it is to be Secretary of State," he argued. "You won't see me on your turf." I frankly wasn't sure about that, but I *was* sure that Dick Cheney would never try to be Secretary of State, and he knew I wouldn't tread on his turf.

The same was true for Brent Scowcroft, who I believe was the ideal National Security Adviser. He'd had the same job under President Ford, and George Bush not only trusted him totally but had enormous personal affection for him. Unlike some of his predecessors in the job, Brent wasn't hampered by a towering ego, and he never peddled a private agenda. Instead, he always bent over backward to be an honest broker for the President.

He also went out of his way to be collegial. Early on, he told me that he wasn't going to go on television talk shows unless I thought he should. Of course, that made it easy to say he could go on damn near anytime he wanted, as far as I was concerned. He also hosted a seven o'clock breakfast every Wednesday in his office, where he and Cheney and I compared notes to make sure we were all singing from the same hymnal. Oftentimes, when our staffs were warring over a given issue, we'd read our prepared talking points to one another, and discover in the process just how much the State, Pentagon, and NSC bureaucracies distrusted each other.

In formal meetings of the National Security Council, Brent would sometimes remain silent when I spoke rather than present a countervailing view on a foreign-policy issue. It wasn't because I was the President's close friend or out of timidity—Brent had forceful opinions and was never shy about disagreeing with his colleagues—but rather out of respect for the way the system was supposed to work. Brent saw himself as a coordinator, a view reinforced by his unassuming style as well as by his experience as chairman of the presidential commission examining the Iran-contra scandal. The Scowcroft Commission concluded that the core of the problem had been that the NSC had become operational, mucking around in matters that should have been handled by the Cabinet departments, particularly

State. As NSC Adviser, Brent practiced what he preached. With a few exceptions, such as Brent's trip to China in 1989 with my deputy Larry Eagleburger, the NSC left the conduct of diplomacy to State—and I was always told about and concurred with those exceptions in advance. For the most part, Brent even went along with an informal agreement among us that his staff should generally refrain from seeing foreign ambassadors.

My first collaboration with Brent, incidentally, was a complete disaster. After that star-crossed debate in San Francisco in 1976, when President Ford said that Poland was not dominated by the Soviet Union, Brent and I were sent out to the press room to explain how the President had nevertheless wiped the floor with candidate Carter. The first questioner wanted to know how many Soviet divisions were stationed in Poland. About six, Brent glumly replied. For the next half hour, he and I tried our best to accentuate the positive. We failed miserably. But I admired Brent's loyalty and good cheer in the face of adversity, traits I would see time and again in the Bush years.

Colin Powell and I were the only two senior alumni from the Reagan administration—other than President Bush himself, of course.* From the start, a simpatico relationship existed between us. Many times, when we were waiting in Brent's office for some meeting to start, Colin and I would reminisce on our shared experiences when he was President Reagan's NSC Adviser and I was Secretary of the Treasury. The most talented military officer of his generation, Powell had a keen mind, a smooth, appealing personal style, and an instinctive feel for the politics of governance. We often found ourselves on the same side of the barricades.

Early on I had told Cheney that I would not call the Chairman of the Joint Chiefs of Staff without telling him, and with maybe only one or two exceptions, I didn't. But occasionally, when he and Dick saw things differently on a major policy matter, Colin would call me for some private counsel. It happened most notably during the Gulf War, when Cheney's views were sometimes more muscular than Powell's. But the relationships between us all were such that an informal back channel like that didn't threaten any of us.

By contrast, I do not think President Reagan's foreign policy apparatus served him the way it should have. It was often a witches' brew of intrigue, elbows, egos, and separate agendas. From day one, the level of suspicion and mutual distrust was utterly out of control among many of the major players. I can't remember any extended period of time when someone in the National Security cluster wasn't at someone else's throat. In eight years,

*Powell replaced Admiral William Crowe, whose term as JCS Chairman expired on September 30, 1989.

President Reagan had seven National Security Advisers. The National Security Council frequently ran amok, as the Iran-contra scandal documented in embarrassing detail. And sometimes when the President decided a major policy issue, his subordinates would ignore his wishes and pursue their own policy schemes.

I think the Reagan presidency was arguably the most effective in a quarter century, but its national security policy succeeded because of the strength of President Reagan and in spite of a lack of organization and cooperation. The chaos and backbiting served him and the country poorly, and the abortive plan to make me National Security Adviser was advanced by Mike Deaver and me in an effort to inject some sanity and cohesion into the national security process. Predictably, it was torpedoed by some of the very same principals whose small-bore behavior had given rise to the proposal in the first place. George Bush had seen it all unfold in eight years as Vice President, and as President he was determined that the system would work the way it was supposed to. I think it did.

"The Building"

In fourteen years of public service, I've only lost my composure once—on August 13, 1992, the day I announced I was leaving the State Department to become President Bush's Chief of Staff. My farewell speech in the departmental auditorium was an unexpectedly painful experience for me; in fact, I literally almost didn't get through it. There were tears in my eyes as I rode the elevator back up to my seventh-floor office as a now-lame-duck Secretary of State—tears of pride mingled with enormous reluctance to relinquish the most personally satisfying of all my government assignments.

"Any success that we may have achieved is due in considerable part to the hard work, spirit, professionalism, and commitment of all of you," I had said in my valedictory. "You are a fine corps of professionals. It has been an honor to have served with you." I meant every word of it. I was proud of what we had accomplished together in forty-three fleeting months. My sense of loss was all the more acute because I had begun my tenure with a fair measure of uncertainty about what lay ahead for me at State.

While I was extremely comfortable in my relationship with the President and his senior advisers, I had approached the running of the State Department with some apprehension. I was not concerned about managing a large bureaucracy. I had run four presidential campaigns, organized the White House successfully, and built a solid operation at the Treasury Department. So it wasn't running a bureaucracy per se that caused me any trepidation. It was running "the Building."

While to most people, the State Department is just a rather ugly, monolithic post–World War II eight-story monstrosity overlooking the Mall in Foggy Bottom, to its inhabitants it's "the building"—a living, breathing being that has opinions and policies of its own. Before my confirmation, I moved in December 1988 from the Bush transition headquarters on Connecticut Avenue to the first floor of the State Department, where a suite of offices had been generously set aside by George Shultz for me and my personal staff. There, I quickly became aware of "the building" and its views on the matters at hand. I soon found out that different floors of "the building" had their own unique views on events: "The seventh floor won't want it that way." "The sixth floor wants to reclama on that." Indeed, letters of the alphabet seemed to have views, too: "S won't stand for it." "P bounced that." "EUR is out of control." (At State, every office had a letter designation, so one of my first tasks was to learn this shorthand. S is the Secretary, P the Under Secretary for Political Affairs, and EUR the Bureau for European and Canadian Affairs.) At State, in short, the inanimate came alive— and pretty soon I understood why.

Ironically, this was in part a function of the building itself. The secretary, his close aides, and the under secretaries sit on the seventh floor. Most of the assistant secretaries and deputy assistant secretaries sit on the sixth floor, and regional office directors and desks are on the lower floors. Typically, a memo to me would start on the fourth floor, be approved (or "cleared," as per the State lexicon) on the fifth and sixth floors, get final vetting on seventh, and then come to me.

But State's organizational originality came from more than architecture. Without a doubt, the State Department has the most unique bureaucratic culture I've ever encountered. In most of the federal government, the work is guided by a small number of political appointees who work together with civil service—the career bureaucracy that is designed to be above politics and provide institutional memory and substantive expertise. But at State there is also the Foreign Service, the elite corps of foreign affairs officers who staff the Department's country and functional desks in Washington and our embassies abroad. Individuals enter the foreign service after passing the foreign-service exam, a rigorous and painful written test and a series of oral interviews. Officers tend to come from the nation's top colleges, particularly the Ivy League, and have an understanding of and affection for things foreign: languages, geography, history, culture, food, and drink. After a training period, they then enter the Foreign Service and rotate between posts overseas and positions in Washington. Regulations stipulate that a Foreign Service officer (FSO) cannot serve in Washington more than five years, which tends to make FSOs oftentimes more at home overseas than here in the United States. Along with the nature of embassy work, which places a premium on understanding and reporting the host government's views on events, this aspect of the Foreign Service fosters the malady of "clientitis," the tendency for an officer to identify more with the interests of the host country (the "client") than with Washington. There is a fine line between understanding a host country's position and identifying so thoroughly with it that you become essentially an advocate for it in policy discussions. It's a disease not unique to the Foreign Service; some of the worst cases of clientitis I encountered involved politically appointed ambassadors who fell so thoroughly in love with their host country and its government that they sometimes lost sight of what was in the American national interest.

Another danger FSOs face is the tendency to assume that others do not understand foreign affairs as well as the Foreign Service. While this may have been true quite often before World War II, in the last forty years the growth of academic programs, think tanks, and research organizations has developed a number of skilled specialists outside the Foreign Service. As a consequence, in many cases, political appointees could have more understanding of a country than a desk officer who had been involved only with the affairs of a given country for the two or three years they had been on the desk.

Finally, the organizational imperative of an FSO is to become an ambassador. That is the peak of a career, and so FSOs tend to view any political appointment into the ambassadorial ranks as a natural competitor to their rightful claim. Moreover, from a strictly personal standpoint, an American ambassador living overseas can be a very powerful person, a true majordomo who has complete control over his or her domain.

In preparing to organize "the Building," I talked to every ex-President and most ex-Secretaries of State. To a man, they told me the Foreign Service was capable at implementing policy, knowledgeable about international issues, and a resource to be utilized. Yet each, in his own way, left me with a warning.

"They always overdramatize the anticipated reactions of their clients," Ed Muskie recalled. Henry Kissinger's warning was typically more colorful: "They're very ingenious. They give you three choices: nuclear war, unconditional surrender, and their preferred course of action."

Richard Nixon was by far the most emphatic. "In the postwar era," he told me, "there have been only three great Secretaries of State: Acheson, Foster Dulles, and Kissinger. Every one of them was distrusted by the bureaucracy. You must lead them. Don't let them capture you." I was determined not to let that happen.

I headed to State assuming that the President made foreign policy, not the Foreign Service. That's why in a *Time* magazine interview after my appointment, I made a point of saying that I intended to be the President's man at the State Department, not the State Department's man at the White House. It was a deliberate signal on my part. I wanted to send a message to the bureaucracy that my style of management would be different from my predecessor's.

In the Reagan White House, George Shultz was my closest comrade-in-arms in the Cabinet. Our life paths are remarkably parallel: Princeton, the Marine Corps, Treasury, and State. I saw him as something of a role model in those days. He was a friend, and we viewed things pretty much the same way on most policy issues. He served nearly six years with great distinction in an appallingly adversarial environment. I watched it all happen and I still don't know how he stood it. I was very sympathetic to his situation; more than once, I'd been his protector when his antagonists had tried their frequent end runs. There was the time, for instance, when Bill Clark, then the National Security Adviser, hatched a plan to send Jeane Kirkpatrick on a mission to Latin America, unbeknownst to Shultz. "Don't you think your Secretary of State should know about that?" I suggested to President Reagan, who quickly agreed and killed the scheme.

George Shultz had followed an "institutional" approach to running the State Department. He relied first and foremost on the Foreign Service to run the "building" and to guide policy. It worked for him—in great part because his years at State were essentially times of incremental, progressive change. Alexander Haig's stormy tenure had begun the Reagan Revolution in foreign affairs, and by the time Shultz came in, the Foreign Service had adapted to the new policy, and so Shultz, quite understandably, was able to rely heavily on the career service.

For three critical reasons, I faced an entirely different situation requiring a rather different organizational approach. First, we were headed into a time of revolutionary change. While no one would foresee just how revolutionary that change would be, I knew from the outset that, like the Soviets, we would need some "new thinking" in our foreign policy. And new thinking would require new people—with fresh mind-sets, different assumptions, and above all little ego investment in the current policy. It's hard to convey how difficult it is for bureaucracies to adapt to radical change. But generally, government work is like any other line of work; most people will tend to approach tomorrow's problems with the solutions that worked today. Only when those solutions fail will people look for a different way. In the private sector, there's almost always a bottom line—profit—that causes organizations to change their approach. But in political and policy work, there's seldom a clear bottom line, and each faction behind a given policy can almost always rationalize why its plan works best or would work best "if only" this, that, or the other were altered.

Second, the Bush administration was a new administration. That meant many Reagan appointees would either be leaving, if they were political appointees, or rotating, if they were Foreign Service officers. More important, it was time for us to reap the legacy of Ronald Reagan's policy of peace through strength: to begin rolling back global Communism and catalyze democracy's victory in Central and Eastern Europe and the Soviet Union itself. That, in and of itself, was going to require a very different strategy, and that meant new people.

Finally, there was a need to pay greater attention to building a domestic consensus at home. Despite the President's overwhelming victory over Michael Dukakis, the Democrats had reaffirmed their control over both the Senate and the House, and the bitterness of the campaign had some potential to poison the atmosphere for building a truly bipartisan policy. For that reason, I wanted my people and my organizational structure to be much more attentive to domestic audiences, not only on the Hill but also generally across the land.

In this environment, I thought that the institutional rigidity of the Foreign Service, with its separate rules, mores, and bureaucratic hierarchy, precluded a reliance solely on it in order to meet the challenges at hand. Most FSOs are talented and loyal public servants, and any Secretary would be foolish not to harness their strengths. I did so, and was served very ably by many of them. But as with any large group, some of them tend to avoid risk taking or creative thinking.

In fairness, it's not entirely their fault. One reason why some FSOs are reluctant to demonstrate much initiative is that when they do, they're often treated quite shabbily by the Senate confirmation process. There are plenty of instances where Senators on both sides of the philosophical aisle have placed holds on career nominations, and even killed appointments outright, because they didn't like the policy approach of a nominee. In most cases, the victim was simply pursuing the policy of the President or the Secretary of State. It happened very frequently with respect to Central American policy, and after enough of these incidents, you can't blame career diplomats for playing it safe (for example, Jock Covey and John Bushnell were two very talented Foreign Service officers who served their country well during my tenure as Secretary of State, but were denied well-deserved ambassadorial appointments).

Primarily for these reasons, I preferred to centralize policy authority in a small team of talented, loyal aides, and build outward from them. This approach has been a hallmark of my government career. It's been my experience that managers who surround themselves with weak subordinates are doomed to fail, because the jobs at these pay grades are just too damn tough to have anyone less than the best. It's worth noting that in the last two decades, the most successful White House Chiefs of Staff have been those secure enough to surround themselves with senior aides who could take over their jobs.

Beyond talent and personal loyalty to the President and to me, I knew I'd need several qualities in my team. I wanted people who could generate ideas and initiatives and whose first inclination was to say "yes"—not necessarily to me but to action. The natural tendency of any bureaucracy is to do nothing. That is true in spades at State, where doing something can lead to war or, sometimes even worse from the bureaucracy's perspective, conflicts with regional clients. I think that's why people so often talked about "the Building," "the sixth floor," or "EUR." It was a way to depersonalize decision making and, ultimately, to avoid responsibility. My team would need to excel at turning ideas into action, and that meant I needed implementers and enforcers as well. I also wanted people who understood politics, because, quite simply, politics drives diplomacy, not vice versa.

In hindsight, the strength of this organizational concept was that it allowed me to develop initiatives privately and coherently and to use them to break diplomatic deadlocks. So the system was great at offense, but it wasn't quite as strong at defense—that is, avoiding potential crises. My approach placed a tremendous burden on me and my closest aides, who simply couldn't always focus on every potential crisis. On balance, however, I believe it served me and, more important, the Bush administration exceptionally well.

The first "inner circle" of my group consisted of three people: Bob Zoellick, Dennis Ross, and Margaret Tutwiler. Zoellick, a native of Illinois, combined Midwest common sense with the policy sophistication of someone who had been educated at America's most elite schools: Swarthmore, Harvard Law School, and the Kennedy School of Government. He had worked for me at Treasury and was a superb manager, policy analyst, and writer. I had learned at the White House that to control policy you need to control paper, so I made Zoellick Counselor of the Department ("C") and mandated that every piece of paper sent to me go through him first. That made him, as one journalist put it, my "second brain" who could organize, synthesize, and refine ideas, thus ensuring that only quality, fully vetted initiatives and ideas got to my desk. With the possible exception of Richard Darman, it would be hard to find someone more suited to the job. Zoellick's ability to take reams of information and boil it down to one page of "bullets" and "ticks"—standard briefing paper format—was legendary. So were his lists of what needed to be done. If he had a weakness, it was that he was too smart and would come up with ten reasons for doing something when three would have sufficed. Like most of my aides, he did not suffer fools gladly; combined with his position in the bureaucratic food chain—gatekeeper—this made Zoellick one of the most feared people at State.

Dennis Ross, my choice as Director of the Policy Planning Staff ("S/P" for "Secretary's Planning Staff"), could scarcely have been a greater contrast to Zoellick. Ross, a native Californian, was probably the most relaxed person in the State Department. It's a cliché to call someone from California "mellow," but that's the only word that fits. Ross had worked in the Pentagon after doing doctoral work at UCLA, and had gone on to work on the Policy Planning Staff under Haig and then on the Reagan National Security Council staff. (In his college days, Ross had worked on campaigns for both Bobby Kennedy and George McGovern and was still relatively liberal politically, despite having served as George Bush's foreign-policy adviser in the 1988 campaign.) While Zoellick spoke in bullets and ticks, Ross spoke in themes and concepts. His substantive specialties were the Middle East and the Soviet Union, but his common sense was useful across the board, although he was so laid back that only his assistant, Helen Ellis, could keep him on schedule.

Together they formed a formidable and close-knit team. In fact, I moved the director's office in policy planning so that it was just down from Zoellick along "Mahogany Row," the inner corridor on the seventh floor, named after the mahogany paneling, where the Secretary and his aides are housed.

Also along Mahogany Row was Margaret Tutwiler, my Assistant Secretary for Public Affairs and Spokesman ("PA"). She was the first person Bo Callaway hired in managing the Ford campaign in 1976. She later became the campaign chairman in her native Alabama, and two years later was the second employee of George Bush's political action committee in Houston. She began in Washington as my executive assistant in the Reagan White House, and later became the liaison with the 1984 reelection campaign. She came with me to Treasury as spokesman, and despite her reservations, I persuaded her to take the same job at State. "She has that nice, soft southern accent," Nixon had told me. "At the same time, she's tough, mean, and devious. Perfect!" Tutwiler possessed an uncanny ability to sort through the clutter of argument and policy doublespeak to determine the bottom line. And she had an instinctive sense of what would "play" domestically. She was very literal—which may have made her even more feared than Zoellick—but no one had a better political antenna or greater personal loyalty.

Just as important, I wanted to make sure I controlled policy, and at State, that meant controlling words. At the Pentagon, in contrast, weapons programs are what really matter, and that means dollars matter more than words. At State, you need to control what is said about U.S. positions on various issues. Ross—with Zoellick's intense involvement—oversaw the speechwriting operation, and Tutwiler took care of public affairs and the press, assisted by Kim Hoggard (and later Grace Moe) and on the road in particular by Judy O'Neill and Mary Ann Yoden. In this regard, Tutwiler was the perfect spokesperson because, with few exceptions, she always followed her instructions for the noon briefing, and went exactly as far as I wanted her to go in briefing the press and no further. She then would spend much of the afternoon and early evening talking to reporters on the phone on "background," again following her guidance with strict discipline. Certainly, this served a useful political purpose, as I had learned at the White House, but at State, it also served a critical diplomatic purpose. Foreign governments follow State Department briefings very closely, and our nuanced use of the briefings allowed us to send various signals to foreign governments and to calibrate our diplomacy, especially with regard to the Middle East peace process. Tutwiler also controlled my scheduling operation, headed by Karen Groomes, another critical but seldom-noticed function. Who I saw and how long I met with them oftentimes had important diplomatic repercussions, so at State, for all its protocol and pomp, scheduling was substance. (Of course, Groomes didn't do it alone; Ardis Johnson, Clairo Gilbert, and Linda Dewan helped manage an ever-changing and oftentimes controversial schedule. Likewise, protocol was politics—and Joseph Reed, a close friend of George Bush, handled it with style and flair.)

Zoellick, Ross, and Tutwiler became known as the "inner circle," in part because they played critical roles in my most important initiatives but also because they traveled with me. But there was another equally important inner circle—my Deputy Secretary, Lawrence Eagleburger, my Under Secretary for Political Affairs, Robert Kimmitt, and my Assistant Secretary for Congressional Affairs, Janet Mullins. This troika was geared less to unleashing initiatives and more to the difficult work of managing problems.

Deputies in the government get all work and no glory, and no one was more suited to handling intractable problems selflessly than Eagleburger. As "D," Eagleburger knew that his job was to do the dirty work no one else wanted to do or could do, and he dived into his work with a relish that was hard to understand, unless you talked to Richard Nixon, who had known Eagleburger as an aide to Henry Kissinger. "He's utterly loyal," Nixon had told me, "won't have his own agenda, and he's smart as a shithouse rat." All were true, especially the last. Eagleburger had an ability to understand "the Building," and to divine trouble and head it off, that had made him a legend in the Foreign Service, where he had spent nearly a quarter century before leaving to join Kissinger and Associates. I've always had first-rate deputies, but Eagleburger was superb. He was ably assisted in the day-to-day management of the department by Ivan Selin and later by John F. W. Rogers, who had served me so well in senior management positions both at the White House and at Treasury.

I made Kimmitt "P" because I wanted a taskmaster to oversee the five regional bureaus that implement most of the policy. Kimmitt was a West Pointer who had impressed me on the Reagan NSC staff and had done an exceptionally able job for me as general counsel at Treasury. When George Bush asked for someone to handle the delicate task of interviewing prospective vice presidential candidates, I recommended Kimmitt. Contrary to the common wisdom, he did a thorough job, asked all the right questions, and never violated a confidence. As "P," Kimmitt became my crisis manager, a job he performed most brilliantly during the Persian Gulf crisis. "Colonel Bob," as he was known, as much for his demeanor as for his paratrooper background, knew how to run a meeting and get things done—a not inconsequential task in "the building," where standard operating procedure tends to be a caricature ("First, do nothing") of the Hippocratic Oath ("First, do no harm"). Kimmitt was also my point man on the Deputies Committee, the most senior interagency committee dealing with national security issues below the Cabinet secretary level.

Another potential constraint on action was the Congress. As chief of staff to two senators, Janet Mullins knew Capitol Hill very well, and during the Bush campaign had shown a real ability to get things done when she coordinated media buys. She was a natural choice to head congressional liaison ("H"), which I knew would be a critical position following a bitter election campaign. She was absolutely first rate in the job.

These two inner circles were supported by my inner office: Caron Jackson, Liz Lineberry, and Marilyn Newman, whose enthusiasm was so contagious that she and my son Doug ended up getting married.

I rounded out State by filling the remaining under secretary and assistant secretary positions with a mix of Foreign Service officers, political appointees, and civil servants.

Despite the conventional wisdom at the time, the Bush administration appointed more career officers to ambassadorships than the Reagan administration. In addition, I chose career officers as one of the four under secretaries and three of the five key regional assistant secretaries. And I'm proud to have picked Larry Eagleburger as my deputy—the first career FSO ever to have that job—and to have enthusiastically supported him as my successor when I left in response to the President's request that I return to the White House.

With almost three dozen assistant secretaries and agency heads reporting to the Secretary, I thought the existing organization was too unwieldy. So I decided that the four under secretaries, who in previous regimes were often window dressing or relegated to special projects, should report directly to me, with the assistant secretaries reporting through them. This had the perceived effect of diluting the influence of the assistant secretaries. To avoid a potentially serious morale and policy problem, I tried to compensate in several ways. Unlike some of my predecessors, I held a daily senior staff meeting that included the assistant secretaries. I had a standing order that any assistant secretary who asked to see me would be put on the schedule automatically. Furthermore, the vast majority of them had a direct private telephone line to me.

None of this did me much good with "the Building," which relished dumping on the new team. They were aided and abetted in this exercise by some veteran State Department reporters whose sources were drying up as I centralized decision making, and were only too eager to publish the naysaying of some disgruntled careerists. It comes with the turf, but the only complaint that really ever got to me was the common charge that I was a foreign policy neophyte. I had had, after all, eight years of varying degrees of involvement in foreign policy matters over the course of two Reagan terms. In retrospect, I might have been more attentive to the mores of the diplomatic culture. I could have done more to cultivate some of the younger and brighter FSOs—people like Bill Burns, Dan Kurtzer, David Welch, Ken Brill, Nick Burns, Molly Williamson, and Richard Boucher—all of whom worked closely with me and were stars. In truth, I was probably not as attentive to the protocol aspects of the job of Secretary of State as I should have been. But substantive results were what President Bush expected of me, not expertise with respect to the nuances of diplomatic niceties. In a world changing with breathtaking swiftness, results had to be my priority. If I were successful, the carping of some within the Foreign Service and a few disgruntled holdovers from the prior administration wouldn't matter. And if I weren't, their affection wouldn't save me—or the President. The Soviet Union wasn't the only place in need of new thinking. George Bush deserved no less from the State Department he would be inheriting.

CHAPTER 3

THE WORLD ON THE EVE OF A REVOLUTION

If I took your gloomy view, I should commence immediate inquiries as to the most painless form of suicide. But I think you listen too much to the soldiers. No lesson seems to be so deeply inculcated by the experience of life as that you never should trust in experts. If you believe the doctors nothing is wholesome; if you believe the theologians nothing is innocent; if you believe the soldiers nothing is safe. They all require to have their strong wine diluted by a very large admixture of insipid common sense.

—*Lord Salisbury in a letter to Lord Lytton, Viceroy of India, June 15, 1877*

I never intended to become involved in politics, let alone international politics. Law was the tradition in my family. From my great-grandfather to my grandfather, to my dad, to two of my four grown sons, the Bakers have been lawyers—public-spirited attorneys who helped shape the foundations of commerce, business, and education, as the frontier territory of Texas became the nation's second-largest state in the nineteenth century. My family has been involved in civic and public service, too: my great-grandfather was a state judge in the 1860s, and my grandfather, Captain Baker, played a critical role in the founding of Rice University in Houston and in the establishment and growth of many of Houston's premier civic organizations.

But politics was something altogether different. Captain Baker's advice to those who wanted to be good lawyers was, "Work hard, study, and keep out of politics." And for the first forty years of my life, that's exactly what I did.* But when Mary Stuart became ill and died, George Bush reached out

---

*After graduating with honors from the University of Texas School of Law, I might have gone to work in the family law firm, Baker & Botts, but at the time the firm had an anti-nepotism

to me to help with his senatorial campaign, and from then on I was hooked. For the next two decades, politics and public policy were my passion, and by the time I became Secretary of State, I had seen American politics from almost every angle and had learned the art of political strategy from the ground up.

Common Sense and Foreign Policy

All of that stood me in good stead when I became Secretary of State. Not that I approached the international aspects of my job lightly. Despite the practical background in foreign policy I had acquired as President Reagan's Chief of Staff and Secretary of the Treasury, I spent November 1988 through January 1989 assiduously studying the issues. Bob Kimmitt remembers me calling him at 6:30 A.M. on a Sunday, asking what "carry-hard" was, an obscure arms-control concept. He had a chance to utter two explanatory sentences before I said, "That's it, thanks," and hung up. I sat through a briefing by every sitting undersecretary and assistant secretary of state and many prospective ones, had my immediate transition staff (basically my inner circle, plus Jim Cicconi, who went on to be staff secretary at the White House) prepare strategy papers on specific issues, and memorized glossaries on arms control and listings of presidents, prime ministers, and foreign ministers. (There was no way I was going to let any senator embarrass me the way Bill Clark had been embarrassed when he was nominated to be Deputy Secretary of State in 1981 and didn't know the leaders of Zimbabwe and South Africa.)

For all that, however, I would argue that theoretical knowledge is not an absolute necessity for success as Secretary of State, because at its core, the Secretary of State's job is political, just on an international stage. To the untrained eye, foreign policy seems devoid of political considerations. After all, it is far more bipartisan than domestic or economic policy, and diplomatic idioms are intentionally designed to obfuscate conflict. But as Secretary of State, I always had to think of at least three political dimensions to any proposal: Will we be able to build a domestic consensus in support of it?

---

rule, so instead I joined Andrews & Kurth, another major Houston firm, where I worked hard and stayed out of politics. I've often said how disappointed I was at the time not to be offered a job at Baker & Botts because, growing up, I had been convinced that it was the best law firm in the country—and because the firm actually voted at that time (1957) about making a first-time exception to the nepotism rule, since I had an academic record to justify it. I've also said that it would have been the biggest mistake of my life. If I succeeded, it would have been said that I did so because of my father. If I failed, it would've been said: What did you expect? He's only here because of his father.

What kind of political reaction will it create in the capitals of our adversaries and allies? And, finally, how will it change the nature of our political relations internationally?

As a Cabinet secretary, you focus not on the technical side of governing but on the political. You don't resolve questions solely on the basis of their political impact and you don't make decisions solely because of their political popularity, but you do make decisions, push initiatives, avoid disasters, and develop strategies with those consequences firmly in mind. I had been thinking and planning that way at a national level ever since I'd been chairman of President Ford's campaign in 1976, and I believe strongly that most political strategy, whether local, national, or international, is nothing more than common sense—the transformation of ideas into action in light of certain realities and in pursuit of specific goals.

In this regard, I have always been more comfortable with action than with reflection. Personally and professionally, for as long as I can remember, my inclination has been to go out and get things done rather than sit around and think about them. It's not that I disdain the contemplative life or the world of ideas. Indeed, in law school, my professors taught me the raw power of logic through the never-ending Socratic dialogues we held in class. I learned that an argument could be a fine-edged scalpel that could hone down and cut away flabby ideas that obscured the main point. But the important part to me was that there had to be a point: the argument had to have a purpose, a goal, a reason for being. If not, it was just a bunch of idle thought that folded back on itself, and what was the use of that?

If forced into a category, I guess you'd call me a realist. As an undergraduate, I had written my senior thesis on the conflict within the British Labour Party between Aneurin Bevan and Ernest Bevin (who eventually went on to become Foreign Secretary). The split between Bevan and Bevin symbolized the division between the true socialists and what in a European context might be called social democrats, but for me the split was even more fundamental: it was between idealists and realists. I admired Bevin. "Bevin was not interested in theories, but in practicalities," I wrote. "He knew that when men were unemployed they wanted bread and work, not an oration on the coming revolution. Bevin believed in solving the problems of the present before tackling the problems of the future. The solution of the immediate difficulty outweighed consideration of the long-term goal." To Bevan, I was less charitable, arguing that he and his followers' greatest weakness was their "lack of concessions to reality," and stating assuredly, as only an undergraduate can, "One is left with the impression that these left-wingers resolve a planetary crisis by a discussion on the advantages of free false teeth."

My study of the law probably reinforced my emphasis on action over contemplation, and that's how it's been ever since. My legal training left me in good standing when I entered the world of politics and public policy. When you enter government, you do so with certain beliefs and values, and your task is to turn them into enduring realities consistent with your interests. That, of course, inevitably leads to conflicts with others who hold different values and beliefs and have different interests. And it is the clash of ideas (usually in the form of policy) intermixed with battles over interests and values (usually expressed as politics) that are the real battlegrounds of Washington. I found that common sense was an effective guide to action.

Yet in a far more profound way, I was fortunate to become Secretary of State when I did—at a time when long-held beliefs about grand strategy were being turned upside down. The simple fact is that from 1989 to 1992, the world underwent a revolution. The world as we had known it changed markedly, and in the midst of such a revolution, most long-held assumptions and strategies had to be changed radically, if not junked altogether. Coming into office with a relatively open and flexible frame of mind, I think I was ready to roll with the changes better than others might have been. As Dennis Ross wrote me on December 16, 1988, the President-elect "says we should dream big dreams, and he's right. We're entering a period that is really unlike any we've seen through the whole postwar era, and this is not the time to put our thinking in a straitjacket. Perhaps we won't realize our dreams, but we won't even have the potential to explore them if we don't stretch our minds and accept the importance of thinking unconventionally."

Ross was responding to a proposal from Henry Kissinger that we discuss Eastern Europe with Moscow—using Henry, of course, as a back channel. Characteristically, Roz Ridgway, then Assistant Secretary of State for European Affairs, and Tom Simons, her principal deputy, had poured scorn on the idea, whereas Ross had argued that sooner rather than later, we'd have to discuss the region with the Soviets—not to split the area up into "spheres of influence," but to prevent crises and manage the transition to democracy. I ended up favoring this approach and raised Eastern Europe in my second meeting with Shevardnadze in May, even though I myself had poured cold water on the Kissinger proposal in the *New York Times* on March 28. I had done so because I didn't want anyone thinking we were going to pursue the "spheres of influence" approach, which was how most Europeans interpreted Kissinger's proposal. Furthermore, since there are no secrets in Washington, if we were going to have such discussions, we wanted to do them through the front channel, directly with Gorbachev and Shevardnadze, and to make it quite clear that we were *not* opting for a Yalta II approach. The contrast in the advice I received from people within the department gave me an inkling that some of them were not going to keep pace with the events that were about to transform the globe.

What I Hoped to Do

I found one critical distinction between my previous political experience and the task ahead of me as Secretary of State. In my other jobs, the overriding objective had either been set by the structure of the situation or was relatively clear in any case. In political campaigns, it had been to win elections; in the White House, it had been to govern, to implement the President's agenda, to work successfully with Congress to pass legislation, and, finally, to ensure his reelection; and at Treasury, it had been to advance America's financial and economic interests both domestically and internationally.

But at the State Department, the objective of our work was far more amorphous. Foreign policy goals involved everything from trying to whittle down the Soviets' massive conventional military advantage in Europe to attempting to jump-start the Middle East peace process, to pursuing an end to the drift-net fishing that was depleting the fish stocks of the oceans of the world. The danger that my in-box or any day's incoming cable would become the driving force behind our policy was all too real—and I was warned about it by every predecessor with whom I met.

The more I thought about it during the transition, the more I understood that the central focus of my job initially had to be U.S.-Soviet relations. As the first long-term planning paper I read on the Soviets put it, "The Soviet Union is a Great Power in decline. By virtually every indicator, Soviet power is waning. As Secretary of State, your central task in East-West relations will be to manage the international effects of this decline productively and peacefully." If I could assist the Soviet empire in a "soft landing," so to speak, the opportunities for the expansion of democracy and free markets and the resolution of regional conflicts would be almost endless. But if reform stalled or were reversed, at a minimum America would have to contend with a very unstable international environment. In the worst case, we could see a cold war become a hot one.

In the face of these realities, my strategic logic was straightforward. All along, containment had been premised on the notion that the more leverage we could exert on the Soviets, the more we could pressure them to make the hard choice in favor of internal change—what Ambassador George Kennan, the primary author of containment, had called "the gradual mellowing of power." And the path to maximizing our leverage began not in negotiations with Moscow but with a consensus in Washington. The more unified and bipartisan American policy was, the more unified and cohesive would be the Western Alliance writ large. The stronger West-West ties were, the more leverage this would put on Moscow to adapt peacefully to the realities of its decline. And the more we could move the Soviet Union toward our interests and values, the better.

Consequently, in my thinking, I approached the world of 1989 from the "inside out," much the way I had approached politics and government. I started with an overall notion of where we wanted to go, and worked backward from that goal, beginning with those institutions that we had to control or influence the most in order to achieve our objective: first, the immediate bureaucracy; second, the Congress; and third, the press. Once we had done what we could in this regard, we would work on ensuring our "continental base" (relations with Canada, Mexico, and Central America), then strengthening and, where necessary, expanding our alliances across the Atlantic and Pacific. (Bob Zoellick convinced me that thinking in terms of "concentric circles" was the most useful way to proceed.)

Immediate Tasks

The first task, as I told an initial cabinet meeting on January 23, 1989, was to rebuild bipartisanship. That required building strong ties with Congress. My relations there were quite good. I had spent the previous eight years working closely with members of both houses on both sides of the aisle—so much so that, in introducing me at my confirmation hearing, Senator Lloyd Bentsen referred to President Reagan's 1986 tax reform bill, which I had championed as Secretary of the Treasury, and said, "Jim Baker consulted so much with us at times, we'd thought we had quite enough of Jim Baker."

I knew the key to bipartisanship was to resolve the dispute over Central America. In Nicaragua, the seven-year war of the contras against the Sandinistas was at a stalemate, and with Congress continuing to refuse any new military funding for the contras, I knew that there was no acceptable military solution to the conflict. In El Salvador, after nine years of fighting, the rebels held one-third of the country but they, too, seemed incapable of winning. It had been a decade of frustration in the region and in Washington. I knew we had to find a way to get Central America behind us if we were to be able to deal aggressively with the decline of Soviet power. Moreover, it was an obstacle to the continued growth of democracy in all of Latin America. Without doubt, it was my first priority.

My next objective, to put it into political terms, was "securing our base," which meant ensuring good relations with Canada and Mexico. During the Reagan administration, Prime Minister Brian Mulroney had been a steadfast friend of the United States and had grown very close to George Bush. Through our efforts at Treasury, we had concluded the Canadian

Free Trade Agreement in 1987, and even while we had been negotiating the Canadian FTA we had thought about the benefits of expanding it to a continent-wide free-trade zone. Part of our interest was driven by concerns about the European integration slated for 1992, but an even more critical reason was our regard for President Carlos Salinas de Gortari of Mexico. Just elected, President Salinas was an economist by training, and committed to free-market reforms. President Bush agreed to meet with him very early, before either had been sworn in, and on November 22, 1988, at Ellington Air Force Base in Houston, we established what we called the "Spirit of Houston." Salinas was extremely outgoing and friendly, clearly anxious to have the very best of relations with the United States, and told us that he was going to name the finance minister, Gustavo Petrocelli, to be his new Ambassador to the United States. As Treasury Secretary, I had negotiated debt issues with Petrocelli, and it was obvious that Salinas was going out of his way to start the relationship on a positive note.

The President and I also wanted to stress relations with Mexico because it was one foreign-policy issue with a direct connection to domestic politics. Two other issues—South Africa and Middle East peace—were also on my early agenda because of their domestic and international ramifications. During my consultations, Senator Paul Simon told me he felt that South Africa could explode, and if that occurred, it could lead to rioting in New York, Chicago, and other American cities. I wasn't so much worried about that possibility as I was intrigued by the idea of moving beyond sanctions. Two years of congressionally mandated sanctions had done little to bring about a peaceful transition to a nonracial democracy, and I felt there might be a chance to establish a more productive working relationship with the Congress, which in turn could be used to encourage change on the part of the regime in Pretoria. I knew I would also have to keep an early and attentive eye on the Middle East. While I didn't want to become immediately bogged down in shuttle diplomacy, the Middle East had been the world's most conflict-ridden region since World War II, and President Bush planned to continue the Reagan administration's strong support for Israel. Like almost everyone else, I assumed that with Iraq and Iran exhausted and impoverished from their decade-long war, the Persian Gulf would be relatively quiet.

Revitalizing the Western Coalition

Nineteen eighty-nine would be the fortieth anniversary of NATO. Despite the fact that the Atlantic Alliance had been the most successful coalition in history, we were concerned that the more reform advanced (or was perceived to have advanced) in the Soviet Union, the more difficult it would be to maintain Western cohesion. That's why during the 1988 campaign, then–Vice President Bush had proposed an early NATO summit. The world was being transformed from one in which fears of the Soviet threat maintained the unity of the Western Alliance to one in which the centripetal forces operating on the West were likely to be just as strong as the centrifugal ones. I realized that one of my central tasks as Secretary of State would be to manage the transformation.

Obviously, as we went about adapting NATO, we would also have to work with the growing power of the European Community (EC), which was slated to become a single market in 1992. Many Americans (as well as other North Americans and Asians) were quite concerned at the time that "EC92" would lead to an inward-looking European political and economic bloc, walled off from the rest of the West. To avoid this, we looked to establish early links with the EC. I also became convinced that, while nothing could replace our "special relationship" with London, power within Europe was shifting to Bonn, not only economically but also because of the openings being created with the East Europeans. Strong U.S.-German ties, therefore, would also become critical to managing transatlantic relations.

At Treasury, Tokyo had required a lot of my attention, particularly on market-opening and exchange-rate issues. I had called for a "global partnership" with Japan while still Secretary of the Treasury, but now at State I could actually implement it. Of course, I would once again have to be mindful of domestic considerations, as Japan-bashing had become a prominent Democratic campaign theme, notably in the primary campaign of Representative Dick Gephardt. Our goal had to be to try to turn Japan from an inward-looking, mercantilist economic giant to an outward-looking economic and political power with strong ties to the United States.

Elsewhere in the region, China was obviously going to be one of the President's personal priorities since he had served as head of our liaison mission there in the 1970s. Little did we expect China to become such a contentious domestic issue, but then I don't think anyone expected what happened at Tiananmen Square in June 1989.

We were also interested in pursuing a broader pan-Pacific organization that would include the small but economically powerful Asian "tigers": Taiwan, Singapore, Hong Kong, Thailand, South Korea, Indonesia, and Malaysia. At Treasury, we had held trade and currency discussions with three of these governments—Taiwan, Singapore, and Hong Kong—and Zoellick and I had discussions at Treasury in 1988 with one of my key international aides, Bob Fauver, about developing this idea of a Pacific organization further. At State, we brought Fauver into the East Asia and Pacific Bureau (EAP) to develop trans-Pacific cooperation. Consequently, when Bob Hawke, the Australian Prime Minister, proposed APEC—the Asia Pacific

Economic Cooperation forum—we welcomed his initiative and sought to strengthen this nascent group.

The relative paucity of working institutions is often overlooked when discussing international relations. In domestic society, institutions are so prevalent that we take them for granted, but in the global arena, there are really not that many, the United Nations and NATO being the most prominent. Without institutions, it's hard to get work done because all your consultations have to be done bilaterally; with an institution, you create a forum for consultation and can greatly expand cooperation. Thus, much of our time at State was spent creating new institutions (APEC), adapting old ones (NATO), or creating interim quasi-institutional arrangements (for example, the "Two-plus-Four" process for German unification).

Managing the Crumbling of Communism

My working assumption was that once we had developed a bipartisan approach to foreign policy and had forged a Western consensus, we would pursue a tripartite approach to the Soviet empire. The first avenue would be direct discussions with Moscow. Premised on continued Soviet decline, our strategy was one of discreet, measured reciprocity. But we couldn't afford to wait for Soviet initiatives; instead, we would need to advance proposals that made sense strategically, but which would also be understandable and acceptable to Western publics. Gorbachev's strategy was to weaken Western cohesion through high-profile, publicly attractive proposals and thus to gain economic benefits from the West. We wanted to attack his strategy by having proposals of our own—initiatives designed to open the Soviet system to Western influence, to institutionalize stability and predictability and prevent a reversal of reform, and finally to foster what we euphemistically called "legitimate political arrangements" in the USSR. By that we meant "democratization," but we didn't want to set off a political firestorm in Moscow by being so direct about our intentions.

Our push for democratization in Eastern Europe—the second element—was more pronounced. There we wanted to be more aggressive in assisting the reformers—not just with economic assistance (which oftentimes could be counterproductive) but also by supporting reformers politically and by engaging Moscow. Much as Gorbachev was trying to take advantage of Washington by playing to Western Europe, we wanted to "play offense" by focusing on Eastern Europe. From the outset, we saw the potential in Eastern Europe for democracy and free markets. There was an organic link between reform in Eastern Europe and the Soviet Union; rather quickly, we developed at least a tacit division of labor with our Western allies, whereby Germany and others would focus on economic assistance to the East Europeans and Soviets, while we would focus more on ensuring shifts in what the Soviets called the "correlation of forces," by working to demilitarize Soviet foreign policy and push Gorbachev on political reform.

The third element of this strategy involved regional conflicts. The Reagan Doctrine had aimed at rolling back Soviet beachheads around the globe, and had succeeded very well. My sense was that besides continuing the pressure on Soviet clients, we could use elections as a tool to dislodge them. The trend toward democracy in the 1980s had been strong, and Gorbachev's own emphasis on glasnost (or openness) and elections made the Kremlin susceptible to the argument that if elections were good enough for Moscow, they would be good enough for its clients in Nicaragua, Angola, Afghanistan, and Cambodia. In essence, we were reaping the success of the Reagan Doctrine, which called for the rollback of Communist regimes in the Third World—by force, if necessary. With most of these regimes already under siege, we were now able to turn to elections as the mechanism for making a peaceful transition to democracy.

Preparing for the Post–Cold War World

While the President and I realized our central mission was to end the Cold War, we also began preparing for the post–Cold War world. To a great degree, this involved either adapting or creating institutions, but it also meant that we would have to begin developing longer-term strategies for dealing with an emerging class of transnational problems that didn't fit into traditional categories: terrorism, narcotics, the environment, and non-proliferation of weapons of mass destruction. But I knew that if we were going to have any chance of tackling these, we were going to have to have the Congress and the American people behind us—and that meant first dispensing with Central America as the continuing obstacle to bipartisanship.

CHAPTER 4

REBUILDING BIPARTISANSHIP:

LANCING THE CENTRAL AMERICAN BOIL

This has been the most implacable issue of the last eight years. Also the most politically polarizing and personally divisive question on the entire agenda.
—*House Speaker Jim Wright to President-elect Bush, November 18, 1988*

I suspect that every new President and Secretary of State arrive at their posts with the cherished hope that they can pursue diplomacy in the spirit of Senator Arthur Vandenberg's dictum: "In foreign policy, all politics stops at the water's edge." George Bush and I were no different. As we discussed foreign policy plans during the transition, the President made it clear that he wanted to move away from the politics of confrontation between the executive and legislative branches that had characterized much of the diplomatic debate in the previous eight years. I made a point of underscoring his commitment in my confirmation hearings. "In order to succeed," I said, "we simply *must* work together."

In examining American foreign policy throughout the postwar era, one truth certainly shines through: from President Truman's support for the North Atlantic Treaty Organization to President Reagan's agreement on intermediate-range nuclear forces in Europe, every important achievement has enjoyed sustained bipartisan support. With East-West relations ripe for new solutions, bipartisanship seemed even more a necessity.

It was clear to us both, however, that there was one huge stumbling block to any hope of restoring bipartisanship: the bleeding sore of Central America. By any measure, the struggle for democracy in that troubled region, delineated most dramatically in the conflict between the Sandinista government of Nicaragua and the U.S.-funded resistance known as the "contras," was our country's Vietnam of the 1980s.

No other foreign-policy issue was so visceral or polarizing. For much of the decade, it had been the Holy Grail of both the political left and the right. To the conservatives, the Sandinistas were a Soviet beachhead in Central America, and the Monroe Doctrine required their removal. But Democratic opposition to President Reagan's preference for a military solution had resulted in 1983 congressional prohibitions against direct or indirect lethal aid to the contras. An effort to circumvent these bans in turn spawned the disastrous Iran-contra affair which, when it was disclosed in 1986, diminished the Reagan presidency and left George Bush a legacy of enormous suspicion and distrust.

The conflict between the executive and legislative branches was hardly confined to the Democratic opposition, however. I recall one afternoon in 1983, when President Reagan invited the Republican congressional leadership to the White House residence to discuss the legislative agenda. At some point, the discussion turned to Central America. House Minority Leader Bob Michel complained in his quiet, understated midwestern way about CIA director William Casey's relations with Congress. Michel didn't want to say outright that many in Congress mistrusted Bill Casey, so he chose to couch his reservations in a common complaint about Casey's legendary penchant for mumbling. It was hard to know what was really happening with policy, Michel observed, when you could scarcely understand Casey most of the time.

"To tell you the truth, Bob," President Reagan replied, "*I* can't understand Bill half the time myself."

"Mr. President," Senate Majority Leader Howard Baker chimed in, "that's the scariest thing I've ever heard."

As President-elect Bush prepared to assume office, the prevailing view within the foreign policy establishment was that democracy in Nicaragua was a lost cause. Even with military aid (which Congress would never approve anyway), the contras were no match for the Sandinista army. In this view, the best that might be managed was a policy of containment that kept the Sandinistas from exporting their Marxism to neighboring democracies.

I disagreed with this judgment. Containment would never work without the deterrent of an armed contra force just across the border in Honduras. I also believed the Sandinistas would be less adventuresome in their own foreign policy if we tied them up internally with constant pressure for democratic reforms, including free and fair elections. Moreover, with Gorbachev and his policy of "new thinking" firmly in power in the Kremlin, I believed a diplomatic solution to the Central American quagmire might be possible—but not without Moscow's help. Richard Nixon had warned me that Central America was insoluble unless Gorbachev could be induced to stop military aid to Nicaragua. George Bush wanted to test the Soviets, but a unified position at home was a prerequisite. We couldn't credibly argue to the Soviets that their behavior in Central America was the greatest stumbling block to improved relations unless Congress and the President were speaking with one voice on hemispheric policy.

In Search of a New Policy

This, I knew, would be no easy matter. In my courtesy calls with members of Congress during the winter of 1988, I was sobered by the unanimity of advice I received when the subject turned to Central America. To a member, they all told me that if George Bush followed through on his campaign pledge to ask for military aid for the contras, he would be voted down convincingly. The view of Lee Hamilton, the chairman of the House Foreign Affairs Committee, was typical. "I know we have an obligation to the contras," he said, "but they're a weak reed. A request for military aid would precipitate one helluva fight." Bob Michel was even more emphatic, advising me that it was simply hopeless.

At the same time, I was heartened by what seemed to be a genuine sense of good will toward the President-elect. "You have a great chance to reinvigorate a bipartisan foreign policy," Senator Joe Biden told me. "Everybody here likes you and George Bush—in spite of your tough campaign. We have respect for you both. I want you to know I'm ready to be enlisted in a bipartisan foreign policy approach." Biden added that he wanted to work with me to create some mechanism for closer consultation with the White House on foreign policy matters.

Senator John Kerry, a leading liberal and a committed foe of the contras, also urged me to pursue a centrist policy that could achieve a rough consensus on the issue. "Only a united approach will ever sway Ortega," he argued. Even the most ardent opponent of the Reagan policy, Senator Christopher Dodd of Connecticut, impressed me as being prepared to be conciliatory.

Not long after the election, Susan and I were invited to dinner at the home of our old friends Bob and Helen Strauss. The guest list included Speaker of the House Jim Wright and his wife Betty. Wright was every bit as partisan a Democrat as his predecessor, Tip O'Neill. But I'd worked with him for years when he was majority leader and knew he was open to reason. After dinner, the conversation inevitably turned to Central America, where Wright had been a vehement critic of Reagan administration policy in Nicaragua, but supportive of U.S. aid to El Salvador. I told him that the President-elect wanted to get Central America off the domestic political agenda and that he wouldn't ask Congress for military aid to the contras. In that case, Wright said, we had a real chance of forging a bipartisan solution.

I'd supported the Reagan policy of sustaining the contras, and still did. But I returned to my transition offices at the State Department from all these encounters convinced that Central America was first and foremost a domestic political issue. Any hopes for a diplomatic solution, much less achieving a bipartisan foreign policy, were doomed unless Central America was removed from its domestic political context. I also believed that the President had a window of opportunity to do precisely that.

But there was precious little time for maneuver. On March 31, only ten weeks after the President's inauguration, humanitarian aid to the contras would expire. I knew Congress would never approve funds to rearm them. Without humanitarian aid and a prompt resolution of the matter, their survival as a credible counterweight to the Sandinistas was unlikely, and the acrimony of the last decade would continue, poisoning our hopes for a cooperative foreign policy.

A Brief Personal and Diplomatic History

My view of how to approach the Central American issue was shaped not only by my preference for a bipartisan foreign policy that could help lead to free elections in Nicaragua, but also by my experiences as President Reagan's Chief of Staff. From that vantage point, I had observed firsthand the slugfests that were waged among George Shultz, Cap Weinberger, Bill Casey, and Jeane Kirkpatrick for policy dominance. I had also been intimately involved in our legislative efforts to support the government of El Salvador against Cuban- and Sandinista-backed guerrilla forces, and to fund the contras amid enormous congressional opposition. I was also aware, of course, of the covert operations in Nicaragua authorized by the President and run by the Central Intelligence Agency during this period. As required by law, these actions were fully briefed to the appropriate members of Congress—the majority of whom disapproved. This opposition precipitated even more congressional funding restrictions in 1984.

I had no desire to further the debilitating ideological warfare of that period, and neither did my boss. George Bush's support for the contras—and mine—was a principled one, but we recognized that while Central America was in many respects *the* cause of the Republican right, we didn't have the votes to restore military aid. We had also seen firsthand the costs of all the fratricide to a coherent and sustainable policy. He agreed that it was critical to our overall foreign policy goals and our ability to conduct a successful foreign policy to remove this issue from the domestic political arena.

One of my first personnel decisions was designed to reinforce our commitment to bipartisanship in fairly dramatic fashion. Shortly after my appointment, Republican Congressman Henry Hyde of Illinois, a strong conservative and fervent contra supporter, urged me to appoint Bernard Aronson as the Assistant Secretary of State for Inter-American Affairs (ARA). I knew Bernie Aronson was a rare breed—a bona fide Democrat who supported aid to the contras. A former White House aide in the Carter administration, Aronson had traveled to Central America and was quite knowledgeable about the region, and in 1986, at the request of White House communications director Patrick Buchanan, he had written a speech for President Reagan about Central America that called for bipartisanship and a more conciliatory approach. A meeting with Bob Zoellick and a memorandum from Aronson only added to our favorable impression.

"The conventional wisdom that Central America will likely be divisive and contentious for the new administration is not necessarily true," Aronson argued. "On both sides of the aisle, members of Congress are wearied from the divisive battles over contra aid and are not eager to repeat them. The administration, in fact, has a rare opportunity to build a new bipartisan base for its Central American policy in Congress and among opinion leaders, but it needs to seize that opportunity early."

He elaborated on this thesis in a private conversation shortly after I was sworn in as Secretary of State. Aronson told me that both sides were simply too rigid ever to reach a middle ground themselves. The key to defusing the issue was through a bipartisan approach grounded in a commitment to promoting democratic elections in Nicaragua, not simply ousting the Sandinistas. If the administration persisted in pressing forward with military aid to the contras, the President would be embarrassed in his first major foreign-policy test, and lose credibility at home and in the region. But if we gave diplomacy a chance by supporting existing regional agreements, he argued, a compromise with the Democrats was entirely possible, and our policy in the region would be strengthened by unity at home. He also suggested that we make Central America a test of Gorbachev's policy of "new thinking."

In the space of a half hour, Aronson impressed me as a bright, articulate centrist more interested in results than ideology. In style and temperament, he was in stark contrast to Elliott Abrams, his equally bright but pugnacious predecessor who had become a bête noire to congressional Democrats. Halfway through this meeting, I knew that Aronson would be an ideal choice for the ARA job. I offered it to him, and a few days later he accepted.

I knew that a few Republicans would oppose Bernie's nomination, so I talked the idea over with the President, who was enthusiastic, on the merits as well as the symbolism. I was encouraged to learn that most of the congressional Democratic leadership privately urged Aronson to take the job.

In spite of occasional efforts to poison the well against him by some members of the Vice President's staff and the National Security Council, who privately whispered that he was a double agent, Bernie did an excellent job.

Esquipulas Presents a Vehicle

Fortunately, a mechanism already existed around which to create a new diplomatic opening. By the middle of President Reagan's second term, his determination to oust the Sandinistas by force had prompted regional leaders to attempt to broker their own diplomatic solution. Led by President Oscar Arias Sanchez of Costa Rica, this effort culminated in the 1987 accord signed in Esquipulas, Guatemala, by the presidents of Costa Rica, El Salvador, Guatemala, Nicaragua, and Honduras. The most important of its provisions were the calls for a cease-fire between the Sandinistas and the contras and for "free, pluralistic, and fair elections" in all the signatory countries.

On the eve of this declaration, the Reagan administration endorsed the cease-fire concept and said it would suspend aid to the contras if the Soviets halted military aid to the Sandinistas within sixty days. Speaker Wright, who had endorsed the White House initiative forty-eight hours earlier, abruptly shifted his support to the Esquipulas accord.

The Reagan administration had rejected an earlier and slightly different version of Esquipulas as fatally flawed, and asked Congress for more military aid to the contras. Then, apparently believing that Esquipulas would eventually force a diplomatic solution the Reagan administration would be powerless to stop, the Sandinistas began modest steps toward implementing the terms of that accord in late 1987. These measures gave congressional Democrats just enough political camouflage to maintain their opposition to contra aid. In February of 1988, Congress voted down $36 million in aid, even though only $3.6 million had been earmarked for military assistance.

As a result, the contras had little choice but to agree to a cease-fire with the Sandinistas in March. Congress quickly approved $48 million in nonlethal humanitarian aid for the contras through September, then appropriated $27 million more to keep the 12,000 contras supplied in their safe havens in Honduras until March 31, 1989.

Less than a month after President Bush's inauguration, the Arias group met again at Costa del Sol in El Salvador and announced that the Sandinistas had agreed to hold a Presidential election by February 25, 1990. In exchange, the five presidents agreed to formulate a plan within ninety days to demobilize the contras.

The President and I were skeptical that the government of Daniel Ortega would ever permit the sort of free elections envisioned by Arias. But Esquipulas was nevertheless an opportune vehicle around which to fashion a new policy. Its call for democratic reforms, elections, and an end to regional subversion was politically unassailable. The fact that the Sandinistas had agreed to it was at least symbolically significant. Perhaps most important of all, it was an arrangement negotiated by the parties themselves, not something forced upon them by the *norteamericanos*. If the President had proposed such an accord, our congressional opponents would have dismissed it out of hand. But its origin from the region itself gave Esquipulas a pedigree which we could use to our advantage.

Into the Congressional Maelstrom

The magnitude of the problem in selling a new policy was succinctly framed in a February 7 memorandum from Aronson. "There is no trust between the opponents of contra aid and the Executive, just the opposite," Aronson wrote. "There is deep suspicion." I would soon learn that this was in fact an understatement. This debate was like a food fight that had gone on for years. It had degenerated into raw confrontation, with no quarter given or asked. Policy differences had become subordinated by the primal desire of both sides to "get" the other. The degree of mutual hostility and venom between the warring factions was extraordinary. And the philosophical gulf was so enormous that one could argue it was the domestic equivalent of sitting Israel and the Arabs down in the same room and attempting to resolve their differences in nine weeks.

Both sides were populated with members who had enormous personal equity in the issue and absolutely no desire to work anything out. The diehards on the right wanted to force a vote on military aid, calculating that its preordained failure would give them an excuse to blame the liberals for the death of democracy in Nicaragua. They viewed the very idea of a bipartisan approach as a secret plot by the President and me to appease the Sandinistas. Conversely, the liberals thought it was nothing less than a plot to save the contras through some semantic trickery. In many instances, the ideological intensity of the principals paled by comparison to the zeal and rigidity of their staffs, many of whom had been traveling to the region for years, and cutting policy deals on the side with various factions to the dispute.

Bridging this chasm, I knew, would require a creative, centrist blend of idealism and realism. Abandoning the contras was morally and politically unconscionable to me, but we would ask for humanitarian aid only to keep them intact as a credible deterrent in the event of diplomatic stalemate. At the same time, we would embrace the Esquipulas accord and seek to give it teeth through a series of carrots and sticks aimed at the Sandinistas. Our policy would be more or less stringent, depending on the degree to which the Ortega government followed through on its pledges.

These incentives and parallel disincentives had another purpose: to provide a framework for congressional consensus. The list was carefully calibrated to include at least a few measures we believed could be embraced by every member of Congress. Only a menu of actions appealing to the broadest possible constituency had a chance to transcend the enmities of this issue on Capitol Hill.

In concert with these actions, we would also press the Soviets to remove all East Bloc military advisers from Nicaragua and to terminate all military assistance to the Managua government and to press Cuba not to rearm the Sandinistas.

This policy was the only chance I saw to retrieve the moral high ground. With its emphasis on a military solution, the existing policy had in effect ceded the ground of "peace" and "negotiations" to the opposition. President Reagan correctly called the contras "freedom fighters," but it was difficult to maintain public support for a rebel army's effort to overthrow a government, even one as anathema as the Sandinistas. I believed the American people would support a policy that refocused the debate on democratic principles. In simple terms, the Democrats couldn't very well oppose a policy that endorsed elections—and neither could the most ardent contra supporters.

At its tactical core, this approach had the appeal of abandoning the strategy of pure and simple confrontation which had previously characterized—and traumatized—the relationship between the Reagan administration and congressional critics. Moreover, as it turned out, it was a good fit for my skills. This was first and foremost a political dispute requiring delicate and disciplined negotiating, a predilection that two decades of legal experience and my years at the White House had honed. I also believed that I had forged a relationship of trust with many members of Congress in my previous incarnations that might overcome the aura of suspicion and ill will of the past eight years on this issue. It was a huge roll of the dice. But I suspected there was a better than even chance to reach an accommodation.

Shuttle Diplomacy on Capitol Hill

It struck me as ironic that my first major negotiation as Secretary of State was not with a foreign power but with our own legislative branch. But the experience would prove just as arduous and delicate an exercise as anything I would later encounter in my dealings with other countries. The twenty-two days of negotiations with congressional leaders were intense, partisan, and frequently acrimonious. What would stretch into more than forty hours of talks began on the afternoon of March 2, when I unveiled our proposal to a group of ten House Republican leaders and staff in the office of Bob Michel. I handed each of them an eight-page top-secret memorandum summarizing the policy we had in mind. At the end of the meeting, I collected every copy except Michel's, a procedure I'd repeat in every session with congressional leaders.

An appendix to the document laid out a list of twenty "rewards for positive performance" by the Sandinistas and parallel "negative incentives for non-compliance" with the Esquipulas agreement. The list was carefully linked to Sandinista performance. For instance, if Managua revised electoral laws by the end of April as promised, we would allow Nicaraguan diplomats at the United Nations to travel around the country without prior notification. If opposition parties were allowed to register by the end of August, we might scale back U.S. military exercises in Honduras. And if a free and fair election actually occurred in February of 1990, the United States would cease efforts to persuade Japan and our European allies to cut off their aid to Nicaragua. On the other hand, if the election was fraudulent, we would consider asking Congress to renew military aid to the contras. The idea was to put the onus for opposing a democratic solution where it belonged—on the Sandinistas.

I walked from this meeting to the other side of the Capitol to meet with Senate Republicans. Bob Dole began the session by saying, "Now, let Jim tell you what these guys want to do." For the most part they were supportive but subdued. Only Jesse Helms of North Carolina, who wanted military aid for the contras, opposed a diplomatic effort.

"I support military aid to the contras, too," I told Helms. "There's just one problem. You can't get the votes for it and I can't get the votes for it. Even Ronald Reagan couldn't get the votes for it. But we *can* get the votes for this."

The next morning, I met with House and Senate Democratic leaders. Protocol and prudence had dictated that I consult with members of my own party first. But as a practical matter, I understood that the support of the Democrats who were the majority was more critical. If I could persuade the skeptical opposition to go along with this approach, the Republicans would have no choice but to follow, despite any reservations.

"This issue has divided our country and poisoned our politics for many years," I told the Democrats. "We want to and must put that behind us." But for diplomacy to succeed, I said, "we must speak with one voice. We can't have one, two, or three policies towards Central America. That demoralizes our friends and comforts our enemies."

I summarized the policy, emphasizing those elements, such as support for elections and democratization, that I knew would be more appealing than more contra aid. "I know there's a good deal of mistrust left over from the past. Let me lay our cards on the table. We have no hidden agenda. We want this diplomacy to work and we will work hard and in good faith to make it work."

The collective Democratic reactions made it clear they were amenable to compromise, but still suspicious of my motives. As Chris Dodd put it, "The issue is not just a diplomatic approach, but whether it's pursued in good faith."

I knew that the only way to persuade them that the President and I had no ulterior motives was to level with them. "Look," I told Dodd, "I'd actually prefer military aid to the contras. But we realize that's not in the cards, so I'm not even going to ask for it. This is not a scheme or a trick. We want to try diplomacy, but it won't work without the leverage of a unified approach."

I emerged from this first round of meetings with pledges of general support for the President's plan, and cheered by the body language. Even the most ideological Democrats were taking great pains to set a new tone of civility. But there were large gulfs to be navigated and narrowed, and in the next three weeks, as I shuttled between Republican and Democratic caucuses, there were times I was convinced the process would collapse as a result of the ideological rigidity that had inflamed the policy debate for the better part of a decade.

I recall walking out of one negotiating session with one of my team. We were suddenly accosted by two members of Dodd's staff who were so angry that the veins in their necks were bulging. They were enraged that the current version of a draft agreement contained *two* references to the need for democratic reforms in Nicaragua. "This is a direct provocation," one of them sputtered. "You're trying to rub their noses in it." I might as well have been in a corridor at Berkeley in the 1960s.

As I'd expected, nobody objected to squeezing the Soviets and the Sandinistas. The most difficult issue, predictably, was aid to the contras. The Democrats essentially wanted to earmark any such aid only for "relocating" the contras, a euphemism for disbanding them, which Republicans would never accept—and shouldn't. Relocation aid, Jesse Helms thundered, was nothing more than a sellout. My terminology of choice was "reintegration." I wanted funds to help the contras return to their homes in Nicaragua if conditions actually improved, as the Sandinistas had promised. In any event, I thought it necessary to maintain the contras in Honduras in a state of military readiness for at least a year to keep the pressure on Managua.

This impasse required some hard bargaining to finesse. Senator John McCain of Arizona, a swing vote among Republicans, was willing to support "relocation" only if the Democrats agreed to consider military aid to the contras if diplomacy failed. Chris Dodd, on the other hand, rejected any deal that failed to include the principle of relocation.

In the end, after some spirited discussions and even a couple of screaming matches, a middle ground was negotiated. The final agreement called for contra aid funds to support *"voluntary* reintegration or *voluntary* regional relocation"* of the contras. We also pledged to cut off all aid to any contra forces that violated the cease-fire by commencing offensive operations.

The final negotiating hurdle centered on Democratic demands for congressional review of all humanitarian aid. Despite my assurances that the administration had every intention of moving vigorously toward a negotiated settlement, some of the Democrats still wanted to believe that they were being lured into a trap that would force them to renew military aid. I'd received a private commitment from Jim Wright for a one-year extension of humanitarian aid. Just as the final touches were being made to a draft agreement, I learned from Janet Mullins and Peter Madigan, her resourceful deputy, that Wright had lost control of his subcommittee chairman. These Democrats were insistent that a one-year renewal of contra aid without any legislative oversight was out of the question.

A solution ultimately materialized in a compromise proposal by Democratic Congressman David Obey of Wisconsin, chairman of the Appropriations Subcommittee on Foreign Operations. Obey suggested that the Appropriations and Foreign Affairs committees of both chambers review the situation in eight months. For contra funding to continue after November 30, authorization from all four committees would be required.

Such an arrangement might be construed by some as a de facto congressional veto. As a practical matter, however, such a "veto" already existed. The power of the purse is specifically reserved for Congress by the Constitution. Indeed, Congress had already banned all military aid to the contras. I concluded that agreeing to Obey's proposal gave away absolutely none of the President's prerogatives. At the same time, it would be seen as a powerful symbolic gesture of goodwill, testament to the President's desire to have a bipartisan foreign policy. The President agreed to my recommendation that we endorse the Obey offer. In truth, I began the negotiations believing we'd be lucky to get six months of aid for the contras, much less the year Wright had promised me. So an aid reauthorization after eight months was more than acceptable.

Late in the process, I was making some rounds on Capitol Hill when

Republican Congressman Duncan Hunter of California, arguably the most virulent critic of any accommodation, was meeting with other conservatives and was preparing to savage the compromise. I decided to drop in on them unannounced. "I hear you have some questions," I said. Hunter complained that the administration was being too soft on the Sandinistas.

"I agree with you we ought to have a tougher policy," I said once again. "But where are you going to get the votes for it? We both know they aren't there." By the end of the session, they'd swallowed their reservations and reluctantly agreed to go along.

On March 24, congressional leaders from both parties joined the President and me for a signing ceremony at the White House to unveil the agreement. "Now, together, the executive branch and the Congress will work to ensure that the promises of democracy in Nicaragua become democracy in fact," I said.

The deal we struck appropriated $50 million in humanitarian aid for the contras through the Nicaraguan elections, subject to congressional review in eight months. At the same time, the administration tacitly agreed to abandon the previous policy of trying to overthrow the Sandinistas by force and instead to support a democratic election and accept the result. In exchange, congressional Democrats extended us a considerable measure of flexibility to pursue a diplomatic solution. By design, the agreement had its share of constructive ambiguity. But it was, I believe, a statesmanlike compromise of competing interests that could ultimately lead to democracy in Nicaragua. And from a tactical standpoint, all the parties were spared a year of constant wrangling and turmoil over contra aid. One of the most personally satisfying moments came when I heard Senate majority leader George Mitchell utter words that once would have been inconceivable: "I trust the President and the Secretary of State." A debilitating era of mutual antipathy was over.

At the very moment of triumph for the President, however, White House counsel Boyden Gray injected a discordant note into the matter. Gray, who had neither been involved with the negotiations nor consulted about them, told the *New York Times* that the agreement was of dubious constitutionality because it, in effect, amounted to giving Congress a legislative veto. This assessment was as erroneous as it was gratuitous. The agreement was, after all, a negotiated political document more than a routine piece of legislation. In any event, the President was understandably furious with his counsel for diminishing his first political and foreign-policy victory. He summoned Gray to the Oval Office woodshed to express his displeasure and ordered him to stop talking with reporters in this fashion in the future.

Giving Diplomacy
a Chance Finally Bears Fruit

Our bipartisan agreement gave the President and me a powerful piece of leverage with which to challenge the Soviets to apply Gorbachev's new thinking to continued Nicaraguan aid. Two months after we announced the accord, I was in Moscow, able to tell Shevardnadze that the President and Congress were united in the view that warmer relations were impossible until the Soviets stopped their mischief in our hemisphere, but that if the Soviet Union would support free and fair elections in Nicaragua, we would honor the results.

We were now offering the Soviet Union something it had sought but never achieved in its history: the acceptance by the United States of a legitimate role in diplomacy in our hemisphere. But we did so on our terms: challenging the Soviet Union to endorse and support the Esquipulas Treaty as the United States had done, and to press its allies in the region, Nicaragua and Cuba, to do the same.

The timing could not have been better. Coincidentally, the press had made much of our review of U.S.-Soviet relations, suggesting that the new President was taking a hard look at the entire relationship. Thus, our challenge to the Soviet Union to cooperate on Central America appeared to them to be an important test of their relationship with the newly elected President. Moreover, it offered them a face-saving means of reducing their $1 billion-a-year subsidy of the Sandinistas while gaining the prestige of partnership with the United States in Latin America.

I had honed these points in my March meeting with Shevardnadze. As soon as he was confirmed, Bernie Aronson had traveled to Moscow to meet with his Soviet counterpart. He was the first, and no doubt will be the last, Assistant Secretary of State for Inter-American Affairs to travel to Moscow on his first official trip—a symbol of the unique transition period in which the Bush administration conducted its diplomacy.

The Soviets agreed to stop delivery of major military supplies to Nicaragua, to try to keep the Cubans from doing the same, and to press the Sandinistas to accept the electoral outcome. Despite some problems, for the most part they kept their commitments.

We also had to box the Sandinistas in on the ground.

We persuaded the fractured opposition to unite behind a single opposition candidate. We pressed the OAS, the United Nations, the Carter Center, the European Union, and many others to flood Nicaragua with election observers. And we convinced the Congress to provide voter registration and other support through the National Endowment for Democracy to attempt to level out the enormous advantages the Sandinistas enjoyed through their control of government resources and personnel.

We reached out to former President Jimmy Carter, in particular, who played a crucial role as head of the Carter Center, reinforcing in the clearest terms our commitment to a bipartisan policy. Carter helped convince Daniel Ortega to accept his electoral defeat, and telephoned me with that good news at 4:15 A.M. on the morning of February 26, 1990.

The defeat of Daniel Ortega by Violeta Chamorro's UNO coalition was a sweet vindication of the Bipartisan Accord on Central America. But it was something more. It represented a stunning ideological defeat for communism and the left. Once the ordinary people of Nicaragua had a chance to speak their mind in the security of the polling place, they sent the Sandinistas packing with a smaller percentage of the vote than even General Pinochet in Chile had received a year before. So much for the Sandinista apologists who had argued for so many years that the regime had the support of "the people." The triumph of democracy in Nicaragua and peaceful demobilization of the contra army—as well as our successful cooperation with Latin American nations and the Soviet Union—also laid the groundwork for our subsequent diplomacy to end the war in El Salvador and to secure an end to Soviet aid to Cuba.

Working together with Congress, we had shown that for all the bitterness and vituperation of the last decade over Central America, Arthur Vandenberg's testament to bipartisanship not only remained sound advice—it still worked.

CHAPTER 5

THE SOVIET UNION:

GORBACHEV, SHEVARDNADZE, AND
THE ''NEW THINKING''

The West should not stand idly by to permit the ''crash of the century.''
—*Hungarian Foreign Minister Peter Varkonyi to Secretary Baker, March 5, 1989*

Writing these words today in a world where communism has crumbled and the Soviet Union has disintegrated, it is difficult to describe how much the Soviet threat and the danger of communism shaped American foreign policy through the decades of Cold War. Indeed, I think it's fair to say that the mere existence of the Soviet Union altered—however centrally or tangentially—almost all our lives. I know it did mine.

Growing up in Houston in the late 1930s and early 1940s, I found a second home on the tennis courts of the River Oaks Country Club. Every summer until college, I'd spend most of every day playing, watching, or talking tennis with the club pro, Andrew Jitkoff. He had been born in Russia at the turn of the century, and he and his family had been run out by the Bolshevik revolution. He'd somehow found his way to this club in Texas, where he managed the tennis program, supervised a nationally known annual amateur tournament, and taught kids like me how to hit topspin forehands through the heavy hundred-degree heat of a humid Houston summer. Afterward, we'd sit by the courts and sip Barq's root beer or strawberry soda.

He would sometimes reminisce about Russia and the revolution, and I remember wondering how painful it must have been for him to be separated from his family and his homeland. Most of the history went right over my head. But the lessons he taught me about friendship, kindness, and generosity of spirit were easy to understand, and I was honored when, years later, he asked me to be godfather to his son. At the end of the day, after I'd showered off the day's sweat and changed out of my tennis clothes, he'd put Rose Hair Oil on my then very curly black hair. I would go home feeling fairly debonair, only to be met there by my mother, who would ask, "Who put all that grease on you?" If the tennis courts were a second home, Andrew Jitkoff was like a second father—and little could I foresee then how closely my professional life would intersect with the eclipse of the Soviet Union, as my personal life had been altered by its creation and Andrew Jitkoff's journey to America.*

Almost as soon as George Bush had announced he wanted me to be his Secretary of State and well before I was confirmed by the Senate, the Soviets came to gain the measure of the new administration. Shortly after election day in 1988, Anatoly Dobrynin, who had come to Washington as Soviet Ambassador in 1962, when Nikita Khrushchev was in power and had survived for twenty-four years, asked to see me privately. I knew Dobrynin from literally the beginning of my years in government. He had come to my swearing-in as Under Secretary of Commerce in August 1975, and I remember thinking how unusual it was for a dean of the diplomatic corps to come to a ceremony in honor of a sub-Cabinet official. I'd like to think he saw me as a possible rising star, but the reality is he probably thought his attendance would help the Soviets with East-West trade issues in which Commerce was centrally involved. I saw him occasionally while Chief of Staff and Treasury Secretary and understood that his transfer back to Moscow in 1986 as chief of the International Department of the Communist Party's Central Committee made him one of Gorbachev's closest advisers on American affairs. I arranged to meet him at my residence on Foxhall Road in Washington. When he arrived, I took him downstairs to our den. I often held my private meetings there, when I met with Alan Greenspan, Bob Michel, Pat Moynihan, Bob Dole, Bill Bradley, and others to work out issues like Social Security and tax reform.

Dobrynin informed me that in a few days, the Soviet Ambassador, Yuri Dubinin, would deliver a message to the White House requesting a meeting with President Reagan and President-elect Bush. Gorbachev would be coming to New York for the United Nations General Assembly in December, and Moscow hoped to arrange a meeting to coincide with his visit. "What we really want," Dobrynin told me conspiratorially, in his unaccented but stac-

*While a student at Princeton University, I also studied Russian history and wrote my required junior-year paper on the short-lived government of Alexander Kerensky, which was established after the overthrow of Czar Nicholas II and then overthrown by the Bolsheviks.

cato English, "is a meeting with George Bush. We're happy to be dealing with you guys. You are known quantities." This was scarcely an admission that he was a closet Republican. But the Bush administration's ties to the Reagan administration made the Soviets feel there would be a degree of continuity in U.S.-Soviet relations.

I told Dobrynin that I appreciated being told about the forthcoming request for the meeting and took the opportunity to ask him how things were in Moscow.

"The people are worried. Their biggest concern is the economy. Right now, there are high expectations. There is lots of grumbling. Pressures are mounting. We can't lift subsidies like those on food and other staples in order to transfer to a market economy without raising wages. And that will cause inflation," he continued, somewhat dispiritedly.

"What do you think of the political situation?" I asked him.

"The danger is whether Gorbachev can survive," he said, bluntly. It was a question that would dominate much of the next three years of my life.

First Encounter with Shevardnadze:
Vienna in March

Four months later, on Sunday, March 5, 1989, I flew to Vienna, Austria, for the opening of the Conventional Forces in Europe (CFE) talks. The predecessor to CFE—the Mutual Balanced Force Reduction talks (MBFR)—had languished for fourteen years, and produced very little movement, let alone an agreement. We were determined not to allow the same to happen to CFE.

The talks were also an opportunity for me to meet with several of my East European counterparts and hear their views about reform. The Hungarian Foreign Minister, Peter Varkonyi, told me that Hungary had begun reform in 1968, but the "unfavorable international situation," as he delicately put it, had retarded those reforms until Gorbachev had come to power. In short, the Hungarians had learned the painful reality of Moscow's crushing of Alexander Dubček's Prague Spring in Czechoslovakia in 1968: the necessary condition of reform in Eastern Europe was reform in the Soviet Union. "When perestroika began, we were ready to go and we were pursuing ideas more radical than those being pursued by the Soviets," he said, noting that the Hungarians were making preparations to eliminate the barbed wire and security measures separating their border with Austria.

When I asked him how the Soviets viewed these steps, he said, "The Soviets are fully supportive. They see our efforts as a good example for their own." He added, "There is no way out for the Soviet Union other than perestroika, and this is recognized by Gorbachev himself."

I heard much the same later that day from Tadeusz Olechkowski, the Polish Foreign Minister. He briefed me in detail on Polish plans for restructuring their political system. At one point, after I asked him how their senate would fit into the governmental structure, the Polish delegates erupted into a debate among themselves about the relative merits of a U.S.-style presidency versus a French one. It was clear the Poles had moved far beyond democratic theory to the point of trying to fix practical problems, which made it readily apparent that their reforms were, as Olechkowski put it, "revolutionary." It was also clear that the Poles—like the Hungarians— wanted American support for their efforts. "It is not enough for you to be observers," he said. "The time has come to finish with small steps and support our process. You shouldn't be absent, Mr. Secretary," he intoned. It was obvious that while the Hungarians and the Poles had relied on Gorbachev to change the East-West climate so their reforms might be possible, they now wanted the United States to help them so they could continue and consolidate their efforts. Maneuvering so that we supported reform without triggering a backlash was going to be very tricky business.

Above all, the Vienna meeting provided a chance to talk briefly with Eduard Shevardnadze. During the transition, George Shultz had told me that he felt he had a good relationship with Shevardnadze. Shultz thought Shevardnadze was someone with whom I could do business. I had met him once previously as Treasury Secretary at a working lunch hosted by President Reagan shortly after Shevardnadze succeeded Andrei Gromyko. As before, I was struck by Shevardnadze's flowing white hair, his penetrating eyes, and his gentle manner. Then as now, he reminded me a bit of Albert Einstein. When I was an undergraduate at Princeton, Einstein had been a guest lecturer. When he'd been introduced, the lecture hall had erupted in an ovation—and Einstein had clapped along with the rest of us. He then went into a lecture that went far over my head and those of most of the audience. Undoubtedly, he was discussing yet another revolutionary frontier of physics. Shevardnadze, I would learn, was also interested in revolutions—political and social. But he spoke of them in simple and compelling terms all could understand.

Shevardnadze met me that day at the U.S. Ambassador's residence in Vienna—the same place President Kennedy had met Khrushchev in June 1961. I wanted to use our first encounter to set the tone for future meetings, so at first we met alone, with only interpreters present. While the ongoing review of our foreign policy prevented me from getting into many substantive details, I wanted Shevardnadze from the outset to understand two realities—one substantive, one procedural. Substantively, I wanted him to understand that the new administration genuinely supported perestroika and that we believed its success augured well for international stability and productive U.S.-Soviet relations. Already, perestroika was loosening the Soviet stranglehold on Eastern Europe—and that was good for Western interests, regardless of how political events turned out in Moscow. Procedurally, I went out of my way to underscore my long-standing relationship to the President and to assure Shevardnadze that, given the close relations among Scowcroft, Cheney, Crowe, and me, there would be no repeat of the internecine warfare that had made the conduct of foreign policy so difficult in many previous administrations.

Shevardnadze appreciated what I had to say, and noted that President Bush had given Gorbachev the same message at the December 1988 Governor's Island meeting. "This is of exceptional importance, because it defines the fundamental policy. If this is the case," he said, adding that he had no reason to question the sincerity of my words, "then both sides can give serious consideration to how we will develop relations further."

On the way we should conduct business, he told me, "There is no need to address the importance of personal contacts. They are very important to create the kind of businesslike and constructive atmosphere of trust, if not actual friendship, which would make it easy to discuss the most difficult and contentious issues in the spirit of mutual accommodation and with a view to seeking and finding those kinds of solutions."

He went on to discuss perestroika—echoing his Eastern European counterparts in calling it a "revolution"—and stressed that it could turn the Soviet Union into a "reliable partner" for the West. Shevardnadze mentioned that he wanted to discuss perestroika in depth at some future time with me, because "it is important that everyone have a deep understanding of what is currently occurring in the Soviet Union. In a nutshell, both the state and society are being rephased. This process is impossible to stop," he stressed, "because by now it has the support of the general public. The government could not stop it even if it should wish to do so." It was the first but hardly the last time that Shevardnadze would reveal to me his acute understanding of Soviet internal dynamics.

I used his discussion of the Soviet scene to make a broader point concerning our relations, tying it in to his recent trip to Tehran. "You have been referring to the 'new political thinking,' " I said. "I think that our aim should be to see whether we can translate that into concrete actions that serve our mutual interests. It is hard for us to understand," I said by way of example, "that at the time the international community is seeking to isolate Iran for its death threats, the Soviet Union creates the appearance of trying to protect Iran from such pressures." I said the same held true for Central America, where Soviet arms shipments to Nicaragua did not measure up to the rhetoric of the "new political thinking."

"I am pleased you've mentioned Iran," he responded. His visit had been planned some time before the Rushdie "scandal," wherein the Ayatollah had "sentenced" writer Salman Rushdie to death. Moreover, Khomeini had sent Gorbachev a "special message," a letter that discussed his philosophy and views, primarily about the "afterlife," as well as Khomeini's wishes regarding the development of Soviet-Iranian relations.

"I do not believe it is possible to isolate Iran. And even if that were possible, that would be the worst of all possible options. It's true that Iran has extremists and genuine fanatics." But, he continued, in an ironic reminder of the Iran-contra affair, "I have also been able to ascertain that Iran has rational politicians." And Shevardnadze had talked with them quite openly about this entire matter and about the "need for the Soviet Union and Iran, who are neighbors along a 2,500-kilometer border, to have good relations."

I pressed him as to whether I could tell the press that he had discussed the Rushdie affair with Iranian leaders. He was sensitive about this, telling me that if I were to do so, his ability to influence Iran in the future would be restricted.

We then moved into a plenary session, joined by eleven officials on my side, eight on his. We covered a range of issues, but very little was new or particularly interesting. The most intriguing idea I heard was Shevardnadze's proposal to expand our bilateral relations working group into one that covered domestic developments more generally. (Under the Reagan administration, there had been four subcabinet working groups that made preparations between ministerials: arms control, human rights, regional conflicts, and bilateral issues. While slightly altering the focus of each of those four, we also added a fifth: transnational issues.) The bilateral relations working group had in the past been used primarily to take care of purely diplomatic business, such as embassies, consulates, and visas. Looking back on what seemed at the time to be a rather innocuous suggestion, I see now the roots of what in future meetings would become Shevardnadze's long and detailed dissertations on Soviet internal politics, economics, and society. And in another harbinger of things to come, given the special interests of the United States and the USSR in the Middle East, he said, "We can at some point consider the possibility of the Soviet Foreign Minister and the U.S. Secretary of State meeting in the Middle East to discuss the region. I am not proposing this now as an urgent question, since the conditions are not yet appropriate for such a meeting."

I learned very quickly at the State Department—as I had at Treasury—

that it was next to impossible to get any real work done in the large plenary sessions. By their very nature, such meetings led to ritualized presentations, designed as much to reassure one's own bureaucracy and avoid press leaks as to convince and move the other side. I had learned at Treasury—especially on sensitive topics such as currency-exchange-rate negotiations—that these discussions were best done with only the other minister and one or two top aides present. These smaller meetings also encouraged greater dialogue and better, more personal relations with my counterparts. Thus, by the time of the Wyoming ministerial six months later, we were conducting most of our work in "one-on-one" sessions. (Technically, they weren't one on one; we both needed interpreters and, in addition, notetakers—in my case, Dennis Ross, and for Shevardnadze, Sergei Tarasenko, who was not only one of the most able foreign diplomats I ever encountered but also one of the gentlest and most decent people I ever met.)

On Wednesday, March 8, the day after my return from Vienna, I sat down with the President for one of our regular twice-weekly meetings. While President Bush was available by telephone or in person for me to voice my views on any specific issue, I felt that these informal twice-weekly sessions were among the most useful we had. In these freewheeling discussions, we would often discuss—and question—the assumptions and concepts underlying any given policy. We would also think out loud, and I am convinced this helped me in many cases to know almost instinctively where the President would come out on a given issue.

That day, I began with Eastern Europe. "The Poles and Hungarians are moving very far and very fast on reform—both political and economic. The pace may surprise us and create a new reality in Eastern Europe." We agreed that meant exploring how we could support these countries economically, as well as looking for ways to accelerate political liberalization. The President suggested giving thought to a possible presidential visit to Eastern Europe at an early date.

Shevardnadze, I told him, very much wanted to establish a personal relationship and ensure continuity in U.S.-Soviet relations. There was, Shevardnadze had said, "no alternative to success," despite the real difficulties and obstacles that confronted perestroika. The distinct impression I had was that Gorbachev and Shevardnadze felt a real urgency to see perestroika succeed quickly. "They're leaders in a great hurry, possessing a sense of urgency but lacking a plan. As a result, they are searching—searching for ideas, debating what's possible, and scrambling to come up with initiatives," I said to the President. The emphasis on initiatives, I felt, was having a real effect in Europe. I pointed out how I had been able to blunt a Soviet CFE proposal in Vienna with our rather modest initiative on chemical weapons, and stressed, "We need to be sensitive to this, because Gorbachev is likely to come out with a major arms-reduction initiative shortly before or after the NATO summit. You must be able to present a bold, sweeping proposal."

While we could continue to push the Soviets to give "new thinking" content—that is, to match their words with action—I said, "In the military area, I'm less convinced we have ideas, much less the analysis to support them. I'm afraid our review will be too hidebound bureaucratically, too likely to lack innovative ideas to meet the problem." Within a month, I discovered that prediction had come true.

The "Strategic Review"

The so-called strategic review was neither truly strategic nor a proper review. Launched by the President on February 15, 1989, the review was intended to produce a fundamental reassessment of U.S. foreign policy. After eight years as Vice President, the President personally was quite conscious of the need to put his own imprint on policy. The review was designed to signal the bureaucracy, the Congress, the media, and the public at large that it was time for a reassessment of old assumptions. That seemed a rather straightforward proposition during a time of such momentous change.

Unfortunately, we made two mistakes in the way we set up the review. First, since we were building on the Reagan administration—not repudiating it, as a Democratic administration would have—we changed personnel in a rather genteel way. Because of this, much of the review was run by Reagan administration holdovers. Since they were responsible for the development and articulation of the previous policy, these officials naturally had a personal and psychological investment in the status quo. It was pretty much like asking an architect to review his own work; he might change a door here or a window there, but it would be unlikely for him to question the basic foundations on which the structure stood. Needless to say, these officials found themselves incapable of truly thinking things anew. Second, instead of asking for ideas and suggestions from sources without a vested interest in established policy, we asked the bureaucracy itself to produce the papers. This resulted in least-common-denominator thinking, with every potentially controversial—that is, interesting—idea left out in the name of bureaucratic consensus.

In the end, what we received was mush.

On the Soviet Union and Eastern Europe, the President held NSC meetings on March 30, April 4, and April 5. In addition, the President held a session with outside Sovietologists on February 12, and I conducted a seminar at the State Department on April 24 with three experts: Steve Sestanovich of the Center for Strategic and International Studies, Steve Meyer of the Massachusetts Institute of Technology, and George Breslauer of the University of California at Berkeley.

Much of the debate in these meetings focused on arcane issues of Sovietology. The most prominent was, Is perestroika a *peredyshka*—that is, a "breathing space"—or is it a *perekhod*—a "fundamental shift"—in Soviet policy? To the more hawkish analysts, perestroika was just a breathing space, designed by the Soviets to overcome the stagnation and technological backwardness of the Brezhnev era, and to revive the Soviet economy for further competition with democracy and capitalism into the next century. To the more dovish analysts, perestroika was a fundamental shift in Soviet policy. To them, Gorbachev was the Soviet Union's Dubček, a man who would usher in a new era of "socialism with a human face."

To me, this seemed mainly academic theology. At that point (the spring of 1989), both views had analytical strengths and weaknesses. What mattered to me were what actions we could take in the face of these two different possibilities, in order to maximize our diplomatic gains while minimizing risks.

That may be why I remember very little coming out of these sessions, other than the sense that one could break the administration down into two schools of thought. The "status quo plus" school held that everything was going our way because the Soviets were so weak; to this school's way of thinking, we needed only to bide our time, as Gorbachev would make concessions, provided we stood firm. The Department of Defense and some on the NSC staff seemed most inclined to this view.

My senior advisers and I felt more inclined toward what could be called an "activist" view. The experts had told me that *perestroika* could be translated either as "restructuring" or "revolution." My sense was that Gorbachev might actually be prepared to usher in far-reaching, fundamental change—but we would be able to find out how far he was willing to go only by moving forward ourselves. Dennis Ross and Bob Zoellick felt that "glasnost" and the "new thinking" might contain within them philosophical tenets which could be used effectively with Gorbachev to push him in directions that advanced our interests, and I agreed with them. Much like an American presidential candidate, Gorbachev was making powerful promises—and our job was to hold him to his word. The boldness and radical character of Gorbachev's pronouncements made him vulnerable to being hoisted with his own petard. It would not be easy for him to say no to our initiatives, in part because in the middle of a revolution, Gorbachev quite consciously was searching for ideas.

Above all, I reasoned, if we were to sit still, Gorbachev would have all the momentum, and this was what finally convinced me that we needed to move. In international politics, as in domestic politics, a sitting target is usually the easiest target. The more we were moving, the harder it would be for Gorbachev to gain advantage over us. Gorbachev's strategy, I believed, was premised on splitting the alliance and undercutting us in Western Europe, by appealing past Western governments to Western publics. Internally, it was also a way for him to build his own authority and stature. We needed to attack his strategy head-on and to craft initiatives that he would feel obliged to embrace. Standing back and standing pat would limit our options over time, and allow the political terrain to shift against us. Whatever inclinations I had were all the more strengthened by my first visit with Gorbachev.

Preparing for Gorbachev

Before my first visit to Moscow in May 1989, as I prepared in the modern birchwood guest house in Helsinki so kindly provided by the Finnish government, I realized that Gorbachev and Shevardnadze had to view the Bush administration with some concern. In its last months, the Reagan administration had been eager to finalize arms control negotiations. The Bush administration not only had frozen the negotiations in place while we went through the lengthy "review," but on April 29, Dick Cheney, when pushed on a CNN interview, had said his guess was that Gorbachev would "ultimately fail."

I called the President and raised the central problem with Dick's remarks. I didn't disagree at all with his substantive analysis—after all, if forced to vote at that time, most experts would probably have predicted perestroika's demise. But it didn't make sense just then for the administration to be predicting Gorbachev's failure publicly or, particularly, for the Secretary of Defense to be the one doing it. The President and I discussed the problem, and he told Scowcroft to distance the White House from Cheney's comments. It was my only major disagreement with Cheney involving turf in all the time we served President Bush as Secretaries of State and Defense, but I didn't want a precedent set for the Secretary of Defense to feel free to make uncleared public pronouncements on major foreign policy issues. I felt then, and feel now, that administrations that speak with disparate voices in foreign policy do not well serve the national interest. The Secretary of State must be the President's principal adviser and spokesman on U.S. foreign policy. Cheney called me after this incident to let me know he understood my position and had been pressed to say something better left unsaid.

With Gorbachev, the President asked me to reiterate in private what he had been saying in public: We want perestroika to succeed. And he gave me a short handwritten note to hand over. The President was eager to hear from me about my meeting—so eager, in fact, that he wanted to know how things went even if our secure communications broke down. "Right after you see Gorbachev, call me," the President ordered. "If the meeting was really promising, say, 'It reminded me of a trip to Otto's.' If the meeting was good, say, 'It reminded me of a trip to Molina's.'" Otto's had the best barbecue in Houston, while Molina's served excellent Tex-Mex.

"And what if it goes poorly?" I asked.

"Then tell me, 'It reminded me of a tennis game with Bob Murray.'" Murray was a Houston acquaintance whose self-promotion drove the President crazy.

Trying to look at the broader state of U.S.-Soviet relations from Gorbachev's perspective, I realized that Gorbachev and Shevardnadze might also be nervous that our emphasis on "testing" the Soviets in regional conflicts played against one of their weaknesses, that it might require them to turn "new thinking" into reality in regions where they'd rather avoid tough choices. I was wary of humiliating the Soviets as they retreated from their global empire because I didn't want to give hard-liners in Moscow the psychological basis for stalling retrenchment.

Internally, I knew the economic situation continued to stagnate. And in the March 26 elections, while the vast majority of Communist Party candidates won, some 20 percent lost—a shocking number in Soviet politics—and many of these were senior members of the Central Committee or party bosses in places such as Moscow, Kiev, and Minsk. The biggest winner had been Boris Yeltsin, who had been expelled from the Politburo in the fall of 1987 after accusing Gorbachev of a "cult of personality." He won an "at-large" Moscow seat in the Congress of People's Deputies with over five million votes—close to 90 percent of those voting in his district. More recently, on April 9, an uprising in Tbilisi, Georgia, was brutally suppressed. Twenty protesters were killed, and it appeared that Soviet troops might have used poison gas. It was just the first of what would become a summer of mass action, driven either by nationalism or economic grievances.

My overriding objective in Moscow was to reassure Gorbachev and Shevardnadze that we supported their reform efforts. But I also wanted to use my meetings to move away from what I felt was an overemphasis on arms control, to strengthen our relations by focusing more on regional and transnational issues, and to redefine our dialogue on human rights into discussions about "institutionalizing democracy." My emphasis on regional conflicts was driven partly by necessity, partly by choice. By necessity, I had to continue pushing the Soviets on Central America. It was the single most vexing regional conflict on our agenda—diplomatically and politically. By choice, I wanted to broaden our agenda, because I felt the political changes taking place in Moscow might allow for greater progress in areas that by their nature were more political than arms control. At the time, my feeling was that arms-control negotiations tended to be dominated by esoteric, technical factors and by positions that deeply entrenched bureaucracies on both sides embraced almost as theology. These negotiations seemed to me to have little relevance to what was taking place in our broader political relations. If we were going to make decisive breakthroughs with the Soviets, they would be driven by broader political considerations. I wanted our overall diplomatic and political relations to drive progress in arms control, not vice versa.

I also wanted to broaden our talks to include transnational issues such as nonproliferation, counterterrorism, and the environment. This was an additional way to signal that we were open to East-West cooperation, and were willing to give the Soviets every chance to show that the "new thinking" could be turned into practice.

On human rights, relations with the Soviet Union had been so poor that the Secretary of State seldom had anything approaching a real discussion; usually, the time reserved for human-rights discussions was devoted to turning over a list of refuseniks and others who had been most egregiously deprived of their rights by the regime, in hopes of getting these few individuals out of the Soviet Union. My aim was to use the opening created by glasnost to transform these sessions into genuine discussions about the ways the Soviets could "institutionalize" democracy in a state founded on the rule of law. Obviously, the notion of "rule of law" was utterly foreign, even threatening, to the primacy of the Communist Party, but I felt the more we could do to change the mind-set of the leadership on this issue, the more a grassroots democratic movement might have a chance of taking hold. We stressed the notion of "institutionalizing" such changes out of the belief that, for a revolution to be consolidated, it must have its ideas reflected in the institutions that govern society.

Stepping Back in Time:
My First Visit to Moscow

With these thoughts on my mind and two planeloads of experts accompanying me, on May 10, I left Helsinki on a foggy, overcast morning for the short hour-and-thirty-five-minute flight to Moscow. Arriving at Sheremetyevo Airport, I stepped onto Soviet soil for the first time in my life. As we rolled into the city, I felt that I had been transported back in time. The yellowing, chipped buildings seemed shrouded in the fog and mist, but even through the dreary morning light, one could see the deterioration and decay of the infrastructure. Stalinesque buildings that seemed to have been built in the 1930s and 1940s looked as though they hadn't been repaired or painted since then. The few cars and trucks on the streets appeared to have come from the 1950s and 1960s. And while the pedestrians were well dressed and well groomed, their clothes, too, seemed somewhat dated, especially in contrast to the modness of Helsinki. At night, the city grew older, lit only by extremely dim and infrequent streetlights. Motorists turned on their headlights only when they came to a particularly busy or dark intersection, and when it rained, cars would scurry to the side so drivers could reattach their windshield wipers, which were an especially scarce commodity and would be stolen if they were left on an unattended car. The only sharp color that intruded on this otherwise colorless scene could be found on the massive billboards that stood above many buildings. In bright red, they advertised not the latest cigarette but "All Glory to the Soviets!"

Thirty-five minutes later, we arrived at the Foreign Ministry's Osobnyak Guest House and were met by Shevardnadze. He was graciously waiting outside to greet us. This was a measure not only of his politeness, but also his guile. Invariably, he would use this brief time to "spin" the waiting press as to the results he expected from our meetings.

The Osobnyak (which many of my non-Russian-speaking staff came to call the "Insomniac," partly because it sounded similar to the Russian pronunciation and partly out of recognition of the hours we worked in Moscow) was a massive and ancient guest house in the middle of Moscow. It had been the home of a well-to-do family and a place where Lenin had held an early meeting. It was more Russian than Soviet in style, and I always found it somewhat ironic to be discussing the most technical of modern nuclear arms control issues while sitting in large, gilded chairs covered with petit point, with ornate wood carvings and artwork from the eighteenth century adorning the fifteen-foot-high walls.

After exchanging pleasantries, I was ushered rather appropriately into the "Red Room" for our initial one-on-one. I began by telling Shevardnadze that in the two months since we had met, we had already seen great changes, and noted that elections were definitely a positive step on the road toward greater democratization. "We have no interest in seeing perestroika fail," I said. "Indeed, we'd like to see it succeed, for it constitutes a potentially revolutionary restructuring of your political philosophy and approach to the world." With that broad introduction, I then tried to set his mind at ease about the strategic review. "There will be no change in our attitude for continuity," I said, "but we all need to recognize that there will be new approaches in some areas. We see great potential for improved cooperation and want an active, constructive, positive, and expanding relationship." I made clear my bottom line: We believed the changes taking place created a real opportunity. And we wanted to use it to build a more stable and predictable relationship.

Moving into a more philosophical discussion about security issues, I stressed once again that we wanted to approach these issues more from a political than a technical angle. I wanted him to understand that we were not going to sidetrack arms control, but that we wanted to go beyond the formalized and ritualized negotiations of the past. We wanted a more creative approach to these issues: by taking unilateral steps (such as their publishing a real defense budget); by addressing sources of war, such as regional disputes, rather than just the means of war, such as weapons; and by focusing on "strategic stability" rather than just numbers. Given Soviet massive advantages in almost every type of weapons system, we felt the numbers game was a losing game; we preferred the concept of arms "control" to arms "reduction." He responded with an equally philosophical discussion of his own.

I then began the custom of using part of our one-on-one to discuss sensitive issues—in this session, two espionage cases and Afghanistan. It is no secret that during the Cold War, the CIA and KGB engaged in numerous cat-and-mouse games with each other. On occasion, I would be asked by the Agency to discuss a specific case, oftentimes outlining how a problem might be resolved if the Soviets were willing to deal. More often than not, this would involve a spy swap that would be done very quietly. On Afghanistan, I told Shevardnadze that we had no interest in a regime that was hostile to the Soviet Union. What we wanted was a peaceful, independent, nonaligned Afghanistan. This wasn't giving him much; it was clear by then that the Afghans were going to be quite anti-Soviet for a long time to come. "But there will be no peace in Afghanistan as long as Najibullah stays. The mujahedin will never accept him. So if peace comes, it won't come with Najibullah in power," I said.

After fifty minutes and a brief plenary session, held as much for the press as for any other reason, we sat down to our first small group meeting. (The small groups were a compromise between the massive plenary sessions and the one-on-ones; into each small group session—arms control, regional conflicts, democratization and human rights, bilateral issues, and transnational problems—we would rotate relevant experts. For example, Dick Schifter, the Assistant Secretary of State for Human Rights, would sit in at the democratization meetings, while Curt Kammen, the Deputy Assistant Secretary of State for European Affairs, whose portfolio covered the Soviet Union, would join us for bilateral issues.)

Shevardnadze began by stressing what he called the "organic interrelationship" across our agenda. "Regional conflicts are very important. But I would like to make a different point about them: regional problems cannot be treated in isolation; there is a direct relationship among settlement of regional problems, disarmament, and the solution of transnational problems such as economic development and the ecological crisis. If we fail to admit the organic interrelationship, it will be difficult for us to reach a global solution to all these problems," he observed.

"I am aware that people in the United States and the rest of the world do not view perestroika in an unambiguous way. We know your basic view and that of the President; we keenly follow what you have been saying and accept it. But there are other views. For example, I'd take issue with the points expressed by your Secretary of Defense," referring indirectly to Cheney's comment about Gorbachev's failure. He went on to say, as he had in Vienna, that he hoped to discuss internal developments further. It was becoming obvious to me that Shevardnadze saw the key to future progress in our relations in the advancement of perestroika internally—and that he wanted me to understand these internal dynamics.

In response, I made three overarching points before moving on to Central America. First was our hope that in the long term, we could remove the competitive East-West dynamic from regional conflicts in the Third World.

Second was that the United States had no surprises in store in Eastern Europe, and that the President would be going to Poland and Hungary in July. "We would be interested, in particular, in hearing from you how you compare the development of perestroika in the Soviet Union to reform in Eastern Europe," I said.

Third, "While there is a body of opinion in the United States that believes it would be good for the United States if perestroika were to fail, because it would mean a weaker USSR, no one in the administration subscribes to that view. Everyone is anxious for perestroika to succeed. Our Secretary of Defense was just expressing his own views regarding the prognosis for success. And you should note that the President made clear he did not share this view."

"I was not surprised by the Secretary of Defense's statement," Shevardnadze responded. "I know the Secretary of Defense needs money. How would he finance his defense programs if there were no Soviet threat? He risks being deprived of his main argument. In this light, we should not view his reaction as bitter." From the beginning, Shevardnadze showed his understanding of bureaucratic politics abroad—and at home. His political infighting with his own Ministry of Defense, especially on arms control, would become legion and, I suspect, left Shevardnadze far more bitter with his own military than with America's.

Taking the opening I had provided him, Shevardnadze began to talk about Eastern Europe. "I believe the President's trip to Poland and Hungary is undoubtedly positive. Visits are an ordinary thing. It is rather surprising when there are no such visits." He said he didn't think we were surprised when Gorbachev went to Western Europe. The more routine the contacts between Western leaders and East Europeans, the better. "Such contacts," he said, "help in building the Common Europe Home. This concept should not be terrifying. It simply symbolizes the need for common efforts to build a single Europe, which," he stressed, "includes the United States and Canada. Europe cannot stay divided. This was one of the biggest blunders made by the East's political leaders."

"What are your views on the differing prospects for reform in the different countries?" I asked. "Why are Hungary and Poland moving toward reform, whereas the GDR, Romania, and Czechoslovakia are not?"

"That's a legitimate question," he replied quickly, obviously having spent a lot of time thinking about it as reform heated up in Eastern Europe. "It seems simple at first blush but is, in fact, very complicated. The processes in each country are not equivalent. New thinking has one principle of fundamental importance: freedom of choice. Every nation has the right to determine its own destiny, to choose the sociopolitical system it considers best.

"Different peoples have different ways of life," he said philosophically, before going on to compare the various countries of Eastern Europe. "There was a time," he added, "when Moscow had encouraged the application of the Soviet model in Eastern Europe; the consequences were not very positive." Even in this understated way, this was the first time a senior Soviet official had repudiated the Stalinist system of puppet states, as well as the Brezhnev Doctrine's central tenet of using force to ensure conformity. Shevardnadze concluded, "The only correct way to proceed is to respect their choices."

After our meeting, I took some time out to meet with three recently elected members of the Congress of Peoples' Deputies. The mere fact of their election was significant. The powers of the Congress of Peoples' Deputies at the time were minimal. But now there was a genuine forum for voicing opposing views, and soon the legislative body would no longer be a rubber stamp.

The rest of my meetings that day with Shevardnadze were uneventful. I raised Central America again, stressing that continuing questions about Soviet arms shipments to Managua could impede progress elsewhere. Shevardnadze took great interest in our elections-centered approach. He noted that he'd recently had several contacts with the Nicaraguans, and "I can assure you that they are ready to conduct the elections on a truly democratic basis, even if they are going to lose." While at the time it seemed he was referring to the Nicaraguan election reform law (which would still have given the Sandinistas major advantages), in retrospect Shevardnadze may have foreseen the eventual peaceful defeat of the Sandinistas more perceptively than most Western observers. On the Middle East, he again raised the idea of meeting in the Middle East, saying, "We like to dream about such things." We also had our first extended, post-strategic review discussion of arms control issues and agreed that the START talks in Geneva would resume shortly.

That evening my wife, Susan, and I joined Shevardnadze and his wife, Nanuli, at their apartment to begin what has become and remains a close and warm friendship. While the exterior of Shevardnadze's building looked like every other in Moscow and we had to use a tiny, dingy elevator that held only three people, the apartment itself was very, very neat. It was decorated in a Georgian motif, and much of the food, most of it prepared by Nanuli, was Georgian, too. Shevardnadze had done his homework on my interests, and presented me with a shotgun as a gift.

From a diplomatic standpoint, the dinner gave me insight into the depth of Shevardnadze's understanding of the changes taking place in the Soviet Union. He obviously understood the immense challenges facing perestroika and was blunt about the regime's ability to manage that change. "When Gorbachev came into office, none of us had any idea of just what we were facing in terms of the economy," he told us. They had seen how far the Soviet Union was lagging behind in science and technology, and had come to the realization that there would be no real economic reform if there were no reform of the political system. "Unless the people are politically enfranchised, no changes can be achieved. There cannot and will not be any perestroika if individuals do not become masters of the country politically," he said. But when I pressed him on whether this would lead to a multiparty democracy, he said that the regime hoped to bring the changes about within a one-party state. The contradiction was evident, but Shevardnadze seemed to have great faith in the Communist Party's ability to renew itself and include new political forces. It was one of the few domestic political issues on which he seemed to have blinders, though over time his position shifted.

He had no difficulties explaining the nationalities problems the leadership faced. He began his discussion delicately, noting that both the United States and the Soviet Union had "multinational populations," then used this rather innocuous point to tell us that while the Soviet Union supposedly consisted of fifteen separate governments, "much that is officially said on this score is simply words." The theory had not been put into practice, and he asked rhetorically, "What is this Soviet 'Union' of republics and nations now?" He reiterated that the nationalities question was the "most subtle and troublesome" problem facing the Soviet Union. He told me that when he had visited his home republic of Georgia after the violence in Tbilisi, he had found his people were totally different now.

It was the first time we had discussed the issue in any depth. I would quickly learn—in my meetings with Shevardnadze later that summer and fall—how acutely he understood the nationalities problem. He intuitively realized that perestroika, glasnost, and the new thinking had the potential not only to unleash economic rejuvenation but also the historic national passions and tensions, which did not lie far below the surface of Soviet society. He was consistently more concerned with nationalities than with the economy. It was not a concern shared equally by Gorbachev, who always emphasized the economy first and foremost, and then in a theoretical and abstract way. Gorbachev seemed not to sufficiently appreciate the nationalist impulses that were being unleashed by his very policies.

Nanuli Shevardnadze's reactions to our conversation gave me ample evidence of how events were viewed through a nationalist lens. Prompted by a brief conversation regarding Iran, she said the Persians had been enemies of the Georgian people for centuries. She told us that she had had a chill when she saw a picture of her husband with the Ayatollah. Despite Shevardnadze's protest, she wanted to discuss some episodes from Persian history. "I have my own attitude about Iran," she said, in her strong-willed and honest way that was always so refreshing. He tried gingerly to cut her off by pointing out that her views probably didn't coincide with most Soviets'. "You're correct. My attitude is the Georgian attitude," she retorted. She went on to tell a story from the seventeenth century about how the Persians had gained control of Georgia. They had taken the Georgian king and queen prisoner. After trying to get the queen to renounce Christianity, the Persians had burned her at the stake. According to Nanuli, half a million Georgians had been killed by the Persians and, in a famous instance in the seventeenth century, the Shah had sent back the severed heads of a Georgian's family.

What struck me was the passion with which she recounted the stories. There I was in the Moscow apartment of the Soviet Foreign Minister, meeting with his articulate and intelligent wife who didn't have to be provoked into revealing that at heart she was truly a Georgian nationalist. I remember thinking that if a Politburo member's wife can be so passionate about her nationality, what is the proverbial man in the street thinking—and doing?

Gorbachev

The next morning, May 11, I traveled the short distance to the Kremlin from Spaso House—the U.S. Ambassador's residence in Moscow where I was staying. While I preferred to stay with our traveling staff, due to the work that always had to be done in the evenings before the next day's meetings, our counterintelligence experts were wary of the bugs in Soviet hotels and wanted me to stay at the Ambassador's residence. I had been briefed about Soviet eavesdropping on (and in) our embassy, but I was still amazed by the sight of the Russian Orthodox church right across the street. It seemed to have more electronic gear sprouting from its roof than the Pentagon, and we began facetiously referring to it as either "Our Lady of Telemetry" or "The Church of the Immaculate Reception."

Crossing into the Kremlin was almost like leaving Moscow. Outside and inside, the Kremlin was utterly beautiful. The minarets of its churches gleamed, and the brick roads and walkways glistened. Everything seemed spanking clean and bright.

At 10:00 A.M., I was ushered into St. Catherine's Hall for my session with Mikhail Gorbachev. While I had been perfunctorily introduced to him on previous occasions, most recently at the state dinner in Washington in honor of the INF Treaty in December 1987, this was the first meeting in which I would be his primary interlocutor. He was joined only by Shevardnadze and his longtime interpreter, Pavel Palazchenko, who was a dead ringer for President Salinas of Mexico. (Later, as our meetings grew more frequent, we would joke about Gorbachev using the President of Mexico to interpret for him. Palazchenko always took the kidding good-naturedly.) I was accompanied only by my interpreter, Dmitri Zarechnak, a longtime State Department employee and fine public servant.

Gorbachev bounded into the room, beaming as always with energy and confidence. While he was neither a tall nor a large man, Gorbachev had an actor's gift to fill a stage with his presence. Indeed, he tended to fill a room as much with his upbeat attitude as with anything else. Whenever we met, he exuded optimism, and in this regard, he reminded me time and again of Ronald Reagan. President Reagan filled a room with his upbeat outlook, buoying everyone in it. Like Reagan, Gorbachev was invariably positive. Perhaps this was one reason Gorbachev and Reagan were able to work together so successfully. While the task the reformers faced was daunting, it was hard not to feel that Gorbachev's confidence alone might carry perestroika to success.

The contrast with Shevardnadze was stark. Shevardnadze carried an aura of wisdom and insight into just how difficult the task was before them. Sometimes it seemed such wisdom carried a psychic cost. As reform became more difficult, his shoulders seemed to carry the burdens of the world, his grandfatherly hair made him look older than he was, and the patches under his eyes seemed to darken and lengthen, reflecting, it seemed, the true tragedy of Soviet history. The more I would work with these two men, the more

I would see this difference—and the more I came to believe that Shevardnadze was perhaps the more realistic of the two.

In what I would realize later was a clear indicator of Gorbachev's priorities, he opened our one-on-one conversation by discussing the American press. "I've gotten to know your journalists fairly well by now, since I encounter them everywhere," he said. "The atmosphere of my relationship with them has changed over time. In the past, they would ask more sensational questions, but now their questions are more thoughtful—although they are, of course," he said somewhat conspiratorially, "still interested in getting hot items."

"You need to feed them to make them happy," I said, and explained how I felt, understandably, that the State Department press corps was more into substance and less into politics than its White House counterparts.

When I thanked him for the small meeting, he told me, "This is sort of an icebreaker, after which the ice will start flowing down the river as it does anew every spring." I would learn that Gorbachev loved a metaphor and metaphysical discussions more than Shevardnadze. Sometimes this approach would throw me off, and I would have to find a tortuous way to get back to the detail of the issues themselves.

This time, I just moved ahead and raised three issues very quickly: the President's interest in developing an active, constructive, and positive relationship between our countries; the President's concerns regarding Central America; and the possible timing of a summit.

"You're right, there are indeed exactly three questions," he quipped, indicating that he, too, wanted to discuss those same three issues.

"That's because we're both lawyers by education," I said.

"That is true, but we both have also studied economics, although you have been engaged in this area more than have I," he responded. He used his mention of economics to turn to the issue foremost on his mind: the approach the United States should take to perestroika. He went through what he saw as two schools of thought—which roughly mirrored the debate in Washington. In his view, perestroika would make for a better U.S.-Soviet relationship. "Only when the feeling of confidence disappears do difficulties arise—this is true for any country—and possible dangers may arise," he cautioned. I thought about how the Reagan administration's policy of "peace through strength" must have eroded Soviet confidence in the late Brezhnev years and the short Andropov and Chernenko eras. Moscow's confidence had "disappeared" and Soviet fears of the West—as many analysts suspected—had risen.

"I know you're being given a lot of advice, and that some of this advice is that the United States should not hurry and should wait until the Soviet Union has become destabilized and disintegrated. It would then be like a ripe apple that will fall to the ground by itself. But things are not that sim-ple." He stressed that our relationship was a "special" one, and "it would not be good if there were to be no progress in the relationship, albeit grad-ual. There need not necessarily be great leaps in the relationship, but it should be active, constructive, positive, and growing."

On Central America, he had written the President, telling him that So-viet arms shipments had ceased as of the first of the year. When I asked him whether we could tell the press about this, he parried me by asking whether we might announce a "moratorium on arms transfers to the region from all sources." It was a double dose of trying to get something for nothing. He knew that Congress had effectively ended our military assistance to the contras anyway, and that our congressionally centered approach to Central America had taken U.S. military support out of the equation in any case. Moreover, it turned out that while Soviet arms shipments to Nicaragua had stopped, shipments to Cuba had not, and Cuban transshipments to Mana-gua continued.

On summitry, Gorbachev wanted "regular" meetings. "These meetings should not always be viewed as something sensational. Extraordinary ac-complishments should not be expected from each one. They should rather be considered an important part of the process and an impetus for new steps." Gorbachev understood the need to control press and public expecta-tions, and he thought—as did many in the U.S. government—that regular meetings would be one way to do that. I favored more, but not necessarily regular, rigidly scheduled high-level meetings. By the end of 1989, this be-came a nonissue. With arms control, German unification, and later the Gulf crisis, the President and I both were seeing Gorbachev and Shevardnadze so often that it was clear that high-level meetings were the norm, not the exception.

We ended our one-on-one session, and the rest of our larger group of senior officials joined us.

Gorbachev began the meeting with a long soliloquy on the nature of perestroika. "First of all, perestroika is a reality," he said. "It used to be a policy or a reflection of what we wanted to achieve under our own philoso-phy; but now we view it as a reality. In any complex country like the USSR, one could not hope to have an easy life, particularly in a period of revolu-tionary change." Outside observers have spoken of a "group of reformers led by Gorbachev" and of "grassroots support." This was an accurate char-acterization of the nature of what was going on inside the USSR, but Gorba-chev stressed that at its core, perestroika was aimed at changing the role of the individual, particularly in terms of the economy. But political change had to take place, too. "To break up the old managerial attitudes and to defeat the old administrative system, some kind of move to political reform is necessary. . . . People are walking tall and speaking out. New people are coming to the forefront.

"Some people want an overnight fix," he continued. "I say to them: You should remember the great Soviet breakthroughs of the 1930s and the Chinese Great Leap Forward of the 1950s; these ultimately led to great leaps backward." He stressed that it was essential to avoid extremes and "stay the course."

I was struck by how easily he moved into Western vernacular, and reminded him that "stay the course" had been President Reagan's campaign slogan in 1984, when he had overwhelmingly won reelection by carrying forty-nine of the fifty states. I told him that I understood from my years as Secretary of the Treasury that the political leadership of a country was far and away the best judge of what the traffic would bear in terms of economic reform, but that in my experience, it was better to move sooner rather than later on issues such as price reform.

"We were twenty years late on price reform, so two or three more years won't hurt," he replied.

On START, he raised questions concerning air-launched cruise missiles (ALCMs), sea-launched cruise missiles (SLCMs), and the link between START and the ABM Treaty which was, in his words, "fundamental." He then moved quickly to preview the position the Warsaw Pact would soon adopt in the CFE talks. He proposed large cuts in troops, tanks, armored personnel carriers, and artillery pieces. The stickler was that he also wanted cuts in strike aircraft and helicopters, in which NATO had a large advantage in order to offset the Soviet asymmetry on the ground. While the proposal was essentially overlooked by the press, in retrospect it further presaged Soviet willingness to draw down the military confrontation in Europe.

Then Gorbachev dropped his customary "surprise." In an almost off-handed sort of way, he told me that the Soviets had decided to withdraw 500 tactical nuclear weapons this year from Eastern Europe. And if the United States was prepared to undertake more radical steps, the Soviets would consider withdrawing all tactical nuclear weapons from Eastern Europe by 1991. He went on to lecture me, saying, "The United States does not believe this is an urgent problem, but we in Europe feel differently."

It was a patently one-sided offer. Even after the INF Treaty was implemented, the Soviets would have a huge tactical nuclear weapon advantage in Europe. More important, Gorbachev knew that we were in sensitive discussions with the Germans, British, and other allies on short-range nuclear forces (SNF). It was a clear attempt to wrap a strategically insignificant proposal in a broader political context, and score public relations points with European publics.

After walking Gorbachev through several clarifications that showed the transparent nature of his proposal, I decided to lecture him in return. "You said we should not let suspicions arise that one side was seeking an advantage. We agreed with that. In fact, Foreign Minister Shevardnadze and I discussed it last night. We understand the political appeal of negotiations on tactical nuclear weapons, but we also understand that you have recently modernized your forces. We also know you have an advantage of 1,400 to 88 in SNF launchers. The Soviet Union also has a large advantage in conventional forces, notwithstanding your good intentions," I added, somewhat sarcastically. "So the fact remains, until we actually reach agreement, there is a major imbalance in SNF and conventional forces favoring the Warsaw Pact." I went on to read to him from a CIA assessment of Soviet SNF modernization efforts. And I reiterated two more times that we understood the "political appeal" behind his proposals.

The Real Test: Western Cohesion

That night, as I flew to Brussels to brief our NATO allies, I reflected on my first encounter with the Soviet leader. Gorbachev had pulled another of his public-relations coups, as the press—always entranced by nuclear issues—gave prominent play to the SNF initiative while downplaying the more substantial conventional-forces proposal. "Gorbachev Hands a Surprised Baker an Arms Proposal," headlined the *New York Times* the next day; "Gorbachev Rolls Baker," read Rowland Evans and Robert Novak's column. Gorbachev's confidence bordered on cockiness, and the reception he had received in Washington in 1987 and in New York in 1988, as well as his trips to Europe, had clearly reinforced his natural instinct to play to the street. But while he was playing to the crowds abroad, the crowds at home were far less enthusiastic. Gorbachev was using victories on the outside to maintain his authority at home—and unless we could come up with a bold and politically imaginative proposal for the NATO Summit, which was now less than a month away, George Bush risked being upstaged diplomatically by Gorbachev.

My meeting with Gorbachev, I later told the President, reminded me of Molina's. The President's summit in Brussels in three weeks, I said, better remind us of Otto's—or we'd be in real diplomatic trouble.

CHAPTER 6

A "EUROPE WHOLE AND FREE"

All your strength is in union, All your danger is in discord.

—*Longfellow, "Hiawatha"*

In statecraft and strategy, paradoxes abound. Almost every achievement contains within its success the seeds of a future problem. This was certainly the case with the trump card Gorbachev had played in Moscow: short-range nuclear forces (SNF). Through the "zero option" provision of the Intermediate Nuclear Forces (INF) Treaty, which had been signed in Washington in December 1987, the USSR and the United States had agreed to eliminate an entire class of theater weapons—but that still left the short-range forces, and it immediately became clear that this would become the most contentious European issue we faced as we took office.*

The NATO plan had been to modernize the alliance's short-range nuclear missile, called the Lance, and for one simple reason: with the Warsaw Pact maintaining a massive advantage in conventional forces in Europe, the

---

*I was Ronald Reagan's Chief of Staff when he proposed the "zero option" in November 1981, and while I didn't play any role in negotiating the INF Treaty, I thought George Schultz had done a magnificent job turning the President's vision into a historic agreement. The INF Treaty was a breakthrough in that it not only eliminated an entire class of nuclear weapons, it codified two principles that would become critical to Bush administration arms-control policy. To get to zero weapons, the Kremlin, which had much higher levels of forces, had to make larger cuts than the West. This concept of "asymmetrical reductions" became critical when we discussed conventional arms, in which Soviet advantages were even greater. In addition, the treaty also required extensive, intrusive verification regimes. Previously, arms control had generally relied on "national technical means"—namely, spy satellites. The INF Treaty made on-site inspection a reality.

West needed to rely on nuclear weapons to deter an attack. Yet since SNF missiles had a range of less than 500 kilometers, and were based in West Germany, that meant that if they were ever used, they were likely to hit targets only in East Germany or Poland. Or as the Germans began to say, "The shorter the missile, the deader the German."

Everyone assumed that the incoming Bush administration was going to pursue the same plan, and avoid any negotiations on this subject, but that was before Gorbachev's speech to the United Nations in December 1989 outlined large unilateral conventional weapons cuts. Once again, Gorbachev had taken the political initiative, and we were losing the battle for public opinion. We had to do something to shake things up.

Moreover, SNF was only the most visible of what seemed to me to be a five-part challenge to transatlantic relations. The most important of these parts was our response to Gorbachev and perestroika. But I felt we would never get East-West relations right unless we first had West-West unity, not only with respect to this response but to the other four parts as well. Besides SNF, that meant developing a unified alliance position on conventional arms control, economic and political liberalization in Eastern Europe, and Western Europe's drive for integration.

If It's Wednesday, We Must Be in Spain

For these reasons, and because the President had pledged in the campaign to send his Secretary of State to alliance capitals to demonstrate the importance we attached to Europe and the North Atlantic Alliance, I left for Europe right after taking office in early February. In addition to wanting to work out a coherent strategy by hearing directly from the Europeans, I also felt that I would be far more credible in future dealings if early on I had met in person with the leaders of the alliance. (I knew that while the President had directed the CIA and read the "Company's" products voraciously, he valued judgments based on personal contact the most.) This intelligence gathering aspect of the trip was complemented by a more practical angle. If negotiations over SNF modernization were heading my way, I knew I would need strong personal bonds with my foreign minister counterparts in NATO, and I wanted to go out of my way by visiting them first. We also wanted to show that the United States—the largest member of the alliance—cared about the smallest. I knew London, Bonn, and Paris were of course the pillars of the alliance, but we also felt that many of the smaller capitals would be willing to be supportive of U.S. positions—if they felt we were taking our consultations with them seriously. That required visiting all fifteen allied capitals—and in just eight days!

It created a logistical nightmare for Karen Groomes and Pat Kennedy.

Karen had worked for me at both the White House and Treasury and was unparalleled as a scheduler. In fact, Dennis Ross always said that Karen Groomes and Caron Jackson, my executive assistant, were two of the most competent people he had met anywhere. Pat was a foreign service officer who had become a legend during George Shultz's tenure by getting Shultz's entire entourage into Moscow by train from Helsinki when the Soviet capital was fogbound. George had urged me to keep him on, and by the end of the first trip, I knew why. Pat just got things done. (On this trip, for example, I remember staying in a magnificent Teutonic castle in Bonn, Schloss Gymnich, where I had the usual high-tech secure telecommunications in my room. I only learned later that Pat's staff had been forced to tie the phone lines to a brick and throw them over the moat to get them into the castle.)

The trip started with a bang, in Ottawa on February 10, when Canadian Prime Minister Brian Mulroney, Foreign Minister Joe Clark, and Mulroney's able Chief of Staff, Derek Burney, in a meeting with the President and me, pointed out in their typical, straight-talking manner just what the problem was. "They sit in Moscow and go right to the heart of our weaknesses like you did to Dukakis with the Boston Harbor speech. On the other hand, we're great on policy but lousy on politics. Mr. President, you have to take the initiative—maybe with a trip to Eastern Europe," Mulroney said. At Treasury, I had spent a large amount of time negotiating the U.S.-Canada Free Trade Agreement, so I knew our Canadian interlocutors well. The United States was fortunate to have them as solid and supportive friends.

The President agreed, "You're right. We must take the offensive. We cannot just be seen as reacting to yet another Gorbachev move. We need to do it to keep public opinion behind the alliance. Maybe Eastern Europe is it—get in there in his end zone. Not to stir up revolution, but we're right on human rights, democracy, and freedom." It was the first of many meetings where Mulroney would play a critical role in shaping our thinking. In Iceland, Foreign Minister John Baldwin Hannibalsson reiterated the theme that was to become dominant in all my meetings with the Europeans: "We need to take the initiative."

England's Prime Minister Margaret Thatcher and her Foreign Minister, Sir Geoffrey Howe, were next. Thatcher had been Ronald Reagan's philosophical soul mate. A remarkably effective leader of her country, she was President Reagan's closest international counterpart, and I knew her well. She was best known for speaking bluntly and resolutely, but her warmth and grace in private contrasted sharply with the public image. As usual, she went right to the point. "We have to have SNF modernization," she said. It was crucial to maintaining deterrence, even though Germany opposed it.

"Kohl's actions are misguided, even in his own domestic terms. Leaders must not be afraid to lead. They must not follow their electorates and follow the mood of the moment. That's a prescription for defeat." Kohl had been arguing that his coalition government would collapse if we pushed modernization. While I was sympathetic to the substance of her argument, my inclination almost invariably was not to second-guess the instincts of others with respect to their own domestic politics. I always figured they probably knew their countries better than any foreigner could. But she pressed ahead: "If we're firm with Kohl, we could restore his natural instinct and encourage him to go ahead and work out the issue prior to the NATO Summit."

On Gorbachev, she was very pessimistic. She felt the forces aligned against him, both psychologically and politically, would prevent him from succeeding. Geoffrey Howe had been Chancellor of the Exchequer when I was White House Chief of Staff, and Foreign Secretary when I was Treasury Secretary. I knew him well as a first-rate intellect, and liked him. I told Howe that we needed to push Gorbachev to make hard choices in favor of reform and new thinking. "We must work together to find initiatives to correct the public perception that we are reacting to Gorbachev," I said, echoing my earlier meetings. Howe agreed, but was convinced Gorbachev had more initiatives to come: "He's got a well-stocked hat full of well-armed rabbits."

Needless to say, my trip to Bonn produced a diametrically opposite position on SNF. Flying across the channel to Bonn, I might as well have crossed into another world. Helmut Kohl, a superb politician, with a quick wit and engaging manner, had been as staunch an ally of Ronald Reagan as Margaret Thatcher had been during the 1982–83 Euromissile crisis. But now he was under strong domestic pressure, and wanted us to agree to negotiate with the Soviets on SNF levels, irrespective of modernization. The public row was also a private dispute. He clearly was in no mood to take London's counsel. "Mrs. Thatcher is rid of *her* missiles," he said. The divide between Britain and Germany on this issue put us in an extraordinarily difficult position, and finding a satisfactory solution to it that did not diminish our "special relationship" with our closest ally or strain our good relations with our German friends was an imperative.

Foreign Minister Hans-Dietrich Genscher took a more indirect route than Kohl. He wrapped the issue in a larger context and stressed that SNF should not be made a test of Germany's loyalty. Moving ahead on modernization in 1989 or 1990 would cause the government to fall in the December 1990 elections, he said, and a decision could be put off until 1991 or 1992. During the past few months, the State Department's European Bureau had warned me about what it perceived as the dangers of "Genscherism"—the purported tendency for Genscher to be soft on the Soviets, which had grown out of his remarks in Davos, Switzerland, in 1987, when he had said the Soviet leader could be taken "at his word." He had not been trusted during the Reagan administration, but I was willing to give him the benefit of the doubt, urged on in part by our then-Ambassador to Germany, Rick Burt. I remember later in the spring, standing on the eighth-floor balcony at the State Department, asking Hans-Dietrich, "How come everyone over here thinks you're such a bad guy? I don't think you're such a bad guy." He took the kidding well. I grew to have great respect for him, and for his intelligence, his political skills, and his ability to get things done. We went on to become fast friends, and after we had successfully worked closely on German unification issues (which included questions concerning Germany's eastern borders), I would tease him in front of others about our next effort: solving the "German-Chinese border problem."

From Germany I traveled to the Nordic countries, where the leaders were as blunt about the disadvantages of SNF modernization as Margaret Thatcher had been about its advantages. When I argued that modernization was a question of showing resolve, the Norwegian Prime Minister Gro Bruntland asked, "What does 'showing resolve' mean in terms of our specific agenda?" Both she and the Danish Foreign Minister Uffe Ellmann Jensen argued that this debate over a weapons system really had nothing to do with military requirements, but it had everything to do with politics—and their politics were distinctly not Britain's. The situation in Greece and Turkey was substantially the same—I was really getting an earful by then—but with a regional twist. The talk of European unity made both the Turks and the Greeks concerned that a unified Europe wouldn't include them, and they were getting nervous. Actually, the most interesting aspects of Athens had little to do with policy. I told Prime Minister Andreas Papandreou that, while in the Marines, I had been stationed with NATO forces for a short time in 1953 in Drama in northern Greece. There, I had befriended a Greek commando whose last name I could not remember. I just remembered that his rank was captain and his first name was Peter. He was a sculptor who had done a beautiful copy of the Venus de Milo and given it to me, a sculpture I still keep in my living room. Papandreou told me (quite rightly as it turned out) that we should be able to find the unusual combination of a commando captain named Peter who was also a sculptor and had served in Drama in 1953. And find him we did—living in Athens, but blind now and no longer able to sculpt. His last name was Moriatis, and we still correspond by letter.

Kim Hoggard, Margaret Tutwiler's deputy, became the center of another interesting scene. Kim had worked in the Reagan White House in the press office, and at State, one of her responsibilities was managing the press who traveled with me. On trips, Kim would shepherd her horde of fourth-estaters to photo ops and press conferences. That required dealing with the host government—and its security services. Reporters have many skills, but taking instructions and waiting patiently are not among them. On this trip, this tendency resulted in a bit of a mess.

As I was ushered into an elevator in an ornate palace high on a hill to meet with the Prime Minister, Kim was playing her "mother hen" role and steering the chosen handful of pool reporters to the photo opportunity. Unfortunately, she ran straight into an Athenian guard, armed with an Uzi and a bandolier of bullets, who moved to stop her. She began with her usual professional demeanor. "Sir, I need to get these people into the elevator for the Secretary's meeting." No response. "I really need to get up there. You see these people travel with the Secretary." The guard just lifted his machine gun, not so much threateningly as fearfully. It was an incongruous picture. On one side, the guard, replete with regalia and arms; on the other, Kim standing firm, with her journalists circling behind her. Finally, Kim simply walked around the guard, who just stood there, undoubtedly shocked by her temerity. When Kim arrived at the photo op, I was none the wiser to the altercation she had just been through.

Rome, Madrid, and Lisbon produced strong opinions of their own, with the leaders especially noting the ironic dichotomy in which the alliance found itself. On the one hand, there was Gorbachev, presiding over a failing system, with very real resistance internally and no formula for handling ferment in Eastern Europe. On the other hand, there was the vibrant, successful, and dynamic Western world that, nevertheless, felt itself on the defensive in the face of Gorbachev's proposals. Each leader emphasized Gorbachev's ability to play to Western publics, and it was becoming obvious to me that we had to counter his skills somehow. As Bob Zoellick liked to term it, we needed to be "playing offense" by pushing liberalization in Eastern Europe. If Gorbachev was going to try to split our alliance, we should certainly be working to play off the Eastern Europeans against Moscow. Prime Minister Cavaco Silva of Portugal reinforced the view by stressing that it would not be possible for the Communist countries to move ahead with economic reform without also moving ahead with democracy. You give people economic freedom and they will want political freedom, he said. Give them political freedom and they will want economic freedom.

Yet of all my stops, which also included France, the Benelux countries, and NATO headquarters, it was my meeting in the Netherlands with Foreign Minister Hans Van Den Broek that may have been the most important of all. "We talk too much about 'modernization,' which just creates problems for Germany," he said, "and not enough about what we actually need." He said he understood our resistance to SNF negotiations, but there had to be an arms control element in the plan that the alliance would issue at the summit. "Why not go for an integrated approach that would encompass both our modernization *and* our arms control needs?" he asked. He passed me a paper with some ideas. Conceptually, he was right, and it was the first time, but far from the last, that I would see this astute statesman suggest a solution to diplomatic deadlock. Now at last, I felt I had a valid angle of attack.

At NATO headquarters, the Secretary-General, Manfred Woerner, a staunch Atlanticist and strong supporter of U.S. leadership within NATO, made it clear he would be willing to help us find a compromise with Bonn. Even though he was a German himself, he understood the need to make hard choices. It was the first of many times where his principled approach won my admiration, and when he died of cancer in 1994, it was a great loss to the Atlantic Alliance.

On the last day of my whirlwind tour, I began the day in Brussels (again) to meet with Jacques Delors, President of the EC, and the Vice President, Hans Andriessen, before going on to Paris to meet with Roland Dumas. While my meetings were far from cold, the staunchly European-centered approach of Dumas and Delors (also a Frenchman) was a clear reminder that American leadership of the Atlantic Alliance would need to be asserted and earned. It could not be taken for granted. Dumas and I were both lawyers by training. The positions of our two countries naturally differed in many respects when it came to NATO, and so we disagreed on many issues. But Dumas was unfailingly courteous and we always disagreed agreeably, contrary to some press reports suggesting otherwise.

Unity or Discord?

I returned to Washington with a far better sense of how Gorbachev affected our European policy. The SNF debate was at heart a psychological dilemma. Modernization would, indeed, show the alliance's resolve, yet it would simultaneously create a public and, above all, nuclear symbol that the Kremlin could use with the Western European people against their governments. Moscow would split the alliance, not by pitting Kohl against Thatcher, but by creating political tensions within Germany that would prevent Kohl's fragile coalition from maintaining unity with the alliance.

The key to solving this nuclear dilemma lay in conventional arms control. Militarily, we wanted nuclear modernization to make up for the continuing imbalance in conventional forces. Despite the sweeping breadth of Gorbachev's U.N. proposal, the Soviets still would maintain their major advantages in troops, tanks, artillery, and armored personnel carriers, even after his unilateral cuts went into effect. If we could eliminate the asymmetry in conventional forces, we could put off the need to modernize Lance. A simple message underpinned everything I had heard: NATO could not afford another crisis over deploying nuclear weapons. The alliance may have been able to endure such a crisis in 1983, when the former KGB chief Yuri Andropov ran the Kremlin, but it would not be able to survive with the wily Mikhail Gorbachev in power. Thus, in my mind, progress on CFE was a prerequisite for solving SNF. (Even though this was the position to which I knew we were headed, publicly we kept up the pressure on the Germans and the alliance for modernization.)

Lowering conventional-force levels would also have two other useful effects. First, in Eastern Europe: the sight of withdrawing Soviet troops would have a positive effect on political liberalization. Each Red Army soldier that was redeployed back in the USSR would help lift a generation-old weight that had been holding down democracy and freedom. Second, in the West: in many states, particularly Germany, a barely conscious and growing resentment had grown against what was perceived to be an overly intrusive American military presence. Lowering American troop levels would certainly help dampen this sentiment.

All of this would have the important effect of demilitarizing Soviet foreign policy in Europe. It could also have positive effects on Soviet internal developments. The intrusive verification regime that we were planning for CFE would cultivate openness in Soviet society. Cuts in conventional forces would be hard to reverse, thereby institutionalizing change. And the military's role in Kremlin politics would diminish as the balance in Europe stabilized.

My European journey reinforced for me practically what I had known all along intellectually: The road to success with the Kremlin began not in Moscow, but in the capitals of Western Europe and Canada. Indeed, I said as much publicly in a speech before the American Society of Newspaper Editors in New York on April 14, arguing, "Ultimately, the success of our East-West policy depends on our West-West policy—the ability of the United States and its allies to work together."

The necessity for coalition building and management of alliances is a reality of almost all political activity. I suppose my first introduction to this fact came through research on my senior thesis at Princeton. My study of the conflict between Aneurin Bevan and Ernest Bevin in the British Labour Party after World War II showed amply the difficulties of maintaining the unity of any political coalition. Whatever academic knowledge of alliances and coalitions I had acquired as an undergraduate, however, had been supplemented by my work in electoral politics and my time at the White House and Treasury. Success in public service in our pluralistic society demands, above all, coalition building. During the Reagan administrations, I had worked closely with diverse congressional leaders such as Howard Baker, Bob Dole, Alan Simpson, Bob Packwood, Bob Michel, Trent Lott, Newt Gingrich, Bill Bradley, David Obey, Pat Moynihan, Dan Rostenkowski, Lloyd Bentsen, George Mitchell, Chris Dodd, Sam Nunn, Robert Byrd, Tom Foley, Jim Wright, and many others, to ensure Republican Party discipline on key votes and build coalitions with diverse and constantly changing blocs of Democrats.

In foreign policy, President Reagan had resolutely managed the Euro-missile crisis in the first years of his presidency. He had shown that the key to alliance unity was consistent American leadership. During the Cold War, that was the persistent paradox in transatlantic relations: While Europeans publicly complained about the imposing nature of American leadership, in private the political elite was consistently far more worried about a leadership vacuum caused by American disengagement or vacillation.

The danger was growing that NATO would fragment in the face of Gorbachev's charm offensive and a diminishing Soviet military threat. The centripetal forces working on the U.S.-European concord were increasing, while the centrifugal forces were diminishing. Without West-West unity, East-West relations would be controlled primarily by the Soviets, as Gorbachev played one side of the Atlantic off against the other.

Returning to Washington, however, I was stymied in efforts throughout the rest of February, and into March and April, to get any movement on a serious conventional-forces proposal. The bureaucratic impediments to movement were great. I knew that Scowcroft was working on Cheney and on Admiral Crowe, Chairman of the Joint Chiefs of Staff, to be more expansive in how they looked at the CFE negotiations. There was little point in pushing too hard in the first hundred days of the administration, anyway. Those are some of the most hectic times for any administration, and I knew, with everything else he had to deal with, the President would not focus on the arms control issues until the summit was closer at hand. My sense of timing also made me believe that as the May 29–30 dates for the NATO Summit approached, the President's competitive instincts would come to the fore, and we'd be able to break the logjam then.

Time for Some "New Thinking" of Our Own

The time became ripe in early May as three events converged.

First, on May 5, Chancellor Kohl and the President spoke by phone. Kohl asked the President to send a special emissary to Bonn to try and solve SNF. He was blunt about his objectives: "First, I want the summit to be successful. Second, I want you to have a success. It will be your first trip to Europe as President. You are a proven friend of the Europeans and, in particular, the Germans. I have never forgotten this fact and never will forget it."

Speaking as a friend, he went on to set the context for George Bush. "We are in a historical position," he said. "It is far from my mind to see Gorbachev as the new hero, and I do not mistake words for deeds. However, you and I are witnessing events beyond our wildest dreams, the ideological breakdown of a political and economic system. This is the hour of our triumph. A triumph, due not least to the efforts of the United States. This is why I think your role should be brought to the fore. This is linked to the cohesion of NATO, and to the success of the NATO Summit."

Second, on May 12, the President gave a speech on Soviet affairs. He argued that we should move "beyond containment," but he presented no new proposals other than to resuscitate an Eisenhower proposal for "open skies" over Europe. The press coverage was less than enthusiastic, and it was clear we would need to do more if the summit were to be a success.

The third event was Gorbachev's SNF ploy in Moscow. It may have irritated me, but it also catalyzed the President. George Bush knew that with the Soviets' massive advantage in short-range nuclear forces (1,400 launchers for the Warsaw Pact to 88 for NATO!), the Kremlin might present yet another proposal before the NATO Summit, and upstage his first venture into Europe as President.

By the time the President and I sat down for lunch on May 17, he was primed. He had already asked Brent to talk to Cheney and Admiral Crowe to put together a bold CFE proposal. "You need to get ahead of the power curve," I told the President, which meant starting from the standpoint that any proposal had to have political impact first and foremost. I suggested a cut of 25 percent in both equipment and manpower made sense. Twenty-five percent would, I thought, generate the kind of political effect we were looking for, while not endangering us militarily.

Over the next week, in a series of meetings at the White House and at the Bush family home in Kennebunkport, Maine, the President listened to his senior advisers thrash out possible proposals. Crowe acted as though Leonid Brezhnev were still running the Kremlin, and he fought virtually every proposal tooth and nail. Cheney was far less dogmatic, but Dick felt Gorbachev was going to come our way anyway, so why move? I argued that we needed a radical initiative for three reasons: First, the President needed to exert leadership over the alliance. Second, a bold CFE proposal would make SNF basically irrelevant, allowing us to resolve the issue and ensure alliance unity. And, finally, Gorbachev's conventional proposal to me in Moscow (which received little press play) showed that he wanted CFE quite badly, and we could move him even further if we were forthcoming. Scowcroft and I were in fundamental agreement. He had been pushing all along to get Soviet troops out of Eastern Europe and realized, too, that the "beyond containment" speech was being interpreted as just a "status quo plus" policy.

With the summit less than two weeks away, the President told Crowe and Cheney, "I want this done. Don't keep telling me why it can't be done. Tell me how it can be done."

The proposal as we finally formed it marked several major departures for NATO. Most important, it included a cut of U.S. and Soviet troops in Europe to 20 percent below current levels. That would require us to cut something on the order of 30,000 troops, but it would require Moscow to withdraw roughly 325,000 troops from Eastern Europe. Moreover, the President proposed that the treaty be negotiated within six months and that it be implemented at the latest by 1993. That meant SNF would essentially become irrelevant within a year or two at most. It was a bold move. The President sent Larry Eagleburger, Bob Gates (Brent Scowcroft's deputy at the NSC), and Jim Timbie, an unsung and unassuming arms control specialist, to preview the proposal with key allies. (Timbie, to my mind, was the epitome of what America needs in its senior civil servants: unfailingly knowledgeable, unerringly loyal, incredibly organized, and invariably creative.)

Meanwhile, SNF had been basically deadlocked. The President had taken Kohl up on his offer to send a special emissary, and Gates and Zoellick had gone to Bonn on the margins of my trip to the Soviet Union. But they couldn't make much progress, as the Germans were too dug in. The German government clearly had a domestic political problem with modernization that had no arms control component to it whatsoever. So some compromise between the German and British positions had to be found. The Germans had indicated a willingness to compromise by accepting modernization accompanied by some arms control component. Thatcher had no domestic political constraint and could be flexible if she were willing, so she was the one we were going to have to work on.

I met with the President on May 19. "You've got to lead the alliance, and that means getting Margaret to compromise on SNF," I said. "If you don't, she won't pay the cost. You will." After seeing his determination to push SNF despite the objections of Crowe and Cheney, I sensed he would be willing to sit down, have a straight talk, and assert American leadership.

My job, as we flew across the Atlantic for the summit, would be to eliminate as many obstacles to that discussion as I could. The first day in Brussels, May 29, while President Bush and I sat down with the other leaders and foreign ministers, Bob Zoellick went to work trying to eliminate the brackets remaining on the "Comprehensive Concept"—the sixty-four-paragraph text that NATO would issue as a communiqué. Of course, by the time we arrived, most of the language had been finalized, leaving only the most contentious issues to be handled at the summit itself. After six or seven hours, Zoellick had done a great job, eliminating most of the brackets.

At 5:00 P.M., I sat down next to Bob, taking the chair for the United States as Geoffrey Howe, Hans-Dietrich Genscher, Hans Van Den Broek and the other foreign ministers took over the negotiation. As the discussion droned on through dinner and into the evening, Zoellick became more and more frustrated with me because I was simply listening or, occasionally, resisting changes that might have been acceptable to London.

"Why is he being so passive? It's there to be done," Dennis Ross whispered to Zoellick.

"Why are you holding back?" Zoellick finally asked.

"At some point, either very late tonight or early this morning," I began, "George Bush, as the leader of the alliance, is going to have to get Margaret Thatcher to compromise. I want him to be able to say to her, 'Jim stayed with Geoffrey the whole way. There was no daylight between Britain and America. This is the best we can do.' " I wanted to ease the President's task if I could. I was also thinking ahead to the next day, when Thatcher might try to bump the decision up to the heads of state in the event the President couldn't get her to accept the compromise. The closer I stayed to Howe, the harder it would be to argue that there was more to be gained.

I must admit the scene was rather surreal. The foreign ministers had been scheduled to join the heads of government at a formal dinner, so we were all dressed in tuxedos, yet we were forced to eat the NATO cafeteria's infamous cheese sandwiches. Moreover, there were really only four players involved in the game: Howe, Genscher, Van Den Broek, and me. So while someone else was speaking, going through their formal remarks, I would walk up to Genscher and pull him aside for a tête-à-tête. Then Howe and I would pair off for a discussion about what Genscher and I had discussed. Occasionally, Van Den Broek would join in, ever the problem solver. Twice during the negotiations, at 11:00 P.M. and 12:15 A.M., I spoke to the President to ensure that we were in complete agreement on negotiating tactics.

At one point, I tried to indicate to Genscher that we had gone as far as we could. "It's my suspicion that Geoffrey has no flexibility. The PermRep had [Charles] Powell's job." Powell was Thatcher's personal National Security Adviser, and Michael Alexander, his predecessor and now the U.K.'s Permanent Representative to NATO, was obviously staying in the room to keep an eye on Howe and ensure he didn't give anything away.

Finally, we had agreement on everything but one crucial issue: the question of the third zero. The United States was willing to delay modernization, but not kill the prospect of modernization completely. Zoellick had worked out four or five different formulations, and Joe Clark had come up with the idea of putting the adverb "partially" before the verb "reduce," to show that while we would negotiate down, we wouldn't by implication allow total elimination of SNF. We ended up with the phrase, "partial reductions," and I suggested underlining it to emphasize that there would be no zero. Of such fine, if boring, nuances are diplomatic negotiations concluded.

The Vision "Thing" Unveiled

Later that morning, the President unveiled his CFE proposal to the alliance as a whole. It caused a massive stir in the room. Thatcher told the group it had "transformed" their discussions, and she readily acceded to the SNF compromise we had worked out the night before. President François Mitterrand took the floor and said, "We need innovation. The President of the United States has displayed imagination—indeed, intellectual audacity of the rarest kind." The press, which the week before had accused the President of being hapless and inarticulate for talking about the "vision thing," was now hailing him. George Bush could only laugh. As he told Ann Devroy and Don Oberdorfer of the *Washington Post,* he was the same man he had been a few days before. But now he was understood, correctly, to be *the* leader of the alliance.

As we left Europe, I reflected back on the paradox that had led to our success. Gorbachev's publicity stunt on May 11 had allowed me to come back to the White House and argue more vehemently for movement on CFE, which, in turn, had been made possible by Gorbachev's substantively more important conventional-forces proposal that same day. The President had already been moving in that direction and was more than receptive to going further. His instructions to Cheney and Crowe, in turn, not only advanced CFE, but allowed us to negotiate a satisfactory conclusion to the dilemmas created by SNF. These achievements showed that we were indeed moving to a "Europe whole and free," as the President put it in his speech in Mainz, Germany, immediately after the summit. We wouldn't have much time to savor our success in Europe, however. On the other side of the globe, events were about to take a dangerous turn for the worse.

CHAPTER 7

CHINA: A GREAT LEAP BACKWARD

This is China's internal affair.
> —*Chinese Foreign Minister Qichen Qian to Secretary Baker regarding the massacre in Tiananmen Square*

The morning of Saturday, June 3, 1989, dawned clear and sunny in Washington. It was perfect golf weather, one of those fleeting early-summer days before the suffocating humidity of July and August saps the spirit and enervates all but the hardiest natives. On the spur of the moment, I called the Chevy Chase Country Club, then telephoned my eldest son, Jamie, at his home in suburban Alexandria, Virginia. It was about 9:30 A.M.

"I've got a great deal for you," I told him. "I've got a tee time at Chevy Chase in forty-five minutes. Grab your sticks and come on over right now and we'll play some golf."

"I don't think you're going to be playing any golf today," Jamie replied.

"What do you mean?"

"Well, I'm sitting here watching tanks rolling through Tiananmen Square on CNN."

"You're kidding me."

"No."

After a few startled seconds of silence, I understood he wasn't. "Okay," I said. "I've got to go."

As I hung up, my other phone line rang. It was a duty officer at the State Department Operations Center, informing me that heavily armed units of the People's Liberation Army had indeed begun firing on demonstrators in the heart of Beijing. Casualties were expected to be heavy, I was told.

The Tiananmen massacre was without question the greatest blow to normalization since Richard Nixon's historic 1972 overture began the process. The crackdown ordered by an anachronistic regime of gerontocrats shattered the bipartisan consensus in the United States that had been carefully constructed over two decades by five administrations for engagement with China. Almost overnight, one of America's most striking Cold War strategic successes was shaken to its core.

As the unflinching lens of television news brought home the brutality of the regime in Beijing, the climate of goodwill toward China on the part of average Americans quickly dissipated. The domestic outcry forced a tricky juggling act upon our new administration. Suddenly, we were challenged to defend a policy encompassing geostrategic, commercial, and human rights interests that in large measure conflicted. In the end, I believe we crafted a middle course that enabled the relationship to survive, but not without repercussions from which both nations have yet to recover fully.

First Encounters with the Middle Kingdom

My first substantial exposure to the People's Republic of China occurred in the spring of 1977, shortly after I'd returned to Houston to resume my law practice after President Ford's defeat by Jimmy Carter. George Bush called me one day to say that he'd been invited by the Chinese government to visit in October, and wanted Susan and me to accompany him. Susan was pregnant with our daughter Mary Bonner, who was expected to arrive in September, so she couldn't go, much to her great disappointment. But I was eager to visit the sprawling Communist behemoth, about which I knew very little, other than Chiang Kai-shek, the Flying Tigers of World War II, and the sobering realization that many Marine buddies from my Basic class at Quantico had been killed by Chinese "volunteers" in Korea.

Our party of ten, which included the radio commentator Lowell Thomas, was entertained like royalty by our hosts. We met with a multitude of government leaders, including Deng Xiaoping, and were allowed into parts of the country normally forbidden to Westerners. We were among the few Americans, for example, who had been allowed into Tibet since the 1959 uprising in support of the Dalai Lama had prompted a Chinese crackdown in Tibet and led the Dalai Lama to flee to India. We reached the capital of Lhasa after an unnerving plane ride—upon breaking through a cloud bank at 25,000 feet, I peered out my window to see Himalayan peaks towering even higher than we were. Then, at the airport, our Chinese hosts met us with small canvas bags filled with oxygen to help us adjust to the 12,000-foot elevation. Tibet seemed like an occupied country, with People's Liberation Army soldiers outnumbering native Tibetans. My other enduring memories include feasting on cold sea slugs for breakfast, and seeing a photograph of a young Lowell Thomas in a museum exhibit that depicted American imperialists banned from Tibet for corrupting the country.

The warmth of our reception and the scope of our itinerary were testaments to the affection held by the Chinese for Barbara and George Bush—he had been the United States envoy to China from 1974 to 1976, before formal diplomatic relations had been established. They knew George Bush was a genuine friend, someone who understood and admired their culture and had sought to expand and solidify Sino-American relations during his tour in Beijing. I had no inkling, of course, that twelve years later his credibility with Chinese leaders and the personal relations he'd developed would be instrumental in sustaining the bilateral relationship through the darkest hours it would endure since Nixon's historic visit to China, seventeen years before.

I traveled to China with President Reagan in 1984, then visited again briefly in 1986, when, as Secretary of the Treasury, I negotiated a taxation treaty with the Chinese government. And in February of 1989, I returned for a fourth time, this time to accompany President Bush on his first trip abroad to attend the funeral of Japanese Emperor Hirohito.

It was the President's idea to expand that trip to include stops in Korea and China. In addition to reinforcing the U.S. security commitment to the South Koreans, he was particularly intent on using the opportunity of an early visit to underscore to the Chinese the importance he attached to improving bilateral relations, and his determination to demonstrate that the United States was a Pacific power as well as an Atlantic one.

During that trip, I met Chinese Foreign Minister Qian Qichen at the Diaoyutai guest house. I'd been told that the chain-smoking Qian was one of the few unabashed Anglophiles in the Chinese leadership. His passion for American culture was well known within the diplomatic corps—particularly his fondness for country-and-western music and the Great Smoky Mountains of Tennessee. It was a friendly and relaxed meeting, with both of us reiterating our commitment to strengthening and expanding bilateral ties. Much of this session focused on economic issues. I told Qian that, since leaving Treasury, "I have been struck by the extent to which economic relations between our two countries have blossomed over the past year." I could not have suspected that little more than 100 days later, our overall relations would be at great risk.

Our Top China Hand—
the President of the United States

Normally, the State Department is an institution in which the process of intellectual fermentation keeps a steady stream of policy papers routinely bubbling up through the bureaucracy, to be vetted at the senior policy levels of government. In the case of China policy, however, it's fair to say that very few policy initiatives were generated either by State or the National Security Council staff during my tenure. There was no real need. George Bush was so knowledgeable about China, and so hands-on in managing most aspects of our policy, that even some of our leading Sinologists began referring to him as the government's desk officer for China.

He was, after all, a bona fide China hand. After two years as our liaison officer with Beijing in the mid-1970s, he understood the Chinese psyche well, and had used his talents for personal diplomacy to forge strong ties with virtually all the senior officials in the Chinese leadership. From the instant of his inauguration, he took an unusually personal interest in China policy and drove its development to an unprecedented degree. His choice for U.S. Ambassador to Beijing, James Lilley, exemplified the President's hands-on approach. Lilley spoke the language fluently and had accompanied us on our 1977 visit. He'd also been the Central Intelligence Agency's station chief in Beijing during Ambassador Bush's tenure, and was, like the President, well versed in the subtleties of Chinese politics and culture.

I wholeheartedly agreed with the President's fundamental philosophy toward China of building on the Reagan administration's policy of broad engagement. There was no question that China was an emerging Pacific colossus that could not be ignored. As in Europe, a new order was taking shape in Asia, largely grounded in a stunning expansion of economic growth and trade. Having fought three wars in Asia in a single generation, the United States was destined to play a crucial role in designing the architecture of this emerging order, and China was a linchpin of these developments.

We recognized, of course, that China's eagerness for economic development was considerably more pronounced than its commitment to political reform. Beijing's record on human rights had contributed to a fair amount of congressional reluctance toward warming relations. The Chinese performance on human rights in fact had been quite dismal by Western standards. I saw this firsthand as Secretary of the Treasury, a department involved in enforcing restrictions against the importation of goods manufactured in Chinese slave labor camps. Nevertheless, it was our judgment that some progress was being made, and we further believed that expanding our ties would encourage the Chinese toward more progress. History shows that economic and political reform are but two sides of the same coin. Give someone economic freedom and they will want political freedom. The reverse is true as well. In pressing the Chinese on human rights matters, we wanted to do what we could to convince an aging leadership that, while they were moving from a Soviet-style economy, they should also recognize that political change must keep pace with the aspirations of the Chinese people. We also understood that they needed our help to sustain their economic growth. We were prepared to use this leverage to encourage greater progress toward political reform.

For all these reasons, the President was determined to engage the Chinese aggressively. He was also intent on ushering in a new level of stability to our bilateral dealings. During more than 150 years of Sino-American contacts, the nature of the relationship could be fairly described as a compass with only two headings. In the McCarthy era of the 1950s, the Chinese were godless Communists who killed our sons in Korea and repressed their own people. In the 1970s, they were a hardworking and long-suffering people, whose exotic and mysterious culture was romanticized by American popular opinion and deemed worthy of intensive engagement by Republican and Democratic presidents alike. The President wanted to end the oscillation between these extremes of confrontation and fascination.

A Promising Start Turns Sour

In early 1989, Sino-American relations were at their postnormalization peak. A broad array of diplomatic, economic, military, and cultural exchanges was flourishing. Winston Lord, whose wife, Bette Bao Lord, was a native Chinese, was the American Ambassador to Beijing. Deng Xiaoping's economic reforms were taking hold, and as a result U.S. trade with China was exploding. Several years of quiet groundwork on our behalf to encourage changes in China's trade policies, so that she could join the GATT world trading system, were beginning to show some promise. Geopolitically, the Chinese were becoming increasingly open and frank in their dialogue with us. Their candor about what was happening inside their North Korean client state, for instance, and their willingness to intervene quietly with Pyongyang in behalf of American interests, was nothing less than remarkable. By historical standards, the relationship was quite close, and by general consensus held an enormous amount of promise. With a committed friend of China now in the White House, there was every reason to expect the relationship would attain a new level of maturity and stability.

At the same time, a new round of internal upheaval was stirring in China. Throughout the 1980s, economic reform proceeded in fairly impressive fashion, but political reform was less dramatic, and prompted growing public dissent. As President Bush took office, Sinologists detected growing evidence of a power struggle within the government between party chief Zhao Ziyang, a protégé of Deng (as Treasury Secretary, I had met Zhao in China) and a proponent of greater reform, and a more cautious faction led by Premier Li Peng. The annual meeting of the party congress in March of 1989 was marked by what many Western experts perceived as a diminished interest in political reform.

In the weeks that followed, student demonstrations broke out in several cities, including a series of protests in Beijing's massive Tiananmen Square. These demonstrations gradually escalated to the point where hundreds of thousands of demonstrators, representing a cross section of Chinese society, joined the students in almost daily protests. As these protests escalated, the hard-liners within the leadership gained strength for their view that the demonstrations had taken on a counterrevolutionary aura and must be dealt with forcibly.

On May 19, the government declared martial law and ordered army units to Beijing to restore order. Three days later, by coincidence, I met in Washington with Wan Li, the third-highest member of the Chinese government. In addition to his status as a Politburo member and chairman of the National People's Congress, the elderly, white-haired Wan carried the added cachet of having frequently played tennis with George Bush in 1974 and 1975. As the demonstrations intensified, the administration had repeatedly urged restraint on the government in both public and private exchanges. I reiterated the President's concern to Wan, whom I knew was well positioned to influence the government's policy.

"While instability in China is not something we want," I said, "we hope that the trend toward reform and political tolerance will continue." Any regression, I suggested, would have an "adverse effect" on our relations.

He responded that, in imposing martial law, the government had acted peacefully to restore order and that only a small number of demonstrators were attempting to foment unrest. Then he ominously noted, "Some things are unavoidable. One should not exclude the possibility of unfortunate incidents. There might be a possibility that bloodshed cannot be avoided." I repeated that while the U.S. government applauded Chinese restraint, "It will be significant for Sino-U.S. relations should this restraint give way to violent measures." I sensed that he understood my meaning, but I also understood his. This was, I would grimly recall all too soon, a harbinger of the tragedy to come.

Slaughter of the Innocents

Finally, on the night of June 3, the confrontation reached critical mass. Regular army troops commanded to restore order in the center of Beijing began firing on protesters. In several hours of carnage, at least several hundred demonstrators were killed and thousands wounded. Tiananmen Square, the geographical center of Chinese life, became a killing field for the army. In a matter of hours, the square was cleared and a brutal wave of repression began throughout the country.

It should be noted that the impact of the massacre on Sino-American relations would surely have been compounded if not for the quick reaction and courage of the U.S. embassy staff. As soon as embassy officials learned that heavily armed troops and tanks were on their way to the square, Ambassador Jim Lilley dispatched embassy officers to the square to warn Americans and other foreign nationals to leave immediately. In response to this warning, a number of Americans departed the scene literally minutes before the shooting began.

The terrible tragedy of Tiananmen was a classic demonstration of a powerful new phenomenon: the ability of the global communications revolution to drive policy. Not since the Vietnam War had Americans witnessed such dramatic images in their living rooms. And unlike Vietnam, where war footage was usually delayed for hours or sometimes days, the carnage in Beijing was captured live and relayed instantly via satellite. The single most powerful image of all was surely that of a lone demonstrator courageously stopping a tank literally in its tracks.

Since then, of course, such "eyewitness news" coverage has become commonplace. In Iraq, Bosnia, Somalia, Rwanda, and Chechnya, among others, the real-time coverage of conflict by the electronic media has served to create a powerful new imperative for prompt action that was not present in a less frenetic time. In the future, I suspect that this trend will intensify— along with public outcries for the United States to become involved in situations of great tragedy that may or may not be consonant with our national interest.

It's imperative that the United States remain engaged internationally, but even as the last superpower, we can neither prevent nor solve all the world's traumas. Our leadership must therefore be selective and based on both the requirements of our national interest and our principles and values. The inevitable intrusion of the video camera and satellite link will make it all the more difficult to engage selectively in the decades ahead.

During the Cultural Revolution, American diplomats were largely in the dark about the true extent of the Chinese government's repression. In this reprise of authoritarian excess, however, the brutality of the regime was undeniable. There was no question that a stern response was essential.

The President was appalled by the slaughter, as were all of us, but his personal distress was heightened by his prior association with the Chinese leadership who had ordered the massacre. He knew that the strategic relationship had been dealt a body blow. "It's going to be difficult to manage this problem," he told me on the day the violence erupted. In hopes of containing the damage to bilateral relations and halting the bloodshed, he tried to telephone Deng directly, but was rebuffed. This not only angered him but also fueled his concern about whether the issue could be handled successfully.

By coincidence, I'd previously agreed to be interviewed by Charles Bierbauer and Ralph Begleiter on CNN's "Newsmaker Saturday" on the afternoon of June 3. I acknowledged that "the situation in China is turning ugly and chaotic" and urged the Chinese government to halt the violence. My most vivid recollection of that interview is that it was interrupted by a live telephone dispatch from CNN correspondent Mike Chinoy, who was watching the violence in Tiananmen Square. As Chinoy reported thousands of troops firing into crowds and even bayoneting demonstrators, my mind's eye carried me back to the Hungary of 1956, when, as a law student at the University of Texas, I'd watched the grim newsreel footage of Soviet tanks crushing the freedom fighters of Budapest. A third of a century later, I had a strong sense of déjà vu as I listened to reports of young men and women being murdered by yet another repressive Communist government.

In considering our response to the massacre, there was simply no dispute that we had to strike a delicate balance between the need for decisive steps and the need to safeguard the underlying strategic relationship to the extent possible. As President Bush would later note, "This is not the time for an emotional response, but for a reasoned, careful action that takes into account both our long-term interests and recognition of a complex internal situation in China."

Certainly, it was clear to us all that we could no longer conduct business as usual with the Chinese. President Bush was filled with revulsion by the slaughter, and felt that in terms of principle, as well as policy and politics, he had no choice but to react strongly to the horror of Tiananmen.

Beyond the political realities at home, the Chinese also needed to understand that we weren't paper tigers on the matter of human rights. Strength inevitably irritates the Chinese, but they understand it. And the absence of resolve in dealing with them can lead to serious miscalculation on their part.

Geostrategically, it was also critical to establish a marker with the forces of conservatism in the Soviet Union and Eastern Europe, where similar reversals of democratic stirrings remained a constant possibility—to let them know that there would be serious repercussions to our relations in the event of similar behavior.

On the other hand, we needed to proceed in a measured way. The Chinese leadership was clearly in an embattled frame of mind. Historically, in previous circumstances of internal turmoil, they had blamed foreign "barbarians" and turned even more reactionary. It was important not to respond in a way that played into the hands of the hard-liners who were pushing for even more repressive action, which would inevitably lead to more bloodshed.

And finally, in expressing our outrage and condemnation of the bloody crackdown, it was important for us to do so, if possible, in a way to preempt punitive congressional legislation that might be difficult to reverse and could do needless long-term damage to the relationship.

On June 5, President Bush announced sanctions against the Chinese government. These included a suspension of U.S. military sales and a halt to all visits between American and Chinese military leaders. In addition, he all but invited Chinese students and scholars in the United States to ask for permission to delay their return to China by announcing that any such requests would be given a "sympathetic review." He also met with a group of Chinese students to signal his concern in a more symbolic way.

"The United States cannot condone such repression and cannot ignore its consequences for our relationship with China," he told reporters.

Later that day, the President agreed to my recommendation that we postpone the June 12 visit of the Chinese Foreign Minister to Washington. An interagency working group had recommended that the visit go forward, but I didn't believe that expressing our outrage to Qian, and then receiving him a week after the massacre, sent a sufficiently strong message to the Chinese leadership that business as usual was over. The Chinese promptly announced that the postponement had been their idea.

Within twenty-four hours, we began evacuating dependents of U.S. diplomatic personnel and urging the 8,800 Americans living in China to leave the country immediately.

At the time, we understood that more sanctions would almost certainly be required. The repression in China was surely worse than initially thought. As the full magnitude of the horror in Beijing sank in, it was imperative for us to lead world reaction rather than leave the perception that we were being dragged along by Congress. On the other hand, our cultural, scholarly, and scientific exchanges had helped to keep China open to the forces of change that were so critical to reform, and I believed they should be insulated from U.S. countermeasures if at all possible.

Like the President, I was also adamantly opposed to the idea of revoking China's most-favored-nation trading status. By coincidence, the President had sent the required certification renewing MFN for the Chinese to Congress only three days before the massacre. MFN status had been a critical catalyst in the expansion of our bilateral ties, and an underpinning of Deng's reforms toward a market economy. Of all the instruments of retaliation proposed by our critics, this was clearly the most counterproductive. It would have been detrimental to the United States economically, hurt the forces of reform in China, and isolated the Chinese to a dangerous degree.

First Attempts at Consciousness Raising

On June 7, I summoned Chinese Ambassador Han Xu to my ceremonial office on the seventh floor. I knew him well, having met him on my first trip to China in 1977, at which time he'd been extraordinarily helpful and engaging while serving as the Foreign Ministry's liaison officer with the Bush party. He'd helped Nixon officials plan the historic 1972 visit and was a firm proponent of stronger ties. The President and I considered him a good friend and had been delighted when he was posted to Washington. Although he was completely composed, I sensed that he was in considerable inner turmoil over a policy I was certain he privately viewed with horror and heartbreak. The poignancy of the moment was quite overwhelming.

"The President thought it would be a good idea for you to hear directly from me just how distressed he and I are over what is happening in your country," I told him. "The United States is committed to democracy and freedom of speech and assembly, and we cannot tolerate what we are seeing." I told him that the President expected the lives and property of American citizens to be protected, and that we wanted landing rights for American military planes based in Japan in order to evacuate American citizens on a moment's notice if required. "And I must remind you that while this President is a friend of China," I added, "the actions of your government cast a serious pall over our relations."

The Ambassador had very little to say. He repeated the shopworn argument about such matters being China's internal affair, and promised to pass on my objections to his government. He knew, as did I, that the relationship was on the verge of sliding into an abyss from which it might require years to reemerge. It must not be easy, I thought to myself, to preserve one's dignity in such circumstances, forced to defend a policy as indefensible as this. I couldn't help but feel sorry for him.

I met with Han Xu again on June 10, in an effort to resolve the fate of Fang Lizhi, the astrophysicist whose association with the opposition had made him anathema to the government. Fearing for their lives, Fang and his wife had fled to the safety of the American embassy shortly after the killings began. The Chinese were livid at the President's decision to grant them temporary asylum. A friendly source in the Chinese government had confided to an American official that Deng himself was extremely upset about the matter, and that the government would use force to seize Fang if the United States attempted to spirit him out of the country—a course which Lilley at one point suggested we consider.

Even though Fang had been a continuing source of friction in our relations with the Chinese—they had been furious when he'd been invited to the President's reciprocal dinner during his 1989 trip to Beijing—there was never any question about granting him asylum. However, after we negotiated his safe passage from China, Fang showed his gratitude for our efforts by traveling to the United States and frequently criticizing our refusal to cut off MFN for China.

"We understand how important this issue is to your leadership," I told Han Xu, "but I must stress that it is also a matter of importance for President Bush." I added that the President was open to any suggestion Beijing had on how to resolve the matter "in a manner that respects both our interests," and suggested that sanctuary in a third country was a reasonable compromise. But we would not allow Fang and his wife to be forced out of the embassy.

"Allowing this issue to become a major irritant between our two countries will greatly complicate the larger task of returning our relationship to a sound footing," I argued.

The Chinese, unfortunately, seemed utterly oblivious to our concerns. Their response was more ruthlessness. On June 9, Deng Xiaoping was seen on television endorsing the action of his military commanders. In rapid succession, more than 400 dissidents were arrested in Beijing, and all independent student and worker organizations were ordered to disband. More ominous, we began receiving reports that dissidents were being sentenced to death by show trials. The President formally appealed to the Chinese government for clemency, to no effect. As the executions began, we decided to take more stringent actions.

On June 20, the President announced a second wave of sanctions. He ordered the suspension of all high-level contacts with Beijing and asked international financial institutions such as the World Bank and International Monetary Fund to postpone all new lending to China indefinitely. A trip by Secretary of Commerce Bob Mosbacher planned for July was cancelled. Almost simultaneously, word was received in Washington that twenty-four protesters had been executed. On June 24, Zhao Ziyang was accused of fostering "counterrevolutionary rebellion," ousted as party chairman, and placed under house arrest.

Congress Turns up the Temperature

Our attempts to salvage the strategic relationship by navigating a middle ground were complicated by intense pressure from Congress, where an improbable alliance of liberals who had been disillusioned by China's contempt for human rights and hard-core anti-Communist conservatives joined forces to demand a more muscular attitude towards Beijing. The poles of this coalition were represented by Senator Jesse Helms of North Carolina and Representatives Stephen Solarz of New York and Nancy Pelosi of California, whose district included San Francisco's Chinatown.

Throughout the crisis, the President was peppered with congressional demands to do more, followed by threats to legislate sanctions even more stringent than those he had imposed. I believed such a course would enrage the Chinese, damage the cause of reform, and create a backlash that might well threaten the very foundation of the relationship. In testimony before the House Foreign Affairs Committee on June 22, I made clear that the President's revulsion with his old friends in Beijing was genuine. "They can clear the square," I said, "but they cannot clear their conscience." But I also urged Congress to join with the President in a unified policy instead of insisting upon its own shortsighted approach.

In a speech to the Asia Society in New York four days later, I sought to reinforce this theme. "The hasty dismantling of a constructive U.S.-Chinese relationship, built up so carefully over two decades, would serve neither our interests nor those of the Chinese people," I said. "Above all, it would not help those aspirations for democracy that were so obvious in the millions who marched to support the students in Tiananmen Square."

Despite the results of public opinion surveys that backed the President's centrist approach by huge margins, Congress persisted in demanding tougher measures. On June 30, the House approved an amendment to the foreign aid authorization bill and imposed additional economic sanctions on China by a vote of 418–0. In July, the Senate followed suit by an 81–10 margin. These margins were so overwhelming that it was clearly impossible to sustain a veto, and the President reluctantly signed the bill.

A Secret Overture

Even as we expanded sanctions against the Chinese, we also looked for creative ways to keep the relationship alive, recognizing that there was essentially nothing we could do bilaterally for the foreseeable future. The idea was to make it clear to the Chinese very privately that while their behavior was unacceptable and couldn't be ignored, the administration took no joy in imposing sanctions and was seeking ways to reconcile our estrangement.

The Chinese had to be made to realize, however, that progress was impossible until they ceased their repression.

To reinforce this reality in unmistakable terms, the President proposed to send Brent Scowcroft on a secret trip to China. I agreed with the concept but objected to the idea of sending Brent off without a State Department representative. I'd never liked such secret missions by officials of the National Security Council. In the Reagan era, I'd seen more than once what happened to the conduct of foreign policy when the NSC was allowed to "go operational." The system simply wouldn't work if State were excluded from such endeavors. I would have preferred to go myself, but a mission of this sort had to be conducted in absolute secrecy, and in the modern era there's simply no way for a Secretary of State ever to travel incognito. I suggested to the President that my deputy, Larry Eagleburger, should accompany Brent to Beijing, and he readily agreed. They were old friends and colleagues, and a perfect complement to one another. The President sent Deng Xiaoping a personal letter asking him to receive his two emissaries.

On Sunday, June 25, after a round of golf at Andrews Air Force Base with Australian Prime Minister Bob Hawke, President Bush and I returned to the White House residence, where we were joined by Larry and Brent. The President said that he'd received a response to his letter. Deng had agreed to meet with them, and had pledged to maintain the utmost secrecy about the meeting.

The President's guidance was explicit. The Chinese must be made to understand that while he was committed to maintaining the relationship, he was personally dismayed by the violence and could not in good conscience allow a return to normalcy until the repression ceased.

Given the political climate, it was essential that word of this visit not leak to the press. Congressional hard-liners would promptly accuse us of appeasing the "Butchers of Beijing," and the President's efforts to preserve the relationship would come under even greater pressure. Moreover, the Chinese would stiffen at any new public criticism, and we'd be even worse off than we were before the visit.

The need for absolute secrecy about this mission was so paramount that we recalled Jim Lilley from Beijing to inform him of the visit face-to-face, in order to avoid sending diplomatic cables, which would have increased the chances of premature disclosure.

Under cover of darkness, Eagleburger and Scowcroft left Washington at 5:00 A.M. on June 30. Their trip went off without a hitch. To avoid being spotted when they landed to refuel, their plane was refueled in the air by an Air Force jet tanker. They spent twenty-four hours in China and returned home without ever being discovered. They reported back to the President that the Chinese had been as inscrutable as ever. The leaders complained bitterly about the sanctions and repeated their ritual insistence that the United States was meddling in their internal affairs. But as Eagleburger told me later, "They never said so directly, but I think the smarter ones absorbed the message that we can do a lot more for them when they aren't killing their own people."

First Tango in Paris

Seven weeks after the slaughter, during a Cambodian peace conference sponsored by the United Nations, I met privately with Chinese Foreign Minister Qian in Paris on July 31. French Foreign Minister Roland Dumas had graciously made his office in the Kleber Conference Center available for the meeting.

In this first ministerial contact between our countries since the massacre, I knew the Chinese would be defensive about an American démarche, so by design, I began our meeting with a lengthy discussion of the Cambodian issue. We needed China's help in reaching a negotiated settlement for Cambodia, and I didn't want the tension in our bilateral relations to poison the environment and prompt the Chinese to withhold using their considerable influence with the Khmer Rouge guerrillas. After securing Qian's pledge of help, I gingerly steered the conversation onto more difficult terrain.

"I know you are aware that the President understands China," I said. "He has a special feeling for China and he does not want to see China turn inward. Our strategic interests argue for doing what we can to preserve our ties.

"But I have to be frank with you: it will not be easy. Americans saw what happened in Tiananmen Square, and what they saw violated the principles on which our country was founded. Our national experience has been to expand the boundary of those freedoms that Americans hold most dearly. They have difficulty understanding what you did, and it has created a new and emotional reality in our country." My credibility was reinforced by the fact that the House of Representatives had only the day before approved the sanctions bill by their stunning 418–0 vote.

"We want to restore our relations, but we can't do it alone. If China wants the same thing, you have to help us. The President and I would like to argue that China is turning away from repression. If there are no more show trials and mass arrests, we can honestly portray China in a more positive light. But if you continue the crackdown, it will be difficult to manage our relations."

Qian was even more defensive than I'd expected. "The events in Beijing were not determined by our will," he insisted, blaming the massacre in turn on student hooligans, anarchists, the international media, Taiwanese agents, and the Hong Kong press. His government's patience had been without precedent for two months, he insisted—"the Chinese government showed the greatest restraint"—until finally there was no choice. Even so, he maintained, the reports of deaths were grossly exaggerated.

"You know that China is not afraid of pressure," he told me. "U.S. actions to pressure China have harmed China. China will not yield to pressure." American public opinion was the result of "exaggerated reports of the U.S. media," he contended. "After the situation quiets down, both sides should calmly understand things better."

I attempted to explain to Qian that business as usual was simply out of the question. He retreated to the lame mantra that "this is China's internal affair" and that the President and I should tell Congress to halt its destructive meddling.

"It would not serve any purpose for us to argue what is or is not China's domestic affair," I said. "The fact is that the Tiananmen incident has created a new reality in the United States. I must repeat that we can't do it alone." It would be helpful, I suggested, "if the world knows that you will not punish those who were only expressing their basic human rights."

Qian's calculated ambiguity was hardly reassuring. "Those who only demonstrated, shouted slogans, even the more militant ones, will not be the subjects of reprisal as long as they did not violate the law," he asserted. Although the meeting ended inconclusively, I believed that it did succeed in elevating Qian's consciousness about the seriousness of our position.

Another Try in September

On September 28, during the U.N. General Assembly session, I met Foreign Minister Qian for the second time since the bloodbath. The state of siege in China had seemed to moderate, and as a result the domestic outcry was somewhat less inflamed in the United States. But the Chinese still seemed oblivious to the dangers to the bilateral relationship. "There's a perception developing in the United States that China is closing the Open Door," I told Qian at the start of our conversation. "Anything you can do to preserve the Open Door will be helpful."

"We are not the ones who want to close it," Qian retorted. "Our door is open. But an open door requires two sides."

The art of persuasion is particularly challenging in dealing with the Chinese. Face is unusually important to them, so an interlocutor must negotiate a delicate balance that nudges them toward a preferred course without embarrassing them in the process. Accordingly, I made a bow to their sensibilities by saying that "We know some of this is related to domestic politics in China." But I also suggested it might be advisable to consider lifting martial law and lessen anti-American propaganda "that appears from time to time." Otherwise, I cautioned, "It would be harder for the President and myself and other people who think like us to continue to work at strengthening the relationship if the public perception and mood are adverse." I reminded Qian that the President had decided (but not yet announced publicly) to allow U.S. contractors to resume their work on upgrading the avionics of Chinese F-8 jet fighters. Given such a generous gesture under the circumstances, I said, a reciprocal gesture seemed in order.

Qian replied that his government was extremely annoyed by continuing pressure from the G-7 nations urging an end to the repression. Not since the Boxer Rebellion of 1900, he complained, when military forces of eight Western powers, including the United States, were dispatched to Beijing to protect foreign nationals, had Chinese sovereignty been treated with such disdain. This "unjust attitude" would not be tolerated. "If this continues day after day," he warned, "we could not avoid hurting the feelings of the Chinese people and damaging Sino-American relations."

Qian had no compunction about asking for American concessions while simultaneously ignoring my request for "visible and positive Chinese steps" to make it easier to allay congressional and public anger with Beijing. Harmonious relations required the renewal of our bilateral science-and-technology agreements and the resumption of World Bank loans, he insisted. Moreover, "there is also the problem of satellite launches"—a reference to a then-secret agreement permitting the Chinese to launch three U.S.-made commercial satellites on Chinese rockets beginning in 1991.

"We intend to stand by our commitment," I said, "but this is a very sensitive issue in the U.S., and if it became publicized I fear Congress would require us to prohibit it or refuse to go ahead. Therefore, we need to be very careful about timing."

Standing in Place

For the remainder of 1989—and indeed the rest of the Bush presidency—the Chinese relationship essentially treaded water. Any real chance for forward motion died along with the demonstrators in the square that fateful June evening. Eager to make an issue of China policy with an eye toward the 1992 election, the Democrats continuously pounded the President, alleging he was too lenient over Chinese human-rights atrocities. Their efforts to turn this debate to narrow political advantage were abetted, ironically, by the demise of the Cold War. The collapse of the Soviet Union

had weakened the domestic consensus for engaging the Chinese as a counterweight to the Soviets, notwithstanding their poor human-rights record.

In this context, the height of congressional interference was reached
when Congress passed legislation permitting Chinese citizens in the United
States to remain for an extended period of time. On November 30, the President vetoed the bill. Despite the fact that he then promptly enacted precisely the same provisions in an executive order, the veto was unpopular
with Congress and public opinion. It did, however, help relations to some
degree with the Chinese.

The Democrats, however, never let up. Well aware that the President
was determined to take a principled approach that he felt to be in the national interest, as opposed to the more politically popular course, they repeatedly legislated revocation of China's most-favored-nation trading
status, forcing us to cobble together enough minority support to sustain
Presidential vetoes. The wisdom of the President's adamant and successful
opposition to such shortsighted and partisan attempts from 1990 to 1992
would later become manifest by the actions of his successor. In the 1992
presidential campaign, Governor Bill Clinton castigated the President's
China policy, and alleged he'd sold out to his friends in Beijing. A year later,
President Clinton embraced President Bush's policy by delinking the
renewal of MFN status with China's performance on human rights. In so
doing, he tacitly acknowledged that the Bush policy of doing what we could
to promote human rights in China without destroying the strategic relationship in the process was the proper course for the United States.

In December, the President sent Scowcroft and Eagleburger back to
Beijing. Unfortunately, this trip ignited a new controversy after the Chinese
allowed news coverage of the toasts at a dinner in the Great Hall of the
People. We were accused by our critics once again of consorting with mur-
derers. Had the trip been as invisible as the first, it would have avoided
becoming a domestic sideshow and giving our critics fresh ammunition.*

Nevertheless, the trip was successful in persuading the Chinese that, as
the President had said in his inaugural speech, goodwill begets goodwill. On
December 19, the President waived a congressional ban on Export-Import
Bank loans to U.S. firms doing business with China and publicly announced
the sale of three communications satellites to Beijing. Not at all coinciden-

---

*On December 10, 1989, in an appearance on "This Week with David Brinkley" while Ea-
gleburger and Scowcroft were concluding this second, but public, trip to Beijing, I volunteered
to Brinkley that this was the first time we'd had high-level officials go to China since the
massacre. A week later, the first Eagleburger-Scowcroft trip was reported by CNN. The secrecy
of that first mission was so absolute that I literally had forgotten about it during the broadcast,
much to my subsequent embarrassment.

tally, martial law was lifted in Beijing three weeks later, and Tiananmen Square was reopened to the public for the first time since the crackdown. Our approach to this crisis, while criticized by many, had avoided setting the relationship back for decades. And while there was no way to know this at the time, of course, the wisdom of this approach would be unexpectedly borne out by year's end, when China's vote in the United Nations Security Council was critical to resolving the Persian Gulf crisis.

CHAPTER 8

THE MIDDLE EAST:

FIRST ENCOUNTERS WITH
THE QUAGMIRE

Ship me somewheres East of Suez, where the best is like the worst.
> —*Rudyard Kipling*

We must distinguish between taking the initiative and launching an initiative.
> —*National Security Review 7 on the Middle East, March 29, 1989*

From day one, the last thing I wanted to do was touch the Middle East peace process. With what appeared to be fundamental and historic changes possible in East-West relations, I frankly saw the Arab-Israeli dispute as a pitfall to be avoided rather than an opportunity to be exploited.

This rather bleak and somewhat selfish assessment was anchored in my conclusion that there was no real evidence to believe the climate was ripe for generating any momentum in a conflict that had defied resolution for nearly half a century. But it was also buttressed by my own experience as White House Chief of Staff in the first Reagan term, where aggressive and well-intentioned diplomacy had produced little more than stalemate, and a disastrous intervention in Lebanon haunted by the terrorist bombing of the U.S. Marine barracks in Beirut, which took 241 American lives.

I remember remarking several times to my transition staff that all Secretaries of State are inevitably sucked into the Middle East, where they expend an inordinate amount of time and effort in an enterprise with few prospects for success and an enormous potential for disappointment. I was determined to resist the siren song of Israel and its Arab neighbors—particularly when it seemed that neither side was interested in considering the difficult political choices necessary to create a real peace process.

I was reinforced in this regard by my preconfirmation consultations with former Presidents and Secretaries of State, all of whom discussed the Middle East in the cautionary tones of those who had been burned by their own involvement. Predictably, Richard Nixon was the most blunt: "Reagan has been the most pro-Israeli President in history," he said. "It's time for some evenhandness out there. But basically, the Middle East is insoluble. Stay away from it!"

I knew this was sage advice. But I also understood that the Middle East was a region vital to American interests and a perpetual tinderbox whose crises had invariably demanded the attention of my predecessors. The peace process was also a perpetual fixture of domestic politics because of our special strategic relationship with Israel and the political power of the American Jewish community. I could either manage the issue or let it manage me. Like it or not, I didn't have the luxury of totally ignoring it.

And so, while American diplomacy concentrated on relations with the Soviet Union throughout 1989, we also sought to manage this issue by pursuing what might be described as a moderately activist policy in the Middle East. Because there was no particular reason to believe our efforts would lead anywhere, I decided against any shuttle diplomacy and deferred a visit to the region until conditions seemed more hospitable. Nevertheless, between February 1989 and March 1990, we attempted to promote a dialogue between Israel and the Palestinians and to nurture a modest Israeli proposal for elections in the occupied territories. While we enjoyed some success with the Palestinians, our efforts during this period were repeatedly hamstrung by the reluctance of Israeli Prime Minister Yitzhak Shamir to stand behind his own initiative, and they collapsed entirely when Shamir refused to accept a compromise plan that would have produced a Palestinian delegation from the occupied territories for peace talks. This experience left me rather cynical about the Mideast quagmire, and chagrined at the time that I had not followed my original instincts to steer a wide berth. At the same time, I also learned some valuable lessons that would help refine my strategy for future efforts toward Middle East peace.

In Search of an Opening

In the beginning, the conventional wisdom among the Mideast specialists was unanimous: the prospects for a substantial breakthrough were bleak at best. In Israel, power was wielded by a national unity government headed by a hard-line prime minister who, given his preferences, would have preferred to keep most of the territory captured by Israel in the 1967 war. Egypt and Israel were at peace, but none of the other frontline Arab states appeared interested in searching for common ground. The Palestine Liberation Organization remained committed to the destruction of Israel; Syrian President Hafez al-Assad vowed to achieve strategic parity with the "Zionist entity," and the Arabs continued to demand an international conference on the Middle East under United Nations auspices, which was anathema both to Shamir's Likud-dominated unity government and even to the more pragmatic elements in the Labor Party. All the evidence suggested that even the most intensive application of diplomacy would be a wasted investment.

A memorandum prepared for a meeting of the National Security Council in early 1989 described the reality in these terms: "The United States is in a position to exercise leadership in the region. This does not mean, however, that the time is ripe for a major new diplomatic initiative. A new plan would harden positions on all sides and catalyze opposition around it. Regional actors would focus on the details of a plan rather than on creating the real conditions necessary for progress towards negotiations."

Dennis Ross, however, believed that the Intifada uprising in the territories, then in its second year, had created a modest new dynamic that should be explored gingerly. He was joined in this view by Bill Burns, Dan Kurtzer, and Aaron Miller of the Policy Planning staff, and John Kelly, the Assistant Secretary for Near Eastern Affairs. The Intifada, they argued, was the source of increasing political ferment within Shamir's national unity coalition government. As the uprising raged on, prompting greater repression in the form of administrative detentions and deportations of Palestinian protesters, the domestic debate within Israel was polarizing. The Labor Party demanded compromise with the Palestinians and threatened to bolt the government unless Shamir relented in his dreams of a "Greater Israel" populated by scores of new settlements in the territories. The Israeli Defense Forces and Yitzhak Rabin, the pragmatic Defense Minister, had warned Shamir, moreover, that a military answer wasn't possible; only a political solution could halt the Intifada. All these factors were pressuring Shamir to adopt a more flexible posture toward the territories.

On the ground, the Intifada demonstrated a divergence between the PLO in Tunis and Palestinians living in the territories. The uprising was indigenous, orchestrated not from Tunis but from the towns and villages of the West Bank and Gaza. This simple reality raised the possibility that Palestinians from within the territories might be willing at long last to negotiate their own destiny instead of waiting for the PLO to act. If the Palestinians from within decided to do something for themselves, the PLO's authority would be diminished. And while the Israelis would never talk with the PLO, they might be induced to sit down with Palestinians who were not themselves PLO officials. American strategy should concentrate on brokering an Israeli-Palestinian dialogue.

Fortunately, thanks to the efforts of my predecessor, George Shultz, and Swedish intermediaries, a modest vehicle already existed to this end. Since December of 1988, the American ambassador in Tunis, Robert Pelletreau, had been conducting a dialogue with low-level officials of the PLO. Yasir Arafat was pointedly excluded from this endeavor. His reputation as a terrorist was so ingrained in American public opinion that no administration could deal with him openly. No solution was possible, however, without at least his private acquiescence to a separate dialogue between Israel and Palestinians from the territories.

The policy approved by the President in early 1989 authorized me to search for a common basis on which Israel and the Palestinians could engage. We would continue the inherited U.S.-PLO dialogue at a low level, but the Egyptians would be available to talk directly with Arafat. Our primary tactical objective was to persuade him to accept negotiations between Israel and Palestinians in the territories. In effect, we were asking Arafat to disenfranchise himself on the grounds of political expedience: there was no way a Shamir-led government would ever negotiate with the PLO. To make this medicine more palatable to Arafat, we needed a credible set of ideas from Israel.

During the transition between the Reagan and Bush administrations, Israeli officials had floated some vague references to a new peace plan. I was told at the time that the Israelis were considering a preemptive peace-plan strike because they were uncertain about, and somewhat suspicious of, the President's intentions, and mine. They knew that we had urged President Reagan to call upon Menachem Begin to end his bloody invasion of Lebanon in the summer of 1982. They also knew that as White House Chief of Staff, I'd led the legislative strategy effort to support President Reagan's decision to allow the sale of AWACS radar planes to Saudi Arabia in 1981.

Nevertheless, I felt Israel's fears about the President and me were primarily rooted in the mythology of our inferred links to the Arabs as a result of our Texas backgrounds. In fact, we both saw Israel as a staunch ally and strategic partner whose security and survival we were committed to preserve. But it's also true that we both believed there would never be peace in the Middle East until Israel was willing to accept the principle of exchanging territory for peace as embodied in United Nations Resolution 242, which had served as the foundation of U.S. policy during all previous administrations, Democratic and Republican.

On March 13, I met in my office with Israeli Foreign Minister Moshe Arens, who had come to prepare the way for Shamir's visit to Washington three weeks later. Arens was an American-educated engineer (M.I.T. and Caltech) whom I'd met previously when he was Ambassador to the United States. My briefing paper had predicted that Arens wanted to "determine the minimum Israel must do to co-opt us on the peace process." Beyond reassuring Arens of America's steadfast commitment to Israel's security, my primary purpose was to deliver the message that we expected Shamir to arrive with at least a general statement of intentions toward the territories.

I wanted Arens to know the United States was prepared to be Israel's partner in peacemaking. "But you can't leave us exposed," I told him. "You can't leave us naked. You need to give us something we can work with." Arens was a Likud hard-liner, though not quite so rigid as Shamir. I sensed that, like his boss, he wasn't particularly interested in blazing trails for peace. But I liked him and thought he would deal with me straight up.

To reinforce the message I'd given Arens, I wrote Shamir on March 24 at the President's request, saying that he and the Palestinians must find a way to talk to one another. "The people of Israel have told you to be cautious and tough, and those are sound pieces of advice," I added. "But I think they have also sent a message to your neighbors that peace is possible—provided the Palestinians demonstrate they are responsible partners. This is the measure of commitment which you, as a statesman, can determine through diplomacy. And it is something that the United States and Israel, as strategic partners, can achieve."

Shamir's Murky Four Points

I'd met Yitzhak Shamir only once in passing, in the early Reagan years. Shamir was Foreign Minister in that hard-line Israeli government: Menachem Begin was Prime Minister, and Ariel Sharon was Defense Minister. I'd been warned that Shamir was difficult to talk to, and even harder to reach. Nevertheless, I wanted to try to establish a personal bond of trust, so at our first meeting on April 5, 1989, I began by suggesting some improbable common ground.

"Mr. Prime Minister," I said, "we both know that the media like to pigeonhole people with catchphrases. You've been described to me as a man of principle who is incapable of being practical. I've probably been described to you as a man totally lacking in principle who cares *only* about being practical. Let me tell you, like you, I'm very much a man who believes in principle, but I also think you have to be practical if you're going to realize your principles. I also suspect you're more practical than your reputation. I think that you and I may be able to surprise some people by working together."

Shamir laughed. "Well, maybe so, Mr. Secretary. I'm much more practical than people think."

I then told Shamir that I was aware he'd brought some ideas along. "We want to take what you have and market it with the Arabs," I said, "but you have to give us something."

"I want to give you something," Shamir replied, "but I don't want to give you something that undercuts us. And I don't want the PLO to get anything."

I responded that the only way to make any progress was to offer a plan that was credible to the Palestinians in the territories. "If you constrain it too much," I argued, "you'll put the PLO in a position to block it at a time when there's a certain momentum inside [the territories] to move forward."

I could tell that my logic tempted Shamir. At the same time, it was difficult for him to accept. I sensed an enormous ambivalence in the man. He seemed alternately interested in doing something and scared to death at the very prospect.

After meeting with the President, Shamir unveiled his four-point plan, whose critical component called for elections in the territories to choose representatives for peace talks with Israel. The administration had privately signaled our endorsement at the staff level before Shamir arrived, but we all knew it was a weak plan that would be difficult to sell to the Arabs. There was no real commitment to permanent-status discussions and only generalizations about how the elections would proceed. The Arabs would not be impressed; indeed, during *his* visit to Washington the day before, Hosni Mubarak had said Israel must negotiate with the PLO, not the Palestinians. But at least it had the virtue of being an Israeli plan. With a bit of creative window dressing and diplomatic sleight of hand, we now had *something* with which to challenge the Palestinians and their Egyptian and Jordanian friends to respond to with some equal flexibility. We were under no illusions, but were willing and eager to try.

In the next three years, Shamir and I would engage in some bitter struggles, particularly over the contentious question of Israeli settlements in the occupied territories. But I believed that this first encounter had succeeded symbolically. As I put it in a note to the President, "I think we have established a relationship of trust, something that is essential if we are to have any chance of moving Shamir over time."

It was a start; Shamir had given us something to market and had said he realized the status quo was unacceptable. But there was a long way to go. Following his meeting with Shamir, President Bush reiterated his opposition to unilateral annexation or permanent Israeli occupation of all of the West Bank and Gaza. Shamir promptly retorted that Israel must never give up those territories.

In a "Dear Misha" letter on April 24, I told Arens that Shamir's proposal for elections was "a positive step." But I also told him that "a creative way" should be explored to address the issue of allowing Palestinians no longer living in the territories to participate in the process. And I was quite clear on another point of contention between our governments: "I believe some way must be found to permit East Jerusalem residents the opportunity to participate [in elections]," I wrote. It was apparent to me that the issue of representation would be the most difficult of all to bridge, and even at this early stage I wanted to lay down a marker that some creativity from Israel on this point was essential to any movement.

Into the Lion's Den with AIPAC

On May 14, the Israeli Cabinet formally endorsed Shamir's four-point plan. Almost immediately, the government started backing away from its own handiwork. In a speech to the Knesset two days later, Shamir announced a tougher line against Palestinians in the territories. After Rabin warned that Palestinians might be denied the "privilege" of working in Israel if they rejected the peace plan, thousands of Arab workers in Gaza were briefly sent home from their jobs as a pointed reminder of their occupied status. These actions infuriated the Egyptians and Palestinians, and undermined U.S. efforts to persuade them that Shamir's initiative deserved their embrace.

By coincidence, I was scheduled to address the annual political conference of the American-Israel Public Affairs Committee on May 22. I was urged by my staff to exploit this fortuitous timing to try to repair the damage from these developments in the Arab world, and to restore a sense of momentum to the process—while at the same time reaffirming the President's ironclad commitment to Israel's security.

We wanted to send a message to the Arabs that, while the United States was firmly behind the Israeli plan, we intended to pursue the peace process as an honest broker. We decided to focus on a list of difficult political challenges *both* sides must confront and overcome to reach a comprehensive resolution of the conflict. I understood that my audience would be considerably more enthusiastic about my prescriptions for the Arabs—such as ending the boycott against Israel and renouncing the Intifada—than my suggestions for the Shamir government. But I was determined that the speech be balanced, fully aware that balance in this context might be considered something less than a virtue.

The speech is remembered today primarily for a single sentence that restated long-standing American policy in a deliberately unsentimental formulation: "For Israel, now is the time to lay aside once and for all the unrealistic vision of a Greater Israel." I also said that Israel should "forswear annexation," stop settlement activity, allow schools to reopen in the territories, and "reach out to the Palestinians as neighbors who deserve political rights."

Despite the fact that the audience of 1,200 sat in stony silence during this particular passage, the speech was very well received. After I finished, I was showered with praise from virtually every member of the AIPAC board of directors. Tom Dine, the executive director, was the most effusive of all. "That was a great speech," he told me, "perhaps the best ever." In a time-honored ritual of Washington, however, another "spin" quickly began making the rounds, fueled by a handful of midlevel AIPAC officials who circulated among the tables, complaining that my remarks had been unduly harsh. These pot-stirring dissidents found a willing ally in John Goshko of the *Washington Post*, who told several friends in the audience that it was the toughest speech on Israel he'd heard in two decades of covering the issue. The morning papers concluded that my message was primarily directed at Israel.

Within twenty-four hours, Dine's reaction was suddenly more guarded, the American Jewish community was in an uproar, and Shamir had denounced my remarks as "useless." Four days later, I received a letter from Arens. "I am sure you will not be surprised," he wrote, "that I found the content and tone of your speech gravely disappointing." I found myself equally disappointed by Arens's reaction. During our meeting, I'd given him the benefit of the doubt on several matters—to the point of personally deleting a reference to Resolution 242 at his request from a joint statement we issued after our meeting. By contrast, he didn't extend the same benefit of the doubt to my speech, erroneously choosing to believe it was an effort to distance myself from the Israeli peace initiative.

Finessing the Irritant of Settlements

Throughout this period, American efforts to generate momentum were constantly hampered by the specter of Jewish settlements in the occupied territories. A succession of Israeli governments had steadily increased settlement activities in the West Bank and Gaza despite the repeated concerns of the United States. The Carter administration had declared these settlements illegal. Even Ronald Reagan had agreed they constituted "an obstacle to peace." Early in 1989, there were informal discussions among the President, Brent Scowcroft, and me about toughening the policy. We all agreed there was a strong case to be made that the settlements were in fact illegal. But we also understood that nothing would be gained by a confrontation on this point with the Shamir government. To the contrary, it would create domestic political problems for us, thereby making any peace initiative more difficult.

We therefore decided to retain the Reagan formula. There was no question in my mind that the settlements were indeed at the least a serious obstacle to peace. While restating our unhappiness with the settlements when asked, I believed it was also important to subordinate this disagreement to the larger objective of breathing some life into a moribund peace process.

This was a far easier proposition in the abstract—particularly since the President was of the very strong belief that the settlements were simply wrong. His principled view of the matter was unfortunately bolstered by his belief that Shamir was not being straight with him in this regard, a feeling that probably had its genesis in the President's first meeting with Shamir on April 6, 1989. In that meeting, the President told Shamir that the settlements issue was very important to him. At first, Shamir had suggested that this was strictly an internal matter and not the business of the United States. "You have things that concern you, we have things that concern us," he said. "Don't let it concern you." Given the fact that at the time American taxpayer-financed assistance to Israel amounted to more than $1,000 per Israeli citizen per year, this was not a brush-off George Bush was prepared to accept. When the President persisted with his concerns, Shamir finally said, "Don't worry, they won't be a problem." Afterward, he told me that Shamir had given him the strong impression that the spread of settlements would be halted.

Two weeks later, new settlements sprang up in the West Bank. It was quickly apparent that Shamir, either goaded or bullied by his controversial housing minister Sharon, was intent on *expanding* settlements at a record pace. Throughout this period, as I continued to probe for diplomatic openings between the Israelis and the Palestinians, settlement activity consistently proceeded. Periodically, the President would be shown maps with Israeli settlements marked in violet. As the proportion of violet steadily increased with each new map, the President's sense that Shamir had betrayed him worsened. He was especially disturbed to learn that on May 2 Shamir had told Bill Brown, the American Ambassador to Israel, that settlements weren't "an earth-shaking matter" for the President. On several occasions, each of us repeated our objections to Shamir. Sometimes he would quickly change the subject. On other occasions, he would express his private disapproval or blame Sharon. But he never did anything about it—except permit more settlements. At times, the Israelis were building settlements without anyone to move into them. In time, it was difficult not to believe that the Shamir government was simply expressing its disdain for American interests. The President felt Shamir had not leveled with him, and each new rebuff seemed to deepen the personal distance between them.

Selling His Own Creation Back to Shamir

Over the summer of 1989, U.S. diplomacy was pursued in a less visible fashion. I wrote some letters and made a few phone calls to reinforce what we were saying at various levels. It was now time for the Egyptians and Palestinians to formulate their own plan to demonstrate good faith. In early July, Mubarak proposed a ten-point plan of his own, laying out his conditions for elections, which included an end to new Israeli settlements and the participation of Palestinians from East Jerusalem and outside the territories in the process. Mubarak's proposal was intended to redesign Shamir's plan in a fashion suitable both to moderate Israelis and the Arabs. It had been devised, in fact, with considerable private input from Israelis and members of the PLO. While largely unacceptable to Shamir, the plan had the diplomatic virtue of keeping the process alive.

By early fall, I became persuaded that a basis now existed for further progress, and American diplomatic efforts should be intensified. I believed there was a way to bridge the distance between Shamir's four points and Mubarak's ten. Both sides were now willing to pursue further talks. We decided to propose that the Egyptian and Israeli foreign ministers meet with me to explore ways to solve the question of Palestinian representation. On September 28, I met in New York with Arens and Egyptian Foreign Minister Esmat Abdel-Meguid to lay out what later came to be known as the five-point Baker plan. Its centerpiece was a meeting between Israelis and Palestinians in Cairo to finally launch a face-to-face dialogue. We would all agree that Egypt was no substitute for, but could act as an intermediary with the Palestinians, and that Israel would attend only after approving a list of satisfactory non-PLO Palestinians. Moreover, all sides would accept Shamir's plan as the basis for negotiations, but the Palestinians would be free to raise their own ideas for elections and the negotiating process. Finally, the foreign ministers of Israel and Egypt would meet with me in Washington within two weeks to facilitate the process.

It was an eminently reasonable plan that in fact gave Israel a virtual veto power over the composition of the Palestinian delegation. It also allowed the Palestinians to raise the question of the shape of a permanent status for the territories, something Israel had traditionally opposed because one possible result could be an eventual return of the territories. However, Arens and Meguid both believed the compromise could pass muster at home.

Not soon after, the proposal leaked to the press. On October 16, Shamir rejected it summarily, saying in an interview that he would not compromise with the Palestinians, even if it meant the collapse of his government and a sharper conflict with the United States. I was not happy that his statements directly contradicted Arens's private assurances to me. But I was even more annoyed that Shamir would air his reservations in public before engaging us privately. I thought he was trying to strangle the U.S. initiative in its cradle. The President was equally annoyed. The next morning, he telephoned Shamir, who immediately sought to deflect our irritation by thanking the President for his good efforts and insisting, "We're fully committed to our peace initiative—to the spirit *and* the letter of it." He was not in the least convincing.

"There *is* a perception that Israel is moving away from your own position," the President challenged. "Jim Baker's five points meet your concerns and protect Israel. You know *who* you will be talking to, and what you'll be talking about. We've invested a lot in this initiative. We're not trying to force you to talk with the PLO. But we *do* wish there could be less delay in responding factually to us on these points. If you give us a positive response, then Israel and the United States can move forward together. If you don't respond, we have to interpret that you *don't* want to go forward."

Shamir's tone became even more defensive. "We are not pulling away from our initiative, but we will not meet with the PLO," he insisted. "I'll be glad to have Arens call Secretary Baker to clarify this matter."

"That's fine," the President replied, "because I've just read the wire story quoting you about a confrontation with the United States. If you want that—fine." Shamir did not respond to what I knew was a controlled but nonetheless very annoyed George Bush.

The President then tried to get Shamir to explain what he was prepared to do to keep the process moving. "What's your plan for implementation of your *own* initiative?" he asked. Again, he never got an answer. After he put down the receiver, we shook our heads over Shamir's rigidity. It was beginning to look like Mubarak had been right when he'd described Shamir as a "Dr. No" who would never commit to anything.

Over the next two months, we pressed both sides to accept this compromise. Perhaps because Labor was threatening to bring down his government if the Cabinet failed to endorse the U.S. plan, Shamir started to sound more positive. By early December, both Israel and Egypt had signed on, but Egypt was not yet able to say they had Palestinian acceptance. Israel's agreement, moreover, was highly conditional; the Israelis were demanding an elaborate set of understandings and assurances. I sent word to Arens that anything more than modest changes would open the entire plan to renegotiation and bring it down.

The Process Crashes and Burns

This Kabuki performance continued into 1990, with no concrete resolution. On January 14, 1990, as we were still awaiting word from the Israelis about the U.S. five-point plan, Shamir told the Knesset that the anticipated explosion of hundreds of thousands of Soviet Jewish immigrants would make necessary "a big Israel." The implication of this provocative statement was clear: The Shamir government was not merely determined to erect more settlements, its strategic goal was a policy of expansion designed to render the land-for-peace option academic. Our public reaction was measured; Margaret Tutwiler described the statement as "not helpful" and reiterated U.S. opposition to settlements. Privately, however, we were furious. When Senate Minority Leader Bob Dole promptly proposed taking 5 percent of U.S. foreign aid to Israel and Egypt and diverting it to emerging democracies, we were obliged to oppose the idea. In truth, however, we weren't at all unhappy that Dole had delivered the Israelis a reminder that cooperation with the U.S. must be a two-way street.

Four days later, Rabin was back in Washington with some ideas for breaking the impasse over Palestinian representation. We'd been working quietly with Rabin for months—so quietly that my staff and I referred to him in all our conversations as "the man who smokes" to disguise our "back-channel" conversations with the chain-smoking Defense Minister.

On the matter of Palestinian representation, he believed Shamir might be willing to accept at least one "dual addressee"—a Palestinian who lived in the territories but maintained a second residence in East Jerusalem. The further problem of Diaspora Palestinians could be finessed, he believed, by allowing a deported Palestinian back into the territories and then including him in the delegation. I thought it was an ingenious compromise which both sides could claim satisfied their principled positions.

Rabin had already broached these ideas with Shamir. As usual, the Prime Minister had reservations. But Rabin believed he had obtained an agreement in principle from Shamir. Before trying to obtain Shamir's formal approval, however, I wanted to make sure the ideas would work with the Arabs. I asked Dennis Ross to float the ideas unofficially with Osama el-Baz, Mubarak's National Security Adviser, who happened to be in Washington. After two days of checking, Osama came back and said there would be no problem. I then telephoned Shamir on January 23.

"We've had a discussion with Rabin," I said, "and he's raised a couple of ideas on how to handle the two problems we have. Are you aware of them?"

"I'm familiar with those ideas," Shamir confirmed. We then raised the

ideas officially with the Egyptians and quickly received their official acceptance along with their assurance that the PLO would go along.

When I called Shamir with this news on January 30, however, he was
somewhat less than enthusiastic. "I think you should talk to Misha about
this," he said in a tone suggesting this was a subject he fervently wished to
avoid. I called Arens and was shocked to learn that the Foreign Minister had
no inkling. "This is all news to me," he said. "I know nothing about it."
Arens was irked at having been excluded from these deliberations, particularly when I told him that his fierce rival Rabin was fully aware of the compromise and indeed was one of its architects. "I have to talk to the Prime
Minister," Arens said. I suggested that he come to Washington at the earliest possible moment.

Over the next three weeks, we attempted to fine-tune the proposal to
satisfy Shamir and Likud. We agreed, for instance, to rule out any Palestinian with a Jerusalem identity card even if he currently resided in the
occupied territories. During a meeting in my office on February 23, Arens
tentatively accepted the revised proposal. But he thwarted my hope of
agreeing on a date for the three-way meeting in Washington with the Egyptians to select the Palestinian delegation, saying he would have to consult
with Shamir, Peres, and Rabin. "I'll call you when that's over," he pledged.

I told Arens that as an absolute minimum I needed Shamir's answer to
one simple question: "As regards the participants in the Israeli-Palestinian
dialogue, would the government of Israel be ready to consider on a name-
by-name basis any Palestinian who was a resident of the territories?"

I was concerned when Arens did not telephone promptly, but my aides
said there was little cause for worry. By most private accounts filtering out
of Israel, Shamir had finally been persuaded to agree. Ross received a phone
call from Martin Indyk, a prominent member of the American Jewish community (later named to the National Security Council staff and then as Ambassador to Israel by President Clinton), congratulating the administration
for its perseverance. "You've got it," he was told. "It's done. Shamir has
agreed." I was frankly elated. Shamir's months of stalling had been frustrating.

As we waited for a formal communication from Jerusalem, however,
two events intervened that ultimately proved most inopportune. On March
1, during testimony before a House appropriations subcommittee, I said
that the United States would support a request for $400 million in loan
guarantees to build housing for Soviet Jewish immigrants, provided that
Israel agree to halt the construction of new settlements in the territories.
Shamir was privately reported to have been enraged by my statement,
which he saw as conditioning U.S. economic assistance to Israel.

Two days after my congressional testimony, during a Saturday press conference in Palm Springs with Japanese Prime Minister Toshiki Kaifu, President Bush was asked about reports that the Israeli were planning to create new settlements in East Jerusalem. "The foreign policy of the United States says that we do not believe there should be new settlements in the West Bank or East Jerusalem," he responded. It was a straightforward, measured restatement of long-standing American policy. But in the fevered climate of the moment, the mention of Jerusalem for the first time publicly proved devastating. There was an instant firestorm within the American Jewish community and among Israeli hard-liners.

I'd later learn that the President's comments had been prompted in large measure by White House Chief of Staff John Sununu, whose Lebanese heritage caused many to see him as an unabashed Arabist. During the previous week, Sununu had brought the President maps that showed the ever-expanding nature of Israeli settlements, particularly in East Jerusalem.

Two days later, I telephoned the President to discuss how we could pick up the pieces. "We almost had that Middle East deal worked out," I teased, "but you screwed it up so bad with that statement about settlements that even *I* can't straighten it out." My terminology was exactly the same as he'd used on me dozens of times before, the sort of needling banter the two of us have employed against each other over decades of friendship.

In truth, I did not believe the situation was beyond redemption. At least Arens was passionately committed to the compromise. If anyone could reason with Shamir, I thought, it was Misha. Even if Shamir refused to accept the plan, Labor would almost certainly pull out of the coalition in the belief that it could muster the support to form a new government. Therefore, we reasoned, the plan was almost certain to be approved.

In fact, we were mistaken. My comments and the President's strengthened the hand of the conservatives by diverting attention from the larger issue of peace. More important, they gave Shamir a convenient excuse—his anger at being pressured by the United States—behind which to hide. When Shamir polled his Cabinet on whether to accept the dual-addressee compromise, a clear majority of Likud ministers joined with their Labor counterparts to support the U.S. plan. But Shamir voted against, and dismissed Shimon Peres as Finance Minister. Labor then forced a vote of no confidence in the Knesset, and on March 15 the government fell on a vote of 60 to 55.

I felt battered, beaten, and betrayed. From the outset, I'd tried to give Shamir the benefit of the doubt. I knew he was ambivalent, but I believed he was at least willing to set a process in motion. It was now clear to me that I'd been wrong about him. To let the government fall on the narrow issue of permitting one Palestinian on the delegation who had a second residence in

Jerusalem said to me that Shamir simply must not be serious about peace. The only bright spot at the time was the possibility that a more moderate government might now come to power that would be more committed to efforts to move a peace process forward. (As it turned out, this was not to be.)

I'd spent nearly a year resuscitating Shamir's halfhearted plan, and refining it in order to make it palatable to the Palestinians. Consulting with Israel every step of the way, we'd pressured the Arabs to accept a formula that effectively disenfranchised the PLO and gave Israel a de facto veto over the Palestinian delegation. We'd developed a formula that we were willing to argue met the political needs of the Palestinians and did so without violating Israel's principles. In the end, Shamir wasn't even willing to embrace his own plan. I bitterly recalled Henry Kissinger's warning to me during the transition: "The Israelis are geniuses at dragging you into a procedural negotiation in which they will say at every turn that you've betrayed them." Kissinger had been right. I should have listened to his advice and my own instincts.

A week later, the Israeli Deputy Foreign Minister, Benjamin Netanyahu, was quoted as saying, "It is astonishing that a superpower like the United States, which was supposed to be the symbol of political fairness and international honesty, is building its policy on a foundation of *distortion* and *lies*" (emphasis added). His language was unacceptable for a senior diplomat from a friendly country. I promptly banned him from the State Department. Even after he wrote me claiming to have been misunderstood, I wouldn't see him in the department for the rest of my tenure, although I rescinded the ban against his seeing others in the Building.*

Two weeks after the Israeli government collapsed, Saddam Hussein threatened to "make fire eat half of Israel" if Iraq were attacked. Suddenly there was a sense that public opinion in what the Arabs liked to call "the street" was shifting away from conciliation in the direction of Saddam's truculence. At the same time, there were reports the Egyptians were losing control of the PLO. The dividing line in the Arab world seemed to shift from Cairo toward Baghdad, facilitated perhaps by the perception of an Israeli government tacitly repudiating its own peace overture.

On May 30, Israeli naval forces intercepted two heavily armed boatloads of Palestinians heading toward Tel Aviv. The ensuing battle prevented a major terrorist attack against Israeli civilians. The Palestinian Liberation Front, a radical offshoot of the PLO based in Baghdad under the infamous Abu Abbas, claimed responsibility for the abortive raid. The acting government, still headed by Shamir, demanded that the United States terminate its

---

*Our relations have since mended. During my 1994 visit to Israel as a private citizen, Netanyahu and I had a very cordial meeting.

talks with the PLO. Arafat denied the PLO was responsible, but refused to condemn the raid. Despite the steady deterioration in bilateral relations with Israel, all of us in the government were outraged by the incident, and furious with Arafat's benign reaction. Painfully aware that the U.S.-PLO dialogue was now all that remained of the tattered peace process, neither the President nor I wanted to end it. But when Arafat's silence continued, we had no choice.

Arafat had squandered any chance of establishing his credibility or even a scintilla of moral authority by refusing to renounce the terrorist attack. From a political standpoint, the PLO was no longer a reliable interlocutor. On the afternoon of June 19, the day before the President publicly announced the dialogue's suspension, I was reviewing a cable that would be sent to Ambassador Pelletreau in Tunis. More than a year of frustration got the better of me. Aaron Miller watched in amazement as I flung the cable into the air. "I want you to know, Aaron," I said, "if I had another life, I'd want to be a Middle East specialist just like you, because it would mean guaranteed permanent employment." Our fledgling attempt at finding peace in the Middle East had ended like most of the others—sabotaged by ancient adversaries unable to take even the most measured risks for peace.

Sorry, Wrong Number

On June 11, the Knesset voted to approve a new Likud-dominated government with Shamir remaining as Prime Minister. With Peres and Rabin excluded from the Cabinet, I knew there was virtually no chance to revive the peace process. (In what we took as a calculated slap at the United States, the acting Shamir government had kept building settlements during the interregnum.) The new government's coalition agreement stipulated that Israel would refuse to negotiate even indirectly with anyone affiliated with the PLO, and barred any East Jerusalemites from the negotiations.

Two days later, my fears were confirmed. In a hard-line interview with the *Jerusalem Post*, Shamir laid down more restrictive preconditions for peace talks. Israel would not talk, he said, with any Palestinians who did not accept its views on autonomy. David Levy, the new Foreign Minister, told reporters that the U.S. five-point plan had "distorted" Shamir's four-point initiative and should be scrapped. Adding insult to injury, Misha Arens, now the Defense Minister, visited two settlements in the West Bank in a pointed symbolic rebuff to American diplomacy.

These developments were very much on my mind later that day as I testified before the House Foreign Affairs Committee. I could scarcely control my anger with Shamir and his colleagues, and in truth I really wasn't interested in doing so. When Congressman Mel Levine of California, a fervent supporter of Israel, lauded me for my efforts but then suggested that the process had been sabotaged by the President's remark in Palm Springs about settlements, I had heard enough.

Unless all the parties tempered their inflexibility, I said, "there won't be any dialogue, and there won't be any peace, and the United States of America can't make it happen. . . . It's going to take some really good-faith affirmative effort on the part of our good friends in Israel.

"If we don't get it," I told Levine, "and we can't get it quickly . . . I have to tell you that everybody over there should know that the telephone number is 1-202-456-1414. When you're serious about peace, call us." (My choice of the White House switchboard was simply because after four years there I knew the number. I had never learned the number at the State Department.)

The "call us, we won't call you" language was the inspiration of Tom Friedman, the diplomatic correspondent of the *New York Times,* whose reporting and thoughtful analysis about the Middle East had won the Pulitzer Prize. I occasionally asked Friedman to share his thoughts with me on an off-the-record basis. In one of these sessions, he'd suggested it made no sense to keep pressing for peace if the parties weren't genuinely interested. The best way to get their attention, he thought, was to let them know we wouldn't be available to help unless they called us. The idea of doing it publicly was my refinement. A few weeks earlier, I'd floated the idea with Dennis Ross, who had disagreed. I'd concluded then that he was right; such an incendiary approach wouldn't be helpful in easing tensions with Shamir. As the Israelis continued to demonstrate a lack of seriousness about peace efforts, however, I decided it was time to remind everyone precisely where the problem lay.

The next morning, my old Democratic friend Bob Strauss, a staunch supporter of Israel, left a message for me with Caron Jackson, my executive assistant. He said my remarks were right on target. "You've finally justified my carrying you on my back all these years and getting you elevated to this position of authority," Strauss needled. "It shows that even a yellow rat will fight if you corner him." It was high praise indeed, and no small comfort for me to hear that one of Israel's best friends in this country thought I'd done the right thing. Public opinion polls subsequently quickly showed that a huge majority of the American people also endorsed my sentiments. The White House was so flooded by telephone calls that I sent roses to the beleaguered switchboard operators.

That same day, June 14, the President sent a letter to Shamir which, while nonconfrontational and low key in tone, was nevertheless quite direct. The President said that unless Israel compromised on the two out-standing issues of Palestinian representation, it would be impossible to launch a credible diplomatic effort.

"What I need to know from you," the President wrote, "is whether you are prepared to go forward without new preconditions on the basis of ac-knowledging—privately at first, if need be—that you will meet with a dele-gation of Palestinians from the territories that include a few individuals who fit the deportee and dual-addressee categories." Absent such a pledge, "Jim Baker and I will be forced to conclude that we no longer have any chance of implementing your initiative."

A few days later, Dennis Ross was informed by Elyakim (Ely) Rubin-stein, the Israeli Cabinet Secretary and a senior Shamir adviser, that "this government is not going to accept those two things." The peace process was dead, the victim of a suicide.

On July 12, I met in my office with Robert Maxwell, the prominent British financier and publishing magnate with close ties to Israel. It was a brief meeting which I had agreed to primarily as a courtesy to former Sena-tor Howard Baker of Tennessee, a longtime friend and political colleague who represented Maxwell's interests in the United States. During our con-versation, however, Maxwell unexpectedly told me that Shamir had asked him to deliver a private message to me personally. " 'Please tell Secretary Baker,' " Maxwell quoted Shamir as saying, " 'that I am serious and I am prepared to work for peace.' "

I told Maxwell that I was delighted with this news and hoped there would be opportunities ahead to explore the Prime Minister's intent fur-ther. Privately, however, I remained terminally skeptical. Having been burned repeatedly by Shamir, I was in no mood to test Maxwell's assertion. Before my confirmation hearing, I'd told an interviewer that peace could not be "mandated or delivered by anybody from the outside, including the U.S." Henceforth, I vowed not to make the mistake of ignoring my own prescience. At any rate, my attitude was soon rendered academic. Exactly three weeks after my conversation with Maxwell, Iraq invaded Kuwait. Further efforts to negotiate the tortuous road to peace in the Middle East would have to wait for a more propitious moment—not to mention, I swore to myself at that moment, a new Israeli Prime Minister and another Secre-tary of State.

CHAPTER 9

THE SPIRIT OF JACKSON HOLE

I found it a feeling of almost disbelief that I was there with these people. It was unreal.   —*Norman Shapiro, a volunteer from Jackson Hole, Wyoming, who loaned Eduard Shevardnadze his hat.*

As a young lawyer at Andrews & Kurth in the late 1950s and 1960s, I had more energy than direction—a condition not unknown to most other associates starting the practice of law, then and now. Beginning one's career with a large law firm required a careful balancing act. I tried on various aspects of the firm's practice, looking for a good fit between something I was good at doing (so I could make partner) and something I enjoyed doing (so I could go home content at night). For far too large a number of associates, skill and interest never intersect, and they leave the practice of law either burned out or bored. I was fortunate—I was not among them.

At first, I wasn't so lucky. I began by wanting to be a trial lawyer; I have no clear recollection of why I wanted to try cases, all I know is that I did—probably because the culture in law school when I attended encouraged the fiction that you were somehow incomplete as a lawyer until you had tried lawsuits. But it was disillusioning. I went to the courthouse as a junior associate and sat through several personal-injury cases. It didn't take long to learn that oftentimes the truth and the trial of personal-injury cases had a tenuous connection at best. There seemed to be no real penalty for pushing the envelope on the truth. I don't remember hearing of perjury charges against witnesses in civil cases. It seemed to me that all too often people would get on the witness stand and flat out lie. Having been taught by my family that my name, and the integrity that went along with it, were my most valuable attributes, I decided rather quickly that this was not an area of specialization that I would enjoy. So I left trial law behind, and specialized instead in a general business law practice. I spent my time drafting documents; preparing letter agreements; contracts; securities registration statements; and real estate, oil and gas, and business merger agreements. This may sound dry, but I found it fascinating. First and foremost, the work required painstaking attention to detail. My father had always told me as I grew up, "Prior preparation prevents poor performance." The "Five Ps," as they were known, were drilled into my head at an early age, and I realized that careful preparation and hard work could take you a long way. I've never forgotten those Five Ps. I seldom suffered from lack of confidence, although I knew that many were a good deal brighter than I was. I always felt I could successfully compete by working as hard or harder than anyone else.

Like most associates, I eventually graduated from drafting the agreements to negotiating them. In the entrepreneurial environment of Texas in the 1960s, many companies were looking for lawyers who could help them organize, structure, and often merge their businesses efficiently and effectively, and I acquired my negotiating skills, first by watching my elders, and then by experience itself.

If there was one key to my success in negotiations other than preparation and hard work, it was that, early on, I recognized the importance of understanding my opponent's position. I learned that if I could put myself in the position of the other lawyer and his or her client, understand how they saw the issues, and appreciate the constraints they faced, then I had a better chance of working through the issues and reaching an agreement.

The same is true for politics and diplomacy. Politics is indeed the art of the possible, as many say. For those who say this view is so pragmatic as to be unprincipled, I would argue that principled pragmatism is what succeeds. President Reagan often used to say it was better to get eighty percent of your goal than to stand firm, go over the cliff, and get nothing. And nobody ever accused the Gipper of being unprincipled.

In a sense, international politics can be thought of as an ongoing negotiation. I was taught that any complex negotiation was actually a series of discrete problems that required solutions. How you worked with the other side in developing the solution to the first problem had ramifications far beyond that single issue. Indeed, its resolution could set not just the logical precedents for subsequent issues, but the very tone of the relationship between the negotiators—and in the long run, that relationship could influence the course of events as much as any objective analysis of the points in dispute. If honesty and trust developed, even the most contentious talks could be brought to a successful conclusion. The negotiators feel free to set aside their formal negotiating positions and reveal their informal thinking—the assumptions, strategies, and even fears—that underlie their approach. Most often, I found when I could leave behind my formal brief and speak informally with my counterpart, success for both of us soon followed. But if the relationship soured—if it became infected with distrust and discord—then it mattered little how far apart the parties actually were. The perception of mistrust overwhelmed any objective reality.

In 1989, with the Soviet Union a great power in decline, no more critical negotiation existed than the one over how that decline would occur. Empires do not go quietly into the night. Power is seldom given up easily, and peaceful transitions are the exception. And while it was clear by the middle of the year that the Soviets were retrenching their positions around the globe, the real question was: How far would the Kremlin go?

Consequently, no relationships were more important than those with Gorbachev and Shevardnadze. Following the NATO Summit and the President's triumphant trip to Poland and Hungary in July, I viewed my personal relations with Moscow with mixed emotions. I had left my first encounter with Gorbachev in May somewhat soured, if not bitter, about the prospects. I was not sure how much business we could do if he was more interested in appealing past us to the Western publics. My hope was that the President's CFE proposal, and our successful resolution of SNF, had sent Gorbachev the message that we could play his game—and play it equally well.

With Shevardnadze, I was more optimistic. Operating in Gorbachev's shadow, he left the scoring of diplomatic points to his boss and seemed more interested in discussing the substance of our relations. In two meetings in wildly different settings—in July at the Soviet Ambassador's residence on the Boulevard Lannes in Paris and in September in the cabin of a U.S. Air Force jet over the plains of the Midwest as we flew together to the Tetons in Wyoming—Shevardnadze and I broke through to develop a unique relationship. At first, he was my negotiating partner and counterpart. By the end, he was more than a respected colleague—he was a close friend for whom I had, and have, great affection. It was a relationship on which I would rely again and again to do my part to help steer the Cold War to a peaceful close.

A Breakthrough in Paris

In late July, I was scheduled to go to Paris for peace talks on Cambodia, and wanted to use the occasion to see Shevardnadze. The backdrop for our meeting was a series of remarkable events taking place in the coal-rich Donets Basin in Ukraine and the Kuznetsk Basin in western Siberia. In these two regions—the first and second richest coal regions in the USSR—over 150,000 coal miners had gone on strike, demanding higher wages and improved working conditions. The strikes had gained political momentum, and Gorbachev had been forced to propose formal recognition of the right to strike, something that would have been unheard of just a few years before. And while the Soviet Union did not have a history of independent labor, as had Poland, there was the slim possibility that Solidarity's success in forcing General Wojciech Jaruzelski, the leader of the Polish government, into roundtable talks could become a model for Soviet workers. At the time, my biggest concern was that Gorbachev or some lower-level official would feel the need to stand up to the miners, a confrontation would develop, and the government would use force. The dangers of "Tiananmen Two" were not far from the surface, and I decided to discuss the issue directly with Shevardnadze.

Within the intelligence community in Washington and the rumor mill in Moscow, there was much speculation about a possible purge of the Communist Party. In mid-July, Gorbachev told a closed-door party meeting, "The cadres need renewal, an influx of fresh forces." While Gorbachev was gearing up to oust conservatives with reformers, his Prime Minister, Nikolai Ryzhkov, was bemoaning the Party's loss of prestige, saying, "If the Party does not find a way out of this situation, then it may lose its influence over the state government."

To me, the most intriguing rumor concerned Shevardnadze. Many felt that, given his domestic difficulties, Gorbachev was likely to replace Ryzhkov with Shevardnadze. Some thought Gorbachev would make Shevardnadze General Secretary of the Party. In either case, the point would be for Gorbachev to signal his commitment to reform by putting one of the two most reformist members of the Politburo in one of these key domestic positions (the other well-known reformer was Alexander Yakovlev). At the time, I was ambivalent, as I felt that Shevardnadze and I had gotten off to a good start. In retrospect, I'm glad Shevardnadze stayed where he was—though he probably could have served Gorbachev's parochial political interests more effectively if he had taken up a position with a domestic portfolio. (Later, Gorbachev did offer the vice presidency to Shevardnadze, who turned it down. He mentioned it to me in confidence, saying that his work in foreign policy was more critical.)

I knew that Shevardnadze was coming to our meeting preoccupied with internal matters. What I could not have predicted was how eloquent and passionate he would be with me in laying out his concerns.

We met late in the afternoon of Saturday, July 29. After opening pleasantries, I wanted to begin this meeting by talking about our next meeting; I thought Shevardnadze would be more relaxed if he knew from the outset that I was looking forward to another full-blown ministerial. Margaret Tut-wiler had suggested, however, that we break past the formalistic, expert-laden approach to ministerials, to meet in a more relaxed setting; that, of course, meant getting out of Washington. Just that year, I had bought a ranch in Wyoming and planned to try to spend part of August relaxing there. Wyoming's breathtaking vistas would symbolize the new openness in our relations, I thought, and something more. At the time, because Moscow imposed travel restrictions on our diplomats, we imposed similar restrictions on theirs: the ministerial would give Shevardnadze and his delegation their first opportunity to see the American heartland. (I had cleared the idea with the President first, as he had been giving some thought to inviting Gorbachev to Kennebunkport, but protocol required that the next summit be either in the Soviet Union or on neutral ground.)

Shevardnadze visibly brightened as soon as I mentioned the idea.* Without a word, his body language signaled his approval: that was our first step together.

He began his reply by handing me a letter of appreciation from Gorbachev to President Bush regarding a Soviet submarine that had sunk in the Norwegian Sea. The President had sent Gorbachev a letter expressing his sympathies and offering the Soviets our help in raising the submarine. In beginning his presentation by thanking us on such an emotional issue, Shevardnadze seemed to be signaling me that he—like I—wanted to break past formal negotiations, and he quickly followed up by agreeing to the meeting in Wyoming in September.

I then moved on to my key concern: the dangers associated with Moscow's using force against the miners. "The President and I want to remain in a position that will permit us to move the U.S.-Soviet relationship forward. In light of that, I hope that your response to your difficulties will be formulated in such a way as to avoid, to the extent possible, any use of force. Avoiding the use of force would be important if one were to avoid an emotional outburst in the U.S. that might well be triggered by those who do not want to see perestroika succeed."

I tried to draw a critical distinction. "We obviously recognize the importance of maintaining order and stability, and there are clear differences between [the actions of] people associated with communal violence involving the killing of innocent people on the one hand, and peaceful strikes carried out by workers on the other. I mention this only because of our fervent desire to move our relationship forward in a positive way. I want to flag this

---

*I showed him a few snapshots of my recently purchased ranch, with its dramatic scenery. At the end of my meeting, he put them in his pocket and I had to request their return, since they were the only copies I had.

for you, because it is important that you understand the kinds of pressures our administration could be subjected to, should events develop in an unfortunate way." In retrospect, it's obvious to me that Gorbachev and Shevardnadze had thought much about the implications of the Tiananmen tragedy for their own reforms. After all, Gorbachev's first day in Beijing had been disrupted as the Chinese government changed his schedule to avoid student protesters. He'd left Beijing with cautious praise for the students, and the protests continued to grow—only to be cut down just two and a half weeks later.

Shevardnadze replied by saying that he was glad I had raised this issue, because he had been planning to if I hadn't. After expressing appreciation for the interest the President and I had shown in perestroika and our supportive statements, he said bluntly, "The trends developing in the Soviet Union have been difficult. Democratization, perestroika, and renewal are affecting every part of our society, and every person and every family, too. We are now in the most crucial stage in what we call our revolution. Indeed, we are having a revolution. The old mechanism and the old machine have been abandoned, and unfortunately the new one is not yet able to function at full strength. We are at a most difficult time, because our renewal of the political system is running well ahead of the renewal of the economic system. Changes in the minds of the people are far more rapid than changes in the minds of many leading officials."

In a few, focused minutes, he had fundamentally changed our relationship. These were not the words of a government minister reading off a prepared briefing paper. They were the words of a man involved in an historic struggle. He had conveyed not just the political position in which the Gorbachev government found itself, but also the emotional struggle in which it was engaged. In March, he had called perestroika "revolutionary," but now he was indicating that it was truly a mass movement—and by implication, raising the question whether Gorbachev was leading it or being led by it. What had begun as a classic Soviet "revolution from above"—inspired and directed by the Soviet leadership—was being transformed into a revolt from below, a fact Shevardnadze acknowledged.

"The strike by workers is, of course," he said, "a very unusual phenomenon in the USSR. But it is interesting and important that they have not issued a single statement against perestroika and the process of renewal. Instead, their protests are against the bureaucracy. The people responsible for the strike are well organized and have a very high level of consciousness. Their demands for better social and economic conditions are quite responsible, and it is also important to understand that they showed in the end an appreciation for what the system could support at this time.

"Our country's social and economic problems are enormous. The financial situation is in very grave condition. There are big imbalances in our markets and money supply, and goods are also vastly out of balance. Sometimes we say we have a real crisis. This is not to say there is no way out." He identified several areas—in the northern Caucasus and Kazakhstan—where he felt real progress was being made, but then pointed to other areas where economic reform was stagnating.

"We know that only we can solve our own problems. We agree with what both President Bush and you have said about the Soviet people being responsible for themselves and for making perestroika work. Of course," he added, "cooperation helps, and we seek it from the United States, Europe, and Asia. We also know that the capability of our partners is limited especially with regard to our needs—and we are not about to require you to take 300 million Soviet people under your wing. We don't want to create that problem for you," he said, laughing.

Getting back to ethnic strife, he said, "Soviet nationality problems are real and have accumulated and been built up over the course of decades. It's time for them to be addressed," he said resolutely. "There is no question that a gap has emerged between the reality and these principles.

"It is hard to recognize our own people these days. Their thinking is unfettered, it's original, it's bold, and it's honest." He had spoken informally for almost an hour.

I began by reassuring him. "I want to repeat that we are strongly committed to the success of perestroika, recognizing that this very much depends on what you do and how you respond to the challenges you face. The vast majority of Americans support your efforts. But how effective we can be in trying to assist you depends on our public opinion continuing in this favorable direction. That's the only reason I alluded earlier to the different responses you might take with regard to your difficulties."

He nodded and said, "I appreciate your comment. I know it is not always easy for you to defend your policy. I know that there are some in your society, like Brzezinski,* who would like to exploit Soviet troubles. His forecast of the end of socialism and the need to take advantage of this is shared by others. Look, for example, at Congress's adoption of the resolution on captive nations. We understand our responsibility to our people and to the world. We won't allow destabilization in the Soviet Union—destabilization in such a huge country with enormous military and economic potential would be a grave thing for the Soviet Union and the world. The same is true for Eastern Europe. It is one thing to speak of renewal, but destabilization is harmful, and it could be catastrophic."

"When we have spoken of the difficulties in the Soviet Union," I inter-

---

*Zbigniew Brzezinski had been President Carter's National Security Adviser.

jected, "we have also made very clear that we do not wish to see instability, but you are right that there is a segment in the U.S. that believes you are not seriously committed." I was concerned that "preventing instability" might become a cover for suppressing legitimate protest and dissent; in fact, in public I always spoke about the need to move toward legitimacy, and tried to leave stability to its narrow arms-control connotation. In a time of such great change, being for stability sounded too much like being for the status quo. I decided to draw the point out with Shevardnadze, and explain how the use of force would reverberate in the United States.

"That's why I suggested that the nature of your response to instability, if it should occur, could have an effect on the public attitudes of Americans. If your response to the difficulties is perceived as being brutal and repressive, those forces in the U.S. who oppose you will argue that perestroika was a fraud from the beginning. And in that kind of environment, it would be difficult for us to continue to respond positively to perestroika. Our whole system and culture are built around the right of the individual to express dissent peacefully. That's why there is such public outrage in the U.S. over what happened in Tiananmen Square. It runs counter to the basic values of the American people."

I told him that I agreed with his concern about instability in Eastern Europe. "That's why the President was so careful to emphasize on his trip that we support the reform process but in no way want to create problems for the Soviet Union. Like you, we believe that movement toward greater openness will continue in both the Soviet Union and Eastern Europe. And we applaud that. We strongly believe that one can't reverse the process once the fruits of freedom have been tasted."

"On the use of force," he responded, "let me assure you that our policy is designed to build a democratic and humanistic basis for our society. We are not going to abandon that as our guiding principle. As for the practical situation, we have had to use force when there was no other way out in dealing with violent clashes between different ethnic groups in places like Georgia. As you know, this is my native republic. Some extremists there have tried to foment trouble, but I must tell you that when I was sent down to Georgia, I categorically denounced the use of force, and I lifted the curfew. Please understand that our most sacred objective right now is to build a rule of law in our society, and we are simply not going to rely upon the use of force in dealing with our citizens."

"I'm glad to hear that," I said, and before I could add anything more, Shevardnadze said he had an additional point on Eastern Europe. "The issue of stability is a very serious one. Let's imagine the economic mechanism for cooperation between Eastern Europe and the Soviet Union had collapsed. That could mean anarchy. The bilateral system of economic ties can't disappear overnight; perhaps they should be replaced in ten or fifteen years by other mechanisms, but at the current point there is no alternative to evolution in these countries. Reform will continue in our country and should not be stopped, but reform must proceed in a stable way."

My impression was that the pace of reform in Eastern Europe had become a growing concern in Moscow. I wanted to make the point with Shevardnadze that change was probably going to come faster than anyone expected. "The President made clear that he was not in Poland and Hungary to foment unrest or make life difficult for the Soviet Union. That said, I want to be sure I understand what you are saying: Our view has been that several countries are trying to move toward a free-market economy, and that necessarily would mean that the tight linkage with the Soviet Union should begin to diminish. I don't believe that should cause a problem from the Soviet standpoint. Am I right in believing that?" I asked.

"You are," he told me. "It is up to these countries and their peoples to decide for themselves how their reform process should proceed and with whom they should have ties. If they conclude that it is advantageous for them to increase their cooperation with the West, and especially in economic areas, that is for them to decide. But no one should doubt that it will take time."

That night I informed the President that I didn't doubt Shevardnadze's commitment to avoid using force internally and to allow the Eastern Europeans to go their own way. But as I wrote, "I had the impression that I was dealing with a man who was preoccupied and more harried than I'd seen before. He lacked his earlier degree of confidence, and I had the sense that he would have been happy to discuss and reassure me about perestroika for the entire time we met. If nothing else, his preoccupation is a reminder of what Gorbachev is focusing on now, and a reminder, as well, that Shevardnadze's role and attention are being diverted increasingly to domestic issues."

As I left Paris, I realized that my relationship with Shevardnadze was evolving on two rather different dimensions. There was the formal level, at which we discussed arms control, regional conflicts, and other diplomatic topics, oftentimes in small group sessions with experts present. Our objective at this level was to eliminate such topics as points of contention and look for grounds for cooperation.

But at the more critical, informal level—centered around discussions of the domestic transformation of the Soviet Union and, by implication, its relationship to Eastern Europe—we were not so much foreign ministers as social commentators, sharing private worries and thoughts. Shevardnadze would reflect on the revolution sweeping the Communist bloc. It became my role to comment on his observations, hoping that my arguments would influence his views, however marginally, so as to help avoid the potential catastrophe that was so worrisome to him—and to me.

Two Controversies

After a two-week vacation with my family at the ranch in Wyoming, I returned to Washington at the end of August to begin preparations for the Jackson Hole ministerial. I wanted the ministerial to mark a departure in our relations with the Soviets, but first I had to endure two controversies—one diplomatic, one political.

The first revolved around Boris Yeltsin's visit to Washington on September 12. When I met him at the State Department at 2:00 P.M. that day, my first impression was of a large, physically intimidating man who reminded me more of an NFL tackle than a legislator. His bull-like physical size was reinforced by his tendency to grand gestures. His axlike hands cut the air, and he was extraordinarily ebullient. I had the genuine sense that this was a man of action who would rather break china than sip tea from it, a maverick who would rather smash the status quo than exchange diplomatic niceties.

He was concerned that perestroika and reform in general in the USSR were stalled. While he professed support for Gorbachev, he told me that the Soviet leadership did not have much more than a year to energize its efforts. On economic matters, he exhibited some typical Soviet misunderstandings of how free-market economics worked. He recognized that foreign investment was key to their economic reforms, and without any prompting, he noted that the Soviets themselves needed to change their laws and permit private property.

In a note that night to the President, headed "Boris Yeltsin: Not Just a Soviet Eccentric," I wrote that "Yeltsin spoke gravely, and despite the current press play, I found many of his critical observations to be on point."

Unfortunately, Yeltsin's visit to the White House had not gone as well. He wanted an Oval Office meeting with the President, balked at meeting just Brent Scowcroft, and then proceeded to put Scowcroft to sleep with an almost hour-long monologue. This led several White House aides—I was never sure exactly which ones—to criticize Yeltsin off the record with the press. Backgrounding and trashing Yeltsin in the media served no purpose whatsoever. While it created no long-run damage, it later was used against us as a sign of our alleged overly pro-Gorbachev tendencies.

In fact, at that time, we were engaged in a serious assessment of our relations with Gorbachev. In a note to me entitled "Growing Turmoil in the USSR: An Impending Crisis?" on July 25, Dennis Ross told me he was going to prepare alternative scenarios for the Soviet future. He had his staff develop a series of papers, the first of which came to me on September 11. It identified four possible scenarios: (1) authoritarian modernization; (2) a military coup; (3) post-Gorbachev paralysis; and (4) post-Gorbachev collapse. The wide range of potential scenarios made it clear that we needed a strategy that could manage the growing uncertainties regarding the Soviet future. I was already sensitive to the precariousness of Gorbachev's hold on power from Shevardnadze's analysis of the Soviet internal situation. What these papers did was reinforce my inclination from earlier that summer that we should do as much as we could to make progress with Gorbachev—to "lock in" change, as Bob Zoellick put it—while he was still in power. We knew Gorbachev was willing to make concessions. We couldn't be certain about his successor. So it made sense to build strong ties to advance our interests, without frivolously irritating potential successors to Gorbachev, such as Yeltsin. My view all along was that Yeltsin understood that we had to deal with Gorbachev, and after the Soviet Union collapsed he never indicated that he resented in any way the approach we had taken.

The second controversy was of my own making. On September 19, I scheduled a press conference to preview the Shevardnadze visit and to try to shape the "expectations" atmosphere for the visit. Everything went well, until I was asked for the third time about comments that Senate Majority Leader George Mitchell had made accusing us of a "wait-and-see" attitude to the changes in the Soviet Union and Eastern Europe. In part, Mitchell's remarks seemed to have been driven by a speech Larry Eagleburger had given at Georgetown University on September 13. In his address, Eagleburger had correctly pointed out that there was a certain stability associated with the bipolarity of the Cold War. Simply stating that fact, however, offered our critics an opportunity to accuse us of being nostalgic for the Cold War.

The first time I was questioned about Mitchell's comment, I gave a nicely nuanced diplomatic response; the second time, I said I just disagreed with that criticism. But by the third time, when pressed to address "an unusually harsh assessment of overall administration policy," I decided to call a spade a spade, and make it clear that Mitchell was just playing politics. "Well, let me address it this way by saying that when the President of the United States is rocking along with a 70 percent approval rating on his handling of foreign policy and I were the leader of the opposition party, I might have something similar to say," I said. It was a mistake. The press understood the truth in what I'd said—but they also knew that I had slipped and given them a nice sound bite that would make their stories more newsworthy. And that's because the Secretary of State is somehow expected to remain above partisan politics, regardless of how truly political the job actually is or how much experience he might have had in the political arena.

This is ironic, given the fact that in a democracy any foreign policy that cannot attract a domestic political consensus will have difficulty succeeding.

Jackson Hole

Shevardnadze arrived in Washington on Thursday, September 21. The two months since I had seen him in Paris had resulted in an even more explosive Soviet internal situation.

If July had been the month of labor unrest in the Soviet Union, August had been dominated by nationalities. In the Baltics, mass demonstrations had greeted the fiftieth anniversary of the Molotov-Ribbentrop pact, and the Central Committee of the CPSU had responded by condemning the "virus of nationalism" in the region. Political movements also stirred in the Central Asian republics and the Caucasus, particularly the Popular Front in Azerbaijan.

Then, on the eve of our meeting, Gorbachev followed through with his summer threat and purged the Politburo. Three conservatives—Vladimir Shcherbitsky, Victor Chebrikov, and Viktor Nikonov—were ousted from the twelve-man body, leaving Gorbachev's most ardent critic, Yegor Ligachev, isolated.

I joined the President that Thursday at 2:00 P.M. for his first meeting with Shevardnadze. "I'm pleased with the way we've moved from confrontation to dialogue," the President began. "We want you to succeed—and want your reforms to go forward to build a better relationship between the U.S. and the USSR."

"Thank you," said Shevardnadze. "We want to move to partnership with you. Over the past few years, we have signed over forty Soviet-U.S. agreements. There have been many exchanges. We understand and appreciate your interest in what is happening in the USSR. We are reassessing things. But we don't want to totally eradicate what we've done in the history of the USSR. Without it, there could be no reform. It is only on the basis of serious and fundamental achievements that we can plan what comes next.

"We fought together in World War II—we saved civilization. Reforms are now covering everything in the USSR. We are a union of fifteen states and of diverse nationalities. Now, we have a nationalities policy that will enable us to stabilize things. Each republic is sovereign and self-managing— or will be. We've just finished a plenum on this. There is great politicization in the Soviet Union, and we think this political awareness is good enough, though it's creating problems for us.

"We've traversed a very important stage," he continued. "We are working to overcome the incompatibility of our economic system with

ABOVE, LEFT: Here I am, on the move.
RIGHT: My father, James A. Baker, Jr. *(Gittings.)*
BELOW: The young Marine second lieutenant, Quantico, Virginia, 1952. I'm in
the center with the cigarette.

ABOVE: Mary Stuart and our four boys, in Houston. From left to right, Mike, Jamie, Doug, and John. *(Lester Kierstead Henderson.)*

BELOW: In the Oval Office with the President, my mother, and my daughter Mary Bonner Baker, 1981. *(White House/Reagan Library.)*

ABOVE: Appearing on "Face the Nation," 1981. Mary Bonner appears more interested in her juice. *(REM Newsphoto.)*
BELOW: Hard at work on the steps outside the Oval Office, facing the Rose Garden, 1981. *(White House/Reagan Library.)*

ABOVE: Asleep on Air Force One, 1982. *(White House/Reagan Library.)*
BELOW: Situation Room briefing. Clockwise: Ed Meese, General John Vessey, Caspar Weinberger, Vice President Bush, President Reagan, George Shultz, John McMahon of the CIA, and me. *(White House/Reagan Library.)*

ABOVE: Horseback riding with Ronald Reagan, Quantico, Virginia. *(White House/
Reagan Library.)*
BELOW: In my office as Secretary of the Treasury, 1985. *(David Woo.)*

ABOVE: White House East Room, my swearing in as Secretary of State, January 27, 1989. With me is my wife, Susan, Chief Justice Rehnquist, and President Bush. *(White House/Bush Library.)*

BELOW: Rose Garden signing of the Central American Bipartisan Accord, April 8, 1989. Surrounding the President and me are congressional leaders Foley, Michel, Dodd, Wright, Pell, Bonior, and McCain. *(White House/Bush Library.)*

ABOVE: My first meeting with Mikhail Gorbachev, May 11, 1989. *(AP/Wide World.)*

BELOW, LEFT: With the President and Soviet Foreign Minister Eduard Shevardnadze at the White House, on the eve of the Jackson Hole Ministerial, September 21, 1989. At the time, the situation in the USSR was difficult: demonstrations, political unrest, and Politburo purges. *(White House/Bush Library.)*

RIGHT: At Jackson Hole, Wyoming: a one-on-one walk in the woods.

ABOVE: A break in the ministerial for some fishing on the Snake River. *(AP/Wide World.)*

BELOW: In my private office at State, the day the Berlin Wall fell, November 9, 1989. *(Paul Hosefros, New York Times.)*

LEFT: Peering through a crack in the Berlin Wall, December 12, 1989. *(Reuters/Bettmann.)*
BELOW: Meeting with Romanian opposition leaders in Bucharest, February 1990.

ABOVE, LEFT: In Wenceslas
Square, waving to the crowd.
RIGHT: With President Havel in
Prague, February 1990.
(AP/Wide World.)
BELOW: Pro-democracy
demonstrators greeting us in
Sofia, Bulgaria.
(Reuters/Bettmann.)

RIGHT: Addressing a crowd estimated at over 400,000 in Tirana, Albania, a town of less than 250,000. *(David Hoffman, Washington Post.)*

LEFT: With Lech Walesa on the grounds of the U.S. Ambassador's residence in Warsaw.

BELOW: Addressing the Supreme Soviet, February 10, 1990—the first foreigner ever to do so.

The Africa trip: in Capetown, South Africa, with President de Klerk and Foreign Minister Botha, March 1990. *(Eckley Bykman.)*

In Soweto, with African National Congress leader Walter Sisulu, at a nursery school. *(AP/Wide World.)*

ABOVE: With Nelson Mandela in Namibia, shortly after his release from jail. *(Reuters/Bettmann.)*
BELOW: Exchanging pens with Shevardnadze in the East Room after a treaty signing, June 1, 1990. *(White House/Bush Library.)*

ABOVE: In Bonn with Chancellor Kohl during the "Two-plus-Four" talks, May 1990.

BELOW: In Germany, with Foreign Minister Genscher, on a visit to his home in Halle, in the former German Democratic Republic.

ABOVE: A landmark event: Checkpoint Charlie is no more, June 22, 1990.
BELOW: A "Two-plus-Four" Ministerial family photo, with our guest Polish
Foreign Minister Skubiszewski. From left to right: Genscher, me, Skubiszewski,
Dumas of France, Shevardnadze, Hurd of Great Britain, and Meckel of the
GDR.

In Mongolia, August 2, 1990. A deceptively lighthearted picture. Saddam had just invaded Kuwait, and some of my top policy advisers were already in Moscow, working on a joint statement. Shortly, I would be, too. *(David Hoffman,* Washington Post.*)*

An historic press conference at Vnukovo II Airport, outside Moscow, August 3, 1990. Shevardnadze is announcing that the USSR will be joining with the United States to condemn Iraq's invasion of Kuwait. *(Caron Jackson.)*

those of Western countries. We don't seek unilateral assistance. We want economic cooperation. Perestroika *will* succeed," he said emphatically. "We have some so-called friends who say we have very little time left. This is not a serious viewpoint. I know my country. I know my people. We will prevail."

He then turned over a long-awaited letter to the President from Gorbachev on arms control. The President had written Gorbachev on June 20, summarizing the outcome of the review of our various arms control positions. Gorbachev's six-page single-spaced response represented, in my view, a marked change in his approach to arms control. It was clearly far more directed at advancing the negotiations themselves than at making public relations points. Most important, the language was vague enough to indicate that the Soviets might be willing to drop their linkage between START and the Defense and Space talks. The President thanked him, and we agreed to discuss the arms control issues in detail in Wyoming.

That evening at 6:30 P.M., Shevardnadze joined me at Andrews Air Force Base for the flight to Wyoming. Instead of flying on the 707 Air Force jet I usually used, we took a DC-9 because of the short runway at the Jackson Hole airport, which is located in the Grand Teton National Park. In the rather noisy cabin of the plane, Shevardnadze and I were joined, as usual, by Sergei Tarasenko and Dennis Ross and our interpreters, along with Ambassador Dubinin and our ambassador to Moscow, Jack Matlock.

After a dinner of chicken parmesan, rice, peas with mushrooms, and cheesecake, prepared on board by the U.S. Air Force, I began our discussion by asking Shevardnadze for his assessment of the nationalities plenum. What I received was a nuanced and impassioned analysis.

"The nationality problems are one of the most sensitive and difficult problems we face," he began. He went on to explain their historical roots, noting that, in principle, under Lenin the Union government was only supposed to have dealt with defense and diplomacy, with all other powers and rights vested in the republics. But in practice, things had turned out rather differently. "There was great centralization of power," Shevardnadze said. "That centralization came, not only because of the subjective views of our leaders at the time, but because of the difficulty of the conditions in which our country found itself. Centralization was needed if a weak country was to be transformed into a strong one. This served us well," he continued, "during a very difficult period because I can't imagine us going to war without centralization. And maybe there even was some justification after the war to maintain a highly centralized economy. We did, after all, have to rebuild. But in the 1960s and 1970s, it's clear that the actual gap between our constitutional rights and the actual practice in the republics was great and was also harmful.

"At that time, we misled ourselves into thinking that the nationality problem had been definitely resolved. That was a mistake, and it was wrong to think that way. Every nation is a living entity. It grows, it evolves, and it was a mistake to think the nationality problem could be solved once and for all." In his words, I heard strong echoes of Nanuli's impassioned comments in May.

He went on to say that they were developing a new nationalities policy, but they should have done it twenty-five years before. Decentralization would be the new organizing principle, and with it would come a new political arrangement between the center and the republics. "We are in the process of searching for a political solution for the relations between the republics and the center. If I were to speak from a purely formal standpoint, I might tell you that everything seems okay. After all, each republic has its own parliament, can discuss questions relating to the budget of the republic, and other related issues. Also, each republic has the attributes of state power. Unfortunately, these attributes are not translated into reality. The truth is that all important problems have to be taken to the center. Now we are going to reverse this process. All these decisions will be sent back to the republics."

It was a revealing moment, not so much for its honesty—Shevardnadze had been open before—as for its admission that we were speaking "informally." It was a turning point in our relationship, because from that point on, we tended to speak "informally" in all our one-on-one sessions—unless either one of us felt duty-bound to present the bureaucratic logic behind our government's position on a contentious issue such as arms control.

The more Shevardnadze and I talked, the more I realized that the Soviets had not defined many of the key aspects of these new center-republics relations. They seemed to have little sense of how they were going to move from an overly centralized, stagnant system to a decentralized, rejuvenated one. It seemed to me that the tendency was for events to take on a momentum of their own once the regime loosened controls.

I took the occasion to make our position on the Baltics abundantly clear. "I know that this is a sensitive area for you," I began, "but I have to tell you that we have a problem vis-à-vis the Baltics. You have heard me say we really want the reform effort to succeed, and we will do nothing to complicate that process. I have said publicly that we do not want to see instability in the Soviet Union. But let me also tell you that it has been U.S. policy for over forty years not to recognize the incorporation of the Baltic republics into the Soviet Union. These Baltic states were independent. There remains a very strong public sentiment in our country that identifies with these Baltic states." I wanted him to understand that our Baltics policy was rooted in historical and domestic political realities, and that the President could not shift away from this position even if he wanted to (which he didn't in any case).

"We are very aware about your concern regarding sovereignty and borders, and will do nothing to exacerbate the problem," I continued. "Nevertheless, as hard as we might try to move our relations forward with you, it would be very hard to sustain positive relations if you were to find it necessary to use force in the Baltics. Let me just say to you that a strong reaction by us would be a given. So I am very hopeful that a peaceful way would be found to solve the nationality problem generally, and especially in the Baltics. I raise this only so that you will understand the extraordinary pressure on us. I don't raise this to pressure you or to hector you." Saying that allowed me to soften the message's personal content, while keeping the strictness of the policy line abundantly obvious. It was always a good idea with one's interlocutor to deemphasize any personal dimension on issues which were in conflict.

He responded with a short discussion on how the use of force would imperil perestroika. "As to your concern about the use of violence, let me just say that this is ruled out by us. That would mean an end to perestroika. It would restore what we used to call the 'dictatorship of the proletariat.' [This was a bit of revisionist Marxism on Shevardnadze's part; the Bolsheviks had taken control in the name of the "dictatorship of the proletariat."] We can't reverse our course. We can't go back to the past. In some areas we were compelled to use force, but this was only in circumstances where different ethnic groups like the Azerbaijanis and the Armenians were practically engaging in genocide. Here force was required to restore order. In the Baltics, no one intends to use force. As you know, in Georgia force was used and there were tragic consequences. Gorbachev and I were out of the country when that decision was made. That decision was taken by republican authorities. When we came back and saw this, we sacked the people responsible. We condemned their decision, and we made it clear that the use of force is inconsistent with our principles."

He went on to discuss what he said were practical difficulties and real dangers that would be created in Estonia if separatists wanted to leave the union, in a situation where one-third of the people in Estonia were Russian-speaking. He went on to say that most people didn't want to secede and, in any case, secession was impractical.

I pushed him, trying to get him to think about how Moscow might create a political process that would get past the impasse that existed with the Baltics. Taking his side for the sake of argument, I asked, "First, if it's totally impractical and the majority in any given republic would choose to stay in the Union, why not solve the problem by having a referendum? If you grant people the right of self-determination and they can vote on what they want to do, and if the majority vote to stay, then the separatists will no longer have a basis on which to push for separation." I had no doubt that most people would in fact vote for independence, but I felt that by putting the stress on elections and referenda, then independence could be achieved in a peaceful, step-by-step process.

"Second," I said, "isn't there a difference between the Baltic republics, which were once independent countries, and the others, which were never independent?"

I knew I had pushed him too far when he responded with a legalistic obfuscation: the question of a referendum was, he said, "a constitutional question. This is a question for the national or union constitution and for each republican constitution. In the current constitutions, there are no provisions for referenda." On this subject, our informal conversation was over. He was stuck in a formal defense of his position. He knew as well as I that the details of the Brezhnevite constitution were irrelevant.

On the broader question I raised, he responded more as a former leader of Georgia and less as Soviet Foreign Minister. "You might note that the Transcaucasus republics were independent for three years after the October Revolution. There were separate governments in Baku and in Yerevan. These governments were in fact set up under Kerensky. So there might not be as much a difference here as you think and, indeed, if the Baltics were to leave, people in the Transcaucasus might say, Why shouldn't we leave also? Frankly, it is okay for this to be part of our open debate. We don't fear debate." Two years later, in the aftermath of the failed coup, as every Soviet republic declared independence, I'd remember Shevardnadze's words as an uncanny prophesy.

Finding myself at a dead end when it came to the Baltics, I turned the discussion to Eastern Europe. I told Shevardnadze we did not want to be troublesome to the Soviets in the region. I said that we did not desire to stir things up or foment unrest, but that we were going to help the Eastern Europeans to develop democracy and free markets.

Shevardnadze suggested that an "unstable Poland would be good neither for you nor for us." He cautioned me about the dangers associated with abruptly breaking economic links between the Soviet Union and Eastern Europe. "So if you rupture all links, it would be suicide, just like it would be suicide for the Baltic states. No one could take Poland under its wing, certainly not Germany. Yes, they could work with Poland, but no one could throw the kind of money at Poland that it really needs. Only we've done that. Only we've wasted our money."

When asked about our respective security and economic organizations, he made a proposal. "Let's disband both NATO and the Warsaw Pact. Let's release your allies and ours. While NATO exists, the Warsaw Pact also exists. As for CEMA, it needs reconstruction. [CEMA was the Soviet abbreviation for COMECON, the economic organization that tied together the Warsaw Pact states.] If that organization rebuilds itself into a sufficient organization, it will exist. If it continues working the way it does now, it will serve neither our allies nor us. We are working to reform it but will have to see how it does. Could I mention a statement Kohl made at the congress of his party? If you haven't read it, it might be worth your reading it.

"It is very similar to statements made by German leaders in the 1930s, and it created a serious concern for us. . . . He spoke in terms of ultimatum, and he also said that the Soviet Union is on the verge of crumbling; CEMA is on the verge of crumbling; and the task in the West, Kohl said, was to see what it should be doing under such circumstances."

I hadn't heard about the statement he was talking about, but even then it was obvious that the German question was on Soviet minds—and touched emotional chords other European issues did not. I responded by saying that we didn't want to see instability anywhere in the region, that "what we would like to see in Eastern Europe is a Europe that is whole and free, where the divisions have been ended, and all this is accomplished in a peaceful fashion."

Shevardnadze agreed, but, he said, "It's important to respect existing realities." He was referring patently to East Germany.

"As perestroika advances and gets applied to the GDR," I responded, "perhaps one won't see so many people wanting to leave the GDR. As you know, perestroika has been lagging in the GDR."

He fell back on his homily: "That's true, but it is up to every country to decide how it wants to live."

I fell back on logic: "When you have thousands of people seeking to leave, however, they obviously are saying something about the system and how it is working."

"Well, that's not always true," he responded. "We in the Soviet Union are going through a period when we are allowing much greater freedom, and yet we are having almost 100,000 people a year leaving. You know, from the standpoint of the freedom of expression, we have never had it so good, and yet people want to leave." It was a rare case in which Shevardnadze's roots in the Soviet system kept him anchored in its defense.

"As for the GDR," he continued, "one has to admit they have a high standard of living. They have a well-developed social infrastructure. Their housing problem is largely solved. They have day-care centers. They produce lots of athletic champions."

"So how do you explain all of those people leaving?" I said, continuing to press him.

"Well, it could be a division of families, relatives, that could be playing a part." Finally his "informal" common sense overcame his "formal" logic. "But, let me say, it is not up to us to solve this problem, it is up to them. If I were in their shoes, I'd let everybody who wants to go, leave. Of course, it is true that if as many as one million people leave, that would be a serious problem for Eastern Europe, but I would let them go." While our discussion of Germany had taken only a few minutes, the internal contradictions and tensions in Shevardnadze's words were obvious. Without doubt, working with the Soviets to manage change in Germany was going to be far more difficult and contentious than in any other state in Eastern Europe.

The Meaning of Jackson Hole

We landed in the clear, brisk mountain air of Jackson Hole, then walked down a red carpet and were presented with cowboy hats and trail slickers by the Governor, Mike Sullivan. Shevardnadze and the rest of his entourage seemed genuinely thrilled to be in the American West.

Over the next three days, we held a total of nine meetings on the full range of our relations. In each area, we made progress, and I'd like to think that the Tetons towering nearby, the Snake River running past us, and the rustic openness of Jackson Lake Lodge facilitated much of it. (Of course, holding the meeting had been a logistical nightmare, and only the hard work of Karen Groomes and Matthew Smith, who was our political liaison to the White House and logistical troubleshooter, made it all possible. They even managed to get a pair of moose to graze on the river at the foot of the mountains as a backdrop for our photo opportunity.)

It was obvious from his style of operation that Shevardnadze was preoccupied with domestic matters. As always, he was fully in charge and self-assured, but he read far more frequently from notes than he had previously, and called on members of his delegation far more often. No doubt, his preoccupation with the just-completed nationalities plenum explained much of it.

Our discussion of economic reform reinforced this impression. For these talks, Shevardnadze brought in Nikolai Shmelyev, a bright, young "radical" (i.e., market-oriented) economist. We focused on what might be done to soak up the ruble overhang, increase competitiveness internally, create a social safety net, and develop a price system. All these were necessary steps for them to move ahead with real economic reform and, eventually, ruble convertibility. Sometimes it seemed that Shevardnadze had brought Shmelyev along as much to give Shevardnadze an economic tutorial as to engage us. Undoubtedly, Shevardnadze also hoped that

Shmelyev's stock in Moscow would rise because of his involvement in this ministerial.

On arms control, I asked Shevardnadze point-blank if the Soviet Union was no longer conditioning or linking a START agreement to an agreement in the defense and space talks. He said that was true (which had been implied in Gorbachev's letter), and that an agreement reducing strategic offensive arms could be concluded even if no understanding had yet been achieved on a defense and space treaty or on what was permitted under the ABM Treaty. This was a dramatic breakthrough. Until we severed that linkage, any progress we made on specific START issues would have been purely hypothetical. Shevardnadze also agreed at Jackson Hole with our position that sea-launched cruise missiles should not be included in a START Treaty—though he suggested they should be addressed as part of a broader effort on naval arms control.

We also reached agreement on the major remaining issues on the nuclear-testing talks and a bilateral chemical-weapons accord. Progress in these areas was a signal that our cooperation could not only close out old issues—such as nuclear testing, which had languished for fifteen years—but also make significant progress on new ones. The President had personally tabled the chemical-weapons treaty when he'd been Vice President, had devoted a whole speech during the campaign to the dangers of proliferation, and was personally determined to see chemical weapons banished. Every time I had needed him to weigh in to break a logjam on chemical weapons within the U.S. government bureaucracy, he had. My work with Shevardnadze in Wyoming became a useful stepping-stone to the President's broader chemical-weapons initiative at the United Nations General Assembly a few days later.

On regional conflicts, Shevardnadze had told the President in Washington, "We are good to our words. *We* are not sending weapons to Nicaragua." In Jackson Hole, he stuck to his guns in arguing that the Soviets were no longer providing lethal aid to Nicaragua. He said he could not speak for Cuba, but he felt their supplies would diminish. Most important, he told me that if I had hard data on arms supplies by the Cubans to the Sandinistas, or by Havana or Managua to the FMLN in El Salvador, that I should give it to him and he would raise it with the parties. He said, "The Soviet Union would not consider it the act of a friend if these countries had violated commitments made to the USSR."

Above all, these achievements occurred in an open and informal atmosphere. Not only had Shevardnadze and I broken down the formal barriers in our talks, but so had many members of our delegations. My sense was that Wyoming ushered in a new tone in our personal relations—and that those ties became the key to much of the progress we made during the dramatic events later in the fall, as Soviet internal problems multiplied and Eastern Europe liberated itself from the USSR.

At an informal barbecue during our last night in Wyoming, Shevardnadze surprised everyone, and touched many, by presenting me with an enamel picture of Christ teaching the people, which had been made in Russia, saying, "You see, even we Communists are changing our worldview." I, in turn, presented Shevardnadze with a pair of cowboy boots, telling him these boots "help folks out here negotiate their way across some very difficult ground sometimes. And you know sometimes I think in our line of work, a person might have to watch where he steps and keep his feet firmly planted on the ground as well. So it occurred to me that some cowboy boots might come in mighty handy for you in Moscow." Little could I know how slippery the ground would become for all of us.

CHAPTER 10

THE FALL OF THE WALL

God bless America. Thank you for everything, sir.
Hans-Dietrich Genscher's secretary to Secretary Baker, November 10, 1989

In politics, words are the coin of the realm. Used judiciously, they can build political capital, coalesce a public consensus, or enrich a nation. But when frittered away or ineffectively employed, words in political life can bankrupt a candidate, sell out a policy, or even dissolve a government. Politics, after all, is mainly persuasion, and even in an age of modems, microprocessors, cellular phones, and faxes, what matters is the written and spoken word.

This is all the more true in international politics. Between states, dialogue occurs at several levels. Foremost are the private discussions conducted in secret between governments, but also critical is the dialogue that takes place publicly. On a typical morning as Secretary of State, my security detail picked me up between 6:45 A.M. and 7:15 A.M. for the short ten-to-twelve-minute ride to "the Building." On my way in, I would scan my day book, prepared the night before, covering the scheduled events for that day, both procedurally and substantively. Once there, I would be greeted by John Crowley, who has been the Secretary's confidential assistant since Henry Kissinger. John invariably would share a smile that helped me ease into my day. Over breakfast, I would read the overnight intelligence from the CIA and State's own intelligence bureau (INR), as well as a thick sheaf of daily press clips about foreign policy matters from a wide range of American newspapers and magazines. In addition, I would scan the daily *White House News Summary*.

This was much more than simply a way to keep informed of world events, because much of my work as Secretary of State was done through that public dialogue. It has often been said that I tended to pay a lot of attention to the press, and that's true. It's a necessity when you're a senior decision maker in the U.S. government. Journalists are an indispensable link between national security policy makers and their audiences, which include foreign governments and publics as well as the U.S. Congress and the American people.

In terms of fine-tuning our own work, staying abreast of the press commentary was particularly important. If I had given a speech or testified on Capitol Hill, for example, it was critical to see how Don Oberdorfer or David Hoffman of the *Washington Post,* Doyle McManus or Norm Kempster of the *Los Angeles Times,* Tom Friedman of the *New York Times,* Walt Mossberg or Bob Greenberger of the *Wall Street Journal,* and their colleagues had reported it, because their headline, their story, and the quotes they'd use received much wider circulation in diplomatic circles than the speech itself. Knowing the message I had intended to send, I could read the news clips and determine whether I had succeeded in my task—and then use the feedback to adjust what we were saying publicly (and privately) to shade or shift the policy in one direction or another.

Other governments did the same, of course—particularly in countries such as Germany and Israel, where foreign policy issues receive extensive scrutiny by the press. Oftentimes, before communicating a proposal, they'd try floating an idea by "letting" it leak into the press. We, of course, did the same. Thus is diplomacy conducted.

This "open source" literature, as the intelligence community called it, was of course complemented by the intelligence community's various products: the *President's Daily Brief* (PDB) and the *National Intelligence Daily* (NID) produced by the CIA, and the *Secretary of State's Morning Summary,* prepared by INR, headed very ably by Doug Mulholland, who had worked for me at Treasury. Even in these oftentimes top-secret publications, much of the analysis and information would revolve around public statements by foreign officials and assessments of the extent to which these public statements accurately reflected the confidential plans of the government involved.

Beyond what governments say privately and publicly, of course, there is the level of what governments do. The most obvious involve the use of military force. This is where foreign policy and defense policy intersect. War is the ultimate and last solution to any international conflict. It is also, of course, the least used. That's why it's often said in Washington that while the State Department manages policy (that is, words), the Defense Department develops programs (that is, weapons systems and military forces).

Long before states go to war—or even contemplate it—their governments will usually have exchanged literally thousands of words, privately and publicly, directly and indirectly. During the Cold War, the danger of a catastrophic war between the superpowers was so great that diplomats used words as surrogates for force, sending sharply worded démarches rather than well-armed Marines to make their points. Paradoxically, in an age of intercontinental missiles and hot lines, words became even more important. And this was just as true for the Cold War's end as for any crisis during its decades-long tenure.

"Points of Mutual Advantage"

It was obvious to me after the Wyoming ministerial that U.S.-Soviet relations had moved to a qualitatively new stage. At Jackson Hole, we had made progress on every part of our agenda. We had turned a corner—as I had put it during the ministerial—"from confrontation to dialogue, to cooperation." I was determined to do what I could to consolidate this change—not only in terms of offical U.S. government policy but also with the Congress and the American public at large. My sense was that the public debate was not coming to a close; if anything, those who supported Gorbachev were becoming more strident in calling for Western assistance to the Soviets, and those who felt Gorbachev was nothing more than a wolf in sheep's clothing were becoming all the more intractable. In this circumstance, I felt that it was critical to articulate our administration's position in a high-profile way, in an effort to coalesce a majority around a sensible policy that could receive bipartisan support and carry the day in the public debate.

So, in a series of three statements in October, I laid out the administration's own "new thinking" on perestroika and the nature of U.S.-Soviet relations. Each statement examined a slightly different aspect of the problem. On October 4, in testimony before Lloyd Bentsen's Senate Finance Committee, I focused on economic reform. Twelve days later, on October 16, in a speech before the Foreign Policy Association in New York, I focused on the overall relationship. And, delivering a speech that had been delayed due to the Loma Prieta earthquake, I spoke on October 23 before the Commonwealth Club in San Francisco on strategy and arms control.

The logic chain of the speeches was straightforward. It represented a public airing of what we had been thinking internally since the time of the Paris ministerial. I argued that perestroika was a "true revolution" that transcended economics to encompass globally all of Soviet society and its relations. "It is an ongoing experiment," I told the Senate, "relying on a fair amount of 'seat of the pants' logic." The fate of perestroika's success would be determined by what the Soviets themselves did, I said, but there was room for a new relationship. I said that the President and I wanted perestroika to succeed "not because it is our business to reform Soviet society or to keep a particular Soviet leader in power—we can really do neither—but because perestroika promises Soviet actions more advantageous to our interests. Our task is to search creatively for those points of mutual U.S.-Soviet advantage that may be possible—and many more may be possible because of perestroika."

I identified five areas in which we would pursue the search for mutual advantage: the determination to make Europe whole and free; the resolution of regional conflicts; the expansion of arms control; the institutionalization of glasnost and democratization; and the providing of technical assistance to support economic reform. In so doing, I fundamentally redefined what had theretofore been our agenda with the Soviet Union. I put Europe and regional conflicts *ahead* of arms control, transformed the issue of human rights into the democratization of Soviet society, and turned the matter of bilateral relations into a U.S. effort to see economic reform succeed.

Moreover, I made the case that this all made strategic sense, even if Gorbachev's position deteriorated. As I said in San Francisco, "Any uncertainty about the fate of reform in the Soviet Union, however, is all the more reason, not less, for us to seize the present opportunity. For the works of our labor—a diminished Soviet threat and effectively verifiable agreements—can endure even if perestroika does not." In short, my position was: "Let's get what we can now and lock in as much change as possible." I didn't want anyone in the future to be able to look back and say, "If only . . ."

The response to the speeches was gratifying. Domestically, the press coverage was almost universally favorable, with editorialists congratulating the administration for moving ahead. Internationally, our allies were reassured, and the Soviets saw that the internal bickering from the spring had been decisively ended.

Or so it seemed. I had not even given the speech in San Francisco when a draft speech that Bob Gates planned to give landed on my desk. I asked Dennis Ross to look at it while I read it myself. Ross was alarmed. "He can't give this speech. It will totally undercut Wyoming and the statements you've just given. This is ridiculous." I agreed. My feeling was that Bob had made a fundamental mistake by failing to distinguish between what the administration thought privately and what we said publicly about those views. His speech was extremely pessimistic about Gorbachev's chances for survival. While that view was shared by most of us, highlighting it in our public comments would have had the effect of pulling the rug out from under the President's statements that we supported perestroika. Analytically, I didn't have any serious disagreements with Gates's assessments. In fact, it would have been fine as closed congressional testimony from the CIA's Deputy Director of Intelligence, which is what Bob had been during the Reagan administration.

But in terms of the policy approach of our new administration, it would be a disaster. It would create a debate over who spoke for the administration, revive concerns in Congress, Europe, and Moscow that there were two rival schools of thought, and in my view undercut much of what the President and I had written or said to Gorbachev and Shevardnadze.

I called Scowcroft and told him it didn't make sense for the speech to be given, and thought the matter was closed. But the day after my speech in San Francisco, I received a memo from Scowcroft, making the case for a revised speech, which he had attached. Gates had cleverly raided my New York speech for quotations, but in Washington diplomatic and press circles, everyone would know that the quotations were intended only to obfuscate the differences in our views. "I believe his text as revised is basically a complement to your speeches, and provides a useful perspective in the current environment in a way that is helpful to the President," wrote Scowcroft. "No way," I wrote in a marginal notation.

Before I called Scowcroft to tell him the second version wasn't any better than the first, I wrote out my reasoning in clipped notes to myself: "(0) Worst possible timing (same week as mine). (1) No way press won't find something different—even if he were reading my speech. (2) This speech is very somber in tone and emphasis—different emphasis as he acknowledges and in some places directly contradicts—'new thinking just grows out of need for breathing space'—for example. (3) Can't fix it; Dennis tried; the inclination to find differences will be reinforced by small differences. (4) Will create view—two schools of thought in administration (should not have). (5) And right at the time we're getting high marks for laying out our coherent framework. (6) Will undo that and look like White House trying to reel Secretary of State back. (7) Lastly—why does Deputy Director of NSC feel need to be so visible on record regarding USSR? (8) Gates has studied Soviet Union—gives detailed speech—and has to deal with naïveté of Secretary of State (timing atrocious). (9) My speech was cleared! (10) We want to give impression that we are a solid phalanx. (11) Major mistake— even if could fix, can't fix—Q&A."

By the time I was done, I was even more worked up. When Gates had been at the CIA, he had given a speech that had completely undercut George Shultz on Soviet policy. That had hurt President Reagan then, and this would hurt George Bush now. I called Scowcroft, killed the speech, and then mentioned it the next day to the President to make sure the controversy wasn't reopened. The President agreed with what I'd done, though he said, "It's caused some heartburn over here."

In retrospect, I'm certain I did the right thing. In the weeks ahead, the crumbling of communism would accelerate markedly in Europe. Tensions would grow as Soviet clients in Eastern Europe fell like dominoes and the unification of Germany became the central diplomatic problem in East-West relations. In that environment, we needed the best possible relations with Gorbachev and Shevardnadze to steer the Soviet ejection from Eastern Europe to a peaceful conclusion. Gates's speech would have poisoned the atmosphere at precisely the wrong time. In international politics, it's not always wise to say exactly what you think.*

The Fall of the Wall

On November 9, 1989, I was hosting a luncheon for Philippine President Corazon Aquino in the Ben Franklin Room on the State Department's eighth floor when Eric Hoghaug, one of my staff assistants, passed me a note from Stapleton Roy, our executive secretary. At the end of a rambling news conference, Günter Schabowski, a Politburo member of the East German Communist Party, had made a vague statement about a new visa procedure that was being interpreted to mean that travel to the West would be completely unrestricted and unregulated. As Roy's note put it, "The East German government has just announced that it has fully opened its borders to the West. The implication from the announcement is full freedom of travel via current East German/West German links between borders." With some emotion, I must confess, I read the note aloud to my table, then I raised my glass and proposed a toast to this moment the West had been anticipating for over twenty-eight years—a truly astonishing turn of events.

Since the breakdown of the four-power talks in 1953, the United States and other Western allies had officially supported the goal of German reunification. At that time, the United States had joined with Britain and France in issuing a statement urging that "the reunification of Germany should be achieved through free elections, leading to the creation of an all-German government with which a peace treaty could be concluded." With the erection of the Berlin Wall in October 1961, the division of Berlin and Germany hardened, and in the ensuing two decades, most Europeans and many Americans began to believe that a divided Germany was an irre-

*Bob sent me a handwritten note a few days later that noted, "I *do* agree with you that, whether or not reform succeeds in the USSR, we cannot stand on the sidelines for years waiting for the final outcome. The process of reform itself offers too many opportunities for us— and history would condemn us harshly for doing nothing."

versible historical reality that actually improved European stability. When Ronald Reagan stood before the Brandenburg Gate in 1987, and said, "Mr. Gorbachev, tear down this wall!" he received much applause, but few Europeans were as enthusiastic about seeing a unified Germany.

In the spring of 1989, the Bush administration began to consider possible approaches to the looming reunification issue. In my time at the Treasury Department, I had worked closely with both the German Finance Ministry and the Bundesbank. My friendships with people such as Gerhard Stoltenberg, then Finance Minister and later Defense Minister, and Karl Otto Pohl, the Bundesbank chairman, had been critical to the negotiations that brought about the Plaza and Louvre accords. Although my father had fought Germans in the First World War, and I still remembered vividly the chilling newsreel footage of Hitler, I had no personal animosity to the German people, or any intimation that history was preordained to be repeated in the center of Europe. Coming into office, my sense was that West Germany had shown itself to be a vibrant free-market democracy—and despite being physically the size of Oregon, it had fully one-fourth the population of the United States and was the third most dominant power in the world economically. In a time of diplomatic upheaval in Europe, we didn't want Germany sliding around of its own weight.

On Wednesday, May 17, I had gone to the White House to discuss the upcoming NATO Summit with the President over lunch. On the list of initiatives and themes Bob Zoellick had prepared for me was one called simply "Germany."

"This is the real opportunity to get ahead of the curve and exceed expectations," I told the President. NATO documents in the 1950s and 1960s had always emphasized NATO's commitment to reunification, but Ostpolitik in the 1970s and the Euromissile crisis in the 1980s had essentially submerged the idea. But now, I told the President, "There's no doubt the topic is coming back. The real question is whether Gorbachev will grab it first." I knew George Bush's competitiveness from our days as doubles partners in Houston, and as his campaign manager I had learned that it was always useful to engage his competitive instincts when you wanted to convince him to move on an issue. "We need to move out ahead in a way that establishes a Western anchor for this process," I continued. I added that we should call it "normalization," not reunification.

His instinct was to emphasize the issue, building on Ronald Reagan's eloquent call. He agreed that the unity of Germany should be a central theme to his European trip. And in Mainz, on May 31—in one of his best foreign-policy speeches—he went beyond our discussion, calling the United States and the Federal Republic of Germany "partners in leadership." He went on to say, "Just as the barriers are coming down in Hungary, so they must fall throughout all of Eastern Europe. Let Berlin be next. Let Berlin be next! Nowhere is the division between East and West seen more clearly than in Berlin. And there this brutal wall cuts neighbor from neighbor, brother from brother. And that wall stands as a monument to the failure of communism. It must come down.''

By the end of the summer, thousands of East Germans who had traveled to Hungary began to demand that they be allowed to cross into the West. On August 24, Chancellor Kohl met with Hungary's Prime Minister Nemeth and Foreign Minister Horn, and they made a dramatic decision: They agreed to open Hungary's border with Austria, which, in effect, opened a back door around the Berlin Wall. For the old East German regime, it was the beginning of the end.

When George Bush had visited Budapest in July, Nemeth had given the President and me each a piece of barbed wire (some of the very first parts of the Iron Curtain to be dismantled), mounted on a plaque inscribed, ''This piece of barbed wire is a part of the 'Iron Curtain' alongside the Hungarian-Austro border, that palpably represented the division of the European continent into two halves. Its dismantling was made possible by the will of the Hungarian people and the recognition of peaceful co-existence and mutual interdependence. We believe that the artificial, physical, and spiritual walls still existing in the world, some day shall collapse everywhere!'' By late September, his prophesy was coming true, and very quickly at that.

Throughout the month, in an effort to make it to the West, East Germans had been flooding into the West German embassies in Budapest and Prague, creating a major refugee crisis. During the United Nations General Assembly in New York, in the last week of September, I asked Hans-Dietrich Genscher, ''What can I do for you?'' He suggested I meet with the Hungarians and the Czechs. Meeting with the Hungarians was straightforward; Budapest had moved far down the path of reform and was already doing quite a bit to help. But meeting with Czech Foreign Minister Johansen created a dilemma. Prague remained reactionary, not reformist, and meeting with Prague's highest diplomat would confer some legitimacy upon a regime that had little. But that adverse effect, I believed, would be offset by the opportunity to put pressure on the Czechs to cooperate in facilitating East German emigration.

The Saturday of that week, Genscher visited Prague, where 6,000 East German refugees were camped out at the Federal Republic's embassy. Speaking from the embassy's balcony, Genscher announced that the refugees would be allowed to travel to West Germany via trains that would cross through the GDR. The East German leader, Erich Honecker, wanted the refugees cleared out before the October 7 Communist jubilee in East Berlin, so he had agreed that they could travel to West Germany as long as they "left from" the GDR—hence the train route. The first trains with East German refugees from Prague and Warsaw began arriving in the FRG on October 1.

The reaction to Honecker's decision was far greater than he had anticipated, however. Three nights later, I informed the President, "The East German population hemorrhage has acutely embarrassed the GDR regime." In the face of 130,000 legal and illegal departures to date, they tried to impose new travel restrictions again, but that only fed domestic discontent. Events were beginning to move rapidly now, and that brought up a new danger.

Throughout the summer, as Poland and Hungary outbid each other in an attempt to be the first to dismantle communism, we became concerned about whether Gorbachev would draw the line against change in East Germany. Besides having 400,000 elite troops in the GDR, the Soviet Union had during the "Great Patriotic War" (as they called World War II) paid an immense historical and emotional price to defeat the Nazis. Moscow had shown consistently during the Cold War that it would not tolerate a revived German threat. This psycho-historical aspect made any change in East Germany potentially far more dangerous in terms of Soviet reactions than in any other country in Eastern Europe. As an adolescent, I had been amazed by the Soviet defense of Stalingrad in the winter of 1942–43. They had fought for seven months and had seen hundreds of thousands killed or injured, yet they had not given up. How do these people manage to endure? I had thought. Having listened to Shevardnadze's impassioned concerns on the way to Jackson Hole, I now began to wonder how much Gorbachev would endure in the GDR.

I didn't have to wait long to find out. On October 7, Gorbachev visited East Berlin to celebrate the fortieth anniversary of the GDR. In his speech before the jubilee, Gorbachev dropped a bombshell. Policy for East Germany, he said, is made "not in Moscow but in Berlin." It was the clearest public signal we could hope for that the Kremlin was not going to intervene.

The next day, during an interview on NBC's *Meet the Press*, I decided to send a signal of our own. When *New Yorker* writer Elizabeth Drew asked me about the future of East Germany and the possibility of reunification, I responded, "It's been the policy of the United States to support the concept of reunification of Germany, provided it is done in peace and freedom. And it seems to us that there should be no concern about a unified Germany which is integrated into the democratic community of European nations."

With Gorbachev basically ruling out Soviet intervention in his public statement, the next greatest danger was that Honecker would attempt to hold on by using his own forces to quash dissent. Throughout this period, rumors in the press and intelligence circles persisted of preparations for a crackdown by the National People's Army (NVA) and the Stasi, the East German secret police. It was ironic that fears of another Tiananmen again came to the fore on the very day—Monday, October 9—that Chinese Deputy Premier Yao Yilin flew in to Berlin for a meeting with Honecker.

That night, large demonstrations—the first since 1953—continued in the GDR. Fifty thousand people marched peacefully in Leipzig. Smaller protests occurred in a number of other cities, and most were broken up by police. The demonstrators vowed to stay and work for reform. The scope and spontaneity of the protests were extraordinary, but the security forces maintained control without resorting to widespread use of force. However, even though pressure was building on the GDR leadership, as I put it in my October 14 night note to the President, "The GDR leadership shows no sign of give. The regime continues to blame its problems on reactionary rowdies and Western interference, singling out West Germany. Gorbachev, during his weekend visit, did his best not to destabilize further a key ally, but also dropped hints about the need for change. Honecker in a speech avowed that any hope of reform is 'built on sand.' Unless Honecker addresses the deep unhappiness sparking the demonstrations, his problems seem sure to multiply."

The following afternoon, Gerhard Stoltenberg came to the State Department for a long-scheduled visit. He told me that Honecker's regime was at a turning point: "If they do not move toward reform, the use of force to suppress unrest cannot be ruled out," he said.

The following Monday, I was due to give the "Points of Mutual Advantage" speech in New York. While the speech was focused on U.S.-Soviet relations, I knew most of the press would be paying particular attention to anything I had to say about Germany. So I decided to send another public signal: "In East Germany, the people themselves are taking bold steps. As I said last week, it is time for perestroika and glasnost to come to East Germany. The status quo is as unacceptable to the people of that nation as it is to the peoples of Poland and Hungary. The people of East Germany cannot be forever denied at home the better life they now seek by fleeing to the West. Of course, the United States and our NATO partners have long supported the reconciliation of the German people. Their legitimate rights must someday be met. But let me be clear: Reconciliation through self-determination can only be achieved in peace and freedom. Normalization must occur on the basis of Western values with the end result being a people integrated into the community of democratic nations."

At Brent Scowcroft's suggestion, I had deliberately avoided the words *unification* and *reunification*. He was concerned that those words, with their emotional connotations, would be used by conservatives in the GDR and the USSR as an argument that the West was trying to stir up trouble. So I used *reconciliation* instead. I hoped that European capitals and Moscow would understand that *reconciliation* implied a two-step process: first, an internal reconciliation between the East German regime and its people; and second, an external reconciliation between West Germany and the GDR. My aim was to keep the heat on the East German regime to continue to allow peaceful change.*

Two days later, all of Honecker's stubborn attempts to cling to power went for nothing, as he was ousted from office by the tide of unrest, and replaced by Egon Krenz, the former Stasi chief turned Communist reformer. And one week later, on October 25, Gorbachev gave the clearest green light possible, when in Helsinki, he announced that the USSR would allow its satellite states to reform in their own way, a policy that Soviet Foreign Ministry spokesman Gennadi Gerasimov called the "Sinatra Doctrine," as he noted about Eastern Europe, "We have no right, moral or political, to interfere in events happening there. We assume others will not interfere, either."†

The Cold War order was crumbling before our eyes—and then, on November 9, came Günter Schabowski's offhand announcement. After finishing my luncheon with Aquino, I went over to the White House to discuss our response with the President. As we talked, we watched live broadcasts on CNN of young Germans chipping away at the Berlin Wall. The Communist glacis had been breached, the Iron Curtain ripped asunder. Later that night, when I finally had time to reflect back on the day's events, I would find it hard to hold back tears of joy as the trickle of people seeking freedom in the West turned into a torrent.

Yet that afternoon, I must admit, I was torn between what I felt as an American and what I was concerned about as a statesman. As an American, I felt an overwhelming euphoria that what we had always worked for had come true, that this truly was freedom's victory. But as a statesman, I had to hold my feelings in check and keep myself from becoming carried away by emotion. At times, I had a gnawing sense that this was too good to be true, for the day seemed rich in historical irony; it was the fifty-first anniversary of Kristallnacht—the start of Hitler's savage attack against the Jews—and the seventy-first anniversary of imperial Germany's collapse in World War I.

While the crowds massing in East Berlin seemed good-natured, they

---

*At the time, the President had already endorsed a "reunified Germany" during a press conference in Montana, but Brent felt that using *reunification* in a formal speech would be too forward leaning. So drawing on a memo from Roger George, the Policy Planning Staff's European expert, I used *reconciliation* and *normalization* instead.

†Gerasimov was, of course, referring to Frank Sinatra's classic song, "My Way."

were very boisterous, and we were concerned that some drunken or euphoric East German might create an incident that would escalate out of
control. Throughout October, our contacts with Moscow had been routine
diplomatic interchanges. My sense was that what we said publicly was
going to matter more to the Kremlin than any private message. We decided
that the President would bring reporters into the Oval Office, and that I
would do all the networks that evening and the morning shows the next
day. We wanted to welcome the change diplomatically, almost clinically—
and try as best we could not to be overly emotional, so that Gorbachev,
Shevardnadze, and other Soviets who saw our reaction would not feel, as
the President put it, "that we were sticking our thumb in their eye."

Nevertheless, it was hard to remain low-key the next day. At 11:30
A.M., Stape Roy informed me that Todor Zhivkov, the Bulgarian party chief,
had been replaced. The most emotional moment for me came at 4:59 P.M.,
when I spoke to Genscher, who called by telephone. Before he came on the
line, his secretary breathlessly told me, "God bless America. Thank you for
everything, sir." Genscher told me, "It's a moving moment for our nation.
Thank you for what you've done and said. I want to thank the American
people for what you've done for Germany since World War II, particularly
for Berlin." He went on to say that Germany would remain in NATO and
the EC.

"What you've said about NATO and your resolve to continue your
present policy in conjunction with the Western allies is very important," I
told him.

"I told a rally of ten thousand people that we will continue with our
alliances and commitments. Germany will not go its own way," he reiterated, adding, "We will develop our policy together with our allies."

"The United States welcomes these dramatic events, but it's a long way
from free travel to reunification. Perhaps it's premature to address reunification now," I said, wanting to see how he'd react.

"The people of the GDR are exercising their right of freedom of movement now; next will come free elections," he said, implicitly endorsing the
notion that "internal" reconciliation in East Germany was a prerequisite to
"external" reconciliation between the Germanies. Little could I know how
quickly that could happen. He continued by assuring me, "Germany will
never be a threat to its neighbors when it is free and democratic. It was only
a danger when under totalitarian rule." We ended the call by agreeing that
it was not time for a Four Powers Conference.*

The emotional roller coaster we were riding continued the next day,

---

*Britain, France, the Soviet Union, and the United States had certain legal rights as the occupying powers of Germany following World War II.

when I talked to our ambassador to West Germany, Vernon Walters, who happened to be visiting East Berlin. My hopes went up when he told me that Walter Momper, the governing mayor of West Berlin, had talked to Schabowski, who had told him, "There will be no Tiananmen Square solution here." But then Walters told me, "The USSR is indicating great concern that nothing happen at the Brandenburg Gate." The Soviets also had a war memorial nearby at the street called "17th of July," and a German celebration juxtaposed with a memorial to Soviet war dead could strike an emotional chord in Moscow.*

Indeed, the mood in the Kremlin was readily apparent in a letter Gorbachev had sent President Bush. The Soviet leader warned that "a chaotic situation may emerge with unforeseeable consequences," and there was a danger of "political extremism" in West Germany. Gorbachev wanted a Four Powers meeting—a request we quickly rejected—but it was clear he was weighing in heavily behind what he called certain "postwar realities, that is, the existence of two German states."

Later that day, I placed a call to Douglas Hurd, who had replaced John Major as British Foreign Secretary. After congratulating him on his new position, we discussed the need to coordinate positions with each other and with the French. He stressed the need for stability, noting dryly, "The British media will likely report an unrealistic version of possible future developments." Obviously, the leadership in the Kremlin were not the only ones keeping an attentive eye on public opinion.

On November 13, Brent and I joined the President in the residence for dinner with Henry Kissinger. Kissinger expressed what we all felt: German unification was "inevitable" and the United States would pay a price if the Germans felt that the United States was obstructing their aspirations. The President said he wanted a "prudent evolution." Our job was to turn the inevitable into that evolution.

The Diplomatic Debate: The Public Dimension

The end of November ushered in a very contentious public debate over unification among Bonn, Berlin, Moscow, London, and Paris. At the same

---

*Although a veteran diplomat, Walters's approach to the unification process was not always productive. On several occasions during the fall of 1989, he assumed a public, unauthorized role either forecasting reunification or pressing it forward. While we shared his sentiment, we had to remind him that such unauthorized, public pronouncements muddled our message and undermined our efforts to effectively manage unification with other countries, particularly with Moscow. Ambassadors frequently complain about Washington guidance or control, but the fact is that they are often too focused only on the effect a strategy might have on their particular post.

time, there was very little private discussion in diplomatic channels. This wasn't altogether surprising. The shock of the Wall's collapse had sent governments scurrying to review contingency plans, and the sheer emotionalism of the event had changed many people's assumptions about German unification, so it was understandable that they wanted to develop their own thinking and form at least a government-wide consensus before raising ideas internationally.

Many of the statements were sparked by a proposal from Chancellor Kohl on November 28. In a surprise move, Kohl outlined a ten-point plan for German unity in a speech before the Bundestag. Kohl's plan was a relatively modest proposal that called for the establishment of several joint environmental, economic, and other commissions, and held out the prospect of a federation after a period of confederation. The plan cautiously set an outline for reunification of the Germanies and encouraged Germans in both East and West to take reunification seriously. While we would have preferred to have heard about the plan before it was announced, Kohl called the President after the speech to reassure him.

The same day, we received a letter from Krenz. He wanted to thank us for our interest in developments in East Germany and to reassure us that they would continue to implement far-reaching changes, but "within a socialist context." In other words, the post-Honecker government *was* going to bring perestroika to the GDR, but not democracy. The message also contained a restatement of the East German view that the existence of two German states was an important factor for European stability. That was where they were going to draw the line. We were told that a similar message was going to Gorbachev. In a note I sent the President that night, I wrote, "Our analysis is that Krenz's letter is the GDR's marker in advance of any discussion of Germany's future at Malta." (The President and Gorbachev were scheduled to meet in Malta the next week.)

While the East German message probably reassured Moscow, the Kremlin was forced to react to the more important public statement by Kohl. Given the chaos in the GDR, it wasn't clear that the regime would be around long enough to implement its policy. Kohl's government had been boosted internally by the prospect of unification, and the Soviets were going to have to deal with him in the months ahead. Shevardnadze complained that Kohl's plan would prematurely accelerate a process that could cause confusion and lead to unforeseen consequences. Foreign Ministry spokesman Gennadi Gerasimov said on November 30 that "there is not one country in Europe today that would thirst for German reunification, because of the questions it raises for stability. It is not on the agenda." During a press conference in Milan prior to his arrival in Malta, Gorbachev said that while German reunification should not be ruled out for the long term, it is "not of urgent international importance. . . . Let's not push or force the issue. History itself will decide this question."

Both London and Paris were skeptical. Reflecting some dismay at Kohl's decision not to consult them prior to announcing his plan, Douglas Hurd said, "I think we are pleased with the ten points. I believe that there is a need for an eleventh point which says that nothing will be done to destroy the balance and stability of Europe or create anxiety in the minds of people who have a right to be worried." Margaret Thatcher recommended that until democracy in the GDR developed deeper roots, existing borders should remain unchanged.

Paris seemed the most irritated by Bonn's announcement, as Kohl had given no hint of his plan during a private dinner with Mitterrand only three days before. Immediately after Kohl's Bundestag speech, Mitterrand announced that he would visit the new East German Prime Minister, Hans Modrow, in December. In a conspicuous jab at Kohl, Mitterrand told the press before telling Kohl of his plans.

Our reaction was far more relaxed. Genscher had visited the week before, and I was confident Bonn and Washington would be able to manage German unification without discord. The real question was how to bring along Moscow and, to a lesser degree, London and Paris. This argued for restraining our enthusiasm over the fall of the Wall—something for which America had labored for decades. Our domestic critics began saying that the President's muted response showed that he had no "vision." Never mind that no good could possibly have come of gloating, or that now was an extremely delicate time in European affairs, requiring a cool head and calm manner if we were to have any chance of staying on track.

I tried to cope with both these concerns the next day when I briefed the White House press corps on the upcoming Malta Summit. I began by making clear that this was not going to be Yalta II. "No negotiation will be held, no deals made, no limits set." I went on to say, "Change is not necessarily destabilizing. On the contrary, it is the only way legitimacy can be restored and stability ensured, both regionally and in East-West relations. Nevertheless, we need to manage this change in a way that encourages the reform process to proceed and succeed." That meant, I said, not pursuing unilateral advantage against the Soviets. But it also led to the conclusion that "any attempts to forcibly intervene and prevent continued reform will be extremely destabilizing and dangerous."

When asked about German unification, I "suggested" four points of our own: One, self-determination must be pursued without prejudice to its outcome. We should not at this time endorse or exclude any particular vision of unity. Two, unification should occur in the context of Germany's continued commitment to NATO and an increasingly integrated EC, and with due regard for the legal role and responsibilities of the allied powers. Three, unification should be gradual, peaceful, and part of a step-by-step process. And, four, the inviolability of borders must be respected as stated in the Helsinki Final Act. While we had discussed these points generally in a 5:15 P.M. Oval Office meeting the day before, we hadn't fully agreed that they would represent the U.S. policy approach. So I added, "This is my view." The points had not come out of thin air. Frank Fukuyama, a deputy director of the Policy Planning Staff who would later write a much-debated article on the "end of history," had prepared a memo days before, arguing that the United States could exercise leadership and influence the debate by laying out such "principles" publicly. The day after the Malta Summit, the President announced the four principles as U.S. policy. We cabled them to all European posts to guide our ambassadors, and a few days later, the European Community adopted them as well. This was a classic case where words weighed heavily. The four principles became a vital interim framework through which we were able to pursue radical change in Europe in a stable way. I'm convinced that our principles calmed Moscow, London, and Paris, while at the same time they reassured Bonn that we were not going to join in a Four Powers attempt to derail unification.

Malta

The Malta Summit grew out of a discussion among the President, Brent Scowcroft, and me in Paris on the margins of the G-7 Summit in July. Having unified NATO behind his Summit initiatives in May and now having seen firsthand the pace of reform in Poland and Hungary, the President felt the groundwork had been set for a face-to-face meeting with Gorbachev. "I think we should meet sooner rather than later," he said. "What good would it do to hold back now?" he asked. Informality, he felt, would be key. I readily agreed, but Brent was initially concerned about raising expectations about what such a meeting could or would accomplish, and about confusing our support for the principles of perestroika with the personality of Gorbachev. The President concluded our discussion of the matter by saying, "Look, this guy *is* perestroika!" making it clear that he had little time for the somewhat academic distinction between principles and personalities.

On December 2, after a series of secret communications regarding scheduling and arrangements, President Bush sat down in the stateroom of the Soviet cruise liner *Maxim Gorky*, docked in Marsaxlokk Bay off Malta, for his first face-to-face encounter with Gorbachev.* The original reason for the meeting—having the two leaders, as Gorbachev put it, "leave behind the cumbersome retinue of aides and, without haste or protocol ceremony, talk about everything that we must discuss by virtue of our position"—was now overshadowed by the political earthquake in Eastern Europe, and the question on everyone's mind was: Would Malta become Yalta II? Would the superpowers form a condominium and decide the German question by themselves? Ironically, the President's proposal for a shipboard summit had originally flowed out of a combination of Gorbachev's insistence on meeting at a neutral site, and President Bush's love for the sea and his fascination with FDR's practice of meeting foreign leaders on ships—for example, FDR's own Malta meeting with Churchill in February 1945. Unfortunately, the weather at Malta was atrocious, and we had to cancel several sessions, as twenty-foot waves and gale-force winds pinned us down on the U.S.S. *Belknap,* a guided-missile cruiser. (In fact, the ship's captain, John F. Sigler, told the President that in twenty-five years in the Navy, he had never experienced such rough seas in harbor.)

In the aftermath of ensuing events—the unification of Germany, U.S.-Soviet cooperation during the Gulf crisis, the collapse of the Soviet Union itself—it's easy to downplay the significance of Malta. Unlike most other summits, it did not have the obligatory signing ceremony, yet I believe it was critical to the marked improvement in U.S.-Soviet cooperation that became so crucial in 1990.

At the personal level, Malta did for George Bush's relationship with Gorbachev what Jackson Hole had done for my relationship with Shevardnadze: enabled it to break through to establish a personal bond. Before the meeting, the President's understanding of Gorbachev naturally had been theoretical. As Richard Nixon trenchantly put it in a letter of advice he sent

---

*In a July Oval Office meeting, the President had given a letter of invitation for Gorbachev's eyes to Marshal Sergei Akhromeyev, Gorbachev's arms control adviser. While I was aware and approved of this approach, Shevardnadze was not, and when he learned of this, he was furious at being undercut, and I had to apologize; Akhromeyev was an acquaintance of Scowcroft's, and we had no idea he would try to keep Shevardnadze in the dark. In August, Gorbachev responded by sending then-Deputy Foreign Minister Alexander Bessmertnykh to Washington for what we publicly announced were talks regarding Wyoming. Ironically, the press was hounding the President for not seeing Gorbachev precisely at the time we were working out the details of the meeting.

President Bush initially invited Gorbachev to his family home on Walker's Point in Kennebunkport or the presidential retreat at Camp David in late September in conjunction with the United Nations General Assembly. Gorbachev countered with Spain, which, he wrote, "has islands, too." The President proposed Malta, based on a suggestion from his brother Bucky Bush, who had recently vacationed there.

the President two weeks before Malta, "There is no question but that he is a remarkable new kind of leader of the Soviet Union, and we welcome the initiatives at home and abroad that he had already taken. But when you examine the evidence, it is clear that what he is doing is making a virtue of necessity. This does not make him a virtuous leader."

But with Malta, the relationship became human and personal, and through the spring of 1990, as we worked to bring a unified Germany into NATO, the President's personal relationship with Gorbachev was critical.

Clearly, Gorbachev's approach to the United States had also evolved. As we prepared in late November, we had expected Gorbachev to spring one of his patented surprises on the President. In order to counter that, we decided to put together a list of twenty initiatives which the President would use in his initial presentation, essentially showing Gorbachev that we had come armed to play his game.

But for Gorbachev, these initiatives revealed something else—that the long "pause" was over and that the President, not just the Secretary of State, was fully engaged in support of perestroika. I don't know whether Gorbachev had a set of initiatives of his own that he decided not to use, but it became obvious from his remarks following the President's presentation that we had moved from conflictual and competitive politics to a more co-operative relationship. In responding to the President's list of ideas, Gorbachev said that he expected to hear of the President's support for perestroika, but added, "I was prepared to say, 'We want to hear specific steps'—and you have done this today, even before I could say it." The proposals, he said, reflected "a political will at the top of your government to move ahead positively." (The initiatives were rapidly eclipsed by further progress in the relationship.)

As for the future, he continued, "all of us feel today we're at an historic watershed. We have to address problems we didn't expect to become so acute. Should we address these problems in the same way as in the past?" he asked then, answering his own question, "No—or else we'll fail. Strategically and philosophically, the way of the Cold War has been defeated. Everyone is aware of this. We know how people have an impact on policy—the people in the street, and in Congress, and in the Supreme Soviet."

At the level of principles, the President reassured him on Eastern Europe, "I hope you've noticed that as change has accelerated in Eastern Europe recently, we haven't responded with flamboyance or arrogance so as to make your situation difficult. They say, 'Bush is too timid, too cautious.' I *am* cautious," said the President, "but not timid. I've tried to conduct myself in a way so as not to complicate your difficulties."

Gorbachev said that he'd noticed that and appreciated it. But he also made a broader point: "We accept your role in Europe. It is very important that you be there." Europe was integrating, he believed, and "as this change moves forward, we shouldn't do anything to undermine it—and we should work together and not lose an opportunity."

His greatest irritation, it seemed, was with our use of the phrase "Western values" in our speeches and public statements. The President explained, "It's not in hostility that the term *Western values* is used." But Gorbachev felt *Western* implied that reformers in the Soviet Union had not embraced or subscribed to some of those values, when in fact he felt they had. In his concern, I saw the classic Russian tension between the Slavophiles and the Westernizers. "Why not call them 'democratic values'?" I asked. "That's fine," said Gorbachev, and with that understanding, we had forged a new degree of cooperation, at the level of both personalities and principles.

Diplomacy as Architecture

As I traveled to work on Friday, December 8, Washington was preparing for the first snowstorm of the winter. By noon, the snow was so high (albeit by Washington standards, which are much lower than others) that the General Services Administration released nonessential personnel. The State Department was a relatively deserted place that afternoon when I received the Soviet chargé, Sergei Chetverikov, who came with an urgent démarche. Moscow was asking London, Paris, and Washington to have their ambassadors to West Germany meet "within the shortest possible time" with their Soviet counterpart to "exchange views on German affairs." Four days before, 200,000 people had poured into Prague's Wenceslas Square to demand the Communist Party's ouster. Two days before, Egon Krenz, less than two months in office, had been forced to follow the way of Honecker, his attempts to hold on to socialism doomed. There were attacks by reformers on military installations in the GDR. Change was, if anything, accelerating, and Moscow was becoming agitated by democracy's success.

In this tense atmosphere, I was scheduled to visit Berlin to give a speech on Europe. Just prior to my arrival, we acceded to the Soviet request and held the first formal Four Powers meeting in eighteen years. It was at that meeting that we had completed work on the landmark Quadripartite Agreement that regulated the status of Berlin and spelled out the rights of powers in the city. On Wednesday, December 12, Soviet GDR Ambassador Vyascheslav met with French Ambassador Boidevaix, British Ambassador Mallaby, and Ambassador Walters at the former Allied Control Authority Building in West Berlin, and began a preliminary discussion concerning Berlin and its possible future status.

I started that day in Berlin at breakfast with a somewhat irritated Helmut Kohl. He told me that he planned to see Gorbachev soon and realized Moscow would be the hardest sell for Bonn. And he understood, as he put it, "change in Germany means change in the math of Europe, and that means change in the structure of Europe and the world."

But what obviously bothered him were the go-slow signals coming out of Paris and especially London. He felt that Western efforts to put the brakes on reunification or to channel the desires of the East Germans into something short of unification, like a federation, would be very dangerous. In the "slalom course" the leaders faced, he said, public opinion in the GDR was the most dangerous gate. If the people felt their aspirations would not be achieved, they might turn violent. The peoples of the two Germanies wanted to grow together, and they needed a "perspective" on how this might occur.

He had no problems with our approach, having obviously been reassured by the President's "four principles." But Thatcher clearly had upset him. "She thinks that by avoiding the phrase *reunification*, it will just fade away," he said. But I noted that the Germans, too, sometimes seemed to avoid the phrase, and that "just fuels people's suspicions," I said. "That's why we've clearly set forth reunification as our objective."

From breakfast, I went to a brief meeting with West Berlin's Mayor Momper before going to visit the Wall near the Reichstag Building. It was a foggy, overcast day, and in my raincoat, I felt like a character in a John Le Carré novel. But as I peered through a crack in the Wall and saw the high-resolution drabness that characterizes East Berlin, I realized that the ordinary men and women of East Germany, peacefully and persistently, had taken matters into their own hands. This was their revolution, and it was the job of men like me to help them secure the freedom they were working so hard to win.

In this tumultuous atmosphere, my speech before the Berlin Press Association took on a new significance. Put bluntly, a political earthquake had leveled forty years of European diplomatic "architecture"—as social scientists liked to call political institutions. And most of Europe was looking to the United States for direction.

In a speech that Bob Zoellick wrote, drawing on competing drafts from the Policy Planning Staff and the European Bureau, I made a conscious attempt to reassure Europeans that we didn't need to start completely afresh. I went through the three major institutions that dominated Europe—NATO, the EC, and CSCE (Conference on Security and Cooperation in Europe)—and showed how each one needed to evolve to promote what I called a "new Atlanticism for a new era," a phrase that Rick Burt, our START negotiator and former Ambassador to Germany, had suggested.

In arguing that NATO needed to become a more "political" alliance, I began the process of conditioning the Soviets to accept NATO's continued existence even as the Warsaw Pact disappeared, and to accept a unified Germany in NATO. For the EC, I had nothing but praise, which the Europeans found very comforting, as they were afraid the United States was going to oppose their attempts at integration. And for CSCE (which I personally found an extremely unwieldy and frustrating organization) I developed a series of initiatives that would make it an instrument for promoting continued internal change in Eastern Europe. I ended the speech by reiterating our four principles on German unification.

The reaction to the speech far exceeded my expectations. I knew that its straightforward language would be reassuring and that the list of initiatives would show that we had serious ideas. But as with most things in politics, it was the timing that made it a spectacular success. In the anxious diplomatic atmosphere of the time, my speech gave diplomats and journalists a clear structure to latch on to, as they sought to explain the changes rocking the Continent. Once again, it showed that even while we were withdrawing troops from Europe, we could increase our influence through a few well-chosen ideas. Above all, the speech affirmed that the United States would remain a European power and set forth the principles that continue to guide transatlantic relations.

Following my speech, I left the Steigenberger Hotel for an unscheduled visit to Potsdam in East Germany. I had made the decision to go only the night before. Ambassador Walters and Harry Gilmore, our minister in Berlin, had opposed the idea, but I knew President Mitterrand was planning to visit the GDR the next week, and I wanted to demonstrate American leadership by going there first. More important, I felt my visit could help support the process of peaceful change, and after hearing an impassioned plea from Richard Barkley, our Ambassador to the GDR, that my visit would do just that, and after checking with Kohl and Genscher, I had Pat Kennedy and Karen Groomes make the arrangements for what would be the *first and last* visit ever made to the GDR proper by an American Secretary of State.

The drive to Potsdam turned out to be one of the most surreal trips I took as Secretary of State, when, beginning at twilight, we crossed into the southeast corner of West Berlin and approached the Glienicke Bridge. It is a stark, rusting steel structure that spans the Havel River and was most famous as a scene of numerous spy swaps. After he was shot down over Siberia in 1960, the U-2 pilot Francis Gary Powers was released across that bridge, and more recently, Anatoly Shcharansky, the courageous refusenik, had crossed into the West there.

But I was headed in the opposite direction, and as we approached the bridge, my West German police escort gave way, much like a caterpillar shedding its cocoon, and my motorcade crossed over, to be picked up and escorted by East German police.

For a fleeting moment, I was reminded that Potsdam had been the site of the last postwar conference of the victorious powers—Britain, the Soviet Union, and the United States. (John Foster Dulles in the 1950s and William Rogers in the 1970s had visited East Berlin.) And I remembered from my Princeton thesis how Ernest Bevin, a Bristol truck driver, had made his first trip as the British Foreign Secretary to the Potsdam Conference by airplane, and here I was driving to Potsdam almost forty-five years later. (Bevin was a last-minute choice of Prime Minister Clement Attlee, as Winston Church- ill had already been defeated in that year's election, despite having won the war. Looking back on it now, it's hard not to miss an eerie parallel to George Bush's fate. He, too, won a war, and he, too, was defeated in its immediate aftermath.)

But these reminiscences quickly gave way to the stark scenery of the eastern side. As Caron Jackson, my executive assistant, put it to me later, "It was like going from color to black and white." To my eyes, Berlin is not the most colorful of cities, perhaps because I have been there during the dark German winter. But West Berlin was like Times Square or Piccadilly Circus compared to the scene that awaited us as we headed for the Inter- Hotel in Potsdam. Everything was gray: the clothing, the buildings, the peo- ple, the mood. The roads were empty, except for a few tiny Trabants with very dim lights that scurried about like roaches on a dark, unclean kitchen floor.

Not much more than an hour after my speech, I was sitting in the Inter- Hotel, meeting with Hans Modrow. My memories of the meeting are as fleeting as Modrow's regime itself, except for the emphasis I put upon the importance of holding free elections. The one highlight was the entrance of a man who at first glance seemed to be Egon Krenz, the Communist party leader. For a second, I thought we had been sandbagged, but when the man offered us mineral water, I realized he was just the waiter.

We then traveled several blocks to the St. Nikolai Church for a meeting with six Lutheran church leaders. Our meeting there was ironic, as the church had been destroyed by Allied bombs and Soviet artillery shells in 1945 and rebuilt only in 1980.

I was struck by how responsible the leaders were and how clearly inter- ested they were in pursuing peaceful change. Echoing what Kohl had told me that morning, one leader told me, "This is a time of great emotionalism in our country, expectations have been raised and made public for the first time. The first question is whether we can control these developments."

Having taken part in the mass demonstrations that had brought down Honecker and Krenz, they knew the power and volatility of mass action. They feared a vacuum of authority and recognized that they represented the only real moral authority in the country.

On reunification, they emphasized that economics, not nationalism, was the driving force behind the popular desire to join the FRG. "We have a right to the same way of life as in the West," one said. "This is not built out of a sense of nationalism but more the sense of, 'We want a better life.' " As another put it, "Our people don't see why they should wait, when unification will mean an immediate improvement in their living standards."

That night, I cabled the President, "Perhaps more than anything else, I am struck by the commitment to reform and peaceful change." Modrow's vocabulary had come from Gorbachev and Shevardnadze: "There's no going back on the process of renewal. The process is irreversible." Modrow had implied that nothing could hold these forces back and that his job was to manage the process until the March elections.

I went on: "It's my view that there will be a de facto economic unification between the GDR and FRG in any event. . . . But I don't see the average East German spending much time considering this option: He just sees greener grass to the West.

"There's obviously a dilemma here. Some way is going to have to be found to build a sense of hope about economic improvement if the pressure for unification is to be managed. . . . What's clear is that the process of peaceful change in the GDR, and the ability to sustain an incremental approach to unification again, comes back to a credible approach to structural and political reform on the inside and perceptible economic help from the outside. The FRG has to lead the way on outside help, but we and the rest of the alliance will need to be supportive.

"Our involvement may give Kohl some cover for taking the necessary economic steps to support a reformed but shaky GDR without raising his neighbors' anxieties too high. (Then Kohl is freer to get some political credit at home, which is fine with us.) Frankly, our activity—politically and economically—in the GDR also serves our own interests by keeping us in the game as the Germanies rapidly move closer together. And I suspect the Soviets will be more willing to see increased ties between the German states if they believe we're keeping a watch on the scene."

My return to the United States took a roundabout route: First to Brussels, then via the Azores to St. Martin in the Caribbean to join the President's meeting with François Mitterrand. Meeting in casual clothes under a striped tent on the beach at L'Habitation de Lonvilliers, a luxury hotel on the French side of the Dutch-French resort island, we discussed the future of Europe. Following the hour-long meeting, Mitterrand in the press conference said that we must deal with the "German problem" in a "harmonious way." As he delicately put it, "If the horses of the team don't move at the same speed, there'll be an accident." Avoiding that accident—and seeing Germany united peacefully as a member of NATO—would become my central diplomatic project in the new year.

CHAPTER 11

PANAMA:

THE DAY OF THE DICTATOR IS OVER

The instability generated by the lack of movement from an authoritarian and corrupt military dictatorship to an open electoral democracy places long-standing U.S. interests at risk. —*State Department policy memorandum on Panama, May 1989*

From the start of my tenure, I was privately concerned that one trouble spot confronting our new administration might eventually require a military solution: the Isthmus of Panama. General Manuel Antonio Noriega, the Panamanian strongman, was a case of what we in Texas call "bad chili." An erstwhile ally of the United States, Noriega had become increasingly dangerous as his collusion with international drug trafficking deepened, and assaults by his armed forces against American servicemen and their families stationed in Panama escalated. In the Reagan years, he'd spurned every effort to reach a negotiated settlement with the United States. Even an offer to drop Federal drug indictments against him had failed to secure his departure from power. I feared that Noriega had been emboldened by the inability of our government to force his ouster through economic sanctions, and that military action might prove necessary.

This was a view not universally shared within the government. The Pentagon in particular had been opposed to military action during the Reagan administration and was certain to resist the notion again. Obviously, I preferred a political solution. But having witnessed Noriega's growing obstinacy, I doubted that diplomacy alone would be enough.

177

Neither maintaining the status quo nor accommodating Noriega's continued presence in Panama was an acceptable alternative to me. His dictatorship threatened the transfer of the canal to Panamanian sovereignty, as required by the treaty, and our capacity to defend its security. His corrupt and repressive military regime undermined our efforts both to promote democracy in the hemisphere and to combat narcotics trafficking. And first and foremost, Noriega was a threat to the lives and well-being of the 40,000 American servicemen and citizens living in Panama. I hoped we could deal with Noriega through a policy of escalating political, economic, and covert pressures. But the bottom line was clear: One way or another, Noriega's rule had to end.

In early February of 1989, I pulled Michael Kozak aside after a meeting on Latin American policy. I knew Mike Kozak from several National Security Council meetings involving Panama that I'd attended as Secretary of the Treasury. A career civil servant and attorney who had negotiated face-to-face with Noriega on several occasions, Kozak was an exceptionally capable diplomat and was the acting Assistant Secretary for Inter-American Affairs, pending Bernie Aronson's confirmation. During the transition, I'd asked him to prepare a policy paper for me discussing what more we could do to persuade Noriega to step aside. That paper had recommended increasing our diplomatic, economic, and political pressure, a course the Pentagon was resisting. I remember being struck by the stark bottom line of that document. "The status quo cannot be sustained," it had argued. "A fundamental policy choice can no longer be deferred." I had reluctantly concurred in that sobering judgment.

"I've felt for a long time that it might come to using force to get this guy out," I told Kozak. "The problem we've had is that Defense hasn't been willing to do it. If it comes to that, we need to be able to make the case that we've gone as far as we can with other means."

As it turned out, my premonition unfortunately proved correct. After months of negotiations foundered, an uneasy status quo was shattered by the cold-blooded murder of an American Marine officer by Noriega's forces in December of 1989. In response, U.S. troops launched combat operations five days before Christmas to oust his illegal government, restore democracy to Panama, and bring Noriega to justice in the United States. Within twenty-four hours, Noriega's reign of terror was over, and two weeks later the general was in the custody of U.S. marshals and was awaiting trial for drug trafficking. The President's decision to strike a blow for democracy sent a powerful signal that, like his predecessor, George Bush was willing to commit the military might of our country to protect vital American interests and support democratic principles in the Americas.

A Dubious Inheritance

For nearly a century, America's overriding interest in Panama has been to maintain a stable political environment for the operation of the Panama Canal and U.S. military installations. This quest for stability has prompted a variety of controversial actions by American Presidents, which have run the gamut from President Theodore Roosevelt's decision to order military intervention in 1903 to the decision by the Carter administration to sign the 1977 treaty transferring the Canal to Panamanian control by the end of the century.

As the treaty's provisions began to be implemented, bilateral relations predictably improved. Matters took a turn for the worse in June of 1987, however, when Noriega failed to honor a 1981 agreement to turn over command of the military to a designated successor. This action prompted several months of demonstrations and general strikes and a constitutional crisis, during which the United States sought to be an honest broker between the military and the civilian government of Eric Arturo Delvalle. In February of 1988, shortly after two federal grand juries in Florida indicted Noriega on drug-trafficking charges, he effectively seized control of the government from Delvalle.

Until this de facto coup, U.S. policy was aimed at maintaining pressure on Panama's political and military leadership to honor the commitment to democratization made by the late General Omar Torrijos Herrera. With his usurpation of power and the indictments, Noriega became persona non grata to American policy makers overnight.

In March of 1988, a coup against Noriega failed, triggering a purge of nearly one-quarter of the officer corps of the Panama Defense Forces (PDF) and solidifying Noriega's hold on power. A month later, President Reagan imposed stringent economic sanctions on Panama in order to increase pressure on Noriega's illegal regime. Simultaneously, he authorized negotiations aimed at brokering Noriega's departure from Panama. The terms of the deal offered to Noriega as an inducement to leave were hotly contested within a government already deeply divided over the appropriate policy course. Indeed, it was one of the more contentious internal debates I recall during my twelve years of government service.

At a meeting of the National Security Council in May of 1988 in the Yellow Room on the second floor of the White House residence, then–Vice President Bush adamantly opposed dropping the indictments against Noriega if he agreed to go into exile. "How can we make the argument we're getting tough on drug dealers if we let this guy off?" he argued.

I supported him on both policy and political grounds. As a nation, we couldn't be in the posture of cutting a deal with one of the worst drug dealers in the world. As a presidential candidate, the Vice President would also suffer politically from such a perception. It was bad policy—and bad politics.

After a vigorous debate, President Reagan rejected this advice, concluding that American national interests were best served by getting Noriega out of Panama. In his view, dropping the drug indictments was a small price to pay in exchange. It was a decision that failed to achieve the desired result. After first claiming he would take the deal, Noriega rejected it, deciding he was safer in Panama than in exile.

When the Bush administration took office eight months later, the question of what to do about him was one of our most pressing problems. Unfortunately, despite some hopeful initial signs, our diplomatic efforts to persuade Noriega to leave were similarly unsuccessful. Throughout early 1989, several feelers were transmitted from Noriega through intermediaries. He claimed to be interested in improving relations. The return message from President Bush, delivered in several meetings between Kozak and Noriega's lawyers, was always the same. The United States was prepared to negotiate, but only if he were willing to discuss his departure from Panama with specificity. Moreover, he was told, the indictments against him were non-negotiable.

While I agreed with the President's position, his principled refusal to drop the indictments substantially lessened any chance for a peaceful resolution of the matter. During his negotiations with Kozak the previous year, Noriega had made clear he would never consider leaving Panama unless the indictments were dismissed. "You'll find some guy like me to come and put me on a plane to Miami," he told Kozak at one point. I couldn't quarrel with his logic because, paradoxically, while Noriega was up to his epaulets in drug trafficking, he had for years cooperated with U.S. drug-enforcement authorities. On several occasions, in fact, he'd handed over Panamanian traffickers to us. As long as he was under the threat of indictment, I thought he'd prefer to take his chances in Panama rather than go to another country and risk being kidnapped by American agents. Since we knew the President would never drop the indictments, the negotiating track was at an impasse. It was clear to me that Noriega had concluded that the United States would never intervene militarily and that his internal opponents were too weak to oust him on their own. He was unquestionably correct in the latter, and absent some action-forcing event, he was likely correct about the prospects of a U.S. invasion.

In April of 1989, U.S. Ambassador Arthur Davis, a political appointee who had served previously in Paraguay and was a favorite of Senator Jesse Helms, sent a strongly worded cable to the department urging a more aggressive policy to break the stalemate. The 1988 negotiations had given Noriega "breathing space" with which to recoup his position, and had created a "policy bind" for the United States. "[Our] policy has stagnated," he asserted. "We have gone on officially ignoring the regime while relying on sanctions to weaken it." Sterner measures were now required. "Ruling out all application of U.S. military power in defense of our interests here is an open invitation to Noriega to maintain his current behavior, which is the surest path to a fatal incident." Subsequent events would unhappily prove Art Davis unusually prescient.

This cable prompted an even more direct internal memorandum from Kozak on April 14, which was discussed by my key aides. "If we want Noriega out, we must act ourselves," he argued. "We should understand clearly that he will not leave without a stronger U.S. effort than we have mounted to date. And while we don't think U.S. military force would be necessary, the President must be prepared to use force as a last resort. The credible threat represented by our willingness to use force opens other options and is the only wedge which will separate Noriega from the Panama Defense Forces."

The preferred strategic alternative, Kozak maintained, was to incite a PDF coup through a series of actions making the threat of U.S. military action credible. "If the PDF has not acted by September 1," he added, "the President should order Noriega's removal by a snatch or U.S. military action."*

The idea of "snatching" Noriega was a topic of some discussion throughout 1989. In researching legal precedent, the administration had determined that the U.S. government could try a suspect who had been kidnapped from a country with which we had an extradition treaty. As a result, a prohibition against such incidents imposed by President Carter was overturned by President Bush. There was no doubt in my mind that if the President had ordered a "snatch" of Noriega, it would have been legal. In fact, the U.S. Supreme Court so ruled in a separate case in June of 1992.

Nevertheless, the President was not interested in kidnapping Noriega, either from Panama or another country. He was, however, insistent that we be prepared to seek Noriega's extradition vigorously if he were foolish enough to leave Panama. Such an opportunity unexpectedly surfaced in the summer of 1989, when U.S. intelligence received what was considered a highly reliable tip that Noriega was about to make an unannounced visit to the Dominican Republic to attend the wedding of a friend's daughter. Armed with standing authority from the President, U.S. diplomats quickly prepared extradition papers and worked out a plan

*September 1 was the date that Noriega's puppet candidates were to be installed in office.

whereby Dominican officials would grab Noriega the moment he arrived in the country and put him on a plane to Miami. Unfortunately, the tip proved to be a false alarm.

On August 4, after a similarly erroneous tip that Noriega had briefly entered U.S. property in Panama, I discussed with the President and Brent Scowcroft in the Oval Office the possibility of apprehending Noriega in such a future circumstance. There was a general consensus that if such an opportunity presented itself, Noriega should be taken into custody by U.S. troops and brought to the United States to stand trial. On August 17, the State Department outlined a series of steps to ensure that a Presidential order to seize Noriega could be carried out swiftly. The mechanics were in place, but the opportunity never arose.

A Stolen Election

Presidential elections were scheduled for May 7 in Panama. As the date approached, however, it became apparent that a campaign of systematic fraud had turned the process into a sham. Noriega's allies had manipulated voter lists, disenfranchised opposition voters, arranged for multiple voting by Noriega partisans, and intimidated opposition candidates and their supporters. Noriega's contempt for democratic processes presented us with a significant opportunity to increase pressure on him and bring to an end the policy drift within our government.

Two days before the election, I summarized the state of play in a memorandum to the President. "From all reports, Noriega has already rigged the results and will steal the election massively," I predicted. In that case, it was important to take immediate steps "to send a clear, decisive signal to Noriega that it is not business as usual with the United States once he steals the election." To step up the pressure, I recommended that he approve a series of policy decisions that had been reached with near-total consensus through interagency consultations led by Aronson and Kozak.

"We are setting out on a road that increases the possibility of confrontation," I cautioned. "You need to be aware that once you take these steps a momentum will build up. Hopefully, Noriega will feel the pressure and be convinced to step down. But if he doesn't, and that is a possibility, you will be faced with pressures to take additional, stronger steps."

Such steps, I cautioned, would increase the risks of a military confrontation. "However, we have seen over the last year that halfway measures are the worst policy choice: we do damage to the Panamanian economy and U.S. businesses there, but we don't look serious enough to convince Noriega to step down."

In rapid order, State pressed for international observers to flood Panama, while the President and I focused international attention on the elections in a series of public statements. If Noriega was going to steal the elections, we wanted the world to be a witness, in order to help prepare public opinion for a stronger U.S. and international response.

As expected, Noriega stole the election from opposition candidate Guillermo Endara. An international group of observers, headed by former President Jimmy Carter, whom we had urged to go to Panama, documented widespread instances of blatant electoral fraud. Their denunciation of Noriega's naked theft of democracy was indelibly reinforced by a photograph of one of Endara's two vice-presidential running mates, Guillermo (Billy) Ford, bleeding profusely from a head wound inflicted by Noriega's thugs, and drenched in the blood of his murdered bodyguard.

The next day, May 11, the President told reporters that "the days of the dictators are over" and then announced the withdrawal of American dependents not living on military bases; the recall of Ambassador Davis; the reduction of embassy staff by two-thirds, and the dispatch of an Army infantry brigade to bolster the 12,000 personnel of the U.S. Southern Command (Southcom) permanently stationed in Panama.

In addition, and most important, the President decided to invoke a provision of the canal treaty that allowed U.S. troops unlimited training exercises, in order to increase the frequency and scope of our troop movements within Panama. Some of these exercises would be staged in areas the Panamanians considered their exclusive domain. It was psychological warfare. We wanted Noriega to believe we were coming if he didn't leave first. More to the point, we also wanted to send the PDF a message: Noriega is the problem; either you remove him, or the U.S. military will.

We also took our case to the Organization of American States. With strong U.S. backing, Venezuela took the lead in convening an emergency meeting of OAS foreign ministers in Washington on May 17. Aronson and I lobbied for a tough resolution, but it took some arm-twisting to convince the Latins to denounce Noriega by name for stealing the election. The old doctrine of non-interventionism and fear of U.S. power still paralyzed the organization. Although the ministers dispatched a mission to meet regularly over the next months, the OAS proved incapable of resolving the crisis. Still, I felt it was important to give the OAS a chance—if for no other reason than to make it clear, should force be necessary, that the United States had exhausted every peaceful, diplomatic alternative.

The only internal disagreement about our tougher stance involved a timetable for the withdrawal from Panama of 6,000 dependents of American servicemen not living on U.S. bases. State, the CIA, and the NSC agreed that a rapid drawdown should be completed within thirty days. Defense wanted a four-month process. Even after the President overruled this leisurely timetable, Southcom dragged its feet. When the U.S. election observers had met with General Frederick Woerner, Southcom's commander, he'd told them a shortage of cardboard boxes for packing personal belongings would likely delay getting dependents out of Panama. Senator John McCain of Arizona, a member of the delegation, was appalled by this explanation, and later complained to the President that Southcom was part of the problem, not part of the solution. For months, many of us had believed that, while he was a fine soldier whose career had been one of exemplary service, Woerner had developed a severe case of "clientitis" with Noriega, and was opposing the President's get-tough policy. Each time a new recommendation for stronger action was considered, Southcom objected. This vignette was the final straw that led the President, at the strong recommendation of Cheney, Scowcroft, and me, to replace Woerner with General Maxwell Thurman in July of 1989.

All these measures were designed to shake Noriega's confidence, to convince him and his military that U.S. patience was wearing thin, and persuade him that his most sensible course was a safe, honorable exit from Panama. By then, there was no doubt in my mind that Noriega couldn't be allowed to remain in power. By January 1, 1990, a Panamanian was to be appointed chairman of the Panama Canal Commission under the terms of the 1977 treaty. There was simply no way the United States could turn the canal over to Noriega's patently illegitimate government. On the other hand, we'd create a regional firestorm if we abrogated the treaty.

Noriega was becoming increasingly radicalized as well. He was getting financial help from Libya, running weapons to the Marxist guerrillas in El Salvador, and supporting the Sandinistas. Moreover, Fidel Castro was arming and training Noriega's paramilitary "Dignity Battalions." He was in effect becoming the Muammar Qaddafi of Latin America—a hostile, radical militant running drugs, allied with our enemies, and in absolute control of a country where American soldiers were stationed to protect and defend the canal.

Three weeks after the May election, I directed the embassy in Panama City to deliver this very blunt message in person to Noriega:

"The attacks you have made against the leadership of the opposition and other Panamanians, including U.S. employees, are despicable and cowardly. Nothing angered President Bush more personally than the sight of your thugs attacking the unarmed opposition candidates while the PDF troops looked on. The President is receiving detailed reports of every act of violence and harassment your people undertake. The message for you is 'lay off.' The President said the crisis will not end until you give up power. The President meant what he said."

Simultaneously, all American officials in Panama were directed to deliver a similar message to their contacts in the PDF. This message reiterated that while the United States had no quarrel with the military, Noriega had tarnished its integrity by using the PDF to brutalize Panamanian citizens. The time had come for the PDF to restore its reputation by joining in partnership with the democratic opposition. "We will respect any agreement worked out between the winners of the election and the PDF," the message concluded. "There will be no place in Panama for those who remain with Noriega until the end. This crisis will not be resolved until he gives up power. It can only get worse and worse."

In truth, we were doing our best to foment a coup. The policy we were pursuing was steadily increasing pressure across the board. The message to be conveyed at every level was simple: either the Panamanian defense forces took Noriega out, or we might.

The Abortive October Surprise

On the evening of October 1, the wife of a Panamanian army major named Moises Giroldi made contact with a U.S. intelligence agent attached to Southcom headquarters at Quarry Heights. Her husband, she said, was organizing a coup against Noriega and needed a modest amount of help from the U.S. military. Specifically, he wanted American troops to block two critical routes so Noriega couldn't call in reinforcements once the coup began. She refused to divulge any details of the operational plan to her American interlocutor.

We didn't know much about Giroldi, but what we did know made us skeptical. He was a member of Noriega's security detail and had helped quash the March 1988 coup. We therefore presumed he was a Noriega loyalist. As we belatedly learned, it turned out that he was for real.

Southcom dismissed the coup report as a provocation designed to test or embarrass Max Thurman, who had assumed command the previous day. They believed these reports should be ignored. Colin Powell—who had assumed the chairmanship of the Joint Chiefs of Staff that very day—and the service chiefs were wary of getting involved in what appeared to be a poorly organized effort. The President, however, was more open to a U.S. role. "Look, you've had me out there for the last couple of months begging these guys to start a coup," he said during a brief Oval Office meeting the next morning. "If someone's actually willing to do one, we have to help them."

Then we heard the coup was delayed for a couple of days. This intelligence increased our skepticism. Coups against Noriega had been frequently rumored before, never to materialize. We assumed this was just more wishful thinking on the part of midlevel PDF officers.

When the coup in fact began on October 3, the President reiterated his earlier sentiments even more emphatically. "If somebody's willing to start a coup," he said, "we go with them." His wishes were carried out. As a result, U.S. troops blocked the exit from Fort Amador and the Bridge of the Americas across the canal, the action that had been requested of us.

U.S. intelligence was sketchy, and arrived in contradictory bits and pieces. At one point, we were told by the embassy in Panama City that Giroldi wanted to turn Noriega over to U.S. troops. A few hours later, the embassy reported that the plotters had no intention of relinquishing their quarry.

All this unfolded while the President was hosting President Salinas of Mexico in the Oval Office. By the time we had enough information to order U.S. troops to block a key reinforcement route, the coup had already failed.

It was, in retrospect, a comic-opera coup, poorly planned and even more clumsily executed. Giroldi apparently believed that once he had captured the Comandancia, Noriega's headquarters, and taken Noriega into custody, Noriega would be more than happy to step down and leave the country with an honorable retirement. Instead, Noriega taunted his captor, and Giroldi actually allowed Noriega to use the telephone to call in reinforcements. He could have easily executed Noriega on the spot. Instead, in a matter of hours Giroldi himself was dead. Unable to move troops by land because of the U.S. blocking action, and unwilling to risk a firefight with American forces, Noriega loyalists shrewdly commandeered commercial airliners and flew reinforcements from a nearby military airfield to the international airport, where they rushed to the Comandancia and quickly overwhelmed Giroldi and his sympathizers.

The collapse of the coup prompted considerable soul-searching within the administration, and public criticism. In retrospect, it was apparent that a prime opportunity to remove Noriega had been squandered. Our reaction had been wholly defensive. Instead of being so skeptical, we should have gone to Giroldi, demanded to know his plan in exchange for our help, assessed his scheme and quietly assisted in its execution.

It's an understatement to say that administration decision making was less than crisp. As a result, we revamped our entire crisis-management processes. The role of the Deputies' Committee was strengthened to assure that policy making in moments of crisis was well coordinated and promptly vetted among all the appropriate agencies of the government. These changes stood us in good stead later during the Persian Gulf crisis.

Our collective performance generated tremendous heat from Capitol Hill for failing to respond more aggressively. Even normally supportive Republicans attacked the administration. Senator Jesse Helms called us "a bunch of Keystone Kops, bumping into each other." Congressman Henry Hyde of Illinois, ranking member of the House Intelligence Committee, complained that "we look indecisive, vacillating, and weak." The President was particularly unhappy that a serious target of opportunity had been lost.

The failed coup crystallized many of the frustrations felt within the administration among those charged with moving the policy forward day by day. Even when the policy was clear, there was often bureaucratic resistance. Southcom had been ordered to engage in vigorous troops exercises in May, for example, but many had been canceled or watered down. Aronson in particular shared these frustrations and wanted to move more forcefully. "These things take time," I told Aronson one day. "We've got to wait for public opinion to build." Or, I recall musing to myself, a blatant provocation against American citizens that would arouse public sentiment and make intervention more palatable.

The October coup was a watershed for American policy toward Panama and Noriega. All of us vowed never to let another such opportunity pass us by. If an opening ever presented itself again, the United States wouldn't be caught unprepared. The President ordered intensive contingency planning to make sure the next chance to topple Noriega wasn't wasted. Within two weeks, seven different scenarios had been vetted. Most of them envisioned another coup attempt by the PDF. None provided for the possibility of a preemptive unilateral U.S. military invasion—although General Thurman stepped up Southcom's contingency planning for a possible military intervention in the event of a coup.

As it turned out—contrary to public statements by me and several of my colleagues—Noriega's hold on power was *not* diminished by the coup. Instead, he unleashed his intelligence operatives on the PDF, and within a matter of days they'd turned up evidence that at least two other coups were being plotted. These ringleaders, who were more senior and considerably more capable than the luckless Major Giroldi, were tortured and jailed. The end result was that contrary to public impression, the October coup strengthened Noriega's position instead of undermining it. He was now an even bigger problem than before.

Paradoxically, even as Noriega tightened his stranglehold on Panama, the diplomatic track unexpectedly resurfaced. A Miami lawyer named Frank Rubino sent word to Kozak that "my client wants to retire." When Kozak reiterated that Noriega's willingness to discuss the terms of his departure was a precondition to talks, Rubino acknowledged that his client was prepared to do so. Significantly, Rubino wanted to know if "the Spain option" was still on the table.

In early 1988, the Spanish government had volunteered that it would be willing to grant Noriega political asylum. As the mother country of most nations in the hemisphere, Spain had a tradition of offering political refuge for leaders of its former colonies.

When I learned of this new overture, I raised it immediately with the President and Brent Scowcroft. We agreed that it was acceptable. Given Spain's strict extradition laws, we would effectively surrender any chance ever to bring Noriega to trial. But at least he would be out of Panama. Moreover, the indictments against him would remain in effect; he could never travel outside of Spain without risk. It was, I felt, a practical solution which met the President's insistence on retaining the indictments while resolving the more critical issue of protecting American interests and returning democracy to Panama. I told Kozak he was authorized to propose the deal. During a subsequent meeting with Noriega's lawyers, Kozak was told they would recommend that their client accept it. But we never heard back. By then Noriega was surrounded by sycophants who had persuaded him that he'd stared down the *gringos*. Indeed, Noriega's behavior became more erratic and irrational.

Operation Blue Spoon

For over a year, Panamanian troops had been harassing American servicemen and their families. Hundreds of these incidents were downplayed by Southcom. In January of 1989 alone, for instance, eighty-seven incidents were reported. We were concerned that Noriega would escalate this violence against Americans in the aftermath of the October coup. Shortly thereafter, the CIA station chief in Panama City paid a visit to Noriega to deliver another blunt personal message from the President. George Bush wanted Noriega to know that if any Americans were harmed or harassed in any way, he would be held personally responsible by the President of the United States. As a result of this démarche, the incidents against U.S. nationals stopped—until Saturday, December 16.

The day before, in a speech to his puppet National Assembly, Noriega had boasted that "we will sit along the banks of the canal to watch the dead bodies of our enemies pass by." At his instigation, the assembly then declared a state of war against the United States and bestowed the title of "maximum leader" on Noriega. Our initial reaction was to downplay these actions as rhetorical posturing. But the next day, an unarmed U.S. Marine lieutenant was shot and killed by Panamanian soldiers. In a second incident that night, a U.S. Navy officer and his wife were detained by PDF troops. The officer was interrogated and beaten, and his wife was sexually threatened.

The wanton murder of an American serviceman was a tragedy that sickened me, but I also knew that our confrontation with Noriega had reached a turning point. We'd just been handed the reason for doing what we should have done in October. There would be no internal debate over our course this time. The death of one of its own had finally brought the military around. A telling indicator of the change at the Pentagon came from a general who attended a late-night meeting in the State Department operations center. At one point, he pointedly asked, "If we decide to use force on this, will you try to tell us how to do it?" After years of reluctance, the Pentagon was ready to fight.

The next afternoon, Sunday, December 17, the President called an emergency meeting of his senior advisers in the residence immediately after a White House Christmas party. At his insistence, the meeting was for principals only—no staff. Before leaving for the White House, I telephoned Aronson on a secure line to solicit his advice. He pushed for a strong response. "If it's possible to send in a Delta team to arrest Noriega and bring him to the States, do it," Aronson said. "If it isn't, we have to go in." "I agree we have to go," I replied. "If we wait, he'll kill twenty more Americans or take them hostage."*

The meeting itself was anticlimactic. I recall very little if any debate over the merits of invading Panama. "This is just going to go on and on," the President said. We all agreed. Most of the discussion centered instead upon the myriad diplomatic and logistical details linked to military action. In addition to consultations with congressional leaders, the Soviets and Cubans would have to be notified, as well as the Organization of American States. We'd need to make certain Endara and Ford were willing to take over the government. Additional electronic surveillance was ordered to help track Noriega's whereabouts. The necessary paperwork to abolish economic sanctions against Panama and to appoint an Endara nominee head of the canal administration was set in motion. For public consumption, White House press secretary Marlin Fitzwater would say only that the President was extremely concerned that a climate of aggression had developed in Panama that placed American lives further at risk. As always, the President was concerned about estimates of American deaths in a combat operation. "There will be a few dozen casualties if we go," Colin Powell estimated. "If we don't go, there will be a few dozen casualties over the next few weeks and we'll still have Noriega."

I knew the President had already decided on his course of action, but one by one, he polled his advisers. I said, "Let's take them up on their declaration of war. We shouldn't wait. He'll kill twenty more Americans or take them hostage." Cheney, Powell, and Scowcroft quickly agreed that the time for diplomacy had passed, and at 3:50 P.M., the President said, "Let's do

---

*My hunch proved correct. After the President ordered the invasion but before it commenced, we received an intelligence report that said Noriega had ordered his Dignity Battalions to kidnap American soldiers and dependents and hold them for ransom.

it." He ordered the implementation of Operation Blue Spoon, the contingency plan for the invasion of Panama by Army and Marine forces. Since Powell had said the Pentagon needed forty-eight hours to prepare for the invasion, the launch date was established for an hour past midnight on December 20. For the first time since the Grenada operation, American troops would soon be at war.

At 5:30, I telephoned John Bushnell, our embassy's chargé in Panama City, on a secure line, and reported the President's decision. I told him that he and I were the only two officials in the department who knew the invasion had been approved. I directed him to contact Endara and begin assembling a Panamanian government that could be sworn in and operational within hours of the invasion. I told Bushnell that we'd decided not to evacuate the embassy staff in order to maintain the element of surprise, so that he could not tell his colleagues about the invasion.

The President directed that an interagency policy committee be tasked to consider economic and diplomatic options and report back early Monday morning. This was essentially a smoke screen; the die had been cast. I wasn't surprised to hear the next morning that the task force had concluded the obvious: there *were* no economic or diplomatic solutions left to consider.

Afterward, I asked to be driven directly home rather than to the Department. The President was determined that word of the invasion not leak, so I made the difficult decision not to confide in any of my staff. I suspected they'd figure out the obvious from my disappearing act, but the President had been adamant about not jeopardizing operational security.

On Monday morning, Aronson asked to see me. "I'm not going to ask you anything you may not be in a position to answer," he said. "But if we're going in, there are some things we need to do to get ready. Would you like me to give you a recommendation of steps we'll have to take?" I told Aronson I thought that might be prudent. For the rest of the day, I kept my closest associates in the dark. But the next morning, December 19, I told Eagleburger, Kimmitt, and Aronson, "We're going in." I asked Kimmitt and Aronson to coordinate planning for a presidential statement, diplomatic messages, and congressional consultations. Later in the day I alerted Margaret Tutwiler and Janet Mullins.

Less than six hours before H-Hour, I spoke again with Bushnell, who had invited an unsuspecting Endara and his two vice presidents to dinner at Howard Air Force Base and told them what was happening. "They're in a state of shock," he told me. "They never expected we'd do this much. They'll do everything they can to make this work."

Around ten o'clock, I joined Tutwiler and Mullins for pizza and Chinese food in Tutwiler's office. Earlier in the evening, they'd stopped answering their telephones, lest their presence in the Building after hours tip some resourceful reporter to the invasion. The military operations orders had been issued, and there was nothing to do but wait. I found it a lonely time of no small anguish. I knew the President's decision was the right one, reached after months of pursuing lesser remedies.

"These are the really tough issues," I said, "because whatever you do, some people are going to die. You just have to hope to God you're right."

The last of my four conversations with Bushnell that day occurred at 11:55 P.M. from the U.S. Army base at Fort Clayton. "There will be a considerable degree of surprise," he said, "but not as much as we would have liked." Word had finally begun leaking, and CNN was airing videotape of U.S. aircraft taking off from Pope Air Force Base, North Carolina, which adjoins Fort Bragg, home of the 82d Airborne Division.

Six minutes later, at one minute past midnight on December 20, Endara and his two vice presidents were sworn in. Within the hour, the largest deployment of American military force since Vietnam began.

Searching for "Maximum Leader"

Just as Powell had predicted, the operation unfolded smoothly. The PDF was no match for American firepower and training, and except for a fierce firefight at Noriega's headquarters, the amount of resistance was less than anticipated.

The next day, Kimmitt, Aronson, and I went to the Pentagon to meet with Cheney and Powell. This wasn't the sort of trip I normally made. I wholeheartedly agreed with the President's view, forged by his World War II combat experience in the Pacific, that once a decision to commit forces is made by the commander in chief, civilian authorities should draw back and let the professional soldiers do their job. In this case, however, I felt it was essential to settle quickly what appeared to be a bureaucratic disagreement over the priority of targets. In order to restore Panamanian civilian authority as quickly as possible, the State Department wanted the military to secure important government buildings such as the central bank headquarters. In addition, my experts believed it was important to destroy or capture transmitter facilities to keep Noriega off the airwaves of Radio Nacional. Some in the Pentagon had different ideas, but Powell and Cheney readily agreed. They also were willing to alter their battle plans to rescue journalists trapped in the Marriott Hotel by the fighting.

With the PDF subdued and civilian authority reestablishing control, the hunt for Noriega intensified. On Christmas Eve, U.S. intelligence reported that Noriega had been spotted in a Dairy Queen in Panama City. By the time American troops arrived on the scene, Noriega had vanished. A few minutes later, we learned that he'd taken refuge in the nunciature, the residence of Monsignor Sebastian Laboa, the papal nuncio to Panama. From the start of the operation, U.S. troops had placed several locations under surveillance where Noriega might seek refuge, including the Soviet and Nicaraguan embassies. Ironically, although the Catholic Church has a rich tradition of harboring political refugees, nobody had thought to shadow the nunciature.

Kimmitt oversaw the preparation of a diplomatic note formally requesting the Vatican to surrender Noriega, but he also recommended that I personally contact Vatican diplomatic officials to make sure the Pope understood the importance we attached to the matter. At 5:30 P.M. on Christmas Eve from the library of my mother's home in Houston, I telephoned Agostino Cardinal Casaroli, the Vatican's Secretary of State, but he was on his way to celebrate midnight Mass at St. Peter's Basilica when he learned of my call. He sent a message through Jim Creagan, deputy chief of the U.S. mission to the Vatican, that the Holy See's usual course in such circumstances was to arrange political exile in a third country. "This could be messy," Casaroli observed.

On Christmas Day, Casaroli called me back to say that the Vatican was genuinely undecided on the appropriate course of action and was consulting international law experts. "He's waging a political fight," he said, "and this request comes from the United States, and not from Panama. That presents us with a problem."

I asked Casaroli to turn Noriega over as a fugitive from justice. "It's not a political matter, Your Eminence," I argued. "This is an exception to diplomatic immunity. We've indicted him as a drug dealer. He's a common criminal. We will not let him go because he's a threat to public security. He's a temporary refugee, but he's not entitled to political asylum. And you must understand that, having lost American lives to restore democracy in Panama, we cannot allow Noriega to go to any other country than the United States."

"We've giving very serious consideration to your request," the cardinal reiterated.

I knew that international law was in our favor, but as it turned out, Noriega proved to be a terrible house guest. He moved a number of unsavory characters into the nunciature with him, and Laboa was distressed to learn that his residence had also become a makeshift arsenal filled with a sizable number of weapons. To increase the psychological warfare against him, U.S. troops blared rock music at the compound around the clock.

On the night of January 3, Laboa met with Mike Kozak, Brigadier General Marc Cisneros, Thurman's senior Army commander, and Major General Wayne Downing at a school across the street from the nunciature. Laboa said that Noriega's loyalists were fearful that a huge demonstration the next morning would overwhelm security forces and tear Noriega and his lieutenants to pieces. He asked Downing what his troops would do if protesters broke through the barricades. He was told that U.S. soldiers would fire in the air. Laboa wanted to know what would happen if they kept coming. "Sir," Downing said, "I'm not going to kill a single innocent person to protect that SOB." Our negotiators didn't tell Laboa that the demonstration had been arranged with the knowledge of U.S. officials to escalate the pressure both on Noriega and the monsignor.

This dose of reality was the final straw for the nuncio. He said he would urge Noriega to agree to leave. In a matter of hours, Noriega walked out of the nunciature to a soccer field and surrendered to U.S. forces. He was whisked by helicopter to Howard Air Force Base, where he was read his rights and remanded into the custody of the U.S. Drug Enforcement Administration.

Noriega believed up until the night we came in that he'd stared us down. Another dictator had underestimated the resolve of the United States to protect its vital interests. He thought he could weather the storm. Instead, in the space of two weeks, he'd gone from being a self-styled "Maximum Leader" to "Hunted Fugitive."

Reflections on a Just Cause

Ordinarily, an American military intervention in Latin America would provoke howls of outrage from our hemispheric neighbors and criticism from the political opposition at home. In the aftermath of the Panama operation, however, the political flak was surprisingly light from all quarters. On Capitol Hill, for instance, such ideological opposites as Senators John Kerry and Jesse Helms, who had urged tougher action for months, praised the President's stand.

In part, this absence of opprobrium was due to the fact that Noriega was a bad character, plain and simple, and even his neighbors knew it. He was also an indicted drug trafficker, which helped rob him of any sympathy. And while its strategic importance has diminished over time, the Panama Canal endures as an icon of the American experience, built by American sweat and ingenuity and whose security remains in the national interest.

Emotional ties notwithstanding, the reason Panama worked was more fundamental. In the hours before the operation began, Dick Cheney changed its code name from Blue Spoon to Operation Just Cause. If ever a military endeavor were aptly named, this was it. At its core, Just Cause was an exercise in supporting democracy and the rule of law in the hemisphere. Noriega was a dictator who had stolen an election and thwarted the will of the Panamanian people. The United States was simply enforcing the will of the Panamanians by restoring the legitimately elected government to authority.

Moreover, the President has a constitutional duty to protect American citizens. Noriega crossed a line when he started killing American servicemen. Our administration was not going to wait until more were dead or held hostage, as in Iran, to respond. In a loftier sense, we were also following the time-honored admonition of the national anthem, whose little-noticed fourth stanza exhorts us to conquer "when our cause it is just. . . ."

The salutary effects of Just Cause extended well beyond the isthmus, however. It made a crucial difference in Colombia, where the Medellín cartel's campaign of political assassination had just claimed its third presidential candidate, and democracy's survival was by no means certain. The President's resolve in Panama was a tonic that gave the Colombian government the courage to stand up to the cartel. It also convinced the Sandinista government that there were consequences to stealing an election, and strengthened the resolve of Nicaraguan citizens to stand up and be counted on *their* election day.

The invasion also had a profound effect on the Organization of American States and was directly responsible for the historic Santiago declaration in June of 1991, in which the nations of the hemisphere endorsed a U.S.-drafted resolution committing the OAS to collective action anywhere democracy was threatened in the region. Without that declaration, the OAS would have been extremely reluctant to have endorsed economic and political sanctions against Haiti, or to have opposed coups in Peru and Guatemala.

I also believe that in breaking the mind-set of the American people about the use of force in the post-Vietnam era, Panama established an emotional predicate that permitted us to build the public support so essential to the success of Operation Desert Storm thirteen months later.

All this flowed from a single event: the President's determination that a naked assault on democracy wouldn't be tolerated. In dramatic fashion, the United States had demonstrated once more that it would stand up for democracy, and behind its friends in the hemisphere.

CHAPTER 12

THE ARITHMETIC OF UNIFICATION

We must find some way of persuading Russia to play ball.
—*Secretary of War Henry Stimson to President Truman, May 16, 1945*

G ianni De Michelis was usually the most exuberant and outgoing diplomat in any setting. The Italian Foreign Minister had a well-deserved reputation as a man about town and bon vivant, who spent a good bit of his free time dancing in discos. He had even written a guide to dance clubs. But that February day in Ottawa he was almost the antithesis of his normal self—and with good reason. Along with several others in the NATO caucus, De Michelis was unenthusiastic about our proposal to manage German unification through what came to be known as the "Two-plus-Four"—an ad hoc forum that included only the two Germanies and the Four Powers (Britain, France, the Soviet Union, and the United States), but no other NATO countries. He began to voice his objections, when Hans-Dietrich Genscher cut him off sharply. "You're not in the game," said Genscher.

The story behind the creation of Two-plus-Four on February 13, 1990, is a classic tale of "great power" diplomacy—and one in which I was reminded forcefully that, as location is to real estate, timing is to statecraft.

Who Should Play?

After leaving Potsdam in December, my thoughts had returned there many times in the ensuing weeks. The site of the last of the three great power meetings that ended World War II, Potsdam symbolized the centrality of the German question in the Cold War. In fact, for many, Potsdam had marked the beginning of the Cold War. There had been a drama to the two and a half weeks of the Potsdam Conference that had been absent during the meetings between Stalin, Churchill, and Roosevelt at Tehran and Yalta. With Roosevelt's death, his successor, Harry Truman, had stepped into the breach—his first performance on the world stage. Meanwhile, Stalin arrived at Potsdam even more paranoid than usual, and argued that Hitler was alive and well and living in Germany. Stalin loathed the press, who kept trying to push themselves into the proceedings. Churchill became upset about the condition of British representatives in occupied Romania, and complained to the Soviet dictator that an iron fence had come down around them. "All fairy tales," Stalin replied, thus dismissing Churchill diplomatically much like the British people would dismiss him electorally on July 26. And while the Four Powers decided the fate of Europe and Germany, scientists in Alamogordo, New Mexico, tested the atomic bomb, Truman approved the attack on Hiroshima, and a new era in world politics was born.

Of course, I was not alone in thinking about Potsdam and its implications in the winter of 1989–90. The German question was on everyone's mind, and during December and January, a raft of proposals was floated in diplomatic circles and in the media. These proposals generally fell into three categories.

First were the initiatives that sought to answer the German question through a grand conference. This would be an all-European affair that would come together for the final peace settlement of World War II. CSCE was the natural avenue for this, since its thirty-five members included all the states of Europe, Canada, and the United States. It was a somewhat romantic approach, one that harked back to the Congress of Vienna, which settled the map of Europe following the Napoleonic Wars, or the Treaty of Versailles after the First World War. From our perspective, a CSCE conference on German unification was a non-starter. It was difficult to understand how such delicate diplomatic negotiations could be managed with thirty-five participants, and CSCE's rule of consensus would give the smaller states of Europe veto power over issues far beyond their standing. Such a large conference would inevitably resurrect memories of Versailles and the peace that had been imposed on Germany following World War I. The last thing we wanted to do was create a basis for resentment in the new Germany. Finally, such a conference would take time to organize and could lead to delay, confusion, and even breakdown as events on the ground sped along.

The second category of proposals grew directly out of the World War II conferences and the fact that the Four Powers had agreed at Potsdam that all arrangements regarding Germany were provisional, pending a final "peace settlement." For Moscow and, to a lesser degree, London and Paris, a Four Powers conference was the best method for slowing and managing unification. Legally, the Four Powers had residual rights that would have to be negotiated in any unification scheme, but the Soviets—as they had during the early days of the Cold War—saw the Four Powers as a political club, not an entity of international law. While the Kremlin was the most insistent on using the Four Powers, Paris and London saw it as a way to moderate, and perhaps influence, Germany's movement toward primacy on the Continent.

Indeed, throughout January, Moscow pressed for a Four Powers meeting. On January 10, Ambassador Dubinin came to the State Department to deliver an oral message from Shevardnadze. Noting that "a consensus is emerging about the desirability of maintaining within the 'Big Four' an exchange of views on German affairs," Shevardnadze argued for a series of exchanges among Moscow, London, Paris, and Washington. "We proceed from the importance of those affairs for all Europe, if not for the whole world," he continued, and cited the "understandable responsibility" resting with the Four Powers. A little over two weeks later, on January 26, Chetverikov delivered a paper drawing attention to "recently intensified activities of right-wing extremist and neo-fascist forces in the FRG, the GDR, and some other West European countries." This threat was "mushrooming," and Moscow looked to concerted international efforts to cope with this "brown" danger.

To us, the Four Powers was largely an anachronism from World War II. The President believed that for four decades the West German people had shown that they were committed to democracy and to the Western alliance. Our belief in self-determination, and the fact that reunification had been a formal, if understated, goal of the alliance for forty years, required that we do everything we could to see that a unified Germany became a reality in a context that provided stability in Europe after the Cold War. Now that the East German people were voting with their feet, George Bush did not want diplomats to get in their way. That was the reason we deliberately downplayed the Soviet's initial demand for a Four Powers session in December, and continued to deflect their calls for meetings in the ensuing weeks.

That left a third category: namely, a German-only solution, in which the FRG and the GDR would merge without any outside interference. Since most of the critical issues involved solely inter-German concerns, many Germans felt there was no need for any serious diplomatic engagement by others. They should just stay out of the way, and once the two Germanies were united, the Four Powers could get together to dissolve their residual legal rights. This, quite naturally, was the process most favored in Bonn, particularly by Chancellor Kohl. But it also found support in Washington, notably in the NSC staff.

I wasn't comfortable with any of these. Following my visit to Potsdam, I was convinced that the pace of unification was going to exceed everyone's predictions. The people of the GDR had tasted freedom and the material benefits that went along with it, and their emigration west and the hemorrhaging of the East German economy would increase. That, in turn, would put pressure on Kohl and Genscher to hasten the political steps necessary to merge the two states. With the train of unification barreling down the tracks, I became concerned that Moscow, and perhaps even London and Paris, might try to slow it down by stepping in front of it. The Soviets still had 380,000 troops in the GDR, Gorbachev was under increasing pressure for having "lost" Eastern Europe, and London and Paris were less than enthusiastic for unification. Allowing the two Germanies to work things out on their own in that kind of situation was, in my view, a recipe for a train wreck. That's ultimately why I disagreed with the laissez-faire approach that Bonn and the White House preferred initially. I felt we needed a process that could help steer the two Germanies to unification, while also giving Gorbachev a place at the table, so he could explain to hard-liners that Moscow was still in the game. I also wanted a process that would maximize the leverage of internal events on the external dimension of unification—I didn't want the Soviets to use their leverage to cause trouble and disrupt our goals.

I found the formula in a memo that Dennis Ross and Bob Zoellick discussed with me on January 30. That had been developed by the Policy Planning Staff, and it combined the German-only approach favored by Bonn and the White House with the Four Powers forum suggested by Moscow, and supported by London and Paris. It was called "Two-plus-Four," and its aim was to have the United States "use Two-plus-Four Power talks to bring German unity to fruition." The advantages of this formula were clear. It would give the Germans (the "two") control over internal matters, but would allow the Four Powers to play a role in the external aspects of unification. The Two-plus-Four would also give great-power legitimacy to unification—a point the Germans recognized. It would keep Moscow, London, and Paris in the game—with Washington participation. Most important, it would create a diplomatic process for unification that could keep pace with events. Without such a process, the odds of the Germans and the Soviets going off alone and cutting a private deal disadvantageous to Western interests (as they had with the agreements of Brest-Litovsk in 1918, Rapallo in 1922, and the Molotov-Ribbentrop Accord in 1939) would increase. I felt it was important to have the major powers at one table, where we could all see the cards that each of us was playing.

While Ross and Zoellick thought Two-plus-Four was ingenious, it had its critics, not only at the NSC, but in the Department of State as well. On February 1, Ray Seitz, the Assistant Secretary of State for European Affairs, raised fundamental objections to Two-plus-Four, all of which flowed from his view that German unification was not moving as fast as the Two-plus-Four memo warned ("We are not facing a stampede"), that we should let the Germanies handle unification themselves, and that we could be involved best through our bilateral channel to Bonn. I had no difficulty making up my mind. Whether the metaphor was that of a runaway train or a stampede didn't matter to me; I didn't think we should chance being run over by it.

Preliminary Consultations

On January 29, Douglas Hurd came to Washington for his first visit as Foreign Secretary. Two-plus-Four was in the front of my mind, if not on the tip of my tongue. I told him that in my upcoming ministerial with Shevardnadze, I planned to let the Soviets know, "Now is not the time to talk about the future of Germany in a Four Powers context. We need to find a special mechanism—a quiet place—where we can address the question in a way that does not appear to be going around Germany and which does not threaten Soviet security worries."

Hurd agreed. Having just seen Modrow, he, too, felt unification was inevitable. "There is virtually one German television, one German airline, and the most popular politician in East Germany is Helmut Kohl." But he cautioned, "No one is thinking of the consequences." He suggested dusting off some of the ideas the Allies had had in the 1950s, when the idea of a unified Germany had been a possibility. He told the President that Thatcher was "a reluctant unifier. Not against, but reluctant."

Four days later, an enthusiastic unifier, Hans-Dietrich Genscher, arrived in Washington. Genscher told me that, following the March 18 elections in the GDR, Bonn would negotiate a treaty that spelled out the path to unification. I asked Genscher what he thought of Two-plus-Four, having already asked Zoellick to preview it with Genscher's key aide, Frank Elbe. (The Zoellick-Elbe channel would become for Germany what the Ross-Tarasenko link was for Soviet policy: my own private back channel to my counterpart.) Genscher liked the concept, provided the "Two" preceded the "Four." This wasn't just semantics. To the Germans, "Two-plus-Four" symbolized that they would take the lead on unification; they saw "Four-plus-Two," on the other hand, as just a wider variant of a Four Powers *diktat,* and so it was unacceptable, politically and emotionally. Genscher also felt that such a mechanism could not come into play until after the March 18 elections in East Germany (he didn't want to do anything to legitimize Modrow's collapsing regime in the GDR).

On February 5, I left Andrews Air Force Base for a trip that would hopscotch from Prague to Moscow, to Sofia, and to Bucharest, before returning across the Atlantic to Ottawa. My first meeting was in Shannon, Ireland. Usually just a refueling stop, this time it was the only mutually convenient place where the French Foreign Minister, Roland Dumas, and I could meet to discuss Germany—and at 5:20 A.M. to boot. Dumas seemed intrigued by the idea of the Two-plus-Four, though he admitted he preferred a Four-plus-Zero. He said he'd check with Mitterrand and get back to me.

After landing in a heavy fog in Prague, I caught a catnap and then traveled to Hradčany Castle to meet with President Václav Havel, the noted playwright and dissident. The Husák regime had interned him in jails for years, but the Communists had never broken his spirit. Indeed, "free spirit" was—and is—the only way to capture Havel's unrestrained enthusiasm for life. He had been on the job only several weeks, but he wanted to offer some ideas, noting, "We are not trying to make Czechoslovakia or Havel famous. It's unimportant who is the author of ideas, whether it is Bush or Gorbachev." I told him Ronald Reagan used to have a sign on his desk that said, "There's no end to what a man can accomplish if he doesn't care who gets the credit." Havel told me he'd have the same statement put on his desk, and then turned to discuss Europe and Germany.

"Czechoslovakia, like a number of other countries, is interested in returning to Europe," he began. He felt that another Helsinki Conference was the way to coordinate it, but more important, he suggested a peace conference to finally settle World War II and the division of Europe. Obviously, he said, the dissolution of Four Power rights and German reunification would be at the center of such a conference, for, in his words, "There can be no united Germany in a divided Europe, nor a divided Germany in a united Europe." Yet, simultaneously, he felt that while some Germans would like to reunite immediately, that would be impossible. As for Soviet troops, he found it difficult to understand how in August 1968, when Brezhnev crushed the Prague Spring, "half a million Soviet troops came here overnight, and yet they keep saying it's difficult to remove seventy thousand here today." But he felt this was something he could work out with Gorbachev.

I began by going through several intelligence and espionage issues. The Communist regimes in Eastern Europe had, for the most part, held only tenuous control over their intelligence agencies. Since the KGB had trained, supplied, and consequently penetrated these agencies, the security services remained as reactionary as ever, even though the governments may have changed in the revolutions of 1989. So with the help of our own contacts, we tried to help the new governments gain control over their own spy services.

I then moved quickly into a broad discussion of German unification. I pointed out how German unification was moving faster than anyone had predicted, and tried to steer him away from the idea of a large conference. I also told him a neutral Germany was not something that appealed to the United States. He told me that Modrow was coming by to see him that afternoon, and "he's speaking of a neutral Germany as part of his reelection campaign. This is nonsense." In sum, Havel exhibited the tension toward Germany felt in almost all the small states of Europe. On the one hand, he thought unification should go slow and that a large peace conference should be the proper forum for deciding the issue. Simultaneously, he was wary of a neutral Germany—which by implication meant that we needed to move quickly to keep Germany in NATO and see it unified before there could be any reversal of reform in Moscow.

I left Havel to visit with ninety-one-year-old Cardinal Tomašek. As the cardinal graciously recounted America's role in the founding of Czechoslovakia in 1918, our efforts to help the Czechs in 1945, and the importance of my visit, I told him simply, "You can continue to count on the United States to be with your people." At that point, my interpreter broke down sobbing. He was a Czech who had been forced to flee the country in 1973, and the regime had retaliated against him by ousting his father from his job. Now, he had come back to a free Prague, and my meeting with the cardinal just overwhelmed him. It was as if his life had come full circle. I was touched that the mere fact of my trip played a small part in his own personal journey.

That evening, at a reception, I met another man who had been redeemed: Alexander Dubček. The father of the Prague Spring, Dubček had been deposed following the Soviet invasion and humiliated by the regime imposed by Moscow. But it was clear that, like Havel, he too had never lost his spirit. Indeed, he told me he also was going to see Modrow, and asked what he should tell him. I said, "Free elections and free markets." "That's what I've always supported," said Dubček. "I know," I replied, "because I remember, and I've always admired you so." It was a great honor to meet such a courageous individual—a man who unfortunately had been twenty-one years ahead of what history would allow.

The next morning, before my speech at Charles University, I visited Wenceslas Square to lay a wreath at the memorial to Jan Palach, a student who had immolated himself in 1969 protesting Communist repression.

While there were large numbers of people in the square, I was struck by how deserted it was, in contrast to the crowds of 200,000 and more who had surged through during December's "Velvet Revolution." It was a stark reminder that the headiness of a revolution quickly gives way to the hard work of building democracy, a theme I built upon in my address that was broadcast across the country.

"If 1989 was the year of sweeping away," I told the students, "1990 must become the year of building anew." While outlining thirteen concrete American initiatives to help the Czechs secure their new democracy, I stressed the need for all the new regimes in Eastern Europe to bolster their legitimacy by holding free elections, and noted that without legitimacy, there would be no stability in the region. Indeed, we felt free elections were so crucial to building up a firewall against a Communist reversal that we made the adoption of free elections, as a principle, one of our prerequisites to the holding of a new CSCE Summit to update the Helsinki Final Act. I also made the case for having Prague, Warsaw, Budapest, and the other new democracies work together in a new regional association. I felt this would be one way to help them deal with fears of German unification to the west and the possibility of Gorbachev's failure to the east.

I made a particular plea to the students to stay involved, because they had played such a key role in bringing down the Communists. Later, talking with Dennis Ross and Margaret Tutwiler, we realized we needed to find a way to get the American people involved in helping these students build democracy. "What about a democracy corps modeled after the Peace Corps?" Margaret and Dennis proposed. So was born the Citizens' Democracy Corps—President Bush's grassroots effort to support democracy in the region.

Kremlin Concerns

As I flew from Prague to Moscow, the afternoon of February 7, I focused on how the revolution in Eastern Europe had moved east, and how the Moscow of 1990 barely resembled the city I had visited the previous May. Over a quarter million people had marched on the Kremlin the previous Sunday in support of democratic reform. Gorbachev and Shevardnadze were embroiled in a Communist Party Plenum, and Yuri Dubinin told me on our arrival that the Plenum was running over and that Shevardnadze had to delay our first meeting for a short period.

When Shevardnadze arrived at the Osobnyak at 8:00 P.M., he was relaxed and confident, despite what I knew had been a grueling Plenum. The Party had adopted the goal, he said, "to build a humane, democratic socialism, and develop a process that takes us to that objective and then produces democracy and freedom." He felt that perestroika had so changed Soviet society that "we can't even recognize our own society, changes are so profound. Democracy, democratization, and glasnost are not just words. They characterize everyday life." Nonetheless, he was concerned because, while "the old mechanisms have ceased to operate . . . the new ones haven't taken their place." We went through the economic reforms Gorbachev was introducing, including changes in the credit system, property and ownership, and prices. "Bread is so cheap that people buy it and use it as feed for cattle," he said incredulously. "We need to have real prices that mean something."

But the greatest changes were reserved for politics. Political reform was "moving at a very rapid pace" and was "outstripping" economic reform. He welcomed the new pluralism in the Soviet Union and recognized that the leadership had to take advantage of it. "The Party at a minimum has to abandon its monopoly on power. It has to accept that there are new parties. This is a very difficult decision. This is a decision, frankly, that was a problem for us and that is meeting a lot of resistance right now." As he spoke, I recalled how, just a few months before, Shevardnadze had told me there was no need for a multiparty system in the USSR. Now, Gorbachev's initiative to repeal Article VI of the Soviet constitution, which gave the "leading role" to the Communist Party, had been the biggest battle of the Plenum. "These kinds of people," Shevardnadze said, referring to the Central Committee members, "are just not used to having to work to get everyone's vote. They assume they could just have it—now what we're telling them is that you will have to earn a position, you may have to engage in debate."

"Welcome to democracy," I said. "Democracy can be messy." I pressed him on Lithuania, where the local Communist Party had declared its independence from Moscow on December 22, 1989, as well as on Azerbaijan, where Moscow had cracked down violently in January against the Azeri Popular Front. As I had in Wyoming, I pushed the idea of a referendum, because I was convinced that it was the most peaceful and democratic way for the Baltics to achieve de facto independence. I went a bit further, however, and asked him, "Speaking obviously off the top of my head, what would be lost if Azerbaijan decided it wanted to be an independent republic? Why, you both might be better off if that were the case."

Still wrestling with the nationalities question, he said again that it was the "greatest problem" Gorbachev faced. He agreed in principle with the idea of a referendum—which was a step forward from where he had been in the fall—but feared that, practically speaking, a referendum could ignite a civil war. He was especially concerned about his native region, the Caucasus, where "people are far more temperamental and weapons have been used," than in the Baltics, "where people are generally pretty calm."

We used the rest of the session and our small group meetings the next day to make progress on other parts of our agenda, especially arms control. I brought proposals on everything from CFE and chemical weapons to air-launched cruise missiles (ALCMs) and sea-launched cruise missiles (SLCMs), as well as such esoterica as non-deployed missiles and anti-telemetry encryption. I told Shevardnadze, "You will be able to tell your bureaucracy that the United States has come in your direction. . . . I hope that when you see the detail you will appreciate our movements because, let me tell you, I have got the scars on my back to show you this took some real effort."

"You know, I've got quite a few of those scars myself," Eduard replied. While, in retrospect, arms control was overwhelmed by the revolutionary political changes we had to manage, issues like ALCMs took days of our time and required long and oftentimes intense bureaucratic fights in both our capitals. Nuclear arms control had its own writ, and the high priests of the atomic era guarded their secrets jealously. More than once, I thought I had an agreement with Shevardnadze, only to see the Soviet military undo it the next time we met.

On Germany, I previewed Two-plus-Four in another one-on-one meeting Friday morning, after first raising our concerns about growing anti-Semitism in the Soviet Union. Shevardnadze had several different, even contradictory, ideas about how to manage unification. He was concerned by moves in East Germany against the Soviet presence, and warned, "We do believe that some political figures in Europe are perhaps moving too fast on unification and want to move forward too quickly." The Kremlin wanted unification to occur in "designated phases," to ensure stability, and that was why the Soviets preferred CSCE. "But," he admitted, "while we think that that's an appropriate mechanism, we're not saying that it's the only one." A few moments later, however, he said, "My basic feeling is that history will not forgive us if we do not effectively use the Four Powers mechanism." Then, almost in the same sentence, he added, "The question of unification will be decided by the German nation and the German people but they should know what is the opinion of others." That's why he felt "there should be some sort of referendum," but was utterly vague about how such a referendum might be organized, and summarized his ambivalence by saying, "We believe that all options ought to be considered. After all, the reality is that our action is late, given the way events are moving."

He seemed overwhelmed by the emotional weight of the issue, in part no doubt because he had been attacked personally during the Plenum for "losing" Eastern Europe and Germany, but also because he had lost a brother in the war. "Maybe because of our instincts and our remembrance of the war, and of the need twice to have to fight Germany, maybe that's the reason we are more sensitive to this. We know very well the scourge of war and we cannot forget the lessons of the past."

In contrast, Gorbachev was almost matter-of-fact, even legalistic. This was no doubt partly due to his success in the Plenum, where he had scored a major political victory over his conservative opponents by ending the Party's monopoly on power, creating a working presidency, and reforming property rights. "As you can see," he told me, "we took on an awful lot. Put simply, the radicalization of perestroika was affirmed by the Plenum." Indeed, he was so buoyed by success that he dismissed Western and even Soviet press reports about his political position. "Well, at least I can say they are never boring. Unfortunately, they also are not enlightening. They are also not useful."

He appeared to have much more use for our approach to German unification, and after my initial presentation asked simply, "I say Four-plus-Two; you say Two-plus-Four. How do you look at this formula?"

"Two-plus-Four is a better way. I said to Eduard that we think the Four Powers mechanism alone cannot work. CSCE is too unwieldy," I responded. "We fought a war together to bring peace to Europe. We didn't do so well handling the peace in the Cold War. And now we are faced with rapid and fundamental change. And we are in a better position to cooperate in preserving peace."

"Basically," Gorbachev replied, "I share the course of your thinking. The process is under way. We have to adjust to this process. We have to adjust to this new reality and not be passive in ensuring that stability in Europe is not upset. Well, for us and for you, regardless of the differences, there is nothing terrifying in the prospect of a unified Germany." It was an odd reversal. For the first time, I had seen Shevardnadze in denial on an issue that Gorbachev was facing head-on. But maybe that flowed from Gorbachev's denial of an even greater reality: the decline of the Soviet Union as a great power. "For France and for Britain," Gorbachev told me, "the question is who is going to be the major player in Europe. We have it easier. We are big countries and have our own weight. We also see how Kohl and his team are talking to us—very carefully knowing what our two countries mean." Gorbachev seemed to believe that the Soviet Union would always be a preeminent power in Europe—even with a unified Germany. I began to think that possibly Shevardnadze saw the future more clearly, and was wary of codifying continued Soviet decline.

Nonetheless, I was more concerned with getting Soviet agreement to Two-plus-Four than with discerning the Kremlin's motivations, so when Gorbachev told me that "Four-plus-Two or Two-plus-Four, assuming it relies on an international legal basis, is suitable for the situation," I pocketed his assent quietly and quickly.

The next morning, I became the first foreigner ever to testify before the Supreme Soviet. I continue to this day to marvel at the change in the U.S.-Soviet relationship that led to the United States Secretary of State being the first such witness. In the Kremlin's Sverdlov Hall—a cavernous, white room with a beautiful, blue-domed ceiling—I spoke to the International Affairs Committee for twenty minutes and then answered the members' questions for over an hour, including questions from Marshal Akhromeyev and Yevgeny Primakov. (Later in the year, Primakov would become a central irritant during the Persian Gulf crisis.) Many of the questions were rather pointed, but the hardest part of the whole affair was keeping my focus, knowing that Lenin—in spirit and in a large white marble bust—was looking over my shoulder.

As I left Moscow, Helmut Kohl was arriving. We did not meet in Moscow before he met Gorbachev. We didn't want to create the public impression in the Soviet Union that somehow the Americans and the Germans were conspiring against them. In private, of course, we were consulting continuously, and that morning I wrote Kohl a letter debriefing him on my talks. I told the Chancellor that I had made the case with Gorbachev against handling unification through CSCE or the Four Powers, and had raised Two-plus-Four as an alternative. I wrote, "While he clearly has real concerns about German unification—some of which may be related to the passions this issue evokes in the Soviet Union—he may be willing to go along with a sensible approach that gives him some cover or explanation for his actions."

Bulgaria and Romania

From the Soviet Union, I headed for Sofia and Bucharest—stops that had been added just forty-eight hours before (in fact, the newest Bulgarian government had fallen the same day I had made the decision to visit there). I had wanted to visit both countries from the outset, but until Chris Liebengood, the head of my security detail, was satisfied he could guarantee my safety in Bucharest, I had had to hold off on making a final decision.

The highlights of Sofia were the rather large number of people that had gathered in the square outside the Sheraton Hotel to await my arrival, and the opposition leaders with whom I met late that night. In the crowd were signs that bore slogans like, "The Communists Must Go," and "Welcome, Secretary of State." And as I arrived, the crowd started yelling and clapping. It was a spontaneous demonstration that would have been unheard of just a few weeks before. Meanwhile, a continent away, President de Klerk announced that Nelson Mandela would soon be a free man in South Africa. Truly, we were living through a global revolution.

The opposition told me things that illustrated what I had realized in Prague: Much work was still needed to consolidate the revolutions of 1989 into lasting democracy. I asked them if they were allowed fair access to the media, noting that government leaders had told me the government had less access to the media than the opposition. "The government has a good sense of humor," replied one of the opposition leaders. "The Communist newspaper has a circulation of 760,000. We were given paper enough for only 70,000." Another told me, "Roosevelt said you should not have fear, but we have it here. During the nightmare days of Stalin, we knew of your great country and of your democracy, and you stood with us." Bibles, one religious leader said, were especially hard to come by, and they could be found only at four to five times the published price. (Later, I heard from Pat Kennedy how difficult it had been to get rooms for our traveling party in Sofia, because the secret police continued to control many of the rooms they had used for eavesdropping on foreigners.)

Sunday, February 11, began with a brief trip to Bucharest. It was a bit unnerving to land at the airport and be met on the runway by armored personnel carriers. The ride in from the airport was something out of George Orwell's worst nightmare: a series of nondescript, impersonal apartment buildings whose monotony was exceeded only by their mind-numbing regularity. They just went on, row after row, silent testimony to a central planner gone mad or, as Shevardnadze had put it in Moscow, an "extreme dictatorship" that produced a "deformed society."

At the Ministry of Foreign Affairs, the building was ringed with militia in green uniforms, carrying AK-47s and standing shoulder to shoulder. I had to swallow and remind myself, These are the good guys. Clearly, the government was still worried about the remnants of Ceaușescu's secret police. In fact, as I had in Prague, I passed information regarding the old Romanian intelligence services to Prime Minister Roman, in order to help the government secure its hold on power. In my meeting with President Iliescu, he ended the meeting by asking, "Do you want to see the Parliament room that has not been used for one hundred years?" I told him I would, and he showed me a magnificent round room with a beautiful glass-dome ceiling. Behind the dais was a Romanian flag, where before had hung a portrait of Ceaușescu.

The Romanian opposition was more scared but, paradoxically, more outspoken than the Bulgarians. I suppose they figured that if they could live through the firefights of the civil war, they could live through anything. "Our telephones are tapped," one opposition leader began. "Our letters are intercepted. There are car accidents that cannot be explained. We are threatened with expulsion from the country, and the secret police harass us." His colleague made an important distinction: "On December 22, we were terrorized. We are not terrorized anymore, we are intimidated. There is a difference. Our police can change their name overnight, but they do not understand democracy. When someone attacks you in the name of democracy, the police say they can do whatever they wish, because they are being democratic." Clearly, the real battle was now within the Romanian people themselves. As one leader put it, "You say we are the opposition. Against what? We are fighting against the Communist world within our people. Psychologically, our people have no concept of democracy." Romanian society had been totally atomized, making it very difficult to start rudimentary associations of any kind and all the harder to build democracy as a result. As we left for the airport, I looked up and saw a single man in one of the nondescript apartment buildings clasp his hands together in a salute to victory. It was moving to see the human spirit survive in such an inhuman place.

Ottawa and the Birth of Two-plus-Four

President Bush's "Open Skies" proposal, which he had put forth the previous May in his "Beyond Containment" speech, was the ostensible reason for the Ottawa Conference, the first meeting of the twenty-three members of NATO and the Warsaw Pact since the revolutions of 1989. But very quickly, it became apparent that German unification was the main game in town—and everyone wanted in on the action.

I began Monday, February 12, with a working breakfast with Prime Minister Mulroney, Foreign Minister Clark, and Shevardnadze. Having had time to reflect back on it, the Plenum now seemed to weigh more heavily on Shevardnadze. "It was a real fight," he said. "This time the fight was among the leadership."

Clark said it sounded like the fights in the House of Commons.

"It was worse. Some even made political accusations," Shevardnadze said. I knew that Yegor Ligachev—Gorbachev's remaining conservative rival in the Politburo—had warned of "a new Munich," but it was obvious that Shevardnadze had been singled out as a target. He told us that one Central Committee member had argued, "The Soviet Union was strong at one time. It was monolithic. It had Eastern Europe in its hands, which provided the USSR with a guarantee of security. Now all of this is crumbling." Shevardnadze had responded by asking the member about the Prague Spring—"that wonderful time in 1968 when all people wanted to do was to live differently"—and how the Soviets had crushed it by force. "What do you say about that?" he had questioned his accuser. And when Mulroney asked him what signs the West could give that would be useful, Shevardnadze said the old guard had twisted Western support for Gorbachev against the reformers. To these "old revolutionaries," Shevardnadze said, "when class enemies applaud, one has to be on guard." He told us he was relating all of this because he wanted to stress the importance of the question of German unification.

And given what he had been through politically at home, it was no wonder he still seemed caught in confusion about a process for managing this "very, very important" question. "We are trying to think things out, to find variants and solutions. I just don't know," he said, almost plaintively. "It is only natural for the Germans to want to unite. On the other hand, no one knows what might be the consequences."

It had become apparent that events had moved beyond the Soviets, although they still had many opportunities to be disruptive. With the Kremlin off balance, we had to keep pushing to set the agenda and pull the Soviets along. We had momentum on the ground, and it was necessary to maintain intellectual momentum.

Following the opening session of the conference, I sat down with Genscher. He reiterated again that the Germans would not attend a meeting where the Four Powers would dictate conditions of unification. I reassured him again that the "two" would lead the "four." Genscher felt that the Germanies should just issue invitations to initiate the Two-plus-Four.

Later that afternoon, Dumas told me that Paris liked the mechanism, though the French preferred that the "four" take the lead on the "two". He also told me that he was going to discuss the mechanism with Shevardnadze, whom he was scheduled to see at 4:15. That made me nervous, because I felt there was a real symbolic problem for the Germans with the French preference for "Four-plus-Two" as opposed to our proposal of "Two-plus-Four." There was also a crucial substantive difference; we needed the pressure of the two Germanies unifying on the ground to pull the British, French, and especially Soviets along. I didn't want Dumas to get Moscow to agree to an approach that the Germans wouldn't accept. So I sent Karen Groomes scrambling to find Shevardnadze, so I could see him before Dumas did.

Meanwhile, I met with Douglas Hurd and told him we needed to move on Two-plus-Four. "Otherwise, we will be getting pressure from others who will want to participate. But we need to be sure the Soviets are on board. They seem to want desperately to be part of the process. But if we delay on the Two-plus-Four formula, other formulas will be introduced, such as CSCE."

"I just saw Shevardnadze," replied Hurd, "and he's in a melancholy mood. But in the end, he acknowledged that the Two-plus-Four formula was 'the best we can do' and that we ought to proceed with it."

"That's my impression, too," I said. "We should move to lock it in.

Dumas agrees, though he prefers a Four-plus-Two formula—which would cause us trouble, as the Germans say they can't accept it."

"What is the difference between 'Four-plus-Two' and 'Two-plus-Four'?" Douglas asked.

It wasn't critical to us, but from a German viewpoint, Ray Seitz added, it was important that the Germans issue the invitations. The Two-plus-Four "fits with the Germans' sense of sequence," added Bob Zoellick. "The two Germanies would work internal issues, then the others would address external issues with them."

Hurd thought that made sense.

Thinking out loud, I said, "Now that it's clear the U.K. and France share essentially the same view as the U.S., I wonder whether I should go to Shevardnadze and tell him that the three Western powers agree with the Soviets on moving ahead with the mechanism."

"That's a good idea," said Hurd, pointing out that such a move was wise now, given Shevardnadze's "gloomy mood."

At 4:25, I met Shevardnadze in a "pull-aside" meeting at the conference. Luckily, virtually everyone was running late, and the meeting with Dumas had been pushed back. I explained in more detail my understanding of Two-plus-Four, and told him we were in agreement that we needed to move ahead. I also tried to buck him up psychologically. He still seemed to be drifting, and I knew we would need him to make the case with Moscow.

My next meeting with the Polish Foreign Minister, Krzysztof Skubiszewski, was a clear reminder why it wasn't in our interest to allow the two Germanies to go it alone on unification. The Minister said he realized unification was under way, and "Warsaw does not wish to disturb its course. After all, one should be realistic. We are neighbors. The last war started in Poland. We need good relations, and we are squeezed between two big countries." Thus, while the Poles did not wish to be "contrary" on unification, it was a subject of real concern.

Poland's primary problem was borders—or, as Skubiszewski called them, "frontiers." At the end of World War II, Stalin had moved Poland's border with Germany farther west and taken a slice of Poland, and there was some concern in Warsaw that a unified Germany would want those lands back. If this issue were not resolved, there were at least a dozen other European border disputes that could flare up, he pointed out, and that would be "regrettable." He recognized that the responsibilities of the Four Powers were largely confined to Berlin, but "once there are talks between the Four and the Two, it would be helpful to have an early statement regarding frontiers so as to remove this poisoning element." His reference to "the Four and the Two" slightly startled me, but then I realized he had conferred with the Soviets. It was another illustration that if we didn't get agreement on our concept in Ottawa, we would lose what might be our only opportunity.

I began an icy Tuesday morning at a Quad meeting over breakfast. Genscher, Dumas, Hurd, and I all agreed that events were proceeding more quickly than we had expected, and that we should move ahead with Two-plus-Four that day. By making a public announcement, I felt, we could shift the debate from whether there would be unification to how fast and under what conditions German unity would occur. With a statement, no one would be able to retreat. Bob Zoellick was asked to prepare a brief statement. He did so in just three handwritten sentences:

> The Foreign Ministers of (list 6) had talks in Ottawa. They agreed that shortly after the March 18 elections in the GDR, the Ministers of the two German states would meet with (list 4) to discuss external aspects of German unification. Preliminary exchanges at the official level will begin shortly.

Genscher asked us to change the end of the second sentence to read "the external aspects of *the establishment* of German *unity.*" That change made it explicit that this forum would end up endorsing, not delaying, unification. Hurd, Dumas, and I readily agreed, and the four of us decided that I would approach Shevardnadze during the Open Skies session later that morning.

Once I got to the conference center, I asked Shevardnadze for a pull-aside meeting. With only his interpreter, Pavel Palazchenko, and my interpreter, Peter Afanasenko, present, I previewed with him the final statement we wanted to issue. He told me he would call Gorbachev immediately and get back to me as soon as he had an answer. I sensed a certain reluctance on Shevardnadze's part, probably from a realization that unification would lead to a political firestorm in Moscow, and this was most definitely an issue on which he did not want to be taking the lead.

Shortly before noon, Shevardnadze invited me to a small meeting room off the conference hall. If we could make two changes, Gorbachev would agree to the Two-plus-Four statement. First, he wanted to delete the reference to the GDR election. Since everyone assumed that the election would ratify a pro-unification government, Gorbachev didn't want it emphasized. I believed also that Gorbachev wanted some flexibility to hold a meeting of the Two-plus-Four before the elections. Given that any meeting would require the assent of all six, I wasn't concerned, because I felt we could veto any proposed meeting just by working with Bonn, London, and Paris, and agreeing not to show up. Second, Moscow wanted to add a phrase referring to the "issue of security of neighboring states." My hunch was that this phrase probably came from Shevardnadze, not Gorbachev, and was an effort on his part to both use and court the Poles. I had the distinct impression that he hoped to use Warsaw's concerns at least to delay Two-plus-Four, and if that failed, he seemed intent on becoming the leading advocate of the Polish border question among the Four Powers. That question would have to be resolved in any unification process, so I had little problem with this change. A less benign interpretation was that this was Moscow's way to blur the lines between a Two-plus-Four forum and CSCE conference, but since no other states were named as participants, this change didn't concern me. I told Shevardnadze that I would have to talk to Genscher, Hurd, and Dumas, but that I would get back to him soon.

Before I could leave, however, he told me that Gorbachev had a new counteroffer on President Bush's CFE manpower initiative. In his State of the Union address two weeks before, the President had proposed cutting U.S. and Soviet troops to 195,000 in what was defined as the CFE "Central Zone." The main thrust of this proposal would be to equalize troop levels in Central Europe, while allowing the United States an advantage elsewhere in Europe. Since the Soviets stationed troops on foreign territory only in the Central Zone, and we planned to have 30,000 additional troops in the rest of Europe, the practical effect would be to reverse a central reality of the Cold War (namely, turning a Soviet advantage in conventional forces into a disadvantage). In Moscow, Gorbachev had told me that he would offer to reduce to an equal limit of either 195,000 or 225,000 for *all of Europe.* In short, he had been willing to go to lower levels of forces, but he did not want to allow the United States to have an advantage.

Shevardnadze told me that Gorbachev, having thought about it over the weekend, was now willing to agree to the equal levels of 195,000 troops in the Central Zone, provided that the United States put its plans to station an additional 30,000 troops elsewhere in Europe in legally binding language in the treaty. I was stunned. After our discussions in Moscow, I had assumed Gorbachev would need more time on CFE, but apparently he felt emboldened by his victories in the Party Plenum and wanted to maintain the momentum of U.S.-Soviet relations.

To ensure there would be no misunderstanding, I asked Shevardnadze, "Are you agreeing there will be an asymmetry in our respective forces in Europe?" Eduard responded, and Pavel began the interpretation. "That's not what he said," interjected Dennis Ross. (Our meeting had been arranged so hurriedly that Peter Afanasenko hadn't been able to get back to the conference hall in time.) Ross, whose spoken Russian was rusty at best, had caught a critical confusion in Pavel's usually errorless translation. Pavel conferred with Shevardnadze briefly and then told me, "There will be symmetry in the Central Zone, but, yes, there will be an asymmetry in the rest of Europe."

I returned to the plenary feeling that the momentum was on our side. We had the opportunity to close out one of the most critical issues in conventional arms control and get the diplomatic process of German unification into a forum that played to our strengths. I asked Phil Zelikow, the NSC staffer on the trip, to put together a short statement, approved his handwritten version on the spot, and asked him to check it with Jim Woolsey, our CFE negotiator. Reggie Bartholomew, the Under Secretary for International Security Affairs and head of our arms control team, and Ron Lehman, the Director of the Arms Control and Disarmament Agency, looked at it as well. I also asked them to check with Washington, to make sure no one there had any problems with it. (It turned out that some in Washington had problems with putting the language into the treaty—as opposed to just a unilateral commitment which had been the President's proposal. But these were ironed out in time for Joe Clark to announce the agreement at 6:00 P.M. that day.) All of us were delighted with this breakthrough. For the first time since World War II, Moscow was going to have fewer troops in Europe than the United States and, moreover, the Soviet limits would be set forth in a verifiable and legally binding treaty.

I left the conference center for my hotel room, arriving there shortly after noon. My first task was to brief the President on where things stood. I got both President Bush and Brent Scowcroft on the line and began explaining the Two-plus-Four statement.

Brent was less than enthusiastic. "I'm not sure this is a good idea. We're moving too fast," he said.

"It's too late for that," I replied. "Everybody has agreed to this."

"Kohl hasn't," interjected Scowcroft.

"Jim, are you sure Kohl accepts this?" the President asked.

"Genscher wouldn't be doing this if he didn't have Kohl with him," I said.

"Well, I talked to Teltschik, and I'm not sure the chancellery is on board," Brent said. Horst Teltschik was Kohl's personal national security adviser, and he and Genscher did not get along.

"We really need to make sure Kohl agrees with this," concluded the President.

"All right," I said, "I will check with Genscher." I knew we had to issue the statement then. Any delay would allow opposition to form in Moscow, London, Paris, or other capitals and resurrect any one of the host of ill-advised fora that had been circulating in diplomatic circles. From the standpoint of public diplomacy, the statement would make it explicit that the

Two-plus-Four would be working toward German unity, and that would change the baseline for future negotiations and prevent any Soviet backtracking.

Convinced that the President and Brent had misunderstood Kohl's position, I asked Genscher to come to my room. "Hans-Dietrich, the White House is not certain that the Chancellery supports Two-plus-Four." "Why, that's not correct," Genscher replied. "I will call the Chancellor." "Fine," I said, "and then ask him to confirm his concurrence with President Bush."

He borrowed the phone in my bedroom to make a private call to Kohl. After a few minutes, he came into the living room and told me, "There's no problem. Kohl's completely on board and is calling Bush right now." We decided that Genscher would call Kohl again in a few minutes to ensure the two leaders connected. Meanwhile, I waited and listened as Genscher told us how emotional unification had become. "You know I was born in what is now East Germany, and I'm going back Friday to give a speech in my hometown. They're naming my old high school after me: The Hans-Dietrich Genscher High School. My old teachers would faint to think that the school was being named after me!" He went on to tell us how East German troops were showing up and asking for jobs in the Bundeswehr, and how the rolls of the East German military were replete with troops who had reported in sick but who had already defected. "The people just keep coming," he said, reminding me once again that events on the ground were moving and we needed to keep up. Finally, he called Kohl back and confirmed that the Chancellor had talked to President Bush and had assured him that he, too, was in favor of Two-plus-Four.

I called the President and Brent back. "Did you speak with Kohl?" I asked. The President said he had, but Kohl hadn't clearly backed Two-plus-Four and hadn't mentioned his support for the statement.

"Kohl and Genscher talked," I said. "I *know* Kohl's on board. You need to call him back," I told the President. I also asked Genscher to call Kohl again to warn him that Bush would be calling back.

Around 3:15 P.M., the President called me back. "I called Kohl. He's okay with Two-plus-Four. Go ahead."

Later, I found out what had caused the confusion. In Kohl's first call to the President at 1:49 P.M. that afternoon, the Chancellor hadn't been clear in his support of Two-plus-Four. Referring to his meetings with Gorbachev in Moscow, he told the President, "We also discussed the same points Jim Baker had been discussing, that the two German states should be working together with the Four Powers—the U.S., the U.K., France, and the USSR. I was informed by Hans-Dietrich Genscher, who called me from Ottawa an hour ago, that the foreign ministers are discussing the same things." In the President's call to Kohl at 3:01 P.M., Kohl made his support explicit.

"George," he began, "I have a feeling there is a misunderstanding. I'm in agreement with what the foreign ministers are talking about in Ottawa." He also told the President, "I worry if this question remains open. Then we may find ourselves in a situation again where others in the East and the West want to join up with the Four. Then we will have a big problem."

Having finally received a clear green light from our capitals, Genscher and I decided to go ahead and issue the Two-plus-Four statement. We didn't want to give anyone time for any more second thoughts. While we were waiting on Chancellor Kohl and President Bush, I had phoned Hurd and Dumas, and received their go-ahead for Shevardnadze's fixes to the statement. In the second sentence, we deleted the phrase "shortly after the March 18 elections in the German Democratic Republic," and we inserted the phrase "including the issues of security of the neighboring states" at its end.*

We went ahead and posed for the requisite photograph of the six ministers upstairs in the room I had been using for bilaterals. The scene was completely chaotic until Kim Hoggard, always cool under pressure, physically cleared out the extra security guards and hangers-on, in the process adjusting Douglas Hurd's collar, which was out of kilter.

During all the back and forth about whether Kohl had really approved of what we were doing, it became obvious to me that NSC staff were not only opposed to Two-plus-Four, but working on the President to decline to approve it, even though I'd convinced London, Paris, and Moscow to go along, and the Germans, too, were on board.

I felt I had fully explained Two-plus-Four even before leaving Washington. I had given the President the Policy Planning Staff paper that outlined the mechanics on January 31, and Zoellick had consulted extensively with Bob Blackwill, the Special Assistant to the President for European Affairs. Moreover, the White House had cleared the letter I sent Kohl from Moscow that made a pitch for this formula.

So before I went back downstairs to the conference, I made my third call of the day to the President from my suite, and this time I made sure it was just the two of us on the line. "We had a good day here," I said. "In fact, this was an historic achievement. But, frankly, it was more difficult than it had to be, just because some there were biased against the Two-plus-

---

*The final statement read: "The Foreign Ministers of the Federal Republic of Germany, the German Democratic Republic, France, the United Kingdom, the Soviet Union, and the United States had talks in Ottawa. They agreed that the Foreign Ministers of the Federal Republic of Germany and the German Democratic Republic would meet with the Foreign Ministers of France, the United Kingdom, the Soviet Union, and the United States to discuss external aspects of the establishment of German unity, including the issues of security of the neighboring states. Preliminary discussions at the official level will begin shortly."

Four idea." George Bush was his usual magnanimous self and told me he understood my point. I'm confident that he feels now as I do that the way we handled German unification was one of the major foreign policy accomplishments of his presidency.

I then went back downstairs to join a NATO caucus that had been going on for some time. The meeting was tense. None of the other ministers had been privy to the discussions leading up to the Two-plus-Four, and to top it off, they had heard about it from journalists before Genscher, Hurd, Dumas, or I could make it back to the conference center to brief them about it. The allies were upset that they had not been consulted. "We have worked together within the Alliance for forty years," De Michelis said. Hans Van Den Broek echoed that complaint, as did the representatives from Luxembourg, Norway, Belgium, Spain, and Canada.*

We tried to let them down gently by pointing out that the Four Powers had legal rights that had to be taken into consideration. But given the hassle we had gone through in getting the statement, Genscher was in no mood for nit-picking. As he brusquely shut down De Michelis, Joe Clark gaveled the meeting to a close.

That night, as we waited for the press to file their stories, I thought to myself: If it's this hard just to get agreement on who is in the game, what's the game going to be like when we start playing with substantive issues?

---

*The allies then pointed out that they didn't like the language on "the issues of security of the neighboring states," because it implied the Two-plus-Four might discuss issues involving their security without them and they were concerned with Soviet meddling. They wanted a "where appropriate" inserted before "issues," so they could issue unilateral statements that made it clear *their* security was not an appropriate subject for this forum. I told them that change was impossible since the statement had already been released in English to the press. But we agreed that Joe Clark could announce publicly that "neighboring states" did not refer to any members of NATO, and the allies asked if I could talk to Shevardnadze about removing from the Russian-language version the "the's" from before "issues" and "neighboring," since each "the" could be interpreted to mean "all." I left the caucus and found Shevardnadze. "Some of the allies want a small fix in the statement. Can you remove the 'the's' in the phrase we added at your request concerning neighboring states?" I asked. "That'll be easy," he said, smiling. "We don't have definite articles in Russian, so they won't be in our statement anyway."

CHAPTER 13

AFRICA: THE END OF APARTHEID

. . . I've studied his speeches. They have a ring of honesty. I feel I am dealing with a man of integrity. But all the pillars of apartheid are still in existence.
—Nelson Mandela on F.W. de Klerk to Secretary Baker, March 21, 1990

For as long as I can remember, I've been an ardent hunter. My father was responsible for instilling in me a love of the outdoors and for nurturing a lifelong avocation that has provided me with many rewarding moments. When I was six years old, he took me out with him on duck-hunting trips. He saw it as a way for a father and son to spend good time together. He was right about that; some of our very best moments were spent in duck blinds. In due course I graduated to hunting other types of game, and by the time I was fourteen, he'd decided I was proficient enough to accompany him on an elk-hunting expedition to Wyoming. It was during that trip in the summer of 1944 that I developed the strong affection for Wyoming that led me to acquire a ranch there in 1988.

Like most avid hunters, I'd always wanted to pursue big game in Africa, and in 1974, I finally got my chance. Susan and I decided to spend a delayed honeymoon on safari, and we spent a magnificent three weeks in Botswana, a relatively stable country with a small population, little development, and large expanses of trackless wilderness in the southern part of the continent. Because of their sublime beauty and relative rarity, the big cats—lions, leopards, and cheetahs—had no interest for me. However, I did hunt the antelope family, including kudu, impala, lechwe, sable antelope, and sitatunga, a marsh antelope.

Of all the animals I hunted on that trip, however, none was more thrilling than the Cape buffalo, because of its unpredictable nature—a nature I experienced the hard way. One afternoon, we suddenly came upon a buffalo that had been wounded by a lion, and without warning, it charged us from a dangerously short distance away. My hunter quickly raised his gun, shot the animal on the run squarely between the eyes, and dropped him a scant seven yards away from me. It happened so quickly that I never even got my gun to my shoulder. The experts always say you should never venture into the African bush without an experienced hunter. That afternoon made a believer of me.

I was ambivalent about shooting elephants, however. I'd bought an elephant license, because friends had told me the ivory tusks alone would cover almost one-half the entire cost of our safari, but even though my hunter put me on several nice bulls that I could easily have killed, I just couldn't bring myself to do it.*

We literally blazed trails on that adventure. We were the first ever to hunt in that particular area, which had just been opened to hunting by the Botswanan government. The terrain was so unspoiled that we had to mark trees every day just to find our way back to camp at night.

Thus, it was with special emotion that, sixteen years later, I would return to a southern Africa where new political trails were being blazed. Historically, the continent had been a pawn on the East-West chessboard. For more than a generation, U.S. policy toward Africa had been driven by our competition with the Soviet Union, but with the end of the Cold War and the rise of Mikhail Gorbachev, new opportunities had materialized to clear away some of the regional underbrush from the U.S.-Soviet relationship. As a result, independence was fast becoming reality in Namibia, and in Angola, a decade of superpower confrontation was showing signs of terminal fatigue.

As tensions eased in those parts of the continent, however, the threat of conflagration flourished in South Africa, where the festering sore of apartheid persisted. As I prepared to become Secretary of State, I remember thinking that while apartheid was a policy of such abiding repugnance throughout the civilized world that it would be dismantled sooner rather than later, it was also such an emotional and fractious issue that its demise

---

*In June of 1989, as Secretary of State, I recommended that President Bush announce a unilateral U.S. ban on the importation of ivory. This initiative paved the way for the international ban that was agreed to at the October 1989 meeting of the Convention on International Trade in Endangered Species in Lausanne, Switzerland. I also urged the Department of Defense to provide surplus Army helicopters to Kenya to help in Dr. Richard Leakey's fight against elephant poachers. When prohibitive maintenance costs made that idea unfeasible, I directed that $2 million in Agency for International Development funds be given to the Kenyan Wildlife Service instead.

would most likely occur only through a bloodbath. In a country of surpassing beauty, where violence had become commonplace and threatened to explode in racial holocaust, the challenge for American diplomacy was to fashion a policy that reduced the chances of such a catastrophic outcome.

Moving Beyond Constructive Engagement

Like Central America, South Africa had engendered bitter policy divisions in Congress and the American public during the 1980s. The Reagan administration had firmly opposed legislative sanctions against the white minority government in Pretoria, preferring instead a policy of "constructive engagement" in order to persuade the Afrikaners of the ruling National Party to end apartheid. After Congress passed the Comprehensive Anti-Apartheid Act (CAAA) in 1986, which imposed strong economic and diplomatic sanctions against South Africa, President Reagan vetoed the bill. Congress promptly overrode his veto—perhaps the most dramatic rebuff of presidential authority to conduct foreign policy during the Reagan years.

I believed it was time to find a bipartisan solution in order to get this divisive and emotional issue off the table. Like his predecessor, President Bush was opposed to sanctions, believed they were counterproductive, and preferred negotiation to isolation. I agreed with him. But I also agreed with his view that it was a moral issue as well. More than anything else, the American experience is defined by our belief in the equality of all people. Apartheid was simply indefensible to most Americans, and its survival would increase pressure on the new administration for even more stringent sanctions, which I believed would only inflame the domestic debate and harden attitudes in South Africa.

Within the State Department, South Africa was viewed as a foreign policy issue with major domestic implications. In the real world, I believed it was more of a domestic civil-rights issue in an overseas venue. A successful policy would need to address both perspectives aggressively.

It was obvious, however, that neither constructive engagement with Pretoria nor congressional sanctions had solved the core problem. "I think we all ought to be candid enough to recognize the sanctions we have imposed have not produced the desired results," I said during my confirmation hearings. "[They] have not weakened the resolve of the Afrikaners. They have not increased black bargaining power. White voters have shifted to the right, and repression has intensified." The euphoric predictions of anti-apartheid militants that the regime was on its last legs had proven hopelessly naive. Government oppression against blacks had become even more iron fisted, and the state of emergency imposed in 1985 was a permanent fixture of South African life. Privately, government officials acknowledged to American diplomats that a revolutionary climate now existed in South Africa. As the threat of wholesale violence escalated, it was time for a policy shift away from an evenhanded posture with Pretoria and the black opposition, in favor of one that strengthened the standing of the majority of white and black South Africans in the middle who supported negotiations.

U.S. policy remained officially under review through the first year of the Bush administration. In reality, however, a new approach toward resolving this conflict was defined during the spring of 1989. In reviewing existing policy, it was apparent to me that a widespread perception had developed in both the United States and South Africa—both sides felt that past administrations had failed to establish meaningful contacts at the presidential level with credible black South African leaders. "I believe that one of your first acts with regard to South Africa should be to rectify this omission," I wrote in a memorandum to the President dated May 2, 1989.*

I recommended that he invite Albertina Sisulu to meet with him at the White House. Mrs. Sisulu was the matriarch of one of black South Africa's leading political families. Her husband was serving a life sentence with Nelson Mandela and had been imprisoned since 1964. Her son, a former Nieman Fellow at Harvard, was one of the most widely respected members of a new generation of black leaders and had himself served two years in detention. Her militant but nonviolent leadership of the United Democratic Front, the premier anti-apartheid movement in the country, made her the perfect choice to signal the President's decision to reach out to moderate black leaders—and to send a powerful message to the South African government that President Bush was not neutral when it came to apartheid, and that more would be required of Pretoria before he would recommend lifting U.S. sanctions.

I knew that the South African government would be sensitive to any perception that we were accentuating high-level contacts with the opposition, and might well balk at issuing Mrs. Sisulu a passport. This obstacle could be overcome, I suggested, by issuing a quiet invitation to F. W. de Klerk to meet with me during a private visit to the United States he planned to make before his likely election as state president later in September.

"While a meeting with you would be inappropriate at this stage," I noted, "we believe de Klerk would be satisfied if he were received at the State Department." Even without a Presidential meeting, de Klerk would

---

*In 1984, President Reagan had met with Desmond Tutu, the Anglican archbishop of South Africa. The meeting accomplished nothing; Tutu lectured the President on the errors of American policy and then trashed both the President and our policy with reporters in the driveway of the West Wing. President Reagan, who had not wanted to meet with Tutu in the first place, displayed his ever-present sense of humor the next day when reporters asked him how the meeting had gone with Tutu. Without batting an eye, the President said: "So-so."

be the first major South African leader to visit the United States in the forty-one years since apartheid had been instituted.

Predictably, the South Africans were not at all pleased about the Sisulu invitation. After being told about it by Ed Perkins, the U.S. Ambassador to Pretoria, they requested that de Klerk also be allowed to meet with the President. Perkins bluntly replied that the reforms of the outgoing government of ailing P. W. Botha, while substantial, weren't sufficient to warrant a presidential invitation for de Klerk. Our policy took the form of a classic carrot-and-stick strategy: by having the President meet with moderate black leaders, we intended to push the Afrikaners toward greater and swifter reform, which could result in what they wanted most of all—an end to U.S. sanctions.

Laying Down a New Marker

On May 27, I met with South African Foreign Minister R. F. "Pik" Botha in Rome while accompanying the President on his trip to Italy, Belgium, and Germany. Our meeting was the first high-level contact with South Africa in the Bush administration. By South African standards, Botha was almost a liberal. He was immensely popular with his Johannesburg constituency, which made it easier for him to punch away at the government to ease the policy of apartheid. He was a gregarious, swashbuckling, flamboyant sort—Hank Cohen, the Assistant Secretary for African Affairs, liked to describe him as the Huey Long of South African politics—but he had also been invaluable in helping Cohen's predecessor, Chester Crocker, broker the deal for Namibian independence. I liked him.

It was a friendly but correct meeting. I told Botha that while the administration was opposed to additional economic sanctions against South Africa, the President's opposition to apartheid was uncompromising. While progress had been made toward reform, I acknowledged, "fundamental changes are required before any normalization of our relations is possible." I pressed him to lift the state of emergency, relax censorship and political restrictions, and most important, release Nelson Mandela. "This would help us argue that further sanctions are counterproductive," I said.

Botha was defensive and complained that his government's commitment to ending apartheid had been essentially ignored by the West. He appealed for assistance, not ostracism, likening the situation to that of Mikhail Gorbachev, "who is also in trouble for trying to change his country." The previous U.S. administration had never recognized that South Africa was changing for the better, he stated. "My government has the impression that your government will be satisfied with nothing less than handing South Africa over to a mass which will run the country down," he said.

"There is no understanding of the complexities of this situation." The government, he assured me, would have more flexibility for moving ahead with reforms after the elections.

The matter of Mandela's release was being actively considered by the Cabinet, he added. Botha said that he and several other leaders favored Mandela's release, but the security forces were adamantly opposed. "Mandela himself does not want to be released at the moment," he told me. "He has serious difficulties with his wife and some ANC leaders to resolve first."

The invitation to Mrs. Sisulu had plainly struck a nerve with Pretoria, particularly since it was paired with the invitation for de Klerk. "An impression of linkage has been created" that was not helpful, he said. I told him as benignly as I could that the United States intended to reach out to blacks and whites, and that it was important his government grant Mrs. Sisulu a visa to travel to Washington. Botha volunteered to be helpful. He gave me the distinct impression that he could be considerably *more* helpful if de Klerk were invited to meet with President Bush instead of me. I gave him no encouragement on this score.

"We're sensitive to your domestic political concerns," I countered. "We ask that you take ours into consideration also. We should not force the pace of our bilateral relationship. You must also understand that this is not just a foreign policy issue, but a moral and serious domestic political issue in the United States. We believe apartheid is immoral." "I can assure you," Botha insisted, "that we have decided to get rid of apartheid."

I was somewhat dubious, but I nevertheless came away from this meeting with Botha believing that new winds were blowing in South Africa, and that once de Klerk got past the elections, he might well accelerate the pace of reforms. That pace was absolutely critical to convincing U.S. public opinion, and particularly the Congress, that the death rattle of apartheid was beginning to be heard throughout the veld and the townships of that fractured nation. It was therefore important to keep the pressure on the government to follow through on the promises de Klerk was making.

Over the next few months, mixed signals emanated from Pretoria. On June 8, twelve days after my meeting with Pik Botha, the state of emergency was renewed indefinitely by the government. Nevertheless, Albertina Sisulu was granted a travel visa, and met with President Bush at the White House on June 30. Five days later, P. W. Botha met with Mandela in prison to discuss terms for his eventual release.

Rescinding a Controversial Invitation

The decision to invite de Klerk to meet with me had been a subject of some controversy within the department. Hank Cohen and the African bureau had supported the idea strongly, and argued that my meeting with de Klerk should be upgraded to include the President. But Dennis Ross and Bob Zoellick were dubious. On June 12, they sent me a carefully worded five-page memorandum that laid out the case against a presidential meeting. "The positive impression that Mrs. Sisulu's meeting with the President is certain to create domestically and among democratic forces in South Africa would likely be undercut if the de Klerk visit does not have some hard news about the prospects for reform and the U.S. role in this process," they argued.

Pik Botha had told me in Rome that, while de Klerk wanted to visit Washington, he was in a delicate position. Not yet in power and therefore lacking a mandate for reform, he could not risk being perceived at home as giving private assurances to Washington in advance of the election. Given this reality, Ross and Zoellick believed that a visit guaranteed to create no results might actually weaken U.S. policy.

To make de Klerk accountable, they suggested, a presidential visit could be made conditional: de Klerk would have to give a private assurance that within six months of assuming office, he would release Mandela and terminate the state of emergency.

"Our failure to take a strong position could damage the President's credibility," they cautioned.

I thought the arguments pro and con made the issue a close call, so I directed Cohen to meet with de Klerk and ask point-blank if he was prepared privately, with the President, to lay out his plans for ending apartheid. In a meeting in Durban, de Klerk told Cohen, "I have no apologies for apartheid, but over the years I've come to feel it's become unworkable. Unless we bring blacks in as full partners, my country won't be fit for my grandchild." He was prepared to move dramatically in early 1990, de Klerk said, and he *would* lay out his blueprint for the President. "I am going to dismantle apartheid and bring about full democracy through negotiations as soon as possible," he told Cohen. "But I cannot go public with this," he reiterated. "We can't be seen as taking orders from the Americans." He declined to disclose specific reforms, but said he understood that he would be expected to assure the President that "important, visible actions" toward ending apartheid would occur in the first six months after he took power.

Based on this conversation, Cohen recommended that the President meet with de Klerk. "It would be a shame to deal ourselves out of the game just when the situation in South Africa is beginning to develop some fluidity," Cohen cabled from Libreville, Gabon, on July 6. "I believe de Klerk's visit would be worth the domestic risk."

I subsequently raised this matter privately with the President. Ultimately, we decided that given the emotionally charged nature of the political debate at home, secret assurances from de Klerk weren't sufficient. A meeting without visible progress that could be announced would surely inflame the anti-apartheid opposition and lend impetus to the drive for more sanctions. The President concluded that he shouldn't see de Klerk unless Mandela were released before the meeting—which we knew was an impossible condition for de Klerk to fulfill until *after* his election. After being informed that it was impossible to see the President, de Klerk canceled his visit to Washington. Pik Botha took the characteristically statesmanlike high road, and announced simply that, given the intense opposition in Congress, his government didn't want to create difficulties for President Bush. The day before, more than 100 members of Congress had urged the President not to meet with de Klerk.

Back to a New Africa

By late 1989, however, even many skeptics had been forced to concede that a new order was taking root in South Africa. On October 15, less than a month after de Klerk was sworn in as state President on September 20, Walter Sisulu and seven ANC colleagues were released from prison. On November 16, de Klerk ordered the desegregation of all beaches. A week later, the last contingent of South African troops withdrew from Namibia, after an occupation of seventy-five years. On December 13, de Klerk met with Mandela in Cape Town to discuss issues of black-white power sharing. On February 2, 1990, de Klerk legalized the ANC and other anti-apartheid political parties. And on February 11, Nelson Mandela was released from incarceration after twenty-seven years.

When I'd met Pik Botha in Rome, he'd told me de Klerk would run for state president on a platform of abolishing apartheid. I hadn't been sure whether to believe him. By now, however, de Klerk had persuaded me. Without question, much remained to be done, but the climate had changed so dramatically that I believed it was now possible to visit both sides in the region in hopes of encouraging further reform. There were many South Africans to the right of de Klerk and to the left of Mandela who were still hostile to compromise. I knew that ceremonies marking the independence of Namibia were coming up soon. I decided to use the occasion to meet with Mandela and de Klerk to strengthen the hand of those in the middle who were committed to moving forward. On March 13, the White House announced that I would meet with Mandela in Windhoek, Namibia, on March 21, and then with de Klerk in Cape Town the following day. I would be the first Secretary of State to visit South Africa since 1978.

Before leaving for Africa, I conducted a series of meetings with congressional leaders and with members of TransAfrica, the African-American group that was fervently committed to ending apartheid. Their representatives included the Reverend Jesse Jackson and Coretta Scott King. Although some of them had problems with my meeting de Klerk, it was a powerful testament to the progress being made that none of my interlocutors objected to my setting foot in South Africa.

After refueling stops in French Guiana and Ascension Island in the Atlantic Ocean, I arrived in Windhoek early in the evening of March 19. As I deplaned, I couldn't miss a huge sign that read Welcome to the Republic of Namibia. With the December 1988 agreement by which Cuba agreed to withdraw its troops from Angola, and South Africa pledged to do the same in Namibia, the independence of Namibia effectively marked the end of colonialism in Africa. In concert with several of our allies, this achievement had been the product of effective American diplomacy led by my predecessor George Shultz and by Chet Crocker, whom I invited to be part of the American delegation to the independence ceremonies.

Making History with Mandela and de Klerk

The Namibian independence ceremonies were attended by representatives of 164 countries, so I took the opportunity to arrange bilateral meetings with eleven world leaders, including President Mubarak of Egypt and Eduard Shevardnadze. I also met with Angolan President Jose Eduardo dos Santos, making the point that a military victory over U.S.-backed UNITA forces was impossible and urging him to begin peace talks. After a morning meeting on March 21 with Hans-Dietrich Genscher at the palatial home built for the German Ambassador when Namibia had been the German protectorate known as South West Africa, I returned to my residence to prepare for my meeting with Nelson Mandela. Five minutes before he was to arrive, however, Mandela sent an aide to ask if I could come to him instead. Glad to comply, I arrived at the house where he was staying just as Shevardnadze's gold Mercedes-Benz limousine was driving away. Mandela and his wife Winnie greeted me in the driveway and ushered me inside, where several of his ANC colleagues had assembled. "It's an honor to be here," I began, and I really meant it.

Mandela is a man of great dignity, soft-spoken and reserved. He impressed me as an individual of strong character and conviction. The stoicism born of twenty-seven years of unjust confinement may have tempered his rhetoric, but there was no doubting his determination to complete the revolution that had consumed his adult life. Neither was there any doubt who was in charge: none of his colleagues in the ANC uttered a word during our meeting. He had great stature and presence as an interlocutor.

He began by reiterating that the ANC was opposed to violence and had dropped its insistence that the end of apartheid was a precondition for negotiations. "It is unrealistic to expect the government to dismantle the system overnight," he said. "It needs some time to phase it out.

"I've talked twice to Mr. de Klerk and I've studied his speeches," he added. "They have a ring of honesty. I feel I am dealing with a man of integrity. But all the pillars of apartheid are still in existence. That is why we are asking to intensify sanctions."

I was disappointed to learn that he was still clinging to long-discredited socialist economic theories. When I talked about the importance of free markets, he'd counter with the need for nationalization of industry. "It's important to redistribute wealth to give people whom apartheid has denied a chance," he argued.*

The only discordant note in a very friendly meeting was his unhappiness over my meeting with de Klerk the next afternoon. "One cannot base the approach to South Africa on one man," he argued. "You should not be offering him greater legitimacy through high-level visits until we see more change in his party and the system." I was a little surprised that he seemed to have already discounted his own release from prison only five weeks earlier. I replied that the United States would maintain its sanctions until the state of emergency was ended and all political prisoners released. From a tactical standpoint, however, I suggested to Mandela that de Klerk's courage argued for trying to bolster him symbolically. "Positive steps are likely to encourage further steps," I suggested.

It was a good meeting more for its tone and form than for its substance. Mandela was rushed but gracious throughout. "He's a natural-born politician, knowing how to play to his constituency, but clearly being pragmatic and level-headed at the same time," I cabled the President. "So long as he retains his moral authority, there may be hope for progress in South Africa."

The next morning, I left Windhoek for the two-hour flight to Cape Town, South Africa, which I'd visited on my honeymoon on the way to Botswana. I had forgotten just how breathtakingly beautiful a place it is, a verdant city with a stunning harbor encircled by majestic mountains.

By symbolic design, my first meeting in South Africa was with black leaders. Many of them were in their seventies and had been imprisoned for as long as twenty-five years. "We will continue to keep the pressure on the government," I pledged, "but we will also recognize positive changes and

---

*During his meeting with President Bush in December 1991, Mandela returned to this shop-worn theme. I told him flatly that even a partial nationalization of South African industry would deal a body blow to prospects for foreign investment. I also told him that American corporate executives in particular would avoid investing in South Africa. I was pleased to learn that by the time he returned home, Mandela had stopped talking about nationalizing his industry.

provide incentives to keep it moving in the right direction." I was struck by their calls for peaceful change and by their concerns about the black-on-black violence in the townships. It was a moving experience to be with these people, and their quiet eloquence and absence of recrimination was an inspiration to all of us.

After lunch with Pik Botha, I met with de Klerk at Tuynhuys, the former official residence of the governors of what was founded as the Cape Colony. He struck me as a sincere, honest man, exceedingly friendly, who smoked with a Rooseveltian cigarette holder.

I began by lauding his political courage in making good on his agenda, and pledging that the United States would "help you maintain the dynamic change you have set in motion." The sanctions mandated by the CAAA were quite specific, I reminded him, and would not be lifted until apartheid was dismantled. "But we *are* considering how to exercise our discretion as circumstances allow," I added.

At the same time, I pressed de Klerk hard on lifting the state of emergency, particularly because it was such a symbol of practices abhorrent to democratic principles. He wondered why his government was being given so little credit for the changes already implemented. "The state of emergency is now strictly an instrument for maintaining law and order," he said. "Perception shapes reality, Mr. President," I replied. "And the perception of the state of emergency is that it violates basic human rights." The way to gain the high moral and political ground, I suggested, was to lift the state of emergency and at the same time call on black leaders to exercise the very authority they were seeking by helping to stop the violence and to restore order to the townships. De Klerk seemed to be taken with this argument.

I came away convinced that the South African government was committed to the process of change, anxious to move quickly and determined to pursue it to its conclusion. A lawyer by training, de Klerk seemed to see his mission as one of devising a practical solution for the cancer of apartheid. Clearly, he understood that the future of South African whites depended upon a political solution reached through negotiations.

De Klerk ended our meeting with a powerful statement of purpose. "We are on a ship that cannot and should not be turned around," he said. "The process we have begun is irreversible. We will follow it to its logical conclusion." Then he asked to see me alone. These "pull-asides" are a staple of diplomacy, a device where matters of extreme sensitivity can be conveyed from principal to principal in an utterly discreet fashion.

"I'm going to be the last white President of South Africa," he said in a voice brimming with conviction. Afterward, I mentioned de Klerk's prediction to Bill Swing, our ambassador, who assured me that de Klerk was a man of his word.

My meetings with Mandela and de Klerk persuaded me that the winds of change were indeed finally sweeping both the anti-apartheid opposition and the de Klerk government, to the point where the rest of the world might well be lagging behind in recognizing their potential. For all the rhetoric, and despite pressure from radicals on the left and right, I sensed that the balance of power on both sides rested with practical moderates who recognized the core political reality: each side needed to offer concessions so the other could reassure their constituencies they were delivering. Two consummate balancers were now dealing directly with one another, which I believed augured well for future progress.

"While the political pressures may be difficult on each side," I cabled the President that evening, "both revealed seriousness and commitment today. If intelligence and determination are the prerequisites for success, we may really have a chance to make headway."

After meetings with black leaders in Johannesburg, I flew to Kinshasa, Zaire, for meetings on Angola with President Mobutu Sese Seko and UNITA leader Jonas Savimbi. I told Savimbi about my conversation with dos Santos at Windhoek, and urged him to accept peace talks despite his temporary military advantage. I arrived back in Washington just after midnight on March 25, and subsequently recommended to the President that we purposely avoid pushing de Klerk for more change. My hope was to avoid anything that could inflame the extremists on both sides. Left to their own devices, I believed that de Klerk and Mandela possessed the political leverage and, more important, the personal and political courage to make progress toward a peaceful resolution of differences.

The Winds of Peace

The rest, as they say, is history—literally. On June 8, de Klerk lifted the state of emergency, except for Natal province. Later that month, Mandela began a world tour and met with President Bush in Washington on June 24. On August 6, the ANC formally ended its policy of armed struggle against the government. On October 18, the state of emergency in Natal was ended.

On July 11, 1991, citing "profound and irreversible" change by the white minority government, President Bush lifted U.S. sanctions against South Africa. Pretoria was now on an irrevocable course toward the nonracial, multiparty democracy the United States had sought for decades.

And, finally, on May 10, 1994, Nelson Mandela was sworn in as President of the country that had sent him to jail for more than a third of his life. F.W. de Klerk became Mandela's Vice President. It was a moment I'd not expected to see in my lifetime, and one in its own way as dramatic and exhilarating as the collapse of communism in Eastern Europe. After nearly a half-century of bigotry and oppression, profound revolutionary changes were at last sweeping through South Africa. And the peaceful nature of these remarkable developments had been assisted and encouraged by steady and measured American diplomacy.

CHAPTER 14

SPRING OF TUMULT:

GERMAN UNIFICATION, LITHUANIAN

INDEPENDENCE, AND SOVIET UPHEAVAL

This is the question of questions.   —*Eduard Shevardnadze, February 10, 1990*

We are going to win the game, but we must be clever while we are doing it.
    —*President Bush to Chancellor Kohl, February 25, 1990*

T en days after the February 14 Ottawa announcement of Two-plus-Four, and only weeks before my trip to Africa, Helmut Kohl arrived in Washington for a weekend of talks with President Bush. In the relaxed setting of Camp David, there was only one real topic and one fundamental issue: German unification—and what it meant for NATO.

"Germany doesn't want neutrality in any way," Kohl assured us. "This would be a deadly decision. There is no serious interest in it. A united Germany will be a member of NATO."

The President was still concerned about Moscow, however. "They're saying that Germany must not stay in NATO. To hell with that. We prevailed, and they didn't. We can't let the Soviets snatch victory from the jaws of defeat."

With the Two-plus-Four announcement, Moscow had implicitly admitted that German unification was an impending reality, but the circumstances of that event were still murky, and the Kremlin had been weighing in. Just five days before, Gorbachev had told *Pravda*, "The unification of Germany concerns not only the Germans. . . . There are fundamental things which the international community has a right to know and upon which there must be no room for ambiguity." With regard to NATO and the Warsaw Pact, reunification "must take place with due consideration . . . that violation of the military-strategic balance of these two international organizations is impermissible. Here, there must be complete clarity." The Soviet hard line remained intact: no united Germany in NATO.

Kohl was confident, however. "The Soviets are negotiating. But this may end up as a matter of cash. They need money. . . . There will be security concerns for the Soviets if Germany remains in NATO. And they will want to get something in return."

"You've got deep pockets," the President observed, not altogether kiddingly.

The Chancellor predicted that Moscow would come around by the time of the U.S.-Soviet Summit that was scheduled for the end of May. "I have a feeling that will be Gorbachev's approach. . . . He wants to make a deal with the other superpower," he guessed. "The central question is the membership of Germany in NATO. In the end, Gorbachev will make that concession to the President of the United States."

"What will he need to make that deal?" President Bush asked.

"Two things," I volunteered. "First, Gorbachev needs to know that Germany remains steadfast behind full NATO membership. Second, he will want to see that legitimate Soviet security interests are being taken into account."

Kohl's blunt commitments took care of the first condition, but the second was an entirely different matter. I knew that ensuring a unified Germany in NATO would require every ounce of our skills in the months to come, and indeed much of that time—in locations as varied as Windhoek, Namibia, and Turnberry, Scotland—was consumed with two tasks. Both were primarily psychological, one oriented toward the Kremlin, the other toward the international environment. The first was to play my part in convincing Gorbachev and Shevardnadze that a united Germany in NATO would not compromise Soviet security and, indeed, could enhance it. This would require assuaging over a generation's worth of Soviet pain. I had seen the war memorials and knew the issue struck deep chords in the Soviet people. Moreover, it was complicated by the increasingly polarized internal politics of the USSR: the reactionaries were counterattacking, the military was reasserting itself, and the dispute with Lithuania was threatening to turn violent. Lithuania was more than just an internal problem for Gorbachev; the Lithuanian struggle for independence resonated with the American people and with the Congress, and any attempt by Moscow to curb Vilnius would limit our room for maneuver on the broader U.S.-Soviet agenda.

The second task—to reshape the international environment by adapting NATO and strengthening CSCE—grew in part out of the first. I knew that Gorbachev and Shevardnadze needed arguments that they could use to combat their critics internally and to provide them the political cover they needed to make hard choices. That meant we had to work with our Western partners to adapt NATO and CSCE to make them appear less threatening to the Soviet people. But even aside from that, there was a broader question. A unified Germany would alter the fundamental geostrategic, political, and economic architecture of Europe. That meant that NATO had to become a more political institution, CSCE had to be strengthened, and a clear and complementary division of responsibilities among these institutions and the European Community would have to be defined. It was a big task.

February in Camp David:
Fixing the U.S.-German Position

At Camp David, Kohl was in an expansive mood. "If things go well, we will have enormous changes occurring in Europe, even if Gorbachev fails," he said. "His successor will have to pursue similar policies. This is an obligatory development in the Soviet Union. I told Gorbachev, 'You cannot go back to Stalin. There will be no Tiananmen Square in Europe,' I told him, 'not in Dresden, Budapest, or Warsaw.' The consequences of such an event would be beyond comprehension. Hitler killed people who listened to radio broadcasts, but now German TV programs can be seen in Kiev. The world has changed beyond recognition, and mass communication has been an important cause of these changes. I told Rakowski, the former Prime Minister of Poland, he and the Communists would be finished when the Pope visited his country. These changes are the reality in which we live."

The realities in the GDR were even starker. "Communism in the German Democratic Republic has collapsed like a house of cards," the Chancellor said. "It looked like a giant, but it was hollow." Now, in the largest leveraged buyout in history, West Germany was going to take over that hollow giant, and with Kohl, we focused on the two most contentious external issues: the Polish border and Germany's alliance membership.

Three days before the Kohl meeting, Polish Prime Minister Tadeusz Mazowiecki had written the President and argued, "The unification of the German nation in a single state opens up a new period in the history of Europe. We cannot possibly enter that period with the security of all the states on the continent, particularly the neighbors of Germany, in their current borders, unassured." The Kremlin was likely to try to position itself as the champion of the Poles, and to use this as an issue with which to slow down unification. London and Paris were also likely to join the Polish bandwagon, and the combined effect could have had the potential of pushing the Germans into a corner—which would only complicate any resolution of this problem.*

Kohl outlined the domestic problem he faced. The vast majority of Germans knew that the present demarcation—the Oder-Neisse line—would remain the border, he said, but the Poles had been pushed west and the Germans were expelled. This was a reaction to Nazi crimes, but the Germans who were affected were innocent—this was twelve to fourteen million people. One-third of the 1937 Reich was cut off. In 1945, two million German civilians were killed fleeing from Eastern Europe. We have to deal with this psychological problem in my country." The best way to handle the issue was to rely on the Helsinki Final Act, which recognized the inviolability of borders, President Bush decided, and to note publicly that we recognized the present Polish-German border. This would put us on the right side of the issue, while giving Bonn time to work things out with Warsaw.

On NATO membership, the Chancellor asserted his general commitment to the alliance, but also raised certain specific issues. How would the GDR, as part of a unified Germany, fit into NATO? What effects would expansion of NATO have on the alliance's future military posture and requirements? That, quite naturally, would require consultations with the other alliance members. "Let's make damn sure we don't leave our allies out, as if we are carving up Europe," the President noted.

In addition, the Chancellor said, "NATO units, including Bundeswehr forces dedicated to NATO, cannot be stationed on East German soil. It wouldn't work to have the Soviet Group of Force in East Germany remain there indefinitely, because it would compromise German sovereignty."

"I hate to think of another France in NATO. We need full participation for Germany," the President stressed.†

We agreed that when referring to GDR territory, we should use the term *forces*, not *jurisdiction*. Following my meeting with Hans-Dietrich Genscher in Washington earlier in the month, I had begun to say that "NATO jurisdiction" or "jurisdiction of forces" would not apply to the GDR. I had continued to use the phrase or variants of it with Gorbachev and Shevardnadze, in part because it was rather vague and seemed a softer version for them to accept. By the time we got to Bulgaria, however, we realized it was creating potential confusion. Stating that "NATO jurisdiction"

---

*Indeed, we received reports a few weeks later that senior chancellery officials believed that the French had been encouraging Mazowiecki to increase his public demands on the issue. And Kohl had called Mitterrand to complain after the French President had sent a letter to the twenty-nine CSCE members who were *not* part of the Two-plus-Four, assuring them that they would have a voice in the process.

†France is not part of NATO's integrated military command.

would not apply to the territory of the GDR might be equated with saying that Articles 5 and 6 of the North Atlantic Treaty would not apply—in effect, leaving the GDR out of NATO's security guarantee. So I began to use "forces" instead, and we agreed to that formulation with Kohl. To reinforce the point and ensure that Genscher was in agreement, I sent a follow-up letter to him on February 28, noting this distinction.

Overall, Kohl was supremely confident. "Everyone is confused but me," he said, noting that Genscher was having problems with his own political party. However, the Chancellor was concerned about opinion in the rest of Europe. Mitterrand, he said, "has been holding firm. Most of the French people are on our side, but the political class is against us. But we have to keep working the problem. Copenhagen and Norway are also hard cases. The Netherlands and the U.K. are also problems.

"Margaret Thatcher: I can't do anything about her. I can't understand her. Mrs. Thatcher talks to me in a way I wouldn't accept from anyone else."

"We don't look at it that way," the President assured him. "We don't fear the ghosts of the past; Margaret does. But you and we must bend over backwards to consult, recognizing our unique role in history."

"In the FRG," the Chancellor jumped in, "there is anger among Germans because we have been reliable partners for over forty years. Why doesn't that help? Logic doesn't help."

March in Windhoek:
Making the Case with Shevardnadze

The intelligence community believed that, in the end, Moscow was likely to acquiesce in a unified Germany's membership in NATO, with certain restrictions. But "the German question is a visceral one among the Soviet population," the National Intelligence Officer for the Soviet Union, Bob Blackwell, wrote on March 1, "and criticism of Gorbachev's policy is beginning to emerge from people like Politburo member Ligachev and from some military officials.

"Such criticism is no major threat to Gorbachev now. But if it were to appear that Soviet troops were being forced to retreat from the GDR, he had 'lost' Germany, and the security environment for the USSR was now more threatening, the domestic fallout—when combined with other complaints—could pose a threat to his position. *Gorbachev at least has to have one eye on this contingency.*" (Emphasis in original.)

In Moscow in February, Gorbachev and Shevardnadze expressed both concern and confusion about the unified Germany's alliance membership.

Saying he was going to hold a "seminar" to discuss options, Gorbachev said, "Certainly, any extension of the zone of NATO is unacceptable." But he also said, "I believe the presence of U.S. troops could be very constructive and be positive in the situation as it evolves. . . . We really don't want to see a replay of Versailles, where the Germans were able to arm themselves. The lessons of the past tell us that Germany must stay within European structures."

Shevardnadze was blunt. "We believe also that unification does raise the question of whether NATO is going to exist as it has," he said. Both of them seemed to envision a Europe in which CSCE was strengthened and NATO and the Warsaw Pact just faded away or melded into one another.

By March, the rush of events seemed to have heightened their anxieties. In a letter to the Two-plus-Four foreign ministers on March 2, Shevardnadze noted that, in the GDR, "certain unforeseen circumstances might arise that will require a reaction" and "it is extremely important, in my view, that no one party among our 'six' act unilaterally."* He went on to outline a procedure for notification—"otherwise we may find ourselves in a difficult situation, for undesirable misunderstandings could then become possible."

Four days later, Gorbachev was asked point-blank by the press, "What is the USSR's attitude to any form of participation by a united Germany in NATO?"

"We cannot agree to that. It is absolutely ruled out," he said bluntly. And on March 8, Shevardnadze reinforced his boss, stating in an interview that Germany in NATO would be inconsistent with Moscow's view of its "own national interests and the security structure of the Common European Home." He also stressed that all security aspects of a German settlement had to be worked out in the Two-plus-Four.

The following week I sent Bob Zoellick, Ray Seitz, and Condi Rice, the President's Special Assistant for Soviet Affairs, to Bonn for the first meeting of the Two-plus-Four at the political directors' level. For the most part, the British and the French sided with the West Germans and us, and the Soviets and East Germans were relatively cooperative. The six agreed on four agenda items: borders; political-military questions; Berlin; and the Four Powers' rights and responsibilities. Moscow wanted to add four topics proposed by the GDR: "synchronization," which was a code word for changes in European security structures; property questions in the GDR; treaty obli-

---

*When Ambassador Matlock in Moscow asked First Deputy Foreign Minister Anatoliy Kovalev what "unforeseen circumstances" might mean, Kovalev, in a neat catch-22, noted that "unforeseen circumstances" by their very nature could not be described or predicted. He did, however, argue that the situation in the GDR was "charged" and "sudden turns of events there could damage all our interests."

gations; and peace settlement. Our team quite correctly resisted all four. All in all, it was a successful first meeting, and went some distance to assuage any concerns that Two-plus-Four could be used by the Soviets as an instrument to block unification. Nonetheless, the meeting revealed that we had a lot of work ahead of us if we were going to bring Moscow around to accept Germany in NATO—a task I undertook in person on March 19, when I met Shevardnadze during the independence celebrations in Windhoek, Namibia. (While the celebration itself was wonderful, the accommodations were tight; our staff doubled and quadrupled up, and our press corps had to sleep in a railroad car.)

We began on START—a subject I thought would be less controversial than Germany. Shevardnadze said he thought we would be able to resolve all the major issues for the U.S.-Soviet Summit. He then ran through several issues he thought we could settle quickly: ACLMs, SLCMs, the duration of the treaty, and the non-circumvention clause. Of these, he felt he had a problem on ALCMs, where he said the Soviets had no fallback position on the range issue. I told him if that was the case, then our two presidents would have to resolve it, because I had no further room to move. "But we will be scolded if we do that," he joked. "Presidents shouldn't have to spend their valuable time on such specifics." I felt we shouldn't have to spend *our* time on issues that could be resolved by our negotiators in Geneva. But I suspected the issue wouldn't be resolved until Gorbachev overruled Marshal Akhromeyev, who was playing an increasingly prominent and unproductive role in arms control negotiations.

I then raised a new START initiative. Throughout the 1980s, analysts had become very concerned about the development of intercontinental ballistic missiles (ICBMs) with highly accurate multiple independently targetable reentry vehicles (MIRVs). They were viewed as the most destabilizing weapons of all, because one MIRVed ICBM could destroy several targets, thus making it a highly effective first-strike weapon. With Shevardnadze, I proposed a two-stage solution. First, we would enact a total ban on mobile MIRVed ICBMs. (This would have required the Soviets to dismantle their rail garrison system for the SS-24, and would have required us to stop work on our efforts to deploy a rail garrison system for the MX or Peacekeeper—which was running into tough sledding in Congress, in any case.) In the second stage, which would be far more ambitious and take more time, we would agree to eliminate silo-based MIRVed ICBMs. We were doubtful that Gorbachev would be interested in the proposal, since he was under such pressure from hard-liners, but "this could be seen as a major step toward enhancing strategic stability," I told Shevardnadze, "and it could answer the critics who claim that the current START negotiations really now amount to business as usual, and do not really reflect the changes that have been taking place in the world."

Shevardnadze told me he would try to have an answer in a few weeks. He emphasized that he very much "valued" our presenting new ideas, especially in a private, quiet way. (Given Gorbachev's political position, a high-profile public initiative would have only created a target for the conservatives.) Shevardnadze added that they were working on new ideas on strategic stability, but none had crystallized yet. However, the military and the Supreme Soviet were also "scrutinizing everything that we are doing, and they tend to get emotional." But, he said, "our first objective is to complete the START agreement," and when the Soviets ended up declining our proposal, I wasn't surprised. De-MIRVing would have to wait for another day.

The backdrop for our talks on Germany had been set two days before by the GDR elections. In what had been the first—and would certainly become the last—free election in GDR history, the people had voted in the ballot box the same way they had been voting with their feet: for the West and for rapid unification. Parties affiliated with counterparts in the FRG (who were all promoting unification) received over seventy-five percent of the vote. There could no longer be any question that all Germans wanted unification—and soon.

Shevardnadze, possibly influenced by the election rout, chose not to get into specifics, but instead focused on some general concerns. "You know how proficient the Germans are," he began. "They have tremendous creative potential. But they also, as we have seen in the past, have tremendous destructive potential." He felt that the process of unification was moving too quickly, outstripping arms control and efforts to build a new European security structure. "Unification is a fact," he recognized. "Therefore, what we do has to have some influence on its pace. It is important that it not be speeded up. In the time that remains, I think we need to seek some guarantees for security."

While making clear that the Two-plus-Four process helped meet some Soviet needs, he had a perceptual problem: the Soviet people couldn't accept a unified Germany in NATO. "Really, it is not so much what I think or believe or even what Gorbachev thinks or believes. . . . We don't believe the U.S. and the Soviet Union are ever going to go to war against each other unless something extraordinary happens. But the image of the enemy is in the minds of our people. That took decades to develop." And while he believed times were changing, the clear implication was that they weren't changing fast enough.

Yet at the same time that he said Germany couldn't be in NATO, he also said, "I recognize that a neutral Germany is a problem and one can't have that." He understood that Moscow's position was illogical. "We don't know the answer to the problem," he admitted. "You and I will have to discuss this more, and our presidents will have to discuss this as well."

When I went through the logic of anchoring Germany in NATO, thus ensuring that Germany wouldn't have to be responsible for its own security, and guaranteeing an ongoing U.S. military presence in Germany, he had an interesting and revealing response: "You have to consider what is going to happen tomorrow. Say we left East Germany. It could well be that you would still be in Germany, and we would have no problems with that. We would not object to your presence. But what if you would have to withdraw also?"

"We can't retain a presence," I interjected, "except if we have NATO."

But he was focused on the Germany of the future. "What if they say to you, 'We don't want to be in the alliance'? I have said to Genscher that if he or Kohl or Brandt were the leader of a united Germany, we would have no problem. But look at the young men waiting in the wings, the Republikaners. . . . I might be mistaken, other scenarios might be possible, but we have bitter lessons from history. And we have shown that when we move together, we've saved the world."

After START and Germany, tensions in the Baltics were the next item on the agenda. In Vilnius, the Lithuanian parliament had declared independence the previous week, and I was receiving reports in Windhoek that the Soviets were buzzing the Lithuanian capital with military aircraft. We were becoming increasingly concerned that Gorbachev would use force in Lithuania. From the start of our meetings, I had stressed with Shevardnadze that the Baltics were markedly different in American eyes. Besides their legal status, there was strong support for them on Capitol Hill, and they resonated in the American psyche as little guys who had been taken over by a bully who now seemed poised to shed blood.

"No, we are not going to use force," Shevardnadze reassured me. "Of course," he added, "it could be different if there were an attack on our garrisons there, but this is not the sort of thing that is done in Lithuania. It might be done where I come from, in the Caucasus, but not there." He said the only answer was a serious, substantive dialogue. He felt that the Lithuanians had become caught in the euphoria of independence. Becoming emotional, he said that the Kremlin had analyzed the situation carefully. "Our conclusion is that if Lithuania withdrew from the Soviet Union today, if anything, there might even be a collapse in that republic. The economic links took shape over a period of decades. All their factories, their plants, their railroads—they wouldn't be able to operate. Do they have a right to take that kind of irresponsible decision?"

Now he felt that many Lithuanians were realizing there were consequences. He believed they would now be able to have the kind of quiet,
civilized dialogue needed to decide the future relationship. He referred indirectly to the movement of Soviet troops, by noting that the Kremlin had
taken precautions to protect the nuclear power plant and defense production plants in Lithuania. Lastly, he said Moscow had noted the nuances of
our public statements and appreciated our restraint.

I told him we had tried not to exacerbate the situation, but we felt
strongly about the use of force or threat of its use. I was glad to hear him
commit not to use force, but I said we would be watching things closely.
More generally, I suggested that the draft secession law needed to be passed
quickly, and Moscow needed to create a credible mechanism for its implementation (probably referenda in each republic). "That's really the only
answer I see to many of the nationality problems that face you," I said.
"Some republics may choose to go their own way. But Mother Russia, as
you say, is strong, has been there historically, and will continue to be
there."

Shevardnadze said he agreed with me. He said they were trying to finalize the secession law; as painful as it was, he said they had to do it. He added
that he had come to accept the referendum idea as well, but that it just
wasn't possible to move as quickly as I was suggesting.

"But time is of the essence, unless you can show a pathway or mechanism that people can look to," I reiterated. "This whole thing can spin out
of control if you don't."

Four days later, it did, when Soviet paratroopers seized the Communist
Party headquarters in Vilnius. In response, I wrote Shevardnadze that our
ability to maintain a balanced posture was "now rapidly diminishing. You
should know," I continued, "as President Bush has said, that use of force, or
coercion, is bound to backfire. With your decision to expel two U.S. diplomats and the international media, you are forcing us to adopt a tougher
public position. We have little choice. Continued actions of this nature will
inevitably have an adverse effect on our relations." A few days later, the
President sent a similar message to Gorbachev. But neither had any noticeable effect on the Kremlin's behavior, and for the first time since the Bush
administration took office, I felt U.S.-Soviet relations were headed on a
negative, downward trajectory.

April in Washington: Two Steps Back

My apprehensiveness grew with the arrival of Shevardnadze at Andrews
Air Force Base on April 3 for a ministerial to finalize preparations for the
summit. Upon his arrival, Shevardnadze compared the situation in Lith-

uania to an earthquake, telling the press "cataclysms happen not only in nature." In three days of talks, Shevardnadze seemed utterly distracted. Even worse, he sometimes fell back on formalistic, ideological arguments or deferred to hard-liners such as Marshal Akhromeyev. Indeed, I had the image of a diplomat with a political gun to his head. Any step forward could lead to suicide.

"I have got to tell you that I am worried," I told him in our first three-and-one-half-hour session, in which Lithuania was the only substantive topic covered. "I am deeply and genuinely worried. We do not want to see this deteriorate, because it is going to have a direct effect on our relations. We have come so far in the last fourteen months. I do not want to see that undermined."

Since he had been going out of his way to point to the political constraints the Soviet leadership faced on Germany, I tried to make him understand what we faced in Washington concerning the Baltics, first by pointing out a 93–0 vote in the Senate condemning Soviet actions, then by making an argument he'd personally find more compelling. "The foreign press has been told to leave, armored personnel carriers (APCs) move through the streets and are seen on our TV. Now, all of these moves normally presage a use of force. And that is disturbing to everybody. And I must tell you that everyone who doesn't like the fact that our relations are moving from confrontation to cooperation are using what you are doing as a vehicle to beat up on us." Shevardnadze nodded in understanding. "I just don't know how long we are going to be able to hold the line," I concluded, "unless we can point to a process that gives the Lithuanians a chance for self-determination."

His response was a combination of irritation and dogmatism. "We want a serious dialogue," he said. "We know that the Lithuanians are at an impasse, and we know that they do not know how to get out of it. They didn't come when we asked them to come a week ago Friday. Gorbachev had even sent a personal invitation to come, and there were also telephone calls from senior Soviet leaders, asking them to come and discuss the issue." Vytautas Landsbergis, the former music professor turned Lithuanian President, had clearly exasperated the Kremlin. ("He is considered to be inexperienced, naive—and therefore, politically speaking, dangerous," Shevardnadze noted later.)

At one point, Shevardnadze tried to deflect me by pointing to the criticism Gorbachev was receiving. He tried to draw on our invasion of Panama to support his case. "Of course," he added dogmatically, "the comparison between Panama and Lithuania is not necessarily appropriate—Panama was a different country, Lithuania is part of our country. But still we acted, and were able to act and speak with some restraint." He hadn't raised Panama as a major problem in any of our conversations in the previous three months, yet now he was falling back on it. Moreover, he was worried about greater dangers. "I have told U.S. reporters in the past," he said, "that there is no alternative to perestroika. Well, the truth is, that's a mistake. There is an alternative to perestroika. If perestroika doesn't succeed, then you are going to have the destabilization of the Soviet Union. And if that happens, there will be a dictator."

Dennis Ross interrupted to ask Shevardnadze, "What in your eyes would it take right now to begin the process or a dialogue? What prevents it from starting now?"

"Well, speaking strictly or legally," Shevardnadze answered, "they have to return to the status quo ante. Their decision has no legal force. On that basis, we will be able to discuss anything."

"You answered Dennis's question in a legal way, in a kind of formal way," I noted. "But why don't you approach it politically, and not legally? Politically, couldn't you overlook or ignore the illegal act? You say it doesn't have the force of law. Why not simply agree to start a dialogue and announce you will go to a referendum and have talks about future relations? If this very act that you say is illegal doesn't have the force of law in your eyes, then why do you have to pay any attention to it?"

"First of all, they have to come to Moscow," he responded. "Gorbachev can't go there. You know, they know how to get there. They can buy tickets and come on the train or we will send a plane for them."

Following our session, Dennis told Sergei Tarasenko, "The Minister talks about the importance of a dialogue, but avoids any mention of how such a dialogue could begin. What's it going to take to get a dialogue started?"

"This has become a matter of face for Gorbachev," Sergei replied. "When Landsbergis didn't come to Moscow when he was invited, that caused Gorbachev serious problems. This is the code word for getting over the hump: Landsbergis to Moscow."

The next night at a private dinner at my residence, I asked Shevardnadze, "If President Landsbergis were to go to Moscow and agree to suspend—as opposed to annul—actions taken in Lithuania, would that be sufficient to lead to the beginning of a dialogue?"

Shevardnadze paused for a long moment, and began his answer by noting that such questions require a decision by the "collective leadership" in Moscow. But, speaking personally, he felt that if Landsbergis were to come to Moscow, it would be "very positive and helpful."

The remainder of the ministerial was a combination of treading water on Germany and backtracking on arms control. Our only discussion of unification was in a massive fifteen-on-fifteen discussion of regional issues,

in which Shevardnadze allowed Aleksandr Bondarenko, a German specialist and hard-liner, to dominate the discussion. I felt Shevardnadze had two
reasons for conducting business that way: first, he needed to bide time,
because he was too exposed politically at home to make any forward progress on his own (or as Margaret Thatcher so aptly put it when the President
met with her in Bermuda a week later, "Shevardnadze has been knocked to
the sidings by criticism"). Second, he wanted his colleagues to be exposed
to our arguments. His bureaucracy, particularly the military, was strangling
any initiative, and he wanted to put them in the position of having to defend Soviet policy. In effect, he was telling them, "If you're so smart, you
argue with the Americans." Arms control was even worse. Whereas previously Shevardnadze and I had conducted much of our work one-on-one,
now we were joined by Akhromeyev and Major General Aleksandr Peresypkin of the Soviet general staff, whose grim visage led some of my staff to
call him "Mr. Smiley." The Soviets were walking away from several understandings we had reached in Moscow in February.* I decided that, under
the circumstances, pushing Shevardnadze was pointless. He had no room to
maneuver, and we were going to have to go back to Moscow to get Gorbachev to make decisions that would stick. As I reported at a Cabinet meeting
shortly afterward, "The further we get in our discussions and negotiations,
the more difficult the issues become to resolve."

A week later, April 13, Gorbachev threatened Vilnius with an economic
embargo unless the Parliament annulled its independence declaration
within forty-eight hours.† Four days later, we started receiving sketchy reports that oil and gas flows into Lithuania were being interrupted. At a 5:00
P.M. NSC meeting, the President made it clear he didn't want to move
precipitously. With the sides seemingly caught in a game of chicken, I called
Shevardnadze on April 18, and told him, "Of course, we would consider an
economic blockade on oil or gas to be coercion, and it could adversely affect
our drive to establish better commercial relations"—a signal that the U.S.-
USSR trade agreement would be in jeopardy if Gorbachev followed through
with his threat. Shevardnadze reiterated that the Lithuanians needed to
move first. In an effort to broker the beginning of a dialogue, I asked him if
he would have a problem if we contacted the Lithuanians. "We would have

---

*We had agreed to deal with SLCMs in parallel, politically binding declarations; now the Sovi-
ets wanted legally binding numerical limits in a protocol to START. Verification had been set
aside; now they wanted it included. On ALCMs, we had reached agreement on everything but
range; the Soviets wanted to reopen counting rules and a host of other elements.

†Our concerns were heightened when the British told us that Gorbachev had not ruled out
force in a meeting with Douglas Hurd in Moscow on April 10, and had threatened "presidential rule" over Lithuania.

no objections," he responded, "but I do want this conversation with you to be confidential." Shevardnadze and I both knew that to have the United States act as an intermediary could be political dynamite—both in Moscow *and* in Washington.

Because of the danger that any formal approach to the Lithuanians could backfire on us domestically, as well as harm our relations with Moscow diplomatically, we spoke to Senator Richard Lugar and asked him to be our intermediary. The next day, Dennis Ross went to Capitol Hill to brief Lugar and to outline what we thought the Lithuanians needed to do to get Moscow into a dialogue that could lead to independence peacefully: they had to suspend their declaration of independence, pending negotiations, and go back to Moscow to begin talks. Meanwhile, I learned from the U.S. embassy in Moscow that the Lithuanian natural gas supply had been cut back, but not cut off completely, and that the fax lines were down.

I had no qualms about our approach. Notwithstanding the fact that the United States did not consider Lithuania to be part of the Soviet Union, I knew that, given the political situation in Moscow, the Lithuanians were not going to achieve de facto independence unless they first made these insignificant symbolic concessions to the Kremlin. I hoped the Lithuanian leadership would take the practical steps necessary to realize their dream.

On April 20, I called Shevardnadze again. I told him that I had been "surprised and frankly disturbed" by the fact that the cutoff of oil and gas had coincided with my phone call to him. It may not have been an airtight embargo, but it was close enough. I wanted him to know that he was now putting me in a difficult position.

I shared with him Landsbergis's response, which I had received from Lugar. While the President of Lithuania had been far from positive, he had said that if a freeze didn't have to be permanent (i.e., a suspension of the declaration of independence rather than a revocation), then the Lithuanians might be able to go along. Shevardnadze said he felt that, in principle, a dialogue could begin with a freeze or suspension, but he needed to check with Gorbachev. We talked again the next day, and I learned that while Gorbachev had sent a harshly worded telegram to the Lithuanians, a lower-ranking Soviet official had met with a group of Lithuanian women and cited the need to suspend the declaration of independence. It was becoming obvious that Moscow was pursuing both coercive and cooperative tracks with Vilnius simultaneously, but I was doubtful the delicate balance could be maintained.

On Monday morning, April 23, I learned that Gorbachev's chief spokesman had said that Lithuania could keep its declaration of independence "for history," as long as Vilnius either rescinded the independence laws or froze them. However slight, Moscow's position was shifting. At an NSC

meeting that evening, the President decided that a key goal must be to try
and protect the continually improving overall relationship with the USSR. I
had found little support among our European allies for stern measures to
register our disapproval of Soviet coercive economic measures toward Lithuania, and hence any actions we would take would probably have to be
unilateral. The President decided that "any response should be proportion-
ate to the crime." That meant that the U.S.-Soviet trade agreement we were
finalizing would be put on hold—and the President wrote Gorbachev a letter to that effect on April 30.*

May in Bonn, Moscow, and Washington: Finally, a Breakthrough

Bonn, on a beautiful, sunny spring day in the first week of May, was the site
for the first ministerial meeting of Two-plus-Four. Having spent the day
conferring with Genscher and then Kohl, I met with Shevardnadze in the
early evening for almost four hours of talks in my suite in the Maritim
Koenigswinter Hotel overlooking the Rhine south of Bonn.

Once again, we covered Germany, Lithuania, and arms control. I
began, however, by raising two other issues. First, I proposed a joint U.S.-
Soviet cooperative effort to help feed starving people in Ethiopia—using
our food and their planes. Senator David Boren was pushing this idea,
and I thought it could become an example of U.S.-Soviet cooperation toward solving global problems. Second, I raised concerns about rumors
we'd heard of a pogrom scheduled for May 5, organized by the reactionary group Pamyat, against Jews throughout the Soviet Union. Interestingly, Shevardnadze basically acknowledged that these were not just
rumors, by saying that the Soviet leadership had taken all the steps they
could to prevent it. There could be individual incidents, he said, but the
Ministry of the Interior and other security elements were on high alert,
and had called in the Pamyat ringleaders and warned them regarding violence against Jews.

Shevardnadze created the distinct impression that Moscow was more
relaxed and confident that its strategy on Lithuania was working. He implied no sense of urgency, saying, "We must show patience." Indeed, when
I emphasized the importance of the Soviets' not simply talking about the
need for dialogue, but actually taking steps to produce one, he said he

---

*The Senate reinforced the President's message on May 1, when it voted 73–24 to withhold
any U.S. trade benefits from the USSR until the Lithuanian standoff was resolved and the
economic embargo lifted.

thought one would be possible in time. He referred to the growing debate among the Lithuanian leadership over the need for compromise, and implied they would come around. He repeated that the Soviets would be willing to start a dialogue if the Lithuanian leaders announced that they were freezing their declaration of independence and the laws that followed from it, and were willing to come to Moscow to begin talks. But he said the initiative, the first step, had to come from Vilnius.

"Sometimes I feel," I said, "that when I look at the situation in Lithuania, there are two ships that are passing in the night, that they are going right past each other. What I see is both you and the Lithuanians saying the right things about resolving the problem through peaceful dialogue, but I also don't see a dialogue beginning." I asked if Landsbergis and the rest of the Lithuanian leadership clearly understood from the Soviets what they needed to do to get Moscow to lift its economic blockade, and what they would get in return—namely, a dialogue on independence. He said he was confident that they did, "but at this point, they haven't done anything. They talk, but they don't act." He noted again that the Kremlin would be patient and "wait a little longer" as the Lithuanians debated the issue. I warned him that our room to maneuver was limited and raised the possibility that we might be pushed to economic sanctions. He said that wouldn't be a tragedy, but it would be unfortunate, as it would indicate where our relationship was headed. He also handed me a letter from Gorbachev to the President that made the same point: "I wish to say quite frankly that the emerging retreat of the U.S. administration from its former reasonable position cannot possibly do a good turn either to the normalization of the situation in Lithuania or to Soviet-U.S. relations," Gorbachev wrote, tellingly describing it as a problem that fell within the USSR's "internal competence."

I moved the discussion to German unification by saying, "It is very important that there be no winners and losers in the unification process." I outlined the principles that guided us on unification. On the one hand, we did not want to singularize or discriminate against the Germans; that approach had been followed after the First World War, had sown the seeds of resentment, and had been one of the causes for Hitler's rise to power. On the other hand, we wanted to take into account the legitimate security needs of others. Besides the border with Poland, that meant ensuring that Germany would not be untethered in the center of Europe, thus creating a dangerous instability. I outlined for him our view of Two-plus-Four as a "steering group" able to decide a limited number of issues, but able to discuss many others. I used the President's speech at Oklahoma State, on May 4, on European security issues as an illustration that we heard what they were saying.* I told him, "We know the lessons of 1871, 1914, and 1939. We have had to fight two wars on this continent in this country. In the most devastating one, we fought alongside you as an ally. We don't want to have to repeat that. So we want to see Germany tied in to as many institutions as possible."

Shevardnadze responded by saying that Moscow welcomed our new ideas. Indeed, our discussion of the new European architecture was compatible with much of their thinking, though they were still developing their ideas. He said they agreed there should be no discrimination against the two Germanies or, in time, one Germany. That was the meaning of Two-plus-Four, where, after all, the two Germanies were sitting as full and equal partners.

In answer to my characterization of Two-plus-Four as a steering group that would decide some issues, but discuss and direct other issues to different fora, Shevardnadze said he needed to think more about this. He noted that the Soviets really thought of Two-plus-Four as a decision-making body, not merely as an advisory group. Moreover, he also felt that it should not rush to make decisions and complete its work. Two-plus-Four needed to address many complex issues and needed time to do that. The Soviets would not encourage delay, but felt Two-plus-Four should be working in parallel with CSCE and with the ongoing CFE talks. As he put it, the three should be seen as a kind of single complex.

In sum, I wrote the President that night, "While the Soviets are not on the same wavelength, I think our concept of Two-plus-Four as a steering group might yet have some appeal to them. Moving them on Germany in NATO will probably prove more difficult. Shevardnadze emphasized again the psychological difficulty they have—especially the Soviet public has—of accepting a unified Germany in NATO. He did this while implicitly accepting the logic of our position—agreeing that neutrality was not the answer for long-term stability and stating clearly that the Soviets want a U.S. military (not just political and economic) presence in Europe. Indeed, he said the U.S. military presence must remain in Europe for at least seven to ten years, probably longer.

"What comes through is that the Soviets don't know how to square the circle. They're wrestling with it. I suspect that Gorbachev doesn't want to take on this kind of an emotionally charged political issue now, and almost

---

*The President's speech that day had been designed to show Moscow that we were moving forward with a serious effort to make NATO more of a political alliance and to strengthen CSCE. The President had also written Manfred Woerner to begin an intra-alliance process to change NATO—a process we intended to complete at a NATO summit by early summer. We wanted that meeting to showcase how much NATO had changed—and provide Gorbachev and Shevardnadze ammunition against their domestic critics.

certainly not before the Party Congress." Shevardnadze had stressed that the Congress, slated for July, would be a political watershed in the Soviet Union. I could only hope so, because we were making little progress in the meantime.

The Two-plus-Four Ministerial on May 5 was rich with historical parallels. On that same day in 1955, the postwar occupation regime in Germany had come to an end, and on May 7, 1945, the first armistice of World War II had been signed. I began my presentation by saying, "Today, we engage in an act of reconciliation—of a people too long separated, of a continent too long divided. In helping Germany achieve freedom and unity, I believe all the states of Europe can be the winners." Genscher struck the right note by saying, "We wish to create not a German Europe, but a European Germany." But Shevardnadze took a hard line that reflected none of the self-doubt he shared with me privately, concluding, "Let us play this new, and last, game in German affairs in a businesslike way, and with a full awareness of all the dangers that lie in wait for Europe on its path into the twenty-first century." That night, we watched a fireworks show over Bonn, as the Germans celebrated "River Rhine in Flame." It was a beautiful display, but one that I feared might be a bit premature. Germany in NATO was still not in sight.

On the way home, I stopped for the day in Warsaw to reassure the Poles and to invite the Polish Foreign Minister to attend the Two-plus-Four Ministerial in Paris in July. Both Mazowiecki and Skubiszewski were appreciative of our position and were glad the United States had delivered the invitation on behalf of the Two-plus-Four delegations.

Ten days later, I arrived in Moscow for four days of talks to prepare for the U.S.-Soviet Summit at the end of May. Uncharacteristically, I had some free time on my hands, so I went for a walk around town, visiting the new McDonald's with its massive lines, then a butcher shop, a ladies' garment store, and a drugstore. There seemed to be more activity on the streets and in shops. The infrastructure hadn't changed. It was still run down, and the quality of goods in the shops was still not the very best. McDonald's was very popular and had two sets of lines—one for rubles, the other for dollars.

At the ministerial, we continued on arms control where we had left off in Washington: going nowhere slowly. Shevardnadze felt compelled to begin by reading his entire arms control brief in front of his whole delegation—as if to show he could be trusted to make the points. He seemed unwilling to make decisions or show initiative, as he had done in the past. "I feel Shevardnadze is distracted and a little overwhelmed by everything," I wrote the President after our first day of talks. "The economic problems, the public mistrust, the sense of losing control, the heat of the nationality issue, and concerns about Germany, all are weighing very heavily. Again, you have to ask, with these kinds of monumental problems, how easy is it to think about ALCMs? And do they really believe they can manage?"

Shevardnadze was less interested in discussing the Baltics than in discussing the broader problem of nationalities. "Let's hypothesize that we can have withdrawal from the union with Lithuania," he said. "What happens next? What could happen next? I'll tell you. The Moldavians say the same thing; the Georgians, the Armenians, the Azerbaijanis, the Ukrainians. . . . Here you can have a worst-case scenario, and I think that's why you have to take a serious, responsible position. The whole situation not only in Europe but also in Asia and the Middle East can be affected by this. Maybe not today, but in ten to fifteen years." Coming from the Caucasus, Shevardnadze understood the explosiveness of ethnicity and, I felt, foresaw long-term political trends better than anyone else, including Gorbachev. I tried to suggest a solution. Why not let the republics go and establish relations with them, like the USSR had with Finland? Shevardnadze didn't respond.

To give me a better sense of Russia and get out of the hustle and bustle of Moscow, Shevardnadze took me to Zagorsk, a town about ninety minutes outside the capital, and to the Russian Orthodox seminary there. Shevardnadze introduced me to the archbishop of the Russian Orthodox Church, and at one point, we lit candles together. I found it odd to be involved in a religious ceremony with the Foreign Minister of a state that had railed against religion. I always found Shevardnadze a deeply mystical man, and I oftentimes wondered if these exhibitions of faith, like the religious icon he gave me in Wyoming, weren't his way of showing me that we had more in common than politics. (In 1993, Shevardnadze was baptized Gregory in his native Georgia.)

The second day of the ministerial, I spent five hours with Gorbachev. He talked at length about Moscow's relationship with us, Soviet financial deficits, Germany, and Lithuania, particularly his just-concluded meeting with the Lithuanian Prime Minister, Kazimiera Prunskiene, whom the Soviets saw as more reasonable than Landsbergis.

For the first time ever in our meetings, Gorbachev raised some questions about our real attitude toward the Soviet Union. While acknowledging that President Bush had shown "amazing restraint" despite severe domestic pressures, Gorbachev felt we were taking some steps that indicated we hadn't fully made up our minds about perestroika. "As I watch the critical points of our relations, sometimes I have a sense that you want an edge, you may seek an advantage," he said. "In the past, I would note this, and I would watch this. Now I think our relations are such that I have an obligation to share my view with you." He cited Eastern Europe, Germany, and Lithuania as examples. "I have information that a part of your policy is driven by trying to disassociate Eastern Europe from the Soviet Union. You know my attitude is that if these countries seek to disassociate themselves, if that's what they want, let them do so. That's okay. But it's not okay if they are being pushed in this regard." As for a united Germany in NATO, "that's going to mean a very serious development in the strategic balance; it's going to mean a serious shift in the balance." He also cited the conditions we imposed on Soviet participation in the European Bank for Reconstruction and Development (EBRD) as an indication that we were trying to block others from helping the Soviet Union.

Domestically, he continued, "there are others who say the Soviet Union is conceding everything unilaterally. There's a lot of resistance but we are moving forward, and we expect you to move forward as well, and not just wait for the apples to fall into the barrel."

"We aren't," I said.

He cut me off. "First we have to produce a few apples, don't we?"

"Well, if there aren't apples at the end of the road, we're both going to be in trouble," I concluded.

He almost seemed to be saying that in his hour of need, he didn't need us to complicate his life. So much of his domestic program had been premised on his international achievements, but now the world outside seemed to be turning on him, and Gorbachev was beginning to sound like a jilted lover who had been left unexpectedly at the altar.

I made it clear that we were seeking neither to exploit Moscow's troubles nor to push the East Europeans away. I noted that it was difficult for us to justify using U.S. taxpayer money to help finance Soviet loans through the EBRD when the Soviets were still subsidizing countries such as Cuba, Vietnam, and Cambodia to the tune of ten to fifteen billion dollars a year, while maintaining very high defense expenditures. Moreover, Moscow still had not come forward with a credible economic-reform program.

Gorbachev said the Soviet Union was facing a significant funding gap over the next few years, and would need $20 billion in loans and credits. He said he needed the symbol of our involvement in the loan effort—in large part, I suspected, so he could demonstrate how his policies were succeeding in getting the United States to contribute to Soviet needs. Gorbachev said the next few years would be critical, because Moscow was going to move to a market-based economy. To cushion the impact and expedite the transition, he needed resources to buy consumer goods and to invest in the conversion of defense plants to civilian output.

Gorbachev told me he was under a lot of pressure to do more against Lithuania, to invoke direct presidential rule over the republic. "I've got telegrams from all over the country—maybe I'll show them to President Bush. Because what they do is protest and say American Presidents act very quickly to protect American citizens, why don't you, as the Soviet President, act quickly to protect Russian citizens in Lithuania?" Nonetheless, he was determined to find a peaceful way to untie the knot. The Lithuanians had made this very difficult, but if they would suspend their declaration of independence, he would begin the dialogue and lift the sanctions immediately. Then all the difficult issues—future economic ties, military installations, territorial claims of the Belorussians—could be unraveled and resolved. If the Lithuanians wanted independence, he'd accept that as long as it emerged from a peaceful negotiation.

Prunskiene had been prepared to suspend the implementation of the laws, not the declaration. This wasn't sufficient in his eyes. He would not force the Lithuanians to nullify the declaration—that would be too humiliating for them—but he did require that the declaration be frozen. In answer to my question, he said he thought Prunskiene understood what was required, and would return to Vilnius to persuade the Lithuanian Supreme Soviet to act accordingly.

I saw Prunskiene immediately after Gorbachev, and she was taking a tough line on the need to preserve the declaration. While assuring her we were committed to Lithuanian independence, I also said the challenge for the Lithuanians was to take steps that would translate their aspirations for de facto independence into reality. Without offering advice, I mentioned the actions that would produce an immediate dialogue. I also asked what the Lithuanians lost by offering a temporary freeze of their declaration—a freeze that could always be revoked if the Soviets exhibited bad faith.

Prunskiene and her colleagues said that freezing the declaration would mean having to act according to Soviet laws. While in practical terms I didn't see much of a substantive gap between what Gorbachev wanted and what the Lithuanians were prepared to do, there was a real gap in symbols. It was beginning to remind me of the Middle East, where symbols constantly wrecked substance. I informed the President that, even with the Gorbachev-Prunskiene meeting, "We're not out of the woods on this one yet."

The bulk of my time with Gorbachev was devoted to Germany. I sought to demonstrate that we had tried to respond to Soviet concerns. Two-plus-Four had provided the Soviets a process that gave them a place at the table and allowed them to show they were helping to manage the issue. Moreover, we were using Two-plus-Four to steer some issues to other fora—for example, the CFE negotiations—where the Soviets had a role.

Most important, I presented Gorbachev with what we called the "nine assurances"—nine concrete steps that formed a comprehensive package the West was willing to take to meet Soviet security concerns: (1) limiting the Bundeswehr in CFE II; (2) accelerating SNF negotiations; (3) ensuring that the Germans would not develop, possess, or acquire either nuclear, biological, or chemical weapons; (4) keeping NATO forces out of the GDR for a transition period; (5) developing a transition period for Soviet forces to leave the GDR; (6) adapting NATO politically and militarily; (7) getting an agreement on the Polish-German border; (8) institutionalizing and developing CSCE; and (9) developing economic relations with the Germans, while ensuring that GDR economic obligations to the USSR would be fulfilled.*

Gorbachev took copious notes as I went through the list and made clear he approved of it very much. At the same time, he said that a unified Germany in NATO was impossible. "It is going to mean the end of perestroika," Shevardnadze chimed in. "And people will say that we are the losers, we're not the victors." Gorbachev felt that our problem was that we banked everything on one premise: namely, that Germany would want to stay in NATO. "What if one day a unified Germany says it wants to be out of NATO? What will we do then?" he asked. "If that happens, we would have lost our ability to affect events. We won't have done anything in the interim period to try and shape the new system. Currently, we have the Four Power rights, the unification process—these give us a means to do something."

I asked him if, in his view, Germany had to be outside NATO. "Yes," he said. "It is outside, and it should be outside a military grouping."

"Are you talking about a neutral Germany?" I asked.

"I don't know if I'd call it that. Maybe I'd call it nonaligned," he responded somewhat illogically. He said he would think the issue over, but "let me just add that if in the end we aren't able to persuade you of our argument, then I will say to President Bush that we want to enter NATO. After all, you said that NATO wasn't directed against us, you said it was a new Europe, so why shouldn't we apply?"

I pointed out that I had been asked that question in a news conference. "Well, it's not such a hypothetical question," said Gorbachev. "It's also not so far-fetched."

I returned to one of my major themes: the Helsinki Final Act guaranteed every country the right to make its own choice of alliances. Trying to tell the Germans that they had to be in this or that alliance, or neutral or nonaligned, would be singling them out, and creating the basis for resentment in the future. "The resentment would arise in having someone else impose their will on the Germans," I said.

---

*We had already planned to take all these steps individually, but by wrapping them in a package and calling them the "nine assurances," we greatly enhanced their political effect and assured the Kremlin that it would see their full impact. The package was designed so that Germany would not be singularized and the Soviets would not be handed an abject defeat. Above all, it was an effort on our part to stand in Gorbachev's shoes and help frame the issue so that he would have a domestic explanation.

"But what if they want to join the Warsaw Pact?" asked Gorbachev. "Can I note from your statement that you say it would be okay if they join the Warsaw Pact?"

"Helsinki says that any country can choose its own alliance," I answered.

"Well," Gorbachev said, "am I specifically to conclude that if a unified Germany wanted to be a member of the Warsaw Pact, the U.S. would say okay?"

"Our position," I responded, "is that the best prescription for stability is that a unified Germany ought to be part of NATO. But in the end that's a matter of choice for the Germans."

Gorbachev concluded our tête-à-tête by saying, "In principle, you're for free choice for the Germans, a right that is fundamental in international relations. So if Germany wants this, you will treat it with understanding."

I left Moscow on Saturday, May 19, with an overriding impression that Gorbachev was feeling squeezed and was likely to react strongly to any step that could cause him political problems at home. In particular, the military now seemed in charge of arms control.* But above all, Germany was overloading his circuits. I had believed that Shevardnadze was more emotional and less logical on Germany than his boss, but it was obvious that both of them were having trouble squaring the circle. I felt they trusted us and trusted the German leadership and oftentimes seemed on the verge of accepting Germany in NATO, only to have their political sense or historical memories pull them back.

On May 30, Gorbachev arrived in Washington with his entourage for his second summit on U.S. soil. The next day, I joined President Bush in the Cabinet Room for a small group discussion on Germany. The President began by walking Gorbachev again through the "nine assurances," and then made the case for Germany in NATO. Gorbachev's thinking had developed since I had seen him in Moscow, but in an odd way. The united Germany could either be in the Warsaw Pact *and* NATO or it could be in neither, he believed. That made no sense to anyone on the American side, but Gorbachev made a personal plea to the President. "You're a sailor. You will understand that if one anchor is good, two anchors are better."

The President said that Moscow was deeply suspicious of Germany

---

*Following the Gorbachev meeting, we were on the verge of closing out ALCMs and SLCMs and the remaining START issues. Unfortunately, after I had recived Gorbachev's explicit agreement to grandfather Tacit Rainbow, the Soviet delegation tried to introduce a number of new constraints. (Tacit Rainbow was a conventionally armed ALCM.) I ended up staying another day in Moscow to resolve the problem with Tacit Rainbow—and then, ironically, we fired off all our Tacit Rainbows in the first hours of the Gulf War, thus eliminating it as an issue in START.

while the United States was not. Germany was a true democracy, a good friend of the United States, and had the potential to be a powerful friend of the USSR.

Gorbachev said he understood German feelings, but added, "I cannot forget the attitudes of my own people."

At the alliance summit in July, I said, we had plans to unveil a new, changed NATO.

Shevardnadze, reiterating what was clearly the Kremlin's theme for the day, then also tried the idea of Germany in both alliances. "Perhaps any country could join either alliance," Gorbachev cut in. "Stalin, Roosevelt, and Churchill, after all, had been one coalition." Maybe the Soviet Union could join NATO, wondered Gorbachev. The President couldn't help teasing Akhromeyev, asking how he'd like to have an American commander.

After more fruitless back-and-forth, the President tried a different tack. Under CSCE principles, he said, all countries had a right to choose their own alliances. Thus, Germany should be able to decide which alliance it would join, he noted. "Isn't that so?" he asked Gorbachev.

"Yes," Gorbachev said, nodding in agreement.

The President was as startled as anyone. "I'm glad that you and I seem to agree that nations can choose their own alliances," he said, trying to get Gorbachev to reaffirm his new position.

"So we will put it this way," Gorbachev responded. "The U.S. and the USSR are in favor of Germany deciding herself in which alliance she would like to participate," following a Two-plus-Four settlement.

The President didn't want such a neutral formulation. He suggested instead, "The United States is unequivocally advocating Germany's membership in NATO. However, should Germany prefer to make a different choice, we will respect it."

"I agree," said Gorbachev. Several of his aides seemed genuinely shocked that their President had agreed to this, which was the practical equivalent of agreeing to a unified Germany in NATO.

Gorbachev then seemed to shift back toward his previous line of argument, and talked about the need for a prolonged transition period. He turned to Shevardnadze and asked him to get together with me to discuss Germany. In a bizarre twist, Shevardnadze defied Gorbachev. He said, right then and there, that this was an issue that needed to be discussed by the two presidents. Finally, after Gorbachev continued to push him, Shevardnadze agreed reluctantly. My guess was that he understood the concession Gorbachev had made and didn't want the responsibility for it to be in any way on him. He had carried enough burdens.

In retrospect, I believe Gorbachev shifted for several reasons. First, the reality of German unification was imposing itself, and Moscow was being left behind. Second, he was far too legalistic and logical a thinker to overlook the gaping holes in reasoning that peppered his own argument. But, third, CSCE had long been the Kremlin's preferred security institution, and when the President relied on CSCE principles to explain a united Germany's choice of NATO as its alliance, Gorbachev was in the difficult position of having to refute an argument that depended on CSCE principles.

With the breakthrough on Germany—or what many in the Soviet delegation, notably Akhromeyev, might have been calling a breakdown—I felt we had regained momentum in U.S.-Soviet relations. But from Gorbachev's perspective, progress required that he return to Moscow with tangible economic benefits—and that meant the trade agreement. "We can't go home without this," Shevardnadze told me on Friday afternoon, just hours before the leaders were to hold an East Room signing ceremony. I called the President. He had heard almost the same message—"I need this"—from Gorbachev. "Let's go ahead and do it," said President Bush. So I had Dennis Ross meet with Alexander Bessmertnykh to work out a formula. Shevardnadze and I approved it, and we gave it to our leaders for signing, delaying the East Room ceremony in the process as we finalized the details.

The President, Scowcroft, and I spent the next day at Camp David, discussing regional issues with Gorbachev, Shevardnadze, and Akhromeyev in a very relaxed way and in casual attire. Gorbachev was in fine form. "Drinking decaffeinated coffee is like licking sugar through a glass," he joked. Emboldened by our guffaws, he reeled off another one-liner about more intimate functions which, while hilariously funny, was more appropriate to the relaxed conversation we six men were having than to publication in a book with "Diplomacy" in its title.

We covered conflicts from Kashmir to Cuba and Ethiopia, to North Korea. It was almost as if Gorbachev's acceptance of Germany in NATO, and the President's decision on the trade agreement, had moved our relations to a higher, more cooperative and more personal plane. The discussion reminded me of some of the talks the President had held with Kohl and Thatcher—thinking out loud, comparing notes, and creating stronger personal relationships.

June in Copenhagen, Turnberry, and Berlin:
One Step Forward, Two Steps Back

Forty-eight hours after the end of the Washington Summit, I saw Shevardnadze once again, this time on the margins of a CSCE ministerial in Copenhagen. The summit seemed to have transformed him. With Gorbachev's acknowledgment that Moscow would no longer oppose a unified Germany in NATO if that were Germany's choice, Shevardnadze and I discussed the remaining critical issues associated with unification. Most important in these discussions, Moscow shifted its approach toward the Bundeswehr. At first, the Kremlin had wanted to decide German troop levels in the Two-plus-Four talks, but on May 23, Moscow had changed its position when Shevardnadze had met Genscher in Geneva, and told him that the issue could be covered in CFE. Now, Shevardnadze told me, the Soviets were willing to accept a unilateral German commitment on the Bundeswehr outside of the CFE talks. This was such a breakthrough that I wanted to tell Hans-Dietrich Genscher about it immediately—even though it was late in the evening. After getting through to Genscher's staff, I went over to his hotel to fill him in. He was delighted, even though it had meant getting out of bed to hear the news.

From Copenhagen, I traveled to Turnberry, Scotland—a windblown golf resort that had been the site of the British Open golf tournament—for a North Atlantic Council meeting. I used the session to reinforce an alliance consensus behind our position on German unification, and to lay the groundwork for the London Summit, by then only a month away. Simultaneously, the Warsaw Pact was meeting in Moscow. In an unmistakable signal to us, the Pact stated in its communiqué that the member states positively assessed "some of the steps taken recently by NATO. They expect the new trend of changes in NATO to be accelerated and deepened."*

On June 12, Genscher called to debrief me on his most recent visit to Moscow. He said the Germans had pledged large cash infusions to help meet Moscow's financial gap: $5 billion now, $20 billion later. He felt Gorbachev's position on NATO was now "yes but," whereas before it had been simply "no." But Genscher believed that it was critical for NATO to show that it was changing. I agreed and said we were looking to do that at the London Summit.

Ten days later, I joined the other five ministers in Berlin for a ceremony commemorating the dismantlement of Checkpoint Charlie—or as Douglas Hurd so tellingly put it, "At long last, we're bringing Charlie in from the cold." For twenty-nine years, the checkpoint had stood as a stark symbol of a divided world. Eight people had been shot trying to escape at that site, and at least twenty East Germans had escaped there. Now, as a huge crane lifted the small building that was Checkpoint Charlie away, the dismantling of the checkpoint could become a symbol of our unity. Or so I thought.

My optimism was cut short almost as soon as we arrived at the Nieder-schoenhausen Palace in the Pankow district of East Berlin for that day's

---

*The President's May 4 speech had promised a more political NATO, and there was much talk of adapting NATO to new realities in European diplomatic circles.

Two-plus-Four session. Noting that the date was June 22, the forty-ninth anniversary of the "fascist" attack on the Soviet Union, Shevardnadze made a lengthy and detailed intervention that basically undercut the progress we had made in the previous month. The Soviet proposal called for retention of Four Power rights after unification; a five-year transition period in which the united Germany would remain essentially split between NATO and the Warsaw Pact; ceilings on the Bundeswehr, both quantitatively and qualitatively; and a host of other restrictions.

While Shevardnadze was making his presentation, I wrote a note to Genscher: "What does this mean?"

"Window dressing" was his reply, but I wasn't so sure. Given the chaotic political situation in Moscow, we couldn't be sure that there hadn't been a reversal against the reformers.

When it came time for my intervention, I said bluntly, "So much for German sovereignty." But rather than take Shevardnadze on right there, I sent Bob Zoellick and Dennis Ross scrambling to prepare new talking points for what would have to be a very different kind of meeting. Dennis cornered Sergei Tarasenko after the meeting broke up. "This is a total reversal," he said. "You guys just screwed us. What the hell is going on?"

Tarasenko said that the document Shevardnadze had presented was a Politburo document, which had been "overtaken by events" but was not retractable before the Party Congress. All movement would be "frozen" until July 15, when the Party Congress would end. Shevardnadze had instructed Tarasenko to come up with ideas for the post–July 15 period.

Later that night, I went over to the Soviet Ambassador's residence to meet with Shevardnadze. "What's happened between Copenhagen and here?" I asked. "The paper you presented definitely tends to singularize Germany. It's going to drag out the process, it's going to impede sovereignty. I must say that it represents such a dramatic departure from what I understood in Copenhagen that I'd really like you to tell me what's going on. . . . I can deal with the true picture, but I need to know what it is."

"Let me tell you frankly that in working on this draft document, we were guided by our domestic situation," Shevardnadze emphasized. "The mood in the country is not shaping up in our favor. And not taking this into account is not only unreasonable, but irresponsible."

He went on to say there was a "moral, psychological, political factor" that had to be considered. "We need to be able to tell our people that we face no threat—not from Germany, not from the U.S., not from NATO. Your Secretary of Defense recently made a statement about reductions of defense spending in this decade. Such statements really help in showing that we're not engaging in military confrontation in the same way with the United States anymore."

"We're very conscious of the political constraints that are on you, and we are aware of your need for some political explanation for domestic consumption," I responded. "And that's one reason why I pulled together the nine assurances." I told Shevardnadze that we were proposing the adoption of a declaration at the London NATO Summit that would highlight the alliance's adaptation to a new, radically different world. In this connection, I also told him of the President's recent decisions on CSCE—including approval of a small secretariat and a conflict-reduction center. All indicated our seriousness about transforming CSCE into an institution and our commitment to a new, inclusive Europe.

While I thought that Gorbachev and Shevardnadze were on the defensive domestically and needed cover on Germany, I also felt they were pushing to see what they could get from us and to ascertain if they could affect German public opinion. We had always been concerned that the Soviets would try to force the Germans to choose between unity and NATO, so I decided to lay down a clear marker of our own. In the end, I said, "Germany will unify, and we are prepared, with others, to grant Germany the sovereignty it deserves, and it is due." I didn't want him to be under any illusion. If push came to shove, we were going to admit a unified Germany into NATO over Soviet objections. "Maybe it is true that you have interests that are more vitally affected than anyone else. But let me say that we, too, have interests."

He said four times that the London Declaration would be critical to the reformers' ability to explain their position on Germany. He emphasized it in part because the declaration would be issued during the Party Congress, and could well affect not only the Soviet posture on Germany, but Gorbachev's political position.

Shevardnadze was as beleaguered as I'd seen him. The domestic political situation was clearly overwhelming him. When I asked him about Gorbachev's status as General Secretary, he said he couldn't predict it. Although saying he was sure Gorbachev could stay if he wanted, he wasn't certain what would happen. He kept emphasizing the crisis atmosphere in Moscow, and I sensed great fatigue in his face.

However, there was some good news that came out of my meetings with Shevardnadze in Berlin. He was hopeful about the Baltics. The Baltic leaders had gone to Moscow to attend a Federation Council meeting, and Shevardnadze saw this as a sign of their seriousness. He was not particularly concerned about the Lithuanian parliament's slow movement, because he said there was a willingness to work things out. At least, this was dropping away as an issue of contention, and Moscow and Vilnius seemed to be moving toward a peaceful negotiation of differences. (Indeed, Moscow lifted its embargo on June 30.)

July in London: A New NATO,
a New Soviet Approach

In May, we had begun preparations in detail for the London Summit. The NSC staff, working closely with a small group of State and Defense aides, prepared a succinct draft declaration that contained several radical initiatives that included declaring nuclear weapons as "truly weapons of last resort"; eliminating U.S. nuclear artillery; proposing a new military strategy; seeking further cuts in CFE II; inviting former enemies to open liaison missions to NATO; and strengthening CSCE by institutionalizing it.

On June 19, I joined Dick Cheney and Colin Powell in Brent Scowcroft's office to go through the text. With one small addition—a paragraph in which NATO made a commitment to non-aggression, and invited the Warsaw Pact to reciprocate—and a few minor fixes, we approved the draft declaration. It was just twenty-two paragraphs long—exactly the kind of succinct political statement that would play well in Moscow. But first we had to gain agreement from the other fifteen members of NATO.

Breaking with tradition, we decided to hold the text closely, and have the President send it to fellow heads of state just days before the summit, and to allow it to be negotiated only by foreign ministers and leaders at the summit itself. NATO, like any institution, has its own bureaucracy, and we couldn't afford to allow bureaucrats to water down what was a critical political document. Moreover, we didn't want any leaks. We wanted the maximum political impact in Moscow when the declaration would finally be released, and that meant following this unusual, and somewhat high-risk, strategy.

Finally, on June 21, the President began circulating the draft to his counterparts. The reaction was uniformly positive, with the exception of Margaret Thatcher and the French. When I met with Douglas Hurd in Brussels on the summit's eve, July 4, he said that Margaret was "very unhappy," particularly with the language on "last resort." I told him we felt it was essential to have "last resort"; a shift in nuclear strategy would do more than anything else to show the Soviets that the world had been transformed. "The Prime Minister is not anxious to cross swords with the President," Hurd stressed, "but she feels very passionately about this."

The next day, we joined the leaders in London for the Summit, and from 2:30 P.M. to 6:30 P.M., I worked with the other NATO foreign ministers as we slogged through the declaration. At times, I was concerned that the negotiations would bog down. "Gentlemen," I was forced to say at one point, "we should keep our eye on the ball. The reason we are here, the reason we are working on this declaration, is to get Germany unified. We do not need to water down this document. It would be a mistake. We have one shot at this. These are different times. This is not business as usual." Unfortunately, it was business as usual for the French, as Roland Dumas objected to almost everything. As we broke for a formal dinner with the Queen and the heads of state, we agreed to reconvene at 10:30. Finally, at 12:30 A.M., and in black tie, we finished. The declaration was fundamentally intact.

From London, we flew to Houston for the annual G-7 Summit. There we agreed to task the International Monetary Fund with a serious study of the Soviet economy in order to lay the groundwork for Western assistance. Kohl made clear that the Germans would unilaterally funnel massive amounts of assistance to Moscow.

Meanwhile, the Communist Party Congress was unfolding in Moscow. Gorbachev came under severe criticism, but fought back. And in the middle of the Congress, the elements of the London Declaration—which was printed in full in the *New York Times*—filtered back to Moscow. With concrete evidence that NATO had changed and European security structures were being strengthened, Gorbachev and Shevardnadze held off the conservatives.*

A week later, we were refueling in Shannon Airport in Ireland on our way back to Paris for another Two-plus-Four Ministerial, which would become almost anticlimactic. Several members of my traveling press told me that they had just checked in with their offices, and the Soviets and Germans had come to an agreement. Gorbachev and Kohl, meeting in the Soviet leader's hometown of Stavropol, had issued a joint statement that acknowledged Soviet readiness to accept German membership in NATO, that agreed to limit the size of the Bundeswehr to 370,000 within CFE, and that resolved virtually all remaining major issues in Soviet-German relations. Everyone declared the statement an "historic breakthrough." The question of questions, as Shevardnadze had described it five months before, had been answered.

And just in the nick of time. For, only weeks away, another, equally momentous question awaited us—in fact, a whole storm of them.

*To help Shevardnadze, I sent him a draft of the declaration, hoping to put the reformers a step ahead of the reactionaries as the Party Congress heated up. Later in the month, Shevardnadze told me, "Without the declaration, it would have been a very difficult thing for us to take our decisions on Germany. . . . If you compare what we're saying to you and to Kohl now with our Berlin document, it's like day and night. Really, it's like heaven and earth."

CHAPTER 15

PRELUDE TO AN INVASION

War is dependent on the interplay of possibilities and probabilities, of good and bad luck, conditions in which strictly logical reasoning plays no part at all.
—*Clausewitz*, On War

I left for Iraq and had a long discussion on this issue with President Saddam Hussein. I believe he is interested in resolving this issue and has no intention of attacking Kuwait or any other party.
—*Egyptian President Hosni Mubarak, July 25, 1990*

Nothing will happen.
—*King Hussein of Jordan, in a phone call to President Bush, July 29, 1990*

On January 20, 1953, just over a month after we'd become engaged to be married, Mary Stuart and I drove the thirty miles up to Washington from Quantico, Virginia, where I was a Marine Corps second lieutenant about to finish my six months of Officer's Basic Training. Quantico was only about an hour's drive from the nation's capital, and I thought I'd probably never have another chance to be an eyewitness to the history of a presidential inauguration.

As we walked down Pennsylvania Avenue, not far from the Capitol, we were approached quite unexpectedly by an executive of a large corporation. As it turned out, his son was a Marine in Korea, and my uniform had caught his attention. He had a couple of extra tickets to the inaugural parade, and wondered if we'd like them. We thanked him for his generosity and quickly made our way to our assigned seats in the temporary grandstands erected along both sides of Pennsylvania Avenue, so caught up in the excitement that we were oblivious to the afternoon chill. Our seats were spectacular—directly opposite the presidential reviewing stand in front of the White House. I still have the color slides I took of the event.

Almost forty years later, on June 8, 1991, I found myself just as unexpectedly sitting in yet *another* grandstand helping to celebrate another authentic American triumph—the end of the war in the Persian Gulf. More than 800,000 Americans had assembled along the Mall to pay tribute to the sacrifice of our troops—the 550,000 who had served and the 390 who had died in the campaign to liberate Kuwait from Iraq's brutal occupation. The parade featured 9,000 troops from all the armed services, led by General H. Norman Schwarzkopf, the commander of U.S. forces in Desert Storm. As they marched proudly down Constitution Avenue past the presidential reviewing stand, accompanied overhead by an aerial armada ranging from a sleek F-117 Stealth fighter to a giant C-5 Galaxy cargo jet, I felt grateful to have played a part in one of the proudest moments in American military and diplomatic history. I recalled what Dick Cheney had said to me as the President was addressing a joint session of Congress to thunderous applause three months earlier: "Baker, it doesn't get any better than this."

And yet the moment was tinged with more than a little irony. Eighteen months earlier, as President Bush assumed office, it was inconceivable that the United States would soon be at war with Iraq. After eight years of brutal fighting with Iran, Saddam Hussein presided over a battered and demoralized nation. Iraq's industry was wrecked and its cities were pockmarked by the damage inflicted by hundreds of Iranian Scud missiles. Iraq, a nation of only 18 million, had suffered more than half a million deaths. None of us would have guessed that this country America had sought to engage could muster the capacity to set the world on a course for war in August 1990.

The Tilt Toward Iraq

The policy toward Iraq that President Bush had inherited from the Reagan administration was grounded in a determination to thwart the expansionist aspirations of the revolutionary government of Iran. The Ayatollah Khomeini's dream of exporting radical Islamic fundamentalism throughout the Middle East was correctly seen as a grave threat to regional stability and American strategic interests. If key American allies such as Israel, Egypt, and Saudi Arabia were threatened by radical fervor fomented from Tehran, the entire region could well be engulfed in turmoil, jeopardizing a steady supply of oil to the West and increasing the chances for another Mideast war.

The decision to contain Iran embodied emotional and political components as well. The Iranian hostage crisis of 1979 contributed greatly to the election of Ronald Reagan in 1980. Jimmy Carter's inability to secure the release of American diplomats held hostage by Iran for 444 days had become a metaphor for a paralyzed presidency and the decline of American power throughout the world. As the electoral beneficiaries of this unhappy period in American diplomacy, and having witnessed the unfortunate consequences of the Iran-contra scandal in 1986, we were all too well aware of the Ayatollah's destructive capacities in terms of domestic politics.

Four months before President Reagan took office, Iraq had invaded Iran, beginning a war that would last for eight years, end in stalemate, and devastate both nations. The war provided the Reagan administration a convenient vehicle by which to contain Iran—helping Iraq. By the end of 1982, President Reagan had concluded it was in the national interest to develop closer ties with Iraq. In 1983, after Saddam Hussein broke with the infamous terrorist Abu Nidal, the Reagan administration removed Iraq from the list of nations engaged in state-sponsored terrorism. A year later, diplomatic relations were resumed after seventeen years. In this same period, the United States began extending credit guarantees that enabled Baghdad to buy American grain. Throughout the Iran-Iraq war, military intelligence was shared with the Iraqis, and in 1987, when Iran began attacking oil tankers in hopes of denying Iraq critical revenues from its oil exports, the United States "reflagged" neutral tankers and deployed American warships to protect them against Iranian assaults.

When the Iran-Iraq war ended in August 1988, the Reagan administration was in its final months. Understandably, President Reagan decided that any serious reappraisal of Persian Gulf policy should be left to his successor. Accordingly, President Bush ordered a strategic review shortly after being sworn in. A preliminary review was completed in April 1989, but final approval was delayed until October.

Iraq had emerged from the war in desperate straits. Its economy had virtually collapsed, and many of its cities and much of its infrastructure were in ruins. Saddam needed capital to rebuild his ravaged country, which in turn required friendly relations not only with the rich Arab states of the Gulf, but also the West.

Saddam's Arab neighbors, notably Egypt, were grateful to him for containing the Iranian menace. They believed he would now focus on domestic reconstruction, and encouraged the United States to reach out to him. Our European allies, especially the French and Germans, were more interested in selling technology than erecting barriers. The Soviets were still a superpower, and Saddam was a primary client. Given the regional and international environment of the time, the United States could have pursued a policy of dual containment against Iran *and* Iraq only by going it alone. And going it alone would not have worked.

THE POLITICS OF DIPLOMACY

At the time, we saw Iraq as a potentially helpful Arab ally in moving the moribund Middle East peace process forward. We assumed that a less divisive and radical Iraq would be marginally helpful to Mideast peace. Conversely, we were convinced that, if it chose, Iraq could encourage and influence the Palestinians, and we wanted to explore the proposition that closer political and economic ties with Iraq might persuade it at the very least to be less of a stumbling block. I'd been personally encouraged in this view, incidentally, not only by several Middle East leaders but also by some very good friends of Israel, including a Republican senator who had privately urged me to reach out to Iraq.

Meanwhile, our new administration was grappling with one of the most revolutionary periods in world history. The demise of the Soviet empire, the dissolution of the Warsaw Pact, and the unification of Germany represented the greatest shifts in the strategic environment since the advent of the atomic bomb. The Middle East peace process and developments in Central America, as well as such unanticipated events as the June massacre of Chinese dissidents in Tiananmen Square in Beijing, also commanded large amounts of time and attention. In this environment, at that time, none of us considered policy toward Iraq to be an urgent priority. And it was simply not prominent on my radar screen, or the President's.

Our administration's review of the previous Iraq policy was not immune from domestic economic considerations. From its modest inception in the Reagan administration, the policy of extending grain credit guarantees to Iraq had expanded dramatically. The Department of Agriculture's Commodity Credit Corporation (CCC) was now extending more than $1 billion a year in credit guarantees to Iraq to buy American foodstuffs. By 1989, Iraq had become the ninth-largest purchaser of U.S. agricultural products. These programs were immensely popular on Capitol Hill and with farm state politicians.

It's also worth noting that Iraq's repayment record on these loans was spotless. Had we attempted to isolate Iraq, we would have also isolated American businesses, particularly agricultural interests, from significant commercial opportunities. And we would surely have been castigated by such ardent congressional supporters as Democrats Jack Brooks of Texas and Charlie Rose of North Carolina, both of whom would later become vociferous critics of the very policies they had so enthusiastically endorsed.

For the next six months, Iraq policy remained on the back burner. On October 2, 1989, however, the President signed National Security Directive 26 (NSD-26), codifying American policy in the Persian Gulf. With respect to Iraq, the directive concluded that "normal relations between the United States and Iraq would serve our longer-term interests and promote stability in both the Gulf and the Middle East." As a means of testing the premise that friendlier relations might prompt Iraq to moderate its behavior on such issues as terrorism, human rights, and chemical and biological weapons, we were prepared to expand our "economic and political incentives" with Baghdad. In that regard, we agreed to "pursue, and seek to facilitate, opportunities for U.S. firms to participate in the reconstruction of the Iraqi economy."

The directive also explicitly envisioned a policy of disincentives if our overtures proved unsuccessful. We were under no illusions about Saddam's brutality toward his own people or his capacity for escalating tensions with his neighbors. We fully recognized at the time that it was entirely possible any carrots we offered him would fail to produce the desired result. If that occurred, NSD-26 provided for rescinding or curtailing our ties. "The Iraqi leadership must understand," the directive noted, "that any illegal use of chemical and/or biological weapons will lead to economic and political sanctions, for which we would seek the broadest possible support from our allies and friends." This flexibility to move quickly from incentives to disincentives has been overlooked by many, but in fact it was a central component of the strategy.

It was well worth exploring the possibility that better relations might stem nuclear proliferation, bring economic benefits, and enhance prospects for Arab-Israeli peace. Just as important, we could always pursue containment later if engagement did not work.

Early Efforts at Engagement

My first direct exposure to Iraq had occurred two months after being sworn in. I met on March 24, 1989, with Nizar Hamdoon, a former ambassador to the United States who was then the Iraqi Under Secretary for Foreign Affairs. I told Hamdoon that the United States attached great importance to its relations with Iraq and hoped to develop closer bilateral ties. I also emphasized that Iraq's uses of chemical weapons during the war with Iran and against its Kurdish population were a serious impediment to doing so.

On October 6, four days after NSD-26 spelled out our policy toward Iraq, I met for the first time with Tariq Aziz, the Iraqi Foreign Minister. Like most initial contacts, it was a diplomatically cordial meeting, with both of us attempting to size up the other and develop a foundation for future contacts. I remember being impressed with Aziz. An urbane, cosmopolitan man, he spoke very good English and had an excellent command of his brief. He was, in fact, a latter-day von Ribbentrop.

My primary interest in meeting with Aziz was to seek his help in moving along the peace process in the Middle East. My proposal for talks between Israel and Palestinians from the occupied territories had been rebuffed. Meetings with PLO representatives in the summer failed to reach any agreement. Around the same time, Mubarak had issued his ten-point proposal aimed at breaking the deadlock. When I asked Aziz to endorse Mubarak's ten points, he replied that Iraq's support for the plan was well known in the region. It was his government's policy, however, to refrain from public statements on the peace process. Such talks might "complicate" matters. I saw his remarks as a polite brush-off, but I still hoped that Iraq might eventually be persuaded to help in reaching a solution.

During our opening colloquy, I'd told him the United States valued its relationship with Iraq and wanted to see it strengthened and broadened. There was every reason to believe the potential existed to move the relationship in a positive direction. Aziz said Saddam Hussein had instructed him to state unequivocally that Iraq was similarly eager for good relations "on the basis of mutual respect and understanding."

Then, quite unexpectedly, his tone changed. He accused the United States of interfering in Iraq's internal affairs and of conducting clandestine efforts to subvert their government. His evidence was sketchy. Iraq had received reports that senior American diplomats were approaching Arab counterparts, "raising suspicion and fear" about Iraqi intentions, which he said were wholly peaceful. Moreover, these officials had questioned Iraqi efforts to develop its "technological base"—a euphemistic reference to Iraq's troublesome military buildup. "Everything that we are doing is for our people," he insisted. Finally, he charged that "some American agencies," presumably the CIA, were attempting to destabilize Iraq. I told him I was surprised by his complaints. This was my first direct exposure to the paranoia that I would later learn permeated the upper echelons of the Iraqi government, fueling a host of miscalculations about America and the West that would later have tragic consequences.

Aziz then complained that Iraq's CCC credits were being reduced from $1 billion to $400 million in the coming year. He claimed this action, which he said would "sour relations," was an unwarranted linkage to the BNL affair, "in which we have played no part." This was a reference, of course, to the revelations that an Atlanta branch of an Italian bank, Banca Nazionale del Lavoro (BNL), had granted more than $3 billion in unauthorized letters of credit to Iraq. His country placed great pride in eliminating corruption, Aziz said. If Iraqi government officials were implicated in BNL, he wanted to know immediately. When I asked him if his government would make available any officials suspected of wrongdoing, he was less than forthcoming; that would depend on what information was made available to Iraq, he said.

As I was privy to current covert operations of the U.S. government, I knew that Aziz's allegations of American destabilization efforts against Iraq were wholly unfounded. Nevertheless, I checked personally with the President and Scowcroft to be certain. Later that month, I told Aziz in a written message that the President had asked me to say that "the United States is not involved in any effort to weaken or destabilize Iraq. I can tell you this with the highest authority."

I added, however, that it was important to address "some serious allegations that need to be explored further" about the administration of the CCC program. I was referring, of course, to the possible complicity of Iraqi government officials in BNL's activities. I hoped that it would be possible to resolve these problems and continue the program, and I reiterated that the President was "personally committed to build an increasingly solid foundation despite inevitable differences." Aziz informed our ambassador to Baghdad, April Glaspie, that he considered the tone of my letter positive.

On October 26, John Kelly, the Assistant Secretary of State for Near Eastern and South Asian Affairs (NEA), and Abraham Sofaer, the department's legal adviser, sent me an "action memorandum" recommending that we push for continuation of CCC credit guarantees for Iraq. Their recommendation was endorsed by Bob Kimmitt and Dick McCormack, the Under Secretary for Economic Affairs, respectively. The memo referred to charges of Iraqi corruption and the implications of the BNL scandal, noting that lawyers from State had consulted with their counterparts at Agriculture who had looked into the BNL investigation and separately with the U.S. attorney's office in Atlanta. (The lawyers had also consulted with the Department of Justice.) While it was possible that several high-ranking Iraqi officials might be involved in the BNL affair, they pointed out, "our information about the investigation indicates that the prosecutor does not now intend to indict Iraqi officials." They recommended that, "provided the review process turns up no evidence of Iraqi wrongdoing," the CCC credits be extended, but administered with "built-in, periodic reviews and related disbursement in tranches to ensure Iraqi compliance with CCC obligations and cooperation with the BNL investigation." They cited Aziz's promise of full cooperation in the BNL matter as "an unprecedented step for Iraq" and argued against going back to the Iraqis with a lesser amount they had previously rejected, "especially when it seems clear they would accept other reviews and other reasonable safeguards." They also included a rationale that Kelly, in particular, knew would appeal to me: "Our ability to influence Iraqi policies in areas important to us, from Lebanon to the Middle East, will be heavily influenced by the outcome of the CCC negotiations."

This position was squarely within the parameters of NSD-26. On October 31, I approved their recommendation that I urge Secretary of Agriculture Clayton Yeutter to go forward with a $1 billion program of credits in tranches. That same day, I called Yeutter and urged him to implement the full program—along with sufficient safeguards to make sure previous irregularities did not recur. "I think we're seeing it the same way your guys are," he told me. "I'll get right into it."

Three days later, Agriculture decided to proceed with the full program of $1 billion in credits in two tranches with the safeguards I'd discussed with Yeutter. The proposal was presented to the National Advisory Council on International and Financial Policies (NAC), an interagency group that coordinated policies such as CCC credits that cut across jurisdictional lines. On November 6, the entire $1 billion program was approved by NAC, with a first tranche of $500 million. Before releasing a second tranche, the program would be reviewed for Iraqi compliance and to consider any new developments in the BNL affair.

In a letter to Tariq Aziz the next day, I said the decision "reflects the importance we attach to our relationship with Iraq." I also told him that I was glad to have learned of his pledge of full cooperation in the BNL affair. "Our cooperation in this area must be free from any taint of illegality," I noted.

On January 17, 1990, the President overrode congressional opposition and signed a directive authorizing an Export-Import Bank line of credit of nearly $200 million for Iraqi grain purchases. Denying these credits, he said, was "not in the best interests of the United States." This decision, which I fully supported, turned out to be the high-water mark of our efforts to moderate Iraqi behavior.

Saddam's Ominous Turn

Despite our pursuit of a course of incentives, our relations with Iraq turned worse as we entered the new year. Almost immediately, the Iraqis embarked on a pattern of conduct that John Kelly has aptly described as Saddam's "spring of bad behavior." By April, it had become clear that our policy had not produced the results we had hoped for. A more confrontational stance toward Baghdad was now necessary.

There's no question Saddam's behavior changed for the worse in early 1990. His rhetoric grew more inflammatory and threatening. He executed an Iranian-born British journalist for espionage, complained bitterly about a Voice of America editorial that made fleeting reference to Iraq's police state, and publicly accused the United States of meddling in the Gulf. He built six Scud missile launchers in western Iraq within range of Israeli cities, and accelerated his efforts to obtain sophisticated technology that could be converted for use in his military and nuclear programs.

Parenthetically, it should be noted that there wasn't much intelligence on what was going on inside Iraq. Much as Winston Churchill had described the Stalinist Soviet Union, Iraq was a riddle wrapped in a mystery inside an enigma. As a result, it was extremely difficult to determine the extent to which Saddam was making strategic shifts or mere tactical changes. Factors that in retrospect seem easily understandable—the extent to which Iraq was impoverished and needed to rob a bank like Kuwait, or Saddam's paranoia over another attack on his nuclear facilities—were open to varying interpretations at the time.

Saddam's increasingly outrageous public behavior, however, contrasted with his private diplomacy, which was considerably more conciliatory. On February 12, Kelly and April Glaspie met for ninety minutes with Saddam Hussein in Baghdad. By all accounts, it was a friendly meeting. Saddam said that with the Soviet Union in decline as a world power, the United States had an opportunity to help stabilize the Middle East. The thrust of his message was that he preferred peace to war in the Middle East, but doubted the United States would exert sufficient pressure on Israel to move the peace process forward. For his part, Kelly reiterated that the President was committed to what he paraphrased as "warm and true friendship for our mutual benefit." However, Kelly also informed Saddam that the State Department's annual report on human rights, to be issued within a fortnight, would be sharply critical of the Baghdad regime.

As Saddam's mischief intensified, we expressed our concerns more aggressively. On February 27, Brent Scowcroft made clear to the Iraqi ambassador the President's unhappiness with Saddam's recent criticisms of the United States. Three days later, the State Department sent a strong démarche to our embassies in Arab capitals instructing our ambassadors to make clear our "fundamental differences" with Iraq on nuclear proliferation, chemical weapons, Scud deployments, and human rights. On March 3, Kelly's deputy, Skip Gnehm, told the Iraqi ambassador that Saddam's statements were "atrocious."

Our strategic calculation changed irrevocably on April 2, when Saddam explicitly threatened Israel in a speech to the General Command of his armed forces. For the first time, Saddam confirmed that Iraq possessed chemical weapons and vowed that if he were attacked, "By God, we will make fire eat up half of Israel." These remarks set off alarms throughout the Western world and in Middle East capitals, and were quickly denounced by the administration. I instructed Margaret Tutwiler to term them "inflammatory, irresponsible, and outrageous." When asked, however, she responded that the bilateral relationship was not under review as a result of Saddam's verbal pyrotechnics. While that was true at that moment, it wouldn't remain so for long.

The day after the speech, Kimmitt and Ross remained after a morning staff meeting to discuss this new development with me. They told me the "Burn Israel" speech couldn't be treated as an isolated outburst. "Our policy is based on an illusion that we can moderate this guy," Ross said. "We can't." Kimmitt echoed, "I'm not comfortable with the policy anymore. These are tough guys. We have to deal with them toughly. Incentives haven't worked; it's time to go to disincentives." I agreed with them that our policy should change, and approved Kimmitt's recommendation that State request a meeting of the Deputies' Committee to consider ratcheting our Iraq policy up to one of containment. I also decided that a démarche should be delivered to the Iraqi Foreign Ministry. On April 11, Kimmitt cabled this guidance to Glaspie to pass on to the Iraqis: "Iraq will be on a collision course with the U.S. if it continues to engage in actions that threaten the stability of the region, undermine global arms efforts, and flout U.S. laws."

The next day, Saddam met with Senators Robert Dole, James McClure, Howard Metzenbaum, Frank Murkowski, and Alan Simpson in the northern city of Mosul. At their request, the department sent new policy guidance to the embassy in Baghdad so the senators would have the benefit of our thinking before this meeting. The guidance was unusually undiplomatic in its tone. It said that recent Iraqi actions had caused a "sharp deterioration" in bilateral relations and repeated the verbatim language of Kimmitt's message to Glaspie. The senators were given specifics of questionable Iraqi behavior and were urged to tell Saddam that he must take concrete steps to correct human-rights abuses and illegal procurement activities. "Without such measures on your part," the cable suggested Saddam be advised, "what little support that is left in the U.S. for Iraq may further erode."

The senators returned to Washington and announced that Saddam was a leader with whom the United States could work. Their private counsel to the President and me was no less optimistic than their public utterances. Nevertheless, we were sufficiently troubled by Saddam's speech that I used it the next day to press Eduard Shevardnadze in a private meeting in my office to support the President's call for an international convention reducing chemical weapons. "The fact that you have people like Saddam Hussein is reason enough to create an incentive to get all the chemical weapons states on board," I told Shevardnadze.

Initially, Kimmitt had encountered some resistance to a policy shift from the National Security Council staff, which was in favor of maintaining the existing policy approach. "We may have some different views over here," one NSC official told Kimmitt. Nonetheless, four days after the senatorial delegation saw Saddam, the Deputies' Committee met at the White House on April 16 to confront a practical dilemma: how to respond aggres-

sively to Iraq's unacceptable behavior and Saddam's threats while also preserving an ability to rebuild the relationship gradually if Baghdad's behavior improved. The DC agreed that the CCC program would remain intact,
but the second tranche of credits would be suspended. An interagency committee was created to coordinate efforts to combat Iraq's nuclear proliferation activities, and an options paper was commissioned. A decision on
Ex-Im credits was deferred. While the decision to suspend the second tranche was a significant policy shift, the issue of what to do then about Iraq
policy probably should have been "kicked up" to the principals for a more
comprehensive policy review.

After the DC meeting, Kimmitt sent me a note arguing that State
should push to cancel all credit programs. "If we go forward with CCC and
Ex-Im," he said, "I think Saddam Hussein will regard the decision as a positive political signal, which will lead him to downplay other efforts we might
undertake to stop his proliferation campaign."

On May 1, I testified before a Senate Foreign Relations subcommittee.
In response to a question from Senator Robert Kasten of Wisconsin, I said it
was "a little bit premature" to discuss possible sanctions against Iraq. My
opposition was primarily institutional. Several members had introduced
bills calling for mandatory sanctions against Iraq. I believed that such legislation would have robbed us of any flexibility in dealing with Iraq and
would also have impinged upon the President's right to conduct foreign
policy.

Moreover, while relations had taken a significant turn for the worse, I
didn't think it wise to take irrevocable actions at that moment. Several of
our Arab allies, including Egypt and Saudi Arabia, had urged us to pursue
this middle-ground approach. On April 30, King Fahd sent a message to the
President saying that his government was seeking to "cool things down"
with Iraq. At the same time, a visiting group of Arab ambassadors, including
Egyptian and Kuwaiti envoys, weighed in to the same effect. Outrageous
rhetoric from radical Arab leaders wasn't exactly a rare occurrence, and at
that point there was no compelling reason to believe that Saddam was engaging in anything more than verbal intimidation.

Furthermore, maintaining the old policy still had its proponents. On
May 18, a senior NSC staffer cabled his thoughts from Baghdad, where he
was on a fact-finding visit. In a memorandum many have erroneously at-
tributed to Glaspie, he emphatically argued that the second tranche should
go forward. He and the senatorial delegation had just told the Iraqis there
was no conspiracy to punish Iraq and that the United States was still open to
"a decent working relationship if Iraq cleans up its act." He wrote that "unless Agriculture has uncovered a legal hornet's nest, we will want to proceed with the second tranche of credits." The Agriculture inspection team

had in effect given the Iraqis a clean bill of health; to punish Iraq under those circumstances "would be seen by the Iraqis as purely political—part of the U.S. conspiracy against Iraq."

Within days, the DC met for the second time (on May 29) to review policy options. After receiving an update on the CCC and BNL investigations, there was unanimous sentiment for suspending all economic credit programs for Iraq, and this was done. The next day, at an Arab League meeting in Baghdad, Saddam denounced Kuwait for engaging in "economic warfare" and confronted the Emir of Kuwait, who rejected Saddam's demands for billions of dollars in reparations and territorial concessions.

The Situation Worsens

By early summer, the administration was increasingly concerned about Saddam's belligerence, which continued to escalate. On July 16, Tariq Aziz complained in a letter to the Arab League that Kuwait and the United Arab Emirates were guilty of "direct aggression" against Iraq by exceeding oil-production quotas, a charge made publicly by Saddam in a speech the next day commemorating the twenty-second anniversary of the Ba'ath Party's revolution. Accusing the United States of abetting the "poison dagger" of his enemies, Saddam warned that if words had no impact, "something effective must be done."

Two days later, on July 19, a brief cable was sent to American embassies throughout the Middle East, with new policy guidance on the Iraq-Kuwait dispute. In all contacts with Arab counterparts, American diplomats were instructed to stress two points. First, "disputes should be settled by peaceful means, not intimidation and threats of use of force. Second, the United States takes no position on the substance of bilateral issues concerning Iraq and Kuwait. However, U.S. policy is unchanged. We remain committed to ensure the free flow of oil from the Gulf and to support the sovereignty and integrity of the Gulf states . . . we will continue to defend our vital interests in the Gulf."

On July 21—two days after American satellites detected a huge movement of troops and equipment toward the Kuwaiti border—the UAE asked the United States to participate in a joint military exercise as a show of solidarity against Saddam's new threats. Fearful of antagonizing Saddam, State's Near Eastern bureau initially opposed the idea. Saudi Arabia was also dubious, fearing such an exercise would provoke Saddam. I thought a joint exercise was an adequate way of signaling American displeasure with Saddam and demonstrating our commitment to protect U.S. vital interests in the region, and the President approved the exercise on July 23.

By this time, we were receiving intelligence reports of an ominous Iraqi buildup near the Kuwaiti border. The preponderance of expert opinion at home and abroad nevertheless believed that Saddam was merely bluffing in hopes of intimidating Kuwait into making economic concessions. At the time, this was not an unreasonable supposition, and our strategy of strengthening our rhetoric and engaging in military exercises was appropriate to counter mere intimidation.

On July 25, I left Washington at 7:15 A.M. for Jakarta to begin a week of consultations in Asia. Later that day, Glaspie was summoned to the Foreign Ministry in Baghdad and, without warning, was ushered into Saddam's office for an extraordinary two-hour audience. Because her meeting was arranged so suddenly, Glaspie was operating without specific instructions but with the general guidance of July 19.

In her eight-page reporting cable of the meeting, which by diplomatic custom was properly weighted toward Saddam's rambling monologue, Glaspie noted that Saddam wished to assure the President that his intentions were peaceful and that he therefore hoped American criticism of Iraq would be tempered. He had agreed to negotiations with the Saudis and Kuwaitis beginning very shortly. He was "very emotional" in criticizing the Kuwaitis for refusing to help ease Iraq's financial crisis. While "some circles" in the American government sought to undermine Iraq, he believed neither the President nor I were guilty of such behavior.

In her analysis, Glaspie contended that our joint maneuvers with the emirates had created the desired effect. Saddam was now worried about American intentions and anxious to avoid antagonizing the United States further. "We have fully caught his attention, and that is good," she concluded. "I believe we would now be well-advised to ease off on public criticism of Iraq until we see how the negotiations develop."

We still hoped the crisis could be defused. On July 28, the NSC staff drafted, and State routinely cleared, the following presidential message to Saddam: "I was pleased to learn of the agreement between Iraq and Kuwait to begin negotiations in Jeddah to find a peaceful solution to the current tensions between you. The United States and Iraq both have a strong interest in preserving the peace and stability of the Middle East. For this reason, we believe these difficulties are best resolved by peaceful means and not by threats involving military force or conflict." It's clear this message was not sufficiently firm and, coming three days after Glaspie's meeting, may have been interpreted by Saddam to mean that we weren't overly concerned.

During this period, State recommended that we take the additional step of moving a carrier task force, which was steaming toward Diego Garcia in the Indian Ocean into the northern Arabian Sea as a sign of our concern—an idea the military opposed. In fairness, however, there was a rough consensus within the government that the crisis may have eased. Despite the ominous Iraqi buildup along the border, the news that Iraqi and Kuwaiti diplomats would meet in Jeddah on July 31 was seen as a hopeful development. Two days later, however, Iraqi forces invaded a defenseless Kuwait.

Reflections on an Invasion

With the benefit of hindsight, it's easy to argue that we should have recognized earlier that we weren't going to moderate Saddam's behavior, and shifted our policy approach sooner and to a greater degree than we did. At the least, we should have given Iraqi policy a more prominent place on our radar screen at an earlier date. I believe the reasons we didn't change our policy approach earlier and to a greater extent are myriad and complex. And while I wish we'd focused more attention on Iraq earlier, given what happened, I remain unpersuaded that anything we might have done, short of actually moving armed forces to the region, would have deterred Iraq's invasion of Kuwait.

Perhaps more than anything else, this entire episode demonstrates the difficulty of altering any long-established diplomatic approach. In the best of circumstances, this is oftentimes an arduous and time-consuming task. Furthermore, diplomacy—as well as the American psyche—is fundamentally biased toward "improving relations." Shifting a policy away from cooperation toward confrontation is always a more difficult proposition—particularly when support for the existing policy is as firmly embedded among various constituencies and bureaucratic interests as was the policy toward Iraq.

For example, a shift would have prompted a considerable outcry from many who later criticized us for not changing our policy sooner. Key members of Congress would have fought us tooth and nail if we'd threatened to cut off grain credits. Similarly, many skeptics who in hindsight criticized us for not being more assertive with Iraq also chastised us for threatening use of force when we did. I continue to believe that if the President had said prior to August 1990 that we were willing to go to war to protect Kuwait, many members of Congress would have been muttering impeachment. Even after Saddam had invaded Kuwait, there was little, if any, domestic support for using our military. We had to build that support painstakingly. And no American President should ever threaten the use of military force unless he's prepared to follow through.

As I've indicated, during this period the administration was preoccupied with the fundamentally more important strategic shift in East-West relations and global politics brought on by the collapse of communism in Eastern Europe. For forty years, the West had sought this development. Ironically, the collapse of the Soviet empire, which so consumed our energies, was the identical event that obsessed Saddam—to the point that by February 1990 he saw the United States as a dominant power and threat to his regional ambitions.

Furthermore, without exception, our friends in the region consistently argued that Saddam was only posturing and that confrontation would simply make matters worse. Simply put, the reason why nobody believed Saddam would attack is because no realistic calculation of his interests could have foreseen a full-scale invasion of Kuwait. Shevardnadze had put it correctly in Moscow on the third day following the invasion: this was an irrational act that made no sense. As Saddam himself told April Glaspie a week before the invasion, "Do not push us to [war]. Do not make it the only option left with which we can protect our dignity. If Iraq is publicly humiliated by the United States, it will have no choice but to respond, however illogical and self-destructive that would prove." Unfortunately, Saddam was true to his words.

Even the Israelis believed that Saddam was bluffing to bully the Kuwaitis into economic concessions. Israel's intelligence service, the Mossad, told U.S. intelligence counterparts that Saddam's rhetoric was designed to deter an Israeli attack, not threaten one of his own. As late as July 31, King Hussein and President Mubarak reassured us that Saddam was engaged in verbal bluster, not literal threats. Ironically, most of our allies privately worried throughout the spring and summer of 1990 that the United States might *overreact* to Saddam's new aggressiveness!

In my view the only realistic chance to deter Saddam would have been to introduce U.S. forces into the region—and neither the Kuwaitis, the Saudis, the Soviets, nor the Congress would have supported that course before August 2. Indeed, it was only the shock of the invasion that allowed us to intervene militarily at all.

The ultimate irony, of course, is that if we *had* succeeded in deterring Iraq's aggression, the West would now be debating how to contain an emboldened Saddam with a substantially stronger military machine and a nuclear and chemical arsenal even more lethal than Western intelligence had imagined. In the final analysis, our "failure" to deter Saddam may well have prevented a far more sinister result.

CHAPTER 16

BUILDING THE COALITION

If it doesn't work . . . if it can't work in a collective way to reverse the aggression, I don't know how we're going to prevent this from happening again.
　　—Secretary Baker to Eduard Shevardnadze during the Bush-Gorbachev Summit, September 9, 1991, Helsinki, Finland

My father was an authentic American hero in World War I, a captain of infantry in the Ninetieth Division in France. He was highly decorated for bravery, but like most soldiers who have watched their friends die, he didn't like to talk about it much. However, he did tell me about the day he ordered his men into a bunker that had been occupied by the Germans. They reported back that the trench was clear of enemy soldiers. He had a very strong sense that his troops were simply too afraid to enter the bunker. So he pulled out his .45 pistol and descended into the trenches himself. A few minutes later, he emerged with three German prisoners. It was a lesson in leadership and bravery I carry with me to this day, and which helped shape my view of the primacy of American leadership throughout the world.

I grew up believing that America had led the free world during World War I, when my dad was "over there" fighting in the trenches against the Kaiser, and I lived through America's leadership in World War II. Every American of my generation remembers what he or she was doing on December 7, 1941. I was an eleven-year-old tennis fanatic. That Sunday afternoon, I had just finished playing a match at the River Oaks Country Club in Houston and was walking from the tennis courts to the clubhouse. As I passed the golf shop, I heard a voice on a radio say, "Pearl Harbor has just been bombed." My parents were not fond of President Roosevelt; my father voted for him in 1932, but never again. He was a fervent opponent of the New Deal, which he considered tantamount to socialism. Sometimes when my parents had guests in their home, I would be asked to recite anti-Roosevelt doggerel I had memorized. But it never occurred to my dad—or to me—to question Roosevelt's leadership in the conduct of foreign affairs. Like George Bush, I was of a generation that embraced wholeheartedly the concept of Pax Americana, an America engaged as a force for creative and constructive change around the world. I still believe that in global affairs over the last fifty years, many things of enduring value have occurred in large part as a consequence of the dynamic involvement of American leadership. In my mind, this has always simply been a given.

And that leadership was challenged once again on August 2, 1990. With his flagrant move into Kuwait, Saddam Hussein's ambitions revealed themselves in all their grandiosity. While most believed Iraq's military buildup on the Kuwaiti border in late July was intended to frighten Kuwait into opening its coffers, and some thought Iraq might take the Rumaila oil field and perhaps Bubiyan and Al-Wadah islands as bargaining chips to extract concessions from the Emir, almost no one predicted a full-scale invasion. By sending his armored columns all the way to the Kuwait-Saudi border, Saddam showed both his appetite and his willingness to run risks. Despite the unprecedented joint statement the United States and the Soviet Union had issued at Vnukovo II Airport on the second day of the crisis and the unanimous vote in the Security Council condemning the invasion, Iraq continued to pour forces into Kuwait over the weekend following the invasion.

In response, as he stepped off Marine One on the White House lawn on Sunday afternoon, August 5, George Bush uttered what was arguably the most famous—and courageous—line of his Presidency: "This will not stand, this aggression against Kuwait." Some critics have fixed on this statement—and the resolute manner in which the President issued it—as an indication of the President's intention from the very beginning to go to war.

That, however, would be a serious misreading, both of George Bush the man and of the situation in which the United States, as the world's remaining superpower, found itself that August. The President's statement reflected his instinctive sense, very early on, that this was no ordinary crisis, that it truly would become a hinge point in history. His statement also showed his determination to undo Iraq's aggression. At every stage in the conflict, from that sunny August afternoon through the blustery days of February, whenever the President made a decision, his choice invariably revealed that determination once again. And with every decision, the world community would be one step closer to ejecting Iraq from Kuwait. What the President's statement did not reveal was how he would go about doing that.

It's doubtful anyone could quite have predicted how this crisis would unfold. Few could have foreseen the critical role the Soviet Union, led mostly by its farsighted Foreign Minister Eduard Shevardnadze, would play in redressing a Soviet client state's aggression. Almost no one could have seen the extent to which Arabs would work with Americans and Europeans in isolating an Arab state whose leader believed he was the natural heir to Nasser. And only with the benefit of hindsight can we fully appreciate how the end of the Cold War made possible the unprecedented international coalition of Desert Shield and the military marvel of Desert Storm—and how they in turn made possible the movement on Middle East peace that allowed Israel finally to sit down in Madrid and talk peace face-to-face with her Arab neighbors. Without these catalytic events, Israel would not today be at peace with Jordan or negotiating for peace with Palestinians, Lebanon, and Syria.

What the President did in the Gulf was simply the right thing to do. George Bush took the difficult choices the world expects of American leadership, even when some of our friends publicly complain when we do exercise that leadership. But none of us was oblivious to the formidable political realities of this crisis for a President who I was sure would be running for reelection in two years. Sometime in August, he and I were alone in the Oval Office. I said to him, "I know you're aware of the fact that this has all the ingredients that brought down three of the last five Presidents: a hostage crisis, body bags, and a full-fledged economic recession caused by forty-dollar oil." The President understood it full well. "I know that, Jimmy, I know that," he said. "But we're doing what's right; we're doing what is clearly in the national interest of the United States. Whatever else happens, so be it."

Coercive Diplomacy and Coalition Building

At a meeting of the National Security Council at Camp David on August 4, the President had decided the first imperative was to deter an Iraqi move into Saudi Arabia. In combination with that mission, however, was the undoing of Iraq's invasion of Kuwait by the pursuit of a policy of coercive diplomacy against Saddam Hussein. We would begin with diplomatic pressure, then add economic pressure, to a great degree organized through the United Nations, and finally move toward military pressure by gradually increasing American troop strength in the Gulf. The strategy was to lead a global political alliance aimed at isolating Iraq. Through the use of economic sanctions, we hoped to make Saddam pay such a high price for his aggression that in time he would be forced to release his Western hostages and withdraw from Kuwait. If he didn't, we would expel him by military force.

To pursue this strategy, I had no doubt we needed a coalition of partners, and in fact told Shevardnadze as much when we met on August 3. Consider what might have come of our diplomatic offensive if we had ignored the Soviets, Iraq's traditional patron. Our strategy of economic pressure would have been doomed if Turkey had refused to shut off its oil pipeline from Iraq. And in the case of military action, we would need the support of the American people and Congress to sustain a war. To win that support, we would have to demonstrate that we had first pursued all reasonable nonlethal remedies; had acted as the leader of the world community, not the Lone Ranger; were insisting on other nations sharing our burden, especially the financial cost; and that war in the Persian Gulf would not trigger war with the Soviets because they were acting in concert with us. Under these circumstances, there was simply no percentage in deciding at the outset to go it alone. I thought that to do so would significantly lessen our chances of overall success because it would mean almost certain political failure, both internationally and domestically.

Almost by definition, the first stop for coalition building was the United Nations. On August 2, at our behest, the Security Council had passed the first of what would become twelve resolutions. Resolution 660 not only condemned Saddam's invasion, but demanded a complete and unconditional withdrawal. The language was simple and crystal clear, purposely designed by us to frame the vote as being for or against aggression. We believed it was imperative to keep the debate from turning into an Iraq-versus-the–United States confrontation, which would have made it more difficult to build and maintain a coalition. The blatant nature of Saddam's invasion certainly helped; even Cuba surprised us by joining in the unanimous 14–0 vote, with only Yemen abstaining. The next day in Moscow, the Soviet Union and the United States joined in condemning the invasion and cutting off arms supplies to Baghdad. Three days later, the Saudis agreed to allow 100,000 American troops to deploy to the kingdom. In less than a week, three of the crucial building blocks of the coalition were already in place.

Desert Storm could have been a unilateral American initiative. Legally, the President was within his prerogatives to act under Article 51 of the United Nations Charter, which allows member states the right of self-defense to protect their national interests. Some of our allies thought that we should invoke Article 51, begin deploying American troops in the Gulf, and launch combat operations as soon as possible. Not surprisingly, the most prominent of these hawks was British Prime Minister Margaret Thatcher.

On August 6, the President met in the Oval Office with the Prime Minister. Much has been written about the special relationship between the United States and Great Britain, and the bilateral ties forged between us over two centuries are every bit as durable as advertised. We have no better friends than the British. And the relationship *is* special. This gives the British a license others don't have—the license of occasionally flexing *our* muscles. And sometimes they are quite adept at it. As her gutsy leadership during the 1982 Falklands war had amply demonstrated, Margaret Thatcher is a charter member of the do-what-you-must-now-and-worry-about-it-later school. She's never been reluctant to say what she thinks, and in this case she wasn't the least bit shy in expressing her serious misgivings about our preference for pursuing a multilateral course against Saddam. "We simply can't let this stand," she argued. "We've got to take care of it now." We agreed that Article 51 of the U.N. Charter gave us the right to proceed unilaterally. But she believed that asking the U.N. Security Council to impose sanctions on Iraq, which was happening that very day, would preclude our later taking military action under Article 51. Bob Kimmitt had convinced me she was wrong on the legal merits, and some time later she conceded the point. But to my way of thinking, our disagreement about legalities was academic. As a practical matter, the United States had no real choice initially but to try a coalition approach in dealing with the crisis. Otherwise we'd never attract the breadth of support to convince Saddam he was confronting the entire civilized world, not just a single superpower he might be able to demonize. We would never have achieved the sort of solidarity from Arab nations that was crucial to isolating Saddam diplomatically. The credibility of our cause would be suspect, not just in the Arab world, but even to some in the West, including the United States. At this point in time, we did not have the necessary domestic political support to do what we ultimately had to do to eject Iraq from Kuwait—move 550,000 Americans to the Persian Gulf and go to war. There are times when great powers must forswear even trying collective action and go it alone in the first instance, as we had done in Grenada in 1983 and Panama in 1989. This was definitely not one of them.

Having decided on building a coalition, we turned our attention to the practical and arduous task of actually putting one together and maintaining it throughout the crisis. Revolutionary changes were buffeting the Soviet Union, and on the eve of war, Shevardnadze resigned, depriving the United States of its strongest ally within the Soviet government.

Our sanctions policy placed enormous financial burdens on many countries, and many nations within the coalition, even some of our staunchest allies, were initially skittish about actually going to war with Iraq. In retrospect, I believe maintaining the coalition's solidarity was even more difficult than assembling it in the first place.

In managing the regional implications of the crisis, we needed to consider a host of major players in the region besides the Saudis: Turkey, a country where civilian government had often been weak and which had genuine concerns about Kurdish nationalism undermining national stability; Syria, where President Assad hated Saddam but was loath to give comfort to Israel; Egypt, the primary voice of Arab moderation in the region; Israel, which could have undermined the coalition at any moment by moving preemptively against Saddam; Iran, whose enmity for Iraq was surpassed only by its hatred of the United States; Jordan, whose King pursued a policy of equivocation to keep from alienating his stronger neighbor, Saddam; the Palestinians, whose support for Saddam threatened our hopes for forging an anti-Iraq Arab majority; the Gulf states, whose sheikhdoms were Saddam's next dominoes; and Yemen, whose support of Saddam splintered anti-Saddam Arab solidarity.

First and foremost, however, Desert Shield was a global confrontation. Suddenly, on the doorstep of a declining Soviet superpower, two of the world's largest armies were poised to square off in a region where three continents, civilizations, and cultures meet, with potentially grave implications for regional stability and worldwide economic security. This latter imperative, along with the need to raise billions of dollars to finance our efforts, underscored the necessity of involving emerging global powers such as Japan and West Germany. The decision to go to the United Nations from the beginning clearly underscored the global nature of the crisis.

On paper, the process of putting together a diplomatic alliance within the Security Council might seem a deceptively simple exercise. On any given matter, we usually started with our counterparts among the "Permanent Five"—Great Britain, France, the Soviet Union, and China—any of whom could thwart our aims with a veto. We would invariably begin with the British, perennially our most reliable allies. Next we'd approach the French, followed by the Soviets. In this case, because of my meeting with Shevardnadze in Moscow on August 2, we already had the Soviets committed to an arms embargo. The French had long been a heavy supplier of weapons to Iraq, and the government was under considerable commercial pressure from domestic arms merchants. But the French could not appear softer than the Soviets. Once we had at least a rough consensus among those three, it was easier to deal with the Chinese. The only thing Beijing liked less than not getting its way on a policy matter was being the odd man out in what Kimmitt liked to call "the big-guys club." Simply put, they hated being isolated. They were particularly loath to appear more obstructionist than the Soviets—partly since the 1989 massacre of hundreds of dissidents in Tiananmen Square had isolated them diplomatically. Our strategy in the Security Council was a permutation of our overall coercive diplomacy approach, and more often than not it worked.

The Soviets were critical, not only as a superpower in demise, but as an important regional player, a longtime patron and weapons procurer for Iraq and Syria. Britain and France also had a long and checkered history in the Middle East; the British, after all, were responsible for creating Iraq, which became independent in 1932. Despite their post-Suez journey away from the region, Britain and France saw in this crisis an opportunity to empha- size their heritage as global powers. Beijing was always more of a wild card, unlikely to support our efforts but in the end not willing to undercut us.

With the Perm Five on board, our focus could then turn to the ten other seats on the Security Council. Many of these nations were nominally non- aligned, small countries whose votes were up for grabs. With them, our strategy beyond the merits was to point out that we had taken our case to the United Nations, traditionally a haven for the world's have-nots, instead of striking out alone. We were also able to exploit another reality: As com- munism collapsed, America's status as the preeminent superpower was magnified. As a result, everyone wanted to get closer to the United States. This gave us formidable leverage, which we didn't hesitate to wield throughout the crisis.

The Soviets

From the start, I had viewed the Soviets as key. In every strategy calcu- lation, I considered their support a prerequisite to a credible coalition. They had to be courted, nurtured, and included to a degree once unthinkable by American policy makers. Indeed, Shevardnadze and I exchanged eleven phone calls and five letters in August alone—a level of consultation that would have been unimaginable just a year before. Their endorsement was so critical, and my relationship with Shevardnadze was sufficiently credible, that I was willing and able to go many an extra mile to keep them on board—even in the face of objections from time to time by some of my colleagues in the national security apparatus. Yet their support was often as difficult as it was indispensable. I was reminded of that by a letter from Shevardnadze only two days after our meeting at Vnukovo II Airport. Its tone was notably different from the tenor of our meeting. He wrote that his government would resist any further U.N. resolutions until the Iraqis were given ample time to withdraw from Kuwait. Clearly, the Arabists were in an uproar over the U.S.-Soviet joint statement, and Shevardnadze was pay- ing the price.

The morning of August 5, I met at the White House with Brent Scowcroft and the President to discuss the delicate task of breaking the news to the Soviets that King Fahd had invited our troops into Saudi Arabia. Given Shevardnadze's letter, they were certain to be unhappy. We decided that I should telephone Shevardnadze and put the most benign face possible on the news; the Saudis had asked us in, but we had no intention of expanding our influence in the Gulf.

On the morning of August 7 in Washington, I reached Shevardnadze at his dacha outside Moscow. I discussed the latest intelligence reports of the Iraqi occupation and said that at the request of King Fahd, the President was dispatching American troops to the Gulf. I informed him that the troops would begin deploying the next day and that the President would make a public announcement on Wednesday, August 8. I went out of my way to make clear that this deployment was temporary and that our troops would leave Saudi Arabia once the crisis had been resolved. We had no intention of seeking a permanent U.S. presence.

I could feel the coolness on the other end of the telephone line; the Soviets were hypersensitive about their status. Even with forty-eight hours' advance notice of our decisions, Shevardnadze was furious. "Are you *consulting* us or are you *informing* us?" he demanded to know.

"Well, Eduard, I'm *talking* with you, because this is not something we want to do by ourselves," I said. "I would like to explore with you whether Soviet forces would want to participate with us in the multinational force. That would demonstrate resolve and make the use of force less likely."

I had learned by then that it's often more useful to avoid answering an unpleasant question directly in hopes of moving the discussion onto more familiar, comfortable ground. It was an improvisation, but it seemed to work. I could sense a change in his tone as he then asked, "How about the military staff committee of the Security Council?" For years, the Soviets had sought to revive this moribund U.N. appendage as a vehicle for giving themselves a greater hand in peacekeeping operations. Despite my assurances to Shevardnadze in Moscow three days earlier, his Arabists seemed convinced that the President was plotting a unilateral strike against Iraq, and so had been pushing the military staff committee idea aggressively since the invasion, hoping they could use it to avert an attack we had no intention then of launching. I told him that I would raise the idea promptly with the President.

Predictably, my suggestion regarding Soviet participation in a multilateral force and Shevardnadze's suggestion to give life to the military staff committee went nowhere with the bureaucracy at State, which argued that inviting the Soviets to establish a U.S.-sanctioned military presence in the Gulf ran counter to forty years of American diplomacy designed to keep the Soviets from meddling in the region. The President, Powell, Cheney, and

Scowcroft all expressed initial misgivings as well. Powell especially worried about giving the Soviets a role in a possible attack on Iraq in the future.

My view was that we needed the Soviets more than anyone else. Period. Gorbachev and Shevardnadze had taken great risks in agreeing to a joint statement with us. It was naive, as well as dangerous to our interests, to believe we could continue to shut them out of the Middle East. Ultimately, a consensus developed that it might well be a significant plus to have the Soviets in our military coalition. It would certainly ruin Saddam's day to learn that his primary arms supplier might now be prepared to join in military operations with the Americans. I telephoned Shevardnadze on August 8 to report that the President had "absolutely no problem" with Soviet military participation in a multilateral force in the Gulf. He promised to raise the idea with Gorbachev. A few hours later, he called back to say the Soviets would not join the military coalition. I later learned that memories of the Soviet debacle in Afghanistan, where Moscow had become embroiled in a guerrilla war against a Muslim insurgency, had helped kill the idea. I knew our strategic interests had been well served regardless. Their refusal to participate damaged the credibility of the hard-liners who opposed a solution involving the use of force. In the meantime, fragile Soviet sensibilities had been assuaged by our offer to include them in the coalition. I knew the overall relationship hadn't suffered when Shevardnadze told me the Soviets would support us on a new resolution at the United Nations.

The Turkish Connection

Later that day, the Security Council passed Resolution 661, which imposed severe economic sanctions against Iraq. The resolution effectively ordered a total embargo on all commercial dealings with Saddam and his puppet government in Kuwait. It was the first step in our strategy not only to isolate Iraq diplomatically but also to apply a stranglehold to its economy. Saddam had invaded in part in order to replenish his own depleted coffers with Kuwait's massive oil revenues. To deny him that wealth, and to underscore the credibility of the sanctions, it was imperative that the oil pipeline flowing from Iraq across Turkey into the Mediterranean be shut down. Three days after the U.N. vote, I flew to Ankara for meetings with President Ozal of Turkey, the first of twenty countries I would visit during the crisis.

I'd known Turgut Ozal since my years at Treasury. He was a skilled economist, had been Turkey's representative to the World Bank and the International Monetary Fund, and spoke fluent English. He was a friendly man, quick with a smile. His firm style of decision making frequently relied on his own visceral instincts rather than his governmental bureaucracy. It was characteristic of Ozal that he had already ordered the pipeline closed the day before I arrived to ask him to shut it down. He told me he knew the decision would be unpopular in his country, but that it was the right thing to do and that he would not let "one drop" of oil through. He also said that he thought Saddam was a madman and that if it came to war, Iraq's army wouldn't fight. He called it a "hollow army." Throughout our meeting, he clicked the television on and off, getting updates from CNN.

Ozal believed that, like most bullies, Saddam would reverse course when confronted. He guessed that the sanctions would have the desired effect in as little as six weeks. I wanted to believe he was right, but if he weren't, we would eventually have to ask even more from Turkey. Since 1966, the U.S. Air Force had maintained a tactical fighter wing at the Turkish air base near Incirlik. The American military presence in Turkey had always been controversial; because of domestic political opposition, the Turks had refused to let us fly missions from Incirlik during the 1980 Iranian hostage crisis or the ill-fated U.S. Marine deployment to Lebanon in 1983. If we went to war with Iraq, we would need Ozal's permission to deploy more of our warplanes in Turkey and launch air strikes from Incirlik and other Turkish bases. Despite his optimism, I suspect Ozal privately knew full well we would eventually need his bases. To help him counter his own nervous diplomats as well as Turkish public opinion, I told him that the United States was committed to finding the money to offset the estimated $1 billion in annual revenues Turkey would lose from the trade embargo. I also knew that Turkey's psychological needs were in many ways more important than its economic requirements. For years, Turkey had chafed at what it considered a lack of respect from some of its colleagues in the North Atlantic Treaty Organization. It was anxious to be treated more as a full NATO partner and it wanted badly to join the European Community. I told Ozal that I had already consulted with key NATO allies and was authorized to reaffirm the alliance's treaty obligations to Turkey's defense if it were attacked by Iraq in retaliation for closing the pipeline. I also told him that, while it was a decision for European Community members, the United States had formally endorsed, and would be strongly supportive of, Turkey's application to join the EC.

Ozal was appreciative, but had a wish list of his own. He said that his economists had estimated Turkey would lose $2.5 billion in receipts from the pipeline. It would be most helpful, he suggested, if the World Bank could be persuaded to increase its loans to Turkey from $400 million to perhaps $1 billion. Anticipating his request, I had talked the week before to President Bush's and my old friend Barber Conable, a former Republican congressman from New York whom President Reagan had appointed President of the World Bank on my recommendation as Secretary of the Treasury. I was happy to inform Ozal that the World Bank was prepared to extend Turkey between $1 billion and $1.5 billion in loans for each of the next two years.

I believe all of these sweeteners were justified on the merits. But they were also pragmatic manifestations of political reality. We needed Ozal's support, and we might well need his staging rights later. His willingness to go out on a limb for the United States at the very outset gave us more of a personal incentive to deliver for him. Throughout the crisis, Ozal was stalwart in his support for the United States. He was a leader of great heart and courage; like Shevardnadze, time and again he was willing to rise above the reticence of his foreign ministry and do the right thing. America is fortunate to have friends and allies like him, and I was proud when as a private citizen and at President Clinton's request, I represented my country at his funeral in 1993.

Toward the end of the meeting, Ozal reiterated a recurring theme that Saddam was the world's most dangerous despot. At a minimum, Ozal said, his Scud missiles and chemical warfare facilities must be destroyed, and he must be expelled from Kuwait, by force of arms if necessary. But these steps, he emphasized, were not nearly enough to deal with the menace. Ozal came right to the point: "Are we going to get rid of Saddam Hussein?" "Mr. President, we are prevented by law from taking actions to assassinate foreign officials," I replied. "Our focus now is to strangle him through political and economic sanctions." Ozal was not fazed. "We need to finish him off," he argued. "Every state is vulnerable if Saddam Hussein continues to exist. We will be in perpetual danger. Please tell President Bush that he has to go."

The Soviets—Again

In the next weeks, I talked almost daily with Shevardnadze, who was being hammered by the Arabists who were still furious with the Vnukovo joint statement. The so-called experts who'd assured Shevardnadze that Saddam wouldn't attack were now arguing they could control him. Threatening the use of force wasn't necessary to bring a client state around and would in fact destroy the relationship, they argued. I knew he was dubious and wanted to side with us, but he was under enormous pressure. I kept making the case that we weren't looking for an excuse to use force, but needed to demonstrate our willingness to use force to coerce Saddam out of Kuwait. During this time, Shevardnadze agreed to support two new U.N. resolutions—one declaring Iraq's annexation of Kuwait null and void, the other demanding the immediate release of all foreign nationals, who had in effect been taken hostage by Saddam. But superpower cooperation almost came apart in mid-August, when American intelligence reported that a merchant tanker was steaming toward Aden, Yemen, with a cargo of Iraqi oil.

The debate over whether to stop the tanker with military force was one of the few times I found myself completely isolated from my colleagues. Cheney, Powell, and Scowcroft all believed the ship should be promptly stopped, disabled, and boarded. There was even some sentiment for sinking the vessel if it ignored our warning shots. Some in the State Department began to refer to those who supported this approach as "the Article 51 crowd." I agreed that we had the right under Article 51 to stop the ship. But from conversations with Shevardnadze, I was sure that unilateral action at that point would be disastrous. The Security Council had voted sanctions against Iraq, but had only authorized nonmilitary measures to enforce them. Without more explicit U.N. authorization, I was sure the Soviets would bolt from the coalition, a calamity that would surely threaten our entire strategy.

Speaking on a portable satellite communications link set atop a huge granite boulder (which was home to a family of marmots) a few yards from the front porch of my ranch cabin in Pinedale, Wyoming, I told Shevardnadze that I had recommended to the President that we hold off from intercepting the tanker, but only if the Soviets agreed to a new U.N. resolution authorizing military action to enforce the trade embargo. He was not pleased, and said the Soviets wanted to be sure the Iraqis were violating the embargo before going any further.

On August 20, Shevardnadze told me he thought the Soviets could persuade Saddam to withdraw unconditionally and asked for five days to pursue the matter. It was too long. By then, the tanker would already be in port. I agreed to raise his request with the President, but suggested that Shevardnadze might best speed up his timetable.

I called the President in Kennebunkport, who was clearly frustrated with my request for a delay. Everyone else was telling him that procrastination would undermine the perception of American resolve. "We're going to be much worse off losing the Soviets than losing that ship," I told him. After a meeting with Cheney, Powell, Scowcroft, and Larry Eagleburger he reluctantly sided with me. On Wednesday, August 22, I called Shevardnadze to say that the Soviets had three days. The President had agreed to delay a vote on a new U.N. resolution until Saturday, August 25. "But will you promise me now that if we *do* move on Saturday, we'll have your support?" I asked. Shevardnadze said he would have to check.

On August 24, Shevardnadze called to say that Gorbachev had sent a blunt message to Saddam asking for a categorical answer within twenty-four hours on whether he would withdraw from Kuwait. The next afternoon, a letter arrived for me at the State Department.

> James:
>   I promised to call you at 11:00 Moscow time. But since I am busy at the Kremlin, I am asking the help of Ambassador Matlock to pass my message.
>   An answer has come from the Iraqis. I think it would not be worth commenting on. Therefore we have decided to instruct our representative in the Security Council to get in contact with Ambassador Pickering and other representatives of the Perm 5. As I already told you, we will suggest certain amendments to the draft resolution, not changing its substance, but widening the range of means which can be used for the purposes of control. I think that now our representatives can begin consultations with each other and with other members of the Security Council to bring about passage of the resolution.
>   If you have any questions which arise then if necessary I will be ready tomorrow to get in contact with you.
>   Sincerely, E. Shevardnadze

I knew Shevardnadze well enough to understand that the language of his letter meant that he was totally fed up—not only with his own Arabists but with the Iraqis. Saddam had made another serious miscalculation by failing to be responsive to the Soviets, thereby undermining the influence of his patrons in the Soviet Foreign Ministry on Gorbachev and Shevardnadze.

Early the next morning, August 25, the Security Council passed Resolution 665, outlawing all trade with Iraq by any means, and authorizing the military enforcement of these sanctions. The vote was 13–0, with two abstentions by Yemen and Cuba. In retrospect, I believe that Soviet support for this resolution was the pivotal moment in the entire diplomatic process—a tougher vote for them, in my opinion, than the use of force resolution in November. If we had invoked Article 51 and boarded or sunk that ship, I believe we never would have gotten the Soviets to come with us on that resolution authorizing military action to enforce the trade embargo, as well as subsequent ones that permitted military force to eject Iraq from Kuwait. The coalition might well have collapsed right then and there. Ultimately, the ship was allowed to reach port.

The Tin Cup Trip

Saddam's diplomatic isolation was now proceeding. By early September, the United Nations had passed five resolutions. But diplomatic support at the United Nations, though crucial, wasn't enough. From a domestic political standpoint as well as a moral one, we needed to insist upon substantial financial commitments from other countries to help underwrite the costs of the operation. The President was prepared to bear the brunt of the burden, in that if force were required to eject Iraq from Kuwait, Americans would die in the Gulf. The very least we could expect in return was that the countries we were helping, and all our other allies with stakes in the crisis, should join not only in supplying forces to the extent they could, but also in financing the costs of Operation Desert Shield.

We knew that, even without going to war, those costs would be staggering. We were mobilizing hundreds of thousands of soldiers and shipping them and their equipment to the Gulf by air and by sea. Once we had them there, we had to keep them in everything from missiles to mouthwash for months on end. Our preliminary projections of the direct costs to the United States Treasury ran into the tens of billions of dollars. Moreover, we felt an obligation to come up with the money to help offset the severe economic hardship the trade embargo would impose on several of our coalition partners, especially Egypt and Turkey. And at a time of economic uncertainty at home, it would be politically impossible to sustain domestic support for the operation unless we demonstrated that Uncle Sam wasn't footing the bill while others with pockets as deep as ours sat on the sidelines.

Thus was the genesis of what came to be known in the press as my "tin cup trip." It was an eleven-day journey to nine countries that also encompassed a Bush-Gorbachev summit in Helsinki, critical talks in Moscow on German unification, and a visit to Damascus to persuade Syrian President Hafez al-Assad to join the coalition. But it began and ended with stops in two countries whose financial support for our effort was essential: Saudi Arabia and West Germany.

On the twelve-hour flight from Washington to Saudi Arabia, my staff and I discussed precisely how much we would ask from our Arab partners. We went over pages and pages of financial analysis from the Pentagon, Treasury, and State, trying to estimate the costs of Desert Shield. It would be more politic to suggest that we painstakingly scrubbed the data, trying to reach a good-faith consensus on what the likely costs would be and what would constitute a fair share for Saudi Arabia and Kuwait. But the truth is we all understood that at this early stage in the crisis, burden sharing was primarily a political challenge rather than an economic one. We had to demonstrate to our domestic audience that everyone, not just us, was taking risks and making sacrifices. The figures before us had some basis in fact, but they were narrowly drawn accountant's numbers, as opposed to what might be loosely defined as politically acceptable ones. From a symbolic standpoint, they were unacceptably low. So we simply doubled them all on the spot. More precise figures were calculated many months later, in some cases after the crisis and war were over. They were remarkably close to our rough "guesstimates."

On September 6, I arrived in Jeddah and met with King Fahd at 9:00 P.M. I felt before I arrived in the kingdom that we would have the full cooperation of the Saudis. Like his subjects, the King was properly concerned by the threat of an unfettered Saddam sitting a few hundred miles from his border. He saw the very existence of his country at stake. From the outset, the Saudis were the most aggressive member of the coalition. When Cheney had arrived to ask permission to send American troops, the King had clearly made up his mind before the meeting began. The Saudis not only wanted American troops on their soil; they privately hoped a diplomatic resolution couldn't be reached. They didn't just want Saddam ejected from Kuwait; they wanted him destroyed. For them, the *only* solution was an American-led war that would annihilate Saddam's military machine once and for all. From the start, they were always advocates for the massive use of force. We knew that if it came to war, permission to launch from Saudi bases would be automatic. And we suspected that the King was also willing to bear any financial burden asked by his American benefactors. Even so, I was urged by our Ambassador, Chas Freeman, to go easy on the numbers. "They're strapped for money," he told me before the meeting. "Don't press for too much right now." I disagreed.

In our meeting, the King was very grateful for what America had done. He said that we were all that stood between peace and disaster for his country. He was belligerent and harsh in his comments about Saddam, something to be expected, given the threat to the kingdom.

"We are prepared to put not just treasure but blood on the line for your country," I told him, "and we need you to do your fair share." I told him that I thought $15 billion was an appropriate contribution. King Fahd was instantly responsive. "Just tell us what you want and what you need for us to do," he suggested, "and go talk to the Foreign Minister," he said. Such was the King's gratitude for what America was prepared to do for his country that I left the meeting feeling he would have blessed virtually any number I had proposed. The next morning, I had breakfast with Foreign Minister Prince Saud, a fellow Princetonian, and Prince Bandar, the Saudi Ambassador to the United States, who bluntly surfaced their own concept of burden sharing. "Don't ask us for $15 billion unless you get $15 billion from the Kuwaitis," Bandar suggested. "They can afford it, too. They have all these assets. What good are they if they don't have their country? So ask as much from them as you ask from us. You'll find that you'll get it."

The next morning, I flew to Taif, Saudi Arabia, to meet with the Emir of Kuwait, a quiet man who grows roses and has taken thirteen wives. The

Iraqi occupation had taken a heavy toll on the Emir. Here was a feudal prince who had been summarily ejected from his country, and forced to take refuge in a Sheraton hotel in a neighboring country. Still worse, he had to subject himself to visits from a Secretary of State asking him for billions of dollars, and which invariably concluded with a battery of questions from American reporters—an indignity he had never experienced in his life. The first time it happened, I had to suppress a smile as I watched a startled look cross his face. "This is not our tradition," he told me after the press departed. "I'm sure you'll get used to it, Your Highness," I couldn't resist saying. In time, he became fairly comfortable with what must have been for him a thoroughly distasteful experience. But like King Fahd, the Emir readily agreed to the $15 billion the Saudis had told me he could easily afford.

After a brief visit to the United Arab Emirates, I then flew to Cairo to see an old friend. I had first met Hosni Mubarak during the Reagan transition of 1980, when I was White House Chief of Staff–designate. I can still remember the first words he ever spoke to me. He strode briskly into the room, shook my hand warmly, and demanded to know, "Where are my tanks?" The Carter administration had pledged him some tanks, and they hadn't arrived. "You've promised me some tanks," he politely lectured. "We need those tanks. Where are they?" I had liked Mubarak ever since. His garrulous, sunny disposition, so typical of the Egyptian people, complemented a tough, courageous personal style reminiscent of Anwar Sadat, his predecessor and mentor. The day I met him for breakfast in Alexandria, however, Mubarak was still fuming at being misled by Saddam Hussein, who had told him before August 2 that he had no intention of invading Kuwait. Mubarak's assurances had contributed to what turned out to be a gross underestimation of Saddam in the U.S. government and elsewhere, and he was chagrined at having let down his friends.

Predictably, he was furious with Saddam. "Jim, I tell you, he's a crazy man," Mubarak said, waving an index finger in the air, as is his custom when he's worked up. "How could he be so crazy? How can he delude himself this way? He doesn't listen to anybody." I was surprised to learn that Mubarak's contempt for Saddam was matched by his disdain for King Hussein of Jordan, whom he accused of engaging in a conspiracy with Saddam to take over Kuwait and divide the spoils of occupation. Saddam was legendary for buying neighbors off, Mubarak maintained. In 1989, he had persuaded Mubarak to join with Iraq, Jordan, and North Yemen to form the Arab Cooperation Council (ACC) to foster stronger economic ties. After the invasion, however, it was apparent to Mubarak that Saddam had intended to exploit the ACC to further his strategic regional aspirations. At one point during this collaboration, Saddam had offered Mubarak and some of his Cabinet the gift of a number of Mercedes-Benz limousines. Mubarak had refused for himself and his ministers, but others had been less circumspect. "You go to Amman," he told me, "and you'll see all the new Mercedeses." He was convinced that King Hussein had allowed himself to be co-opted by Saddam. To his mind, that explained the King's refusal to condemn the invasion of Kuwait. "I told the King, 'What's going on, what are you doing?' " Mubarak said.

Mubarak was almost as hawkish in his anti-Saddam fervor as the Saudis. He believed Saddam's ability to threaten his neighbors must be destroyed, and he was prepared to commit his troops to the coalition. Understandably, he was delighted to learn that the United States was prepared to forgive his $7.1 billion in debt. He wanted Saddam dealt with, and he didn't think it would take long. In six weeks, he predicted, the sanctions would force a humiliated Saddam to retreat in disgrace.

"Let's hope you're right, Mr. President," I said, "but we can't plan on the basis of that being true. We have to plan on the basis of it being necessary to continue to build the pressure against him."

Helsinki and Moscow Interludes

From Cairo, I flew to Helsinki to join the President for a hastily arranged summit with President Gorbachev to coordinate superpower positions on the Gulf crisis. The meeting followed logically from my talks with Shevardnadze at Vnukovo II Airport a month earlier. In the interim, Saddam had been busy trying to split the Arabs and was also working his apologists hard within the Soviet Foreign Ministry. It was time to demonstrate afresh that the superpowers were still together on the crisis. Meeting with the President and Scowcroft the night before the one-day summit, I stressed that having Bush and Gorbachev meet and reiterate what their ministers had already said at Vnukovo wasn't enough. There needed to be a new joint statement ratcheting up the language of the previous communiqué, and I had asked my staff to work up a draft statement on the flight from Cairo to Helsinki. A stronger joint statement would demonstrate in a dramatic way that despite Saddam's efforts, the leaders of the coalition were even more firmly unified and, if necessary, were willing to consider tougher measures to force Saddam from Iraq. The President also wanted to make a personal appeal to Gorbachev, who was clearly more concerned about U.S. policy intentions and the prospect of force than Shevardnadze was.

On the morning of September 9, while the President and Gorbachev were meeting at the presidential palace, I met with Shevardnadze. Predictably, the Soviets were still pushing their long-held dream of convening an international conference on the Middle East. Gorbachev and Shevardnadze had both made speeches a few days earlier linking a resolution in the Gulf with the Palestinian problem. "Eduard, that would be a disaster," I argued. "It would look like Saddam had delivered, that he would have gotten something nobody else could have. It would be a great victory for him and would send the message that his way of doing business works. It would put the moderate Arabs on the defensive and cause all kinds of problems with the Israelis. We simply can't do this." After quite a long discussion, Shevardnadze said, "Okay, but let's talk about peace in some way." I said, "We should emphasize our stake in a peaceful solution, our stake in guaranteeing that we succeed and our willingness to spell out that if sanctions don't work we're prepared to take additional steps. I would hope that if sanctions don't work and don't get the job done, that you would feel free to join us in the Security Council to get authority to go further along the lines of the resolution that we passed on naval interdiction. Here we're talking about using appropriate measures. I'm not asking you to sign a blank check, and I'm not asking you to do it today. I'm just outlining, in response to your question about next steps, the direction we might want to go in. . . ."

Shevardnadze replied, "I'm in total agreement with you. Everything that we've done so far has been correct. It can fail, and I must say I would feel less concerned if I thought we were dealing with a more predictable person. But he may try to gamble."

I then pulled out the draft of the proposed joint statement that my staff had worked up and read it to Shevardnadze. The language included a reference to "additional steps" that Bush and Gorbachev would consider if Saddam refused to leave Kuwait. "That's good, that's very good, let's get Dennis [Ross] and Sergei [Tarasenko] to work on the draft," he said.

When I rejoined the President to report on the results of my meeting, however, it quickly became aparent that Gorbachev had pushed him very hard about a Mideast peace conference. When I heard him say, "Well, I think he's going to require that we have an international conference," I was worried that he might agree to the idea. A small group of us, including Scowcroft, Sununu, Ross, John Kelly, Condi Rice, and Richard Haass, the President's Special Assistant for Near Eastern Affairs, began to discuss the issue.

Ross was impassioned almost to the point of intemperance. "You can't do that," he said. "This will absolutely undercut what we're trying to do. We'll put the moderate Arabs in a position where Saddam is delivering for the Palestinians and they're not. If we create linkage, he can claim victory. And if he does that, we're going to face a Middle East that is far more dangerous than we've ever seen."

"Well," the President responded, "I just don't think he's gonna accept anything less than that." We pointed out that Shevardnadze had already accepted our draft that said nothing about a conference.

"We don't have a choice," I interjected. "We cannot be talking about an international conference. That would be a big victory for him and it would be a disaster for our friends in the Arab world."

"Well," the President replied, "I am afraid we're going to find we have to do this. We need a joint statement, and Gorbachev is gonna want that in there."

"We've already *got* a draft, and it's not even mentioned," I reminded him. "Don't worry about it."

"Well, I've *got* to worry about it," he came back at me, with a poignancy I will never forget. "I put all those kids out there. Nobody else did it—*I* did it. And I've gotta take every step to be sure that I don't put their lives at risk needlessly. If I can get them out of there without fighting, I'll do it." The room was suddenly very quiet; the President had spoken from the heart about the loneliness and responsibility that only the commander in chief can ever feel.

After a few moments, Sununu broke the silence. "Well," he said, "maybe we can put a reference to an international conference in there." I flared. "Get off of it, John," I said. Finally the President said, "Look, Jimmy, if you can get the statement without it, fine."

Ross and Tarasenko had worked out a joint draft statement that made no mention of an international conference, but included vague references to working together in the region after the crisis "to resolve all remaining conflicts in the Middle East and the Persian Gulf." After Shevardnadze and I approved it, the draft was brought into the second Bush-Gorbachev meeting in progress. Gorbachev went through the text line by line, asking only for modest changes, such as adding some language about the humanitarian needs of Iraq's citizens. After I summarized the changes, Gorbachev was satisfied. "Fine," he said, "let's clean it up." As it turned out, the Arabists in the next room were still hoping to eviscerate the text Gorbachev had just accepted. In a reprise of my experience at Vnukovo II, they had drawn up a new draft watering down the language. The commitment to additional steps had been softened, and a demand for Saddam's unconditional withdrawal had disappeared. When this end run was pointed out to me by Ross, I interrupted the meeting and raised the matter directly with Gorbachev. "Mr. President, isn't this what you have agreed to?" I asked, reading Gorbachev the original language. "*Da,*" he replied. At least for the moment, that took care of the Arabists.

Constructive ambiguity, of course, can be useful in the practice of diplomacy. But for the most part, it's a dangerous tool, to be used sparingly. More often than not, absolute precision is the more preferable device. I generally preferred to leave a meeting with a discordant air rather than with a misunderstanding that would lead to wider problems down the road.

Nothing made me angrier than interlocutors who tried to revisit an agreement laboriously worked out.

The final communiqué issued by Presidents Bush and Gorbachev gave us far more than half a loaf. The Soviets had agreed that "we are determined to see this aggression end, and if the current steps fail to end it, we are prepared to consider additional ones." In exchange, without having to acknowledge it publicly, we had privately committed to try to work with the Soviets on a regional Mideast peace conference after Iraq had left Kuwait, while denying both Saddam and his friends in the Soviet Foreign Ministry the explicit commitment to linkage they had sought. It was a good bargain. Soviet cooperation with our strategy had been significantly reinforced.*

Two days later, on September 12, I met with my counterparts in Moscow to sign the documents sealing the historic reunification of Germany. After the Two-plus-Four ministerial, I stayed on an additional day to meet with Gorbachev and Shevardnadze at the Kremlin to discuss various bilateral issues left over from Helsinki. Afterward, Gorbachev asked if he and Shevardnadze could meet privately with Dennis Ross and me. We adjourned to a small conference room and sat around a tiny circular table. I had no idea what was on Gorbachev's mind as he began his soliloquy about the status of his dreams of transforming the Soviet system into a market economy.

"We need help," he began. "We're in the middle of the transition right now. As we move toward implementing these reforms, there's going to be great dissatisfaction. It's very difficult for us now. The domestic situation is getting much worse.

"In six to nine months, things will get better for us. But we need help now. We have to meet the people's needs during this period of transition. I understand there's a limit to what you can do, but can you help get some money from the Saudis for us?" He mentioned a figure of $4 billion to $5 billion.

I told Gorbachev that I would see what I could do. (This very serious meeting ended on a note of levity when I showed Gorbachev something someone had given me as a joke in the United States. It was a small packet with a single condom inside. On its front was a picture of Saddam. On the back was written "For big pricks who don't know when to withdraw." Gorbachev and Shevardnadze both roared with laughter when the translation came and Gorbachev put the packet in his pocket.)

---

*We kept this private commitment by working immediately after the war to put together such a regional conference under U.S.-Soviet sponsorship. The result was Madrid, October 30, 1991.

Back in Washington, after having researched the legalities to make sure there were no impediments to asking the Saudis for financial help for the Soviets, I checked with the President, who agreed that there was no downside. We needed the continuing help of the Soviets, and it cost us nothing to ask the Saudis for money on their behalf.

Two weeks later, during the United Nations General Assembly meetings in New York, I raised the matter in a private meeting with Prince Saud and Prince Bandar. "I can't tell you what to do," I told them, "but Gorbachev's situation is difficult. He's under a lot of pressure from the old guard, and it's important to help sustain him in the face of that pressure."

"I understand," Saud replied. "We will do something." He was true to his word. That something turned out to be a very generous $4 billion line of credit to get the Soviets through the winter. Gorbachev was grateful to the Saudis, and later telephoned the President to thank him for his support. I believe that our role in arranging the line of credit was instrumental in solidifying Soviet support for the use-of-force resolution and keeping them firmly in the coalition throughout the crisis.

Finishing Touches: Damascus and Bonn

After the Gorbachev meeting, I flew from Moscow to Syria, a visit so controversial within the department that it almost didn't happen. Dennis Ross was vehemently opposed to my visiting Damascus. His view was that for his own reasons, President Assad would join our coalition regardless. Assad had a deep personal enmity toward Saddam, who, despite their common Ba'athist heritage, was Assad's primary rival in the region. Their relationship had understandably not been helped by Assad's belief that Saddam had been trying to kill him for years. Bringing Saddam to heel would suit Assad's purposes nicely. There was little doubt Assad was prepared to send Syrian forces to Saudi Arabia. We knew from Mubarak that Assad had already promised at least one division, and the Saudis had promised to underwrite his expeditionary costs. Moreover, Assad had already agreed at our request to send a representative to the Arab League meeting in Cairo in August in which the Arab coalition had been formalized. As a practical matter, Assad was already very much on board. "When you go to Damascus," Ross argued, "you're doing something he wants very badly, and you won't get anything from him that he isn't already prepared to do."

From the start, I had wanted to go to Syria despite Ross's objections. Notwithstanding the merits of all his arguments, I felt that the symbolic importance of Syrian participation was far more crucial than their literal presence. With Syria represented, the credibility of our Arab coalition partners was immeasurably strengthened. But I had a more long-term purpose

in mind. There was no way to move a comprehensive Mideast peace process forward without the active involvement of Syria, and I believed that
there could well be an opportunity to begin laying the groundwork with
Assad for a new effort to revive the peace process. The only question was
timing. I also knew that President Bush was anxious to engage the Syrians.
He had always believed that George Shultz had made a serious mistake by
cutting off contacts with Syria after the disastrous 1983 bombing of the U.S.
Marine barracks in Beirut. In 1986, Vice President Bush had wanted to visit
Damascus on his trip to the Middle East, but had been reluctantly dissuaded
by aides fearful of the potential political fallout. How would it look, he'd
been told, if terrorists harbored by Syria blew up an airplane? The photographs of Bush with Assad could come back to haunt him and President
Reagan. He had grudgingly accepted that he shouldn't visit Syria, but he
always believed that the United States had dropped the ball and should
have engaged Assad, despite serious disagreements over Syria's support of
international terrorism and heavy involvement in narcotics trafficking.
Now, here was an instance where strategic American interests coincided
with the President's belief that we had already missed critical opportunities
to reach out to Syria.

Because of Ross's adamant opposition, I had dropped Damascus from
the itinerary in the early planning for my September trip. But one day in
August, the President told me, "I think you should consider going to Syria.
I don't want to miss the boat again." Since I favored going to Syria at some
point, I instructed Margaret Tutwiler to have Damascus penciled into the
end of the trip. Ultimately, the President's instincts were proved right about
the importance of Syria, in the contexts both of the Gulf war and Mideast
peace as well.

I made the announcement that I would be going to Damascus myself
during the course of a press conference following a NATO ministerial meeting in Brussels. The announcement created quite a stir in the American
press, as this would be the first high-level meeting between an American
Secretary of State and the Syrian President in over two years. I met with
Assad in Damascus on September 14 in a rather nondescript building on a
residential street across from the building in which Assad lived. The fur-
nishings were comfortable but spartan. The room was a long rectangle with
two large overstuffed chairs separated by a small table at one end. Olive-
colored velvet curtains covered one long wall of the room, and behind them
were bulletproof windows which could not be opened even when the room
became quite warm (as it often did). At the other end of the room were two
doors, which led into Assad's working office, where he spent most of his
waking hours. The major decoration in the room was a large painting of the

Battle of Hittin, in which the Muslim leader Salah-ad-Din defeated the Crusaders.

After the obligatory pleasantries, I told him a little about myself and stressed that the President and I had been close friends for thirty-five years. "We are very close," I said. "I share everything with him and he shares everything with me." I wanted Assad to view me as an extension of the President, someone whose characterizations of George Bush's views could be accepted as gospel and whose word was good. Ambassador Ed Djerejian had told me that Assad attached enormous importance to the credibility, or lack thereof, of his interlocutors. I told him that I had heard he was a difficult bargainer but could be counted upon to keep his word once given.

"Well, we've heard things about you, too," Assad said with a smile. "We have been watching reports of your opinions very carefully. We have come to the conclusion that you are strong and decisive, you say what you mean, and this makes us believe that you are a straightforward man. Perhaps it would be better for us to say this behind your back, but this is an important trait. It's very important to be straightforward. It's important that a person be frank and direct, whether or not we agree. When these qualities are there, even if there is no agreement, there is trust. There should be no hidden issues between us." I made a mental note of Assad's grammar; he preferred the imperial "we" in his diplomatic conversations.

I described the situation in the Gulf as the first real crisis of the post–Cold War era. "A new order is going to evolve in an important way out of how we handle this crisis," I said. "This is why it's important that Saddam Hussein not succeed. And even in defeat, he cannot be seen as a hero." I gave Assad a summary of our military preparations and told him that the primary purpose of my visit was to find out if he was willing to allow his division to participate in the military coalition in a meaningful way. Sending troops was an important symbolic gesture, but if it came to war, we wanted Assad's troops engaged in combat along with the Egyptians.

"In the event of military action, we will need to know what you will be willing to do with your troops that are going to Saudi Arabia, and with your troops on the Syrian-Iraqi border," I said. "We think it's important that we do not have a public discussion of that possibility, except to say that we have not ruled out any options." As I would come to learn was frequently his habit, Assad avoided a direct response. He said he hoped the sanctions would weaken Saddam's resolve. "They are severe ones, and they should bite," he mused. But when I asked him how long he thought it would take for sanctions to take hold, he said he didn't have reliable information on Iraq's internal situation. But he left no doubt that he had no brief for his bitter enemy. He indicated that Saddam's invasion was wrong, and therefore Syria was adopting the principled position of supporting the coalition's efforts. But he remained studiedly vague on the extent of Syria's involvement. After considerable prodding, he finally said that he had not decided how many troops he would send to Saudi Arabia. "We will commit as many as is required," he pledged, up to 100,000 troops. With only one Syrian armored division firmly committed, it was an encouraging signal that Assad was even then prepared to expand his participation. "We will do the right thing," he said, "but it is not easy to do because of our own public opinion."

"It isn't so easy for *us* to be there, Mr. President," I said. "We have our own public opinion, and many people are critical that I am in Syria today, but it is important to be here in the context of this crisis, and hopefully in the future as well." Assad had lectured me on American timidity, but it was a positive exchange. With the benefit of reflection, I now believe it was probably my first inkling that Assad might be willing to consider shouldering some of the considerable risks necessary to revive the moribund peace process.

Above all, Assad is a realist. He didn't have to be told that joining the coalition would reinforce his clout in the Arab world and help settle old grudges with Saddam. He also understood intuitively that it would make it easier for the United States to deal with Syria. But I wanted him to recognize that the stakes were much higher than simply a warming in bilateral relations. In my view, a successful outcome in the Gulf would open up new avenues for reviving the prospects for peace in the region. "We're optimistic that the circumstances that bring Syria, Egypt, and the Gulf states together in a major Arab coalition can augur well for the future of the Arab-Israeli peace process," I said.

At the end of the meeting, Assad remarked, "We are satisfied with the discussion. There is no substitute for such one-on-one encounters. Hopefully, this will enable us to accomplish more in the future. It is in the interest of all our countries and peace in the Middle East. I want peace in a real way." It was far too early to know if he meant it; like most Arab leaders, he'd been saying it for years. But the most urgent objective had been achieved. Syria was firmly committed to the coalition.

I flew from Damascus to Rome for a brief consultation with the Italians, who agreed to send a squadron of Tornados to the Gulf, then to Germany, where late in the afternoon of September 15, I met with Chancellor Kohl at his home in Ludwigshafen, not far from the giant U.S. Air Force base at Ramstein. Although the German constitution prohibited Kohl from sending military forces to the Gulf, securing a hefty German financial commitment was symbolically mandatory. Just before leaving Washington, I'd been peppered with complaints during my testimony before the Senate Foreign Relations Committee about other nations not pulling their share of the load. Germany had been singled out for special criticism, and while I didn't say so publicly, I shared the view that Germany's response to the crisis up to then had been disappointing. Their reluctance was even more perplexing because, two days earlier in Moscow, I had participated in the treaty ceremony where the four Allied victors in World War II had terminated their occupation rights in West Germany, clearing the way for the reunification of Germany after nearly a half-century. It was essentially an American-brokered agreement, and the Germans knew it. Now we needed some help in return.

Before I arrived, the Foreign Ministry had begun leaking word that Germany was prepared to be more responsive, but I wanted to make sure Chancellor Kohl understood the stakes. It was just the two of us and interpreters.

"We've worked very closely in the last year to meet your needs," I said. "I think we've done a good job, and it wasn't always easy. We worked closely together, and we kept you informed every step of the way. It's a wonderful achievement for all of us, but *we* have some needs now.

"You're not going to contribute any forces because your constitution prohibits it, and then if it looks like you're being skimpy on the money, you're getting all the benefits of this and you're not contributing. And even if I don't believe it, that's the way it's perceived. You have to put me in the position where I can argue when I appear before the Congress that Germany is doing its fair share. I know how important the U.S.-German relationship is to you, and you know how important it is to me. But you can't leave me hanging out there."

The Chancellor was a confirmed Atlanticist, a strong supporter of the United States and its presence in Europe, a close friend of President Bush, and a leader who was very grateful for what America had just done. He showed it by providing assistance of almost $2 billion in value. In addition to providing millions of dollars' worth of support equipment for U.S. forces in the Gulf, the Chancellor agreed to substantially increase the amount of German military and economic aid to Turkey, and to provide German ships to transport Egyptian armored troops and their heavy tanks to the Gulf.

When I returned to Washington at three in the morning on September 16, I believed there was ample evidence that our diplomacy was working. Later that day, the U.N. would pass its seventh resolution condemning the invasion. The diplomatic coalition was hanging together. Sanctions were beginning to take hold in Iraq, and our partners had pledged billions of dollars to share the financial burdens of Desert Shield. But Saddam was still in Kuwait, and his rhetoric suggested he was in no hurry to withdraw.

CHAPTER 17

ALL NECESSARY MEANS

Saddam is a man losing his balance . . . a man with no understanding of morality, a person who disregards every human value accepted by every society. Perhaps Allah has contrived these events to rid us of Saddam.

—*King Fahd to Secretary Baker, Jeddah, Saudi Arabia, November 5, 1990*

By October, American deterrence had succeeded in the Gulf. If Saddam Hussein had been planning to invade Saudi Arabia, the President's initial deployment of troops in August had erased that threat.* Our diplomatic efforts, helped along by Saddam's intransigence, had also isolated him from the diplomatic mainstream. There was no support anywhere in the world for his invasion of Kuwait. But he remained there nonetheless, impervious to our pressure. The President believed it was now necessary for American policy to adopt a more coercive cast.

Unfortunately, our bullish friends in the region had been proved wrong about Iraq's vulnerability to economic measures. From the outset, Mubarak and Ozal had been convinced sanctions would bring Saddam to his knees and out of Kuwait within six weeks. Gorbachev and Shevardnadze had agreed with them. Initially, we'd been persuaded by their optimistic assess-

*Indeed, a few weeks after the end of the Gulf War, I learned something that indicated that Saddam might well have intended to move aggressively beyond Kuwait. I was told that on the eve of the invasion, Saddam sent a personal message to Hashemi Rafsanjani, Iran's leader, describing his intention of living in peace with Iran on land, which he referred to as "our 840-kilometer seacoast." Rafsanjani had evidently taken out a map, measured the Gulf, and realized Saddam was describing a new frontier extending from present-day Iraq to the United Arab Emirates—which, of course, would include Saudi Arabia's Persian Gulf seacoast.

ments; they knew their quarry better than we. Two months later, however, while the embargo was proving quite effective in an economic sense, I had come to believe, as did most of my colleagues in the government, that sanctions alone would never succeed in ejecting Iraq from Kuwait.

In many respects, Iraq was the perfect candidate for economic sanctions. It relied heavily on imports to feed its people and keep its industry running. Its essential export—oil—could be effectively cut by closing pipelines into Turkey and Saudi Arabia and by enforcing a naval blockade in the Persian Gulf. Geographically, Iraq was relatively isolated. While there was some leakage through the Hashemite kingdom of Jordan, even it, along with the other countries bordering Iraq, was essentially honoring the embargo against its domineering neighbor.

Politically, however, it was unlikely sanctions would ever work to force Saddam out of Kuwait. In the first place, the nature of Saddam's totalitarian regime enabled him, without fear of public protest, to reallocate critical resources around the country to keep his military and security apparatus well fed and supplied. Second, a leader desperate enough to invade a neighbor was probably desperate enough to hold on in the face of sanctions. Kuwait was an enormous prize for Saddam, and he was going to have to be forced to pay a very large price to give it back. Eight years of war with Iran had exacted a monumental economic and human toll on Iraq. It was doubtful short-term sanctions could ever come close to duplicating that cost. Third, as a practical matter, time was on Saddam's side. Those arguing for more time to let sanctions work repeatedly underestimated the difficulty of holding the coalition together for an extended period. Eventually, a key partner was likely to bolt, in which case the coalition would likely disintegrate. It was also a fair bet that having been willing to use force to win Kuwait, Saddam was unlikely to surrender Kuwait without at least a clear threat of force being used against him.

There was, however, still a modest chance that the sanctions, coupled with the threat of military action, might persuade Saddam to leave Kuwait. But for such a threat to be credible, our forces in the Gulf required a major augmentation. At the same time, we needed to begin quietly exploring the prospects for obtaining a United Nations resolution authorizing the use of force against Saddam if he failed to leave Kuwait by early 1991.

Augmenting the Force

In mid-October, Colin Powell telephoned me and said, "I'd like to have a little private chat with you." So on the afternoon of October 19, we met for forty-five minutes in my office. Since Powell had asked that the meeting be private, I respected his wishes and dispensed with my usual custom of informing Dick Cheney of any such contacts. Some have suggested that Powell and I knew that we were both opposed to the use of force and that he was soliciting my help in opposing the development of any such course of action. This is not the case and, in fact, this meeting produced a consensus that both a more aggressive military *and* diplomatic policy was required if there was any hope of getting Iraq out of Kuwait.

We had worked closely together in the second Reagan term, when Powell was the National Security Adviser and I was Secretary of the Treasury. He knew that I had a close personal relationship with the President. He also recognized that sanctions were having no substantial effect on Saddam, and understood that the President would soon have to decide whether sterner options were necessary. I think his purpose was simply to get a better sense of what I was feeling about the situation.

On October 15, I had met with Bob Kimmitt and discussed steps that needed to be taken if a military option were to be pursued. These included additional Security Council resolutions, a major diplomatic effort to develop support for the use of force, augmentation of our forces in the Gulf, establishment of effective command and control arrangements, and an early November trip by me to consult on these steps with our coalition partners.

As it turned out, Powell and I were pretty much of one mind. I agreed with his concern that existing policy was "drifting." Our military deployment had contained Saddam's designs on Saudi Arabia but would not be sufficient to persuade him to leave Kuwait. It was obvious to both of us that more would be required in order to do that, and as we talked we agreed that, absent some further provocation by Saddam, our choices boiled down to three: just keeping all options open, which would perpetuate the drift; consciously opting for a policy of declared containment, in which the sanctions would be strengthened and U.S. military forces would remain in the Gulf indefinitely but in an essentially defensive role; or building a deliberate offensive capability sufficient to eject Iraq from Kuwait if necessary.

We favored the third course. "We have the capability to put together a real offensive force," Powell said. This should persuade Saddam Hussein we were serious. Such a force augmentation would require at least four more divisions of ground troops. But we both felt that we probably couldn't survive politically if the United States were taking 75 percent of the casualties in the event of war. A force buildup should include the deployment of a substantial number of additional forces from other countries, particularly Arab states. This expanded force could be ready to fight in three months. Powell agreed with my belief that the military option had to be linked with a diplomatic offensive to authorize the use of force if necessary.

At home the next day, I summarized a course of action based on the options Powell and I had discussed, in notes to myself written on the back of an envelope. I noted that to "get ahead of erosion of support," the President should announce a date after which military force would be used. I was thinking perhaps February 1 or March 1, but "whatever date (we pick) we need to be ready." In the meantime, we should immediately begin marshaling "a massive force" in the Gulf. As justification, I wrote: "New world order—Have to be principled & stand up to aggression. Don't make same mistake we did in 30s; *nor* same as in Vietnam—uncertain, tentative, etc.— if we go in we have to have *massive* force. At the same time, we should go to the Congress and the U.N. to ask their support for possible use of force.

"If they (Congress) do and he won't leave—go in!" I wrote. "If they *won't* then announce we will *contain* him—keep sanctions on and keep forces there as we have in Germany and Korea." In this event, we would need to consider an eventual evacuation of American diplomats remaining in Kuwait.

The next day, I called the President and said I wanted to speak with him privately about something. "Why don't you come over and we'll have a drink," he said. That afternoon, a Sunday, I summarized my views with him at the White House. He said he found them interesting and was generally sympathetic, but as was his custom, wanted time to think about it. We left it that the matter should be discussed with his senior advisers. While I was pursuing the idea with the President, Powell had gone to Riyadh to confer with Schwarzkopf about what he needed for a viable offensive threat.

Over the next three days, the President pondered these issues with Cheney, Powell, Scowcroft, and me on several occasions. On October 24, he told us he was leaning toward a major new deployment of American troops to the region. On October 31, the day after a two-hour meeting in the Situation Room, the President officially approved a force augmentation of 200,000 troops to Saudi Arabia, subject to Saudi approval. This deployment effectively doubled U.S. troop strength and would provide the heavy armor capability required to fight a ground war. Once these reinforcements arrived from the United States and Germany, our defensive force would pack a potent offensive capability. If the United States needed to go to war, the muscle would be in place to fight and win.

Although some have charged that the force augmentation was tantamount to deciding to go to war, the President and his senior advisers still hoped our buildup would persuade Saddam to leave peacefully—that our coercive diplomacy would work. In retrospect, the war may seem to have been a clinical and relatively straightforward affair. At the time, however, we were confronted with very sobering casualty figures, estimated by the Pentagon to be in the thousands; the specter of possible chemical and bio-

logical attacks; and a war expected to last for months, not days. There was
no doubt in my mind the President would authorize force if necessary—and
we were very careful all along to preserve our options under Article 51 of
the U.N. Charter. But from the very beginning, the President recognized the
importance of having the express approval of the international community
if at all possible. For years our allies had complained about America's cowboy mentality. Our brief expeditions in Grenada and Panama had reinforced this impression. In opting to assemble an international political
coalition against Iraq, George Bush had proved he was mindful of these
criticisms. Primarily, though, he correctly believed that the threat to use
force would be even more credible if formally sanctioned by most of the
civilized world. That's why he had decided by late October not only to escalate U.S. troop levels but also to seek another resolution in the United Nations authorizing the coalition to go to war if necessary.

   This decision was by no means cut and dried. Margaret Thatcher opposed the idea, believing that if we failed to get the resolution, the coalition's ability to use force under Article 51 would be seriously undermined.
She was also of the opinion that the United Nations would reject any such
resolution we offered, and therefore that the risk of trying for it and losing
outweighed any possible gain. Dick Cheney and Brent Scowcroft supported
her in this view. I agreed with all of them that it would be extremely damaging to lose such a crucial vote. It made no sense to try for the resolution
unless we were certain the votes were there for approval. I believed, however, that intensive diplomacy could enable us to obtain the necessary support. I argued that it could be done in such a way that we would never
submit the issue to the Security Council for a vote unless we were certain
we had sufficient commitments to know the ultimate result. In the end, the
President agreed it was a risk worth pursuing. It was my task to sell that
resolution—to the Security Council as well as to our coalition partners.

All Necessary Means

Our diplomatic timetable was driven by a simple, unyielding reality. By
sheer coincidence and under a long-standing arrangement, the United
States would chair the Security Council in the month of November. Thereafter, the rotating chairmanship would pass to Yemen, an ally of Iraq unal-
terably opposed to the coalition. As a practical matter, any vote on a
use-of-force resolution would need to occur no later than November 30.

   In October, well before the force augmentation decision, I had asked
the interagency Deputies' Committee to draw up some proposed language
for a resolution. I wanted the resolution to include a clean, unambiguous
statement that authorized the use of force but didn't mandate it. My sug-

gested language was "all necessary means, including the use of force." Skillful diplomacy, however, is grounded in the art of the possible. So we had a backup position. At my request, Bob Kimmitt had researched the legalities and concluded that if the Soviets and other allies objected to such specificity, the simple phrase "all necessary means" conferred sufficient authority to wage war. I was much less interested in grammatical purity, however, than in overwhelming numerical superiority in the Security Council. With Yemen and Cuba on the Council in November, a unanimous vote was quite unlikely. But a sharply divided vote in the Council would make it easier for Saddam to argue that he was the victim of an American-Zionist vendetta, and thus undermine the credibility of a military operation.

I was determined to meet personally with the head of state or foreign minister of every Council member in the weeks before the vote. U.N. ambassadors are notorious for their freelancing. Negotiating directly with their superiors would make it less likely for an agreement to be undone in New York. I also wanted the foreign ministers from each of the Council's fifteen member states to be there for the vote. We were asking the Council to authorize the use of force for the first time since Korea. It was simply too momentous a decision to be handled at anything less than the highest levels.

A Thirty-seven-Hour Day

I left Washington on November 3. In the next three weeks, I spent eighteen days traveling to twelve countries on three continents. On the day after Thanksgiving, my Air Force crew told me I had set a personal record with a thirty-seven-hour day that took me from Jeddah, Saudi Arabia, to Bogotá, Colombia, to Los Angeles, then home to Houston. Working against an end-of-the-month deadline, I met personally with all my Security Council counterparts in an intricate process of cajoling, extracting, threatening, and occasionally buying votes. Such are the politics of diplomacy.

If the resolution ran into resistance, the President had authorized me to make some concessions to win over recalcitrant Council members. Throughout my November globe-trotting. I kept in my pocket a list of diplomatic sweeteners that we could have committed to in exchange for support. We were willing, for example, to commit to withdrawing a fixed percentage of American troops from Saudi Arabia if the Iraqis withdrew. We were also ready to call for the creation of an Iraq-Kuwait claims tribunal at The Hague to deal with the border dispute in an impartial fashion. As it turned out, neither of these became necessary.

During my travels, I also met with most members of the military coalition to update them on our preparations and obtain three critical assurances from each of them. In the event that military force became necessary, we had to be sure that all combat operations remained firmly under the control of American commanders. We also needed to know that they had no objections to bombing Iraq, and that they would remain with us if Israel retaliated if attacked by Iraq.

At my first stop in Manama, Bahrain, I met the Emir, Sheikh Isa bin Sulman al-Khalifa, at the Bapco Hospital, where he was recuperating from a heart attack. His family had led Bahrain since 1782. As I had expected, he was totally supportive. "If and when the shooting starts, we want to be able to call the shots," I told him. "We also need to know if our Arab and Muslim coalition partners would have a problem if we undertake offensive operations against Iraq, including the bombing of Baghdad. And if Saddam Hussein strikes Israel, would our Arab partners remain committed to a military response against Iraq?" The Emir was unequivocal on all three points. "Bahrain will support any effort against Iraq," he pledged. "Peace would never work with Saddam. A rabid dog bites anyone who comes his way."

I left Manama to visit the troops of the Army's First Cavalry Division, who were then stationed in the middle of the Saudi desert. At the end of a noisy seventy-five-minute ride in an open helicopter, the sight of 4,200 soldiers of the First Cav emerging in formation over the horizon was impressive and moving. I spoke to them while standing under an enormous camouflage net, from a lectern flanked by two soldiers dressed in nineteenth-century frontier uniforms. I reminded them that they and their efforts were constantly on our minds, and that without their courage, this whole effort would be impossible. I found their morale high and that they were eager to face whatever lay ahead. As I mixed and mingled in the ranks, a captain told me that he had gone to school and played football with my son Mike at Northwest Academy in Houston. When I left, the troops presented me with a packet of what many consider one of the least attractive parts of military life—field rations. (In my Marine Corps days, I had learned that the rations were much better doused in hot sauce. I carried a bottle with me at all times.)

In Taif, the Emir of Kuwait was equally agreeable. Of course, he wanted his country back and Saddam defeated, the sooner the better. He suggested that I discuss my three questions in my subsequent meeting with the Crown Prince, who had no problem with the first two, but found the third troublesome. I reassured him that "we will not accept a partial solution. But we do need to know what Arabs will be there if Saddam Hussein attacks Israel. We need to know you will be with us." It was apparent that my question caused tension among the Kuwaitis. There was dead silence for a time. "Can you guarantee that Israel will not take the first step in attacking Iraq?" the Crown Prince parried. "Assume the opposite point," I replied.

"We need to put these issues on the table. We need to know if Saddam Hussein attacks Israel, where will you be?" "You are right to raise this question," the Crown Prince acknowledged. "Our position is clear." But it wasn't. All that was clear was the difficulty he was having in formulating a response. The Crown Prince kept turning to his advisers and conversing in Arabic.

"We know this is a very hard subject," I gently prodded. "I will be talking to all of the Arabs that I am seeing on this trip and asking the same question. I must know the answer."

Finally, I got the only acceptable response. "With regard to the position of the Kuwaiti people, if Saddam Hussein attacks Israel, since you are trying to liberate our country, I do not believe that any Kuwaiti will say anything. If he starts it—okay."

"That's all we need to hear," I replied.

That afternoon in the lobby of the Sheraton, I talked briefly with four Kuwaitis who had managed to escape their occupied homeland. All had been tortured and mutilated. One man had been shot in the back of the head; his tongue had been blown away and his face was horribly deformed. Another had been sexually assaulted so badly that he could no longer walk. I remember thinking that this was the first time I had ever seen firsthand victims of man's inhumanity to man. I was shocked, repulsed, and outraged by what had happened to them.

Before seeing King Fahd in Jeddah, I met for two hours with Prince Saud and Prince Bandar, who pressed me for an early start to the war. Bandar was particularly insistent on moving swiftly. "He goes," he quipped, "or we go by January." "The President has yet to make a decision," I told them, "but I know the direction in which he's headed." I previewed for them the three questions I would ask the King. They predicted he would have no problems with a U.S. command structure and offensive operations against Iraq. "United States aircraft will be killing Arabs in Iraq," I reminded them. "Iraq has not killed Americans in Kuwait, it has killed Arabs," Saud replied, "so this is no problem." They were divided on the matter of an Israeli attack on Iraq. "No problem," Bandar assured me, in the idiomatic English he'd perfected in his years in Washington. But Saud thought it might be "a complicated problem," which the King would have to decide personally.

I met with the King at the al-Salaam Palace from 10:00 P.M. until midnight. He served carrot juice from Taif, which he noted was a favorite libation of Margaret Thatcher. The King was as hawkish as Saud and Bandar. He now believed that Saddam had originally planned to attack the kingdom's Eastern Province and had been deterred only by the quick response of American forces. "True friends are those you can count on when you

need them," he said. "The U.S. and the kingdom are in the same bunker."
He described Saddam as "a man losing his balance . . . a man with no understanding of morality, a person who disregards every human value accepted
by every society. Perhaps Allah has contrived these events to rid us of Saddam."

As I had expected, the King wasn't hard to sell on the need to respond
more forcefully to the crisis. He endorsed the idea of a use-of-force resolution at the United Nations. When I asked him for permission to deploy
200,000 more U.S. troops beginning immediately, he simply nodded his
assent. I asked him to allow American commanders, not his generals, to
control the conduct of the war. "These arrangements are only natural," he
said, smiling. He was even agreeable on the delicate issue of Israel.

I told him as politely as I could that I needed to ask him for more financial aid. "Nothing is impossible to discuss between partners," he smiled. I
reminded him that on my earlier visit, he had agreed to cover up to $2.5
billion in costs for fuel, water, construction, and in-country transportation
for American troops. Now, I said, I believed it was reasonable for him to also
pay the cost of transporting our troops from the United States to Saudi Arabia. "There is now a cancer in the region," he replied. "For everyone's sake,
we must eliminate it. So okay, no problem."

I flew to Cairo for a quick meeting with President Mubarak at the It-
tihadiya Palace in the suburb of Heliopolis. His answers to my three questions were predictably positive. Mubarak wasn't sure, however, if he could
send a third Egyptian division to the Gulf as I requested. The Egyptian people, he said, didn't want to see the destruction of another Arab state. He also
reserved judgment on my request to allow U.S. warplanes to use two of his
air bases for offensive operations. In the end, however, I was sure he would
agree.

Skeptical Chinese and Soviets

Afterward, I spent ninety minutes in the VIP lounge at the Cairo airport
lobbying Chinese Foreign Minister Qian Qichen, who was on his way to see
Saddam Hussein. Our meeting had been arranged a few days earlier, when
we'd learned that by coincidence Qian and I would be in the region at the
same time. I was encouraged when Qian told me he planned to tell Saddam
that China was committed to full implementation of all U.N. resolutions,
and that unconditional withdrawal was the only way to avoid bloodshed. I
explained the use-of-force resolution to him and added, "The best thing
you can do to help a peaceful solution of this crisis is to tell Saddam that
China will support this resolution."

Qian was noncommittal. China believed the sanctions were beginning to work, he said, and so long as that was the case, talk of force was premature. War would alter the balance of power in the Gulf and must be averted at all costs, he argued. "So long as there is a ray of hope for peace, China will do its best to strive for a peaceful settlement." I pressed him again on the resolution. "Unless we convince Saddam we are serious," I said, "there is little or no chance he will leave Kuwait peacefully."

The Chinese were still angry that neither the President nor I had visited Beijing. I explained that such a visit would prompt domestic criticism that would inevitably set back our bilateral relations. To reinforce the point, I read from two recent letters from members of Congress angry that in their view George Bush was coddling the Chinese. Qian was a wily negotiator; he wanted to link support for the resolution with a pledge for a presidential visit. I told him that I would agree to send Bob Kimmitt to Beijing by the end of the year with instructions to discuss a possible visit by me in 1991.

I thought Qian understood that a Chinese veto would be disastrous for improving Sino-American relations, but I wanted to make sure he got the message. "We don't hold it against our friends that they are not joining us," I pointedly noted. "But we *do* ask that they do not stand in the way." Qian didn't respond, but his body language, and the tone of his opening comments, led me to believe the Chinese wouldn't be an obstacle. I cabled the President with this report: "My sense is that following Qian's return to China, they will conclude it is in their interests to either support a resolution or at worst abstain. . . . I do not think we need a visit by me to obtain their support or acquiescence on the U.N. resolution."

In Ankara the next day, November 7, I met for two hours with President Ozal, who, like Qian, believed the economic embargo was working. A trained economist, he was keeping track of commodity prices in Baghdad. The price of a fifty-kilogram sack of rice had soared from six dinars on the day before the invasion, he noted, to more than two hundred dinars. Similarly, eighty kilograms of flour now cost more than senior Iraqi officials earned in a month. "I know you think sanctions will work," I said. "Shevardnadze said they would work in two months, and we're now in the fourth month." Ozal agreed to support the resolution and to consider my request to send an armored brigade to Saudi Arabia. He agreed to permit an increase in the number of U.S. jets at Turkish bases from 48 to 130, but said he was unsure if he would permit those planes to bomb Iraq. Like Mubarak, I was sure Ozal's support would be forthcoming if it came to war, which seemed ever more likely. "We are very pessimistic about a peaceful resolution of this crisis," I confided to Ozal. "There is no sign that Saddam Hussein is going to pull out."

From Ankara I flew to cold and snowy Moscow on November 7, the seventy-third anniversary of the Bolshevik Revolution, for what turned out to be thirteen hours of talks with Shevardnadze and Gorbachev, beginning at nine o'clock on the morning of November 8. I knew that in a few hours the President would be announcing our force augmentation, so I began by giving Shevardnadze the details as a courtesy. I laid out the case for a use-of-force resolution, but Shevardnadze wasn't persuaded the time was right. Threatening force might make Saddam a hero, he thought. "Maybe we should just tighten the sanctions," Shevardnadze suggested. "Tightening the sanctions isn't the problem, Eduard," I replied. "This guy will let everybody in the country starve before he'll give this up." I reminded him that our Arab partners were adamant that hostilities couldn't begin after mid-March, when the holy season of Ramadan began, and thereafter, we would be constrained by the searing summer heat. As a practical matter, further delay might force us to postpone military action into the fall. "The likelihood of being able to sustain the coalition that long is very suspect," I argued.

As soon as I finished, Shevardnadze said, "I understand." He had spent months fighting off the Arabists in the Foreign Ministry. He understood just how fragile an animal the coalition was in reality. Instantly, his whole approach changed. "The only thing that's critical, then, is that if you're going to use force, you have to know that you will succeed," he said. "We learned from Afghanistan. Don't listen to military men who give you these simplistic views that you'll succeed. You need to *know* that you'll succeed. Are you really sure you've thought this through?" Clearly, the Soviets were still suffering from their own Vietnam-style hangover.

"I want you to hear from our military," I replied. "I'm going to bring Howard Graves in. It's a measure of our relationship that I'm going to bring him in and have him talk to you. We're doing something that we never would have done before." The room was cleared of everyone except the interpreters, and General Graves delivered a highly detailed classified briefing on our war plan. Graves was careful not to be too specific about what our weapons could do in battle, but his presentation of our tactical concept for conducting the war was nevertheless an extraordinary exchange of military information from one former foe to another. In another era, it would have been the most far-fetched thing imaginable that a high-ranking U.S. military officer would be authorized to brief the Soviet Foreign Minister on our war plans against a Soviet client state.

"Our concept first of all is to make sure we destroy the ability of the Iraqis to communicate strategic instructions to their own forces," Graves began. "In that way, we will deny them the capability to wage war against our forces or to mount an effective defense against our attacks. Then we will destroy their air defenses, both aircraft and missiles. Once this is done, we will then be able to move with impunity to the destruction of their ground forces in Kuwait and Iraq." In his dispassionate, understated style, Graves summarized the array of lethal weaponry available to the coalition, and stressed the overwhelming technological superiority of American ground forces. "Our tanks can destroy enemy tanks while traveling at high rates of speed," he said. "The Iraqis have no way of protecting themselves." For obvious reasons, it was left unspoken that these inferior Iraqi tanks were Soviet built. In a worst-case scenario, Graves estimated, the combined air and ground campaign would be over in no more than three months.

I knew that Graves's timetable was fairly disingenuous. In the previous two weeks, Dick Cheney and Colin Powell had briefed me in detail on the Pentagon's contingency planning if force became necessary. Those war plans estimated that the coalition would win the war in three to four weeks. I'd been assured that was an honest assessment of the military reality, but I feared Shevardnadze might think it too rose colored. I had told Graves that if and when he were called upon to give that briefing, he should low-ball the scenario and say the war would be over in three months. When I heard Shevardnadze's admonition against overly optimistic military scenarios, I was relieved that we had decided to err on the side of caution.

Shevardnadze seemed absorbed by the detail and the confidence of Graves's brief. He had only a single question: "Aren't you concerned about the Scuds?" he wondered. "No, we're not concerned about them at all, because they're just not very accurate," Graves replied. "They're not a threat to our forces." It took a moment for the enormity of Graves's mild-mannered insult to sink in. The Soviet Foreign Minister had just been informed that one of his military's best missiles was a worthless piece of junk. Shevardnadze was silent for a moment, then broke out into a broad grin. He'd at least been persuaded we knew what we were doing.

"We have to be prepared to use the force, because we don't know that this [resolution] will work," I said. Shevardnadze agreed. "Once you've done this, you have to be prepared and you have to succeed." Shevardnadze was finally reconciled. He had first been convinced that Saddam would never invade. Then he'd concluded that once the sanctions took hold, Saddam would come to his senses. For the first time, I sensed he knew better.

"Look, I want to go out and prepare the President first," he said. He picked up the telephone and told Gorbachev he should receive me and should endorse my proposal. Then he left for Gorbachev's dacha at Novo-Ogarevo, arriving there twenty minutes before I did to argue my case directly.

Our small motorcade then left for Novo-Ogarevo—which is similar to our Camp David—on what was a beautiful half-hour drive through the heavily wooded, snow-covered Russian steppe. The scenery was truly soothing; the light snow seemed to soften the landscape and deer could be seen from the road.

When we arrived at the large mustard-colored main building of the secluded complex, Gorbachev met me in the entry hall under an impressive chandelier. I was the first high-level American official ever to visit here. The building was comfortable and relatively modern—I later learned that the TV in the staff room had MTV, but not CNN! Gorbachev escorted me down the hall to his library to start what would be a two-hour meeting. When the press photographers came in for the obligatory pre-meeting photo op, the crush was so great that they smashed into a wooden table, breaking glasses and overturning water pitchers. Gorbachev began the meeting by crossing the index and third fingers of both hands and saying, "What's really important is that we stick together. We can't let a thug like this get away with what he's done." It was an encouraging gesture, but Gorbachev quickly made clear he wasn't enthused about the resolution. It was one thing to ask for Soviet support, he said, but quite another to ask for help in going to war against a client state. Moreover, he thought a deadline would backfire. The Arab mentality becomes intransigent in the face of an ultimatum, he said.

Gorbachev's tone hardened. "You understand, now, that if we pass a resolution authorizing the use of force, and if Saddam does not move, you will actually have to use force. If you do it, you have to use it. Are you really ready to do that right now?"

"The President understands that perfectly," I said. "He is reluctant to use force, but prepared to do so."

Still searching for a diplomatic middle ground, Gorbachev unexpectedly proposed two resolutions, the first authorizing the use of force, but only after a six-week hiatus, the second ordering the start of hostilities if Saddam were still in Kuwait. It was a dreadful idea. "It would look like we were backing down from unconditional withdrawal," I told Gorbachev. "We'd never get a second resolution, and we'd embolden Saddam to make a token withdrawal which could result in a partial solution." I proposed to split the difference—a single resolution embracing Gorbachev's pause, with a date certain after which the use of force was authorized. Gorbachev didn't want to make a commitment at that time. "It's just a thought," he said of his two-tiered idea. "I'll have to think more about this." He promised to give the President an answer in eleven days, when they would meet at the CSCE Summit in Paris.

On the ride back to the Osobnyak guest house, I told Dennis Ross and Margaret Tutwiler that I felt the meeting had gone very well and that Gorbachev would support us in the end. The Soviet President had seemed at ease in this country setting, and was noticeably warm and gracious to my staff.

Tutwiler, Ross, and I discussed in the car what we should do with the huge contingent of media understandably anxious to know what had taken place during what was already a long and busy day. When we arrived back in Moscow, Shevardnadze was reluctant to meet the press before all of our meetings had been completed, citing unfinished business on the CFE talks. "Sir," Margaret Tutwiler pleaded, "our press is not interested in CFE. They are interested in the Gulf; they believe that is the reason we are here."

Thus, even before the end of what had already been a grueling day, Shevardnadze and I held a joint press conference. He was asked if he saw a situation where force might be required to expel Saddam from Kuwait. "Well, probably this could not be ruled out," he said. "And a situation may emerge which effectively would require such a move." I couldn't resist an undiplomatic smile. Once again, Shevardnadze had shown the courage to get out ahead and stare down his opponents in acknowledging the inevitable.

Over supper we went straight to another meeting, which primarily concerned the final stages of the CFE talks. Since we wanted to complete these negotiations by the CSCE Summit, Shevardnadze at one point offered to meet all night. Thankfully, we made enough progress to break for the day a little after ten o'clock.

The next morning, I sent a cable to the President entitled "My Day in Moscow, November 8, 1990," summarizing what I felt was considerable progress toward our goal. "I have had long and rather extraordinary discussions with Shevardnadze and Gorbachev today," I began. "Each listened, explained their concerns, and noticeably moved during the course of the discussions. Shevardnadze, in particular, came close to our position that a UNSC resolution authorizing force should be passed this month. Gorbachev is close but not there yet. . . .

"While I think Shevardnadze is not enthusiastic about using force, he is more inclined to think it will have to be used eventually. For his part, Gorbachev's image of the new international order is such that he has a hard time reconciling the fact that we might need to use force in this initial test. . . . I believe their stake in good relations and desire for partnership with us will lead them in the right direction. But it may take some time and effort to get there—Baker."

The Europeans and Africans

On November 9, the first anniversary of the fall of the Berlin Wall, I flew from Moscow to London, where Prime Minister Thatcher was still troubled by the decision to seek a U.N. resolution authorizing force. She did not believe the President needed to do this to help build political support at home and in Congress. "Prime Minister," I politely suggested, "please let us be the judge of domestic political consequences in the U.S." True to form as our staunchest ally and friend, she left no doubt that her country would be there with us whatever the decision was. On November 10, I was in Paris for a meeting with President Mitterrand. By coincidence, my friend and fellow Texan, Lloyd Bentsen and his wife, B. A., were staying at the Royal Monceau Hotel, where I was. We enjoyed morning coffee together before my meeting with President Mitterrand.

The French had been congenitally difficult. As Douglas Hurd liked to observe with characteristic understatement, "They have a special way of approaching things." They had agreed to send their rapid-response force to Saudi Arabia, but insisted initially that it not be under American command. Diplomatically, they favored letting sanctions run for a longer period before considering force, and they also favored linking the crisis to the Middle East peace process, which played into Saddam's hands. I always felt the French would be with us in the Security Council, but as usual they were a labor-intensive proposition.

Mitterrand was a master at putting his interlocutors on the defensive, so he began by complaining of reports in the French media about unnamed American officials who were saying the United States doubted France's resolve. However, he quickly left little doubt about the need for strong action against Saddam Hussein. "He is a brute," Mitterrand said. "He is intelligent, smart, and more dangerous than any of the others. Saddam Hussein in Kuwait is no different from Assad in Lebanon. France sees no difference between what is going on in Kuwait and what is going on in Lebanon, but we did not come to the defense of Lebanon. You are correct when you say we have a long alliance. If I had asked you to help in Lebanon, no one would have shown up.

"We have good relations with the Emir and Saudi Arabia. I went to Saudi Arabia recently. I received affluent gifts. In their palaces, one sees no women, or ordinary people. It's not the kind of government I would like to send French soldiers to be killed for. A country could not commit itself to the principles of Kuwait. They cannot ask soldiers to die for the way the Kuwaitis have their type of government. How am I going to tell French farmers I've committed their sons' lives to retain a billionaire? The Emir of Kuwait is a very nice man. Can we ensure the use of force is not just protecting the safety of bank safes in Switzerland? It's an idea that leaves me totally cold.

"[Nevertheless] Saddam Hussein is not harmless. He is dangerous. He needs to be contained. We are in Saudi Arabia. We have 6,000 men deployed. Our navy is doing its job in the Persian Gulf and Africa. After the

United States, we are doing the best. If he doesn't feel threatened, he will not yield. The past friendship of France and Iraq was not made personally with Saddam Hussein. He has requested to see me for the last nine years. I have never been to Iraq and I have never seen him. There is a coolness in our relationship, even though we, France, have supported him militarily by selling him things. For nine years I have turned down his offer to rebuild the power plant that the Israelis blew up. Our refusal has jeopardized our relations."

Mitterrand seemed primed for war, but he didn't believe that Article 51 of the U.N. Charter was sufficient to justify an attack in political terms. "Article 51 doesn't mind public opinion," he said. "Fifty-five million French people are not international lawyers. We need that resolution to ensure the consequences it will entail.

"It reduces itself to simple conclusions: peace or war," Mitterrand said. "The U.N. authorizes sending forces to enforce international law, is the way I prefer. I think that war is necessary. Whatever settlement there is should include his disarmament and stripping him of his weapons. I've summed up my view. We will engage ourselves more than some of your friends and allies."

In their own way, the French were in agreement with us. I told Mitterrand that the President would be extremely pleased with his view. France's enthusiasm made it much more likely the use-of-force resolution would prevail.

After three days back in Washington and a quick trip to Bermuda to meet with Canadian Foreign Minister Joe Clark, I resumed my odyssey in Brussels on November 15, where I participated in a meeting of European Community ministers and met with Belgian Foreign Minister Mark Eyskens on November 16. My next session was in Geneva with three non-aligned Council members: Ivory Coast, Ethiopia, and Zaire. My first meeting was with Ethiopian Foreign Minister Dinka Tesfaye. Despite its radical tendencies, Ethiopia had sided with us on ten previous votes in the Security Council. Having been invaded by Mussolini's Italy in 1935, Ethiopia was sensitive to small nations being gobbled up by aggressive neighbors, and was immediately on board. So was Zaire, though its Foreign Minister, Katanya Mushabshwa, expressed unhappiness that Congress had cut off foreign military aid to Zaire. I told him that the President was "deeply disappointed" with the congressional vote, and that the administration would try to maintain U.S. assistance.

The only potential hitch came with the Ivory Coast. When I met with Foreign Minister Simeon Ake, who like Eyskens had been Finance Minister when I was Secretary of the Treasury, he got right to the point. "The major concern in our country right now is really not the Gulf," he said, "it is in development. We are having a financial crisis. The G-7 has looked at debt forgiveness. Forgiveness would be extremely helpful."

As it turned out, Ivory Coast had not been included in a G-7 debt-forgiveness plan agreed to at the Toronto Summit in 1986. "Let me see what if anything can be done," I said. "I will look into what might be done, without promising anything, or tying it to the other subject we have been discussing today—and I know you are not suggesting such." We both knew better, of course.

That evening, after a brief meeting with Jonas Savimbi concerning Angola, I met with my staff to review our diplomatic offensive. We debated about whether we should travel to Malaysia, another Council member. The Chinese would be irritated that we were flying over again without stopping, so we decided to see if we could persuade the Malaysians to meet somewhere else.

On November 18, the day before the CSCE meetings, I met with the Romanian Foreign Minister, Adrian Nastase, in Paris. I encountered no resistance from him, perhaps because the preceding December I had visited Bucharest and delivered $80 million in humanitarian assistance to the new government, notwithstanding some human-rights reservations that we had.

Earlier in the day, I had spent half an hour on the phone with Chinese Foreign Minister Qian from my suite in the Hotel Inter-Continental. The communications equipment that always accompanies the Secretary of State enabled me to speak to Beijing through the department's operations center. I was concerned that Gorbachev's reluctance to announce publicly his support for the resolution would make it easier for the Chinese to veto. I assured Qian that I felt certain the Soviets would be with us on the vote. I asked him to consider saying publicly that they would not veto the resolution. He said he could not respond on the telephone and would have to consult his government. The Chinese were playing diplomatic hardball. In our meeting in Cairo, I had told him that we were willing to receive him in Washington after the Security Council vote. I'd offered him an incentive proposal: the President would see him for a yes vote, but I would meet with him if China abstained. He was insisting on a presidential meeting so long as China didn't cast a veto. "That was not our deal, Minister," I reminded him. I suspected they wouldn't veto, but we wanted a unanimous vote in the Perm Five, and a meeting with the President was the best chip I had to play.

At 11:15 P.M., I met with Shevardnadze, who had arrived late in Paris with Gorbachev. We met until 1:30 A.M., discussing the language of the resolution for what seemed to me the hundredth time in the last few weeks. I showed Shevardnadze a draft of the language that I had written out by hand. As he had insisted, it did not include the phrase "use of force." Gorbachev's language about a pause for goodwill had also been incorporated.

Shevardnadze told me the Soviets would vote for the resolution, and that there hadn't been any substantial question about it since the meeting in Moscow. "But we don't want to say this publicly," he said. "We want to talk to the Iraqis one more time." At about 1:45 A.M., we met the press briefly on the steps of the Hotel Inter-Continental, and I had difficulty not appearing so relaxed and upbeat that my body language gave away the fact that I now finally knew we would get our resolution.

Dead tired, I collapsed in bed well after 2:00 A.M. Fifteen minutes later, I was awakened by a telephone call from Margaret Tutwiler with word that Ivory Coast would indeed vote for the resolution but would not yet say so for the record. That was our ninth affirmative vote.

From San'a to Bogotá

At the conclusion of the CSCE talks where the CFE Treaty was signed, I joined the President on Air Force One and flew to Jeddah on November 21. The next morning, the President began a lengthy Thanksgiving day of activities with our troops in Saudi Arabia. I left for the Yemeni capital of San'a, hoping to persuade the Yemenis to vote with us on the resolution. I knew it was a long shot. There was a long history of bad blood between the Saudis and the Yemenis, made worse by Yemen's condemnation of King Fahd for inviting foreign troops into the kingdom. The Saudis had retaliated by tightening regulations on foreign workers, thus forcing hundreds of thousands of Yemenis to return home. It was pretty clear the Yemenis were not going to vote with us, and the Saudis correctly told me I was wasting my time going there.

Yemen was also the architect of a troublesome attempt within the Security Council to press for a resolution long sought by the Palestinian Liberation Organization to extend U.N. protection for Palestinians living in Israel's occupied territories. Among other elements, they wanted the United Nations to appoint a commissioner to monitor treatment of Palestinians in the West Bank and Gaza Strip. It was an old idea, supported by many nonaligned nations, but its proponents were now pressing for a Security Council vote before the use-of-force resolution. If they were successful in forcing a vote, the United States might well have to exercise a veto. That would cause us difficulties with some of our Arab partners, and lend credibility to Saddam's strategy of couching the crisis in Arab-Israeli terms. While concentrating on the use-of-force resolution, American diplomacy also had to find a means to block early consideration of a territories resolution that was patently obstructionist.

I reminded President Ali Abdullah Saleh that the United States had not put the unified Yemen on the terrorism list, even though South Yemen had been listed before its merger with the north. I also reminded him that we had urged the Saudis to lighten up on the Yemenis, to no avail. "We cannot understand your lack of cooperation with us on the Security Council," I said. I wanted them to know that they would pay a price if they continued to push a course of action at the United Nations that we considered unacceptable. Yemen was risking $70 million a year in U.S. foreign aid by its behavior. He seemed far less concerned about the Gulf crisis than I believed the situation warranted. "This is like a summer storm. It will blow over," he insisted. "The storm, if it comes, will be violent," I replied.

Saleh was an exceedingly gracious host. Prior to our meeting, he had arranged for my entourage to visit the old part of the city, which is more than two thousand years old. The scene was right out of *The Arabian Nights*. Walking through the narrow, cobblestone streets of the souk, we saw men who had just come in from the desert to sell their goods. Almost all wore traditional Arab headdresses and silver daggers. Everyone—man or woman, old or young—seemed to be chewing green leaves of *kat*, which has, we were told, a mildly narcotic effect.

Following our trip to the old city, my traveling party and I had our Thanksgiving Day lunch with President Saleh. He couldn't have been more hospitable, although we had mutton rather than turkey, as might have been expected. Then we went outside to meet the press, where he delivered a resounding no to the resolution. I had not expected his support, but he had given me no indication in private that he would reject my request quite so firmly in public.

I returned to Jeddah that night and received word that the Malaysian Foreign Minister had agreed to meet me in either Los Angeles, Houston, or somewhere in the Pacific. I decided to fly from Bogotá—where I was to meet with President Cesar Gaviria Trujillo, not only to solicit his vote but to let Gaviria know we weren't pleased with the action of his U.N. Ambassador, who had complained publicly about our policy toward Iraq—to Los Angeles and meet the Malaysians at the airport.

After an eight-hour flight to the Azores for refueling, we flew all night to Bogotá, where we rode in from the airport in blue armored Suburbans, a testament to the drug cartels' campaign of terror. "I quite frankly have been dismayed at the ideas advanced in New York by your mission," I said to Gaviria. "These ideas have the potential of undermining all that we in the Council and the coalition arrayed against Saddam have worked so hard to achieve. I encourage you to share your ideas with us before they are put in writing and distributed widely in the U.N. system. Such consultations will avoid the perception that there is a split between the U.S. and Colombia in the Security Council." As Colombia's U.N. Ambassador, who had flown in from New York to join the meeting, squirmed, Gaviria clearly noted my irritation.

I explained the details of our resolution, including the language of all necessary means. "It's important that Colombia and the United States, representing our hemisphere, not be separated. It would be extremely disappointing." "The way this problem is solved is crucial for all humanity," he replied. "We have exactly the same goals as you. At the end, we will vote with you. We will find a way." But he was looking for a fig leaf for Saddam. "It's important that Saddam Hussein feel that he is getting something when he gets out, like the [U.S.] military leaving the area."

"Saving face is hard to distinguish from rewarding brutal aggression," I replied. "We cannot fall into the trap of partial solutions." I left Bogotá with Gaviria's personal commitment to vote with us firmly in hand, secure in the knowledge that the mischief making of the Colombian Ambassador in New York was about to cease.

After refueling in Cartagena, we flew for seven hours to Los Angeles for our airport meeting with Malaysian Foreign Minister Abu Hassan, who I knew would be a hard sell. With a proud and often difficult Islamic government, the Malaysians were also pushing for the occupied-territories resolution. They resented having to fly thirty hours from Malaysia to see me, and were understandably exhausted.

From the moment the Foreign Minister began by dryly noting that "we would have preferred to have seen you in Malaysia," I knew this meeting would be prickly. He had his brief down well; his lengthy instructions had been typed on hotel stationery, then annotated. "I must express frankly our unhappiness with the U.S. approach in west Asia," he scolded. "You are spearheading this move to punish Iraq. We need to talk about Israeli aggression against Palestinians. Malaysia is not opposed to Saddam Hussein being punished. At the same time, Israel must be punished for the way it treats the Palestinians. We will study your resolution very carefully, but we cannot support sanctions for the virtual destruction of Iraq."

"This resolution gives us the only hope for trying to find a peaceful end to the situation," I replied. "We do not want to spill American blood in the desert. There is great risk for Americans and for this administration."

"Are you proposing a threat of war?" he asked.

The resolution we are suggesting at the United Nations, I said, would be general in nature. "It would not mention the word *force*, and it would not mention the word *military*. We are not seeking a resolution that *requires* force." The Malaysians wanted sanctions to be given more time, so I repeated my standard arguments. "I don't believe sanctions will do it for a long time. . . . We cannot maintain our forces at this magnitude in the desert. Big countries should not be allowed to roll over small countries.

"It is meant to say to Saddam Hussein, 'You will be thrown out one way or the other.' I personally spent fourteen months on an Arab-Israeli peace plan, but I believe strongly that you cannot link these two issues or you will make Saddam Hussein a hero."

After an extended discussion on legal points, the Foreign Minister ended a very tough, unyielding presentation by inquiring, "I hope that our position on this will not spill over into our bilateral relationship." I was happy for the opening to suggest that in light of recent world events, it might be prudent to consider one's future relations with the United States very carefully. "The only way to answer that," I replied, "is to say this is really important to us and to the world and should be important to you, Mr. Minister." Suddenly, there was a dead silence in the room. You could have heard a pin drop. For the first time, I thought he had absorbed just how serious we were about this.

After the meeting, I flew to Houston to spend the weekend with my ninety-six-year-old mother. I was exhausted when I arrived, but it would be one of the last times I would see her. En route, I reviewed the cables requesting all members of the Security Council to send their foreign ministers to the meeting on November 29. In the invitation to the Cuban Foreign Minister was a personal note from me asking for a meeting in New York on Wednesday, November 28. The cables also included the draft language of the proposal. It called for the use of all necessary means if Iraq was still in Kuwait on January 1.

On November 26, Douglas Hurd telephoned from London, concerned that it might be a mistake for the resolution to include a date certain for Iraqi withdrawal. An explicit deadline, he said, might cause "excitement" as it approached, and increase the risk of a preemptive strike by Iraq. "It's necessary to keep the Soviets aboard, Douglas," I said. "They feel very strongly about it." I asked him to help with the Colombians. "They owe us one," he confided. "We'll try to help there."

Final Lobbying at the United Nations

On November 28, the day before the vote, I flew to New York and went immediately to the Soviet mission for a two-hour meeting with Shevard-nadze, where I received a disturbing piece of news. "We have talked with Iraq," Shevardnadze confided. "They have told us that if war begins, they will attack Israel." He gave me a readout on a meeting in Baghdad between Soviet diplomats and Tariq Aziz. "I think it's beginning to sink in," he said.

"Will Aziz tell Saddam Hussein the truth?" I asked. "I think he will faithfully communicate," Shevardnadze guessed. I still wasn't sure; more than once, Saddam had been known to respond to bad news with summary executions.

During that meeting, we agreed to the final language of the resolution. Gorbachev had balked at the January 1 date. Led on by the Arabists in his Foreign Ministry, Gorbachev still believed he could somehow persuade Saddam to leave Kuwait, given enough time. He had pushed for a deadline of January 31. A two-month delay after passage of the resolution was simply unacceptable; it allowed too much time for mischief and would raise questions about the credibility of our willingness to use force. France suggested we split the difference. The President agreed; the final deadline was set for January 15.

I drove to the Waldorf-Astoria for my meeting with Cuban Foreign Minister Isidoro Malmierca. It was the first official bilateral meeting at the ministerial level between the two nations in nearly thirty years. Even so, we had to bend the rules to have it. Technically, I was meeting with the Minister in my role as President of the Security Council, not as Secretary of State of the United States.

Cuba's support of six prior U.N. resolutions against Saddam provided some common ground on which to build. "We have our differences, but have some things upon which we can agree," I said. "There are some principles at stake here. Unprovoked aggression against a smaller country cannot be allowed to succeed. Taking hostages is in violation of all international standards and should be condemned. We know your government has had discussions with Iraq saying that they should withdraw and allow the Kuwaiti government to return. Frankly, if we had not agreed on these points, it was not our intention to meet with you.

"We are working for this resolution because we think it is the only chance for peace that is left. I hope you can see that the United States is working through the United Nations. We are acting in a legal way in the international arena. Many people have encouraged us to pursue this under Article 51, but we have resisted. We have ten Security Council resolutions; you have voted for six of them. None of those resolutions has been implemented."

Many small nations such as Cuba see the United Nations as their central forum, so I went out of my way to stress our multilateral strategy. "We see the credibility of the United Nations at stake here," I argued. "It's extremely important that the U.N. Security Council resolutions be implemented if the U.N. is to be an effective body for peace and security. It is perhaps more important that we have an effective, functioning United Nations for smaller countries. No peaceful international order is possible if larger states can devour smaller ones. That is what is at stake here. Thank you for coming. That is my story.''

The Foreign Minister was an elderly man with a crippled leg. Except for an extended tirade against Israel's policies toward the Palestinians, he refrained from the sort of ideological bombast we had all come to expect from Fidel Castro, in favor of a fervent pacifist appeal. The object, he agreed, was to avoid combat. The problem, as he saw it, was that the resolution would all but guarantee war, which would raise oil prices and cause ''an economic catastrophe for the world.''

''We believe many will die of hunger if the war is begun,'' he argued. ''Given time, Iraq will accept the terms. The tendency to use force is not helpful. The threat of force is making Iraq's position stiffen. We believe the adoption of such a resolution would not result in a peaceful outcome. You need to try to find a formula of compliance without military action. We think setting a fixed date is dangerous and could be misinterpreted. It could encourage Iraq to take military action first. We feel the resolution that has been submitted is a process which would move us toward war.'' We were in fundamental disagreement.

''We do not quarrel with all you have said,'' I replied. ''We disagree with you on how best to get there. You say the people of Kuwait will suffer in a war. I say they cannot suffer much more than they are now. We don't think sanctions will work in a short period of time. He will feed his army first, so a great deal of suffering is going on in Iraq as a consequence of his policies. A large neighbor cannot invade and brutalize its smaller neighbor. The bottom line is that we agree on the ultimate goal, but differ on the best way to get there. The international community must not make the same mistakes it made in the 1930s. The Soviets will tell you the same. I hope you will give some thought to not voting against this and being isolated.''

My not-so-subtle argument didn't faze him. ''We don't fear not voting in favor of the resolution tomorrow,'' he shot back. ''We hope we will not be the only one with that position, but we will not hesitate to be alone and try to avoid war.'' It had been a long shot; even in the face of pressure from their longtime Soviet benefactors, Cuba would stand fast.

Foreign Minister Qian was delayed en route, so our meeting began shortly before midnight. By then, our specialists had concluded that the Chinese had decided an abstention was the minimum necessary for us to get relations back on track. They were correct; we had already agreed to allow Qian to visit Washington the day after the vote. But I made one last attempt to persuade him that an abstention would be costly to Chinese interests. ''Anything less than supporting the resolution will weaken our unity, give comfort to Saddam, and therefore draw much criticism from Congress and the American public,'' I argued. ''This could do so much damage to the atmosphere for your visit that it could restrict our flexibility in advancing the bilateral relationship.

"To be honest, many congressmen are assuming that you will vote yes. I don't intend to press you tonight for what your vote is, but a positive vote would be a major factor to move our relationship forward. Still, there is this sentiment in Congress that we have to deal with. It's important to have Permanent Five unity. We have deleted any reference to the use of force from the text. You will be welcome in Washington on Friday regardless of your vote."

The Chinese were still irritated that I had not accepted their offer to visit Beijing. "This is our fifth meeting, but there is still no exchange of visits to capitals," Qian complained. "This is abnormal and is detrimental to our relationship. We will not veto this resolution. We cannot vote in favor because of the use of military force. You have been to several countries recently. We hope you will come to China." An abstention was clearly the best we would get from Beijing.

Totalitarian regimes never seem to think that their internal policies, no matter how repressive, should be of any consequence in bilateral relations. "You have in George Bush someone who understands China and who wants to see an improvement in the relationship," I replied, "but he has political constraints on what he can and cannot do."

I went to bed at around 1:30 A.M. My wake-up call the next morning was from the President, who still wanted to explore ways of persuading the Chinese to vote for the resolution. He said he was willing to have lunch in Washington with the Perm Five foreign ministers, after which he could have a brief "pull aside" meeting with the Chinese minister. That formulation would make it appear as an impromptu meeting, more of a courtesy than a diplomatic quid pro quo. Still in my bathrobe, I convened a meeting of my senior advisers at my suite at the Waldorf to discuss the proposal. It was agreed that I should call the Foreign Minister and pass on the President's invitation, but nobody felt there was much chance they would accept. The Chinese were playing hardball. They knew we knew they wouldn't thwart our resolution with a veto. I suspected a seemingly impromptu meeting wouldn't be acceptable. I telephoned Qian; when he called back in the middle of my meeting with Douglas Hurd, I delivered the President's message. He was noncommittal: "Thank you, I will pass this to Beijing."

The Chinese can be many things when they want to, and unyielding is one of them. A short time later, he called back to say, "We cannot vote yes. My government has instructed me to abstain. We will not vote yes just to get a meeting. We should have a meeting because we abstained." I told him that I was disappointed, but that as I had promised, he would be welcome for a meeting. "Now we need to plan your trip to Washington," I said. What I didn't say was that our planning would include a meeting with me, not the President.

After the vote, a message was relayed to me from Qian in the middle of the night via Bob Kimmitt. The Chinese were furious when they saw that our draft itinerary for his visit to Washington didn't include a presidential meeting. The message was unequivocal: if Qian didn't see the President, he wasn't coming. This time, they had us. For all our problems with the Chinese, we didn't want to isolate them further. Qian's visit had already been announced. A cancellation would set back the relationship even further and would be embarrassing for both sides. I called the President and recommended we capitulate, so as not to exacerbate an already unpleasant situation. "This is a small price to pay for avoiding a veto," I said. He readily agreed. The Chinese would get their presidential meeting. But they didn't get what they *really* wanted: a presidential visit to China, and a commitment to press for the removal of economic sanctions imposed after the Tiananmen Square massacre. That would have won us a yes vote on the resolution, but at a terrible cost to principle.

Throughout the day of the vote, I alternated working on my remarks as chairman of the Security Council with a series of bilateral meetings with ministerial counterparts, including one with Roland Dumas. "This is an historic occasion," he said. "It's not often that the Permanent Five are in one place. What do you think about us meeting while we are here, to give Iraq the impression that the Permanent Five are together in their thinking?"

He and I got along well personally, but once again, we felt the French were being the French. In their view, we were softer on Israel than they believed was warranted. Dumas was angling to make a gesture to the Palestinians in the occupied territories and their allies in the United Nations. "I will be more than willing to do that, Roland, but I am not willing for the five of us to meet to discuss the occupied territories. That would be linkage."

"I understand," he said. "We could just talk about the region generally." In principle, it was a reasonable idea. I set about arranging a private dinner for the Perm Five ministers after the vote.

At 2:00 P.M., I called the President to say that he might have to make one last call to the Malaysian Prime Minister. I also told him that the Soviets, Saudis, and Kuwaitis were still pressing the Chinese to change their mind and vote affirmatively. Forty minutes later, I met briefly with Secretary-General Javier Pérez de Cuéllar. I handed him two checks totaling $186 million in partial payment of the United States' debt to the United Nations. (By law, the Treasury cannot issue a check for more than $100 million.) Many countries ignored their U.N. debt; even the United States was in arrears. But the President wanted to make a symbolic gesture, in appreciation for the help of the United Nations during the crisis. I also had heard that Pérez de Cuéllar was miffed that the U.N. bureaucracy wasn't calling the shots on the Gulf crisis. From the start, this had been our show; we had assembled the coalition, and the President had sent America's sons and daughters into the Gulf.

At 3:00 P.M., I met briefly with the Colombian Foreign Minister, who told me that his nation, along with Cuba, Yemen, and Malaysia, would not press in the meeting for a vote on the occupied territories resolution. I felt that the reason he was being magnanimous was because some adroit diplomacy on the part of the United States and its allies (notably Great Britain) had made sure that the requisite nine votes weren't there to bring the resolution before the Council. I thanked the Minister anyway for his statesmanship. "We are doing the right thing," I told him. "We must deter this aggression."

Ten minutes later, the Malaysian Foreign Minister informed me that his country would vote with us, but that he intended to press for action on the Palestinians. They had been difficult, but I thanked him for his forbearance. "We have 500,000 young Americans in the Gulf," I said, "and I think you can understand my concern."

I was left with less than ten minutes to prepare for the meeting of the Security Council. I received a quick brief from Tom Pickering, our U.N. Ambassador, and one of his parliamentarians, and read over my prepared statement for a final time.

Shortly before the session began, John Kelly told me that Yemen would definitely vote against the resolution. "Well, this will be the most expensive no vote they have ever cast," I said. Several news accounts later reported that I was kidding. I wasn't.

A Historic Vote

At 3:30 P.M., I gaveled the session to order. The chamber was packed, with galleries overflowing, and diplomats sitting and standing several deep around the conference table. It was the 2,963d meeting of the Security Council, and arguably the most important. Thirteen of the fifteen members were represented by their foreign ministers, only the fourth time in history the Council had convened at that level. I knew the votes were there, but I was speaking to a larger audience. The time had come to confront both Iraq *and* the American people with the proposition of war in the desert.

"I would like to begin today's discussion with a quotation that I think aptly sets the context for our discussions today," I said. " 'There is . . . no precedent for a people being the victim of such injustice and of being at present threatened by abandonment to an aggressor. Also there has never before been an example of any government proceeding with the systematic extermination of a nation by barbarous means in violation of the most solemn promises, made to all the nations of the earth, that there should be no resort to a war of conquest and that there should not be used against innocent human beings terrible poison and harmful gases.'

"Those words could have come from the Emir of Kuwait, but they do not. They were spoken instead in 1936, not 1990. They come from Haile Selassie, the leader of Ethiopia, a man who saw his country conquered and occupied, much like Kuwait has been brutalized since August 2. Sadly, his appeal to the League of Nations fell upon deaf ears. The League's efforts to redress aggression failed, and international disorder and war ensued.

"History now has given us another chance. With the Cold War now behind us, we now have the chance to build the world envisioned by the founders of the United Nations. We have the chance to make this Security Council and this United Nations true instruments for peace and justice across the globe.

"We must not let the United Nations go the way of the League of Nations. We must fulfill our common vision of a peaceful and just post–Cold War world. But if we are to do so, we must meet the threat to international peace created by Saddam Hussein's aggression. That's why the debate we are about to begin will rank as one of the most important in the history of the United Nations. It will surely do much to determine the future of this body.

"Our aim today must be to convince Saddam Hussein that the just, humane demands of this council and the international community cannot be ignored. If Iraq does not reverse its course peacefully, then other necessary measures—including the use of force—should be authorized. We should put the choice to Saddam Hussein in unmistakable terms."

By custom, representatives of the countries directly affected by Council action are invited to attend. Even allowing for the niceties of diplomacy, where you're always supposed to say kind things about colleagues you cannot abide, this was not a time for totally equitable treatment. So I invited "the Permanent Representative of Iraq" and "the Distinguished Deputy Premier and Minister for Foreign Affairs of Kuwait" to take their places at the Council table. The Kuwaitis then spoke, followed by Iraq's same tired harangue against "America's imperialistic ambitions" we had all heard for months. At 4:10 P.M., I passed a note to the Secretary-General: "Best defense against doing what's right is to rant and rave against the United States."

In the interest of fairness, the opponents of the resolution deserved to have their say. By prearrangement, Yemen spoke first. Their Foreign Minister complained about a double standard on the Palestinian issue and alleged we were voting on a war resolution. At least he was correct in that regard. He was practically bursting in his desire to rub it in to their ancient enemies, the Saudis. I thought it would be a Pyrrhic victory for Yemen with their larger and wealthier neighbor to the north. I *knew* it would be costly with the United States. I scribbled a quick note to Bob Kimmitt. "Yemen's permanent rep. just enjoyed about $200 to $250 million worth of applause for that speech. Kelly needs to get word to the Kuwaitis and I want to talk to Kelly and Reggie about our aid program to Yemen."*

As I'd expected, Cuba sided with the Iraqis as well. Midway through Foreign Minister Malmierca's speech, I jotted a note to Bernie Aronson, the Assistant Secretary whose responsibilities included Cuban affairs. Aronson was forever teasing me about my efforts to halt drift-net fishing, a noble endeavor he believed consumed too much of my energies. "After hearing the first half of the Cuban F.M.'s speech," I predicted, "I am convinced that Cuba will either (a) vote no, or (b) vote no. You are going to be moved from ARA to Assistant Secretary of State for Drift-net Fishing."

Chinese Foreign Minister Qian was the last of six to speak before the vote. He was personally gracious to me, but all our efforts had failed to sway the Chinese from an abstention. Qian said that such "hasty actions" were contrary to the Chinese belief in solving international disputes through peaceful means. Again, I scribbled a note to myself for the record: "China can't go for military means—except in case of traffic jams—like the one in Tiananmen Square in June of 1989."

At 5:26 P.M., I called for a show of hands. The vote was overwhelming: twelve votes in favor, Cuba and Yemen opposed, China abstaining. Resolution 678 was plain and straightforward. The Council had voted "to allow Iraq one final opportunity, as a pause of goodwill," to withdraw its troops from Kuwait unconditionally by midnight of January 15, 1991. If Saddam were still in Kuwait by then, member states would be authorized "to use all necessary means . . . to restore international peace and security in the area." Not since Korea in 1950 had the United Nations granted such sweeping authority to wage war.

By custom, the Council president is entitled to the last word. "Members of the Council, we meet at the hinge of history," I said. "We can use the end of the Cold War to get beyond the whole pattern of settling conflicts by force, or we can slip back into ever more savage regional conflicts in which might alone makes right. We can take the high road toward peace and the

---

*Our aid program to Yemen was $70 million per year, but other coalition countries also had aid programs.

rule of law, or Saddam Hussein's path of brutal aggression and the law of the jungle. Simply put, it is a choice between right and wrong. I believe we have the courage and the fortitude to choose what's right."

With this vote, both the military and political elements of our plan to force Iraq from Kuwait were now firmly in place. The number of U.S. troops in the region had doubled, making our threat to use force credible. And the coalition now had a U.N. resolution authorizing the use of that force if necessary.

CHAPTER 18

FORGING CONSENSUS AT HOME

It's absolutely essential that we cooperate. We face a very difficult and momentous challenge. We need to send the strongest possible signal to Saddam that he can't divide Americans.

—*Secretary Baker to the congressional leadership at the White House, November 1990*

Public opinion in this country is everything.   —*Abraham Lincoln, 1859*

O n November 7, 1990, the fourth day of an eleven-country trip to lobby coalition partners to support the "all necessary means" resolution, I arrived in Moscow shortly after 5:00 P.M. and was in my suite at the Mezhdunarodnaya Hotel an hour later. I took advantage of an uncharacteristically free evening to have dinner in my suite, followed by a massage. Afterward, before turning in for the evening, I wandered down to Bob Kimmitt's room, where the staff had assembled to compare notes at the end of a day that had begun fourteen hours before in Ankara. Kimmitt was on the phone to Washington. Like most of my staff, I was clad in a running suit and sneakers—the preferred after-hours uniform on the road and on long flights.

Earlier in the day, while flying to Moscow for meetings with Gorbachev and Shevardnadze, I had learned from Richard Haass, the NSC representative on the trip, that the White House planned to announce a huge new deployment of American soldiers to the Persian Gulf the next day. The President had made the decision on October 31, six days before the midterm elections. But to give us a chance to consult with our coalition partners and to keep it from becoming a partisan campaign issue, we had purposely decided to delay a formal announcement until later. The timing was horrible. Neither Congress nor our allies had been adequately prepared for the news. The Soviets wouldn't be pleased, and I knew Shevardnadze, who was viscerally opposed to a military solution, would be particularly furious if once again he felt informed after the fact. It made far more sense to wait a few days to make sure all the parties had been contacted. Upset that I had not been consulted about the decision to move up the announcement, I had vented my irritation with Haass, the most convenient victim. "What the hell do I have an NSC guy on the trip for?" I remember complaining. I ordered Haass to complain directly to Scowcroft on my behalf. Simultaneously, I had cabled my objections back to Scowcroft, adding a symbolic caveat to the merits of delay: an announcement that would almost by definition start the country thinking seriously about war perhaps ought not be unveiled on Veterans' Day.

Kimmitt put down the phone and confirmed what we had learned unofficially on the airplane earlier in the day. The next morning in Washington, the President would announce the force-augmentation decision. My recommendation that the announcement be delayed until after appropriate congressional and coalition consultations had been rejected. Because of its obvious sensitivity, this decision had been held exceedingly close. Now the White House feared the news was about to leak from the Pentagon and had decided to shorten the original timetable.

I had assumed the White House would at least arrange briefings for senior members of Congress shortly before the President's public announcement. I was wrong, as Kimmitt's telephone call made clear. I was surprised and dismayed by this news, but Janet Mullins, my chief congressional liaison officer, was particularly thunderstruck to learn that such a monumental decision would be announced without properly alerting Capitol Hill. "I can't believe we're going to do this without them knowing anything," she said. "They have no idea we're preparing for war. These guys will go crazy. You're going to have a load of crap on your hands when you get back."

Mullins was always sharp in assessing how Congress would respond to a given development. Diplomatic pressure and economic sanctions were hard enough for Congress to endorse. A massive new commitment of military force was quite another matter. I remember thinking that marshaling congressional support for a more aggressive policy in the Gulf would be every bit as difficult as passing comprehensive tax reform in the second Reagan term.

I called the President and urged him to begin telephoning the congressional leadership personally with news they almost surely would be unhappy to hear. I also suggested that we immediately schedule a presidential briefing for the leaders as soon as they returned to Washington the following week.

If anything, Mullins understated the reaction. Even with advance notice, many members would have opposed our decision. But they were furious at being caught by surprise. It took two months of intensive damage control, a United Nations resolution, and a final diplomatic effort by the President, culminating in direct talks between me and the Iraqi Foreign Minister, to persuade legislators to support the option of U.S. military intervention—a policy course Congress has viewed with wariness ever since Lyndon Johnson seized upon the 1964 Tonkin Gulf congressional resolution as justification for the Vietnam buildup.

Ultimately, the Persian Gulf crisis would establish in rather convincing fashion that our country's long and oftentimes debilitating post-Vietnam hangover had at least temporarily run its course. In large measure because Desert Storm was such a resounding success, the American people and their elected representatives now appear more willing to endorse the application of military power under clearly defined circumstances when vital national interests are at stake. (Paradoxically, however, that stunning success may have created its own troubling syndrome. In the future, any application of U.S. military power in situations where massive force is not appropriate might well be far more difficult politically because of Desert Storm.) But at the outset of the crisis, there was no way for any of us to know that. To the contrary, the President's private resolve to order American forces into combat if necessary to expel Saddam Hussein from Kuwait was conspicuously lacking in support—both in Congress and with the public at large.

Although not all of my colleagues agreed, I was convinced that while the President had the legal authority to act unilaterally, as a practical and political matter, we would be making a big mistake to undertake a war as big as this without first securing a resolution of support from Congress. That would prove to be a task no less formidable than assembling the international coalition against Saddam Hussein.

Before Iraq's invasion of Kuwait, we had begun to stiffen our approach toward the regime in Baghdad. The policy of constructive engagement was giving way to a more sober and critical view of Saddam. This tougher line was sufficiently incremental, however, that those few Americans who were paying attention could be excused for having missed the shift. And then, practically overnight, we went from trying to work with Saddam to likening him to Hitler. The apparent contradiction made it more difficult to raise the consciousness of the American people to Saddam's threat.

From a psychological standpoint, we also faced the hurdle of educating the public to a totally new threat. For a generation, Americans had seen the

Soviet Union as the singular adversary. But by 1990, Moscow was receding in the minds of most people as a real and compelling danger. Into this transition suddenly stepped Iraq and Saddam Hussein, who presided over the fourth-largest army in the world, had amassed huge stocks of chemical and biological munitions, and was furiously developing a nuclear capability. Nevertheless, Saddam was a leader unknown to the overwhelming majority of Americans. It was therefore hard to make the case about the danger he posed. This problem was exacerbated by the fact that very few people knew anything about Kuwait, or even where it was. Those who did knew it was a tiny country run by a feudal monarchy not exactly steeped in Western democratic traditions. In the decades since Kuwait had been carved out of Iraq by the British, the ruling al-Sabah family had never permitted a single election.

Typically, Congress's disinterest mirrored the public's apathy. To underscore long-established executive branch policy that vital American interests were at stake in the region, the United States had maintained a naval presence in the Gulf for more than forty years. On Capitol Hill, however, the prevailing view held by a majority of members from both parties was that American military intervention in the Gulf simply wasn't critical to the national interest. Even the initial deployment of U.S. troops to Saudi Arabia in early August was seen as a dangerous overreaction by some in Congress. Moreover, the linkage between oil and a robust American economy was largely an abstraction; it had been more than a decade since American consumers had experienced gas lines. There would be no groundswell from the voters urging Congress to send troops to protect our interests in the Gulf.

Explaining the New Threat

From the outset, our diplomatic offensive at the United Nations was a critical component in winning over a reluctant Congress. Since early August, we had prevailed on the Security Council to pass resolution after resolution tightening Saddam's political and economic isolation. We believed that the cumulative effect of these resolutions would have the added domestic benefit of eventually thrusting congressional fence-sitters into a politically awkward posture. I wanted to be able to ask doubting members of Congress how they could deny their President support that countries like Ethiopia and Malaysia and Zaire had given him in the Security Council. When the United Nations finally passed Resolution 678 on November 29 authorizing "all necessary means" to expel Iraq from Kuwait, an essential building block of our domestic strategy fell into place. Now we not only had the diplomatic authority for waging war, but also the political leverage to, in effect, shame the recalcitrants in Congress into doing the right thing.

For better and worse, there was a synergistic relationship between the international coalition and domestic support. The stronger the coalition, the easier it was to generate consensus at home. Likewise, the more domestic support we had, the more the President was put in a commanding position vis-à-vis other governments. Domestic criticism of Germany and Japan, for example, could be used to push Bonn and Tokyo to make larger financial contributions to compensate for the fact they weren't contributing combat troops to the coalition. The reverse was also apparent—if the coalition began to fray, congressional and domestic support would be undercut. And had Congress tied the President's hands by refusing to support his policy, the coalition might well be undermined.

Ironically, the diplomatic track created an unanticipated early setback to our strategy for mobilizing congressional support. On August 6, at the urging of the United States, the United Nations Security Council passed Resolution 661 imposing economic sanctions against Iraq. Unfortunately, the resolution gave some in Congress an opportunity to indulge in their well-known proclivity for wanting everything both ways. They could continue to denounce Iraq's aggression while using the resolution as cover to avoid coming to grips with the central policy dilemma: What should be done if the sanctions didn't work? The sanctions resolution gave many members an ideal excuse to avoid the hard choices for a year, a time frame heard frequently on Capitol Hill, but one which was totally unrealistic. There was simply no way to hold the international coalition together that long. In fact, I suspect that the reason some congressional leaders expressed an early and strong preference for dealing with the Gulf crisis through the United Nations was because they believed it would never vote for military action, thus taking Congress off the hook politically. Mullins confirmed this in frank discussions with some members and their staffs. Such profiles in timidity are standard operating procedure for many in Congress, who sadly often prefer to associate themselves with a President's triumphs and distance themselves from his failures. By any measure, our Gulf policy was fraught with risk. In yet another refrain of the Vietnam syndrome, members did not wish to be held responsible for sending troops from their states and districts off to what might be a bloody war. So many in Congress preferred the politically safer course of doing nothing if at all possible.

My view that we should seek a congressional mandate was grounded in political realities, not constitutional or legislative legalities. For the most part, the Bush administration strove hard to keep Congress well briefed. George Bush, after all, was a former member of Congress himself, and instinctively understood the wisdom of keeping Congress apprised. For my part, moreover, congressional consultation has always been something of an obsession. Throughout my years in public life, I've enjoyed cordial relations with the legislative branch, in large measure because I worked at it constantly. When I returned to government in 1981 to become Ronald Reagan's Chief of Staff, I resolved never to leave my office at the end of a day without returning every telephone call from a member of Congress, no matter how junior. For twelve years, I religiously stuck to that rule, and I believe it paid dividends for Presidents Reagan and Bush, as well as for me. In America, we judge the success or failure of our Presidents largely on the strength of their legislative records. President Carter's relations with a Congress controlled by his own party were frequently strained, and he paid a price for it in legislative effectiveness, which contributed to his defeat. I knew that President Reagan would have his hands full with a Democratic-controlled House that he had campaigned against vigorously, so it was even more essential to keep the lines of communications open and civil with Capitol Hill. As a result, even though we fought many fierce legislative battles with the Democrats, I believe President Reagan enjoyed better relations with the Congress than most observers had expected.

However, I emphatically believe Congress does *not* enjoy an equivalent right with the President for either the conduct of foreign policy or the deployment of American military forces. The Constitution is unassailable on this point: the authority to conduct foreign policy, particularly when it involves the prerogatives of the commander in chief, is preeminent in the executive. There was absolutely no doubt in my mind that the President didn't legally have to have congressional approval for ordering troops into combat. War in the Gulf, however, wouldn't be a limited engagement like Grenada or Panama. Even if it weren't required by law, I believed that sending hundreds of thousands of soldiers into battle, with the possibility of significant casualties, but *without* legislative imprimatur, could well prove to be a Pyrrhic victory. Privately, I feared that if we did not obtain congressional approval, we would be unable to sustain an attack on Saddam from a practical political standpoint and might have to settle for a policy of containment.

Our task in gathering congressional support, however, was made more complex by the jurisdictional tension that has simmered since Vietnam between the President and Congress over which branch of government can wage war. The 1973 War Powers Resolution, a legislative curb on executive authority to conduct military operations, has been considered unconstitutional and given only lip service by the last six Presidents, much to the irritation of Congress. In October 1983, when I was White House Chief of Staff, President Reagan assembled the congressional leadership in the Yellow Room of the residence one evening and told them American forces would invade the Caribbean island of Grenada the next morning. House Speaker Tip O'Neill said that this courtesy was insufficient under the War Powers Resolution. "This is notification, not consultation," he complained.

"Good luck." He promptly left the White House, leaving behind a tacit message: Don't look to us for any support if things go badly.

Our problems were further complicated by the realization that throughout the fall of 1990, the administration and the Congress had different perceptions of the direction in which policy was evolving. All of us inside the government were reluctantly moving toward a reality the President had sensed early on—that military action might be inevitable. While we hoped the force augmentation would sober Saddam into understanding our resolve and withdrawing from Kuwait, the very act of sending those troops was a tacit acknowledgment that they might eventually have to be ordered into battle if Saddam didn't leave—and so with every passing day, the likelihood of war intensified.

In hopes of conditioning Congress and the public to this new reality, I used the opportunity of a long-scheduled speech to the Los Angeles World Affairs Council on October 29 to treat the possible use of force against Iraq more explicitly than in my previous statements. I said that in a tinderbox like the Middle East, "when you add weapons of mass destruction and much of the world's energy supplies, it becomes an explosive mix." The President was determined, I noted, not to appease Iraq's aggression. I pointed out that "our military forces are also there to provide an effective and decisive military response should the situation warrant it." In words carefully chosen for their impact, I said that while the President was exhausting every diplomatic avenue to achieve a peaceful solution, "let no one doubt: we will not rule out a possible use of force if Iraq continues to occupy Kuwait."

Unfortunately, many members of Congress ignored these signals and focused instead on my remarks about the abusive treatment being endured by American hostages in Iraq. I was publicly and falsely accused, in fact, of overstating the case with regard to the privations of the hostages. Clearly, Congress had no idea the objective reality had shifted. They were still embracing the politically easier let-sanctions-work approach. As a result, the November 8 announcement of the new deployment exploded on Capitol Hill. The bipartisan leadership was predictably upset, particularly Senator Sam Nunn and Representative Les Aspin, chairmen of the respective Armed Services committees. They all felt blindsided; Nunn quickly let it be known that he'd heard about the announcement just hours before at a restaurant. The Democratic leaders were especially apoplectic. The President's commitment to an early meeting to seek the leadership's counsel mollified nobody.

Jobs, Jobs, Jobs

On November 13, the day before that meeting, I flew to Bermuda for a quick bilateral meeting with Joe Clark, Canada's Minister for External Affairs. From the outset of the crisis, the Canadians were stalwart in their support, and Clark told me his government would endorse the use-of-force resolution in the United Nations. After our meeting, I took the opportunity of a joint press conference to explain that while we were determined to stand up to naked aggression, there was also a fundamental domestic imperative to our policy.

"The economic lifeline of the industrial world runs from the Gulf, and we cannot permit a dictator such as this to sit astride that economic lifeline," I said. "And to bring it down to the level of the average American citizen, let me say that means jobs. If you want to sum it up in one word, it's jobs. Because an economic recession worldwide, caused by the control of one nation, one dictator if you will, of the West's economic lifeline will result in the loss of jobs on the part of American citizens."

My words had been chosen deliberately. Three days before, in Moscow, I had said that the standard of living of every American was at stake in the Gulf. My Bermuda comments were designed to reinforce those earlier remarks. In truth, for weeks I'd been frustrated by the administration's collective inability to articulate a single coherent, consistent rationale for the President's policy. Our public pronouncements had ranged from the principled to the esoteric. At times we talked of standing up to aggression and creating a new world order. At others we called Saddam the new Hitler and cited the threat to global stability from rising oil prices. All these arguments were true. We *had* responded to a clear violation of international law, a blatant case of aggression, and the first genuine crisis of the post–Cold War world. And we *were* dealing with a megalomaniacal personality. But it was also true we had vital national interests at stake, something all prior administrations, Democrat and Republican, going all the way back to FDR, had recognized. We had to make sure we could maintain a secure supply of energy. Our swift response in early August had deterred Saddam from invading Saudi Arabia. But if we allowed him to remain in Kuwait, an emboldened Saddam—who, by his own admission, had invaded to replenish his depleted coffers with Kuwaiti oil revenues—would easily be able to influence worldwide oil pricing decisions. Higher crude prices would almost certainly follow, which in turn would likely create not only a global economic downturn but also a recession in the fragile U.S. economy. Inevitably, that would mean the loss of tens of thousands of American jobs. Frankly, we had done a lousy job of explaining not only the fundamental economic ramifications of Iraq's aggression but also the threat to global peace and stability from his weapons of mass destruction, and we were beginning to pay a political price at home as a result of our rhetorical confusion. Public support for Desert Shield was starting to unravel. The President was being heckled by protesters with signs urging "No Blood for Oil." Congress was increasingly skittish about the continued military buildup. I was searching for a formulation that drove home the magnitude of the threat to ordinary Americans, and thereby shored up domestic support for a policy that might end in combat in the desert of Kuwait.

In the end, it came out badly. In trying to bring some coherence to the administration's message, I overreacted to the growing complaints that the only reason we were in the Gulf was because of oil. I took a complex policy decision, which at its heart was a principled stand against unprovoked aggression, and tried to define it as a simple economic calculation—jobs. I still believe I was right, but it didn't work. There *was* a compelling economic component to the policy, and it wasn't just about oil. If I had substituted the phrase "economic prosperity" for "jobs," perhaps my remarks would have been better received.

Immediately after the press conference, I was handed a disturbing piece of wire copy. Richard Lugar of Indiana, a critical Republican on the Senate Foreign Relations Committee, had publicly urged the President to call Congress back from its recess into an immediate special session to consider a resolution authorizing military action against Saddam. Lugar had been pushing this idea for some time, and had just left the Oval Office mistakenly convinced that he'd talked the President into backing it. It was a good-faith effort on Lugar's part. His constituents were saying they didn't understand why more troops were necessary. A resolution of support from Congress, Lugar believed, would deliver a powerful, unequivocal statement of bipartisan support in behalf of the policy. Lugar was joined in his proposal by Bob Dole, who saw, beyond the merits, an opportunity to force the hand of Democrats who were posturing against the policy but who they felt would be understandably reluctant to vote against the commander in chief on what essentially amounted to a declaration of war.

On its face, it was a tempting proposal to deny the Democrats further opportunities to have it both ways. But Lugar's suggestion was a potential disaster. At the time, we didn't have the votes to prevail. Influential members on both sides of the aisle were still furious at our failure to consult on the force augmentation. Seeking a resolution and failing would have been catastrophic. The President's hands would have been tied. Realistically, we couldn't have used force in the face of explicit congressional disapproval. Our international coalition would be left to wonder about the durability of America's resolve, and the President's ability to conduct foreign policy would have been thrown into doubt. Moreover, economic sanctions had been in effect only sixty days. A majority of Congress still believed sanctions would force Iraq out of Kuwait if given sufficient time. Janet Mullins warned me that if we went to the Hill, as Lugar wanted, there was a strong chance Congress would pass a conditional war resolution. We would then have our authorization to go to war—but only after sanctions were given many more months to prove their effectiveness. The idea was prohibitively dangerous. Legally, we felt we had the authority to move in the Gulf, but defying a congressional authorization would have disastrous long-term consequences.

Ironically, our predicament was alleviated in large measure by the co-operation of Democrat George Mitchell, the Senate majority leader. After returning from Bermuda, I had several conversations with Mitchell. Ulti-mately, he agreed with me that a congressional resolution was important—but only after a similar resolution was approved by the United Nations Security Council. Mitchell told me the votes indeed were not there for a "clean" resolution of support, but that a definitive U.N. resolution would provide powerful leverage with which to persuade wavering members. Ul-timately, Mitchell publicly announced that he would not call a special ses-sion to consider the Lugar proposal.

The day after I returned from Bermuda, I attended one of the most contentious meetings I can remember with the bipartisan congressional leaders. The President was resolute, defending his troop decision as a pru-dent precaution and reiterating that the best hope for avoiding war was to convince Saddam we weren't just posturing.

"This is the only possibility of settling this peacefully," I said. "His press is trumpeting that we're short of breath. We have a mutual responsibility not to send him mixed signals." The members were dubious. As I listened to them denounce our policy, the irony was inescapable. I had just returned from a trip where I had prepared the allies for the possibility of war, while the Congress, whose support was just as critical, was not on board.

The escalating legislative turmoil hastened the debate within the ad-ministration about the advisability of asking for a congressional resolution of support at all. I still believed we had to try, and in the end would prevail. For all the conflict between the executive and legislative branches of gov-ernment over war-making powers, Congress usually deferred reluctantly to the wishes of the President in such matters. It would require a considerable amount of consultation and hand-holding, but I thought that if the Presi-dent asked, Congress in the end would not turn him down. The Vice Presi-dent was strongly of the same opinion. Brent Scowcroft was essentially neutral; a resolution would be helpful, he thought, but not mandatory. Dick Cheney opposed the idea, believing the repercussions of losing the vote were simply too dangerous to risk. John Sununu, the White House Chief of Staff, argued that Congress should be ignored; the President should do what he wanted.

If we decided the votes were not there for a resolution of support, the President was always prepared to bypass Congress if necessary, and go to war under Article 51 of the U.N. Charter and a U.N. resolution authorizing use of force. At one point, we even gave some consideration to finessing the matter by actually invoking the War Powers Resolution, which gives a President ninety days to fight a war without congressional approval. The Pentagon was assuring us this war was certain to be over by then. Even if that assessment proved wrong, there was no way Congress would vote to stop the fighting once it began. In the end, we decided that such a stratagem, while clever, would set a terrible constitutional precedent sure to haunt a future President's freedom of action.

At a December meeting with congressional leaders, the internal debate ended when somebody asked George Bush what he wanted to happen. "My preference," the President said, "would be to get the Congress to bless what I'm about to do."

Congressional Confrontation

I believed the outcome of any effort to obtain congressional support was far from certain, a view which would be reinforced by two days of intense testimony before skeptical lawmakers. In late November, I'd received a call from Dante Fascell, chairman of the House Foreign Affairs Committee. Fascell and I had always gotten along well. A conservative Democrat, he was a hawk on most issues of national security, and I knew he would support the President. But he told me in blunt terms that there was a perception on Capitol Hill that I was stiffing Congress by refusing to testify. He was right about that; I *had* been very reluctant to share information with Congress about the delicate negotiations I'd been engaged in and the state of our contingency planning for war. I knew anything I said, even in executive session, would be in the newspapers the next morning. I'd concluded that it made more sense to risk annoying the Congress temporarily than to risk leaks that might derail our policy and threaten the cohesion of our international coalition.

Fascell told me this policy of benign neglect was reaching the point of diminishing returns. "I'm getting beat up by my people," he said. "I think you need to get up here." I'd been hearing the same thing from some Republican allies as well. As a practical matter, I also knew we couldn't ask Congress for a resolution of support without my first agreeing to testify. I decided to appear before both Foreign Affairs committees in early December. By design, those dates were set for a time after the U.N. resolution authorizing use of force came to a vote. That vote would provide us powerful leverage in asking Congress to support the President. I knew that my congressional appearances would be one of our last opportunities to persuade a reluctant Congress that a policy they clearly opposed—preparing for war—in fact offered the only chance of securing the peaceful resolution all of us were seeking. I also knew it would be a very hard sell.

In my testimony before the Senate Foreign Relations Committee on December 5, I restated the moral and historical case for standing up to Saddam's aggression that the President and all of us had been making since August. I also defended our military buildup as a prudent precaution essential to preserving the credibility of our diplomatic efforts. If Saddam thought the military option was just a bluff, he would never get out of Kuwait. But my main purpose was to attack frontally the premise behind which many in Congress were hiding—the misguided notion that, given enough time, economic sanctions would inevitably force Saddam from Kuwait. "We have to face the fact that four months into this conflict, none of our efforts have yet produced any sign of change in Saddam Hussein," I said. "We have to face the difficult fact, I think, that no one can tell you that sanctions alone will ever be able to impose a high enough cost on Saddam Hussein to get him to withdraw. . . . I am personally very pessimistic that they will."

I predicted that Saddam's success in staring down the West "would only guarantee more strife, more conflict, and eventually a wider war. There would be little hope for any effort at peacemaking in the Middle East. Economically, his aggression imperils the world's oil lifelines, threatening recession or depression here and abroad, hitting hardest those fledgling democracies that are least able to cope with it. His aggression is an attempt to mortgage the economic promise of the post–Cold War world to the whims of a single man.

"Politically, Mr. Chairman—finally, politically—we must stand for American leadership, not because we seek it but simply because no one else can do the job. We did not stand united for forty years to bring the Cold War to a peaceful end in order to make the world safe for the likes of Saddam Hussein . . . simply put, it is a choice between what's right and what's wrong. And, Mr. Chairman, I think that we have the courage and the fortitude to do what's right."

I also wanted members to understand that, while they might be reluctant to engage, they should be prepared to pay a political price for sitting on the sidelines as the President searched for a peaceful solution. I laid down this gauntlet in language calculated to make them squirm: "Put bluntly, this is the last best chance for a peaceful solution. If we are to have any chance of success, I must go to Baghdad with the full support of the Congress and the American people behind the message of the international community." (The Friday before, the President had proposed sending me to Baghdad and having Iraq's Foreign Minister Tariq Aziz come to Washington as a last attempt at a peaceful solution.)

As I had expected, the committee was cordial, but the dialogue quickly degenerated into confrontation. It was apparent to me that members were so obsessed with clinging to sanctions as the easy way out that they refused to entertain the premise that sanctions in fact weren't working. There was a distinct accommodationist flavor to their monologues. Republican Frank Murkowski of Alaska wondered whether we should offer a Kuwaiti oil field to Saddam—a terrible "crime pays" idea endorsed by Democrats Paul Simon of Illinois and Christopher Dodd of Connecticut.

The most vocal critic was Paul Sarbanes of Maryland, another Democrat, who told me the administration's view that the President had the right to go to war without congressional approval was "totally contrary to the Constitution," then made an impassioned defense of sanctions.

"It seems to me that you have placed us on a course to war," Sarbanes said, in a voice close to shouting. In effect, he alleged that the force buildup and the deadline proved we weren't really interested in a peaceful solution, because sanctions would require "more than four or six or eight or ten months" to be given a fair chance—a timetable I knew was unrealistic in practical terms.

"This buildup now of the force almost takes you irresistibly down the path of going to war," he charged. "Now, I cannot say to a family that loses a son or daughter in a conflict that may well take place in the next sixty to ninety days, that we exhausted every possibility for a peaceful solution before this happened, because the sanctions option has not been exhausted.

"You had a policy that was working. The sanctions were squeezing him and, obviously, they were going to squeeze him more day by day. Instead, we've abandoned our policy and we've shifted off to a course now which I think is going to take us into conflict. This is the time for the qualities of the long-distance runner—perseverance, stamina, determination. It takes courage to have those qualities as well. . . . The last, best chance for a peaceful solution . . . is to sustain the sanctions policy for a period of time sufficiently long to give it a chance to work."

I thought this line of reasoning naive at best. Sarbanes was a Rhodes scholar with substantial experience in foreign affairs. As a practical matter, he surely knew as well as I that it would be almost impossible to keep the international coalition together as long as he was suggesting.

Sarbanes was so worked up that he hadn't bothered to ask a question, but I didn't want him to get away scot-free. "Let me say, Senator," I said, "that right out my window at the State Department, I look every day at Arlington National Cemetery. I understand very, very well what's at stake here and I think the President of the United States understands very, very well. We have not been precipitous. We have not been reckless. . . . As the Secretary of State of this beloved nation of ours, Senator, I understand the high responsibility that I have, and that we have to spare no effort and leave no stone unturned in the search for a peaceful solution. I would submit to you that that is what we have been doing, and that is what we will continue to do because that is what we want.

"But I will also tell you that I think there is a risk of misjudging what could lead us to a peaceful solution. Unless we can convince this dictator that the threat of the use of force is a credible one and that he runs the risk of being forced out of Kuwait if he doesn't leave peacefully, we will not get a peaceful solution."

The next day, I repeated my testimony to the House Foreign Affairs Committee, which was somewhat less combative. Like their Senate counterparts, however, they were dubious about the troop buildup and made their preference clear for relying on sanctions.

The low point of that hearing occurred shortly before the end, when Fascell and other senior Democratic members had left the room, passing the gavel by default to Peter Kostmayer of Pennsylvania. As a junior member of the committee, Kostmayer, in normal circumstances, would have been allowed only a few minutes of questioning. As acting chairman, however, he was free to grandstand at will. In dozens of appearances before congressional committees over the years, I'd learned to put my guard up when a member of the opposition begins his remarks with lugubrious praise, so I had a hint of what was coming when Kostmayer first paid tribute to "how brilliantly you and the President have managed to marshal and mobilize these international forces and international finances against Saddam Hussein." Then, after a quotation from Clausewitz about the need to balance the cost of war against its political value, he asked, "Are you convinced, as I am not, as Secretary of State, as a citizen, and as a father, that this object is worth the loss of thirty or forty or fifty or sixty thousand American lives?" he asked.

His query was sheer demagoguery, a stunt to garner headlines. Even in the worst-case scenarios, the Pentagon's casualty estimates were a few thousand. I bristled at the crassness of his cheap shot. Aides sitting behind me later said the back of my neck turned bright red during the ensuing exchange.

"That is a hypothetical question that really has no basis in fact that I am aware of," I replied.

"To not ask yourself that question," Kostmayer persisted, "as a person who may be involved in making this decision, to me, would be, I think with all due respect, sir, irresponsible. You must ask yourself, how many Americans will be killed?"

"Of course you must," I replied, my temperature rising. "You must also ask yourself very sensitive questions about how long you think any engagement might last. But you must not do it here in this public forum."

Kostmayer kept at his political game. It was a classic "when did you stop beating your wife" performance. In effect, he wanted me to tell him how many lives a Gulf war would be worth. Congress was intent on still driving the policy in the opposite direction. The easiest way to do that was to conjure up images of body bags on the evening news. He knew, as did I, that there was only one appropriate answer: one life lost was too many.

Still, he kept trying to get a number out of me. "It seems to me that if it's going to cost—and I don't think it will, although I have no idea— 250,000 lives, it isn't worth it," he moralized. "For 250,000 lives it isn't worth it. You've got to speak to that issue."

"Then I would refer you, Mr. Kostmayer, to the military leadership, who are the only people who can make a reasonable estimate in that regard." I was determined not to give him an answer.

Kostmayer countered by claiming that military leaders such as Admiral Crowe had testified that letting sanctions work was the most sensible policy course. "That is at least 50 percent a political judgment," I interjected. I wanted to say that during his tenure as chairman of the Joint Chiefs, Crowe had never wanted to use military force anywhere, anytime, anyhow, regardless of the merits. He always had a reason why force should not be considered. Nearly a decade before, when President Reagan considered whether to send U.S. forces to Grenada, I listened to Crowe privately argue against the invasion he later dutifully carried out. I confined myself to saying that Crowe and other critics were superb military men. "But they are not experts with respect to the political questions," I argued. "Is there a more important question to be asked [than] how many Americans, Mr. Secretary, will die in the Persian Gulf if we go to war?" Kostmayer persisted.

I'd had enough. "Let me tell you when the question ought to be asked," I snapped. "The question ought to be asked if and when there is a decision made to use force. That's when it ought to be asked. And it is appropriate to be addressed, if I may say so, to the military leadership."

With a snide complaint that the issue had still not been addressed, Kostmayer finally gave up. Like most confrontations with Congress, this one ended in a standoff. I hadn't given him a casualty number, but Kostmayer had his sound bite for the television news shows. I thought it was a new low in cheap stunts. I was particularly infuriated by his repeated inferences that we were totally cavalier about sending American soldiers off to die. I wondered to myself, as this tawdry gamesmanship was occurring, how Kostmayer might have acted if our roles had been reversed. Kostmayer had done precisely what he'd accused us of doing—toying with the lives of our GIs. It was a gross disservice to them and an embarrassment to Congress and the administration that I wasn't interested in tolerating in the future.

The next time I was asked to testify before the committee, I sent a message to Fascell politely inquiring whether someone in authority would be in the chair at all times to keep the proceedings under control.

Throughout the rest of December, all of us pressed the case with Congress, which had adjourned in late October for the year. Several factors worked to our advantage, not the least of which was Saddam's intransigence in the face of entreaties from the Soviets and others. The U.N. vote of November 29 authorizing the use of force was a compelling factor. By voting against the President, Congress not only would be turning its back on America's traditional obligation to support U.N. Security Council resolutions for which it voted, but also would be spurning the will of the international community. The several hundred thousand soldiers already in the desert also posed a severe problem for those not inclined to support the President. If war began and difficulties arose, members might well be criticized by refusing to stand with the President.

Help also materialized from Israel's strongest supporters on Capitol Hill. Many of these members were Democrats like Senators Al Gore and Joe Lieberman, and Representatives Les Aspin and Stephen Solarz. Some of them had viewed the President and me with suspicion, believing we had tilted toward the Arabs during our attempt to revive the Middle East peace process the previous year. Ironically, however, they were susceptible to suasion on parochial grounds. From their perspective, war in the Gulf, while perhaps not a desirable prospect, could have a beneficial side effect— the greatest threat to Israel's security would be destroyed. Politics indeed makes strange bedfellows. Many members not normally supportive of administration initiatives stood with us on the Gulf.

The decisive factor, however, was probably the Baker-to-Baghdad/ Aziz-to-Washington offer of November 30. Our main purpose in "going this last mile" was to show Congress, the American people, and history that we were still looking for ways to avert a war, not start one. When my meeting in Geneva on January 9 failed to produce a breakthrough, opposition on Capitol Hill began to crumble.

Three days later, on January 12, Congress voted the President authority to wage war under the terms of the U.N. resolution. The Senate approved the resolution by only a 52–47 margin. A shift of three votes would have reversed the result. For all practical purposes, we now had in hand what Speaker Tom Foley described as the practical equivalent of a declaration of war. All that remained, regrettably, was for us to wield it.

CHAPTER 19

THE LAST, BEST
CHANCE FOR PEACE

Regrettably . . .

> —*Secretary Baker at a press conference after meeting with*
> *Tariq Aziz on January 9, 1991*

When I was an undergraduate studying classics at Princeton, I remember reading the Greek historian Thucydides' *The Peloponnesian War*. No doubt any effort on my part was inspired as much by the fact that this was required reading as by any scholarly pretension. In those days, I was far more inclined to focus on strategy on the rugby field than in the metallic green carrels of Firestone Library. Thucydides' pithy explanation—"What made war inevitable was the growth of Athenian power and the fear which this caused in Sparta"—was a stark expression of political realism. Moreover, Thucydides was one of the first historians to ponder whether and how a war that actually did happen, might not have: What were the specific instances leading to the outbreak of war? What was the last possible opportunity to avoid war? When did human volition and the wish to maintain peace give way to fate and the necessities demanded to prosecute war?

For the scholar, working in retrospect, these are questions of evidence and logic. For the statesman, working in real time, these are questions of emotion and intuition. For the soldier, working in danger, these are not as much questions as moments when a dreaded future becomes a dangerous reality.

During the Gulf crisis, those questions were answered for me that crisp, clear evening in Geneva when my meeting with Tariq Aziz at the Hotel

Inter-Continental ended with President Bush's letter to Saddam Hussein lying on the table between us. Our ultimatum would not forestall the calamity that was about to befall the people of Iraq. Until then, I had believed—as much from dread of war as hopes for peace, and more from wish than logic—that Iraq might leave Kuwait without force. From that evening on, my heart knew what my head had calculated long before: America soon would be at war, and my task as a diplomat would no longer be to try and achieve a political solution and thereby prevent war, but to help wage war and to win it. How I came to that view is a circuitous journey from the United Nations vote on November 29, 1990, authorizing the use of force to reverse Iraq's aggression.

The genesis for my meeting with Tariq Aziz lay in a conversation I had with President Bush on the evening of that historic United Nations vote. I spoke with him by phone from a holding room at the United Nations. He was gratified by the overwhelming support for Resolution 678 and wanted to explore next steps. "I want to talk to you about an idea I have," he said. I thought I knew what he had in mind, since we had discussed it in passing before. But because I was in the room with others and not on a secure line, I responded guardedly. "I've got some ideas on how to win domestic support, now that we've got international support," I said. He suggested that we meet first thing the next morning with Brent Scowcroft.

From that two-hour meeting emerged the proposal that the President had been pondering for three weeks: a face-to-face attempt to avert war in the Gulf. This initiative was easily the biggest surprise of the entire Gulf conflict and arguably the most controversial. It confused and confounded our friends, delighted our critics, and fueled whispers about a weakening of America's resolve. At least momentarily, it undermined our credibility with some of our coalition partners, and handed Saddam Hussein a propaganda opening. It was also unpopular with some of the others in the President's War Cabinet and several members of my immediate staff.

Much as the November 8 force augmentation announcement had been the turning point in the military buildup, and Resolution 678 the key to cementing the international coalition, my meeting with Aziz became the turning point in building domestic consensus. After that meeting, the Congress would authorize force, the coalition would finalize preparations, and the military would be set in motion.

The Offer: Baker to Baghdad, Aziz to Washington

By late November, we still had not formed a domestic consensus behind the use of force. After the U.N. vote, the President found himself in a rather odd position. He had quite literally convinced the world of the necessity for war if Saddam failed to withdraw by January 15, but had so far been unable to get the Congress and U.S. public opinion firmly behind him.

Following my conversation with the President after the U.N. vote on November 29, I sat down for a dinner at the Waldorf-Astoria with the Perm Five foreign ministers. It was principals only; no staff except for interpreters. My aim was to thank Shevardnadze, Hurd, and Dumas for their steadfastness, exert some subtle peer pressure on Qian to stay on board, and explore possible future options.

Relieved of the drama of the moment, we engaged in some lighthearted banter over cocktails as we waited for Qian to arrive. "We're happy that Douglas did not get to become Prime Minister," Dumas quipped, "since we wouldn't want to break up our group that works so well."

"I think the KGB had something to do with it," Hurd shot back. "Didn't it, Eduard?"

"I'm not saying now," Shevardnadze deadpanned, "but when I write my memoirs I'll have a lot to say." As the laughter subsided, Shevardnadze steered the conversation back onto the serious ground we had yet to resolve: How to avert a war we now had the authority to conduct. "We have to stick together, because Saddam knows how to play on contradictions between us. He is dangerous and unpredictable."

"We must let Saddam Hussein know how we feel," Dumas added. "I have gotten information and I now have the impression that Saddam is poorly informed by his aides. This is often consistent with a dictatorship. He doesn't want to hear, and thus he doesn't get told very much."

Hurd argued that Secretary-General de Cuéllar "has been acting obscurely" but was planning a trip to Baghdad in a week. I thought it made sense to support that mission. "Look, we know for the first week Saddam is going to beat his chest and criticize the resolution," I said. "Roland says he feels that Saddam is not well informed and suggests that maybe we get de Cuéllar to give Saddam a copy of Resolution 678 directly."

Shevardnadze was dubious. "Maybe this is the situation, but I don't think so," he said. "I believe he really understands and knows what goes on. Okay, maybe he *is* surrounded by sycophants, but he really knows what is in the world. He knows how to play the contradictions between us. Thus, we five must agree to be together. We must say this either through the Secretary-General or through others, but it is important that Saddam know that implicitly we five are acting in unity."

To that end, Shevardnadze tossed onto the dinner table an idea none of us knew about in advance and which he admitted he hadn't cleared with Gorbachev. Why not convene a summit meeting of the Perm Five heads of state a few days before the January 15 deadline, he proposed.

Hurd was skeptical. "We must know what to expect from a summit of this kind," he interjected. "The mere fact that such a summit is possible would have an enormous impact," Shevardnadze countered. "Just think about it. We need to get instructions from our leaders."

Dumas saw the summit proposal as a way of ensuring that the Chinese didn't split from the group again. Cleverly, he suggested that such a meeting might be held in Beijing—an idea certain to appeal to fragile Chinese egos. If the leaders couldn't be persuaded, he added, perhaps the five of us could meet in China to issue a joint declaration.

"A summit meeting of the Five will be needed to give him guarantees that no one will attack him," Shevardnadze persisted. "It really is worth thinking about. If he leaves and the five leaders of our countries show him they have respect for him, they will touch his self-pride."

It was one of the few times during the crisis I felt Shevardnadze was deluding himself. Through various intermediaries, the Iraqis were passing word that they were fearful of being attacked even if they began to withdraw. I thought it was another hollow ploy by Saddam to stall for time by persuading the coalition that he might actually pull out. "This is not just to save his face," I demurred. "This is to save his ass!"

Qian had sat silently through the dialogue. "Saddam wants a reward for leaving Kuwait," he said. "Then he wants guarantees. He wants a guarantee that no one will attack him. He is afraid of war." It made sense for direct talks between the United States and Iraq, Qian maintained, to deliver the message that if Saddam withdrew from Kuwait, his retreating forces would not be attacked by the coalition.

"Saddam is first and foremost afraid of the U.S., not France, the U.K., or Saudi Arabia," Hurd said. He suggested that the President send a private assurance to that effect to Baghdad, then begin saying the same thing publicly about three weeks before the deadline.

"I still believe he will leave Kuwait," Shevardnadze theorized. "The Secretary-General should go to Baghdad. Then we all give him the same message separately (that he won't be attacked if he leaves). Then around January 1, we five ministers all send the same message together."

Dumas concurred. "What better guarantee is there of not being attacked," he mused, "than hearing it from the countries that are the leaders of the Security Council? He should hope that he will escape the fate that is inherent in what we gave him today."

Our dinner ended inconclusively, as many diplomatic dinners do, with no real action plan, but agreement to consult in the days ahead. It was clear, however, that no one intended to allow the forty-five-day "pause for peace" to become a true pause in Gulf crisis diplomacy. For my part, I thought a Perm Five meeting with the Iraqis was a well-meaning but ill-advised concept, a prescription for losing control of the diplomatic agenda. In such a setting, the United States would surely be pressured to negotiate down from the resolution the full Security Council had just approved.

In our meeting on the morning of November 30 in the Oval Office, the President told Scowcroft and me he felt an obligation to explore the possibilities of direct discussions with Iraq, and had been mulling over a formula for such talks in his mind for several weeks. He had ruled out meeting with Saddam Hussein himself, but he was willing to receive Tariq Aziz, and he wanted me to meet with Saddam. "If he hears it from you, he'll know it's for real," the President reckoned.

The idea of a high-level, "last chance" meeting had been circulating around Washington in various forms. Three days earlier, Lee Hamilton had proposed one variant. Indeed, in retrospect, the President's proposal, if not its timing, was almost predictable. A set of face-to-face talks was the ultimate expression of George Bush's personal style of politics and diplomacy. Having met with Thatcher, Mitterrand, Gorbachev, Fahd, and most of the other heads of state of the coalition, he now wanted to make one last personal push—with the adversary.

The President went on to say that if Saddam watched the congressional hearings on CNN, he might doubt our resolve. I agreed. In fact, during the Security Council session the day before, the Iraqi Ambassador to the U.N. had used a quote by Senator Bob Kerrey of Nebraska in which he said our turning to the use of force "is a mistake because it forsakes the potential for a new world order in favor of the tactics of the old order. Rather than relying on diplomacy, cooperation, and multilateral regulation of arms flows, we will revert primarily to reliance on U.S. troops and U.S. arms sales." Moreover, Saddam may have misread history. He apparently was fixated by our experience in Vietnam and, like Hafez al-Assad, thought our pullout from Lebanon after the Beirut barracks bombing in October 1983 showed Americans were "short of breath." Unlike Assad, however, Saddam was willing to test that proposition in a high-profile, high-risk way.

The President continued by stressing how history would read his actions. With war coming closer, he was reflecting more and more on how his actions would be judged and particularly on whether he had done everything he could to avoid war. George Bush was fully committed to war if necessary, and had crossed that personal Rubicon before any of us. But he never relished the prospect. Going to war *was* the last thing he sought. All he really wanted was to get Iraq out of Kuwait. As I listened, I was reminded of the conversation in Helsinki in September when he had told all of us that we had put our men and women in the desert, that he was ultimately responsible, and that he wasn't going to put their lives on the line unless he absolutely had to.

I felt the proposal had three distinct merits. First, it would give us one last diplomatic opening to avoid war. A face-to-face meeting might create its own psychological and political imperatives that could lead Saddam to withdraw. It certainly would give him an opening he could use to avoid war if he were seeking one. And if we could not convince Iraq to withdraw in direct talks, then no one would be able to question that we had done all we could. This would also help us with the Soviets and others who were reluctant to see force used. In Moscow, in particular, the President's initiative would give Gorbachev an explanation that could hold off hard-liners such as Yevgeny Primakov, who were trying to meddle in the strict line Shevardnadze had pursued toward fulfilling the U.N. resolutions.

Second, the proposal would help us domestically. If the President met with Aziz and I went to Baghdad, not even our critics would be able to say we had not gone, as the President repeatedly put it, the "extra mile for peace." With the United Nations solidly behind us, no congressman could credibly oppose the war if these high-level meetings could not get Iraq to withdraw. Paradoxically, only by offering these meetings could we ever hope to obtain the domestic consensus necessary to wage war.

Finally, the proposal would show that we were doing something other than just preparing for war as the deadline neared. I was still quite concerned by the talk the night before at the Perm Five dinner about a high-level meeting of the Security Council's permanent members. I felt that without a diplomatic initiative of our own during this period, we would be hard put to sustain coalition unity in the face of proposals from all over the world for peaceful resolutions—most of which would of necessity involve diluting the U.N. resolutions.

My concerns about standing still had been amplified earlier that morning when I appeared on ABC's "Good Morning America." Before I went on the air, I had heard the U.N. Secretary-General stress in an interview that no effort at peace should be spared in the period leading up to January 15. When Charlie Gibson asked me what we were going to do in the days before the deadline, I said, "It doesn't mean that we will engage in forty-five days of appeasement . . . but it means that we will engage in forty-five days of serious, honest, good-faith, hard efforts, to try and find a diplomatic, political, and peaceful solution to this problem." Now in the Oval Office, I realized that if we took the initiative, we could maintain control over any high-level discussions. Having struggled to maintain the coalition's cohesion, I was concerned that some other event would intervene to adversely affect the coalition and thereby limit our room for action. Forty-five days could be an eternity.

Scowcroft was nervous about the idea. His stated concern was that such a personal approach could be exploited by Saddam and would only complicate or delay military planning. "What do we do," he asked, "if he pulls out a few thousand troops and offers to withdraw even more if we do the same?" I later learned he and others were also worried that once I got into a discussion with Saddam Hussein, with world attention focused on my meeting, that my natural instinct would be to negotiate and return with a compromise. On this point, they were dead wrong. From the very beginning, I was of the view that we should not and indeed *could* not negotiate down from the Security Council resolutions we had worked so hard to achieve. U.S. credibility was at stake.

Despite Scowcroft's muted objection, the President decided to go ahead with the offer. The three of us quickly reworked a statement the President had personally drafted the night before. To make sure there was no hint that we were willing to compromise with Saddam, I inserted this sentence into the draft: "But let me be clear about what we're *not* going to talk about—walking back from the U.N. resolutions." There was nothing we were willing to do for Saddam unless Iraq withdrew. The United States could not have led the charge in the United Nations for the Security Council resolutions, then turned around and unilaterally watered them down in direct negotiations with the Iraqis.

At 11:00 A.M., the President went to the White House press room and announced that he was willing to meet with Tariq Aziz during the week of December 10, and then would send me to Baghdad to meet Saddam Hussein "at a mutually convenient time" between December 15, 1990, and January 15, 1991, the deadline set by the United Nations for Iraq's withdrawal. There would be no concessions to induce Saddam to get out of Kuwait, no face-saving gestures. Unconditional withdrawal was the only acceptable alternative to war. His overture was simply an effort, as he put it, to the world this time, "to go the extra mile for peace"—for George Bush knew better than anyone else that we owed it to our brave men and women in the Gulf and their families at home that no stone be left unturned in the pursuit of a peaceful outcome.

The Aftermath: Confusion versus Consensus

The President's announcement brought the contradictions between the needs of the international coalition and a domestic consensus to the fore. The decision didn't sit well with some of our friends, who were annoyed they hadn't been alerted in advance. Some of our partners in the military coalition wondered whether the January 15 deadline was genuine. The overture contributed to speculation among many of our European and Arab allies that we really didn't want to use force and were desperately looking for an escape route. The need for secrecy created an aura of confusion it took us a few days to dispel. In retrospect, it's probably true that Saddam mistook our initiative as a sign of weakness. At the same time, it reassured balky allies such as the Soviets and French that the President was not rushing precipitously into war. And it enabled us to argue that the President should not be undercut by Congress before what I began describing as "the last, best chance for peace."

Among our coalition allies, the Saudis and Kuwaitis in particular were very concerned, fearful that talks might lead to the nightmare scenario of Saddam leaving Kuwait with his full military might intact. They were also unhappy about being caught unawares. Three days after the announcement, I met with the Kuwaiti Foreign Minister and Ambassador al-Sabah at the State Department to reassure them that we had no intention of wavering. I told him the need for secrecy was so critical that I had not even told the Perm Five ministers in advance. His anxieties were somewhat relieved when I confided that, despite our desire for a peaceful outcome, "my own sense is that we will probably have to use force."

Domestically, the proposal had startled the Congress. Democrats who were staking out positions in opposition to the war were confounded: How could they oppose a President who was supported by an unprecedented international coalition and was willing to make such a high-profile gamble for peace? I knew the proposal had worked to blunt the damage created by congressional hearings chaired by Sam Nunn, which were marked by the testimony of former Joint Chiefs of Staff Chairman William Crowe in opposition to using force. The first sign that this proposal sparked momentum behind the President's approach came in a meeting that afternoon with the congressional leadership in the White House Cabinet Room. During that meeting, the leadership raised a number of questions—but all the leaders praised the President's initiative privately and, more important, also publicly when they went outside to talk to the press.

Officials in the government were as stunned as the financial markets, which had fluctuated wildly at the news. None of my closest aides knew about the proposal in advance. Predictably, they weren't happy about having been excluded from the decision-making process. They also had misgivings with the concept. Bob Kimmitt warned that the lack of precision in the statement would reinforce the impression in some quarters that we'd caved. Margaret Tutwiler thought it was a no-win proposition. If there were a war, she argued, I'd be blamed for the failure of diplomacy. Even if I negotiated Iraq's unconditional withdrawal, some would accuse me of selling out to dictators. Dennis Ross, too, had not known about it—and when he learned the news, he told me it was a major mistake. He conceded that the initiative itself made good sense, particularly from the standpoint of the need to achieve domestic support for our approach. "But the notion of December 15 to January 15 is a mistake," he argued. "The Iraqis will say January 15 is fine, and you've just lost your deadline." I had inserted the phrase "at a mutually convenient time" into the President's statement, believing it gave us an out. It would be simple enough to say that a date too close to the deadline was not mutually convenient. Ross continued to insist: "They will go for a very late date, and they'll do it so the deadline becomes meaningless." I've always encouraged my staff to speak frankly, but I was not thrilled to be told the President of the United States and his two senior foreign-policy officials had blundered. Nevertheless, I concluded that Ross had a point about the timing. In the next few weeks, we refocused our strategy, and moved the acceptable timeframe toward the front end of the window, to make sure the Iraqis knew the January 15 deadline was real and not subject to slippage.

For the next month, both sides maneuvered for diplomatic advantage. Two days after the President's press conference, the Iraqi government accepted his proposal for talks. On December 3, the Iraqis agreed to our proposal that the talks should be bilateral only. By pushing for limited participation, we quickly headed off Iraq's suggestion that the talks include Palestinian representatives. On December 6, in a calculated move to fragment the international consensus behind the use of force, Saddam began releasing all foreign hostages in Iraq and Kuwait, including about 2,000 Western nationals. Having made a dramatic gesture designed to make himself appear reasonable, Saddam began pressing us again to use broader talks to open a dialogue on larger Middle East issues—a diversionary tactic to change the terms of the debate from "Kuwait" to "Palestine" that he had used throughout the crisis. Once more, we refused. The only acceptable topic for these talks was Iraq's withdrawal from Kuwait.

Tensions escalated over timing. Baghdad wanted me to see Saddam on January 12, only three days from the deadline. We accepted their proposal that Aziz visit Washington on December 17, but ruled out January 12 for my visit. To underscore our flexibility, we proposed fifteen alternative dates between December 20 and January 3, including Christmas Day. In an interview on "This Week with David Brinkley," I said that I would refuse to go to Baghdad any later than January 3. This was disingenuous, since I was prepared to meet at a slightly later date if necessary. But I hoped that my statement would keep the pressure on Baghdad.

On December 14, the President announced that a meeting with Aziz was "on hold." He sharply rebuked Saddam for attempting to manipulate the negotiations. "He can see John Connally, Muhammad Ali, and Ted Heath with fifteen minutes' notice," he told reporters, "but he doesn't have an hour or two between the twentieth of December and January 3 to receive the U.S. Secretary of State." The next day, Saddam canceled Aziz's visit to Washington, saying that if the United States intended to use the meetings to repeat U.N. resolutions, "There will be no reason for us to go."

For the next two weeks, both sides held their ground. On New Year's Day, the President convened his senior advisers over dinner. We agreed that the idea of a Perm Five summit was ill advised, but what the President privately called the "home-and-home" initiative was not discussed at any length. I knew, however, that he was having second thoughts about sending me to Baghdad. During a call that afternoon to chat and wish me a happy new year, he had told me he was worried our allies would believe that a meeting with Saddam was an attempt to make a deal. I replied that we should at least keep the Baghdad option alive a while longer. In the few remaining weeks before the deadline, I felt it was critical for domestic purposes to be seen as involved in further diplomatic efforts to reach a settlement.

This contradiction between our international needs and our domestic ones was resolved over the next two days when the next morning, in a meeting with Scowcroft, Sununu, and me in his small study adjoining the Oval Office, the President said he was ruling out a Baghdad meeting. However, the following day, January 3, he publicly announced that I was willing to meet with Aziz in Geneva on January 7, 8, or 9. The next day, Iraq accepted. Aziz and I would meet in Geneva on January 9.

I had been intrigued by the idea of meeting with Saddam. But when we finally settled on Geneva as a compromise, I wasn't terribly disappointed. A few days after the President's November 30 proposal, Prince Bandar had called me and suggested that Baghdad was the last place I should consider visiting. "You've got to be crazy to go there," he said. "This guy is going to hold you as a hostage." Bandar was convinced that if Saddam were really persuaded we were coming after him, he wouldn't abide by any rules. I still thought it was quite unlikely. Saddam may have been irrational, but he surely understood that taking me hostage would bring down the full wrath and fury of the United States government on his head. My view was confirmed a week later, when Saddam began releasing his Western hostages. Bandar, of course, didn't want me to go in the first place. The Saudis had no desire for a compromise solution that would leave Saddam's military intact. His concern was not a serious risk in my view, and played no part in the decision not to see Saddam. But I will confess that my enthusiasm for going to Baghdad diminished somewhat after my conversation with Bandar, particularly since Dennis Ross raised the same concern. In view of Saddam's assassination attempt against President Bush during our visit to Kuwait in March of 1993, in retrospect I may have given Saddam more credit than he deserved at the time.

On the afternoon of the day that Iraq agreed to the Geneva meeting, I met with Ambassador April Glaspie to pick her brain in advance of my meeting with Aziz. In that conversation, she recounted a very telling story about being invited along with other diplomats to a dam construction site in northern Iraq. Saddam had made disparaging remarks about the Vietnamese laborers who were building the dam, dismissing them as subhuman. "And these are the people who beat the Americans," he marveled. In the four months of the crisis, we had seen repeated evidence of this outmoded mind-set from Saddam. Iraq's leader thought Vietnam had so traumatized the American psyche that we would never fight again.

"A Good Job—With a Very Bad Brief"

I arrived in Geneva shortly after 9:00 P.M. on January 8, exhausted from a day that began in London and included stops in Paris, Bonn, and Milan. Normally the arrival of a Secretary of State in Geneva would be greeted by the two U.S. Ambassadors stationed there: the Ambassador to Switzerland and the U.S. Representative to the U.N. mission. However, we did not want the selection of Geneva as the meeting site to trigger a "business as usual" atmosphere and so we called ahead and asked that they not greet my plane. As my motorcade rolled onto the grounds of the Hotel Inter-Continental, we were met by a cluster of antiwar protesters, standing at the corner across the street, so Swiss in their discipline and deportment that the scene was almost surreal. It did become surreal inside. A big wooden peace dove with an olive branch in its beak perched over the main door of the hotel, and thousands of journalists milled around with literally nothing to do but trade rumors.

In preparing for this meeting, I wanted to have the ability if I thought it advisable to get Aziz to appreciate just how lethal war would be for Iraq. So in London three days before, I had asked Howard Graves to prepare a detailed unclassified summary of our war plan and be ready to deliver it during the meeting. I also asked the Pentagon to provide us a half dozen satellite photographs of potential targets in Baghdad to accompany Graves's briefing. It was essential that Iraq's leadership understand that Iraq would not be allowed to fight a war of attrition, like their eight-year stalemate with Iran. Our forces, not theirs, would define the terms of this engagement. The day before the meeting, however, Dick Cheney and Colin Powell had second thoughts. They worried that the briefing might disclose too much of our tactical scheme. Powell in particular was concerned that if we talked too much about the air war, the Iraqis would simply hunker down, which would make our task of destroying their troop concentrations more difficult and extend the length of the war. As a result, we destroyed the high-tech photographs, and Graves's presentation was carefully scrubbed of any specific detail that might have endangered our forces. The amended version, which he rehearsed for me the night before the meeting, was nevertheless a stark summation of American military power.

"You have so many Scud launchers, and we can eliminate them in so many days," Graves noted. "We know how long it takes you to reload them, and we will be able to target them based on our knowledge of your operational principles. We know you have about 10,000 ground-based attack weapons in the area. We know where they are. We know you've got about 2,100 tanks. You need to know that our tanks can fire effectively while on the move. We can identify your tanks from a distance of more than two kilometers and we can kill them while we're moving at about sixty kilometers an hour. If you don't believe this, wait and see." Graves said that the long-range guns of some of our warships "can level your troop concentrations," and that our Tomahawk missiles were not only quite lethal, but so accurate that they could hit a particular part of a building in downtown Baghdad from their mother ships in the Persian Gulf. He described how our Stealth fighters could appear without any radar warning, and how our weapons would destroy not only the Iraqi military, but "we have the capability to destroy your ability to govern, and we are prepared to use it," he said.

It was a clinical exposition of the coalition's ability to punish Iraq. "Let's wait and see how everything goes," I told Graves. "If it turns out to be a very professional discussion, we may not use your presentation. Just be prepared." My plan was to respond in kind to Aziz. If he were bombastic and belligerent, I would call on Graves and ratchet up my own rhetoric. If he turned out to be Saddam's "good cop," a threatening lecture on military superiority might backfire.

The truth is that I hoped Aziz would be swayed by what he heard from me, but I was under no illusions. I assumed the talks would be unsuccessful and that within a matter of days, we would be at war. Most of the very pessimistic opening statement I delivered at a press conference after the meeting was in fact drafted the day *before* our talks. There was simply little reason for optimism beyond mere hope.

As I went to sleep, chants from the antiwar protesters echoed quietly up to our block of rooms while preparations for the meeting continued. Karen Groomes, Kim Hoggard, and Joe Barnes, our advance team, negotiated with the Iraqis until 3:00 A.M. over protocol issues, including the size of the flags that would be on the table. Even before we began our talks the next morning, I encountered a diplomatic test. It's customary to begin such a meeting with a handshake for press photographers, but I was loath to do so. Aziz may wear suits tailored in Paris and speak English more typical of Oxford, but underneath this veneer, he is as tough as they come and a Ba'ath

Party loyalist through and through. I did not want my handshake to convey the impression that this was just another routine meeting of two foreign ministers. It was, in a deadly serious way, much more than that. Still, both Aziz and I were experienced diplomats, and I did not want to create a slight that some could use to suggest we were not really serious about going the extra mile. So I decided to shake his hand but to do so without smiling, my look of distaste evident.

With the photo opportunity out of the way, we sat down to work in the hotel's Salon de Nations, room D. Across from me, Aziz was joined most prominently by Barzan al-Takriti, Saddam's half brother and a man whose reputation for brutality was supported by his demeanor. Barzan had played a critical role in purging twenty-one senior officials in Saddam's grab for power in 1979 and then headed the secret police, the Mukhabarat, until late 1983, when he had a falling-out with Saddam over a family matter. To get him out of the way, Saddam exiled Barzan to Switzerland as Iraq's Permanent Representative to the United Nations, where, angry about having to wait for his car, Barzan once beat up his chauffeur at a diplomatic reception. Barzan then rehabilitated himself through his secret negotiations with Tehran to end the Iran-Iraq war and by his work on the Iraq covert-arms network. He never uttered a word in the meeting but during the meeting he received several notes brought in by numbers of his Geneva staff, and left the room several times while discussions were in progress. His presence at Aziz's side was an unmistakable sign that Saddam wanted an independent report of the meeting. If there were to be any doubt, Saddam's personal interpreter sat on Aziz's other side—even though the Foreign Minister speaks fluent English. Clearly, Aziz would not be straying from his instructions.

I began my presentation, and Gemal Helal, my new Arabic interpreter, followed. I thought, His first chance at interpreting is also his most important; I hope he gets it right. (He did.)

I had come with no illusions. Even if Saddam planned on withdrawing from Kuwait, Aziz would not present the details. Rather, he would carry with him a set of probing questions and parries—initial feints toward withdrawal with actual steps to be filled in later by Saddam himself. So I wasn't looking for a full-blown proposal. But I was hoping for, while not expecting, a step in the right direction. It never came.

In the time-honored manner of diplomatic exchange, Aziz and I began with general statements. "This is an important meeting," I said. "I hope you agree that we meet as representatives of two sovereign states, albeit states with significant differences. Our purpose ought not to be to put pressure on each other. However, it should be no surprise that I'm not here to negotiate from the resolutions passed by the United Nations. I am here to communicate. Communication involves not just talking, but listening. I'm willing not just to talk, but to listen. I hope you will join me in a spirit of willingness to both talk and listen. I'll proceed in whatever order you like. But before you decide, let me give you a letter from President Bush to President Saddam Hussein and ask you to deliver it. The original is in the envelope, and here's a copy." I pulled out the letter and pushed it across the table.

In our New Year's meeting, the President had decided on the letter as another attempt to reach Saddam directly. We suspected that Aziz might refuse to take the letter, however, so before leaving Washington we had decided to deliver a copy simultaneously to the Iraqi Ambassador in Washington. We also made a conscious decision to seal the original letter but to give Aziz a copy. If he had been instructed not to accept the President's letter, he would be hard-pressed to avoid reading his own copy.

"Thank you, Mr. Secretary," he began. "I truly hope this meeting will be a fruitful one. The way to achieve this is to listen to each other." He asked for time to read the letter.

"Mr. Secretary," he said after finishing, "you said the purpose of this meeting is not to pressure each other. I've read the letter, and it is full of expressions of threat. Indeed, it is alien to the manner of communications between heads of state. I cannot accept it. You may publish it in your media. I hope this will not impede this meeting. We've not talked during the crisis. Our people are poised to confront each other, and we must explore all possibilities for a solution between our countries."

"I want to make it clear I don't see this letter as inappropriate in any way," I responded. "It's important that we clearly understand each other. I can't make you take this letter with you, nor will I try. However, you should know that we may or may not publish it. You are the only person on your side of the table who knows what is in it. That seems a large responsibility for one to take on oneself. If that's what you want, so be it." Aziz's hands seemed to tremble. I left the President's letter and Aziz's copy in the middle of the table, and at our first break told Karen Groomes and Ron Mazer, my security chief, to leave them there.

"Our objective is for you to leave Kuwait. That's the only solution we'll accept. And if you will not do that, then we'll find ourselves at war, and if you do go to war with the coalition, you will surely lose. This will not be a war of attrition like you fought with Iran. It will be fought using the means and weapons that play to our strengths, not to yours. We have the means to define how the battle will be fought, and you do not.

"This is not to threaten, but to inform. You may choose to reject it, or not believe what we say, but we have a responsibility to tell you that we have tremendous technological advantages in forces, and our view is that if conflict comes, your forces will face devastatingly superior firepower. In our view—and you may reject this and disagree—our forces will really destroy your ability to run the country, and they will destroy your ability to command your own forces. . . .

"We owe it to you to tell you that there will be no stalemate . . . no U.N. cease-fire or breathing space for negotiation. . . . If conflict begins, it will be massive. This will not be another Vietnam. Should war begin, God forbid, it will be fought to a swift, decisive conclusion."

I then made a point "on the dark side of this issue" that Colin Powell had specifically asked me to deliver in the bluntest possible terms. "If the conflict involves your use of chemical or biological weapons against our forces," I warned, "the American people will demand vengeance. We have the means to exact it. With regard to this part of my presentation, this is not a threat, it is a promise. If there is any use of weapons like that, our objective won't just be the liberation of Kuwait, but the elimination of the current Iraqi regime, and anyone responsible for using those weapons would be held accountable."

The President had decided, at Camp David in December, that the best deterrent of the use of weapons of mass destruction by Iraq would be a threat to go after the Ba'ath regime itself. He had also decided that U.S. forces would not retaliate with chemical or nuclear weapons if the Iraqis attacked with chemical munitions. There was obviously no reason to inform the Iraqis of this. In hopes of persuading them to consider more soberly the folly of war, I purposely left the impression that the use of chemical or biological agents by Iraq could invite tactical nuclear retaliation. (We do not really know whether this was the reason there appears to have been no confirmed use by Iraq of chemical weapons during the war. My own view is that the calculated ambiguity regarding how we might respond has to be part of the reason.)

"War will destroy everything you fought to build in Iraq," I concluded, "and it will trigger, thanks to your unwillingness to withdraw from Kuwait, a conflict that will turn Iraq into a weak and backward country." I told Aziz that I worried the Iraqis were about to make another serious miscalculation about American resolve. "There have been other leaders who have miscalculated the readiness of the American democracy to fight," I said, "and have paid the ultimate price. Do not repeat their mistake. Don't misinterpret the different voices you hear from American society. We have the strongest system of government in the world. America will unite to fight a war if you give us no other choice."

When I sought to temper my vision of gloom with "the other, brighter side," Aziz quickly interjected, "The carrot *and* the stick." I complimented Aziz on his perceptiveness, which elicited a rare smile from him. "I am told you worry that you may be attacked whether you withdraw or not. Let me repeat the President's assurances face-to-face. You will not be." I was reminding him, in effect, that Americans don't shoot their adversaries in the back. I ended my intervention by saying that we supported Iraq and Kuwait settling their differences peacefully, but only after a withdrawal. "We're glad your President sent you to Geneva," I said. "This is the last, best chance for peace."

Instead of reacting to the substance of my remarks, Aziz began instead with a demand for respect. As though plagued by some inner demon of national inferiority, he felt compelled to insist that Iraq was not governed by fools. He would return to this theme constantly throughout this meeting.

"We have been leading our country for twenty-two years," he reminded me. "The average age of our leadership is in the fifties. I'm fifty-five, my President is fifty-four. I believe you would agree that this is a mature age." Because I was over sixty, I could not pass up this opening to observe in jest, "That's quite young." Aziz missed the levity and even appeared visibly angered. "Not really," he retorted, adopting a much sharper tone after what he clearly mistook as an insult. "Sages say wisdom begins after forty. . . . We understand fully what's happening around us. Since August 2, we have been expecting U.S. military action against Iraq. . . . The U.S. is a superpower, and recently has become the only superpower in the world. So, when we behave as we do, you must have no doubt that this conduct on our part wasn't the result of ignorance. You are an advanced country, and have moved tremendous weapons to our region. I assure you we know exactly what you've moved to the area. We know the efficiency and destructive power of each weapon. We are a diligent, active government. We work hard, read, analyze, and follow up.

"I have no illusions about the cost of war. My youngest son is eleven. All he has seen in his life is war, air raids, and Iranian missiles. War is not a strange thing. There is a verse in the Koran describing war as an abhorrent thing: 'Fighting has been forced on you to do, although you hate to do it.' So we know these facts, and we know your determination that war will be destructive.

"I say this without arrogance, despite the fact that part of your statement contained some insults. The present leadership will continue to lead Iraq now and in the future.* Those who will disappear are not in Iraq, but some of your friends in the region."

Aziz denounced the "Western description" of his country as a totalitar-

---

*In this, of course, Aziz was right. But our threat to the regime in Iraq was conditioned on its use of weapons of mass destruction, which we do not believe occurred. Our conscious decision not to "go to Baghdad" or "take out Saddam" is treated at length in chapter 24.

ian state. "Iraq as a nation is six thousand years old," he said, "and it has witnessed successive kingdoms, empires, and civilizations. We have outlasted coalitions like yours in the past, and we will last longer than your coalition will last. We are not afraid of being attacked by a superior force. Our people not only support us, but they love us. Our population of nineteen million is convinced that once war breaks out between us, we will be victorious. I want to say that war doesn't frighten or intimidate Iraq. . . . The issue of war is not one of fear on our part or yours. I hope you won't miscalculate our capability to endure the costs of war." Aziz spoke of war with the fatalism of someone for whom peace no longer held any real meaning. I realized it would be pointless for Howard Graves to present his apocalyptic vision of this potential conflict.

We broke after two hours and five minutes. Even though no progress had been made whatever, the tone had been thoroughly professional. I called the President from my suite with a brief report. "I can't tell you anything," I said. "We don't have any movement from them yet, but they're going out of their way to try to show that they're reasonable. He wouldn't take your letter but he did read it." I also told him that I expected the Iraqis to continue to stonewall and that expectations for a breakthrough seemed quite slim, but that it was important to give them all the time they wanted to talk.

Downstairs, the media army covering the meeting was in a frenzy. Our talks were lasting longer than expected, spawning rumors of a diplomatic breakthrough we knew were baseless but were powerless to suppress. World financial markets and oil prices gyrated wildly as CNN fed the proceedings live throughout the globe. It was a bizarre way to conduct diplomacy, but unavoidable in an era of instant telecommunications.

When we returned to the conference table at 2:30 P.M., the remainder of the discussion bogged down in largely extraneous issues. Aziz complained repeatedly about an American double standard toward Israel. If its enemy could possess nuclear and chemical weapons, Iraq had every right to acquire them. He predicted that if war began, the Arab coalition would defect before fighting their brothers. He called President Mubarak "ignorant of the history of the region," and complained that the United Nations had moved against Iraq unfairly.

He characterized the invasion as a defensive act against "an alliance among the U.S., Israel, and the former rulers of Kuwait to destroy Iraq." Almost in the same breath, he contradicted himself by asserting that "the events of August and afterwards are one hundred percent connected to the Palestinians." He returned to this theme of Palestinian linkage time and again. "It is the mother of all problems," he argued. "This has been the factor that has caused all the instability in the region."

"In the spirit of frankness," I said, "no one in the world would buy your explanation, including those allied with you, that you acted in self-defense against Kuwait. I don't question your belief, but I tell you that it will not wash with the rest of the world. You can overcome all of these problems by withdrawal from Kuwait."

When I asked if he had read the Amnesty International report detailing Iraqi atrocities in Kuwait, Aziz countered with the most bizarre argument of the entire meeting. He conceded that "some incidents occurred," but implied that Indian servants were responsible for most of the theft and looting during the occupation.

In an earlier exchange, Aziz had been so intent on proving that Iraq's leadership was capable that it seemed to me he was deluding himself. I wanted to remind him again that the American experience in Vietnam and the Iraqi experience with Iran were simply no longer applicable. "Don't let your military commanders convince you that your strategy against Iran will work against us," I countered. "You are facing an entirely different kind of force. I have heard you think that if you can stretch out the conflict and you can cause many casualties, we won't be able to continue. Our very strong belief is that won't happen. Because of the superiority of our forces, we will dictate the terms of the battle, not you."

After another break, this one of twenty minutes, Aziz resumed his dissertation, rebutting my earlier points in random fashion. "Our military commanders are courageous men," he said, "but they're not irrational. They have long experience in war. They follow your deployments and concentrations carefully, and they have accurate studies on your weaponry." A new war would be different from the Iranian experience, he acknowledged, but no less difficult. "The war with Iran was no picnic . . . despite this, we could take the burden and come out of that war victorious.

"We feel unjustly treated. This is our feeling, and when a feeling like this is generated amongst a people and war is imposed upon it, then the people will fight. Don't doubt the determination of our people to stand fast. We are determined that if we have a war, it will take a long time—one to two years." His comments were fresh evidence that the Iraqis were assuming we had learned nothing from Vietnam.

Aziz predicted again that the war would be seen as an American-Arab conflict. "Once a people enter battle and fire prevails and blood is spilled," he said, "then people go back to their origins and behave instinctively. If you were to attack an Arab state, you will be the enemy in many Arab countries."

Aziz then said, quite unexpectedly, "If you are interested in further dialogue, there can be further talks." He resurrected the President's earlier proposal for a meeting between Saddam and me in Baghdad. It was a last-minute dodge to force us to move back the deadline. I reminded him that President Bush had made precisely that proposal six weeks earlier. "It's too late for that, Minister," I said. "This meeting is your chance. If you aren't prepared to act on this now, forget it. Time runs out six days from now. Do not think you can postpone or extend it." I assured Aziz that I would be pleased to visit Baghdad—but only after Iraq's withdrawal from Kuwait.

"Why do you not encourage an Arab solution?" he demanded to know. "There *can* be an Arab solution," I replied, "if Iraq should withdraw from Kuwait." We were going in circles.

I reminded Aziz that he hadn't responded to my earlier request for safe passage for our embassy staff. I asked for his personal assurance that our five remaining diplomats could leave Baghdad on January 12 without any delay. Aziz gave me his personal pledge. It was the only concession I extracted from the Iraqis.

After six hours and forty-five minutes, I finally said, "Minister, I am finished. I have nothing more. How do you want to handle the press?" "Why don't you go first?" Aziz suggested. "Okay, I'll take a few minutes to prepare and then go first," I responded. "Is it your intention not to take the letter?" "Yes," he said.

To his credit, Tariq Aziz was thoroughly professional, from start to finish. It was as cool and as direct a discussion as I can remember—and totally unproductive. Unlike a normal negotiation, Aziz had been given absolutely no latitude and, of course, we were never going to negotiate down from the Security Council resolutions. There was now no question in my mind—we were going to war. I will never forget the look in Aziz's eyes as we shook hands at the end of the meeting. He didn't appear angry or aggressive, but fatalistic. "Good-bye, Mr. Secretary," he said. "Perhaps we'll meet again." "Good-bye, Mr. Minister," I replied. I felt no animus toward him whatsoever. He had done a very credible job with an extraordinarily bad brief.

War Becomes Inevitable

In keeping with my instructions, the President's letter to Saddam and Aziz's copy remained in the middle of the table even after the room had been cleared. They were retrieved by Sandy Charles, an NSC staffer. Aziz had underlined three passages from the President's letter: "calamity for the people of Iraq"; if war came, it would be a far greater tragedy "for you and your country"; and "you will be held directly responsible for terrorist actions."

I went back upstairs to my suite, took off my jacket and shoes, and stretched out on the bed while my call to the President was patched through to the White House. "There's no give," I reported. "They didn't give an inch. They're not prepared to change their position. They offered not one new thing, no single idea, and I told them that." Then I went back downstairs to meet the press.

"Regrettably, ladies and gentlemen," I said, "in over six hours I heard nothing that suggested to me any Iraqi flexibility whatsoever on complying with the United Nations Security Council resolutions." When a reporter asked me to describe the mood, I didn't have to think about my answer. "Somber," I replied. "You've got it."

From a tactical standpoint, the tone of my remarks was intended to reinforce the message that the United States was the reasonable party, not the Iraqis. I knew we would win the war with Iraq, but the battle with Congress and the public was still very much in doubt. My press conference was primarily aimed at the domestic audience and was yet another example of diplomacy via television. Apparently, it was successful. Sam Nunn, who voted against the congressional resolution, would later observe that as soon as I uttered "regrettably," any chance of defeating the use-of-force resolution was lost.

My "regrettably" also caused the stock market to reel. As the meeting had continued on and the White House had issued a statement saying the talks were "substantive," the Dow Jones Industrial Average had risen more than forty points by the time of my press conference. It closed down more than thirty-nine. Oil prices—which had dropped—jumped from $23.35 when I began speaking to $31 five minutes later. If anyone doubted global interdependence and the power of instantaneous communications, those gyrations should have changed their mind.

Afterward, I returned to my suite to watch Aziz's press conference. His eloquence was surpassed only by his intransigence. In a forty-five-minute session, he did not mention Kuwait once, referring just to the "situation in the Gulf." It was especially odd because he talked often about Kuwait during our meeting, only using "Palestinians" more often. The fatalistic attitude he had assumed during the meeting had given way to an almost nihilistic brusqueness. "Yes. Absolutely, yes," Aziz replied when asked if Iraq would attack Israel during the war. "Is war now inevitable?" a reporter asked. "That's up to the American administration to decide," he said. Iraq is "prepared for all expectations. . . . We have been prepared from the very beginning."

I then called Shevardnadze in Moscow to alert him that no progress had been made. We talked for almost forty minutes, about the meeting but also about the rising tensions in the Baltics.

Despite Aziz's admonition that Iraq had invaded because of the al-Sabah monarchy's "conspiracy" to bring Iraq to its knees economically, Kuwait was just a down payment on Saddam's regional, and perhaps even global, ambitions. Here, after all, was a contemporary leader in the Middle

East who was fond of comparing himself to Nebuchadnezzar. Here, as President Mubarak pointed out to me after the war, was a strategist who refused to risk his combat aircraft against Iran when Tehran was losing the war, in order to have them available for his regional hegemonistic goals. Saddam was looking northeast and northwest, not south. To his northeast, he saw his patron, the Soviet Union, in decline, forced to give up its empire in Central and Eastern Europe. More so than most other strategic thinkers, Saddam saw in Soviet decline the danger of a "unipolar moment," a period when the United States would be the only superpower. That could not bode well for Saddam's efforts to dominate the Middle East, given the close American ties to Israel and, to a lesser extent, Egypt, Saudi Arabia, and other Arab moderates. The greatest threat Saddam saw to his grandiose plans to become the new Nasser lay far to his northwest: America. That is certainly one explanation for his paranoid statements in the late spring and early summer of 1990, and in his earlier charges, that the CIA was attempting to destabilize his regime. He may not, unfortunately, have been the focus of our attention, but we were certainly the center of his.

During the meeting, Tariq Aziz had told me, "The issue of war is not one of fear on our part or yours." He was wrong. Thucydides once again was right. For what made the invasion of Kuwait inevitable—and the war to redress it—was the decline of Soviet power, the ascension of American power, and the fear that this caused in Saddam—fear that while America might not react now to his power grab, it would be more and more likely to do so as the unipolar world took shape. Saddam had seen his own window of opportunity, and had tried to leap through it.

The next morning, as I departed Switzerland on a military 707 that had been Air Force One in the Kennedy presidency, the icy shores of Lake Geneva spread out beneath us. Margaret Tutwiler turned to Dennis Ross and summed up the sorry truth of the moment. "This is a beautiful city, Dennis," she observed. "We'll have to come back after the war's over." We wouldn't have much time to wait.

CHAPTER 20

THE SHIELD BECOMES
A SWORD

We all need to appeal to God to help his people. Saddam Hussein stands ready to sacrifice millions of young and old solely for the sake of his own greed.
—*Sheikh Zayed of the United Arab Emirates, Abu Dhabi, UAE, January 10, 1991*

He is a man who cares about himself. Nothing else matters, even the destruction of his country.
—*The Crown Prince of Kuwait, Taif, Saudi Arabia, January 11, 1991*

I cannot predict whether Saddam will change his mind at the last moment and pull out of Kuwait. But I fear the worst.
—*Egyptian President Hosni Mubarak, Cairo, Egypt, January 12, 1991*

Two days after the ill-fated session with Tariq Aziz in Geneva, I arrived in Taif for another meeting with the exiled Emir of Kuwait. Afterward, I visited the pilots and crews of the U.S. Air Force's Forty-eighth Tactical Fighter Wing, whose F-111 fighter-bombers and EF-111 Raven electronic-jamming planes had been redeployed from their home base in England to a Saudi military airfield in the desert outside Taif. Those young men and women were about to become the backdrop for what I knew would be our last attempt to convince the Iraqi leadership that the January 15 deadline was real.

It was my second visit with the "Liberty Wing." When I was there during my September "tin cup" trip, only a few hundred wing personnel had arrived. For the most part, I found them bored, restless, and frustrated. The tone of their questions conveyed a sense that they saw themselves as little more than a cosmetic, show-the-flag presence. The Forty-eighth was battle-tested; its planes had led the American attacks on Libya in 1986. They wanted action, not stalemate. My expressions of gratitude for their service to country had done little for their morale. As one airman had complained, "Let's *do* something."

Now, as January 15 approached, their ranks had swelled to nearly three thousand and their warplanes bristled with armaments. Four months of desert training had honed their readiness, and the failure of the Geneva meeting had galvanized their morale. As I spoke to them in a hangar, their esprit was not merely infectious; it was inspiring. George Marshall had described America's citizen-soldiers best: "Where do we find such men?" Without question, they were America's finest. But on this somber occasion, I was really speaking not to them but to an audience of one in Baghdad.

In the aftermath of the Aziz meeting, I realized the likelihood of avoiding war was probably nonexistent. Saddam appeared intent on making another tragic miscalculation about American resolve. Because we knew Saddam watched CNN, however, there was an opportunity for one last appeal to reason—a public démarche not as easily ignored as the President's letter had been in Geneva. En route from Riyadh to Abu Dhabi that morning, I reworked my draft remarks for the Forty-eighth. I crafted my comments consciously, in stark language whose signal would be crystal clear.

"Time is running out, but the path to peace remains open," I told the troops. "There is still time for Iraq to walk that path . . . they can still choose peace and avert disaster. But the choice is theirs and theirs alone. But even as we hope, and we pray, and we work for peace, America and all of the other nations of the international coalition must be prepared for a conflict that we do not seek, but from which we shall not shrink.

"When I talked to you four months ago, most of you told me that you were ready. But you also asked how long before you would know whether you would be called into action to undo this terrible aggression. Now, as the clock ticks down to midnight, January 15, I cannot give you an absolute, definitive answer. But I can tell you this: you will not have to wait much longer for an answer to that question." The audience exploded in a pent-up frenzy of cheers, whistles, and nervous tension. These troops were ready.

"As I said in Geneva, there have been too many Iraqi miscalculations. And we fear another miscalculation, a truly tragic one. We believe that if Iraq is going to withdraw from Kuwait, Saddam Hussein will probably wait until he is on the very brink before he moves. And our worry is that in his usual style, he will miscalculate where the brink exactly is.

"Just so there is no misunderstanding, let me be absolutely clear: we pass the brink at midnight, January 15." It was the closest I ever came in public to acknowledging when the war would actually begin.

Meeting those pilots caused me to reflect upon my own modest military

experience. In 1952, at the age of twenty-two, I had graduated from Princeton and immediately began officer's training with the Marine Corps—fully
cognizant of the number of Marine second lieutenants who were then
dying in Korea. At the time, I was gung-ho. You didn't join the Marines in
those days unless you were willing to fight. But in retrospect, I was fortunate not to have had to serve in Korea. At Taif that evening, I contrasted the
irony of my own good fortune four decades earlier with the hundreds of
thousands of men and women whose lives and careers had been disrupted
and might even be lost by their unselfish service to country.

I'd been told by Jim Mead, a friend and predecessor at Princeton who
had joined the Marine Corps, to consider naval gunfire spotting as my military specialty. While naval gunfire spotters normally hit the beach in the
first wave, they went in with six to eight men instead of a platoon of forty-
four. You didn't have a platoon leader's responsibilities for forty-four men,
and adjusting gunfire for ships, while equally dangerous, was to me far
more exciting and interesting than the infantry. When I arrived at the Basic
School in Quantico, Virginia, in August 1952, I was told that those of us
who applied ourselves and got the best grades would earn their choice of
duty assignments. So I worked hard at being an overachiever and came in
at around fifteenth in a class of about five hundred officer candidates. I
believe I was close to first in my class among those of us who would be
receiving reserve commissions. So when I was summoned to see the major
who commanded my unit to talk about my first duty assignment, he said,
"Baker, you've done very well. We want you to be a platoon leader. In the
Marine Corps, we need our best as infantry platoon leaders." I felt like I'd
been had. "Major," I remember saying, "this is directly contrary to what
you told me when we first started here, which was that if I busted my tail
and did well, I'd have a better shot at getting my preference in duty assignment. I really want to be a naval gunfire spotter."

I figured my candor would land me a berth on the next troop transport
to Korea. Instead, to my surprise I received the 0840 military occupational
specialty—naval gunfire spotter—and shipped out to an air naval gunfire
liaison company (ANGLICO) with the Fleet Marine Force, Atlantic, at
Camp Lejeune, North Carolina. From there I was assigned as part of the
reinforced battalion of Marines with the Sixth Fleet in the Mediterranean,
where I spent much time heaving over the rail of the U.S.S. *Monrovia*. I fully
expected to go to Korea as a naval gunfire spotter, but the closest I came to
combat was training exercises in the Mediterranean, and later in Puerto
Rico, where I adjusted fire from the mighty sixteen-inch guns of the battleship U.S.S. *Missouri*. The war in Korea was in full force. I assumed that I
could be sent there at any moment, and spent some time thinking about it.
Dozens of lieutenants from my basic class at Quantico ended up dying

ABOVE: With King Fahd of Saudi Arabia (right) and his nephew, Saudi Ambassador to the United States, Prince Bandar. Also, State Department interpreter, Gemal Helal. *(AP/Wide World.)*
BELOW: With the Emir of Kuwait in the Oval Office. *(White House/Bush Library.)*

ABOVE: With President Hosni Mubarak in Cairo.
BELOW: With our troops in the Saudi desert, November 4, 1990. I was
beginning an eighteen-day, twelve-country trip to convince Security Council
members to vote for a "use of force" resolution. *(AP/Wide World.)*

ABOVE, LEFT: Addressing the troops of the renowned First Cavalry Division.
(Caron Jackson.)
RIGHT: At the "use of force" vote, flanked by Bob Kimmitt and U.N. Ambassador
Thomas Pickering. The vote was 12 to 2, with one abstention. Now, Iraq had until
January 15, 1991, to withdraw from Kuwait. *(Reuters/Bettmann.)*
BELOW: My unsmiling handshake with Tariq Aziz, January 9, 1991.
This was Iraq's last chance. *(Reuters/Bettmann.)*

ABOVE: With President Assad of Syria, January 13, 1991. Another marathon session.

BELOW: With British Prime Minister Major at RAF Base Alconbury, January 13. Three days later, the air war would begin.

With Prime Minister Mulroney (center) and Foreign Minister Clark of Canada, that same day in Ottawa.

Silhouetted against an oil fire in Kuwait, March 9, 1991. *(AP/Wide World.)*

ABOVE: Hearing a tale of horror at a Kurdish refugee camp on the Turkish border, April 8, 1991. Tens of thousands of refugees had fled Saddam's troops. *(AP/Wide World.)*

LEFT: The scene at the refugee camp. *(Caron Jackson.)*

ABOVE: Another milestone: crossing the Allenby Bridge from Jordan to Israel—the first Secretary of State ever to do so, May 14, 1991. *(Reuters/Bettmann.)*
BELOW: At the July 1991 London NATO Summit with Margaret Thatcher and George Bush. *(AP/Wide World.)*

ABOVE: With King Hussein in Amman, April 20, 1991. The war was over, and the window of opportunity was open. Was this the time for genuine Arab-Israeli peace talks?

BELOW: With Shamir, toasting each other in his apartment. *(AP/Wide World.)*

ABOVE: With Palestinian representatives Faisal Husseini and Hanan Ashrawi. A difficult dialogue.

BELOW: A Madrid family portrait. In the front row: Gorbachev, Spanish Premier Felipe Gonzalez, and President Bush. *(AP/Wide World.)*

ABOVE: In Beijing, with Premier Li Peng, on the right, November 15, 1991.
BELOW: The Kremlin, nine days before Gorbachev's resignation, December 16, 1991.

With Shevardnadze, and with Yeltsin that same day. *(David Hoffman, Washington Post.)*

ABOVE: Greeted by natives in traditional garb in Turkmenistan, February 12, 1992. *(Reuters/Bettmann.)*
BELOW: A happier meeting with Shevardnadze as the new President of his native Georgia, May 26, 1992. *(Reuters/Bettmann.)*

ABOVE: In Munich, at the Economic Summit with President Bush, July 7, 1991. *(White House/Bush Library.)*
BELOW: Rabin had replaced Shamir as Israeli Prime Minister, and the mood for peace moved forward. In his office, July 19, 1992.

ABOVE: President Bush presenting me with the Medal of Freedom, July 3, 1992. *(White House/Bush Library.)*
BELOW: Susan and me, with our eight children, in 1993. From left to right, Jamie, Bo, Doug, Mary Bonner, Elizabeth, John, Will, and Mike.

ABOVE: Two friends in Wyoming during the Democratic convention in 1988. *(White House/Reagan Library.)*

BELOW: Fly-fishing in Silver Creek on my Wyoming ranch. *(White House photo.)*

With two Presidents: still
on the move. *(White House/
Reagan and Bush libraries.)*

there. I was willing to fight, but that's not to say I wasn't plenty scared about it. And those who have ever faced the prospect, however remote, of going into combat would be lying if they told you they never worried about not coming back.

In that hangar at Taif, I remember thinking to myself that here were some individuals like the guys in Basic School with me who went off to Korea. Like my classmates, they were highly motivated; they had terrific aircraft at their disposal and were itching, as they said to me over and over, to fly off to Iraq and "kick butt." In my heart, I knew that within four or five days at most, these pilots would launch their jets into harm's way, and some would not be returning. For me, and indeed for all of us there, it was a riveting moment of raw emotion. More than once, tears welled up in my eyes. It took everything I had to maintain my composure.

My visit to the hangar was the emotional pinnacle of a nine-day trip that had begun on January 6, my sixth journey abroad since the Gulf crisis had exploded in August. The attention of the world was riveted on my January 9 meeting in Geneva with Tariq Aziz midway through the trip. While we had hoped for a diplomatic breakthrough in Geneva, we had to finalize preparations for war with our coalition partners if that break-through didn't come. We needed to know that they remained steadfast. We had to know that they would send their forces into battle under the command of American generals. And from our Arab partners, it was critical to know, once again, that they would stand fast if Iraq attacked Israel, as Aziz had now publicly confirmed. I also needed to work out notification procedures with other governments regarding the commencement of hostilities, and to secure new commitments of financial support from many of them. My journey took me from the searing heat of the Gulf to the numbing chill of Ottawa, where heavy snows almost prevented my departure to Washington. In all, I traveled 18,240 miles to meet with leaders from fifteen countries and the Secretary-General of NATO. It might be seen in the aggregate, in effect, as a final meeting of the international war cabinet.

Except for the Arabs, who were uniformly eager for war, I encountered a mixture of determination and foreboding at all of my stops. There was considerable concern in many quarters about casualties, particularly the inevitable civilian deaths that would occur from the "collateral damage" of the air campaign. Those leaders I visited before the Aziz meeting were pessimistic about the prospects for a breakthrough in Geneva. Some of them worried that Saddam might offer a deal. I reassured them I had no intention of entertaining anything short of the terms of the U.N. resolutions. The collective mood was one of resignation. Saddam had left us no choice.

The trip began in London, where the British were as stalwart as ever. After meeting on January 7 with Douglas Hurd, who failed to convince us there could be problems with our aircraft attacking Iraqi biological weapons facilities as planned, I concluded a crucial temporary basing agreement with Spanish Foreign Minister Felipe Ordonez, a very capable and well-regarded diplomat known to most of his colleagues as "Paco." (Ordonez has since died, but not before working closely with me once again when we selected Madrid as the site of the Mideast peace conference.) U.S. submarines and jet fighters had been stationed in Spain for decades, but the Madrid government had grown increasingly sensitive about this arrangement. The Pentagon believed it essential that U.S. B-52 heavy bombers and KC-135 aerial tankers be allowed temporary basing rights at Torrejón. Ordonez accepted my argument that these were not ordinary circumstances and told me his government would permit the use of Torrejón as a base for B-52 strikes, as well as refueling operations for other B-52s on their way from American bases to targets in Iraq and Kuwait.

The French Again

After consulting with Foreign Minister Jacques Poos of Luxembourg, then the EC chair, I flew to Paris. When I arrived on January 8, I was still peeved with the French about a meeting of the North Atlantic Council three weeks earlier in Brussels. Roland Dumas, the French Foreign Minister, had arrived late, left early, and ordered his ambassador not to agree to anything. As a result, a series of decisions not related to the Gulf War were passed by votes of 15–1. I had insisted on the unprecedented action of registering each vote to publicly spotlight the French obstructionism within NATO. Manfred Woerner told me later that France's behavior was inappropriate, and his pique fueled my own annoyance. When I saw Dumas before meeting with Mitterrand, I spoke very frankly about what I perceived as French gamesmanship.

"With no other country except France do we have this," I complained. "Nowhere else in Europe do we feel that we have to deal with such antipathy. Woerner was outraged and frankly, I am, too. This is no way to treat a friend. We've been too close for too long to let this happen." While blaming the Brussels snafu on American as well as French bureaucrats, Dumas was conciliatory. "There is in our attitude a measure of misplaced pride," he conceded, "a feeling that the United States imposes things on France." Such sensitivity was the result, he said, of "remnants of the old go-it-alone Gaullist syndrome." Implicitly, he was acknowledging what one European foreign minister used to deride privately as "Gallic gag." Dumas and I had always gotten along well personally. He promised to patch things up, and even rode with me to the airport to signal his good faith.

I began my meeting with Mitterrand by reading to him President

Bush's letter to Saddam and asking for suggestions. Mitterrand thought it excellent: "This is a tough letter, understandably so. It leaves Saddam Hussein no option but total surrender." But he challenged a sentence at the top of the second page pledging that if Saddam withdrew from Kuwait, "Iraq will escape destruction." Imprudent language, he believed. "It is a mistake to announce the destruction of Iraq. It creates a confusion between military and civilian establishments, a point which would certainly be used for propaganda purposes." It was a very pertinent point. We had no quarrel with the people of Iraq. Suggesting the destruction of the entire country might well be seen as a unilateral attempt to broaden the Security Council's resolutions. After consulting with President Bush, the language was changed to say that "if Iraq withdrew, the Iraqi military establishment will escape destruction."

From that point, the dialogue became increasingly difficult as I attempted to obtain a commitment that Mitterrand was plainly reluctant to offer—that in the event of war all coalition forces, including French forces, would be under one unified command with an American at the top. After much back-and-forth on the point, Mitterrand confirmed that while his air forces would not participate in the air campaign, "there is no restriction on the unity of military operations with the United States under U.S. command on the day that ground operations are unleashed."

We then moved on to a discussion of the differences between us regarding an international conference on Middle East peace. He had proposed such a conference for seven years and would continue to do so. In opposing it, he argued, "You are wrong and Israel is making a mistake. On this issue, Shamir is very obstinate and unyielding." (I couldn't resist observing that telling me Shamir was unyielding was like telling Noah about the flood.)

It had been a difficult discussion, but in the end, Mitterrand had delivered. "The French will be with us when it counts," I cabled the President. "It just may be bumpy for the next week or so."

Meeting with Helmut Kohl later that same afternoon, I noted that the Germans had come through on the financial commitments Kohl had given me in September in Ludwigshafen. But as with all our nonmilitary allies, more would be required in 1991.

"I'm not the least bit optimistic about our chances of avoiding a conflict," I said, "though I won't rule it out entirely, either. Perhaps he'll still get the message."

The Chancellor was dubious that we could make good on our pledge that Iraqi units wouldn't be attacked if they withdrew from Kuwait. I told him I could guarantee that we wouldn't attack—"and the U.S. forces are the only forces large enough to cause him serious problems."

As for the money, Kohl said he would give serious consideration to my request for $335 million per month. "I shall have to think about that, but I will do something."

My final stop before Geneva was in Milan, where I met with Gianni De Michelis. The Italians were steadfast supporters of the American presence in Europe and our leading role in NATO, and had already contributed several squadrons of jet fighters to the effort. But they were sensitive that we sometimes paid more attention to the British, French, and Germans. De Michelis had turned down a meeting in Brussels and insisted I come to Italy, where the Italians reiterated their staunch support of our efforts.

The Arabs

After the full, unfruitful day in Geneva with Aziz, I flew to Riyadh on January 10 for consultations with the Saudis. Before seeing King Fahd, I met for dinner with Prince Saud and Prince Bandar, who as might be expected were ebullient at the prospect that their archenemy was about to be challenged. Even Saddam's allies now seemed reconciled to war. Quoting a source he said was very close to King Hussein, Saud confided with a touch of glee that "there's a mood of gloom in Amman over the failure of the coalition to collapse." The kingdom's support, they assured me, was unqualified. "We intend to see this matter through," Saud emphasized. "Saudi Arabia has crossed its Rubicon even as the President has crossed his." Bandar told me that his own brother had always been virulently anti-American. "Now he never sees me without saying he owes me an apology about the United States," Bandar recalled.

There were some urgent details to be finalized. We agreed that if an attack were ordered, Bandar would inform King Fahd by a prearranged code: "Our old friend Suleiman will be coming." Then, the Saudis suggested, the King would convene all senior officials of the government in an underground command center. Once they were assembled, their telephone access to the outside world would be cut. The Saudis were our friends and allies, but their communications security could be charitably described as nonchalant. Given that lives were at stake, no one wanted to risk the chance of some loquacious minister compromising operational security.

I presented the price tag for the Saudi share of Desert Shield costs for 1991: $1.1 billion per month, more if hostilities ensued; $800 million in economic aid to Turkey; $1 billion over five years for a Turkish special defense fund, and $800 million for Eastern Europe, to help offset the dramatic rise in energy costs as a result of the embargo on Iraqi oil. Saud wanted to know how much we were asking of Kuwait. I told him we were asking half as much. As he had done in a previous meeting, Saud urged me to ask the

Kuwaitis for no less than the Saudis. Both countries had paid an equal assessment in 1990, he argued, and Kuwait had greater foreign cash reserves. I agreed to think about it before arriving in Taif to see the Emir.

I thought that Saud's insistence on financial parity was more the result of some internal tensions between the two governments than a discreet hint of Saudi financial difficulties. While waiting to see the King, however, I received an inkling that my hunch could be wrong. Our Ambassador to Saudi Arabia, Chas Freeman, suggested to me that perhaps we shouldn't ask quite so much of the Saudis. As a result of their previous commitments to Desert Shield, he said, they had a liquidity shortage that Saud hadn't wanted to admit to me. It seemed to me to be a classic case of clientitis from one of our very best diplomats. "I'm going in front of the Congress and I'm asking them to go ahead and fund this effort," I said, "and I've got to explain that American blood will be spilled. If you think we're not going to ask the Saudis to pay for this, you've got another think coming." It was the last I ever heard from him about going easy on the Saudis in terms of the costs of the operation.

As I'd expected, King Fahd was very gracious when I told him we needed more financial support. "Of course," he said. "Money is worth much less than lives. What is money for, if not to serve us as we do our duty? How can you put a dollar value on people's lives who are fighting? Your requests will be met. Saudi Arabia will continue to pay its fair share of the Desert Shield operation."

The King had recently received several letters from Saddam asking for a meeting. He had steadfastly dismissed them as political posturing. Two days before Kuwait was invaded, Fahd had sent Prince Saud to Baghdad, where Saddam had asked him to assure the King that reports of an invasion were untrue. As a result of this personal treachery, Fahd would never forgive Saddam. I couldn't resist noting that as I watched Saddam in his elaborate military uniforms on television, he reminded me of the ushers at the Houston movie houses of my youth. The King smiled and said he'd had exactly the same thought. "Saddam and his men are dressed like gaudy clowns," Fahd remarked.

I asked the King for his help in persuading President Assad to commit his troops to the attack if a ground war became necessary. For symbolic and emotional reasons, it was important for Arab soldiers to liberate Kuwait City. "I don't want American troops going into an Arab capital," the President had told me several times, and while we all realized that our forces would inevitably spearhead the ground war, a Syrian combat presence would be very helpful. In a hastily arranged meeting in Geneva on November 17, the President with great effort had persuaded Assad to allow his troops to deploy in defensive operations if war began. But he had failed to get a commitment for Syrian troops to move across the border and join in the attack.

I knew it would be difficult. I'd learned from the Saudis that Syrian commanders were balking at an offensive role. As major Soviet client states, both the Iraqis and Syrians were heavily equipped with Russian armaments. The Syrians feared that if they were involved in frontline fighting, they might be mistaken for the enemy in the confusion of battle, and chewed up by American firepower. The Syrians wanted the political benefits of participating, but only at a discreetly safe distance. To assuage their attack of nerves, I'd sent Howard Graves over to the Saudi defense ministry to ask Norm Schwarzkopf to come up with an offensive role that might pass muster with the Syrians. An hour later, Graves was back with Schwarzkopf's solution: the Syrians would not be asked to move into Iraq, but they would enter Kuwait as a strategic reserve to Egyptian armor, and join the attack if the Egyptians needed help. King Fahd agreed to send Prince Saud to Damascus the next morning to lobby Assad personally before my arrival two days later.

Well after midnight, as our meeting was ending, the King offered a very good tactical suggestion. Iraqi forces would be on their highest state of alert on January 15, he reasoned. If an attack were delayed slightly, their guard would be down. "When nothing happens on the fifteenth," he said, "some people will say that nothing will ever happen. So I think we should wait two days to hit them." His advice essentially coincided with our own tactical calculations.

As my plane lifted off from Riyadh for Abu Dhabi the next morning, I peered out my window and could see hundreds of sleek American warplanes, wingtip to wingtip, filling the tarmac. It was sobering to realize that those planes would almost certainly be ordered into action in a matter of days.

Like Fahd, Sheikh Zayed was an unreconstructed hawk. He believed the war would last three days, and the Iraqis would be out of Kuwait in twenty-four hours. "Saddam Hussein rules with a gun in his hand," he said. "He even shoots his own army officers. We all need to appeal to God to help his people. Saddam Hussein stands ready to sacrifice millions of young and old solely for the sake of his own greed."

He wasn't interested in quibbling when I raised the matter of higher war costs. "Please present us the estimates and we will look at them," he said. "We will commit ourselves to what you are committing." I then met in Taif with the Crown Prince of Kuwait and told him we were requesting $400 million a month in direct costs for the American presence in the Gulf.

In addition, I asked him for $800 million for Turkey, above and beyond the $150 million he'd already pledged, plus $400 million in aid to Eastern European countries. He agreed in principle to everything I proposed financially. On reflection, I'd decided that Prince Saud had a point. The numbers I later presented to the Crown Prince were comparable to what I had asked from the Saudis.

After speaking to the American pilots and crews of the Forty-eighth TFW, I flew on to Cairo, where I found President Mubarak in a foul mood. He had just received what he described as a "rude" response to a conciliatory letter he'd recently sent to Saddam. Given that unpleasant experience, he said he wasn't surprised to learn that Tariq Aziz had refused to accept the President's letter. "He should have accepted the letter and Saddam Hussein should have answered it," Mubarak said. "This is the way civilized people behave." Mubarak dismissed Saddam in epithets strikingly similar to Fahd's. "Saddam is casting himself in the role of the Prophet Mohammed," he charged.

By coincidence, Abdul Kareem Iryani, the Foreign Minister of Yemen, was at that moment in Cairo preparing to fly to Baghdad in hopes of brokering a dramatic last-second deal to avert war. Mubarak told me the minister believed Saddam might agree to withdraw if assured that American troops wouldn't attack his retreating forces. As we say in Texas, I knew that dog wouldn't hunt. I'd offered precisely that to Aziz in Geneva, to no avail. Mubarak asked me to talk to Iryani anyway. I was in no mood to waste my time with Yemen after having been rebuffed in the Security Council. But Mubarak was a staunch ally and friend, and had just reassured me that when war began, "the United States can count on Egypt." As always, Mubarak was solid. America owed it to him to make a gesture I knew was meaningless. I turned down a meeting, but agreed to talk on the telephone. A few moments later, Iryani called on Mubarak's private line. My salutation was deliberately prickly. "I am deeply disappointed with your vote on Resolution 678," I reminded him. But I reiterated the President's policy: If Iraq began an immediate and unconditional withdrawal, the coalition would not attack. The Minister seemed hopeful, and rang off in search of yet another illusory settlement. I sent Bob Kimmitt to Iryani's hotel to deliver a message I hadn't wanted to mention over the telephone: If Iryani *did* go to Baghdad, he'd better make damn sure he was out by midnight on the fifteenth. Kimmitt reported back that Iryani had literally flinched when he heard my warning and made clear that he would stay only a few hours. At least Iryani had gotten the message; hopefully, he would convey his own sense of alarm to Saddam.

As I had done with King Fahd, I asked for Mubarak's help with the

Syrians. "It's hard for me to believe the Syrians would sit down at the table and not ante up," I observed. Mubarak told me not to worry about his friend Assad.

I flew directly from Cairo to Damascus for an afternoon meeting with President Assad, which lasted nearly four hours. Assad had just made a public appeal to Saddam and the Iraqi people to get out of Kuwait, his last effort to avert war. I believe we both knew that by then war was a certainty. But I didn't want Assad to be blindsided. "If we make this decision after the deadline passes," I told him, "this should constitute your consultation. Don't expect that you will hear anything else." Assad is adept at reading between the lines; he understood precisely what I was saying. "That is fine with us," he said.

I told Assad that as the deadline approached, it was necessary to have a clearer sense of Syria's participation in combat operations. "Most people when they come to the table are ready to deal the cards," I said as I outlined the limited offensive mission that Norm Schwarzkopf had devised two days earlier, but it didn't impress Assad, whose reluctance was ostensibly grounded in more strategic calculations. In a lengthy exchange, in which he demonstrated a zest for intellectual combat which can only be described with some irony as Talmudic, Assad reminded me that he had committed his troops only for the defense of Saudi Arabia, not for an assault against brother Arabs. He made no mention of the concerns of his generals I'd heard about in Riyadh, but did surface the red herring of unfriendly weather. "We will not enter into foggy weather, and cannot allow others to do so," he vowed. Moreover, he insinuated that his heretofore minimal participation had caused him trouble with his public.

"What do we say to the Syrian people?" he asked. "There are Syrians who question why we have sent forces to the Gulf."

"I would never suggest to you, Mr. President, what to say to the Syrian people."

"You talked about American public opinion. We have similar problems."

"Maybe what you can say is that your forces are acting as a reserve for Arab forces to liberate your Arab brethren who have been invaded and brutalized, your sole objective is the liberation of Kuwait, and that your forces will not fight on Iraqi soil."

"If you were a Syrian citizen, do you think that would be enough?"

"I think the Syrian people believe you when you speak. If you tell them this, they will believe you."

"Yes, they will believe me, but words will not be sufficient to convince them. I am not giving you a final decision, I am just discussing the issue. We want everything to be clear."

The notion that Assad was somehow accountable to Syrian public opinion was not believable, of course. Assad exercised total control over his country. At this point in a delicate negotiation, it made more sense to humor him than to challenge his analysis of what I felt were nonexistent domestic concerns.

In the end, he refused to be swayed by my arguments about his troops fighting in Kuwait. "Well, we'll be talking to the Saudis," he promised. It was, I knew, the diplomatic equivalent of "don't hold your breath." I've been involved in hundreds of negotiations in my public and private career, and Assad was always one of the toughest. I was learning that he would be a formidable interlocutor in the postwar task of forging peace in the Middle East. Ultimately, the Syrians agreed to enter Kuwait, but only in a militarily meaningless support role well to the rear.

I left Damascus for Ankara, but fog blanketed the Turkish capital. Within a few hundred yards of the runway, the pilot twice aborted his landing attempt. Low visibility invariably renders me a white-knuckled flier; on more than one occasion, I'd told my pilots not to push their luck. We diverted to the Incirlik air base, where U.S. warplanes were being readied for the air war. I spent the night at a bachelor officer's quarters. My senior staff slept on cots in shared rooms, while junior aides and the press were bused to a five-star hotel. When I finally saw Ozal the next day, he was as solid as ever.

My last two stops were with our strongest allies, Great Britain and Canada. In testament to the gravity of the situation, John Major, who had taken over for Margaret Thatcher in November 1990, graciously met me during a refueling stop at the Royal Air Force Base at Alconbury. He was predictably stalwart. When I asked him if anyone else needed to be consulted, he told me only Queen Elizabeth remained to be informed. "I trust she will not," he said, chuckling, "for the first time in three hundred years, withhold approval."

In Ottawa, Brian Mulroney was no less supportive than Major. Ironically, this last stop provided the trip's only uncomfortable moment for me. Before seeing Mulroney, I met with Gareth Evans, Australia's Foreign Minister, who was in Ottawa by coincidence. Evans was very bright, shrewd, and capable—an excellent foreign minister. He was also a friend. I was delighted to learn from him that Australia was firmly with the coalition, but less pleased to be challenged on the delicate issue of prenotification. No doubt my mood was influenced by sheer exhaustion, but I reacted poorly to his insistence that because "Australians are at risk," he must receive advance notice of the attack. "You have one frigate in the Gulf," I replied testily. "We have 500,000 men and women on the ground. I will not risk their security by premature notification." In the heated exchange which ensued, Evans demanded to know on the spot the precise time of the attack and intimated that I was holding back on an ally. His implication as well as his tone were not appreciated. "There's not going to be any prenotification," I snapped. Our friendship survived the meeting, as did our ability to work closely together on a number of important Asian-Pacific issues.

Lithuania Explodes

I returned to Washington at midday on January 14, satisfied that I had touched all the bases. The coalition was solid and prepared for the inevitable. In the meantime, however, I'd been reminded that foreign policy is frequently multidimensional at the most inopportune moments. As we prepared for war in the Gulf, we were simultaneously evacuating American and other foreign diplomats from Somalia, where clan violence threatened to engulf the country in open warfare. Suddenly, a fresh and ugly crisis in the Baltics intruded. This trip pointed up the challenge that faces U.S. policy makers when dealing with multiple crises such as these at a time when some officials are operating in Washington and others are on the road. The world does not rest while you focus on one crisis—almost inevitably another one pops up. To succeed, it is paramount that there be the closest cooperation and coordination among departments and officials. That is why, for example, there was a representative from each relevant agency and department on my airplane. While we had a few instances of busted signals, it is truly a credit to all the participants that we stayed in touch as well as we did. And because we did, the President could spend his time leading the U.S. effort to deal with these multiple crises, not adjudicating our internal differences or misunderstandings.

On January 11, tensions which had been building since the first of the year between Moscow and the independence-minded government in Lithuania erupted in Vilnius. Soviet airborne troops who had been flown in to enforce conscription laws opened fire on a crowd surrounding the government's main printing plant, wounding several citizens. By the end of the day, the paratroopers had surrounded the television station and other government buildings.

I sent a message to Shevardnadze explaining that Mitterrand, Kohl, Dumas, Genscher, and Hurd had all told me that any crackdown would have a negative effect on their willingness to provide continued assistance to the Soviet Union. Clearly the same would be true as to the United States. Although Shevardnadze had resigned on December 20 and had only a few days left in office, I sent the message to provide him an incentive and credible basis on which he could go to Gorbachev and talk to him about the consequences of moves toward imposing presidential rule in the Baltics.

Despite an agreement between Gorbachev and Boris Yeltsin to settle the crisis peacefully, local commanders let the situation get out of hand. On the morning of January 13, "Bloody Sunday," Soviet troops killed fifteen Lithuanians and wounded hundreds more in an assault on the television station. It seemed as though Gorbachev's authority was disintegrating and the Baltics were on the verge of anarchy.

Crafting the appropriate response to the situation was tricky. Certainly, the violence couldn't be condoned, but our rhetoric had to be more than boilerplate. A slap on the wrist would dishearten our friends in the Baltics and embolden our critics in the Congress, who would surely charge that we were looking the other way to keep the Soviets in the Gulf War coalition. More important, if the Soviets were exploiting the January 15 deadline on the assumption that we were preoccupied with the final stages of war planning, they had to be disabused. On the other hand, there was no doubt Gorbachev was under growing pressure from the enemies of reform. Coming down too hard might embolden his critics and weaken his standing, which obviously was contrary to American strategic interests. Moreover, we didn't want to be so harsh that Gorbachev might be tempted, as the President said, to bail out on us. The President and I agreed that our response must be measured, but with sufficient vigor so that all parties understood our seriousness. I believe the President's public statement as well as mine, which was issued in Ankara before my meeting with President Ozal on January 13, struck that delicate balance. In those statements, we emphasized that while we supported and admired the Soviet effort to change through glasnost and perestroika, the use of force in the Baltics fundamentally and tragically contradicted these principles. "Peaceful dialogue, not force," I said, "is the only path to long-term legitimacy and stability."

On the morning of January 15, I registered an official démarche with Soviet chargé d'affaires Sergei Chetverikov, who was running the embassy until a replacement was named for Alexander Bessmertnykh, who himself had succeeded Shevardnadze as Foreign Minister. I told Chetverikov there was absolutely no justification for the use of force against the democratically elected government of Lithuania, and that it was reasonable for us to worry that Soviet policy had changed for the worse. "The violence that has taken place in the three Baltic states invites unhappy comparisons with earlier periods in Soviet history," I said. "They give cause for concern for the reform process and directly contradict Mikhail Gorbachev's assurances, given President Bush at the Washington summit, that he would resolve the Baltic question without violence. The Baltic governments were elected through processes President Gorbachev himself created. We worry that he is threatening his own historic legacy."

Lacking any instructions, Chetverikov began predictably. "I appreciate the clarity of your remarks," he said, wondering whether they represented my personal view or an official statement of the United States government. "The President asked me to convey his concerns," I replied frostily, "so you should consider them official." He called the incidents "tragic and regrettable," and insisted that Gorbachev had dissociated himself from the incidents and had ordered a full investigation. His excuses were uniformly lame. Tensions had been sparked by recent price increases. There was a genuine threat of anarchy and chaos in Lithuania. Troops had moved in to separate warring factions who were threatening public order. "Why were troops needed to seize the television station?" I asked. To quell "inflammatory broadcasts" urging the masses to resist the forces of democratic reform, he claimed.

"We've worked hard on the U.S.-Soviet relationship, and have accomplished a great deal," I reminded him. "Continued violence, however, will inevitably affect our ability to stay the course."

I wasn't sure Chetverikov had absorbed the message, so I repeated it in a midafternoon call to Bessmertnykh that was ostensibly to congratulate him on his appointment as Shevardnadze's replacement. "Our ability to pursue our new relationship depends on your government upholding the principles of perestroika," I said. "I hope what we've seen doesn't represent a return to old thinking and past practices."

Bessmertnykh maintained that "these unfortunate incidents" were isolated and not a change in policy. "This is not the way things should be done," he said. "These conflicts can be resolved. This doesn't constitute a crackdown. The tensions of the moment got out of hand."

I felt Bessmertnykh believed what he was telling me. I also knew that Gorbachev was under extreme pressure from the right. Unless he understood how serious the stakes were, he might be forced into more of a hard line against the Baltics. Bessmertnykh understood American politics quite well. I reminded him that Congress would not tolerate further violence, and neither would the President. "We can't stand by and take no notice of recent developments," I said. "If you don't get something done, Sasha, this is going to end the whole thing." Bessmertnykh assured me that Gorbachev understood the perils to the relationship and would resolve these "difficulties" in a peaceful fashion.

My private view at the time was that Gorbachev had more knowledge about what had gone on than he wished the President to believe, and on some level may have been testing the United States. I also believe he knew what his troops were doing in the Baltics. His power was rapidly eroding. Dissatisfaction with reform was emboldening his critics on the right, and in less than eight months Gorbachev would survive a coup attempt that nevertheless sealed his fate. In desperation, he had made a calculated gamble to tack in the direction of his conservative critics. His Baltic offensive may have temporarily eased his domestic problems, but if pursued would destroy the new relationship with the United States that he and Shevardnadze and the President and I had worked to build. While we couldn't ignore Soviet behavior, neither could we afford to lose the Soviets on the eve of the Gulf War. This was one of many instances where we juggled principles and interests, realism and idealism, in the pursuit of creative diplomacy. I believe our response struck the right balance: tough enough to avert disaster in the Baltics, but not so strident as to alienate the Soviets into bolting the coalition. As I had hoped, Bessmertnykh got the message. The crisis eventually eased—but not in time to salvage a Bush-Gorbachev summit meeting scheduled for February 1991, which was postponed indefinitely.

By the time I finished my call to Bessmertnykh, the Gulf crisis was approaching its climax. In less than eight hours, the deadline for Iraq's withdrawal from Kuwait would expire. In a little more than twenty-four hours, America would be at war. The President had already signed the necessary directives. Saddam's brinksmanship had underestimated America's determination to stand fast. The price for his miscalculation was certain to be cataclysmic. I could only hope that it would be borne by him and his military machine, and not by the men and women who at that instant were preparing to transform Desert Shield into Desert Storm. The only thing left to do was pray for their success and safety.

CHAPTER 21

PASSING THE BRINK

This is the most difficult moment we have reached.
—*Israeli Prime Minister Yitzhak Shamir to Deputy Secretary Eagleburger, in reaction to Iraqi Scud attacks on Israeli cities, January 23, 1991*

Well, times are very tense.
—*Soviet Foreign Minister Alexander Bessmertnykh in a phone call to Secretary Baker, January 24, 1991*

On the morning of January 16, I received a call from the President. "Can you come on over for lunch?" he wanted to know. "I'd like to talk." It was just the two of us in the private dining room of the White House residence. We'd been alone together like this countless times over the last three decades. But this time, I sensed an inner tension not often detectable in a man as gregarious and extroverted as George Bush. Before the day was out, the United States would be at war. He had just made decisions that would send what he'd been told could be hundreds of soldiers, marines and airmen to their deaths. At the moment of truth for his presidency, perhaps the single most important moment in the journey we'd begun together in November of 1978, I knew he was seeking some reassurance.

I found him somber. He was very secure with the tough decisions that he had made. He felt he'd received good advice from Dick Cheney and the generals, and was convinced the troops of Operation Desert Storm were superbly equipped, trained, and motivated. Objectively, there was no way we could lose; it should be over in a matter of weeks, with minimal casualties. Still, as a young Navy pilot in the Pacific, he'd experienced combat up close; he knew that war seldom unfolds according to the textbooks and operations plans—"the fog of war." As Colin Powell had reminded us all more than once, war is always filled with surprises. The tone of the President's voice indicated to me a nagging anxiety about the terrible consequences that somehow might yet result. "I know this *is* the right thing to do," he said, "and I know we've done this right. We've exhausted every opportunity, and I just can't be getting casualty estimates that are far off." If the military assessments were accurate, the coming battle would turn out well. If the estimates were wrong, as they had been in Vietnam, the toll in human life would be higher, the outcome less certain. We both knew there was an enormous amount at stake—in terms of possible consequences for the lives of American soldiers, their families, and the country; and I must confess to feeling the same nagging anxiety as he did about what might be the ultimate result.

"Of course a decision on war is the most difficult a President has to face," I said. "But you've made the right decisions, you've gone about it the right way, and it's going to work out."

I assumed that the toughest part of my job was over. Now it would be essential, of course, to maintain intact the political coalition we'd assembled. The Soviets would surely be tempted to produce some new diplomatic initiative. Such efforts could threaten the cohesion of the coalition and would need to be politely but firmly discouraged. I felt good about the job the President and his administration had done in organizing an international coalition and building a domestic consensus to support our policies. But our coercive diplomacy had failed to get Iraq out of Kuwait. Statecraft, I thought, was moving to the sidelines. The focus of this crisis would now be squarely on the battlefield and at the Pentagon. I was wrong.

Almost immediately, I found myself back in the maelstrom. As Tariq Aziz had promised in Geneva, Iraq swiftly struck at Israel in an effort to provoke the Shamir government into retaliation—a potentially catastrophic escalation that would surely fracture our political and military coalition. As Scud missiles rained down on Israeli cities, we had the additional political task of keeping Israel from entering the war. For the first several days of the air war, I spent most of my energies trying to persuade Israel to do what it had never done before—refrain from retaliating against an aggressor. My efforts to keep the Soviets from new mischief were less successful. A joint statement with the new Soviet Foreign Minister blew up in late January, causing a major problem with the White House.

The War Begins

After lunch with the President on January 16, I returned to the department to prepare for an extensive round of notifications. As American warplanes and Tomahawk missiles closed in on Iraq, I met separately with the ambassadors from Israel, Kuwait, Saudi Arabia, Germany, Syria, and Japan. I made fourteen calls to my ministerial counterparts, as well as the ranking members of the congressional foreign-affairs committees.

At 6:11 P.M. Washington time, I woke up Alexander Bessmertnykh in his Moscow apartment and told him the attack on Iraq would begin "very shortly." Bessmertnykh told me that this was a cataclysmic development and pressed me for a more specific time. I told him to expect an attack within the hour. Bessmertnykh asked for a delay. Gorbachev would want some time for a final plea to Saddam. For that very reason, I had refrained from calling the Soviets until shortly before the bombing commenced. "It's too late for that, Sasha," I said. "We're past that point."

Twenty-seven minutes later, Bessmertnykh called me back. Gorbachev was asking the President as a personal favor to delay the war by at least twenty-four hours. "This is a personal appeal from the President of the Soviet Union," he stressed. I told him his request had been overtaken by events. "We're at H-hour. You can't call off an operation of this size."

Afterward, I sat in my office with a stiff double martini, listening to CNN network anchor Bernard Shaw and correspondent John Holliman, both of whom I had known from my White House days, reporting live from Baghdad that reports of the air war having begun seemed erroneous, because nothing was happening. Seconds later, they were speaking from under their desks as Baghdad erupted with explosions. Here we go, I thought to myself. I remember thinking that I would almost certainly never again be in a situation where I would actually watch the start of a war in which I had played a significant role. My thoughts drifted back to those F-111 pilots at Taif I'd visited only five days before. They were in the first wave now, on their way to Baghdad. I said a silent prayer for their safety.

As I watched the war unfold on television, I realized that several of the reports used maps that unintentionally revealed targets we were planning to hit that night. I asked Margaret Tutwiler to call ABC's John McWethy and CNN's Ralph Begleiter to tell them that some of the maps depicted actual targeting schemes. To their credit, these networks took our suggestions and were careful with future reports. Later in the evening, the President called. "It looks like it's started well," he said. He was euphoric about the first reports from the field; unbelievably, none of our planes was lost in the first wave of attacks.

Our relief over the amazingly low coalition casualties was quickly shattered the next evening, when eight Scud missiles struck Tel Aviv and Haifa. I was getting a haircut at the Sheraton-Carlton Hotel when I learned about the attack. I rode the two short blocks to the White House and went immediately to Brent Scowcroft's West Wing office, arriving at 7:39 P.M. We were joined by Larry Eagleburger, Bob Gates, and several other NSC aides.

The Israeli Conundrum

Throughout the prewar period, keeping Israel out of the conflict had been a central strategic concern of our diplomacy. Our task was complicated by the fact that relations between our countries were not at their best. Still, I believed Israel would understand that restraint would serve its larger interests. Some of her longtime enemies already recognized this reality. The Arab elites understood that Saddam was a greater threat to them than Israel. However, though I had been able to secure agreements from all our Arab coalition partners that if Saddam attacked Israel first, and Israel struck back, they would remain firm, no Arab leader could be sure that the masses wouldn't take to the streets, and threaten the stability of their regimes, if Israel retaliated. In addition, such an escalation would give Iran an opening to bolster its political position in the region by playing to the disaffected masses while watching the coalition destroy its archenemy, Iraq.

In early January, Israeli Foreign Minister David Levy had publicly warned that an Iraqi attack would be considered an act of war and would prompt "terrible retribution." To reinforce our concern that this would be a particularly unwise policy, the President sent Larry Eagleburger and Paul Wolfowitz to Israel to urge restraint. In spite of Levy's hard line, I believe that Prime Minister Yitzhak Shamir had in fact made a strategic calculation well before the war began to break with tradition and refrain from striking back if Israel came under attack. Such a decision was momentous for any Israeli leader. Immediate, massive retaliation had always been the bedrock of Israeli deterrence. It was a cardinal principle of Israeli politics: the Arabs must always know that whenever they attacked the Jewish state, Israel would react with overwhelming force. But Shamir also understood the larger stakes for Israel. The United States had marshaled an unprecedented international coalition, including Arab states, to deal with Israel's gravest threat. It made no sense for Israel to do anything to jeopardize such a welcome prospect. As a practical matter, the Israeli air force could never match the resources the coalition would bring to bear against Saddam. Shamir understood that becoming involved could cause the coalition to splinter, and result in the loss of Israel's larger strategic objective—the destruction of Saddam's military capabilities. From a purely political standpoint, restraint also made sense for Shamir. His intransigence in the peace process had damaged his relations with the administration and with American public opinion. By acting responsibly, his personal standing with both would improve. He may also have felt, with some justification, that Israel would then be owed something for its forbearance.

Moreover, as is now well known, Shamir had been meeting in secret for some time with King Hussein in an effort to find some formula that might lead to peace between Israel and Jordan. Although the King continued to support Iraq during the crisis, he also remained in contact with Shamir. During one of their secret meetings, he told Shamir that if war came, he would be forced to attack any Israeli aircraft entering Jordanian airspace on its way to strike Iraq. Shamir knew Israeli pilots would respond in kind, and suddenly the specter of a wider war between Israel and the Arabs would be realized. Shamir understood full well that Israel must not play into Saddam's hands by allowing itself to be sucked into the conflict.

Once Saddam's missiles began raining down on Israel's cities, however, Shamir's preference for restraint came under ferocious pressure from the Israeli Defense Forces, particularly the air force. Defense Minister Moshe Arens lobbied furiously for permission to launch retaliatory air strikes. Within minutes of the first Scud attack, Arens was on the phone with Dick Cheney, asking for our IFF electronic codes (identification-friend-or-foe), which identified friendly aircraft from enemy planes. Even worse, Arens told Cheney that the counterattacks he was contemplating would require Israeli aircraft and helicopters to enter Saudi Arabian airspace on their way to western Iraq. He asked that President Bush contact the Saudis and secure their permission to permit these overflights.

I telephoned the President in the residence and briefed him on these requests. His relationship with Shamir was strained, so he asked me to call the Prime Minister directly to appeal for restraint and to contact Arens as well. While waiting for my call to Shamir to get through, I telephoned the ambassadors from Saudi Arabia, Egypt, and Syria with identical messages: we would do all we could to keep Israel out of the war, but we expected their countries to remain fast as their leaders had personally promised me in early January. I told Prince Bandar that the Israelis wanted permission to overfly his country to attack Iraq. Bandar said King Fahd was a generous man, but that it would be a waste of time to pass along such a request.

I knew Misha Arens well from his previous posting as Foreign Minister, and we'd always worked together fairly well. While he was very hard-line, I considered him a practical diplomat who did a credible job of balancing prudence with the demands of a volatile Israeli public opinion. When I finally reached him at 9:30 P.M., however, he was in no mood for conciliation, reflecting perhaps the pressure on him as Defense Minister to do something.

"We don't have a choice," Arens bluntly informed me. "We have to go. They've hit us. We have to hit them back. Israel can't sit here and be hit with missiles and do nothing." I told him that on a personal level, "The President and all of us are very sad and sorry about the attacks." Retaliation was certainly understandable, but would be disastrous. "It's not in your interests to complicate our task," I argued. "You have just as much of a stake in this as we do. You can't let this guy off the hook. I hope you can find a way, if at all possible, to keep from responding to the attack. You should take this as a formal request to withhold a response." Arens was adamant; even though I ignored his restated demand for the IFF codes, he was insistent upon Israel's right of self-defense. But he agreed to discuss our request for restraint with Shamir immediately.

In this conversation, Arens repeated his earlier request for permission to enter Saudi airspace. I knew it was out of the question. King Fahd had given us his assurance that he would remain stalwart if Israel struck back after being attacked first by Saddam. But allowing Israeli warplanes to transit Saudi airspace was too much to ask. Then, too, the harder we made it for Israel to respond, the less likely they might actually follow through.

An hour later, I finally reached Shamir. "The President and all of us are outraged by this additional aggression," I told him, "but we hope you will not retaliate." Within minutes of the Scud launches, Schwarzkopf had diverted American and British fighter-bombers to western Iraq with orders to search out and destroy the Scuds. "We now have four F-15s over those launch sites," I assured Shamir. "We are going after western Iraq full bore, Prime Minister. There is nothing your air force can do that we are not doing. If there is, tell us and we'll do it."

I believed Shamir wanted to stay out, despite the pressure from his generals and the Israeli public, so I suggested that his restraint was not only essential but would also help repair bilateral relations, which we both knew were in some considerable disrepair. "We are *very* appreciative of the approach of the government of Israel throughout this crisis," I said. "We will remember it. This is *very* important to us."

Shamir said very little. "This is a terrible problem for us, which we have to face up to," he cautioned me. "Israel has never failed to respond." He thanked me for my concern, and pledged to call me later in the evening. "I need to talk to my Cabinet," he said. I knew that at the very least, Shamir would never order an Israeli attack before calling me back.

At 2:03 A.M., Shamir woke me up at home with an exceedingly sobering message. "Mr. Secretary, the Cabinet has decided to prepare an immediate response to the attacks on Tel Aviv and Haifa," he informed me. I told Shamir bluntly that such an attack would be a disaster for Israel. "No one has more of a stake in this than you do," I said. "Don't make it more difficult for us to do the job for you. Before you do anything, let's see if the attacks persist."

Shamir agreed that it was important for Israel to do everything in its power to keep from provoking other Arab nations, but refused to rule out an attack. "You cannot do this, Prime Minister," I said. "It's not in your interests. We'll respond to whatever needs you have, but you can't do this."

Shamir had sounded as though retaliation were a fait accompli. But I knew both he and Arens understood the military facts of life: for Israel to attack Iraq, coalition forces must either "deconflict"—stop flying missions in a certain area, thus allowing Israel a corridor for its warplanes—or give Israel the identification codes. We had no intention of doing either. As long as that was the case, we believed Israel's vows to attack would probably not be acted upon.

To demonstrate our good faith in finding a solution to the Scud attacks, the President decided to send Eagleburger back to Israel. Essentially, he was given a blank check: whatever Israel needed was a price worth paying to keep them out of the war. "Do whatever you have to do to assure them we have the Scuds under control," I told Eagleburger. "And, Larry, don't come home if you're unsuccessful," I joked. "I won't," he promised.

Shortly after arriving in Tel Aviv on January 20, Eagleburger was informed by Shamir that if the attacks continued, Israel would retaliate. Eagleburger's report to me on the mood of Shamir and Arens was succinct: "Their demeanor was grave and their voices urgent . . . there is a limit to Israeli restraint—and we are close to it." Arens believed the United States was not doing enough to eliminate Saddam's missile launchers. In addition to more air strikes, Arens asked for an electronic downlink with U.S. intelligence satellites so that Israeli planners would have instantaneous information on Iraqi deployments. He requested that a direct communications channel be established with Schwarzkopf's headquarters, and that an Israeli planning group be allowed aboard a U.S. aircraft carrier. At a minimum, he wanted an Israeli general assigned to the Central Command staff.

I agreed with Eagleburger's recommendation that these requests should be politely rebuffed. Arens was essentially asking American forces to help plan Israeli strikes against Iraq. That was out of the question. I believed the best course was to commit more coalition assets against the Scuds. As Eagleburger correctly put it, "The danger to our objectives in Desert Storm posed by doing this . . . [is] dwarfed by the likely impact of an Israeli strike."

Over the next five days, various measures were agreed upon. Schwarzkopf ordered more combat sorties in western Iraq. Although Israel had rejected our offer of Patriot missile batteries before the war, they now were eager to have them. We began sharing intelligence with Israel, and continued to maintain a direct communications link with Israeli defense headquarters. Israeli intelligence helped American commanders with target identification, and the President approved some special forces operations against targets in western Iraq.

Just as we began to believe the threat of an Israeli retaliation was receding, more Scuds hit Tel Aviv on January 22. Eagleburger telephoned me with disturbing news: a close adviser to Shamir had passed word through the American ambassador that "unless you can give us something very big and significant, we will have to go." The Israelis renewed their request for a five-mile-wide air corridor over Saudi Arabia to launch a commando operation against the Scud launchers, and a three-hour "stand-down" of American air operations in the vicinity. Eagleburger was instructed to tell the Israelis we would do nothing to enable them to attack. This view was reinforced by the Pentagon, which had felt insulted when Arens had publicly alleged the U.S. military was doing a poor job of destroying Scud launchers. As a matter of fact, our effort to destroy all of Saddam's Scuds was the only part of the overall campaign in which the military's predictions had been a bit overly optimistic.

Later that day, I received an urgent request from the Pentagon. An American pilot had been shot down over western Iraq. The most direct route for American search-and-rescue helicopters would require a flight plan over Syria. I telephoned Foreign Minister Farouk Shara and asked him to request permission from President Assad on humanitarian grounds. Shara said such a request had political implications that must be considered. I told him we had no time for such diversions; the mission must be launched within the hour or the pilot would be captured by the Iraqis. A few moments later, Shara called back. Assad had agreed to a one-time exception, provided we made no public mention of his cooperation and our aircraft flew without lights. The pilot was eventually rescued. Assad declined, however, to respond to a second request the Pentagon had asked me to pursue. As a result, we were unable to overfly Syrian airspace with Tomahawk cruise missiles.

The new Scud attacks heightened the pressure on Shamir, and on January 23, he sent a letter to the President, formally asking the United States to step aside and allow Israel to retaliate. With all due respect to American forces, Shamir said, "we believe we can, and must, mount an operation that has a chance of carrying out the task and achieving its objectives."

By this time in the crisis, we had done a considerable amount for Israel. The President was prepared to do more, but all of us felt it was time for Israel to respond in kind. Eagleburger was instructed to tell Shamir that the President could not agree to "deconfliction," but that if Israel would refrain from retaliating, the United States was prepared to double the number of Patriots in Israel, send a team of targeting experts to Israel to solicit suggestions for dealing with the Scuds, and provide intelligence to Israel from a sophisticated new communications satellite system being tested in the Gulf. We believed this was a reasonable quid pro quo very much in Israel's interests.

Shamir, however, was upset by what he considered an unacceptable linkage in our offer. The Prime Minister characterized the proposal as "inhuman" and said he did not understand how a friend could utter such words. He was particularly offended by the conditionality of the Patriot offer. Shamir had been struggling with his conscience from the first Scud attack; now he felt his forbearance had been betrayed. "This is the most difficult moment we have reached," he told Eagleburger. Never one to mince words, Eagleburger told me, "We have taken a great step backward from the atmosphere of confidence we have been able to build over the last several weeks."

In his typically selfless fashion, Eagleburger volunteered to take the fall. He asked for permission to go back to Shamir and report he was embarrassed to admit that he had exceeded his instructions by linking additional American help to a commitment not to attack Iraq. Eagleburger would reiterate that while the United States would not deconflict, and while we expected the Israelis to stay their hand, the President's offers of help were unconditional and would be implemented immediately. "Something along those lines will get us most of what we want," Eagleburger advised, "while making it clear to Shamir that we will not deconflict should he ask us to."

Even in the most difficult of moments, Eagleburger never lost his sense of humor. "If the above meets your approval," he cabled me, "I would like to be able to return to Shamir very early Thursday morning Jerusalem time. If the above does not meet with your approval, and I am fired, please wait until I come back; I need the plane to come home on."

Predictably, Eagleburger had devised a creative solution to the impasse. By making more U.S. help unconditional, Shamir was given critical leverage with the hard-liners in his government. Now he could say that he had extracted significant new concessions from us as a result of his restraint.

Ultimately, the Scuds proved to be more of a political weapon than a military threat. In the end, strategic interest won out over visceral impulse. But our refusal to give Israel the electronic codes was critical to this outcome. Shamir headed a shaky coalition government. He might well have been pushed into attacking if he had the codes. Without them, there was simply too much risk of an Israeli pilot inadvertently shooting down an American aircraft, or vice versa, either of which would have been a disaster for both countries. Despite Shamir's pragmatic preference for staying on the sidelines, I believe that if we had given the Israeli government those codes, sooner or later they would have struck back at Iraq.

The Joint Statement That Bombed

Two hours before Eagleburger returned from Tel Aviv on January 26, I met with Bessmertnykh for the first time since his appointment as Foreign Minister. This Saturday session was the first of three in which developments in the Gulf were not foremost on our agenda. On a personal level, I was anxious to cooperate with Bessmertnykh. He'd been Ambassador to the United States, and was a friend of Soviet reform. More important, he had responded quickly to my warnings about the deadly Soviet intervention in the Baltics, and argued successfully with Gorbachev that American support for perestroika would be imperiled if the strong-arm tactics didn't stop. He was more of a friend to the United States than many of his comrades. I wanted to help him consolidate his own power base and keep him personally committed to cooperation with us. After a long discussion in which I reiterated the President's view that more violence in the Baltics would be a disaster for Soviet-American cooperation, we turned to the Gulf. Bessmertnykh assured me that Gorbachev would not renege on the Soviet commitment to force Iraq from Kuwait. "We have to be together with you and work things out," he said. At the same time, however, Soviet policy makers were concerned about the growing destruction of Iraq and escalating civilian casualties. It was apparent the Arabists were up to their old tricks; Bessmertnykh was fishing for a formula that would stop the fighting and give Saddam a face-saving excuse to get out of Kuwait. I reminded him that Saddam had been given every opportunity to withdraw and had spurned all U.N. resolutions. He had imposed war on his own people.

"We've been rather passive when it comes to political steps at the point when military action is going on," he chided me. "There is a growing position in many countries that the bombing is becoming more destructive and there's no search at the same time for anything else." It was even more important to search for political solutions to end the war. "Maybe some kind of gesture would be appropriate," he said, adding that the Soviets were thinking of offering a new resolution in the Security Council urging a pause in the bombing.

It was an unacceptable proposition. "If we give him a pause," I replied, "he'll have a chance to repair some of the damage that's been done, and it will also give him a chance to rearm his forces, and that would cost us lives." We also knew that another U.N. debate would give the Soviets a fresh opportunity to build political momentum for a cease-fire that might allow Saddam to escape Kuwait with his military largely intact.

"We really do need to take some steps," Bessmertnykh persisted. "It's very important that we begin thinking about the post-crisis security structures." He finally stopped talking about a new resolution and suggested we

conclude our meeting with a joint statement, like the joint statements issued earlier in Moscow and Helsinki. I asked that he come back with some
draft language. As an indication of how little importance I attached to this
statement, I did not suggest that my aides prepare the initial draft—as we
had at Vnukovo II and Helsinki.

Two days later on Monday, January 28, Bessmertnykh returned with
drafts of *two* joint statements—one on the Gulf War, the other on the Middle East. The language of both was largely unacceptable, the handiwork of
Saddam's friends in the Foreign Ministry. The Mideast draft was especially
dangerous, because it resurrected the specter of linkage that we had sought
to avoid since the start of the crisis. At the same time, I knew that Saddam's
defeat would bring fresh opportunities for progress on Arab-Israeli matters.
I suggested we try to find some mutually acceptable language that would
satisfy the Soviets, give Bessmertnykh an opening to make the point in
Moscow that he was every bit as formidable as his predecessor, and keep
the pressure on Saddam.

The final version was a compromise that gave us far more in the bargain
than Bessmertnykh. The Soviets had agreed that "Iraq's withdrawal from
Kuwait must remain the goal of the international community." In exchange, we agreed to language the Soviets had wanted: "the ministers continue to believe that a cessation of hostilities would be possible if Iraq would
make an unequivocal commitment to withdraw from Kuwait."

At lunch Tuesday with my staff before meeting with Bessmertnykh to
finalize the deal, we had considered the possibility that this language might
be interpreted as a weakening of our support for unconditional withdrawal.
For that specific purpose, we had attached language designed to reinforce
our resolve. The phrase "continue to believe" was inserted to show there
was no change from existing policy. We also insisted that any Iraqi commitment to withdraw "must be backed by immediate, concrete steps" leading
to full compliance with the U.N. resolution demanding unconditional withdrawal. I concluded that these qualifiers protected us against charges that
we were breaking new ground. It was a compromise I considered fully acceptable, particularly since we had persuaded the Soviets to accept some
new language on the Arab-Israeli conflict that moved beyond the tired diplomatic lexicon of previous statements.

We knew the White House was nervous that the Soviets were preparing to distance themselves from the continued pursuit of the air war, but I
didn't think we needed to vet the statement with the NSC staff. It was only
a ministerial communiqué (not a presidential one), and when it was issued,
I believed the White House would be reassured that we had committed the
Soviets even more firmly to American policy in the Gulf and the Mideast.

I met with Bessmertnykh shortly after 4:00 P.M. on January 29. As we were finishing, he told me. "It would really help if I could put this statement out." From a practical standpoint, I told him that made little sense. The President would be delivering his State of the Union address that night. "Believe me, Sasha, this won't get two lines in any American newspaper," I said. I suggested we wait two days before releasing the statement.

Bessmertnykh was adamant. "If I get back to Moscow and this hasn't been issued yet," he warned, "I'm going to face a lot of opposition." The Arabists might even be able to persuade Gorbachev to insist on revisions. This was particularly true, he added, with respect to the new language on the Middle East. "I want us to be able to put these new words in," he said. "But when I get back to Moscow, they're going to see the old words are missing, and we'll have a problem. Let's finish it now and make it a fact." I somewhat reluctantly agreed that he could do what he wanted with the statement and that we would only post it in the press room at State. I assumed it would be ignored until the next day because of the President's speech. I decided to forgo my usual custom and did not accompany Bessmertnykh downstairs, because I didn't feel we had agreed to anything particularly important. And to compound the error, I never even ran the statement by Margaret Tutwiler, who had left for the day after telling our press corps that there would not be an appearance by Bessmertnykh and me following our meeting. She undoubtedly would have quickly recognized the danger and save me from one of the biggest mistakes I made as Secretary of State.

In the lobby, network film crews were setting up cameras so that diplomatic correspondents could comment on the foreign-policy portion of the President's speech with State as their backdrop. They were also eager to cover Bessmertnykh's departure. As he walked out of the building, a group of reporters routinely asked how our talks had gone. Almost gleefully, Bessmertnykh embraced this unexpected opportunity. He pulled a copy of the joint statement from his coat pocket and read it aloud, on camera.

Suddenly, for the State Department press corps, which was already nervous about the action moving to their counterparts at the Pentagon and White House, there was a story to feed their editors. Journalists are notorious for understandably wishing to view the news in black-and-white terms. So without the benefit of any backgrounding from our press office, they got it wrong. By suggesting that we would accept a cease-fire in exchange for a mere promise by Iraq to withdraw from Kuwait, they erroneously assumed that the principle of conditionality had been injected into the equation for the first time. Moreover, by including a paragraph on the Mideast in the statement, a case could be made that we were linking the two issues, a policy we had adamantly resisted for months.

Not long afterward, Brent Scowcroft was asked about the statement during a White House briefing before the State of the Union speech. He had no inkling of the statement. Reporters now smelled an even juicier story. As White House Chief of Staff, I'd learned on many occasions just how much the press loves what are known as "scuffling in the wheelhouse" stories. In my mind, I could see the headlines in the morning papers: "Administration in Conflict over New Policy Flap."

I couldn't blame Scowcroft for being upset at being caught by surprise. When he called me to ask what was going on, I assured him that I had not agreed to any change in policy. After a relatively sleepless night, I called the President the next day to make my apologies. "You know darn good and well I wouldn't be out there consciously trying to upstage your State of the Union," I said. He knew I wasn't trying to do that, and accepted my explanation with his usual graciousness. But as the media frenzy spun out of hand and threatened to overshadow his speech, it was widely reported that he was in fact furious with me. While he never showed it to me, I certainly wouldn't have blamed him if he had been. Reports of the President's displeasure were fueled with a fair amount of enthusiasm by White House Chief of Staff John Sununu, and by some partisans on the NSC staff anxious to take advantage of my miscalculation. It was a mistake of omission, not commission. I knew the statement represented no change in policy; I also believed—naively, in retrospect—that its innocuous quality would garner only casual attention. I still believe that would have been the case if Bessmertnykh had not been so eager to hype the statement for his own reasons. Newly appointed to his post, he was trying to establish himself as Shevardnadze's legitimate successor. He wanted to demonstrate that he was no less a player on the world stage than his predecessor. In the aftermath, I felt used, but I was angrier with myself than with Bessmertnykh. I should have foreseen what might happen. I had far too much experience in the ways of Washington and the media to have made such a careless error.

The joint statement created a furor at the time. Critics confused the rationale for its creation with the way in which it was handled, which admittedly was poor. But the statement itself was well advised. Its object was to bind the Soviets to us in the coalition. Our greatest ally, Shevardnadze, was gone. Bessmertnykh was new in the job and being tested by the Arabists, who were still lobbying for a new peace initiative. Even before Bessmertnykh's arrival in Washington, talk of a pause had been emanating from Moscow. This was a disastrous notion; if the war were interrupted, it would be almost impossible to resume. I felt that a new formulation recommitting them to the coalition and the existing U.N. mandate would reinforce our existing cooperation.

I still believe, as I said at the time, that this was "not a big deal." Nevertheless, the statement served the purpose I had envisioned. Three weeks later, when Gorbachev was trying to launch his peace initiative before the ground invasion, we used the joint statement to remind them of what they had already committed themselves to. I had been so raked over the coals at the time that I couldn't resist a modest bit of retaliation. At one meeting in February, at which several of my critics were present, I took the occasion to assume a deadpan expression and earnestly tell the President, "It's a good thing we got that statement." But in the weeks ahead, Gorbachev and the Arabists in his government would prove even more troublesome.

CHAPTER 22

GORBACHEV'S GAMBIT

If the [ground] war starts today, it will start and the whole world will see that it
has been started in circumstances where the USSR has indeed accomplished a
tremendous achievement to find a political settlement . . . then those who have
started it will take upon themselves the responsibility.

—Soviet envoy Yevgeny Primakov, February 23, 1991

I'm not here to create any division between us," my interlocutor insisted. "I'm not here to cause any problems." It was early in the afternoon of October 18, 1990. My visitor was Yevgeny Primakov, a Soviet
politician of no small skill and cunning, and I had every reason to be suspicious. A member of the Politburo, and the Foreign Ministry's ranking Arabist, he was a personal friend of, and apologist for, Saddam Hussein.

Primakov was in Washington to present to the President a Soviet peace
initiative he had persuaded Mikhail Gorbachev to embrace in hopes of ending the Gulf crisis. His visit personified the dual nature of Soviet behavior
throughout the Gulf crisis. At key moments, their diplomatic solidarity was
invaluable; indeed, the Soviet Union had at that time endorsed all nine
United Nations resolutions against Iraq and was steadfast in demanding
that Saddam withdraw from Kuwait.

And yet, once the air war began in January 1991, Soviet efforts to avoid
a ground war became without question our greatest political impediment.
Under the guise of restoring Soviet prestige in the world, Primakov sought
to curry favor with Gorbachev while embellishing his own position within
the Foreign Ministry and the Politburo. Diplomatically, his efforts were
aimed less at getting Saddam out of Kuwait unconditionally than at salvag-

ing the USSR's tattered patron-client relationship with Iraq. As a result, the United States now found itself occasionally working at cross purposes with its most important strategic partner in the crisis. By February 1991, Primakov's maneuverings complicated plans for an allied ground offensive to eject Iraq from Kuwait.

During Desert Shield, I had viewed Primakov's meddling with a mixture of annoyance and forbearance. His regional globe-trotting was a nuisance, but one we were willing to tolerate. Anyone and anything that could help us get Saddam out of Kuwait unconditionally without resorting to force was welcome. If anyone could breach Saddam's megalomaniacal delusions, it was Primakov, who had known him for more than two decades and was considered Saddam's favorite Soviet.

Besides, I rather liked Primakov personally. Shevardnadze, who had been a mentor of sorts, had originally vouched for Primakov, but came to resent his intrusion into Shevardnadze's domain. I'd met Primakov for the first time in Moscow in February of 1990, when I spoke before, and took questions from, the International Affairs Committee of the Supreme Soviet. Primakov was chairman of the committee. I got to know him better, however, in May of 1990, at an informal dinner Shevardnadze hosted at the home of his artist friend Zurab Tseretelli, whose daughter provided us with a huge Georgian meal. At the time, Shevardnadze and Primakov were close; diplomatic channels were filled with speculation that Shevardnadze would soon become Prime Minister and be replaced by Primakov. I assumed that by including Primakov as the only other dinner guest, Shevardnadze was signaling me that Primakov might soon be my counterpart. The three of us did serious damage to a half-gallon of Tarkhuna, a potent herb-flavored Georgian vodka that has the color of Scope mouthwash. I enjoyed Primakov's company that evening, and a succession of toasts to Soviet-American friendship, delivered in heavily accented English, led me to conclude that we were of basically one mind on the future direction of bilateral relations. In my subsequent meetings with Soviet officials, Primakov usually made a point of seeking me out for private dialogue in some quiet corner of the meeting room. He seemed committed to perestroika and loyal to Shevardnadze. He was smart, smooth, a good conversationalist, and knew his Arab history well. At the start of the crisis, I had believed Primakov was positioned to help reach a diplomatic settlement.

Primakov's October Surprise

By the time he arrived in Washington in October, however, my illusions had long since evaporated. Our efforts to keep the Soviets in tandem with U.S. diplomacy had been repeatedly threatened by Primakov's inclination toward protecting a Soviet client state. I suspected that he was among those Arabists attempting to water down the language of the first joint statement between Shevardnadze and me in early August. At Helsinki in September, he'd tried to eliminate language from a new joint statement that had already been agreed to by the President and Gorbachev. And he had abetted Saddam's strategy to weaken the Arab coalition by linking the Kuwaiti crisis with the larger Arab-Israeli conflict. Now, after personal lobbying, and against Shevardnadze's wishes, he'd persuaded Gorbachev to send him to Baghdad to broker a deal. There was little doubt that Primakov's plan was a wolf in sheep's clothing, more capitulation than compromise. Shevardnadze had warned me as much; in a private message delivered to Dennis Ross through Sergei Tarasenko, he had alerted me that he vigorously opposed the scheme Primakov was now laying before me. Shevardnadze felt betrayed by Primakov and humiliated by Gorbachev, who by allowing Primakov to peddle a peace initiative, had permitted him to usurp Shevardnadze's authority as Foreign Minister.

Primakov began with what would turn out to be the only words of encouragement I would hear. Gorbachev had instructed him to reaffirm that the Soviets would remain firmly in the political coalition. "Whatever happens, I can tell you we'll be with you," he assured me. But it was nevertheless crucial, he argued, to explore new proposals for reaching a peaceful outcome. I told Primakov that obviously this was a worthy goal, but not at the expense of principle. "We can't reward this behavior," I said. "Nothing less than unconditional withdrawal is acceptable." The President was always willing to listen to any ideas that might avoid bloodshed, but buying Saddam off was nonnegotiable.

"Well, I've known this guy for twenty-two years," Primakov said. "He's got a real Masada complex. If we put him in a corner, we'll have an explosion." If his only options were surrender or war, Saddam was sure to fight. "Threats of force will never dislodge him," Primakov said. I replied somewhat dryly that if threats of force were insufficient, then perhaps actual force would be required. "But a war will create an explosion that will be hard for any of us to recover from," he protested. "If it blows up, it will be terrible. So if we can avoid a war, we need to. Right now, he's painted into a corner. We've got to find a way out for him. I've seen him, and I have the sense that he won't just back down. But I think there's a way to construct an approach where we can get him out."

Briefly, Primakov sketched out what he described as "face-savers" in vague terms. It would be helpful if the United States would commit to an international conference after the war, to deal with the Palestinian question, he suggested. Perhaps Saddam should be allowed to keep two disputed islands and the Rumaila oil field. As interested parties, the Saudis might wish to negotiate the particulars with Iraq. He couldn't be certain, but he believed Saddam would find these terms acceptable and would then agree to withdraw from Kuwait voluntarily. Little wonder. It sounded like a formula Neville Chamberlain might have approved.

Paradoxically, Primakov's apocalyptic view of the war's aftermath would in fact be realized precisely if we gave Saddam the very out Primakov was suggesting. Saddam would continue to dominate the area and would be seen by the Arab masses as the greatest hero since Nasser. No Arab nation would be able to resist the power of a leader who had defied both superpowers. Saddam's triumph would surely embolden him to consider more aggression. Ultimately, the risk of a graver military conflagration in the future would be increased. Primakov's peace plan was a Potemkin village; he was simply trying to protect a client. There was no point in wasting any more time: I was scheduled to testify before the House Foreign Affairs Committee, and nothing in Primakov's face-savers warranted my late arrival on Capitol Hill.

"Well, why don't you continue your talks with Dennis, then he'll fill me in," I said. "But I find it hard to share your optimism. Everything you're suggesting is either a reward for him or will be seen as a reward for him."

Primakov was no fool. Sensing he was getting nowhere, he resurrected Gorbachev's pledge of continued support. "There will be no gap between us," he promised. "We'll support whatever you do. If it means war, so be it. But I think that would be a terrible mistake. I think it would radicalize the area. I think it would damage both of us."

The next morning, Primakov saw the President in the Oval Office. Primakov had been sufficiently chastened by his session with me and his subsequent meeting with Ross that his rhetoric had been muted considerably. I had to suppress a smile when I heard him tell the President that Saddam should not in any way be rewarded. His proposals had also taken on a more cautious tone overnight. But they still amounted to surrender. The President would never have agreed to any of it, but Primakov had the added misfortune of meeting with him just after he'd read a gruesome recounting of Iraq's atrocities in Kuwait compiled by Amnesty International, as well as a book detailing how Hitler's storm troopers had behaved when they occupied countries. Primakov wanted to start a dialogue, but he never had a chance. "They're just like the Nazis," the President said. "They go in there and they loot and they pillage, and we're not going to accept it. You give face-savers to someone who's part of the civilized world. We will not accept this kind of uncivilized behavior in this day and age." The President said he had no objection if Primakov wanted to visit Baghdad for another try at peace. "But tell Saddam that you found an absolute stone wall here."

The Primakov meeting was essentially a cosmetic affair, a courtesy to

Gorbachev to show that we took the Soviets seriously and needed their continued diplomatic cooperation. But Primakov could not be trusted to report our determination faithfully to Moscow, for fear of presiding over failure and thus losing bureaucratic standing. So after the meeting broke up, I suggested to the President that he contact Gorbachev directly to make sure he knew that while we were grateful for his assistance, in our view Primakov's plan was a disaster.

The Soviet Stakes—and Ours

During this period, Primakov's meddling was a major distraction for us— particularly since over time it quickly became obvious that neither he nor Gorbachev had sufficient influence with the Iraqis to moderate their behavior. They produced considerable noise, but to little effect.

On the other hand, a constructive bilateral relationship was vitally important to American strategic interests. Their cooperation was essential on such issues as arms control and European stability. Gorbachev had already been a good partner with us on German unification and in the Gulf. With constructive Soviet participation, reviving the Middle East peace process would be a less formidable task. We also needed their help in other regional conflicts, and it was important for the United States to support economic and political liberalization in the Soviet Union. For all these reasons, it was necessary for us to pay proper heed to Gorbachev. At a minimum, we would listen to his proposals and receive his envoys. I recall frequently observing throughout this period, "We don't want to rub his nose in it." The President was of like mind. In almost every one of his public statements, as well as his private conversations with Gorbachev, he was careful to say that he personally appreciated these efforts, which he privately considered wrong-headed but sincerely motivated. We both wanted to do whatever we could, moreover, to strengthen Gorbachev's tenuous standing at home. The fact that we listened to his proposals and tolerated Primakov's meddlesome initiatives so politely is quiet testimony to just how weak Gorbachev's position actually was.

For his own strategic interests, Gorbachev similarly recognized the necessity of remaining in the American orbit, no matter how personally distasteful he might have found it in this instance. America's continued economic and moral support was important to his controversial and painful program of economic reform. From a political standpoint, he knew the key to unlocking additional backing for his economic program in the months ahead lay in Washington. We had already interceded with the Saudis and other friends to come to Gorbachev's financial aid. In short, he owed us, and needed us. His impulse to remain coordinated with American policy on the Persian Gulf, however, was constantly buffeted by a myriad of countervailing pressures.

Geographically, Iraq was separated from the Soviet Union by only a few hundred miles of Turkish and Iranian territory. So from an emotional perspective, the war was essentially on the Soviet doorstep. Their anxiety in this regard would be roughly comparable to American concerns over a war in Central America, and thereby understandable.

Historically, until its invasion of Kuwait, Iraq had been a showcase Soviet client state. Five months later, that client was being pounded by the largest Western air offensive since World War II—and its former patron was a diplomatic party to the onslaught. This specter was bound to have been chilling to other Soviet client states, who no doubt wondered about the durability and credibility of their association with Moscow.

Militarily, Gorbachev was also under enormous pressure from his generals. The Iraqis had spared no expense in building up their conventional forces. Their modern Soviet equipment was even augmented by some sophisticated Western armaments. Their tactics, honed over the years by thousands of Red Army advisers, were the mirror image of Soviet combat doctrine. By early February, it was apparent that American weaponry and tactics in the air campaign were annihilating Saddam's army. Soviet officers had frequently boasted to American visitors in late 1990 that the Iraqi military would be a credible match for the coalition. In Helsinki, Marshal Sergei Akhromeyev had cautioned me, "You should not underestimate these boys. They will put up a very good fight, and it will not be easy." Now, Akhromeyev and other senior Soviet military officials had to be extremely nervous that a ground war would not simply defeat Saddam, but expose even more starkly the myth of Soviet military power.

The critical impact of internal chaos upon Soviet decision making during this period should not be underestimated. By the fall of 1990, perestroika was under serious assault. Shevardnadze had resigned in December, and Gorbachev's hold on power was becoming increasingly tenuous. On his left were the more radical reformers led by Boris Yeltsin, who were unimpressed by what they considered the leisurely pace of political and economic reform. They were also suspicious of Gorbachev's true commitment. More significant, Gorbachev was besieged by a conservative counteroffensive, which would culminate in the abortive June 1991 parliamentary coup and an attempted putsch two months later. The old guard had become increasingly restless. For them, the unification of Germany, the liberation of Eastern Europe, erosion of the Warsaw Pact, and the CFE treaty were symbols of Soviet capitulation. Iraq's abandonment helped push the conservatives over the brink. Inexorably, they coalesced against Gorbachev. The watershed event in the reemergence of the Soviet right was the January

1991 crackdown in Lithuania. Had Gorbachev been more firmly in control, I doubt whether a crackdown in the Baltic states would have occurred then.

All these tensions were occurring against the backdrop of Soviet self-delusion over its declining geopolitical status. During the 1973 Yom Kippur War, the Soviets had been bona fide participants. The theoretical prospect of a nuclear exchange between the two superpowers threatened to escalate that regional war into a global conflict. In the Gulf crisis, there was no longer even a theoretical prospect of this. The August 3 joint statement had neutralized their freedom of action from a military standpoint, and once the "all necessary means" resolution had been passed by the United Nations in late November, Soviet diplomacy had become far less significant in terms of shaping the final outcome, since there could be no negotiating down from the U.N. resolutions as far as we were concerned. The Arabists in the Soviet Foreign Ministry were beginning to fear that unless something were done to reverse this trend, the Soviets might soon be seen as an afterthought to American hegemony in the region.

In this respect, Primakov's interests coincided with Gorbachev's loftier ambitions to be a peacemaker. With the air war in full fury, the Gulf crisis was clearly an American show. At a minimum, however, a successful peace initiative that prevented a ground war would allow the Soviets to assert that they had shaped the outcome. And Gorbachev's increasing need to show that his crumbling union retained its stature in the international arena would be met.

Gorbachev's Diplomatic Offensive

Almost immediately, these various external considerations and internal pressures coalesced to push Gorbachev into seeking some solution for averting the ground war. Two days after the air campaign began, Gorbachev telephoned the President asking for a pause. The savagery of our attack was horrible, Gorbachev argued. Saddam had clearly gotten the message. Now it was time for the coalition to ease back and allow Soviet diplomacy to arrange a peaceful solution. The President replied that a pause would simply allow Saddam to boast about having once more stared down his enemies. The war would continue.

On February 10, citing "increasingly alarming and dramatic" developments in the Gulf, Gorbachev announced he was sending his personal emissary to Iraq in hopes of stopping the war. Two days later, Primakov arrived in Baghdad to present a plan to his old friend Saddam. The elements were deceptively simple: he urged Saddam to announce his willingness to withdraw from Kuwait, specifying a fixed period of time in which the withdrawal would occur. In exchange, he told Saddam, the coalition could be persuaded to agree on a cease-fire—a deal Primakov had no authority to offer and which was unacceptable on its face. The President had no intention of accepting a formula that walked back from the U.N. resolutions. Such an alternative was never discussed by us, not even in private.

I have no doubt that Primakov had sold this new peace initiative by telling Gorbachev that he could do his friend George Bush a huge political favor by saving the lives of thousands of American soldiers. Gorbachev was probably susceptible to this line of reasoning, since it also encouraged him to believe he could simultaneously preserve his relationship with the United States, shore up his shaky right flank by "saving" Iraq, and enhance his standing as a statesman of the first rank.

On February 15, Bessmertnykh telephoned me in the middle of a meeting with the President. I took the call in the small private study adjacent to the Oval Office. Bessmertnykh said that Gorbachev had just sent the President a letter laying out the particulars of Primakov's proposal. What's more, it was his view that Primakov had discovered some unspecified "encouraging elements in Saddam's behavior" which boded well for a possible breakthrough. In fact, Saddam was sending Tariq Aziz to Moscow to explore the matter with Gorbachev. I told him we would reserve judgment until we had received Gorbachev's letter.

Predictably, Bessmertnykh had attached a far more expansive interpretation to what Primakov had actually produced. And, not surprisingly, he had refrained from telling me that Gorbachev's letter contained a sentence which I knew was not acceptable the instant I read it: "It would not be desirable to conduct any massive ground operations, if they are being planned, during the period of the Moscow talks."

There was no need to debate our response. In a statement subsequently released in Baghdad, Saddam had agreed merely to consider a withdrawal. When the President read Gorbachev's letter, his reaction was succinct: "No way, Jose." Publicly, he dismissed the proposal as "a cruel hoax." I telephoned Bessmertnykh to reiterate the view that Primakov's scheme was a fraud. "We won't accept anything short of the U.N. resolutions without conditions," I told him. I agreed, however, that Saddam might finally have begun to appreciate the precariousness of his situation. "But we need proof," I added, and the only acceptable proof would be if Saddam stopped imposing conditions on any pullback. Bessmertnykh seemed taken aback by my vehemence. He said the Iraqis had in fact eased their position significantly and that the United States should be welcoming this development, not denouncing it.

Three days later, on the afternoon of February 18, Bessmertnykh telephoned again, with more ostensibly encouraging news. The talks between Gorbachev and Tariq Aziz had produced a comprehensive new peace proposal; a cable from Gorbachev would be in Washington within ninety minutes. Its elements, he assured me, were "within the limits of what we've discussed." Tariq Aziz was rushing back to Baghdad and had been asked to obtain a response from Saddam as soon as possible.

Later that afternoon, Chetverikov summarized Gorbachev's plan for me in a twenty-minute call. It had four key elements. First, Iraq would declare its willingness to withdraw and agree to a specific time to begin removing its troops. Second, the withdrawal would start the day after a cease-fire, and third, it would be unconditional. Finally, a point we had already pledged publicly: withdrawing Iraqi troops would not be attacked.

According to Chetverikov, when Tariq Aziz asked about the Arab-Israeli question, Gorbachev had replied that the Soviet Union would insist that the United Nations deal with "the whole complex of Middle East issues and conflicts, including the question of regional security." In the margin of my handwritten notes from this call, I scribbled a single comment: "hooker." Once again, the Soviets were playing with linkage. And the plan contained no provision for an exchange of prisoners of war and ignored the requirements of most of the other eleven U.N. resolutions.

The letter from Gorbachev noted that the Iraqis had responded to his proposals with "resentful objections." However, they had not rejected the plan outright, and had agreed to seek a prompt reply from Saddam. Gorbachev saw "a beginning of a certain shift in the understanding of realities by Hussein and his team."

Gorbachev then suggested that this new flexibility from Baghdad "should be taken into account in conducting the military operations in the next few days." The Iraqis had complained to him that "Baghdad had been subjected to particularly harsh strength at the time when the personal representative of the USSR President was staying there." Primakov was probably making the case to Gorbachev that the United States was more interested in attacking Iraq than making peace. In fact, we had undertaken the former to achieve the latter—for Kuwait and the region as a whole.

Gorbachev's plan contained some new elements; clearly, Saddam was beginning to behave as though he genuinely feared an American ground offensive. But it still wasn't sufficient. I told Chetverikov that we would not even consider the proposal unless Iraq formally agreed to all four points. The President then sent Gorbachev a letter declaring the plan unsatisfactory. Later that day, Tuesday, February 19, he publicly said that the plan "falls well short" of an acceptable solution.

I then called Bessmertnykh to emphasize that any withdrawal must *begin* with a cease-fire, not afterward, as Gorbachev had proposed, and that a POW exchange must occur twenty-four hours thereafter. "We genuinely fear Saddam Hussein will exploit any ambiguity," I said.

In a second "Dear Mikhail" letter sent the next day, the President let Gorbachev down as gently as possible. "I do appreciate your efforts," he wrote, "but I worry that perhaps incompleteness and ambiguities in your proposal may give heart to Saddam Hussein that he can somehow escape the consequences of his actions and obtain an unclear outcome, which he can exploit politically." This letter added a new condition: no cease-fire would be considered before the start of a "massive" Iraqi withdrawal, which must be concluded in ninety-six hours.

In discussions Wednesday afternoon and Thursday, the President's War Cabinet unanimously agreed to deliver a new ultimatum similar to the one we'd issued before launching the air war. After a flurry of telephone conversations with our major coalition allies on Thursday evening and early Friday morning, we were confident our partners were still on board.

But Gorbachev would not be deterred in his quest to prevent a ground war. On the morning of Friday, February 22, as final preparations for the offensive were being readied, he called the President with a refinement of his earlier proposal. The President and I had been assessing recent developments in the Oval Office when the call came in. He was late for a Rose Garden ceremony, and then was scheduled to attend Lynn Martin's swearing-in ceremony as Secretary of Labor. "You talk to him until I can finish this event," he told me. Neither of us had any idea the call would last for an hour and forty minutes.

"I wish to report to you on my urgent meetings with the Iraqi representatives," Gorbachev began. "Iraq has not agreed to these proposals, but Aziz believes Saddam Hussein will accept them." Iraq would now agree to an unconditional and immediate withdrawal—to begin the day after a cease-fire and to be completed in three weeks. Prisoners would be exchanged within three days of a cease-fire, and once the withdrawal was complete under U.N. Resolution 660, all other resolutions would be rescinded. In what he touted as an enormous concession, Gorbachev informed me that he had dropped his preference for linking the crisis to the Middle East peace process.

I pointed out that the withdrawal Gorbachev envisioned was neither immediate nor unconditional. Moreover, this plan would have given Iraq absolute immunity from a variety of sanctions, reparations, and liabilities imposed in other Security Council resolutions as a result of its invasion of Kuwait. The air war had finally pushed Saddam to the edge of reality. Now he wanted to be released from the other consequences of his unprovoked aggression. I told Gorbachev I didn't want to presume to speak for the President, but that I believed that he would find such terms still unacceptable.

Gorbachev wasn't pleased to hear this. "What is our priority?" he asked, in a brusque tone signaling his annoyance. "I have cooperated with you and tried to find a political role to protect your servicemen and the Iraqis. Our task is to find a tough but practical solution. They can't get out in one week." "They went into Kuwait in two days," I replied. When the President returned, Gorbachev repeated the particulars of his plan without avail. Having just been shown pictures of the Kuwaiti oil fields ablaze, the President was particularly offended that Gorbachev was in effect endorsing releasing Saddam from the requirements of all of the other U.N. resolutions. When Gorbachev asked him to give negotiations a few more days, he was in no mood to be generous. "This man will do anything," he complained. "They've set the oil fields afire. We cannot accept that." Gorbachev quickly retreated. "Look," he said, "I'm not defending him." At the end of the conversation, the President put down the telephone and said, simply, "It's totally unacceptable."

One Final Deadline

Within the hour, the President directed spokesman Marlin Fitzwater to issue one last ultimatum "in a final effort to obtain Iraqi compliance with the will of the international community." If a ground war were to be avoided, it stipulated, the Iraqis must agree to all previous U.N. resolutions, begin a full-scale withdrawal by noon New York time the next day, February 23, and complete their withdrawal within a week.

Afterward, the President asked me to join him at Camp David for the weekend. He said he wanted me there when the ground war began. I believe he had another purpose in mind as well. Over the previous month, I had absorbed a fair amount of anonymous criticism from sources in the White House upset with the Bessmertnykh joint statement. I believe it was the President's way, in his typically generous and unspoken fashion, of sending a signal that he did not share in the brickbats being directed at me. He reserved the right to be displeased with me in private, but felt that nobody else had that license, particularly publicly and anonymously.

Despite the President's rejection, Gorbachev attempted one final negotiating flurry. One half hour before 1:00 A.M. on February 23, Bessmertnykh woke me up in my bedroom at Birch Lodge to say that Tariq Aziz would shortly announce Iraq's commitment to an immediate and unconditional withdrawal, so there was no longer any reason for a ground war to begin. The President's ultimatum had "mixed things up," he said, but Soviet diplomacy had brought Saddam around. By now, we were talking past each other. Once more, I reminded Bessmertnykh that this prospective withdrawal offer was neither unconditional—eleven of the twelve U.N. resolutions were to be rescinded—nor immediate. "If Iraq could get into

Kuwait in two days," I suggested, "it can damn sure get out of Kuwait in less than three weeks."

Bessmertnykh's diplomatic reserve was beginning to crumble. "On the eve of a political and military victory," he complained, "our differences are only over legalistic matters. These are like lawyers arguing over words." I responded that our disagreement was substantive, not semantic, and that Saddam was using his talks with the Soviets as a cover for a scorched-earth campaign of destruction in Kuwait even as we spoke. We would not settle for less than full implementation of all U.N. resolutions and full acceptance of the President's terms. If necessary, I said we would also publicly reject Gorbachev's call for a Security Council meeting unless Iraq agreed to our terms in full and began withdrawing. It was apparent to me that for all their alleged influence, the Soviets had still been unable to persuade the Iraqis to agree to anything more than a bare minimum.

Saddam's intractability was a recurring theme of the crisis, one which foiled Gorbachev's peacemaking tendencies and made our task less difficult. To the very end, the Iraqis were just as inflexible with the Soviets as they had been with us in Geneva. Whenever the Arabists appeared to regroup and persuade Gorbachev to authorize some new dialogue, the Iraqis thwarted their traditional benefactors. Consistently, the Iraqis were their own worst enemy. They could have easily complicated our efforts with even some fairly modest gestures. In particular, a partial withdrawal from Kuwait might well have forced us to consider postponing the ground campaign and would have made it infinitely more difficult to keep the Soviets in the coalition.

Gorbachev was relentless. In midafternoon, after the deadline had passed but before ground operations had actually begun, the President and I were interrupted during a game of wallyball, an exhausting variation of volleyball played on a racquetball court. Gorbachev was calling with one final plea. The President took the call in the tiny fitness center. I sat with him on a bench in the men's locker room while he talked. Gorbachev suggested that the differences between the American and Soviet positions had been reduced to "details." Surely a few more days of negotiations were preferable to the carnage of ground combat, he suggested. The President was polite but very firm. He appreciated Gorbachev's efforts, but Saddam was playing games. If Gorbachev were talking with the Iraqis anytime soon, he suggested, he should remind them that the deadline which had just expired should be considered just as credible as the earlier deadline for the onset of the air war. Gorbachev understood the implicit message of the President's "suggestion."

A few minutes later, at 3:25 P.M., Bessmertnykh called me again. We talked for twenty-two minutes. He had been listening in on Gorbachev's call to the President. "We now have the chance to stop the coffins coming home from the Persian Gulf," he pleaded. I complimented Bessmertnykh on what I called a "noble purpose." The President appreciated Gorbachev's efforts. But a fundamental difference remained: we believed Saddam would never leave unless forced out. "They still want to trade," I said. "We have to convince them the bazaar is not open. They have to stand up and say they're beaten and are leaving. They cannot continue trying to trade." Bessmertnykh received this brush-off glumly.

Later that evening, I returned to Washington with the President, who was going to speak to the nation about the beginning of the ground war. At 9:50 P.M., I called Bessmertnykh from the State Department to inform him that ground operations had been in effect for nearly an hour. At 10:00 P.M., the President would publicly announce this, but he had asked that I inform the Soviets in advance as a courtesy. "I regret hearing this news," Bessmertnykh said. I thanked him for his efforts and said I would look forward to working with him in happier circumstances in the future. The call lasted only a single minute; there was really nothing more to say. Bessmertnykh was resigned, and bitterly disappointed at having been unable to stop what he was convinced was a terrible mistake.

As I had done when the air war began, I quickly notified other allies, including the Secretary-General of the United Nations, the Prime Minister of Italy, the Secretary-General of NATO, and the foreign ministers of Spain, the Netherlands, Syria, Japan, Israel, and Luxembourg. Israeli Ambassador Zalman Shoval, clearly delighted with the news, asked if we intended to overthrow Saddam. We had no intention of expanding our war aims or political aims, I replied. But if the Iraqi people drove Saddam from power, "we would not weep."

A Swift Conclusion

Although in many respects it was anticlimactic, I was frankly more nervous about the start of ground operations. The air war had gone far better than anyone had anticipated; only twenty-seven U.S. aircraft had been lost in combat, a figure some had predicted we would lose on the war's first night. I was concerned, however, that casualties could be substantial once we sent two corps of American armor and infantry hurtling into Iraq and Kuwait. The military was still fearful the Iraqis would use chemical weapons against attacking forces, and I knew that, by definition, ground combat would be riskier and inevitably costlier in terms of lives than aerial warfare. I remember at one point looking out my seventh-floor window across the Potomac

River to Arlington National Cemetery. I wondered how many more brave young Americans would soon be lying beneath those hallowed slopes.

There had been no internal debate on the necessity of a ground war to achieve both our war aims and our political aims. All of us would have preferred to avoid a ground campaign if it had been possible. As a former combat aviator, however, the President was particularly aware of the limits of airpower, and he was not interested in second-guessing his generals, who believed there was no alternative.

The preliminary planning for a ground war had not been reassuring. Frequently, in fact, Cheney, Scowcroft, and I had privately complained about a marked reluctance early on within the Pentagon to the use of force to achieve political or diplomatic objectives. As White House Chief of Staff during the first Reagan term, I had heard senior defense officials frequently argue against committing our troops even in places like Grenada. Much has been written about this phenomenon. The first operations plan submitted by the Pentagon in the fall of 1990 reflected this mentality. It was a fighting plan, Scowcroft had dryly observed, designed to show why we shouldn't fight. Its centerpiece was an assault into the teeth of the Iraqi defenses in Kuwait. We called it the Washington Monument plan: straight up the middle. Our troops would have been ground up, and casualties would have been enormous. It was pressure from Cheney and Scowcroft that led to what became enshrined as the "left hook" plan, a bold flanking maneuver into the desert of western Iraq.

Whenever the offensive option was discussed, the Pentagon understandably wanted more men and arms. Cheney's strategy, supported by Scowcroft and me, was to recommend that the President accede to every request. The deployment of six aircraft carriers, a Marine division, a second Army corps from Germany, and the activation of at least 157,000 reservists were all designed to reinforce the credibility of our commitment and produce a quick and overwhelming victory. It had the additional result of ensuring that any reservations on the part of the military were eliminated.

The President had given them whatever assets they needed, and the final war scenario was a brilliant scheme of maneuver. Now satisfied they could do the job, our military leaders were optimistic about the ability of our forces to finish the war quickly with minimum loss of life. We were also reassured by intelligence reports from Marine patrols who had breached Iraqi lines under cover of darkness. Iraqi forward trenches, they found, were either empty or full of bodies. When the attack came, Powell told us, enemy defenses would quickly collapse. I knew we would win, but I confess to being much less convinced the outcome would be as clean or as swift as we were then being told, particularly in view of earlier casualty estimates.

In the end, the optimism was well founded. The ground assault, launched in the predawn darkness of February 24, was a phenomenal success. Iraq's forces were routed, and American casualties were gratifyingly light. Within forty-eight hours, organized resistance was crumbling throughout the theater of operations. The President announced that the war would continue, but that coalition forces would not attack unarmed soldiers in retreat.

On the morning of February 27, we gathered in the Oval Office to assess the situation. The general view among us all was that we had achieved both our war and political aims. I remember Colin Powell saying with a trace of emotion, "We're killing literally *thousands* of people"—Iraqis trying to escape along the "highway of death." The President telephoned Norm Schwarzkopf, who agreed that our war aims had been achieved. That night, the President announced a cease-fire after 100 hours of fighting.

Six weeks after it had begun, Desert Storm was over. The President had made good on his simple pledge that "this will not stand." The first test of the post–Cold War order had ended with American power and diplomacy triumphant. Iraq had been chastened, its strategic threat to regional security largely diminished. Unfortunately, events would quickly prove that Saddam was defeated, but would remain in power.

CHAPTER 23

A POSTWAR VISION FOR THE MIDEAST

We must now begin to look beyond victory and war. We must meet the challenge of securing the peace.
—*From President Bush's Address to the Nation, Washington, D.C., February 27, 1991*

I t was an incredible scene straight from Dante's *Inferno*. As I flew from Taif to Kuwait City on the afternoon of March 9, 1991, less than two weeks after the end of Desert Storm, I could not believe what I saw from the windows of our Air Force jet. The normally brilliant desert sky had been transformed into an eerie darkness by billowing clouds of sulfurous smoke from more than six hundred oil-well fires that had been ignited by Iraqi forces before retreating from Kuwait. For more than a hundred miles, these fires raged out of control. Some were plumes of flame thrusting thousands of feet into the air like fiery orange geysers. Others bubbled up through tiny crevices in the earth for what seemed to be miles on end. By the time we landed at a burned-out Kuwait International Airport, the scene of a fierce firefight between U.S. Marines and Iraqi troops, our gleaming silver jet was covered by a greasy film of oil.

As I peered from the window of my cabin, I found this wanton and deliberate act of destruction difficult to comprehend. I couldn't help but wonder how anyone could order such an uncivilized thing. I remember thinking I'd seen oil-well fires before in Texas—but never *anything* to compare with this. I was so struck by this horrific spectacle that I would later cable the President that I had just seen "a colossal waste and a colossal environmental disaster. Iraq should pay for it."

Before landing, we circled to the north over Highway 6, the main road between Kuwait City and Basra, where coalition pilots had caught retreating Iraqi soldiers in the open on the last day of the war. I saw literally hundreds of burned-out tanks, artillery pieces, personnel carriers, even civilian automobiles that had been commandeered by the Iraqis. When burning vehicles blocked the asphalt, the Iraqis had frantically driven into the desert, where they were even easier prey. For hundreds of yards on either side of the road, wreckage was strewn throughout the sands in a pattern resembling a reverse funnel. Little wonder that it was quickly termed the Highway of Death.

And yet I sensed that this apocalyptic horror of almost Biblical proportions obscured something more positive: the seeds of hope for a region where dreams of peace and reconciliation had been cruelly thwarted for centuries. For all the devastation spread out beneath our flight path, I believed the invasion of Kuwait and its liberation by an American-led coalition had established a dramatic new reality in the region. Arab radicalism had been discredited, thus strengthening the hand of moderate Arab nations such as Egypt and Saudi Arabia. In defeating Iraq, the United States had earned the deep gratitude of all of the Gulf Arabs. At the same time, we had also neutralized the gravest threat to Israel's security. The Soviet Union, long a force for trouble in the area, was now a partner of American diplomacy. And American credibility internationally was higher than at any time since the end of World War II.

It was apparent to me that the Gulf War had created an unprecedented window of opportunity to pursue the possibility of peace between Israel and her Arab neighbors. As Dennis Ross was fond of observing, "We've just seen an earthquake. We have to move before the earth resettles, because it will, and it never takes long." Given the painful history of Mideast diplomacy, I found this analogy particularly compelling.

I was not at all certain we would be able to take advantage of this rare opening. Primordial hatreds would not be as easily conquered as Iraq's military forces had been. Yet I felt very strongly that the effort had to be undertaken. American diplomacy had come close to achieving a breakthrough in 1989–90 under far less favorable circumstances. Our leverage was now infinitely more potent. More significant, it would almost certainly never be so great again.

A Postwar Vision

In testimony to the congressional foreign affairs committees on February 6 and 7, 1991, I had given some inkling of my thoughts about a revived peace process after the war. The committees and the media, however, paid scant attention to that portion of my remarks. They were far more interested in exploring the progress of the air campaign, in demanding reparations from Iraq after the war, and in criticizing Germany and Japan for not contributing more financial assistance to the coalition's effort.

The primary purpose of my testimony was to sketch out in preliminary fashion the President's vision of the postwar Gulf. A revived peace process was the fourth pillar in a five-part agenda to stabilize the balance of power in the region, prevent a resurgence of Iraqi expansionism, and, in my words, to "secure the peace" that we were then in the process of winning, for future generations.

The agenda also included new regional security arrangements, including an Arab peacekeeping force bolstered by an expanded U.S. naval presence in the area; regional arms control agreements to halt the proliferation of conventional weapons and prevent Iraq from rebuilding its weapons of mass destruction program; an ambitious plan for economic reconstruction; and new conservation efforts to reduce American dependence on oil.*

The most controversial aspect of my testimony was the assertion that a post-Saddam Iraq should be included in postwar efforts to build a more stable region. "The time for reconstruction and recovery should not be the occasion for vengeful actions against a nation forced to war as a result of a dictator's ambition," I argued. "The secure and prosperous future everyone hopes to see in the Gulf has got to include Iraq."

On the second day of my testimony, I unveiled the idea of a Middle East Development Bank in my remarks to the Senate Foreign Relations Committee. This bank would collect funds from the more prosperous countries of the region to finance economic development in the region. I advanced this idea without the approval of the Treasury Department, which was cool to it. When the President later publicly stated that U.S. money would not be spent on rebuilding Iraq, the development bank became stillborn. It was a classic case of planting a very good and farsighted idea before it was ready.

I still believe the entire agenda was a worthy concept, notable for its vision and optimism. The development bank in particular was a creative solution. The Middle East, a land of disproportionate wealth, remains the only area of the world without one. With appropriate conditions on any aid to rebuild Iraq (i.e., a post-Saddam Iraq), the bank is *still* a good idea, and I wasn't surprised when it was resurrected by the Clinton administration in 1994.

Unfortunately, as subsequent events have demonstrated, the frame-

---

*The energy pillar was a late addition to the agenda primarily in irritated reaction to a *Washington Post* article that had revealed a four-part agenda several days before my testimony. It was also designed to prod the bureaucracy into engaging on the issue. This injection of a domestic subject into a proposed foreign policy agenda raised a few eyebrows at the White House.

work I sketched out that day was in large measure unfulfilled, with the notable exception of the peace process. The Gulf states initially supported, then quietly walked away from, the idea of an Arab peacekeeping force. In truth, the security of the Gulf today rests squarely where it did before Desert Storm—on the United States.

In part, the demise of this postwar agenda was the result of our underestimating Saddam Hussein's durability. Much of our planning in this regard was predicated on the assumption that Saddam would not survive in power. When he consolidated his authority in the months after the end of hostilities, much of the agenda's rationale was undermined.

During my testimony, I had committed the administration to trying to revive the peace process. "Let's not fool ourselves," I told the House Foreign Affairs Committee. "The course of this crisis has stirred emotions among Israelis and Palestinians that will not yield easily to reconciliation." Nevertheless, I added, "there may be opportunities for peace—if the parties are willing." Three weeks later, Desert Storm was over. It was now time to explore whether such opportunities in fact existed.

The collapse of my first effort at peace-process diplomacy in the spring of 1990 had left me disappointed and somewhat resigned to the conclusion that there was little hope for progress in the foreseeable future. I remember telling myself afterward that my initial reluctance to get involved had been well founded, and that I should have heeded my own counsel. Now, despite the success of American diplomacy, as well as the war itself, some respected voices still believed that American capital should not be expended on the issue. Three days before I left for the Middle East, in fact, one internal memorandum reflecting the views of Harvey Sicherman, a solid member of my Policy Planning Staff, offered this rather downbeat assessment of the situation: "What we have is a brief moment to rearrange some of the furniture in the bawdy house in the hope of making it more comfortable."

My own assessment, however, had been fundamentally altered by the war. As a practical matter, I felt we would be properly criticized if we didn't undertake a renewed effort. In putting together the diplomatic and military coalition against Iraq, I had repeatedly pledged that the United States would address the larger issues of the Middle East after the crisis had been resolved. In large measure, this promise had enabled me to repel efforts to link the invasion of Kuwait with the Arab-Israeli dispute. Having given my word in this regard, I felt a moral obligation to follow through.

There was little doubt that the environment in the region had been drastically altered. It was also apparent that the entire world suddenly wanted to get closer to the United States. The Soviet Empire was gone. The principles and values of the American experience—democracy and free markets—were being embraced around the globe as never before. It seemed as though everyone wanted to be America's best friend. Although we didn't do a good job of explaining the concept, this worldwide advance of democratic ideals represented what we really meant by the phrase "new world order"—not the absence of regional conflicts, as most interpreted it. Our status as the last remaining superpower had been enhanced by the war. We had tremendous strength and credibility around the world, and stood at the zenith of our influence in the Middle East. I believed it was time to seize the moment. If we hesitated, we would lose an historic opportunity.

Brent Scowcroft was initially opposed to the idea. For many of the same reasons which had led me to avoid a peace initiative in the early months after I became Secretary of State, Scowcroft believed any effort was destined to fail. His view was that Israel was the main stumbling block to peace, and that we could not convince Yitzhak Shamir to abandon his staunch opposition to opening a dialogue with the Palestinians. "I just don't think anything can come of it," he said in one of our meetings with the President. "Do we really want to launch something where there's no real chance of success?"

I knew the President was eager for me to try; he had mentioned it to me on several occasions. When I raised it with him in February, he wholeheartedly approved my plan. But if Scowcroft remained opposed to a new initiative, it would make success that much harder to achieve. So I asked my deputy Larry Eagleburger to pay him a visit. In characteristically blunt language, Eagleburger told him that if I were willing to make the effort, he should not oppose it. Eagleburger's friendly démarche to his colleague of long standing worked, and Brent agreed.

The Two-Track Concept

I had learned several important lessons from my previous experience with the peace process. It was now obvious to me, for instance, that any new American initiative would fail if it merely resurrected the diplomatic status quo. A fresh attempt to create a dialogue between the Israelis and Palestinians, as we had done in 1989, would prove both shortsighted and fruitless. During the war, some Palestinians had stood on rooftops cheering as Iraqi Scuds struck Israel's cities. As a result, Israel's position had hardened. As a practical matter, I knew it would be virtually impossible to persuade Shamir to engage the Palestinians without some other inducement. Any new initiative would require an Arab state dimension.

I had also learned another important lesson about how best to deal with Shamir. He was enormously ambivalent. He wished to be a peacemaker, but he was also a "settler," whose policies in the West Bank made peace more difficult. I concluded that the only way to deal with this was to devise some formula which would put him in a position in which he could no longer say no to new initiatives.

The best way to take advantage of the moment, I concluded, was to devise a means of breaking the taboo on direct talks, which had existed since the very creation of Israel in 1948. The Egyptian-Israeli peace treaty of 1979 had not really altered this grim barrier to progress. Other than Egypt, Arab governments simply would not deal directly with Israelis. It was maddeningly simple: you can't make peace if you won't talk. To my mind, we now had our best chance, and possibly our last, to assault this barrier.

In consultation with my senior advisers, I decided that we would try a two-track approach. We would attempt to restart a process leading to an Israeli-Palestinian dialogue, although we recognized that the question of Palestinian representation would ultimately be the most difficult issue of all to resolve. Simultaneously, however, we would propose a second track— direct talks between Israel and the Arab states in the form of a regional conference on the Mideast cosponsored by the United States and Soviet Union, where all the parties would be represented. This format was a calculated exercise in creative ambiguity. The Arabs could claim that this *was* the international conference they had long sought. Similarly, Israel could contend that it was nothing more than the face-to-face discussions they had wanted for forty years, no different than the 1973 Geneva talks in which they had participated, and *not* the larger international conference sponsored by the United Nations that they had consistently opposed.

For the second track to have any chance of success, I would have to persuade both sides that the other side had undergone a significant change in attitude. For this reason, I decided to propose what came to be known as the concept of parallel reciprocity. I would ask Israel and her Arab neighbors to consider certain confidence-building measures as a means of demonstrating that both sides were now willing to break new ground in a quest for peace. I knew that each side would need something from the other for purposes of political cover. The Arabs would have to justify any moves toward Israel by pointing to Israeli flexibility toward the Palestinians. Similarly, the Israelis would have to put any concessions to the Palestinians in the context of a larger reconciliation with Arab states. Moreover, neither side would be willing to move first. Parallel reciprocal steps, I believed, was the logical solution to this impasse.

This would be a high-risk undertaking, but I believed it could be done. My calculation was grounded in the assumption that it would be extremely difficult for the Arabs to say no to the United States after all we had done for them in Desert Storm. I also believed they would not be able to sit on the sidelines, as they had done in 1989. For their own reasons, they now had to demonstrate that they, too, cared about the Palestinian cause. With the

Arab radicals discredited and in disarray, I further believed that Saudi Arabia and the other Gulf Arabs would feel more naturally confident and thus might be willing to take greater risks. And with his Soviet patrons now American partners instead of competitors, Assad might also be prepared to be more flexible.

If I could persuade the Arab states to agree to direct talks, I believed that eventually Shamir could not to refuse to go along, since for over forty years Israel had said she wanted direct negotiations with her Arab neighbors. While my previous experiences had taught me just how difficult it would be to work with Shamir, I also believed he wanted to be the Prime Minister who actually began a process that would someday bring peace to Israel.

Testing the Waters

Since I believed that Shamir was the more immediate hurdle, it was important to demonstrate first that the Gulf War had caused a dramatic change in Arab attitudes. For that reason, I decided that Saudi Arabia should be the first stop on a ten-day, seven-country itinerary that included talks in Moscow and Ankara. In all of my talks in Saudi Arabia, Kuwait, Israel, Egypt, and Syria, I made the case that the United States was prepared to be what the President had called a "catalyst for peace"—but not unless all the parties were willing to take risks. After explaining the two-track concept in detail, I pressed each of my interlocutors to support it, and asked whether they would consider taking conciliatory steps if their counterparts were willing to do likewise.

After arriving in Riyadh on the morning of March 8, I met with Norm Schwarzkopf, who was exuberant over the success of the war, and emphatic in his belief that American troops had done their job and should not be asked to stay in the region one day longer than necessary. "We need to be out of here sooner rather than later," he told me. I told him he didn't have to worry about that; the President had promised an early withdrawal, and I had pledged the same to the Soviets.

Before seeing the King, I met over dinner with Foreign Minister Prince Saud and Prince Bandar. In the aftermath of the coalition's victory, I found them all feeling very comfortable—not only about their position in the region but also with the enhanced bilateral relationship. They were nonetheless troubled that Saddam remained in power despite his defeat. I outlined our plans to keep U.N. sanctions in place to ensure that Saddam could no longer threaten his neighbors. The Saudis were not entirely assuaged by my assurances.

After an expanded meeting, I later met with King Fahd privately to discuss the peace process. "We can take great satisfaction in what we have accomplished together," I said. "But we cannot rest on our achievements in war. Now we must put just as much energy and determination into securing the peace. I do not wish to sound arrogant or immodest," I said, "but the United States has gained credibility on both sides of the Arab-Israeli issue. We are prepared to spend this credit. We are prepared in the aftermath of the war to roll up our sleeves and work just as hard to achieve Arab-Israeli peace as we did to defeat Saddam.

"But let me be very frank: we can work to affect Israel's positions, and shape new opportunities for peace, *only* if you are equally committed to moving forward. That means you have to help give us the means to deliver. We cannot and will not do it on our own." The King seemed unusually pensive, listening carefully and occasionally nodding his head.

I outlined my idea of a two-track approach and listed a variety of confidence-building measures that both Saudi Arabia and Israel might consider. I suggested that the Saudis could drop the economic boycott of Israel, reject the 1975 U.N. resolution equating Zionism with racism, end the formal state of belligerency with Israel, meet with Israeli officials at a low level, or quietly exchange intelligence information on terrorist activities. In turn, I was prepared to urge Shamir to respond in kind by, among other things, halting the deportation and administrative detention of Palestinians in the occupied territories and withdrawing the Israeli army from certain towns in the West Bank and Gaza Strip. I assured the King that any prospective concessions on his part would be held in the strictest confidence. "You must trust me enough to tell me what you can do," I said, "and know I won't put it on the table publicly without knowing what you get in return from Israel."

I told the King in all frankness that I needed something from him with which to leverage Shamir. "The President and I are willing to do our part," I pledged, "and that includes frank discussions with the Israelis. But we need something to work with. What are you prepared to do? What can I say to the Israelis?

"I ask you again to put your trust in me and the President. This is the time to break old taboos and generate a breakthrough for peace. Without it, the odds are high that the Arab world might well return to old assumptions and patterns of behavior. That would justify Israel's refusal to change, and I fear that an historic opportunity to make progress would disappear."

Traditionally, the Saudis preferred a certain timidity in these peace-process matters, but as the King began responding to my remarks, I sensed a sea change in his tone, a confidence that had not been present during my four meetings with him during the crisis. For the first time, he seemed prepared to adopt a leadership position on the peace process. He confided something I had never heard from him before: if a homeland could be found for the Palestinians, he was prepared to approve full economic and diplomatic relations with Israel.

"What you have just said, Mr. Secretary, is what is in my heart," he replied. "I want once and for all to reach a settlement of the Arab-Israeli problem. The Palestinian-Israeli problem is the main headache in the region, the crux of all our problems. It gives Saddam and others, like Qaddafi, material on which to promote themselves. It should no longer linger on. It must be solved."

As I had expected, the King was reluctant to commit to any specific actions, but he acknowledged that it was important to give me something to use with Israel, and promised me an answer before I left the kingdom.

"I consider this one of the best nights of my life," he concluded. "Allah might well have desired Saddam's crisis to serve as a springboard from which to solve this greater problem. Had Saddam Hussein not rejected all of the President's offers prior to January 15, we might never have come to the moment of opportunity now before us."

The King's response was so encouraging in tone that I sent this message to the President: "The proof is in the pudding, and we're a long ways from being able to eat it. But I think it's fair to say that we've piqued their interest."

The next morning, I flew to Taif to visit the Emir of Kuwait, who had not yet returned to his country. I suggested as delicately as I could that it would be wise for him to return home soon to deal with the criticism prompted by his absence. He was clearly still rattled by the invasion and pillage of his homeland, and nervous that the threat from Iraq had not been totally eradicated. He preferred that U.S. military forces remain in Kuwait in large numbers indefinitely. I explained to him that the President believed it was inappropriate to establish a permanent American ground force in the region, but that several thousand troops would remain for a transitional period.

The Emir was far less receptive to my ideas for reviving the peace process. He said that parallel steps were unlikely unless proposed by the U.N. Security Council. I reminded him that the U.S. relationship with Israel made us the only country with substantial influence with them. "Using the U.N., Your Highness," I suggested, "will remove *any* chance of influencing Israel." As we talked, I found myself increasingly unhappy about the Emir's seeming intransigence, particularly since we had just liberated his country. (Shortly thereafter, it should be noted, Kuwait became far more supportive of our efforts and of the peace process.)

Fortunately, his reluctance was not shared by the Crown Prince, whom I met that afternoon in Kuwait City at the residence of a wealthy businessman instead of at the royal palace, which had been damaged during the fighting. The city showed signs of fierce combat. Many buildings were bombed out, and the gutted hulks of Iraqi armor and unusually tight security were grim reminders of battle. In our meeting, the Crown Prince was considerably more positive toward my proposals than his cousin. His reaction was far closer in spirit to that of King Fahd. "The time to move is now," he said, "and we have an opportunity to do so."

I returned to Riyadh and on March 10 met with the foreign ministers of the Gulf Cooperation Council, a confederation of Saudi Arabia and the smaller Gulf states. Also attending were the foreign ministers of Egypt and Syria. The council was unanimously supportive of the President's agenda for regional stability. Privately, they were even more enthusiastic. The Emir of Bahrain told me he wanted an American naval presence for another fifty years. Another foreign minister told me that his country was prepared to grant the United States "anything you need." The reaction of Syrian Foreign Minister Farouk al-Shara was even more significant, however. Shara privately told me that if the Israelis would permit new elections in the occupied territories, Syria and its neighbors would use their considerable leverage to press for the election of a new breed of Palestinian representative more supportive of the peace process.

It was apparent by then that the moderate Arab states, in particular the Saudis, seemed interested in exerting a greater leadership role on regional security issues and the peace process. This was confirmed to me before I left Riyadh, when King Fahd sent me word via Bandar that he supported the two-track approach in principle, and would consider specific steps depending upon Shamir's reaction. I cabled the news to the President immediately, adding this thought: "The basis for this improved Arab attitude is the extraordinary credibility we now have in the area. American standing has never been higher, and the Arabs are impressed enough with the United States' ability to deliver on its word to grant us some room to move forward."

In Cairo, I found President Mubarak in a splendid mood. Within an instant, it was clear he was firmly with the United States. He repeatedly emphasized the importance of his relationship with the President. It was invaluable, he said, to be able to pick up the phone and talk with George Bush. At that point, he actually picked up his telephone and telephoned President Assad in Damascus. Obviously for my benefit, he told Assad that we were the best administration the region had ever had to deal with. "If progress isn't made with this administration," he said, "it will not be made." It was essential, he said, that Assad give me "something to work with" when I visited him. Assad replied that he was looking forward to my visit and would engage seriously. Mubarak supported the two-track concept, but he was not particularly enthused with the idea of a regional conference, and he remained skeptical that any such initiative would ever be accepted by Israel. "Shamir will never change," Mubarak said. "He's not interested in peace." He repeated this dour assessment several times in the conversation.

The Israeli Reaction

From Cairo I flew to Israel, and arrived in Tel Aviv shortly before 3:00 P.M. The day before, four women had been stabbed to death in Jerusalem by a Palestinian terrorist. The murderer had described his act as a personal message to me. Tensions were inflamed as a result of the tragedy, and on the advice of my security agents I reluctantly canceled a walking tour of the Old City with Mayor Teddy Kollek. The next afternoon, in an unsuccessful effort to be unobtrusive out of respect for the families, I drove unannounced to the Givat Shaul Cemetery accompanied only by Dennis Ross and Margaret Tutwiler, to pay my respects at the graves of the four victims. The Israeli press, however, monitors the police frequencies and, overhearing that we were there, hordes of press showed up. The savagery and suddenness of the deaths of these four women starkly brought home to me the human component of the Mideast tragedy, an element all too often obscured by the intensity of the political debate. It was impossible not to be touched and deeply troubled by the experience.

Notwithstanding our previous problems with the Shamir government, I was impressed by the warmth of the welcome on my first visit to Israel. I remember being struck by the neatness of the country, and the stark beauty of the drive up from Tel Aviv to Jerusalem. Susan and I were moved to tears by our visit to Yad Vashem, the searing memorial to the victims of the Holocaust. And as I flew north for an aerial inspection of the Golan Heights, I was able to visualize for the first time Israel's acute sense of vulnerability. From my helicopter, I could see the entire breadth of the country, from the Mediterranean to the west to its border with its enemies to the east. I also thought about the impact of technology on security. The Golan was without question a critical piece of terrain. But as the Scud missiles which struck Israel from hundreds of miles away had demonstrated during the war, Israeli occupation of the heights no longer provided an absolute guarantee against attack from the northeast.

That evening I had dinner with David Levy, the Israeli Foreign Minister. I came away from this first meeting believing that Levy was more moderate and flexible than his boss. Although as a "constraints minister" he'd helped kill my earlier efforts, I sensed in Levy a politician who was now prepared to define himself and his future in terms of the peace issue. I remember at one point suggesting that Arab states rigidly opposed to Israel were now talking peace. "We will talk peace with anyone," Levy assured me. He was totally political and rather impulsive. After our meeting and before I had even met with Shamir, he told reporters that we were on the road to peace! But I came to view Levy as a realist willing to take some risks for peace and to push Shamir, Arens, and others in the same direction.

At eight-thirty the next morning, I met with Shamir. I began by thanking him for his restraint during the war and reaffirming the President's commitment to maintaining Israel's military superiority. Israel's security was nonnegotiable, I reiterated. But I urged him to take advantage of what I called "new opportunities and attitudes" in the region, particularly on the part of Saudi Arabia. "The moderate Arabs of the coalition have demonstrated their worth as partners," I said. "To make progress with them, you have to help them on the Palestinian issue. There will never be a better time to move than now, when the radicals are weak and discredited, when our Arab friends feel strong and confident, when American credibility is at its height." I told Shamir that for the first time I had found King Fahd willing to exert leadership for peace. He was skeptical, reminding me of traditional Saudi reticence in such matters. But when I revealed that the King had told me, "We know there is a state of Israel, and no one could or more importantly *should* deny it," it seemed to have a noticeable effect on him.

"Frankly, Mr. Prime Minister," I said, "the Saudis are not reacting in their traditional cautious way. I believe it's a new day. You are a leader with a chance to seize a strategic moment in history for Israel and the Jewish people, and I want to help you. As long as I have something to work with, I can hold off the Europeans, the Soviets, and others for an international conference. But I need some help."

As I had done in my meetings with Arab leaders, I enumerated my list of confidence-building measures that both sides should ponder. I urged him to consider less oppressive policies in the occupied territories, to declare a willingness to meet Palestinians without new elections, and to think about withdrawing from southern Lebanon within six to twelve months, if during that period we could see to it that there were no terrorist attacks against northern Israel. It was also important, I said, to ponder a commitment to begin negotiations about the Golan Heights with Syria.

Predictably, Shamir was more interested in talking about what the Arabs should do. At a minimum, he insisted, they should suspend the economic boycott and recognize Israel's right to exist. Nevertheless, he made several particularly interesting comments. He accepted my contention that the concept of "autonomy" for residents of the territories was "a loaded term" for the Palestinians. "We need to find more effective terminology," he said at one point. He reacted favorably to my suggestion that "self-government" was perhaps a more useful semantic formulation, especially when I noted that "the Saudis liked the term when I tried it out on them in Riyadh." I was also encouraged by his insistence that the United States should do everything possible to keep King Hussein in power despite his support for Saddam Hussein during the war. A stable Jordan, he said, was crucial to long-term prospects for peace.

Shamir said he realized that negotiations had to move beyond interim steps for self-rule and work out a permanent status for Palestinians in the territories. He repeated his 1989 proposal for a timetable, in which permanent status talks could begin three years after interim arrangements had been implemented. While Shamir clearly was not prepared to modify his opposition to the concept of land for peace, this was a far cry from his traditional position of refusal even to discuss permanent status.

The idea of a conference had some appeal for Shamir, who said he would consider a regional conference with Egypt, Jordan, Saudi Arabia, and Syria. But he opposed a conference with Soviet co-sponsorship. I sensed, however, that his opposition would crumble if the Soviets resumed diplomatic relations with Israel.

"We have to be tough, Mr. Secretary," he interjected at one point. "Mr. Prime Minister," I said, smiling, "nobody would ever accuse you of being otherwise." But he had demonstrated a flexibility of spirit in this meeting which I found both encouraging and surprising. The most hopeful sign of a new reality, however, was his invitation for Susan and me to have dinner with him and his wife at the Prime Minister's residence in Jerusalem that evening.

Despite the unhappiness of the Israeli government, I met with a delegation of ten Palestinians that afternoon at the American Consul-General's residence in Jerusalem, including Faisal Husseini and Hanan Ashrawi, who were to become my principal Palestinian interlocutors. My purpose was to reinforce the President's belief that legitimate Palestinian rights must be included in an enduring peace. I also wanted to remind them, however, that the PLO's support of Iraq in the war had not been helpful to the Palestinian cause. It was a lively and animated discussion and, as expected, they spent considerable time detailing the suffering their people had endured at the hands of the Israelis. Their indignation was tempered to a certain extent by their defensiveness; their tactical position was not good, and they knew it. They gave me a letter from Yasir Arafat stating that he had empowered them to represent his interests. (And I received a similar pro forma letter at every subsequent meeting I had with them.) "I have sat with leaders of eight Arab states, and all said they will not support your leadership," I noted. "You are moderate people of good sense. You have to realize that we're not going to renew a dialogue with the PLO in the face of Arafat's embrace of Saddam Hussein."

They requested a formal resumption of the dialogue, which the Israelis had wanted me to describe as "terminated," but which I had termed "suspended" when we had broken it off earlier. "You've got more to gain or lose than anyone else in this process," I reminded them. "If you stick to your old bottom lines, we won't get anywhere." As if to prove my point, they made the ridiculous suggestion that the same sort of international coalition that enforced U.N. Resolution 678 by liberating Kuwait should now enforce Resolutions 242 and 338 by removing the Israelis from the occupied territories. "If you're asking that we send in the Eighty-second Airborne, forget it," I replied. "That ain't going to happen." I then carefully explained the difference between 678, which was mandatory and unconditional, and 242 and 338, which called for negotiations involving land for peace. For all their posturing, I knew they were clearly relieved at least to be talking directly to us.

My dinner that evening with Shamir was primarily a social occasion, designed in my view to build some bridges between the two of us. In that regard, it succeeded and helped to establish a stronger personal relationship than the conventional wisdom supposes. I knew Prime Minister Shamir to be the one person in the Israeli government with whom I could always share information, confident that it wouldn't leak. By the time we both left office, we had come to recognize that the word of the other was good, regardless of the difficulties of the moment. This dinner was an important part of building that sense of mutual trust.

Afterward, our wives continued their conversation at the dinner table as the Prime Minister took me aside to a small sitting area of his living room. He produced from his files a letter that President Ford had sent then-Prime Minister Yitzhak Rabin on September 1, 1975, reaffirming U.S. support for Israel. He asked me to read the letter with particular emphasis on its final paragraph, which pledged that in formulating future policy with respect to the terms of a peace settlement, the United States would give "great weight to Israel's position that any peace agreement with Syria must be predicated on Israel remaining on the Golan Heights." It was a commitment which I was later called upon to reconfirm in letters of assurances—and did. I knew from my two meetings with President Assad during the Gulf crisis that Syria would never agree to peace with Israel without the return of the Golan. On its face, Shamir seemed to be asserting that Israel would not completely withdraw from the Golan under any circumstances. I concluded, however, that Shamir was signaling at least some degree of flexibility. Otherwise, I don't think he would have raised the subject with me.

"What if there were American troops up there?" I asked him. He paused for a moment, as if he were startled by the notion. "Then it would be different," he said. We would return to this topic later.

Shamir told me that Israel was serious about peace, but that there was nobody with whom to talk. The Palestinians I had met with that afternoon were unacceptable to him. "We know these people," he said. "We know all about them, and they're PLO." I pointed out, without any success, that while many of them had ties to Arafat, none were PLO officials. It was apparent that Shamir would resist most of these Palestinians as part of an official delegation to any talks. He told me he had met secretly with King Hussein, and the King was critical to peace, adding that he believed that some sort of a confederation with Jordan at some distant point in the future was the likeliest solution to the problem of the West Bank.

That night, I found Shamir serious, thoughtful, and at least more willing to entertain difficult choices than before. I sensed that Shamir understood that, since his perennial adversaries were signaling moderation, he would be required to engage, whether he wished to or not. I knew, however, that his tendency would be to proceed very slowly and carefully, if at all.

The Syrian Connection

I was beginning to come to the conclusion that Syria was the key to significant progress. Assad's engagement would signal, in the most dramatic fashion, that our efforts were legitimate in Arab eyes. His participation, in effect, would insulate the process. I hoped that the collective weight of the other Arab states would have an impact on Assad, and my first two meetings with him during the Gulf crisis had persuaded me that, at the very least, he was prepared to reconsider his traditional rigidity toward making peace with Israel.

My aides have told me in hindsight that I had prepared more intently for that first meeting with Assad than for any similar encounter with almost any other leader. There were complex policy issues to absorb, and I wanted to know about his internal political situation and his relations with other Arab leaders. But I remember also trying to get a feel for his personality, his negotiating style, his thinking, how he came at issues. I learned that Assad had a reputation for being thoughtful, serious, determined, and unyielding, and that he loved marathon meetings designed to wear down his interlocutors.

A few months earlier, I had been talking about the Middle East with Yitzhak Rabin, then Israel's Defense Minister. We both knew that any headway toward peace wouldn't happen without Syria's active participation. Rabin had told me that Assad was one fierce adversary, but possibly the smartest player in the Middle East, and above all a man of his word. "He's very tough, but if you do a deal with him, he'll stick absolutely with the letter of the deal," Rabin had said. "Don't assume there will be any spirit, but what he agrees to, you can count on." I was struck by Rabin's assessment, and resolved to test it when I met Assad on September 14, 1990, for the first of what would become eleven meetings. Like all our meetings, it was a marathon session—four and one half hours without a break. I was accompanied only by Ed Djerejian, our Ambassador to Damascus, who spoke fluent Arabic and had become well acquainted with Assad over the previous two years.

After a lengthy discussion of the situation in the Gulf, our discussion had moved to a dialogue on the state of the bilateral relationship, which had been strained for over a decade, primarily because of Syria's support for international terrorist activities. As I would be reminded each time we met, Assad treated my complaints about Syria's terrorism the way one might react to an eccentric uncle at family gatherings—as an unavoidable nuisance to be endured politely. Assad was particularly unyielding on this subject, and barely tolerated what he considered an intrusion on Syria's internal affairs. "We have had extensive discussions on the terrorism issue with the Ambassador," he said. "We don't need to talk about it any more." But I insisted, and we spent more than an hour on the issue anyway. Assad made no apologies for supporting terrorism against Israel, which to him was simply part of an armed struggle for liberation from an unjust occupation, but insisted that he had agreed to condemn acts of violence elsewhere. "Any person in the land of Syria who is carrying out or planning a terrorist operation outside of the occupied territories will be tried, and our laws are indeed severe," he maintained. I brought up the 1988 bombing of Pan American Flight 103 over Lockerbie, Scotland, and preliminary intelligence reports suggesting Syrian complicity. Assad repeatedly insisted that Syria had not been involved in that tragedy but that if the United States had evidence to the contrary, he would look into it. (This was the first of several times I raised this issue with the Syrians until our investigation concluded that this tragedy had been caused by Libyan terrorists.)

Finally, our discussion turned to the peace process. In language I would repeat scores of times throughout my travels, I described to Assad my vision of the ultimate scenario: once Saddam's overriding threat to regional instability was removed, all the parties would feel more comfortable in taking risks for peace. "We're optimistic that the circumstances that bring Syria, Egypt, and the Gulf states together in a major Arab coalition can augur well for the future of the Arab-Israeli peace process," I said.

I told him that the United States would not attempt to impose a settlement on the parties. "In a recent book," I observed, "the writer stated that if you are intent on promoting peace in the Middle East, you have to be ninety percent obstetrician. Peace will not come until the mother is ready."

Assad laughed. Then he said, "Israelis should know that Syria will not agree to peace while any part of its land is under occupation, and that without Syria there will be no Arab-Israeli peace.

"Every Israeli should understand that there can't be peace without a full return of Golan," he predictably insisted. Ironically, what should have been an utterance of utmost gravity was garbled by an error in the translation. "There can't be peace without a full return of hunger," the interpreter said. It was one of only a few amusing moments of this first encounter.

After this meeting, I felt, the dichotomy in the Arab world between moderates and radicals had been breached. On a personal level, I learned later that Assad had told an aide that he was intrigued by what he described as my "Texan-Princetonian mix."

In the practice of law, for all the availability of precedent to guide decision making, you must frequently rely on intuition. After this first meeting with Assad, I instinctively believed that Rabin had been right. Assad *was* intellectually engaging, wily, and one tough customer, not readily prone to take risks in pursuit of his goals. But he probably would stand behind an agreement, once it had been reached. I had no illusions about his ruthlessness and his dismal history of harboring terrorists. He understood power and had in the past used it brutally.

Our second meeting, on January 12, 1991, primarily focused on persuading Assad to allow his troops to participate in offensive operations in Kuwait in the event of a ground war. I took advantage of the occasion, however, to engage Assad in a lengthy dialogue on the peace process as well. By now, Assad understood that Saddam would be neutralized as a regional political force, and that the postwar environment would offer fresh and more promising openings for retrieving the land he had lost in the 1967 war. His body language was notably more positive than in September. "We want to work with you, and are prepared to do so," he said. He made a curious addition to his original bottom line, however. "We must have the Golan back—plus a meter," he insisted. I asked him what he meant. "Well," he said with a smile, "the Israelis are smart." In a joking fashion, this vintage horse trader was serving notice that the price for peace would not diminish as a result of his participation in Desert Storm. I've been involved in hundreds of negotiations in my public and private career, and those with Assad were some of the toughest.

Our third meeting, on March 13, lasting seven hours, was the most positive of the three in terms of atmospherics. Having been briefed in advance by Mubarak on the details of my proposal, he had already digested them. He said it was his desire to make something happen. Therefore he supported the two-track approach, but was less enthused about parallel confidence-building measures. He agreed that Israel should take such steps, but was cool to the idea that Arab states should do likewise. At every other stop in the region, the concept of parallel reciprocity had been embraced. Nevertheless, I concluded that Assad was genuine when he said that he had never seen an American commitment of such credibility before and was prepared to respond to our seriousness of purpose with a seriousness of his own. I cabled this assessment to the President: "Assad gave me the clear impression that he is serious about pursuing peace, but that he will be a tough nut to crack."

I was less concerned about the Soviets, who were delighted at being included in the President's postwar blueprint for the Middle East. In a meeting in Moscow on March 15, however, I cautioned Alexander Bessmertnykh that Moscow must also be willing to make tough choices. I told Bessmertnykh that the President was prepared to accept a regional conference co-sponsored by the Soviets. In exchange, however, Gorbachev would be expected to establish full diplomatic relations with Israel. "There's no point in delaying any longer, Sasha," I said. "This is a critical measure of your good faith. It's a new day, and it's a perfect place to demonstrate to all that new thinking is alive and well in Soviet foreign policy." Bessmertnykh said that Gorbachev was prepared to recognize Israel, but not immediately. That was fine with me. At the appropriate time, I wanted to try and use it as leverage to get something from Shamir in exchange.

I cabled the President, "It's clear to me that Sasha and his boss need to be seen to be involved in this issue to show that new thinking is producing on the outside."

After meeting in Ankara with President Ozal, I returned to Washington at 2:40 A.M. on March 17, satisfied that the environment had indeed been transformed in the region as a result of the war. "There can be no doubt that something potentially significant is stirring among the Arabs," I had reported to the President midway in the trip. "We can't know how long it will last or whether it will be concrete enough to move the Israelis. Even if it does, we can't be sure that it will overcome the division and turmoil among the Palestinians. I suspect things will get worse and become more polarized among Palestinians in the near future. But perhaps that, particularly in this new strategic environment, will set the stage for Palestinians capable of making peace to emerge."

As I flew home, three realities were clear to me. First, concrete Arab concessions would be necessary to bring Shamir along, but I believed that both contingencies were possible. Second, cutting the Gordian knot of Palestinian representation would be even more difficult than I had anticipated. And finally, there would be no effective process without Syria's participation.

In the weeks ahead, it would be my task to persuade both sides to move from generalized assertions of goodwill to concrete steps to break the impasse. Even with the benefit of a new strategic reality and the stirrings of new thinking among the principals, this would remain a daunting objective, just as it was before the war. The ancient taboos remained firmly embedded, but they were without question under the most intensive review in the history of this bitter conflict. In a region as polarized as the Middle East, that was no small foundation upon which to build.

![decorative band]

SADDAM STAYS
IN POWER

Our problem is so great that it needs international efforts.
— *From a letter passed to Secretary Baker by Kurdish refugees, April 8, 1991*

On the morning of August 10, 1953, a violent earthquake struck three Greek islands in the Ionian chain. For the next five days, Cephalonia, Ithaca, and Zante were battered by tidal waves, fires, and 120 major aftershocks. Contemporary accounts compared the devastation to an atomic bomb explosion. Nearly 500 people died, 25,000 homes were destroyed, and 93,000 survivors were left homeless. Several cities simply disappeared from the face of the earth.

As a twenty-three-year-old Marine second lieutenant assigned to the Sixth Fleet, I spent two weeks participating in NATO rescue and relief operations. We dropped supplies, bread, and cans of drinking water from British helicopters to survivors in dozens of towns literally flattened by the tremors. Virtually no buildings were left standing in Zakinthos, the capital of Zante, which had been engulfed by enormous fires that followed the earthquake.

My battalion was assigned the harrowing task of digging out the dead from the rubble. I'd seen dead bodies before; when I had briefly entertained the thought of becoming a doctor, I'd seen cadavers floating in vats of formaldehyde, and later as they were dissected by medical students. But I can remember to this day the stench of the blackened and rotting corpses we pulled from the remains of their homes and businesses. More than forty years later, the beautiful faces of dozens of children orphaned by that earthquake is my most haunting memory of Zakinthos.

I would not see faces of such heartbreaking beauty again until April 8, 1991, beneath snow-capped mountains in southeastern Turkey and northwestern Iraq in an area populated by thousands of Kurdish refugees who had fled the terror of Saddam Hussein's vengeful forces.

Just three days before, the President had announced an ambitious effort to airlift food and supplies to suffering Kurds in northern Iraq. He had asked me to get a firsthand report on the situation from Turgut Ozal in Ankara. But the visit to one of the refugee camps was Margaret Tutwiler's idea. In the days before I left on my second postwar trip to the Middle East, she had urged me to add such a visit to the itinerary. She had watched as the plight of the Kurds worsened and media attention grew. We were all aware that the administration was being criticized for not doing enough to protect the Kurds in the north and the Shia in southern Iraq from attacks by Iraqi forces. It was important to demonstrate in a dramatic way, she argued, that the United States had not abandoned the region in the aftermath of the war.

I agreed to Tutwiler's recommendation, having no idea of the logistical difficulties such a visit would create. The only airfield with runways long enough to accommodate a Boeing 707 jet was a ninety-minute helicopter ride from the Turkish/Iraqi border. My security detail had ruled out using Turkish helicopters, so American military choppers were disassembled, transported from U.S. bases in Europe, and reassembled at the Turkish military airfield at Diyarbakir. After landing there I inspected one of the C-130E aircraft that would be air-dropping emergency food assistance to refugees.

After a helicopter ride at 13,000 feet over snowy mountains, deep valleys, and the muddy Tigris River, I arrived at the Jaudarna Brigade headquarters of the Turkish army near the village of Cukurca. I received a briefing from Turkish military officials and the local governor of the area. Then I met with a delegation of twenty to twenty-five Kurdish refugees representing different factions and wearing turbans and long, flowing robes. They were polite and appreciative of my visit, but made clear to me their belief that neither the United States nor the world had done enough for their people. They presented me with a handwritten letter, signed by ten of them, which thanked the coalition for our efforts in Iraq and requested humanitarian assistance. As I read the letter, I was struck by two sentences in particular: "All Iraqis were waiting for freedom and democratic regime in Iraq. But the mistakes and wrong decisions that allowed the Iraqi regime to use tanks and helicopters caused this tragedy." There was an undercurrent of emotion to this meeting, particularly when they told stories of Iraqi troops slaughtering their friends and family members. But their representations to me were very calm and rational. In no way did they—or the grim videotape that Turgut Ozal had played for me in Ankara the previous day, showing a stream of refugees twelve miles long—prepare me for what I would see next.

After being advised to leave the food that some of our staff had brought to give to refugees, because doing so might trigger a riot, we piled into four-wheel-drive vehicles of the Turkish army, and drove for ten to fifteen minutes up a twisting dirt road toward the crest of a steep ridge at an elevation of about nine thousand feet. As we neared the top, the hillside suddenly seemed to explode with knots of people. The desperation and deprivation of the scene was literally unbearable. Women were hauling dirty water to drink and to wash their clothing, which was drying on the scrub brush and few remaining trees in the area. Most of the trees had been cut down for firewood to combat the freezing nighttime temperatures. A few rickety old tents were scattered along the hillsides. Sanitation conditions were an open invitation to serious disease. Most people were barefoot and few had adequate clothing. Everywhere there were children with what were bound to be empty stomachs.

My mind's eye conjured up the children of Zakinthos, but with a grim difference. Those children had at least survived the catastrophe. Without quick help, these innocents might well die of exposure, starvation, and disease. Two days later, in fact, thirty-seven refugees would die from exposure, twenty-seven of them children. For all practical purposes, there was no shelter from the elements. I have spent a fair amount of time in the outdoors. I know how cold it can become at night close to nine thousand feet in the mountains, even in springtime. I remember wondering to myself what would happen to these people when the winter snows came.

At the top of the ridge, I got out of my vehicle and walked a ways on a dirt road and crossed the border into Iraq. As I looked over the slopes on the Iraqi side of the mountain, the magnitude of the nightmare was immediately apparent. Before me, a huge mountain valley teemed with approximately fifty to sixty thousand refugees—part of an exodus strung out along the border that was estimated at more than a quarter million people. Almost immediately, I was engulfed by a throng of refugees, applauding and pressing up against me and my suddenly very uneasy security detail. From out of nowhere, an urgent voice cried out: "Mr. Baker, Mr. Baker, can I talk to you, please? Please, Mr. Baker. I need to talk to you."

A slightly built man pushed through the horde of humanity and sought unsuccessfully to breach a phalanx of Turkish army troops protecting me. I motioned to the guards to let him through. His name was Sam, and he had left everything he owned in the city of Kirkuk and walked for six days to this forlorn and forbidding place. "We are suffering," he told me. "Our children are suffering from hunger and starvation. We need doctors, we need medicine, we need water. There was heavy bombing and shelling on our heads. You've got to do something to help us."

It is difficult even to this day to describe the eloquence of his poignant plea. I told him that I would do everything possible to expedite relief operations. "It is up to the international community as a whole to do something about this tragic crime," I said. A few minutes later, what began as a murmur became a muffled roar as word went through the crowd that an American dignitary was visiting. A huge mass of humanity scrambled up behind my party, blocking the road and cutting us off from our vehicles as they swarmed around. Turkish officials accompanying us reported that they were losing control of the crowd and insisted that I leave immediately. It was one of the few times that I sensed my own security detail was genuinely worried about the situation. As we turned to walk back into Turkey the entire mountain seemed to stand and explode with rolling applause. I was determined to see us do all we could to prevent this from becoming even more of a humanitarian catastrophe than it already was.

On the helicopter ride back to Diyarbakir, I reflected to myself that the people I had just seen were living examples of the will to be free. They could not be permitted to die. This was no longer simply a political challenge for the United States. It was a true humanitarian emergency of vast proportions.

When I returned to Diyarbakir, I had a press conference with Ahmet Aptemocin, the Turkish Foreign Minister. I used this opportunity to convey a sense of urgency and alarm about what I had just witnessed. After the takeoff, I called John Bolton, who was Assistant Secretary for International Organization Affairs, and Princeton Lyman, our Director of Refugee Programs, up to my cabin and told them in no uncertain terms that I wanted things to happen and to happen fast to alleviate what I was convinced would be massive suffering. Both of these individuals were fine public servants who needed no prodding and who assured me that every effort would be made to eliminate bureaucratic foot-dragging and to mobilize international and private voluntary relief organizations. I then left for a ninety-minute flight to Israel. For several minutes after takeoff, we could see dirt roads and paths filled with refugees streaming out of Iraq. I then telephoned the President from the plane and told him there was no way for me to overstate the scope of the humanitarian tragedy I had just witnessed. "You have no idea of the human nightmare here," I told him. "There's a true disaster in the making if we don't move fast. People are dying every day. We've got to do something and we've got to do it now. If we don't, literally thousands of people are going to die."

To prevent this unspeakable tragedy, I said that the administration had to devote the same effort toward generating emergency relief as we had in putting the international coalition together in the first place. I proposed that the President call the United Nations Secretary-General and urge him to appoint a relief coordinator immediately, and suggested he should also call key coalition leaders and ask them to pledge more for relief operations and to make payments at once. I also recommended that Congress be asked for an urgent supplemental appropriation for Kurdish aid, and that the United Nations be pressed to consider a lien against future Iraqi oil exports to support the relief effort.

"What we've done so far is a pittance," I said. "We have to mobilize the world. We've got to think big. Otherwise, this could be the systematic destruction of a people." The President grasped the urgency in my voice and said he would order action right away.

While en route from Turkey to Israel, I called Bob Kimmitt to tell him to push the interagency process. "I don't care what you have to do. Get something going," I said. He understood, but told me that the DOD bureaucracy was raising some practical and logistical reservations about a relief effort.

Consequently, when I arrived at the King David Hotel in Jerusalem a few hours later, I wanted to follow my call to the President with a personal appeal for action to Dick Cheney. But he was at a Baltimore Orioles game, and so I had Margaret Tutwiler pass on a three-part message to Kathie Embody, Cheney's indispensable assistant ever since we had all worked together in the 1976 presidential campaign: "One, the situation is desperate and urgent. Two, people are going to die. Three, the U.S. military is the only organization that can help, so please cut through all the red tape and turn loose." I learned later from Kimmitt that, after receiving my message, Cheney had told colleagues that in sixteen years he had never known me to be an "alarmist," and so the tone of my message got his attention.

I realized, however, that humanitarian assistance alone would not be sufficient. Once their survival from the elements was assured, the Kurdish refugees eventually had to be able to return home free from future threats of the persecution and harassment that had sent them fleeing for their lives. My experience on that rugged hillside was not only the catalyst for a huge expansion of American and international relief to the Kurds that came to be known as Operation Provide Comfort: it also galvanized me into pressing for a new policy, announced by the President on April 16, of establishing safe havens for the Kurds in northern Iraq—refugee camps secured by U.S. forces and administered by the United Nations under the command of then-Lt. Gen. John Shalikashvili, the deputy commander of U.S. Army forces in Europe (later he would become not only the representative of the Joint Chiefs on my plane but eventually Colin Powell's replacement as the chairman of the Joint Chiefs of Staff). It was the largest military relief operation ever undertaken, and delivered millions of dollars in food and supplies to more than 400,000 refugees.

I believe that American intervention saved the lives of tens of thousands of innocent victims of the Gulf War and its aftermath. These efforts did not spare us, however, from criticism for our postwar policy. Our detractors accused us of inciting the Kurdish and Shiite rebellions against Saddam in the days immediately following the end of the war, then dooming them by refusing to come to their aid, either through U.S. military action or covert assistance. These are many of the same voices who also allege that Desert Storm was halted prematurely for political reasons, and that United States forces should have gone on to Baghdad and occupied large portions of Iraq. We never embraced as a war aim or a political aim the replacement of the Iraqi regime. We did, however, hope and believe that Saddam Hussein would not survive in power after such a crushing defeat. Ironically, the uprisings in the north and south, instead of lessening his grip on power as we felt they would, contributed to it, as he skillfully argued to his army that these events required his continued leadership in order to preserve Iraq. When he managed to consolidate his power, Saddam scrambled our strategic calculations. The result was a sobering reminder that the consequences of success are often far more intricate and unpredictable than anticipated.

Ending the War

The administration's policy in the weeks immediately following the cessation of hostilities was grounded in a complex mix of calculations, designed with one overriding strategic concern clearly in mind: to avoid what we often referred to as the Lebanonization of Iraq, which we believed would create a geopolitical nightmare. But there was a strong emotional component at play as well—and this reality was most apparent in the President's decision, endorsed by all his senior military and political advisers, to end the war when he did, instead of pursuing it for another few days. Of the criticism leveled at our decision making during this period, this has the least merit. Many of those who now complain that we erred badly by halting the war fully supported the decision at the time. The fact is conveniently overlooked that the President's decision to order a cease-fire after 100 hours of fighting was enthusiastically endorsed by the military, our coalition partners, the Congress, and American public opinion.

Within hours of the launch of the ground war, it was apparent to all of us that victory would be swift and total. Powell and Cheney had reported that the Iraqis were being routed at will. U.S. intelligence reported that the once-feared Republican Guard had been decimated, and thousands of tanks and artillery pieces destroyed or captured. The American-led military coalition had achieved both its war aims and political objectives. Kuwait was liberated, and Iraq's military had been so weakened that Saddam's ability to threaten his neighbors in the future was clearly, substantially diminished. It had been a spectacularly successful victory, concluded quickly and with gratifyingly light casualties. There was no operational reason to remain.

The military leadership, understandably, was adamant on this score. They believed that their troops had done their job damn well and should be sent home promptly. Except for some wrenching incidents of American and British deaths from "friendly fire," the war had unfolded amazingly well. But as Clausewitz observed of war, the simplest things become difficult, and uncertainty rules. A longer war—even one lasting only a day or two more—could result in needless American casualties.

Diplomatically and domestically, the political mood also argued in favor of ending the fighting. Increasingly, American fighter pilots were returning from their missions talking about the "turkey shoot" of Iraqis desperately fleeing north along what became aptly known as the Highway of Death. These comments were certain to be followed in short order by grisly news photographs of the carnage. The Soviets had furiously sought to head off the ground war. Now there were genuine fears that they might fracture the coalition by calling on the U.N. Security Council to halt the continuing slaughter. Back home, the thought began to resonate that this war was about to become un-American—that it was, perversely, *too* easy and therefore must be stopped.

From the start of the crisis, we had said repeatedly that the United States had no motives beyond forcing compliance with the U.N. resolutions and ejecting Iraq from Kuwait. We had argued that we had no grand design for a substantial permanent military presence in the region. The simplest way to establish our credibility on this score with all parties was to remain true to our word and withdraw promptly from Iraq. In short, there was no reason to continue, from either a military or political standpoint.

The Marching-to-Baghdad Canard

To this day, controversy endures over whether coalition forces should have continued their offensive all the way to Baghdad and toppled Saddam's regime. I believe this idea is as nonsensical now as it was then, and not merely for the narrow legalistic reason that the U.N. resolutions did not authorize coalition forces to undertake anything beyond the liberation of Kuwait. The entire truth embodies strategic, pragmatic, diplomatic, and political aspects that prompted the President's decision not to go to Baghdad— an absolutely correct judgment on which there was virtually no debate.

Strategically, the real objective was to eject Iraq from Kuwait in a manner that would destroy Saddam's offensive military capabilities and make his fall from power likely. By the time the cease-fire was announced on February 28, the vast bulk of Iraq's military machine, including most of its nuclear, chemical, and biological weapons programs, was destroyed. Our core political and war aims having been achieved, there was literally no reason to contemplate sending our forces further north.

We believed, moreover, that marching on Baghdad was ridiculous from a practical standpoint. At the very least, it would make a nationalist hero out of Saddam. Suddenly, a coalition war to liberate Kuwait from a universally condemned invasion could have been portrayed as a U.S. war of conquest. In addition, even with our massive military superiority, the odds of finding Saddam were quite improbable. Even in Panama, a nation friendly to the United States, where American troops have been stationed for most of this century, it took U.S. invasion forces fifteen days to find and capture General Manuel Noriega in 1989. Unlike Panama, however, where a democratically elected government was available to assume power, there wasn't even an organized opposition to Saddam. More to the point, Iraqi soldiers and civilians could be expected to resist an enemy seizure of their country with a ferocity not previously demonstrated on the battlefield in Kuwait. Even if Saddam were captured and his regime toppled, American forces would still be confronted with the specter of a military occupation of indefinite duration to pacify the country and sustain a new government in power. The ensuing urban warfare would surely result in more casualties to American GIs than the war itself, thus creating a political firestorm at home, criticism from many of our allies, and the dissolution of the coalition. Ironically, while Saddam was wrong in thinking that America's Vietnam and Lebanon hangovers would save him from a war, the painful lessons learned by U.S. policy makers from those conflicts may have actually saved Saddam himself from capture.

Diplomatically, pressing on to Baghdad would have caused not just a rift but an earthquake within the coalition. As a matter of fact, had we opted for this approach, we never would have been in a position to create a meaningful peace process because we would have lost the Arab members of the coalition. Furthermore, as much as Saddam's neighbors wanted to see him gone, they feared that Iraq might fragment in unpredictable ways that would play into the hands of the mullahs in Iran, who could export their brand of Islamic fundamentalism with the help of Iraq's Shiites and quickly transform themselves into the dominant regional power. This was also a genuine concern of the Bush administration and many of our allies as well. Just as fears of Iranian expansionism helped shape U.S. prewar policy toward Iraq, this same phobia was a significant factor in our postwar decision making.

Emotionally, the success of the war was a powerful tonic for the American psyche. In six short weeks, the bitter legacy of Vietnam had been swept away by Desert Storm. Euphoria permeated the country to a degree not seen since World War II. Little wonder that the operative impulse, from the President to the ordinary citizen in the street, was a hearty "bring the boys home."

There was no sentiment at senior levels of the U.S. government for occupying even part of Iraq. In addition, our military was adamantly opposed. Prince Bandar had told me on February 27 that it was important to the Arab world that the pullout occur quickly and in a visible way. At the end of the war, coalition forces controlled a huge swath of territory in southern Iraq, roughly everything south and east of As-Samawah below the Euphrates River almost to Basra. This area was littered with mines and unexploded munitions, and Schwarzkopf was worried about losing men needlessly. When I met with him in Riyadh in March, he said that no military purpose was served by occupying any territory. "My men are living in foxholes. They are in the middle of nowhere. There is no enemy—we beat the enemy. But it is a very dangerous area, full of land mines and cluster bombs. It's time to go," he insisted. I told him President Bush had told me he wanted to see our forces out as soon as possible.

Helping the Kurds

On March 2, two days after the President's cease-fire announcement and the day the U.N. Security Council approved Resolution 686 setting the terms of a formal cease-fire, armed Shia rebels in the south joined with army deserters to capture the town of An-Nasiriyah. Saddam Hussein mobilized the remaining forces of his battered elite Republican Guard to quell this insurrection. Simultaneously, however, he was confronted by another revolt in the north by the Kurds, his longtime adversaries.

While we had been careful not to embrace it as a war aim or political aim, our administration had made it publicly clear for some time that we would shed no tears if Saddam were overthrown. There was reason to hope that an emotionally battered armed forces leadership would rise up against the man responsible for the Kuwaiti debacle. In fact, precisely the reverse occurred. The rebellions provided a convenient excuse for the military to forget their humiliating performance in Desert Storm. Suddenly, there was a new war—one which they could *win*. As the fighting continued, it became apparent that, while weak and ill supplied, the twenty-four Iraqi divisions which had not seen action in Desert Storm were sufficient to subdue the rebellions. From a practical standpoint, nothing short of direct U.S. military operations would have guaranteed success by the insurgents.

We did not assist the insurrections militarily, primarily out of fear of hastening the fragmentation of Iraq and plunging the region into a new cycle of instability. The Shia were quite naturally perceived as being aligned with Iran, and the Kurds, who had demanded an independent state of Kurdistan for decades, were very fragmented in their leadership and were a constant source of concern to Turkey. For these geopolitical reasons, we were wary of supporting either group. We believed it was essential that Iraq remain intact, with or without a more reasonable new leadership. The Lebanonization of Iraq was viewed adversely by all of us. We believed these rebellions would inevitably increase unwelcome pressures within Iraq and the entire region.

Our caution in this regard was further reinforced when the Iranians injected themselves into the fray. Seeking to capitalize on the regional power vacuum created by the war to challenge its arch-rival, Iran quickly moved to support the dissidents. Iranian President Hashemi Rafsanjani called for Saddam to resign, and appealed to the Iraqi citizenry to rise against its discredited leaders. Throughout this period, Iran made several such appeals urging the overthrow of Saddam by the Shia. Worry over Iranian fundamentalism remained strong in the region, and we feared inadvertently helping the ayatollahs in Tehran by helping the Shia in Iraq.

Our political calculations were bolstered by an intense reluctance within the government to do anything that might result in the eventual reinvolvement of U.S. military forces in Iraq. The operative impulse was that the war was over—and it shouldn't be restarted. This mind-set was widespread throughout the Pentagon, which had opposed a recommendation of the Deputies' Committee to establish a demilitarized zone patrolled by U.N. troops in southern Iraq. Institutional reluctance was also a factor in the decision not to shoot down Iraqi helicopters—even after they began attacking the insurgents.

When Schwarzkopf met with his Iraqi counterparts on March 3 to dictate the terms of a cease-fire, he had banned all flights by Iraqi fixed-wing aircraft. Since U.S. bombing had destroyed most of Iraq's bridges, the defeated generals had asked permission to use helicopters to resupply Iraqi troops scattered throughout the country. With coalition air forces in complete control of Iraqi airspace, Schwarzkopf knew the helicopters posed no threat to his soldiers, and agreed to this request. It was a decision made on the spot, and in fairness to Schwarzkopf, it certainly seemed reasonable from a military standpoint. There was no particular reason to be suspicious of what seemed at the time little more than a logistical courtesy from victor to vanquished. Once Iraqi helicopter gunships began pounding Kurdish and Shiite villages, however, all of us knew in retrospect that it had been a mistake not to have explicitly forbidden flights by Iraqi helicopters just as we had for fixed-wing aircraft.

I do not recall any debate among the President and his senior advisers on this issue, either before or after Schwarzkopf's decision. I also believe that Saddam's troops would quickly have gained control of the insurrections with or without them. Intelligence analysts concluded that the combination of numerical superiority and Iraqi armor and artillery were sufficient to prevail rather easily. Shooting down Iraqi helicopters would have made a symbolic statement, but it would not have guaranteed successful insurgencies, and Colin Powell, in particular, believed that shooting down helicopters could suck us into a civil war, a contingency neither our coalition allies nor any of us wanted to happen. There was little if any debate at the time that the most appropriate course of action for the United States was to increase our humanitarian assistance to refugees.

During this period, there was some discussion of supporting the rebellion against Saddam Hussein through covert operations. I vividly remember the arguments advanced by several senior officials from other coalition partners. "We must find a way to help people go after Saddam," one told me. "Now is the time to foment unrest." A few said they were willing to help fund and participate in clandestine operations. "But we need some assistance," they said. I was told also, "You must treat the Iraqi opposition as you did the mujahedin in Afghanistan. This is the only way to separate the Iraqi military from Saddam." If the rebels were supplied with antitank and surface-to-air missiles, this official reasoned, they could not only defend themselves more effectively but could also inflict significant losses on Saddam's divisions. The remnants of the Iraqi army needed a quick victory to restore their battered self-confidence. A difficult and costly insurgency might well be psychologically unacceptable. "The military needs to know that as long as Saddam is in power, the army will have to fight a long and costly internal war," one foreign minister argued. "When that realization sinks in, the military will be more willing to act against Saddam."

For obvious reasons, I cannot go into the details of internal U.S. government discussions regarding these proposals for covert operations. Suffice to say, they raised a host of thorny questions. Could such operations be mounted successfully, given the intelligence assets that the United States and its coalition partners could bring to bear? Would such operations just foment the fragmentation of Iraq and backfire against our desire to see stability restored in the Persian Gulf? If such an effort were tried and failed, could we count on maintaining substantial U.N. economic and political sanctions against Iraq?

With the benefit of hindsight, some critics have suggested that steps such as pursuing these covert operations, shooting down helicopters, or holding on to Iraqi territory might have assisted our long-term goal of ensuring that the Iraqi regime would not pose a threat to stability in the region.

Yet at the time, all of these possible actions raised one kind of risk or another. On the one hand, there was the risk of having the U.S. military bogged down or sucked into an Iraqi civil war. We had made it clear throughout the crisis in discussions with our coalition allies that we had no desire to play a role in preserving order in Iraq. Moreover, we wanted to encourage the Gulf states to work together with the Syrians and Egyptians to develop postwar security structures in the region. The President had repeatedly promised that we were not seeking a permanent military presence, and the faster our forces left, the more pressure there would be on the Gulf states to work together to ensure their own security.

We also were leery of fragmenting Iraq or dissolving the coalition. We needed the coalition as much in the postwar period as we had before the war for at least two primary reasons. First, during the war, we had learned that Saddam Hussein's program to develop weapons of mass destruction was both more substantial and better concealed than we had believed at the outset. We were determined to use our victory in Desert Storm to put the Iraqi regime under the intense glare of the most intrusive weapons-inspections regime ever developed, to root out every last bit of that program. We were also determined to maintain substantial economic and political sanctions against Iraq to restrict its aggressive tendencies—sanctions that remain in effect even today. To put Saddam Hussein in that cage, so to speak, we needed implementation of existing U.N. resolutions (and an additional U.N. resolution enacted), and we needed all our coalition partners to be with us to achieve this. Second, Saddam's defeat was a clear repudiation of Arab radicalism and created a unique opportunity to pursue a lasting peace in the Middle East among Arabs and Israelis. To do that, we needed to keep the coalition intact and focused on building the peace.

Whither Goest Saddam?

While Saddam had been vanquished, other leaders remained nervous over his survival in power. When I met with Yitzhak Shamir in Jerusalem on April 9 to discuss the peace process, he was quite concerned that despite a great victory, Saddam was alive and still in control. "It's not a good lesson for the area," Shamir told me. "Such a man, if you could call him a man, who's cost us so many losses, who has dared to attack us with missiles, is a man that we can't live with. I think everything in the region will be temporary until this fact changes." I responded that all our Arab coalition partners believed that Saddam would be ousted by a coup within six to eight months, but that I was concerned the uprisings in the north and south might have created a rallying cry for him.

The following day in Cairo, President Mubarak expressed similar concerns. During part of our discussion involving the refugee problem, I observed that Saddam was seeking revenge against Turkey and Iran by forcing Kurds to flee across their borders by the tens of thousands. "Saddam is not that intelligent," Mubarak argued. "Simply stated, he would like to kill the Kurds off."

It's important to recall that, while it would have been welcome, Saddam's departure was never a stated objective of our policy. We were always very careful to negate it as a war aim or a political objective. At the same time, we never really expected him to survive a defeat of such magnitude. Perhaps we should have remembered that Saddam had always been a wily survivor, somehow finding a way to confound his enemies. To this day he remains in control of his country, while the administration that defeated him in a textbook case of diplomatic and military skill is no longer in power. In occasionally reflecting on this perverse twist of history, I'm reminded of something Tariq Aziz said to me in Geneva: "We will be here long after you're gone." It was one of the few things he said that proved to be true.

CHAPTER 25

PRELUDE TO A MIDEAST CONFERENCE:

THE DEAD CAT ON THE DOORSTEP

I want to give you my thinking before we head off on this trip. I don't have high expectations, but there are some new realities that make progress possible and we owe it to ourselves and everyone else to make the effort.

—Memorandum from Secretary Baker to President Bush
on the eve of the first of eight peace-process shuttles.

Within two weeks of my return to Washington from the Middle East in mid-March, I'd begun to fear that my guarded optimism about resuscitating the peace process had been misplaced. The brave words and hopeful signs that greeted me at every stop had suddenly fallen victim to that one great leveler—the status quo. At every echelon up to and including the President, American diplomacy had pressed all the parties to go beyond their platitudes, with concrete steps. None had been forthcoming.

By the end of March, it was apparent that unless I broke my promise to myself to avoid shuttle diplomacy, the window of opportunity created by Desert Storm would slam shut out of inertia. Peace would be the loser, but American credibility and prestige would also suffer. Having started this process, I was now determined to try and save it from a premature demise.

In early April, I recommended to the President that I begin an intensive round of personal diplomacy in the region. "I don't have high expectations," I noted in an April 6 memorandum to the President, "but there are some new realities that make progress possible and we owe it to ourselves and everyone else to make the effort."

As in March, my strategic objective was to persuade all the parties to

443

break the ancient taboo against direct talks between Israel and her neighbors. To that end, I intended to press them all for symbolic concessions to assault the legacy of mutual hatred and distrust. I would also ask King Fahd and President Mubarak to help "produce Assad" and "fence out the PLO" from a formal role in the process, and attempt to extract commitments from all of the parties to attend a regional peace conference. The Soviets would be asked to help by joining the United States as co-sponsors, and the Europeans, like the PLO, would be delicately encouraged to stay at home because of Israeli objections.

The crux of my tactical approach was simple enough. "We want everyone to invest in the process so it's not so easy to walk away from it," I wrote. "We want them to build their stake in its success and increase the cost to them of failure."

At that moment, I had no inkling that this next round of Middle East diplomacy would carry me the equivalent of twice around the world in a period of six weeks. Nor did I anticipate that while a degree of progress beyond reasonable expectations would have been achieved by the end of this odyssey, the search for peace would still remain as maddeningly elusive as ever.

Shamir's Cold Shoulder

As always, the tortured road to peace ran through Jerusalem. Contradictory indicators accompanied my arrival in Israel on April 9. Misha Arens announced the release of 1,200 prisoners, including 300 Palestinians held in administrative detention as a result of the Intifada. This welcome confidence-building measure, however, was diminished by the establishment of more settlements in the occupied territories.

I quickly entered my objections to the settlements in a meeting with David Levy, who from the very start had been leaning forward for peace. "We have definite agreements and understandings and they need to be put in a credibility bank," I said. Housing Minister Ariel Sharon's inflammatory rhetoric and expansionist zeal was undercutting the peace process, I complained, especially since his statements "are left to stand as if they represented the official policy of the government of Israel. These actions frankly create an impression that Israel is deliberately misleading us."

"You should have a Ph.D. in land mines and obstacles," Levy said, laughing. "You're very clever at pointing them out and avoiding them." But he gave no ground on settlements, insisting that Israel had not agreed in February to halt them, only to stop populating them with Soviet immigrants.

Before leaving Washington, I had a private meeting at my home with

Dan Meridor, Shamir's former Justice Minister and a rising star in the Likud Party. I told him I'd expect answers to three core questions during my visit: Would Israel attend a regional conference with the Arabs and the Palestinians? Would they agree that the basis for any such meeting would be a comprehensive settlement based on United Nations Resolution 242? And would Israel attend if Palestinians from the territories were present?

I restated these questions in Jerusalem to Shamir in the first of what would become eight meetings with him over the next six weeks. After fifteen minutes of dialogue on other matters, Shamir announced, "Now let's go to your questions, which as you know are not the easiest in the world."

I was relieved to learn that Shamir had moved a little. He had dropped his previous opposition to Soviet co-sponsorship; Israel was now prepared, he said, to attend a regional conference, but not under United Nations auspices, as the Arabs had been insisting for years. He also agreed to Palestinian representation, but wanted the Palestinians to be part of a joint delegation with Jordan. In this way, he believed, the PLO's impact would be diminished. He was uncomfortable about the basis for the conference, however. To the Arabs (and most of the rest of the world), U.N. Resolution 242 envisioned exchanging territory for peace, which Shamir had vowed he would never do. He wanted to insert the phrase "as agreed at Camp David" into the 242 formula, since Israel's position was that Menachem Begin had not agreed to exchange land for peace in the 1978 peace accord hammered out with Anwar Sadat under President Jimmy Carter's auspices at Camp David. I told him this was merely a matter of semantics. Both sides could *interpret* the formula however they wished, but the Arabs would never agree to any *language* modifying Resolution 242 as the basis for a meeting.

My meeting with Palestinians from the territories that afternoon was notably more upbeat than our first encounter in March. I was struck by the almost total absence of polemics and the ritual mention of the PLO. More than anything else, I sensed a poignancy that had been obscured by the posturing of our first meeting. Despite being severely criticized by their brethren for meeting with me again, they each made it clear they wanted to be part of the process. More important, they agreed to the three preconditions Shamir had laid down as the price of meeting with them in a regional conference. They agreed to support a two-track process between Israel and both the Arabs and Palestinians, phased negotiations, and peace with Israel. "That alone," I noted in a message to the President, "is a good indicator of the change of mood and attitude among potential Palestinian leaders in the territories."

I had not wanted to begin these crucial talks with Shamir on a confrontational note, so I waited until the start of our second meeting the next day, April 10, to protest the latest settlement provocation with him directly. On

March 13, Sharon had announced that Israel would build 13,000 new units of housing in the territories over the next three years. At a time when the United States was asking all the parties to make conciliatory gestures in the cause of peace, this was a particularly disappointing development.

"I see it as a deliberate effort to sabotage peace," I told Shamir. "It's really a major problem for us, and I respectfully ask you to repudiate these statements."

As usual, Shamir sought to deflect my complaint. "I am not happy with these statements," he said, "and everyone in the country knows it."

"I'm not asking you to adopt our position," I countered. "But I *am* asking you to keep this man from throwing land mines in the way of peace."

"I don't want to involve you in our internal politics," Shamir demurred.

"I don't want to see your internal politics involve *us,* but it will," if settlement provocations continued to occur, I warned.

"I will deal with it," Shamir said. By now, of course, I felt that he wouldn't—and he never did.

Turning to the peace process, I was pleased to learn that Shamir had decided to drop his language about Camp David, and said he'd consider my proposal to allow a representative of the European Community to attend as an observer. Shamir didn't trust the Europeans, believing they were overwhelmingly Arabist, but I believed some sort of gesture would be important to keep some of them from complicating the process. I wasn't surprised to discover, however, that Shamir had a new request to put on the table. In our first meeting, he'd demanded a U.S. pledge that the Palestinians would never mention the PLO. Now, he wanted a letter from Palestinians attending the conference that formally disavowed the PLO and attested that they weren't representing Yasir Arafat. I turned this idea down flatly. "You're pushing too hard," I cautioned Shamir. "You can't insist that these people commit suicide." I said I would tell the Arabs that trumpeting a PLO connection would scuttle the process, something I firmly believed. Conversely, the process would also die if Israel insisted on the letter. "If you impose a condition which makes it basically impossible to move forward, I'm through," I said, "and I will say exactly what caused the effort to fail."

Before leaving, I wanted to make sure there was no misunderstanding on the issue of Palestinian representation. My bottom line was simple. "I want you to tell me," I said, "if you will not sit down with them if they say that they are representatives of the PLO." I needed an answer before I left the Middle East, and Shamir said he would oblige.

On the whole, I felt these two sessions had been a promising start. I had no doubt Shamir would be difficult to bring around, but he *had* moved—

and now I had something to show Mubarak, who was predictably optimistic when I visited him in Cairo that afternoon. After some initial misgivings, Mubarak was now ready to support the regional conference idea. He also endorsed Shamir's preference for a joint delegation of Jordanians and Palestinians, and predicted that both Israel and the PLO would avoid a rhetorical confrontation.

Afterward, Mubarak asked to see me privately. "I did not want to say this in front of the others," he said, "but, Jim, I'm amazed that Shamir has moved this much." He'd told me previously several times that he thought it would never be possible to make progress with an Israeli government led by Shamir.

Assad's Equally Cold Shoulder

After separate meetings in Cairo with the foreign ministers of Saudi Arabia, Egypt, and Tunisia, I flew to Damascus on April 11 to see Assad. This meeting lasted five and one half hours, excluding a break for Iftar, the traditional breaking of fast during Ramadan. Since I knew that Assad would be the toughest Arab domino to topple, I deliberately sought very little from him at the outset. He would not be asked now to end the state of belligerency or recognize Israel, I told him. "What we would like to see from Syria is that you are committed to the process," I said. I asked that he refrain from criticizing any Palestinians willing to talk with Israel, and to "work on the PLO" to keep their profile low. Most of all, I wanted Assad's agreement to attend the regional conference.

He listened intently to my summary of Shamir's reaction, but basically ignored it, focusing instead on the conference. He was willing to attend, he said, but only if four conditions were met. He insisted on describing it as an international conference. He wanted assurances that the co-sponsors would guarantee all its results. The conference must be continuous to guarantee impetus to the negotiations. And, he added, to ensure that the conference had what he repeatedly called "international legitimacy" and "moral authority," it must be under the aegis of the United Nations.

To varying degrees, three of his particulars posed problems for Israel, but I believed that compromises could be fashioned that Shamir might ultimately be persuaded to accept. In fact, we reached a middle ground on the spot on what to call the conference. Assad had initially rejected the Israeli preference for a "regional conference" out of hand. "This term would belittle the significance of the conference," he said. "Let's give it its due.

"Is it an educational, economic, or cinema conference?" he deadpanned. "It *must* have a name." I told him I preferred the formulation of Esmat Abdel Meguid, Egypt's Foreign Minister: "A conference is a conference is a conference." I reminded him that nothing could prevent him from calling it an international conference—or, I knew, Israel from calling it a regional conference. Assad finally suggested that since the meeting was designed to achieve peace, it should be called a peace conference. Since it was to be in fact a conference to begin face-to-face discussions about peace, I readily agreed.

His fourth requirement concerning U.N. sponsorship, however, was a dagger aimed at the heart of peace. The United Nations had always been perceived, with justification, by Israel as a mortal enemy held at bay only by the American veto in the Security Council. The 1975 resolution equating Zionism with racism had cemented this view. No matter what it was called, I knew Shamir would never attend any conference under U.N. auspices.

"On the issue of the moral authority of the U.N. presence," I warned, "let me say to you that we would refer to that as a deal-breaker. I cannot convince Israel to attend an international conference which is under U.N. sponsorship. It is just a fact of life that I cannot overcome. If you insist, I know I can't make this work."

"If a U.N. umbrella was good enough for the [Gulf] war," Assad shrewdly countered, "why not here?" I replied that the United States had no problem with a U.N. *presence;* in fact, I told him I was willing to press Shamir to agree to allow a U.N. observer to attend. "But we can't put this deal together if it has a U.N. umbrella," I reiterated.

For the most part, I considered Assad's demands little more than a cosmetic smoke screen. These were the arguments of someone, I believed, who really wasn't interested in a dialogue. "The points you make are matters of form rather than substance," I told Assad. "The real issue here is not what we call this conference. It's whether the Palestinians and the Israelis and the Syrians and the Jordanians and the Lebanese have decided it is time for peace. We will never know that if the parties continue to go on without talking to one another." Assad deflected my point by launching into a dissertation on why Syria declined to attend the 1973 Geneva talks, which were also a regional peace conference co-sponsored by the United States and Soviets after the October War in the Mideast.

I tried to appeal to Assad's sense of practicality by pointing out that, by persisting, he would hand Israel a chance to refuse to attend and blame it on Damascus. "Don't give them an excuse not to engage in peace talks and let them say it's the Arabs' fault," I argued. Seemingly impervious to all reason, Assad refused to give ground. My frustration escalating, I asked him what he could possibly lose by attending.

"We will lose Arab domestic public opinion," he said. "They will know what is going on. This would not only be adventurism, it would be a form of suicide. It is one thing to adopt a suicidal policy if it brings benefits to the people, but it is truly foolhardy if there is no positive result."

In the end, we each agreed to consider the other's reservations. "You haven't made it impossible for me, Mr. President," I said, "but you've made it very difficult." Assad feigned disbelief. "That's not my intent," he insisted. "I really want this to work." But it was clear he wanted it to work without any concessions on his part. Privately, I wasn't at all sure we'd ever be able to get around his objections.

My disappointment with Assad coincided with irritation over yet another unwelcome leak from Israel, erroneously claiming I'd agreed to exclude East Jerusalemites from any Palestinian delegation. En route from Damascus to Geneva, where I met with Jordanian Foreign Minister Taher al-Masri, officials of the European Community, and Shimon Peres, head of the Israeli Labor Party, I dictated a letter to Shamir from my aircraft. I accented the positive, telling him that while Assad had been difficult on the matter of the conference, he and the other Arabs had agreed to the two-track concept and at least some kind of conference.

"I want to avoid the land mines," I said, in reference to the leak, "not highlight them. My ability to do so depends on everyone showing restraint on what they publicly say on sensitive issues. That's why the public comments . . . do not help at this time. I'm quite serious about trying to avoid the East Jerusalem issue, but at this point I can't categorically say that no one from East Jerusalem will *ever* take part in this process."

As I flew back on April 12 to Washington from Geneva, I felt I was making slow progress. But in a sentiment I didn't share with my staff, I thought to myself that this process would probably die. With all the conditions Israel and Syria were attaching, there was simply too much distance between the parties.

Back in Washington, I received Shamir's reply to my letter on April 15. I was disheartened to see that he was descending to Assad's level of form over function. "Since the regional meeting will not be the forum for peace negotiations," he said, "it makes no sense to call it a peace conference." He also said that Israel would never accept a Palestinian from East Jerusalem on any delegation. "That will create an untenable situation, because it puts East Jerusalem on the agenda," he argued.

After four days of work back in Washington and an EC ministerial meeting in Luxembourg, I returned to Israel on April 18. In a meeting with Shamir the next day, I told him that I'd taken some pains to structure a process tailored to Israel's concerns and that it was now time for him to begin considering compromises. I said I couldn't produce an agreement limiting the conference to a single meeting. "But I *can* get an agreement where you are protected," I said. The conference would be powerless to take votes, make decisions, or impose solutions on any of the participants. And Israel would retain the option of walking out at any time.

"What I'm asking you to do is give me enough procedural flexibility to make this work," I said. "If this doesn't work, at least put us in a position where together we can leave this dead cat on the Arab doorstep." This wasn't the first or last time I'd use this analogy, whose origin escapes me. From the beginning, it was the main leverage I had.

Shamir and his aides ignored my plea. Instead, they constantly raised procedural roadblocks, debating points, reservations, and new concerns. The haggling seemed endless to me, a calculated exercise in obfuscation to play for time and avoid coming to grips with the hard choices required. My irritation was beginning to get the better of me. By now I had essentially fashioned a process built on Israel's specifications, yet Shamir wasn't satisfied. "If you can't help me," I finally said, "I'll go home."

Rapprochement in Aqaba, Regression in Jeddah

After meeting with the Palestinians again, I decided to stop in Jordan, which I had been avoiding on prior trips to the region due to our displeasure with its support of Iraq. I flew to the Red Sea port of Aqaba, where King Hussein hosted me for lunch at his summer palace. The King was a longtime acquaintance and good friend of President Bush. In early 1977, shortly after George Bush and I had moved back to Houston following Jimmy Carter's election, Hussein had been the guest of honor at a dinner at the home of George and Barbara Bush. Their strong personal bonds forged over nearly two decades had made the King's support of Saddam Hussein during the war an act of personal betrayal that had caused the President enormous anguish. It also elicited uncharacteristic anger from a man who prefers to give friend and foe alike the benefit of the doubt. The President was still so furious with Hussein that he had refused several requests from the King for a meeting. I was just as upset, but we understood there would be no peace process without Jordan's active participation. In particular, the King would be crucial in persuading the Palestinians to come to the table.

We also knew the United States now had considerable leverage to exert. The King had always felt more secure on his precarious throne with an American embrace. More to the point, Jordan's economy was in desperate shape, and his previous financial patrons, the Saudis, were even more enraged with him than we were. His foreign debt had mushroomed. More than 300,000 Palestinian refugees were camped in his country in the aftermath of war, bleeding his beleaguered treasury. Simply stated, the King was broke and needed America's help to persuade his longtime benefactors in Riyadh to bail him out. There was every practical reason to believe the King would be willing to do almost anything to end his political isolation and to reclaim the good graces of the United States.

The King is a very gracious person, and welcomed me warmly to his seaside home. As our entourages exchanged the usual pleasantries before lunch, I thought to myself, Here are people who've been saying terrible things about us and are behaving like nothing has happened. But I was interested in moving the peace process along, so I wanted the King to know that we were willing to move step by step to let bygones be bygones, but only if Jordan enlisted actively in the U.S. peace initiative. By design, before lunch I spent fifteen minutes with him alone to explain this new reality and to outline the terms for an eventual reconciliation.

"Please give my very best to the President," he asked me. "I'll do that, Your Majesty," I said, "but you need to know that it's going to be a tough row to hoe to repair Jordan's relationship with the United States. It's hard to understand some of the things that were said.

"I don't want to go over what divides us. I'm here to try and see if we can move toward peace. But there's much hard feeling in the United States. I hope we can overcome this, but it's going to take a while." I also told him that despite our differences, "We'll do what we can to help you patch things up with the Saudis."

The King showed me some recent photographs of equipment seized from terrorists who had entered Jordan to kill him. He said that he, too, was committed to peace and to repairing his tattered ties with Washington. He made no real attempt to justify his support for Saddam with me. During lunch, however, he launched into an extensive rationalization of his behavior during the war, which our delegation found wholly unconvincing. At one point he even claimed that Saddam was now contemplating a more democratic political system for Iraq. "I guess old habits die hard," I noted in my cable to the President.

But I also told him that I'd found the meeting "very encouraging." From the start of the lunch, it was clear to me the King understood the simple dynamic: for us to help him now, he needed to play on our terms. In fairly short order, he endorsed the conference and declared (somewhat improbably, I felt at the time) that Jordan would attend even if Syria didn't. He also agreed to Shamir's idea of a Jordanian-Palestinian delegation in principle, and endorsed my compromise of U.N. observer status. He pledged to tell the PLO to keep a low profile and to encourage the Palestinians to remain committed to the process. I asked him to say something to the press about breaking old taboos, which he did. The press traveling with me missed the impact of this statement, but I took full advantage of it when I telephoned Shamir before leaving Aqaba, to tell him the King's views were closer to his than to Assad's.

At the end of the day, I sent this summation to the President: "I'm a little more hopeful about our ability to manage the key problems after today's meetings than I was yesterday. But I think the key to Israeli-Palestinian-Arab diplomacy is recognizing that there will be highs and lows and that we just have to work our way through them. We're not just dealing with fears that frequently tend to dominate hopes, but also with an enormous reluctance to make concrete commitments. And the best way to deal with that is to keep pushing everyone to get more and more practical."

On April 21, I saw Mubarak in Cairo again to ask his help with the Saudis and the Syrians. "I'm at a point where we cannot do any more without decisions from Arab governments," I said. "I need help from you and King Fahd. I need help with the PLO. You can tell Arafat not to block this process."

"The Palestinians know this is the only way," Mubarak assured me. "They understand us."

As always, Mubarak was generous with his offer to help persuade what he invariably described as "my brothers." He offered to call Shamir and tell him a continuing U.N. conference would pose no harm to Israel. He also volunteered his personal aircraft so that Osama el-Baz, his National Security Adviser, could visit Assad and King Hussein immediately. I showed him a draft statement of support I hoped King Fahd would issue. "The Saudis will be terrified of this statement," he warned. "During the peace process with Sadat, I went to Saudi fourteen times. I don't believe they will say this." It wasn't what I was hoping to hear. So far, Mubarak had been the only Arab leader wedded to much more than rhetoric.

I arrived in Jeddah later that day in time for dinner with Prince Saud before seeing King Fahd. Saud informed me that while the Saudis would support U.S. efforts, it would not be appropriate for his country to attend a peace conference. I was quite frankly appalled to hear this. Even by the standards of traditional Saudi reluctance, such a rebuff was breathtaking, given all that the United States had just done for the kingdom.

In a late-evening meeting, per his custom, the King was as warm as ever. But his polite evasions were reminiscent of the classic Saudi preference for avoiding risks. I asked him to issue a mild statement in support of peace that I could use to put Shamir on the defensive. He responded with various excuses about not wishing to inflame Arab public opinion. "We're your partners," I reminded the King. "We were there for you. We need you to be there for us. How can we be partners in war but not in peace? If you can't do this, what do I say to your friend George Bush?"

"Tell him that I *am* his friend," the King replied, "but that we will look at this and come back to you."

In the end, the King pledged to lean on the Syrians, the PLO, and even their erstwhile brother King Hussein. The Saudis later issued a mild statement endorsing the U.S. initiative and supporting the idea of a conference. It was better than their standard bland public statements, but several steps short of really leaning forward. The King would have to be further encouraged to produce anything of genuine effect. Ultimately, however, he produced. And there wouldn't be a peace process today without courageous decisions by King Fahd and President Mubarak.

My cable to the President, however, reflected my unhappiness at that moment. "Notwithstanding their words, the Saudis are beginning to revert to form," I wrote. "Despite their earlier pledge, they gave us nothing to work with re Israel. I'm afraid that an argument to Israel that there's been a real change in the Arab world rings a little hollow tonight. I let [the King] know I was disappointed. I sense my disappointment will spur them to do more."

This troubling turnaround brought home to me the indispensable role of Prince Bandar, the Saudi ambassador to the United States. As King Fahd's nephew, Bandar had extraordinary influence with his uncle. He'd been educated in the States, had an idiomatic command of the English language, and understood the American psyche very well. Bandar exuded an aura of charming roguishness, but he possessed a first-rate intellect and was the most progressive of the King's closest advisers.

Before all my previous trips to Saudi Arabia, Bandar would fly home to brief King Fahd before I arrived. His powers of persuasion in these situations were frequently decisive. I'd been unable to avail myself of his services on this visit, however. A former pilot in the Saudi air force, he'd crash-landed an F-5 in 1977, permanently injuring his back. This chronic condition had flared up, and he'd been recuperating for several weeks at his father's chalet near Geneva.

For several days before I arrived in Saudi Arabia, I'd left messages for Bandar, which were never returned. My last one was designed to get his attention: "Tell Prince Bandar I'm just calling to ask about him. I'm busting my commoner's ass out here while he's sitting on his royal butt. I hope he's having a good time. I'll call him when I get to Tel Aviv."

Bandar liked to remind me that Saudi diplomacy was not impulsive, and it was apparent to me that his absence had emboldened the more cautious of the King's ministers. Bad back and all, Bandar would have to be pressed to rejoin the fray if King Fahd were to reciprocate the courage of the President of the United States a mere two months earlier.

Bladder Diplomacy

On April 23, I met President Assad again in Damascus. Without any doubt, this was the most difficult and laborious negotiation I'd ever had. It made some of my marathon arms-control negotiations seem easy. For openers, the meeting lasted nine hours and forty-six minutes without a break, in a room rendered unbearably stifling by too little air conditioning and sealed bulletproof windows concealed behind drab olive-colored drapes. Assad served strong Turkish coffee and ultrasweet lemonade without ice, which because of the oppressive heat was consumed in copious quantities. Six hours into this meeting, the call of nature captured Ambassador Ed Djerejian. Just as Assad launched a favorite monologue on the evils of the Sykes-Picot Treaty, the situation reached critical mass. Djerejian scribbled a message reminding me to raise a certain policy issue that hadn't yet been surfaced. "And of course," he added, "it's perfectly all right for you to take a break now to use the men's room." Inexplicably, *my* kidneys were still operational, so I waved Djerejian off. The anguished look on his face bespoke the obvious. He gestured to the Syrian Foreign Minister that he needed to make an important telephone call. In his absence, I revealed the true nature of Djerejian's mission: "You have to wonder, Mr. President, why the ambassador has gone to the men's room to make an important phone call." Assad roared with laughter. When Djerejian returned, we pretended to be none the wiser.

An hour or so later, I pulled out a white handkerchief and waved it at Assad. "I give up," I confessed. "I have to go to the bathroom." Thus was coined the phrase which I will forever associate with my sixty-three hours of talks with Assad: bladder diplomacy.

Negotiating with Assad was always the ultimate endurance contest, all the more remarkable for the perennial intelligence reports that he was in poor health. His stamina was phenomenal. We always sat side by side in two enormous easy chairs that made me feel like a midget. Assad was sphinxlike, legs riveted to the floor, knees together, hands folded in his lap, never changing his position. I always needed a massage after seeing him; having to look to my left at an angle of ninety degrees gave me a crick in the neck. (After I mentioned this to Mubarak once, he laughed his hearty laugh and said he'd often urged Assad, to no avail, to move the chairs so that they faced each other.) Assad, on the other hand, never demonstrated the slightest discomfort. He seemed to *relish* these grueling sessions, which were a classic case of trying to win by exhaustion.

In this meeting, Assad was unyielding on two demands which I knew would never be accepted by Shamir. He insisted upon "full participation" of the United Nations, with all members of the Security Council present, as well as a continuous conference, one constantly in session.

I tabled a proposal at the very start of the meeting that, in terms of its scope, could be fairly described as significant. I told Assad that in response to his previous insistence that the conference co-sponsors guarantee all its results, I was prepared to explore the concept of a formal American pledge guaranteeing the security of the Israeli-Syrian border along the Golan Heights. I made clear that such a commitment could be offered only *after* Israel and Syria had negotiated a full and complete peace. The look on his face told me that Assad was both surprised and interested by this proposal. I went on to say that it would be a waste of time for me to explore this idea with the President unless he were willing to drop his two objections to the conference modalities. "I'm not even going to check with President Bush unless you're prepared to fall off these two things," I said.

I confess that this posture was pure negotiating tactic. In truth, I'd already discussed this idea with the President and Scowcroft after my first meeting with Assad. Our idea of guaranteeing the border was to offer to station U.S. troops as peacekeepers in a buffer zone along the Golan to guarantee the security of the border between Israel and Syria. This was the ultimate security guarantee. After all, the Gulf War had demonstrated that U.S. military technology was the marvel of the world. Such a major diplomatic and military undertaking would require congressional approval, but we felt that most of Israel's supporters on Capitol Hill would welcome such a direct U.S. military involvement if it could be the linchpin of a secure peace between Israel and her most implacable Arab neighbor. A variant of the idea had worked before—it was a major component of the peace agreement between Israel and Egypt, and U.S. forces continue to serve without incident in the Sinai over fifteen years after that agreement was made. It was further our view that a majority of the Israeli body politic was tired of being a nation perpetually at war and that Israel would never enjoy complete peace until she achieved a full peace with Syria.

"Look, you will *never* get Israel to withdraw from the Golan if its security isn't guaranteed," I said. "This is a security issue in Israel, not an ideological one. The U.N. isn't believed in Israel, but the United States is. This is probably the only way to get Israel to consider withdrawal.

"If we are going to make progress on this issue," I said, "you have to give me more to work with." Assad responded by saying that "the thorns that are in the way are Israeli thorns, not Arab."

"I've spent more than thirty-six hours with you, and I find myself saying *nam* [yes] to your *la* [no]," I challenged. "You're learning Arabic," Assad said with a smile. "This is good."

Assad continued to spar, surfacing peripheral demands that I knew were utterly unrealistic. I groped for an analogy that might force him back to the real world. Finally, I blurted out, "Well, you know, Mr. President, as we say in Texas, if a bullfrog had wings, it wouldn't scrape its ass on the ground."

Djerejian was so aghast that he accidentally plunged his hand into a bowl of hummus, which had been served to help us make it through this marathon meeting. Gemal Helal looked at me in sheer terror. "I can't translate that into *English,* much less Arabic," he pleaded. Assad was totally puzzled. "What does this mean? What does this mean?" he asked. "Ed, I guess that's not translatable," I said. "I think not, Mr. Secretary," Djerejian said. I thought for a moment, then revised my remarks. "I'm reminded of what my father said when I was a young man," I told Assad. "If the dog hadn't stopped running, he would have caught the rabbit." I'm sure he had no idea what I was talking about.

"Mr. President, we need to deal with reality," I suggested. "You gave me four points to deal with. I completely dealt with two of them and I am working to partially deal with the other two." "I feel your sense of purpose," Assad dodged.

"We can handle another ten years of this or another fifty or one hundred, but you are sure passing up a good chance. You haven't moved this far," I said, holding up my thumb and index fingers an inch apart. "I can't keep flying around. At some point we have to count you in or out. That is your decision, not mine. I want you in. I can't see how you can let this opportunity go."

"If you were in my place," Assad countered, "you wouldn't be more flexible than I am now." I tried to contain my growing sense of exasperation. "Mr. President, you haven't given me *any* flexibility," I complained.

"The land is important," he retorted. "It connotes dignity and honor. A man is not chosen to go to paradise unless he can do so in a dignified way. We don't want anyone to say we have given up what we have been talking about for twenty years."

"You can keep saying for twenty *more* years what you have been saying about the land, and the situation will continue to deteriorate," I parried. "It is in the nature of negotiations and creating a peace process that everyone has to move a little bit. I have great respect for your iron kidneys, but you're the *only* one who has not moved—not a bit."

"We are aiming at a midway solution between full sponsorship, as Syria wants, and no U.N. participation, as the Israelis want," he contended. I pressed him to agree to a simple quid pro quo: I would ask the President to endorse the U.S. security guarantee, only if "you can tell me that these two issues will be off the table. Before I go forward, I need to know that if I come back with a yes, you'll help me make a conference happen."

"Frankly, I can't give you an answer without consulting with the institutions of the party and the Progressive National Front," he demurred. "We will do what we can."

It was, I knew, the ultimate brush-off; there was no one in the Syrian Arab Republic with whom Assad needed to consult, except himself. "Okay, let's leave it," I abruptly concluded, slamming my portfolio shut to make sure Assad absorbed my irritation.

Before leaving the room, I decided to raise the stakes for Assad. "Everyone has always told me you're the shrewdest and smartest leader in the Middle East," I said, "and my own conversations with you have suggested as much. But I have to admit I have a hard time understanding how or why you would forgo the chance—even if it's just a chance—to produce Israeli withdrawal from the Golan, for procedural conditions that have no effect and ensure no results.

"I've really enjoyed my discussions here. Our debates have been very interesting. If I get the right answers on these two questions from you, I'll be back in Damascus. If I get the wrong answers, I don't expect to see you again for a long time."

The truth is, my instinct told me that Assad would move, that he was simply waiting to see what happened in my meeting with Shamir on Friday. But I wanted to make sure he understood the ball was in his court.

Unfortunately, when I met Shamir again on April 26, it was apparent the Israelis were becoming more rigid, not less. Not only were they adamant on their objections to conference modalities, they were raising *new* potential roadblocks. By now I'd learned that Henry Kissinger was right—this *was* a standard tactic. Shamir would enunciate a nonnegotiable position—which in Israeli parlance was described as a "red line"—then strew land mines for ten miles in front of that line. Now, Shamir told me, Israel was unhappy that the Saudis wouldn't be at the conference. I recalled that I'd warned King Fahd that his refusal to participate would hand Israel a convenient excuse for further foot-dragging. Predictably, the Israelis were now saying that a conference without the Saudis made little sense.

After an hour or so of sparring, my frustration with Shamir bubbled over. "I'm structuring a meeting right now that meets your requirements on the PLO, on East Jerusalem, on terms that reflect the phases of Camp David," I reminded him. "We're meeting all these things and you're saying the parties can't get together again even when you have the right to veto a reconvening. I've got to tell you I'm *very* disappointed. I'm working my ass off and I'm getting no cooperation from you. I'm finished. I'll tell you, no one has worked harder for you than I have."

"You *are* working very hard," Shamir said, "I admit it. But it doesn't come down only to us. What do we need this for?" I argued that the U.N. observer was merely a symbol which cost Israel nothing. "I can't accept the U.N.," Shamir said. "It's a problem."

I reminded Shamir that I had left three questions for him a week earlier. "What I've got is two nos and a maybe on EC participation," I complained. "I've got to say I'm basically disinclined to come here again. I don't see how we can do this."

"Well, let's think it over and see how we can bridge the gaps," Shamir suggested. "You need to think it over," I said in exasperation.

The tension of the moment was broken by an unexpected development. I was called from the room and told by Susan that my mother had died at her home in Houston at the age of ninety-six. I absorbed this news with a mixture of sorrow as well as the guilt of a son who'd been away from home too long over the years. She'd been terrific about our return to Washington in 1980, but missed us terribly—especially as her health declined. Every time I left her, her advancing frailty made me fear it was the last time I'd ever see her. Even though she'd had a wonderful life, as she used to say often, it was difficult to accept the fact that she was gone. I told Shamir that I would have to leave immediately. He was very gracious in offering what I could tell were truly heartfelt condolences.

My distress over the loss of my mom intermingled with, and may have exacerbated, my unhappiness with the Prime Minister's rigidity. On the way to the airport, my disappointment spilled over. "I'm going to leave this dead cat on *his* doorstep," I vowed to Dennis Ross. "Let's not rush to judgment," Ross counseled. "Let's see how they respond." That was wise advice, but I admit to leaving for home in a mood of serious depression, and fast losing faith in Shamir's credibility.

Perhaps in response to my foul mood, Ross sent me a memo on April 30 accentuating the positive. "In some ways," he said, "we are actually very close to being able to put this together." He conceded that critical differences remained between Israel and Syria on the last two issues. But he reminded me that Shamir and I had worked out the formula on the most difficult issue of all: East Jerusalem. The United States had agreed that East Jerusalem residents would not be included on the Palestinian side of the joint delegation. In turn, Israel had pledged not to challenge any member of the Jordanian side of the delegation with a Jordanian passport, even if they happened to have been born or raised in East Jerusalem. It remained to be seen, however, if this crucial compromise would be accepted by the Palestinians.

On May 3, two days after returning to Washington from my mother's funeral, Ed Djerejian called me to report that Assad had capitulated on the two sticking points from our previous meeting. According to his Foreign Minister, Assad was now willing to accept my compromises of a U.N. observer and reconvening the conference by consensus. I was elated. I now had dramatic new leverage with which to challenge all the other parties, especially Israel and the Saudis, to demonstrate similar flexibility.

The Saudi Backbone Stiffens

This breakthrough with Assad made the Saudi refusal to participate in any way in a peace conference even more troublesome. If Arab moderates like the Saudis remained on the sidelines, Shamir could correctly claim that Arab attitudes really *weren't* changing, and that would reinforce his own reluctance to stay away from the peace table. The Saudi position seemed shortsighted to me, since as a result of their reticence, congressional sentiment was beginning to turn sour against the beneficiaries of Desert Storm.

Armed with this reality, Dennis Ross paid a visit to Prince Bandar's elegant home in the Virginia suburbs. If for no other reason than their own self-interest, Ross argued, the kingdom must make at least some gesture for peace. He proposed that the Saudis send a representative of the Gulf Cooperation Council to attend the conference as an observer. When I learned about the idea later from Ross, I thought it an ingenious way to overcome congenital Saudi caution. Sending a representative of the six-member GCC would give King Fahd some protective cover with his more militant subjects. Conversely, since Saudi Arabia was the dominant force on the council, I could argue to the Israelis that the Saudis were in fact participating in the process. Bandar liked the idea, and agreed to argue it vigorously with King Fahd and with what he would frequently describe with some frustration as "the old thinkers" in his foreign ministry.

On May 7, the President and I met with Bandar at the White House to formally ask him to pass our request to King Fahd. We also asked him to ask the King to announce that Saudi Arabia would participate in multilateral working groups on regional issues such as water and arms control after the political working groups had begun meeting. It was also critical to have the King state publicly that he would suspend the state of belligerency against Israel in exchange for Israel's halting settlement activity. "We've got to get Saudi Arabia leaning forward," the President said. Bandar said he would leave for home that very night. "I'll try my best," he promised. Privately, he told me not to worry. "Relax," he said, "we'll work something out."

Three days later, the Saudis announced that a GCC observer would attend the opening session of a peace conference. Even more important, the

Saudis would attend the multilaterals. It was a stunning development—the custodian of the two holy mosques had agreed to join others in the same room with Israel. Initially, the five other GCC states had refused to go along. But I later learned that King Fahd had awakened the rulers of those countries at two o'clock in the morning to obtain their agreement personally. The King and Bandar had come through on two of our three requests; another crucial Arab domino had fallen into line. Saudi participation now would increase the pressure on Jordan, Syria, and Israel to say yes. The following day, May 11, I left on my fourth trip to the region since the end of the Gulf War. In the fifteen days since leaving Israel, my spirits had done an abrupt turnaround. The mood on my plane was now sky high. Hard bargaining lay ahead, but I had the sense that a tangible momentum for peace was finally beginning to materialize.

Assad's Double Cross

My optimism was short-lived. The first inkling of trouble had come when I arrived in Damascus on the evening of Saturday, May 11, and was greeted by Foreign Minister Shara. This was standard procedure for the Syrians. In addition to being good protocol, it enabled Shara to pick my brain, assess my body language, and report to Assad before our meeting. This modus operandi, of course, also enabled *me* to convey a message in advance of the meeting, particularly with respect to tone. On the ride in from the airport, Shara advised me that Assad had changed his mind on one key point. The United States would need to agree that the conference could be reconvened *without* the approval of all the parties. "That's not what you agreed to, Minister," I said. The next morning, Djerejian brought more bad news. Shara had advised him that Assad had also reneged on his second commitment and was now insisting that the United Nations attend the conference as "a full participant." I asked my staff to annotate a copy of the transcript of my previous meeting, so I would be ready to refute what appeared to be a complete reversal by Assad.

My instinct told me this would be a distinctly unpleasant meeting instead of merely grueling, so at eleven the next morning, I began our session with a quip in hopes of injecting some levity into the situation. "The press has come to refer to these sessions we are having as bladder diplomacy," I joked. Assad ignored me. "What has happened since you last left us?" he asked. For the next five hours and forty-five minutes, the dialogue careened downhill.

In short order, Assad confirmed that he was now spurning the compromises he had previously accepted. Still worse, he was justifying this behavior by maintaining that I had misrepresented the nature of the security guarantee the President was prepared to consider along the Israeli-Syrian border.

I reminded Assad that in our earlier meeting, I'd been very precise in saying that I wouldn't even raise the subject of U.S. security guarantees with President Bush unless Assad first agreed to compromise on the two points in dispute. I wanted him to understand that he was in effect walking away from commitments to the President of the United States. "What should I now tell President Bush?" I inquired. "You should say that I have made a major concession by accepting U.N. full participation as opposed to sponsorship," he replied.

Assad then claimed that in our previous meeting, I had promised to guarantee the *return* of the Golan to Syria in exchange for his two concessions. "I feel you have gone back on the basic matter we discussed at the last meeting," he said. I told him I had done nothing of the sort, and even read aloud from the previous transcript to bolster the point. "You will never find in the transcript that we will guarantee that Israel will return the Golan," I argued. "But the reality is that only with this continuing security guarantee of the border in my opinion would you ever have a chance to get the Golan back." The transcript was unambiguous, and Assad was too smart to have misunderstood. For whatever reasons, he had decided to renege on his word, and now was accusing me of the same, evidently in an effort to mitigate his own conduct.

"Your position is totally unrealistic," I argued. Assad was unfazed. "I did not ask for a guarantee to return the Golan," he insisted. "It was *you* who offered that." In effect, Assad was calling me a liar. "No, sir, I did not," I countered, maintaining my composure with some degree of difficulty.

"I have no doubt or ambiguity that the guarantees referred to in our previous meeting have been withdrawn or backed away from," he reiterated. "Contrary to your views," I replied with a measure of starch, "we are not pulling back *any* guarantees."

Fortunately, Assad then launched into a history lesson, one of his favorite diversionary techniques for deflecting an interlocutor's line of attack and ultimately wearing him down. His lecture was so boring and repetitious that his own vice president, Abdul Halim Khaddam, fell asleep. After about a half hour of this smoke screen, I could take no more. "I'll be frank," I said. "You're really letting Israel off the hook. I'm continuing to try to seek ways to permit us to either hold this conference—or, if not, leave the dead cat on the other doorstep." Assad made no response.

I reminded Assad that an American security guarantee offered a vehicle for gaining Israeli withdrawal from the Golan Heights. Such an offer from the United States was unprecedented and he should not underestimate its importance. "But if you now prefer to focus on form instead of substance,"

I warned, "you will surely be the loser. The Golan will be even more densely settled by Israel, and you'll never get it back."

Finally, I offered a new compromise on the U.N. imbroglio for Assad's consideration: the co-sponsors would keep the Secretary-General regularly informed of the progess of bilateral and multilateral negotiations. In reality, I argued, that would surely have more weight than either Assad's "full participant" formula or my observer compromise. "This is a new idea," Assad replied. "I will consider it." But he refused to budge on the second issue. "On the matter of continuity," he said, "it is a settled matter."

As a matter of principle, I'd insisted on sitting through Assad's interminable soliloquies in each of our previous four meetings, no matter how pedantic or irrelevant to the topic at hand. But now he'd crossed the line in my view. He had given his word, then withdrawn it, accusing me of villainy in the bargain. It was now apparent to me, as we say in Texas, that I was being diddled.

I slammed my portfolio shut with all the intensity I could muster. "We need to get to Cairo," I announced. "We've exhausted the subject. We're back where we started from. I would not be human if I did not tell you I am disappointed. Because of your insistence, there will be no peace negotiations. But I thank you for your time. I hope to see you again sometime." At that moment, I was certain I'd never visit Damascus again. But my dead cat would.

For the first time, Assad seemed a trifle defensive. "I never say anything and go back on it," he maintained. "I must say, Mr. President," I replied, "that I get the feeling that you are so suspicious and untrusting that you will manufacture meanings that don't pertain. This proposal is tailor-made for you, but because of your suspicions, you will pass up this opportunity."

"We'll discuss this here in Syria, but our impression today is not a positive one," Assad said. It was, I realized, a monumental understatement. Assad blamed the Israelis for their intransigence. I replied that he could be right—Israel *might* not be serious—but the only way to know was to test them. "Don't look at it as a question of who is giving what on the issue of symbolism," I suggested. "Look at how it will be judged in the aftermath of failure. Put yourself in the position that Syria is for peace."

On the plane to Cairo, I mused with my aides about why Assad had so brazenly retreated. It was possible that he thought we were getting too close to a deal and wanted to slow down the train. It was also possible that he'd reflected on the possibility of a security guarantee and concluded it wasn't worth the price of concessions. I preferred to believe that he was waiting until he saw if I could extract further concessions from Shamir. Like many Arab leaders, Assad harbored the simplistic notion that the United States could simply deliver Israel whenever we wished because of her dependence on American financial and security commitments. I knew just how false that impression actually was.

I was also irritated with Assad because he'd violated one of my own cardinal precepts of negotiating. I react poorly when an interlocutor reopens an item that's already been resolved. I do not believe in that—a deal is a deal.

During the meeting, I'd consciously tried to modulate my irritation with Assad. I made a point of referring to his retreat as a mere "misunderstanding." But in fact I was furious at what I considered calculated bad faith, and during the ninety-four-minute flight to Cairo to meet with Soviet Foreign Minister Bessmertnykh, I gave a background briefing to reporters traveling with me, in which I unloaded on Assad. Speaking under the protective cloak of "a senior administration official briefing reporters as Secretary Baker flew from Damascus to Cairo," I made it clear that Assad was an impediment to progress and hinted that if he remained intransigent, the United States might pursue the process without Syria. I wanted to leave the impression that Assad might not be up to the challenges required of great leaders, and I apparently succeeded. Two weeks later in Lisbon, Syrian Foreign Minister Shara approached Dennis Ross, whom he believed had been the briefer, and pointedly pleaded with him never to give such a harsh backgrounder again.

In a cable to the President, I admitted that from a personal standpoint, Assad's turnaround had "left a bad taste in my mouth" and dashed my hopes for a breakthrough. "At this point," I conceded, "I have low expectations." I was still bitterly disappointed with Assad when I arrived in Cairo, but I felt somewhat more serene after meeting with Sasha Bessmertnykh in the Gold Room of the Soviet Ambassador's residence. Bessmertnykh had been shuttling around the region for the first time himself and delivered an upbeat appraisal of his talks. "I think Assad is prepared to be more flexible on the U.N. issue than he is revealing now," he told me. Gorbachev would be writing a letter to Assad, and Bessmertnykh would lobby Assad personally two days hence in Damascus. "I believe he is susceptible to the argument of responsibility," Bessmertnykh ventured.

Egypt and Jordan, Again

A night's sleep hadn't helped my temperament, and the next day, on May 13, I unfairly took out my frustrations on Hosni Mubarak, the one Arab leader who had from the beginning demonstrated his courage and commitment to peace, and who deserved far better from his dispirited guest. He had already been briefed by the Syrians, but my demeanor was really all he needed to know. "Jim, I can read the disappointment in your face," he remarked.

"I can't keep flying around here on an airplane," I complained. "We're stuck. Israel won't budge." Mubarak had seen it all before. "Be patient," he counseled. "You'll get the Syrians."

"I'll tell you I am just not going to do it," I replied. "If you want me to stay out here, you better give me a good reason to stay out here. Right now I don't have one."

Mubarak believed Assad was simply stalling for time, expecting to get a better deal. "You're dealing with a rug merchant and a master negotiator," he said. "Assad gives you a little bit of hope and then he changes the ground rules." It was a classic Assad technique which had served him brilliantly in the past, Mubarak told me in a fatherly tone, suggesting that perhaps I was overreacting to the disappointment of the moment. Assad was too smart not to understand the ramifications of intransigence, Mubarak insisted.

I asked him to remind Assad that because of the Gulf War and America's preeminent position in the world, it was unlikely that any other American President would ever be in a position to offer a guarantee of the border along the Golan. "I can't believe he's prepared to throw away this opportunity," I said. As usual, Mubarak was one step ahead of me. He would be leaving for Europe within the week, and had already altered his itinerary to stop in Damascus to reinforce my message personally with Assad. "I will tell my brother that he would be a fool if he chooses not to go along with what is being proposed," Mubarak promised.

After a working lunch with Mubarak and Bessmertnykh, I met with Lebanese Foreign Minister Faris Bouez, who assured me emphatically that Lebanon would participate in the peace process. I welcomed this news with a grain of salt. We both knew that Lebanon wouldn't do *anything* without Assad's approval.

The next afternoon, May 14, I flew to Amman for my second meeting with King Hussein. I reminded him that his participation was critical, regardless of Assad's decision. I pressed him for a commitment, but he said he would need to consult further. He was willing to put together a joint delegation to a peace conference, but only if the Palestinians asked him. I reiterated that Israel privately understood that any Palestinian delegation would have the tacit acquiescence of the PLO, but a visible PLO role was unacceptable. "The Palestinians from the occupied territories need to be visibly working with you," I said, "and you *have* to keep your PLO tie in the background as you work on a delegation. Arafat cannot show up in Amman during this process." The King told me this would be no problem, and agreed to use his private channels to assure the Israelis there would be no surprises with the delegation. As a sweetener to encourage his continued cooperation, I told the King that, despite congressional objections, the administration would shortly deliver $27 million in food assistance to Jordan.

I sensed that the ever-cautious monarch was quite eager to engage but would reserve a decision until he saw how Assad reacted. In his remarks to the press after our meeting, he basically repeated the words in a draft statement I had shown him. While hedging when asked if he would attend a conference, he welcomed the GCC's decision to attend, and urged Assad to participate. "This is the time to move away from clichés and taboos and see exactly who is genuinely committed to the cause of peace," he said. I took as a positive sign the fact that his statement mirrored precisely the formulation I'd been using since my first trip to the region in March.

After my meeting with the King, I was scheduled to travel to Jerusalem. The day before, I had complained to my staff, "Between security, staff, press, and gawkers, I'm a prisoner on these trips. I've barely seen the territory these people are fighting over." In response, Margaret Tutwiler suggested that rather than fly from Amman to Jerusalem, we should drive, crossing the Jordan River into Israel by foot via the Allenby Bridge. The idea was a good one. As the first Secretary of State to make such a journey, it would have a significant emotional and political component.

Following my press conference in Amman, our motorcade left for the forty-minute drive west to the Jordan River. When we arrived at the Allenby Bridge, I was met by two Jordanian army colonels who accompanied me on foot to the midpoint of the bridge. There we were met by Gadi Zohar, a brigadier general in the Israeli army. For a brief moment, the four of us stood in silence. Then, one of the Jordanian colonels turned to me and said, "Sir, I cannot go any further." He and his colleague saluted me, turned and left, and I continued the walk across with General Zohar. As I walked the last few feet into Israel, I reflected on just how short the physical distance really was between these peoples whose differences oftentimes seemed so irreconcilable. If nothing else, this brief walk by the American Secretary of State over an old wooden bridge visually demonstrated the importance of promoting coexistence between these peoples.

My fourth meeting with three Palestinian leaders in Jerusalem that evening was less than satisfactory. Unlike in the previous three sessions, Husseini, Ashrawi, and Zakariah Al-Agha seemed to have reverted to form. They dusted off their old argument that the issue of Jerusalem must be addressed before peace talks could begin. And they insisted that the formation of a Palestinian delegation was a matter for Palestinians only—a position Husseini repeated to the press afterward.

They were always lecturing me about an American double standard. "May I be impolite?" one of them asked, prompting me to ask myself how

I would know the difference. "You've been able to get nothing from Israel on settlements, deportation, and increasing economic strangulation. Things are getting worse, and you have shown you have no clout." By now I was beginning to believe that the Palestinians were more interested in arguing than resolving anything. "Are we going to talk forever?" I interrupted. "Sixty-five percent of what you claim as your land has already been settled by Israel. If we can't begin negotiations, they will take eighty-five percent of it. But we can get you negotiations if you cooperate." I began to feel that I was the crew chief for some vintage aircraft held together with baling wire and chewing gum. Every time a new crack was patched up, another fissure developed elsewhere on the fuselage.

A Bittersweet Denouement in Jerusalem

The next morning, I met Shamir for the fifth time in as many weeks. In truth, my patience with his evasions had by now evaporated. I was loaded for bear. But the Prime Minister totally disarmed me when he began the meeting by handing me a certificate attesting that his government had planted a grove of ninety-six fir trees in the American Independence Park as a living memorial to my mother. I was extremely touched by this thoughtful gesture, and tears filled my eyes as I thanked him for his kindness. My mood changed appreciably. My aides later told me that Shamir's gesture had kept what they had feared might develop into a somewhat ugly meeting from getting out of hand.

Nevertheless, it was a difficult session. I told Shamir that I was still unhappy that he wasn't willing to show any flexibility on the remaining two points in dispute: U.N. observer status and reconvening the conference. I let him know that I was particularly irritated that Yossi Ben Aharon, one of his key assistants, had belittled the Saudi decision to attend the multilaterals, saying in a public statement on the Sunday the Saudi decision was announced that it "contributes nothing" to the peace process. "For over forty years," I said, staring straight at Aharon, "Israelis have called on Arab states to do what Saudi Arabia has done, and then an Israeli official dismisses it. Your reaction sends a terrible signal to the Arabs." Aharon sat silently through this denunciation. Shamir tried to wave it off. "He didn't really mean it," he said, as though that excused it.

I also complained that a premature leak from Israel had killed plans for the symbolically important visit by a brother of King Fahd to East Jerusalem. "Leaks like this are really devastating," I noted. "And of course, the settlements that get set up or expanded each time I arrive in Israel certainly don't send positive signals to Arabs of your intentions."

My greatest disappointment, I told him, was that "you're leaving an impression that you and Syria are in the same boat, that both of you plan to stand fast on modalities." I repeated the practical arguments I made with Shamir time and again: the process had been purposely skewed to Israel's specifications, much to the irritation of the Arabs, to give Israel what it had always wanted—direct talks. Hiding behind peripheral issues which had no effect upon face-to-face negotiations was extremely shortsighted to Israel's interests.

"I frankly don't know whether or not Syria will start moving its position on modalities," I ventured, "but I *do* know that [if we fail] I want Syria to be the party seen as not agreeing to a reasonable process."

I asked again that Shamir drop his objections to the two remaining procedural issues. In exchange, I pledged to tell the Arabs that there could be no East Jerusalemites on the Palestinian side of any joint delegation. "And let me also assure you that I will not allow the goalposts to move," I pledged. "I won't come back to you on these issues and ask for more. You can lock in your position, confident that the onus will now be on the Syrians."

At a minimum, I said that I expected to leave Israel with a written summary spelling out precisely what Israel had agreed to, so that we could show the Arabs with specificity what was required from them to reach an agreement. This "working paper" had a secondary purpose as well. In effect, I wanted it in writing so that if King Hussein and Assad agreed to compromise on the remaining two issues, Israel would have no standing to raise new ones.

Once more, I pressed Shamir to drop his dual objections. "You've got to give me something on the U.N., and you've got to give me something on reconvening," I said. If not, the onus would now be on Israel, not the Arabs.

Shamir was unyielding, so I resorted to some amateur theatrics in hopes of shaming them into softening their position on a U.N. observer. "You've got a guy sitting there like this"—I clasped my hand over my mouth so that I couldn't speak—"you tell me how that's a threat? I don't get it." Even Shamir had to smile. "You're not giving me anything on this," I complained. "You've got to give me *something.*"

In the end, they did. The next morning, Thursday, May 16, Shamir refused to budge on the U.N. observer. But he declared that the multilateral talks that would follow the conference would be considered by Israel as a reconvening of the process. It wasn't much, but in tandem with a twelve-point memorandum of understanding on principles and modalities our staffs had hammered out overnight, at least there was something new I could market with Hussein and Assad.

"I am not disappointed," I told reporters at Ben Gurion Airport. "I think we are making progress." In truth, however, all I had in my pocket after 53,068 miles of shuttling throughout the region were some very modest concessions from Shamir, and a retreat by Assad. On the long flight home to Washington from Tel Aviv, I prepared a memorandum for the President summarizing the trip and mulling future moves. "I come back from this trip disappointed in the attitude I encountered in Syria," I began, "but still hopeful about our prospects. Though the path is still difficult, and the objective may yet prove unattainable, we do have a chance to put this thing together."

I knew that if Assad could be turned around, King Hussein's participation was a given. I was dubious about Assad, but there was still some chance Hussein could be persuaded to participate unilaterally. After learning that he would be visiting Syria shortly, I had called him before leaving Israel. I wanted his commitment to attend the conference regardless of whether Syria came. "I'll be the master of my own destiny," he told me. "I'm going to Damascus only for reasons of form." I wasn't prepared to bet the ranch on it, but if he could be persuaded to attend, it would be time to end his political and economic isolation.

Shortly after returning to Washington, I reviewed the situation with the President and Brent Scowcroft. We agreed that an intensive round of telephone diplomacy involving the President should be followed by some action-forcing event. For some time, we had been considering bringing matters to a head by having the President issue conference invitations to all the parties. I wasn't sure, however, that the time for brinksmanship was quite at hand. If we issued the invitations and someone declined, the entire process might collapse like a house of cards. Given Shamir's intransigence, I wasn't willing to risk everything just at that point. It would be hard for both Israel and Syria to say no to an invitation on the basis of symbols still in dispute.

We decided instead on an interim step. On May 31, the President sent letters to Shamir, Assad, Mubarak, King Hussein, and King Fahd, urging that they all demonstrate new flexibility so that a peace conference could be held. I personally delivered Assad's letter to his Foreign Minister during a meeting in Lisbon the next day. The letter offered some new language, mainly on the role of the United Nations, that we hoped would satisfy Assad's reservations. It also included some carefully veiled warnings to give Assad pause. "We cannot agree," the President wrote, "that a process not proceed even if you choose not to come." Moreover, he pointed out, "our bilateral relationship is dependent on many things; but as with other states in the region a critical part of that relationship depends on Syria's position on peace." I knew Assad would absorb the implication: this train is leaving the station, and there would be repercussions if Syria wasn't aboard. I reiterated that point with Shara, who wanted me to go to Damascus for another marathon session. "That only makes sense if I know the trip will be productive," I responded. "Henry Kissinger came to Damascus thirteen times," Shara protested. "I don't intend to do that," I said.

Six days later, Shamir responded with a very tough letter, rejecting any compromise on either the U.N. or the reconvening issues. I'd expected his reply to be more nuanced, and his strong tone reconfirmed my dark suspicion that Shamir simply was not interested in peace.

While Shamir had avoided saying no—and his letter indicated some nervousness that we might go ahead and issue invitations—I felt we were left with only one last tactical stratagem—persuading Assad somehow to compromise, thereby thrusting Shamir onto the defensive. If Syria showed the flexibility that Israel had now shunned, Shamir would be forced to reconsider to avoid being tarred as the only one not willing to talk peace.

After my meeting in Lisbon with Shara, I'd sent this private assessment to the President: "In the end, I think we have Assad feeling uneasy. He wants to build a relationship with us and he knows he can't if he stiffs us on the peace process. Similarly, he fears being tagged with the responsibility for blocking peace, and he knows we're serious both about movement and about shifting the onus on those who prevent it. That may not be sufficient to move Assad, but for the moment we have positioned ourselves about as well as we can."

The early indications, however, were discouraging. The Syrians took the position that since the Israelis had rejected the President's letter, Assad was under no obligation to do anything. I passed word via Djerejian that when the President of the United States sends a letter to another head of state, a response is mandatory. I also asked Mubarak and King Fahd to remind Assad that simply by agreeing to talk, he now had the priceless opportunity to embellish his own credentials as a statesman, while shifting the onus to his archenemies in Jerusalem. My efforts to move Shamir had failed. Now, I mused with some irony, the last line of defense for salvaging the peace process rested with Damascus. Despite the special relationship between the United States and Israel, only Assad was in a position to move the Israelis. I could only hope that he would grasp the benefits of seizing the moment more clearly than Shamir.

CHAPTER 26

FROM BERLIN TO THE BALKANS

We killed communism, but we are faced with its debris, which is still toxic.
—Albanian opposition leader Sali Berisha, June 22, 1991

Thursday, June 20, 1991, two weeks later, was a sunny, bright day in Berlin, a perfect day to go outside and enjoy the warmth of the sun while doing some work. Sasha Bessmertnykh agreed, so we sat around a table on the back lawn of the U.S. Ambassador's residence and tried to make progress on the START Treaty. This was not easy to do, of course, but Bessmertnykh was, as always, good humored. "By the time we get arms control solved," he joked, "my six-month-old son will be working on it." After two hours of trudging through downloading, perimeter portal monitoring, and the like, we concluded with a brief press conference.

I was in Berlin for a CSCE ministerial and for a speech that would build on my December 1989 Berlin address on Europe's new diplomatic and political architecture. I was looking forward to my first meetings-free evening, when Bob Pearson, the Department's executive secretary, rushed in. "Main State just received a flash cable from Ambassador Matlock in Moscow," Pearson said. My eyebrows went up. "Flash" was a cable designation to be used only in the most extreme emergency—the outbreak of war or an attack on an embassy. "Mayor Popov went to Spaso House to see Matlock on an urgent basis. He penciled on a piece of paper, 'There is going to be a coup against Gorbachev.' Larry Eagleburger's gone over to the White House to see the President," Pearson explained.

"Gorbachev needs to know," I said. "Let's call the President, and if he agrees, I want to see Bessmertnykh now!"

We returned to the Inter-Continental Hotel ten minutes away, and I spoke to the President, using the STU-III secure telephone in my suite. President Bush had already told Larry to instruct Matlock to arrange a meeting with Gorbachev. The President agreed that I should talk to Bessmertnykh, too.

I reached Sasha by phone a few minutes later. "I have something important to tell you, and I want to do it in person. Can you come to my hotel in a few minutes?" I asked.

Bessmertnykh clearly didn't have a clue as to why I wanted to see him. I presumed he thought I wanted to clear up some esoteric arms control issue. In any case, he told me he had an appointment with the Cypriot Foreign Minister. "Can't this wait?" he said.

"Sasha," I said, "I really think this is necessary. What I have for you is new and important."

Maybe, he said, someone else could come over.

"No, Sasha, it has to be you. Alone."

Finally, he got the message. Fifteen minutes later, he arrived at my suite.

"Sasha," I said, "reliable sources have told us that there will be an attempt to remove Gorbachev tomorrow. We understand this effort involves Pavlov, Kryuchkov, Yazov, and Lukyanov.* Matlock is asking to see Gorbachev. You need to call him and tell him it's important to have that meeting—and promptly—but obviously you can't tell him why over the telephone" (because of possible KGB bugging).

Thanking me, and clearly agreeing, Bessmertnykh left immediately to pass word to Gorbachev through his longtime aide, Anatoliy Chernyayev. Meanwhile, the President was informing Russian President Boris Yeltsin, who was at the White House on a long-scheduled visit.

Minutes later, Matlock stepped into Gorbachev's office at the Kremlin and relayed the warning. The Soviet President was far from alarmed. He realized that in the parliamentary maneuverings that week, hard-liners were trying to chip away at his reform program. But he found the idea of a coup fanciful and believed no one could overthrow him. And for the moment, he was right. There was no coup attempt—though Pavlov did make an open attempt to seize power through the Soviet parliament.

In retrospect, we were wise to take the warnings of the coup seriously—Gorbachev was almost toppled in a coup just two months later. But our efforts to warn him and work with him that June day revealed one of

---

*Valentin Pavlov was the Soviet Prime Minister; Vladimir Kryuchkov head of the KGB; Dmitri Yazov Defense Minister; and Anatoliy Lukyanov Speaker of the Parliament and a law school classmate of Gorbachev.

the most critical paradoxes of U.S.-Soviet relations from the onset of the Gulf Crisis through the spring and summer of 1991: just as U.S.-Soviet cooperation was reaching its highest point, Gorbachev's domestic political position and the stability of the Soviet state were reaching their lowest levels.

Soviet Opportunities—and Dangers

Almost a year earlier, on July 18, 1990, on the margins of the last Two-plus-Four Ministerial in Paris, I had met with Eduard Shevardnadze to discuss the state of our relations. I had just come from the London NATO Summit and the Houston Economic Summit. Each had advanced East-West cooperation significantly—London by adopting the political and security declaration that helped us get the unified Germany into NATO, Houston by instructing the international financial institutions to conduct a study of the Soviet economy, a prerequisite to any large-scale Western financial assistance. But it was the political aspect of our relations that I wanted to raise with Shevardnadze.

The week before, at the Communist Party Congress, Boris Yeltsin had stormed out and quit the Party. He'd railed against the Party, arguing that it could never be the engine of real change. He had gone on to stake out a far more radical position than Gorbachev, both on political and economic reform. Mayor Gavril Popov of Moscow and Mayor Anatoliy Sobchak of Leningrad had also resigned. For the first time, it looked as though the nucleus of a viable opposition was forming.

While we remained committed to working through Gorbachev to advance American foreign policy interests, we wanted to begin hedging our position by diversifying the political contacts we were developing in the Soviet Union.

I had said as much to our traveling press on the way to Paris, but now I wanted to preview our evolving approach with Shevardnadze. "We will," I said, "from time to time, be willing to meet with leaders of the opposition in the Soviet Union, just as we meet with the opposition in other countries. When the opposition from other countries come to the United States, we meet with them. It's routine for us." I told him that I didn't want him to misread this as a diminution in our desire to see perestroika succeed. However, "if and when an opposition party develops in the Soviet Union, we'll expect to see the representatives of that party. That's the way we do it with opposition parties from a democratic state, and neither you nor President Gorbachev should misinterpret that. It's really part of our concept of democracy."

Shevardnadze said he was glad to hear this. In fact, he was looking forward to the time when a real opposition existed in the USSR. "For the time being," he observed, "what I could call a responsible opposition does not exist. Now we have adventurists in the political arena—they're not serious because all they want to do is harass Gorbachev."

Jokingly, I noted, "When Gorbachev comes into Washington, he meets Democrats, and we don't have any problem with that; we understand that."

"But I must say I don't remember Democrats saying insulting things about the President of the United States," Shevardnadze responded. "Now that's a real political culture," he exclaimed.

The conversation was over almost as soon as it started. Yet I felt confident that I had laid down the predicate for expanding both the number and type of contacts with the political opposition in the Soviet Union.

Less than a month later, Iraq invaded Kuwait—and our need for not just Soviet cooperation but Gorbachev's personal engagement was greater than ever. Throughout the Gulf crisis and the war to liberate Kuwait, we had to rely again and again on the personal relationships the President and I had carefully developed with Gorbachev and Shevardnadze.

Moreover, we managed to maintain the momentum in U.S.-Soviet relations during this period. At the CSCE Summit in Paris in November, we codified many of the changes that had occurred across Europe during the past year, strengthening CSCE and making it what I came to call "the conscience of the Continent." All members of NATO and the Warsaw Pact joined the other states of Europe in signing the "Charter of Paris," which ended the era of "division and confrontation," declared that "security is indivisible," and agreed to "build new partnerships and extend to each other the hand of friendship."

With much hard work, we completed the CFE Treaty, and heads of state signed it in Paris on November 19. (At one marathon negotiating session with Shevardnadze at the Soviet mission to the United Nations in October, I took a break, playing the Marine Corps hymn on the piano,* and told my colleagues from Moscow, "I bet you'd never thought you'd hear the U.S. Marine Corps hymn played at the Soviet mission, much less by the American Secretary of State.") Completed in less than two years, CFE achieved significant cuts, not only in manpower, but in tanks, armored personnel carriers, and artillery—the very weapons that for a generation had raised fears of a Soviet blitzkrieg into Western Europe. The larger Warsaw Pact members reduced the bulk of their forces, as they were required to cut ten times as many weapons as was NATO.

However, shortly after the Paris signing, several disagreements emerged concerning details of the treaty. The Soviet military was asserting

---

*The only tune I can play on the piano.

itself even more than it had in the spring of 1990, and eventually it took us until June 1991 to resolve these disputes.*

But then in December 1990, thunder struck. In what he called "perhaps the shortest and most difficult speech" of his life, Eduard Shevardnadze resigned as Soviet Foreign Minister, as a "protest against the onset of dictatorship." I was jolted. Two weeks previously, we had met in Houston, and I had shown him Houston's sights—not only the Johnson Space Center, where we talked to U.S. astronauts orbiting the earth, but also the house where I had grown up. I'd introduced both Eduard and Nanuli to my mother. The Shevardnadzes had been very kind to my mother. They'd given her a samovar, and Eduard had held her hand very thoughtfully and graciously as he said nice things to her about me. We'd flown back to Washington on my plane, and had a few vodkas during the trip. Shevardnadze seemed under a good deal of stress—somewhat lost in thought toward the end of the flight, but laughing and joking most of the way. I had no inkling that he was about to resign. I realized Shevardnadze had been under great political pressure at home, but he was *always* on the spot in Moscow. I found it hard to believe he would leave Gorbachev. The two just seemed inseparable.

I went down to the press room on the Department's first floor to say a few words about his resignation. It was not an easy task; he was a respected colleague, but our bonds far exceeded a mere professional relationship. I told the press, "I have known Eduard Shevardnadze to be a man of his word, a man of courage, conviction, and principle." When one of the reporters asked me how I felt personally, I had to answer, "I am proud to call this man a friend. I think that we achieved some significant things during the twenty-three months that we were able to work together, and on a purely personal note, I would have to tell you that I'm going to miss him."

The next day, Matlock received a message from Shevardnadze via Sergei Tarasenko. Shevardnadze asked me to understand that he would not have resigned if he hadn't been confident that the positive course in U.S.-Soviet relations was irreversible. He thought that his successor would be constrained to follow the same course, though improvements would come somewhat more slowly. Gorbachev had refused to accept his resignation,

---

*First, we disagreed with Moscow about the size of the USSR's conventional arsenal. Second, there was reason to suspect that the Soviets had begun to move weapons outside the Atlantic-to-the-Urals zone (ATTU), thus removing them from CFE jurisdiction. And third, we disagreed with the Soviets on their definition of three divisions of troops near the Black Sea. These divisions had been designated as army forces, thus subject to CFE limits. The Soviet military then redefined them as "coastal defense units," placing them outside the scope of the treaty's limits.

but Shevardnadze felt he could not stay on, having announced his departure. To stay, Shevardnadze believed, would be moral suicide. A month later, he wrote me. He said he had been particularly warmed by my public statements concerning his resignation, but "frankly, my feelings and emotions become all the more intense as I realize that this step came to you as a surprise. . . . Of course you have the right to resent that I failed to tell you what I have been pondering this whole past year, even though we have met so frequently. There is, however, a limit beyond which I had no strength to step, and this, I'm sure, you can understand very well." I wrote him that I understood why he couldn't tell me about his pending resignation and saluted him because, "true to your convictions and your values, you took a courageous and difficult step."

Shevardnadze's resignation, the Soviet military's intransigience on arms control, and the crackdown in Lithuania in January 1991 made me all the more wary of Gorbachev's prospects. I well remember a White House session in late January with two of the Agency's Soviet specialists: Bob Blackwell and George Kolt. After their presentations, which were quite pessimistic, I remember saying to them in effect: "What you're telling us, fellas, is that the stock market is heading south. We need to sell."

But in the case of U.S.-Soviet relations, "selling" meant trying to get as much as we could out of the Soviets before there was an even greater turn to the right or shift into disintegration. And the way to do that was to maintain our relations with Mikhail Gorbachev until we could successfully prosecute the Gulf War, which we did; finish the START Treaty, which we did in July; and ensure that CFE didn't unravel, while also advancing other unfinished items on our foreign policy agenda, notably progress toward Middle East peace.

In March, I returned to Moscow for the first time in six months. The political situation was even more polarized. Four days before my visit, Yeltsin and his supporters had taken to the streets of the Soviet capital and the other major cities, producing massive crowds agitating for radical reform. Yeltsin urged his supporters "to declare war on the leadership of this country, which has led us into a quagmire."

When I met with Gorbachev on March 15, he was fixated on problems at home, particularly Yeltsin. An avid reader of translations of the Western press, Gorbachev had read in *Time* magazine that one of our embassy officials had said the Soviet Union was on the verge of a revolution. "That's wrong!" Gorbachev exclaimed. "We're not on the verge of a revolution, we're *in* a revolution!" He said he was stressed, and the pressures were enormous. But small changes or tinkering with the system had been tried and couldn't work. An overhaul was needed, and it had to be fundamental. Nonetheless, Gorbachev said he needed room to maneuver. "Each maneuver is designed not to retreat from perestroika but to preserve it," he said.

In any case, he was more concerned with the economy than with politics. Noting the severe economic downturn, he said, "Hitler exploited a drastic drop in economic production to come to power. Dictators always emerge in circumstances of total economic chaos and depression. Pressures for a dictator are now building in the Soviet Union."

"Why not settle the Center-Republic issues first?" I asked, noting the March 17 date for a referendum on the future of the Union. "Those issues are political. They're more amenable to solution than trying to reshape an economy grounded in seventy years of the traditions and psychology of a command system. Why not take advantage of the referendum to declare victory, reach out to the republics, and modify your laws on secession?"

Gorbachev felt the draft Union Treaty would meet these needs. I was far less sure. The Union Treaty might paper over some of the Center-Republic differences, but power seemed to be shifting to the street, to borrow a phrase from Lenin, and that favored the republics over the longer term.

On Yeltsin, Gorbachev was positively neuralgic. He said Yeltsin was unstable and would use populist rhetoric to become a dictator if he ever had the chance. Shevardnadze echoed this view. I felt Yeltsin was at heart a theatrical, wholesale politician, a man prone to larger-than-life gestures. But, above all, he was a street-smart politician who sensed the democratic mood sweeping the country, and what seemed like instability could just as easily be explained by the political roller coaster Yeltsin was riding. There were going to be ups and downs, but anyone who could turn out hundreds of thousands of people into the street was someone the United States needed to cultivate.

The day I arrived in Moscow, Yeltsin sent word that he wanted to see me privately for ten minutes, either before or after a dinner I was hosting the next evening. I sent the President a note, telling him I planned to see Yeltsin, unless he thought it was unwise. He didn't, so I went ahead and scheduled the meeting. However, just hours before the dinner, and ten minutes before I was supposed to see Gorbachev, I found out that Yeltsin was demanding to see me either at his office, the Russian Republic's guest house, or a neutral site. It was clearly an effort to lift his profile symbolically—and drive Gorbachev up the wall. So while I left for my meeting, I had my staff call the NSC. After consulting the President, Scowcroft sent word back that I should broach the subject with Gorbachev, who naturally went through the roof. But before I could talk to Yeltsin, his staff sent word that he couldn't make the dinner (and therefore the private meeting either before or after) and would send someone else.*

The incident was symptomatic of the complex relationship between Gorbachev and Yeltsin, but it also illustrated the fine balance we had to maintain between the two of them. On the one hand, by the summer of 1991, Gorbachev was one of the most unpopular politicians in the Soviet Union, but he remained President and commander in chief of a country with 30,000 nuclear weapons and was responsible for the Kremlin's decision making on issues vital to our interests, such as START, CFE, and Middle East peace. And it was his decisions on those issues of importance to us that contributed heavily to that unpopularity. On the other hand, by this time, Yeltsin was the fastest-growing political force in the USSR, and in June of that year, he would become the first popularly elected leader in Russian history, and win an overwhelming mandate for radical change. Building ties to him, and supporting him, was undoubtedly consistent with our values, and certainly in our long-term interest of bringing democracy to the Soviet Union.

I don't doubt that our efforts to balance these complex interests and values and maintain ties with both of these men irritated both Gorbachev and Yeltsin from time to time. Yet for U.S. diplomacy, what truly mattered was whether a minor irritant grew into a lasting resentment that adversely affected our interests. I think it's obvious that in the case of Mikhail Gorbachev and Boris Yeltsin, the opposite was the case: Both always valued their relationship with George Bush and the United States, not only in terms of their standing in the world but also their standing at home. And our handling of the transition from Gorbachev to Yeltsin was effective and of substantial benefit to the United States in many ways.

Western support for economic reform was the other major Soviet domestic issue we had to balance in the spring of 1991. Time and again since we had come into office in January 1989, Gorbachev had shown an unwillingness to bite the bullet and adopt a genuine market-reform program. This continued throughout 1990 and well into the spring of 1991. It wasn't for lack of good ideas; in August 1990, Stanislav Shatalin, by Soviet standards a true free-market economist and prominent Gorbachev adviser, had proposed a plan to shift to a market economy in 500 days. But after considering the "500-Day Plan" for a month, Gorbachev had turned it into a "presidential plan" that was more mush than market. By April 1991, the Kremlin

---

*He did—Vladimir Lukin, whom Yeltsin appointed as the Russian Federation's first Ambassador to the United States.

was inhabited by more reactionaries than reformers, and Prime Minister Pavlov proposed an "anti-crisis" program that had far more central planning than market economics in it.

Into the mix entered a close adviser to Yeltsin, Grigory Yavlinsky, who had assisted Shatalin on the "500-Day Plan," and a handful of Harvard professors.* They proposed the idea of a "grand bargain," in which the Soviet Union would move decisively to a free-market system in return for the West's providing billions of dollars to help cushion the shock of the transition.

When I first heard of the idea from Bob Zoellick, I was openly skeptical. I doubted Gorbachev had either the political will or capability to push through such a plan. Moreover, there was no Western consensus behind massive sums of assistance, and I didn't see one developing on the horizon. But I told him to keep working with Yavlinsky, in hopes that there would be some cross-fertilization of ideas that would at least get us beyond the Pavlov plan.

Unfortunately, the whole notion of any bargain was stillborn when Gorbachev decided to send Primakov to Washington in late May to discuss economic issues.† Politically, Primakov's Gulf meddling had severely undermined his credibility in the administration, and economically, he was a neophyte. When I met with him on May 29, I said that for two years, I had been telling Gorbachev and Shevardnadze that they needed to make hard choices with regard to the economy. As a former Secretary of the Treasury, I had told them, there were no shortcuts. There was going to be pain regardless of what they did, so they should do it quickly and right. But Primakov came with nothing new, and as far as I could tell, our meetings did little to change Soviet thinking. Gorbachev continued to equivocate, and while he made the political case for Western assistance quite convincingly, he never established the economic reforms to get such an effort off the ground. The "grand bargain" ended up being neither very grand nor much of a bargain.

Breakdown in Belgrade

Following the "non-coup" and the CSCE Ministerial, I left Berlin on Friday, June 21, for a one-day trip to Belgrade, Yugoslavia. The six Yugoslav republics—Slovenia, Croatia, Bosnia-Herzegovina, Serbia, Montenegro, and

---

*Among them was Bob Blackwill, formerly the President's point man on Europe (not to be confused with Bob Blackwell of the CIA), who had left the NSC staff for academia.

†Both the President and I had tried to support Yavlinsky's approach of radical reform by statements supporting his work and ideas.

Macedonia—were caught in an intricate and intense web of political conflict. In what our Ambassador to Belgrade, Warren Zimmermann, liked to call "top-down" competitive nationalism, the leaders of almost every republic were jockeying for advantage in the rapidly disintegrating Yugoslav federation.

Slovenia and Croatia were bidding for outright independence and had set deadlines in late June to make their moves unilaterally. Yugoslavia was probably the most ethnically heterogenous country in Europe, but efforts to break it up by declaring independence unilaterally, and thereby foreclosing any possibility to negotiate the split peacefully, raised the specter of civil war. At the Berlin CSCE Ministerial, the organization had taken the unprecedented act of involving itself directly in an internal controversy of one of its members, and issued a statement that called for a "peaceful solution of the current crisis." As a positive inducement, CSCE also made it clear that the international community would assist Yugoslavia in its efforts to transform itself economically and politically, if it did so peacefully and consensually. But to complement this positive message, we also needed to deliver a negative signal, to try to shock the various republic leaders into accepting two basic realities: that they needed to negotiate their differences, not act unilaterally; and that under no circumstances would the international community tolerate the use of force. This was the message all of my European colleagues in Berlin had urged me to take to Belgrade, and it was one I was ready to deliver, because the President and I had grown quite concerned that Yugoslavia was about to implode.

My day in Belgrade started ominously. The FBI had a report of threats against me, and, according to the Bureau, their source for the report was credible. Upon arrival, I went directly to the Federation Palace, a monstrous Stalinesque building that housed the Yugoslav government and those of the six republics. Each republic had a huge, cavernous meeting room decorated with artwork from its own ethnic tradition. For the next ten hours, save for a side trip to meet with representatives from Kosovo, I shuttled from room to room, meeting with the heads of each republic. I also began and ended my day in a session with Prime Minister Ante Markovic, the head of the federal government, who was trying in vain to prevent the Balkan powder keg from exploding.

In each meeting, I made the same core points. Coming to Belgrade, not just as a representative of the United States but also as a representative of CSCE, I wanted the leaders of each republic and the Yugoslav Federation to know that all of Europe, Canada, and the United States were extremely concerned about their situation. I asked each representative, "personally and as a political leader," to reaffirm their adherence to the principles of the Helsinki Conference, notably the principles that all disputes must be resolved peacefully, borders must not be changed except by consent, and human rights must be protected, particularly minority rights.

I then went on to lay out four specific concerns. First, I said over and over, "Our critical interest in the Yugoslav question is its peaceful settlement. We will continue to oppose the use of force or intimidation to resolve political differences." Unilateral acts, I reiterated, would lead to disaster, a point I underscored with the Slovenians and Croatians. I also said that while we supported the territorial integrity of Yugoslavia and existing republic borders and would not accept unilateral changes, the international community, of course, recognized that if the republics wanted to change borders by peaceful, consensual means, that was an altogether different matter.

Second, I raised human rights—of Albanians in Kosovo, of Hungarians in Vojvodina, of Serbs in Croatia. These rights could best be protected, I told each of my interlocutors, through what we called a "democratically renewed Yugoslav union." I told Markovic and each republic president that the shape of this union—federal, confederal, or whatever—was up to them, but cautioned that any attempt to split Yugoslavia along ethnic lines would only lead to bloodshed and the denial of minority rights. I went on to note that while we sought to isolate no one in Yugoslavia, those who trampled on minority rights would isolate themselves from the international community. I emphasized this point in particular with the Serbians and the Croatians.

Third, I raised the need to continue the Yugoslav Federation's constitutional rotation of presidential authority. In May, the Serbs had blocked Stipe Mesic, a Croat, from assuming the presidency. This had infuriated both the Croats and Slovenes and was interpreted (rightly) as a power play on Serbia's part.

Finally, since the country's economy was in shambles, I tried to explain the economic ramifications of further conflict. While noting that the international community would not help those who would unilaterally tear the country apart, I stressed that the European Community and the United States would provide economic support toward a peaceful resolution. More important, in the short term, the EC had offered to assist in drafting a new constitution, and I urged the Yugoslavs to pursue that avenue to resolve their disputes.

Going from room to room, I repeated these arguments in each meeting, but I convinced no one. The Bosnian President Alija Izetbegovic and Macedonian President Vladimir Gligorov already understood the international community's position and needed no convincing. More than anyone else I met with that day, those two saw and feared the very real danger of civil war.

By contrast, Milan Kučan, the Slovenian President, was almost metaphysical. "You will see, Mr. Secretary, that in Yugoslavia nobody has a monopoly on the truth," he began, in responding to my presentation. "In Slovenia, eighty-six percent of the population favors independence. The question is not whether the decision is to be carried out, but how. You have said that our act could trigger violence, but spiritual and physical violence exists already. We would like to end it. Violence appears as nationalism and national conflicts. This is an anachronism; Yugoslavia is based on ideology, and therefore belongs to the past."

My next meeting was with Slobodan Miloševic, the President of Serbia, a man whose whole life has been built on using the past to inflame the present. On first appearance, a friendly charmer in a well-tailored suit with a short-cropped haircut, Miloševic is at heart a tough and a liar. Like most toughs, I knew he respected power. I decided not to pull any punches with him, and after beginning, "We want good relations with Serbia—but it is up to you," I said, "I must tell you that we regard your policies as the main cause of Yugoslavia's present crisis. You could be helping lead the way to a prosperous, democratic union that would benefit all the peoples of Yugoslavia. Instead, you are propelling your people, your republic, and Yugoslavia toward civil war and disintegration."

I warned that if force were used, it would lead to ostracism by the international community. Then I went through the list of concerns: exploitation of ethnic resentments, failure to respect human rights in Kosovo, sabotage of Markovic's economic reforms, and blockage of the transfer of power to Mesic.

"If you persist in promoting the breakup of Yugoslavia, Serbia will stand alone," I continued. "The United States and the rest of international community will reject any Serbian claims to territory beyond its borders. Serbia will become an international outcast within Europe for a generation or more."

It was the most contentious meeting of the day. He was clearly a cool customer who didn't like being put on the defensive. He was trying, I could tell, to maintain the typical diplomatic appearance of a "normal exchange of views." Indeed, he spent almost all of the time denying that Serbia had anything to do with Yugoslavia's problems. At times, I felt I was talking to a wall with a crew cut, and suspected I was having no impact whatsoever.

From Miloševic, I went to see Franjo Tudjman, President of Croatia. After I outlined my concerns, he dismissed them almost casually. "Fears of war in Yugoslavia," he contended, "are exaggerated by those with no political roots in any nation, those who want to impose their own solutions on other nations. Dogmatic Communists and unitarists have wanted to involve the army against Croatia." As a former army general, however, Tudjman "knew" that, although two-thirds of the officers were Serbs, their ideology would not allow them to act against Croatia and Slovenia. That seemed far-fetched to me, to say the least, but Tudjman was headstrong. Indeed, obstinacy seemed to be a trait that cut right across ethnic lines—at least so far as Kučan, Tudjman, and Milošević went. Reason was the last thing they wanted to hear.

I ended a long day with Prime Minister Markovic, who was reasonable and quite conscious of the risks of civil war.

"What are your impressions of the meetings you've had with the six republic presidents?" he asked.

"My concern is even greater now than it had been before," I replied bluntly. I went on to make two suggestions: The first was for Markovic to use the EC's offer to help with a new constitution to begin a dialogue. "You badly need a process," I said, "and you need it soon. Otherwise, the republics will continue to take actions that dig themselves in further." My second idea was to try to convince Slovenia and Croatia to make public statements, and possibly parliamentary declarations, that recognized that Yugoslavia's future was a subject for negotiation. That, I felt, might allow the Serbs (and their Montenegrin allies) to permit Mesic to assume the presidency. I was far from optimistic that either of these initiatives would work, but I felt Markovic had to try something.

I then gave him a debrief on my meetings. "I didn't mince words," I began. "Leaders who fail to negotiate will be held responsible if violence breaks out. Neither the U.S. nor any other country will recognize unilateral secession." I explained how I had warned both Milošević and Tudjman about any conspiracy to divide Bosnia, which Izetbegovic and others told me they had considered.

Because of Markovic's ostensible control over and ties to the Yugoslav National Army (JNA), I ended my discussion with him by again warning about any use of force to preserve the federation. "Resorting to force will be exploited by those who want to break up the union. This issue would be portrayed as freedom and democracy on the one hand and force on the other. In the United States, if you force us to choose between unity and democracy, we will always choose democracy." I then switched tacks to appeal to the self-interest of his federal government. "The use of force would also lose for Yugoslavia the support of most of the international community. Of course, the United States will make the argument that self-determination cannot be unilateral and must be pursued by dialogue and peaceful means. But we can only make the argument if there is no use of force."

Markovic didn't respond directly, but instead switched subjects and became philosophical. "In seventy-five years, many structures have been formed which cannot be broken easily. Peoples and nations are intermingled; there are many mixed marriages. It is not at all simple for anyone to carry through with separation," he said.

"I agree that separation will trigger violence and bloodshed," I responded. "Once it starts, you won't be able to get the toothpaste back in the tube. There has to be an agreement among republics; otherwise, there is no way to prevent Slovenia from deciding to take over a border post in six weeks. It might be logical to use the army to prevent this, but that would start an explosion. It only takes one match."

It had been a dispiriting day, one of the most frustrating I'd had as Secretary of State. I'm not sure I had ever been in a situation where self-interest and logic had been discarded so thoroughly by my interlocutors. These people were headed right into a civil war, and yet nothing seemed capable of changing their minds.

In reporting on my day, I wrote the President, "I argued strongly against unilateral steps that would preempt a negotiating process, and basically sought to introduce a heavy dose of reality into the unreal political climate in Yugoslavia. Markovic was very pleased with this message and the thrust of the visit. Frankly I'm dubious about the effect." I felt that way because of the insane psychology of my meetings; the leaders seemed to be sleep-walking into a car wreck, and no matter how loud you yelled—or in the case of Milošević, practically slapped them in the face—they just kept on going.

I told the President that we'd need to work with the Europeans to maintain a collective non-recognition policy against any republic that unilaterally declared independence, as a lever to moderate behavior. "It is the practical steps that begin to implement independence (e.g., setting up customs posts, etc.) that will quickly produce disintegration and warfare. (We'll also want to continue to persuade Markovic to exercise restraint, particularly with regard to the use of the military in response to these declarations.)"

I concluded my report pessimistically, "My gut feeling is that we won't produce a serious dialogue on the future of Yugoslavia until all parties have a greater sense of urgency and danger. We may not be able to impart that from the outside, but we and others should continue to push."*

---

*On June 25, the Croatian and Slovenian parliaments voted for independence. The war in Yugoslavia began the following day. For U.S. policy in this period, see chapter 33.

The Road to Albania

I saw the promise inherent in communism's collapse the next day, when we flew an hour south to Tirana, Albania. Ruled for more than four decades by a committed Stalinist, Enver Hoxa, Albania was the most backward and isolated country in Europe—and the last to throw off the Communist yoke, when it held multiparty elections on March 31, 1991. The week before I arrived, the Communist government had been replaced by an interim government, which included opposition groups, and I wanted to use American prestige (which had been greatly enhanced by Desert Storm) to prod the Albanians toward democracy and free markets.

Following a rather bumpy landing because of potholes in the runway, I stepped off the plane into what passed for a motorcade. Usually, our arrivals were scenes of military precision, but this time it was rather different. An ebullient crowd of a few hundred people was gathered on the tarmac, and as my staff and I got into our cars and buses, the Albanians who had come to greet me got into their antiquated cars and buses and tried to join the motorcade.

As we left the airport, I started to see small knots of people every fifty yards or so. Often, they'd be standing next to a plow whose only engine was an ox or two. Invariably, these men, women, and children were smiling and waving, and one or two would be holding a sign that read, "Welcome Mr. Baker"—or "Becker" or "Beaker." Some held signs that said, "God Bless America!"

After winding quite a distance through the golden Albanian countryside, which reminded me of the California chaparral around President Reagan's ranch in Santa Barbara, we entered the outskirts of Tirana—and crossed into chaos. The small knots of people turned into surging masses, three, five, or seven deep lining the road. Teenage boys and young men jumped into the road to touch and even kiss my car. One man jumped in front of the motorcade and kissed the ground before us. Many threw flowers. Several climbed up on my car's hood or roof, and had to be removed by my security detail. To prevent any injuries, my agents jumped out and jogged alongside my car, trying to fend off small children so that none of them would accidentally slip underneath the wheels. Several times, we came to a standstill and the crowd enveloped us, rocking the car in sheer joy. (That raised the possibility that the crowd would try to *carry* my car, which seemed far-fetched, except some Albanian students had proposed to our advance staff to do exactly that.)

"Just keep going!" said Bill Gaskill, second in command of my security detail. But at times there was nowhere to go, except inch by inch into the sea of humanity before us.

The closer we came to the center of town, the larger the crowds became, and the slower we moved. (It took us almost an hour to travel the four- to five-mile route from the airport.) The street narrowed and on each side stood three- and five-story apartment buildings. In every window and on every roof, I saw smiling faces and Albanians holding placards or handmade American flags. Men gave the V-for-victory sign—which I learned afterward was also the symbol for Albania's democratic opposition—and women lifted their babies for us to see, and threw kisses our way. When we arrived at Skanderbeg Square, where I was to give a speech, we slowly proceeded into sheer bedlam. The square was packed with somewhere between a quarter and a half million people—in a country of just over three million and a town of 250,000.

We had anticipated a large crowd, but this was absolutely incredible. In the fifteen years I had spent in national politics, I had never seen anything like this. With us was John Dancy of NBC News, who had covered American politics for years, and he, too, couldn't believe it. It reminded me of the joyous crowds and the outpouring of emotion that I had seen in newsreel footage of the end of World War II. For the Albanians, having lived under forty-seven years of the most despotic, isolationist Communist regime in the world, I suppose it was like the end of a war. I never felt more privileged to represent my country and never understood better how, for much of the rest of the world, even if we sometimes take it for granted, America is the embodiment of hope and freedom, truly a "shining city on a hill," as President Reagan used to say.

The crowd was so boisterous and so tightly packed together that, in an effort to calm them down I had Sali Berisha, then head of the opposition, speak first. I worried that the joyous surges that threatened to topple the wooden platform from which I was to speak might turn into tragedy, and cause someone to be crushed. "The American way of greeting friends is quieter than ours," he told the crowd. "So please let him speak."

Stepping onto the makeshift stage, I was greeted with chants of, "U.S.A., U.S.A., U.S.A." and "Bushie, Bushie, Bushie." I began simply: "On behalf of President Bush and the American people, I come here today to say to you: Freedom works." After the translation, the crowd went berserk. "At last, you are free to think your own thoughts," I continued. Again, a huge roar. The crowd continued to erupt and to sway back and forth in great waves—it reminded me more of a massive rock concert than anything. I became concerned that the hundred-degree heat would cause cases of heatstroke and decided to cut my remarks short. But that didn't diminish a moment that would forever stay etched in my mind.

My meetings with Albanian politicians could scarcely compete with the crowds I had seen, though Berisha was an impressive man. Like most of the post-Communist leaders I had met in Eastern Europe, he had little political experience; under the old regime, he had been a heart surgeon. But he understood his society acutely, even if he had to explain it in medical terminology: "Albania has a democratic head, a democratic heart," he said, "but a Bolshevik body."* Over the remainder of the summer, I'd spend much of my time on the Middle East, but in August, Berisha's comment about the body of a Bolshevik would apply in spades to Gorbachev's Soviet Union.

*I followed affairs in Albania closely thereafter, and was pleased to see Berisha become President in April 1992. Just as important, I've been pleased to see the Albanian government's commitment to free market principles and privatization. As William Ryerson, our first Ambassador to Albania and an exceptional Foreign Service officer, once wrote me, " 'Freedom works,' indeed, it works perhaps even better than most imagined when you spoke to the Albanian people from Skanderbeg Square."

CHAPTER 27

BREAKTHROUGH FOR PEACE

We have accepted.

—*Yitzhak Shamir, confirming Israel's decision to attend a peace conference, July 31, 1991*

On the afternoon of July 14, 1991, I was meeting with Sasha Bess-mertnykh in my office at the State Department to finalize agreement on the START treaty, when Caron Jackson handed me a note that Ed Djerejian needed to speak with me urgently. I went to another room to take his call. "Ed, what's up?" I inquired, in a tone Djerejian later told me suggested that this had better be *damn* important. "Well, Mr. Secretary," he said, "I have in my hand Assad's response to President Bush that we're putting in a telegram right now to you and the President. It's an unqualified acceptance of our invitation to the peace conference."

I couldn't quite believe there wasn't some loophole. The memory of Assad's maddening twists and turns of May were still too vivid. But Djerejian was an able and very careful diplomat. He explained to me that he'd been so sure there was a catch that he'd read the letter twice to satisfy himself.

"That's great, Ed," I said. "Well done. I look forward to reading the letter." I telephoned the President, then broke the news to the press. "According to our Ambassador in Damascus," I said, "President Assad has accepted the President's invitation."

Djerejian would later chide me good-naturedly for giving myself an out by attributing the positive interpretation to him instead of me. "You know, you really had me hanging out there," he reminded me. He was right. But

the history of Mideast diplomacy is littered with ambiguities and misunderstandings, and I wanted to be certain. When I read the fine print later that
day, I concluded that Djerejian was right. The "assurances and clarifications" in the President's letter "will have a cumulative effect to meet our
requirements for input from the U.N. and to provide a basis of international
legitimacy," it said. As a result, "Syria responds to your invitation to attend
the peace conference in appreciation of your mediation and efforts." There
was no catch: Syria would sit down across the table from Israel, thereby
abandoning a policy position it had held since the beginning of its conflicts
with Israel.

As I read his acceptance again, I knew that Assad had given us the most
critical piece of missing leverage to launch an endgame for peace. The opportunity now existed to create an irresistible momentum toward direct
negotiations. I was already late for the annual summit of the G-7 industrial
nations. The moment that summit in London concluded, however, I would
fly directly to the Middle East. I planned to exploit Assad's participation to
cajole the other Arab states—not simply to follow suit, but also to make
new gestures toward Israel. Armed with these fresh signs of Arab commitments to peace, I could then present Yitzhak Shamir with what I hoped was
a crystal-clear portrait of Arab willingness to engage in direct negotiations,
something they had steadfastly refused to do, and Israel's stated goal for
over forty years. I calculated that neither Shamir nor the Palestinians could
possibly remain intransigent in these circumstances.

Ultimately, my instincts proved correct. I saw Assad in Damascus on
July 18. Precisely three months later, after four more grueling rounds and
an additional 60,000 miles of shuttle diplomacy, the United States and Soviet Union issued carefully worded and laboriously worked-out invitations
to a Mideast peace conference in Madrid beginning October 30. The real
story of how Madrid came to fruition is a rich tale of determination, false
starts, personal and political courage, blind alleys, perseverance, misjudg-
ments, lost tempers, endless negotiations, scores of creative compromises,
and both good faith and bad. In the end, the courage and determination of
the parties themselves to give peace a chance—bolstered by the psychological sustenance, credibility, and catalytic creativity of the last superpower—
somehow prevailed over years of enmity and chaos.

Making Sure Yes Means Yes

The coincidental intervention of the London G-7 summit delayed my arrival in Damascus to nail down Assad's unconditional acceptance and to
pay him the appropriate diplomatic tribute. More important, it also provided a fortuitous vehicle to reinforce our strategy for the peace process by

underscoring the need for reciprocal Arab and Israeli gestures. Responding unanimously to a proposal by President Bush, the G-7 leaders called for an end both to the Arab economic boycott of Israel and to new Israeli settlements in the territories. The Israelis were not happy but American credibility as an honest broker was enhanced with the Arabs, which was our intent.

From the start of our meeting, Assad had but one thing on his mind—to confirm his acceptance of President Bush's proposals. He signaled his intention by choosing to have an uncharacteristically short encounter—a mere 150 minutes, which for Assad was barely a light workout. When he began the session by predicting that "this meeting should prove to be shorter than the previous ones, since we have studied these issues so extensively," I knew that the yes in Assad's letter was genuine. I'd feared another extended meeting would signal that Assad's commitment was more ambiguous than advertised. I needn't have worried. At another point, Assad pointedly reminded me—as though *I* were the cause of our marathon encounters—that "we should not forget the need to have a brief discussion to give a positive impression."

I told Assad that his letter had galvanized the G-7 meeting and was directly responsible for securing the resolution calling for the end of Israeli settlements as well as the Arab boycott. "I cannot overstate the dramatic, profound effect your letter had around the world," I said. "You are now seen to have chosen peace." In negotiations, flattery is almost always useful, and I wanted to appeal to Assad's considerable ego. I also gave him a preview of my tactical approach. "I hope to start here in Syria to build a climate going into Israel that makes it untenable for them to say no," I acknowledged.

As it turned out, we each harbored a parallel concern. I wanted to make sure there was no backtracking from Syria in our subsequent press conference. "There is no question," he replied. "We agreed to the points. It is clear." For his part, Assad wanted to be satisfied "that there be no retreat from President Bush's proposals and points." "On what we propose," I assured him, "there will be no retreat. There will be no *process* before there will be a retreat."

I asked him about his potentially troublesome statement of the previous day that the U.N. observer would have a speaking role at the conference—something I'd already promised Shamir wouldn't occur. It was quickly apparent that while this was his preference, it wasn't a condition for his participation.

"There is no ambiguity," I was delighted to inform President Bush. "They have accepted what we have proposed. We have a yes, and we're going to try to build on that."

Duly reassured, I left for Cairo in an optimistic mood. I wanted Mubarak to issue a statement linking Arab willingness to suspend the boycott to a suspension of settlement activity. This statement would convey a psychological impact beyond measure by demonstrating a clear, unmistakable change in Arab attitudes toward the Jewish state. Tactically, Israel would also be thrust into the uncomfortable position of spurning something of genuine value—lifting the boycott—by adhering to its settlement policy. "We wouldn't simply be making an argument about settlements being an obstacle to peace," I told Mubarak. "The Arabs would be *proving* it." As always, Mubarak was stalwart in his support and issued the statement in the press conference following our meeting.

After a full day of meetings in Cairo the next day, I flew to Jeddah, meeting King Fahd per his nocturnal custom at 9:40 P.M. "I can't leave Saudi Arabia with no result," I told the King, reminding him that his endorsement would make it easier for us to deal with the pressure to be expected from Congress for early action on the Israeli loan guarantees he firmly opposed. With a little editing, he agreed to issue a statement supporting Mubarak's initiative.

"My brother Mubarak is a great leader," the King said. "We will support his initiative. But we must coordinate first with Brother Hafez Assad."

"Hafez Assad doesn't like it," I replied, "but he will look the other way."

The King's endorsement was largely the handiwork of Bandar, who had come up with the idea in the first place, and argued that it would have more impact for Mubarak to propose it and the King to ratify, instead of vice versa. I knew Saudi Foreign Minister Saud felt more comfortable submerged in the mainstream of Arab consensus. But Saud had promised me I wouldn't leave Jeddah empty-handed, and he'd delivered. I also asked Fahd to press King Hussein and the Palestinians to form a joint delegation and to keep the PLO invisible. He agreed to all my requests.

"George Bush and I are grateful to you for this decision," I said. "I know it's not easy, but it's the right thing to do."

"The Middle East has changed," the King said. "If we're going to go for peace, boycotting companies from friendly countries does not make sense."

Frankly, I was still worried about King Hussein. Even as he was asking the United States to repair his ties with Saudi Arabia, he'd released a white paper on the Gulf War that attempted to justify Jordan's policy of support for Saddam Hussein. But it was quickly obvious to me upon my arrival in Amman on July 21 that the courage shown by Mubarak and King Fahd had stiffened his own resolve. In three hours of talks, the King committed to come to the conference, and endorsed the reciprocal gestures proposal for ending both the Arab boycott and new settlements. He also assured me that he was now working seriously on the joint delegation. His Prime Minister had invited Palestinians from the territories to come to Amman to discuss prospective names. I reminded him of the parameters: the delegation could include a Palestinian resident of Jordan from a prominent Jerusalem family, but not a government or PLO official. I stressed that he must also publicly say that talks had begun with Palestinians "from the territories," to ease Israel's concern about PLO involvement. I cabled the President, "The King was better in private than in public. Nevertheless, he said enough in public to be helpful."

The Last Holdouts—the Palestinians and Shamir

As I'd always known, the Palestinians would be the last Arab holdouts. In early July, I'd met in my office in Washington with Faisal Husseini and Hanan Ashrawi, two of the Palestinians with whom I'd been meeting regularly, to press the wisdom of a joint delegation with Jordan. By then, Israel had privately agreed that Palestinians from outside the territories—so-called Diaspora Palestinians—could participate in eventual talks about the permanent status of the territories. Husseini and Ashrawi, however, were still insisting on some PLO representation at the peace conference, which I told them simply would never happen, and resisting the idea of a joint delegation. When I saw them again in Jerusalem on July 21, they were still adamant. Our dinner meeting was intense and emotional. As I later noted to the President, "I told them the train was moving and they'd better not miss it, for it was not likely to come around again soon." Unfortunately, Arafat was still withholding his authorization for the Palestinians to meet with the Jordanians. They asked me for a letter of understanding to push Arafat to a decision, or at least make it more difficult for him to block them from going to Amman. I told them the United States would provide a letter of assurances—but only when work actually began on a joint delegation.

"We need to make a distinction between symbols and substance," I stressed. "I don't mean this disrespectfully, but you know as well as I do that people have said that Palestinians never pass up an opportunity to pass up an opportunity. Please don't pass up this one.

"Who do you think produced the G-7 statement? And who do you think produced the Mubarak statement on settlements and boycott? Who do you think produced the Saudi acceptance? These things didn't come out of thin air.

"Once you and Israel engage," I predicted, "there will be no turning back. But we can't get there unless we crack the representation issue." And the price of getting there, I told them, was little more than a fig leaf. The Israelis would accept a Palestinian from a prominent Jerusalem family now residing in Jordan, but only on the Jordanian side of the joint delegation.

On behalf of the President, I offered them several assurances for future negotiations. The United States would support the inclusion of East Jerusalemites and Diaspora Palestinians on any delegation dealing with the final status of the territories. Moreover, we and the Soviets were agreed that the current exclusion of Palestinian East Jerusalemites wouldn't set a precedent for actual negotiations themselves in the future. But an indirect link to East Jerusalem was the best they could get for now.

None of this seemed to make much difference. Grumpy and testy, they were skeptical that Assad was fully committed. Ashrawi complained that ending the boycott was a reward to Israel for ceasing their illegal settlement activity. "They should do this without being paid off," she maintained. Predictably, they were most angry about losing their Jerusalem card. Understandably, this was most difficult for Husseini. He was a Jerusalemite with a distinguished pedigree. His father was Abd al Kadar al-Husseini, the legendary Palestinian fighter killed in the 1948 war. A nephew of the Mufti, the former religious leader, Husseini had been the sub-rosa chief of Fatah, a political arm in the PLO in the occupied territories for nearly twenty years. His Fatah link had persuaded Shamir that he was a terrorist, a conclusion not justified by evidence that we had, but an article of faith with the Israelis nevertheless. He was arguably the most credible of all the Palestinians, but Israel would never accept him on the Palestinian delegation. I told Husseini that the President would receive him at the White House as the titular leader of the Palestinians from within the territories, but that he would have to accept a Palestinian on the Jordanian side of the joint delegation as the only connection to Jerusalem which I could persuade Israel to swallow. His disenfranchisement, I realized, would be an exceptionally bitter pill for him. And it clearly was, judging from the expression on his face when I told him.

"We can't deal with this," Husseini replied. "It's a matter of principle. It's a red line for us, and we cannot deal with a process in which we have to accept this condition. The absence of East Jerusalemites on the delegation will be seen by Palestinians as a funeral for East Jerusalem." I responded that while the Shamir government was vulnerable politically on the peace issue, it could easily mobilize great strength on the issue of Jerusalem. As a practical matter, the status of Jerusalem must wait for later. "If you highlight it first," I warned, "there will be no peace process, and that would be a pity first and foremost for you, because Palestinians will suffer more than anyone from its absence."

As he frequently did in our meetings, Husseini unfurled maps showing Israeli settlements outlined in orange. "Faisal," I said, appealing to reason, "if you don't get to the table, pretty soon you'll be bringing me a map that's completely orange and this discussion will be moot."

"This is most unfair," Ashrawi thundered. "Israelis who have been here only for a relatively few years will serve in the delegation, whereas Palestinians whose families have lived in East Jerusalem for centuries will be kept off."

"All right," I shouted. "It's not a question of fairness or what might be right. It's a question of reality." We were no closer to solving this imbroglio. I used the excuse of a meeting with Shamir to close off an encounter going nowhere. My instinct told me, however, that I had made some modest headway. I hoped that their common sense—and a belief that I was honestly doing the best I could—would ultimately prevail.

Before calling it a day, I met alone with Shamir later that evening. He knew that my talks with the Arabs had elevated the pressure on him, so during the preliminaries, he sought to place me on the defensive. "There's a lot of suspicion in Israel that the U.S. is determined to force Israel from the territories," he said. "There's a lot of suspicion in the United States," I countered, "that you aren't serious about negotiating peace."

Shamir seemed genuinely shocked, almost thunderstruck, and quite suspicious, over Assad's acceptance. Just as three months earlier, Mubarak had doubted Shamir's willingness to compromise, the Prime Minister now couldn't really believe Assad's acquiescence—particularly since, as Shamir knew, the conference would be conducted essentially on the basis of Israel's specifications. He had a blizzard of questions. It was as though he were relying on me to vouch for a credibility he couldn't bring himself to bestow on his fiercest enemy. "What's the reason for this change?" Shamir asked. "Assad never mentions the word *peace*. What's his goal? This is not dramatic like Sadat." I told him that Mubarak, Fahd, and Hussein had all told Assad that he'd never have another opportunity like this, and he had finally believed it. "What happened this week," I said, "is nothing short of the breakthrough that you have sought for decades." Having produced Arab negotiating partners largely on Israel's terms, time was now of the essence. In ten days, I reminded him, the President would see Mikhail Gorbachev in Moscow, when we would be proposing a date to the Soviets for the conference, and I had every reason to believe the Soviets would agree to a conference in the fall. Israeli vacillation, I told him, must now be concluded.

In a previous meeting with Shamir, before I had broached the issue with Assad, I'd talked to him about the possibility of U.S. troops on the Golan after Israel and Syria had made peace. He'd seemed to like the idea at first but cooled to it later, perhaps because an American military presence would tend to negate any argument that Israel needed to retain the Golan Heights for its own security. He asked me if the United States still stood behind President Ford's 1975 letter, which he'd shown me in March. "We don't want you to support the Syrian position that Israel has to withdraw from the Golan Heights," he said. I reiterated our position that this was a matter for bilateral negotiations between Israel and Syria, and told him I would reaffirm in our letter of assurances to Israel that the United States still stood firmly behind President Ford's commitment.

I could sense from Shamir's tone that he had never expected Assad to say yes. Given that reality, however, he knew the ball was squarely in his court, and that as a practical matter he couldn't say no to the regional conference. At the end of the meeting, I felt I'd reassured him sufficiently. But he said he needed more time to reach a decision. "I will send you an answer very shortly," he promised.

As was usually the case when we met with the standard complement of advisers on both sides, Shamir was slightly more querulous in a second meeting the next morning. At one point, for example, he asked me for a copy of Assad's letter. "Would you expect me to show Assad a letter from you to President Bush?" I replied. I offered, and he settled, for a briefing on its contents instead.

"We need a little time," Shamir said in conclusion. "But you'll get your answers, and you won't be disappointed."

For the next week, I turned my attention to an ASEAN conference in Malaysia, a quick return trip to Mongolia to make up for the shortened one of August 1990, and the President's Moscow summit with Gorbachev beginning on July 30. The Middle East was somewhat peripheral to the main business of the summit, which was highlighted by the signing of the START Treaty. Nevertheless, we reached agreement with the Soviets on an October date for the peace conference. Bessmertnykh had preferred to wait until later in the fall, but we were tantalizingly close to a final agreement, and I feared that any delay might destroy our momentum. The Palestinians in particular were a problem. Without the pressure of a genuine deadline, I doubted they'd ever finally cross the threshold.

Before leaving Jerusalem, I'd passed word that I was prepared to return—but only if Shamir agreed to the conference in advance of my arrival. The Israelis conveyed a message to me in Moscow through Dennis Ross that Shamir had accepted. Their cable, however, stopped just short of an unqualified acceptance. "He wants to save his yes for when you get there," Ross told me. But having been burned more than once, I decided that wasn't good enough. I telephoned Shamir from my suite at the Penta Hotel and thanked him for his positive response. "But I'm not coming unless you tell me yes now," I said.

Shamir again promised that I wouldn't be disappointed, but I was unyielding. "But we have these concerns to discuss," he protested, revisiting some earlier reservations that the Arabs would find a way to bring the United Nations more intimately into the process, to Israel's detriment. He also asked me to help repeal the "Zionism is racism" resolution in the United Nations. I told him I'd consider the points he had raised and call back when I had more time to talk. I was prepared to give him some, but not all, of his shopping list.

After consulting with the President, I called Shamir back early the next morning and pledged the United States to a "serious effort" to repeal the Zionism resolution. I assured him that the United States would not allow the United Nations to create a "competing process" to the conference. But I firmly rejected his request for two years of automatic vetoes in the Security Council on any measure Israel opposed. And I told him I wouldn't come to Jerusalem to negotiate on these items.

"I want you to be able to stand up with me after a short meeting and say you've said yes to our compromise proposals," I said. "There is still the Palestinian representation issue to work out. You will be saying yes to everything but that. The key is, I want you to be out there saying 'yes,' and putting the onus on the Palestinians."

There was a momentary silence on the line. Then at 8:40 A.M. Moscow time, Shamir said in a soft voice, "We've decided to enter the process of negotiations in accord with the American proposal. We have accepted." "That's terrific, Mr. Prime Minister," I said, "I'm really happy to hear that." I informed him that I'd be delighted to visit with him in Jerusalem the next day.

I arrived with a present from Gorbachev I knew would cheer the Israelis. "Jim, you can tell them the USSR will resume diplomatic relations before the conference starts," he told me during the first day of the August summit. I coupled this news, which I'd known and kept secret for months to disclose at the optimum moment, with a restatement of the assurances I'd given Shamir over the telephone. It was a relatively brief meeting, which in truth was pretty anticlimactic.

But the delicate matter of Palestinian representation remained. I asked Shamir to accept the U.S. understandings I'd already given the Palestinians about future negotiations over Jerusalem. "I'm not asking you to sacrifice your principles," I said. "Just give me a little flexibility to tell the Palestinians they don't give up their claims before ever coming to the table." Most of all, I told him, it was critical to refrain from negotiating the representation issue in the press.

Afterward, the Prime Minister and I met with reporters. His tone was gracious, but his countenance betrayed an inner turmoil. Shamir looked as though he'd bitten into an unripe persimmon. He'd confided to me once that he thought he would be the Prime Minister to begin peace discussions with the Arabs, but someone else would see them to fruition. I suspect that he never expected this beginning to arrive so quickly. But now, the United

States had delivered Israel's Arab neighbors to a formula for which she had pressed for forty years—face-to-face, direct negotiations. He had no choice but to say yes. I knew it and so did he.

Fighting Symbols over Substance

Now, at long last, the onus resided on the uncertain shoulders of only one party—the Palestinians. Perhaps because they were intelligent enough to understand that the irresistible momentum I'd hoped to create had now arrived on their doorstep, the Palestinians were edgier than I'd ever seen them when we met on August 2. Husseini and Ashrawi told me they feared being assassinated by right-wing Israeli fanatics. "You're talking to a dead man," Husseini said. "I'm sure extremist Israelis will kill me. Maybe in a week or a month, or two months, but they will get me. Don't let me die without something in my pocket."* During this meeting, which lasted four hours, they read me a truculent, contentious letter from Tunis. I didn't take it seriously—"I hope that was written before this meeting," I said—but it had the effect of dramatizing the pressure they so plainly felt.

I had no choice but to exacerbate their anxiety by reminding them they were the final obstacles to a process that in time might end Israel's occupation of the Palestinians. "Shamir has just accepted our terms for the process—the same ones he said *weren't* acceptable in his letter to the President," I told them. "I don't have his *final* word, because he's able to hide behind the fact that we have no joint delegation."

My appeal to enlightened self-interest failed to assuage them. They remained preoccupied with the representation issue, and unwilling to accept any compromises. They wanted the United States to change long-standing policy opposing an independent Palestinian state. I offered them a letter of assurances which I suggested should meet their concerns. "What I have in mind is a possible formula which would reiterate our support for your legitimate political rights," I said, "not including a separate independent Palestinian state, but not *excluding* self-determination in the context of a confederation with Jordan."

I tried to persuade them that these various statements, assurances, and

---

*I looked into the question of protection for them because I was concerned for their safety. The Palestinians wouldn't accept Israeli protection as a matter of principle and expedience, so at the direction of the President, the U.S. Secret Service quietly provided security training to Palestinian bodyguards. I also asked Shamir to see if there was anything he could do through intelligence channels to reduce any risk. He was quick to respond that he would see what could be done. Ironically, when I later mentioned these concerns to Bethlehem mayor Elias Freij during a meeting in Washington, he told me I shouldn't worry. "There have been threats against all of them for the last twenty years," he said.

gestures so laboriously constructed would have the cumulative effect of demonstrating they hadn't surrendered their claims relating to Jerusalem in advance of negotiations, and that the question of East Jerusalem would be on the agenda at some point. "If you tell me that's not good enough," I said, "then I must tell you that your position is that symbols are more important than substance—and unfortunately, that position has helped to create and sustain the Palestinian tragedy. For God's sake, don't let Israel hide behind symbols." As the meeting concluded, I made one last appeal for them to tell reporters that we were making progress. "You don't want a story," I said, "that the cat died on the Palestinian doorstep."

I made essentially the same arguments with King Hussein later that day in Amman. I asked him to use his private Israeli channel to give Shamir the Palestinian names. At this point, there simply couldn't be any surprises. He assured me he'd do so. I agreed to his request for a separate letter of assurances. The King, I concluded, was at last fully on board. "The time has come to try to get assistance flowing again," I told the President in an overnight cable. I then visited Morocco, Tunisia, and Algeria, and received commitments for their participation in the multilateral talks. In Tunisia, I also received a large silver dove with an olive branch in its mouth from President Abidine Ben Ali. "Let's now see if we can make this bird fly," I observed. I returned to Washington on August 5. I'd been gone so long that my security agents had begun joking they should have filled out absentee ballots beforehand.*

The Nightmare of Multiple Assurances

After the momentous events of the preceding year, culminating in a twenty-three-day trip traversing twelve countries and 33,769 miles, I felt I could justify a vacation. So I left Washington on August 9, expecting to spend some time fly-fishing on my ranch in Wyoming. Ten days later, my reverie was interrupted by the coup against Mikhail Gorbachev by Soviet hard-liners (about which more in the next chapter), which prompted my return to Washington for meetings with the President, a trip to Brussels for an urgent session of NATO foreign ministers, and a visit to the President's summer home at Kennebunkport, Maine, for further discussions of the abortive coup and its aftermath.

When I returned to Wyoming on August 22, crucial work remained on the peace process, despite Israel's conditional acceptance. The Palestinian

---

*At some point during this marathon trip, Lt. Col. Don Jackson, our aircraft commander, sent me this note: "Under our frequent-flyer program, you are entitled to a round-trip flight for two between Washington, D.C., and Hawaii. Please request this crew."

question was still a potentially lethal complication. And then there was the matter of providing all the parties with additional diplomatic camouflage to make their participation in the peace conference more palatable. During my discussions with Shamir in May, I'd committed the United States to providing a side letter elaborating American commitments and understandings. Not surprisingly, the Israelis promptly leaked this news to the press. In rapid order, Syria, Jordan, and the Palestinians all demanded their own "letters of assurances." As a matter of balance, there was no choice but to oblige them. Thus began two months of seemingly interminable haggling with each of the parties to produce these letters.

This proved to be an exasperating exercise in trying to weave through an enormous minefield. Each of the participants wanted specific language assuaging their fears. Inevitably, terminology that reassured one of them would offend another. From the outset, I'd sought to minimize the bickering by laying down three absolutes: The terms of each letter would be made known to all the other parties, and neither American policy nor terms of reference for the conference could be changed by any of the language. (This would prevent us from being hoist with the petard of conflicting secret assurances, as some of my predecessors had been.) Much to my annoyance, this marker was largely ignored in negotiating the terms of the letters. Invariably, they all sought—unsuccessfully—to extract new American policy commitments through these letters.

Confecting generalized language which all the parties could accept— and persuading all of them that leaking the contents would be disastrous— required lapidary skills of the highest order. More than once, my patience ran thin as one or another of my interlocutors attempted a diplomatic end run by asking for a little extra consideration that would disrupt the delicate semantic balance. In the end, however, these letters provided the extra psychological boost of encouragement to the parties, which in my view made the conference possible.

By mid-September, after considerable consultation with all the parties by State Department specialists, draft letters of assurances had been prepared. Before we could issue invitations to the conference, formal acceptance of each letter had to be negotiated. I also wanted to show—but not negotiate—the draft letter of invitation, so none of the participants would be surprised by its terms. The matter of Palestinian representation also remained open, largely because of PLO intransigence. I hoped that my third trip to the Mideast in two months, which began in Jerusalem on September 16, following trips to Mexico and the suddenly transformed Soviet Union, would dispose of these remaining impediments and clear the way for the conference. Not for the first time, my optimism about the peace process would prove misplaced.

My meeting with Shamir was surprisingly uneventful. The Israelis voiced some concerns with the letter of assurances, but by now I had the sense that Shamir posed far less of an obstacle than some of his more militant advisers like Misha Arens and Yossi Ben Aharon. During these discussions, a pattern began to develop in which objections were sometimes surfaced by underlings such as Ely Rubenstein and Yossi Ben Aharon. At one point, I interrupted to say: "I don't want to hear this from staff. I only want to hear objections from the constitutionally elected head of government. The Prime Minister can speak for himself." As I suspected, Shamir did not share all of their objections.

My meeting with the Palestinians at the residence of the U.S. Consul General that evening was as difficult as I'd expected. In an unintended metaphor of the gulf between us, both delegations ate separately at opposite ends of the room during a break in discussions, which proved a frustrating exercise in déjà vu. In the six weeks since our last meeting, they'd remained frozen in place, unable to muster the political resolve to move forward. Zero progress had been made toward forming a joint delegation with Jordan. Cowed by Tunis, the Palestinians hadn't even begun talks with King Hussein. I wanted them to know that I was personally disappointed in their performance and fast losing my patience.

"The time has come to stop talking about action, and act," I said. "You're in danger of squandering the best opportunity to end the Israeli occupation you're ever going to get.

"I've been—pardon my French—busting my ass for you, and I'm extremely frustrated that all our efforts have produced not a shred of evidence that you're doing what I asked you to do—get moving on contacts with Jordan about the joint delegation."

I handed them a letter from the President with twelve assurances, including specific language on Jerusalem I'd promised them previously. "It's the best we can offer," I argued, "the best you've ever had, and in my judgment the best you'll ever get before negotiations."

The next morning, following a contentious meeting with Shamir and his principal advisers that failed to resolve our differences over settlements and loan guarantees, I departed for Cairo, where I found Mubarak his usual steadfast self. He briefed me on his efforts to persuade the PLO to stop hindering the Palestinians. Before leaving for Damascus, I met with Prince Bandar, who told me the Saudis had received intelligence that Saddam Hussein realized all was lost and was contemplating suicide—but not before wreaking vengeance on the kingdom. The Saudis worried he might be able to cobble together one last missile attack with three or four chemical-tipped Scuds. "I hope your reconnaissance is intrusive enough to give us advanced warning," Bandar said. I replied that we were monitoring Saddam's military capability closely and would keep the Saudis informed, but that I thought it was unlikely Saddam would take his own life. Nevertheless, Bandar was relieved to hear that the President had agreed to a previous request for additional Patriot missile batteries. The Patriots would be on their way to the kingdom from Kuwait tomorrow, I promised.

My meeting with Assad the next afternoon was a six-hour marathon. "The biggest obstacle right now," I told him, "is the inability of the Palestinians to do anything." I asked him to send a signal to the Palestinians and to the PLO in Tunis that "if they don't move with you, you may move without them, along with King Hussein."

I then handed Assad a draft of the letter of assurances. It contained eight specific understandings. The sixth was a restatement of America's long-standing opposition to settlements.

At this point, a fresh dispute materialized over President Ford's 1975 letter concerning the Golan. Shamir was insisting that the United States reaffirm Ford's pledge to give "great weight" to Israel's view that a Syrian-Israeli peace treaty "must be predicated on Israel remaining on the Golan Heights." Assad, understandably, took a dim view of this pledge, arguing that it contradicted President Bush's promises in his May 31 letter to Assad. "It is a very strange letter," he complained. "Can we give Ford the right to concede our land?"

I contended that President Bush's offer of a security guarantee was in fact the ultimate proof of giving "great weight" to Israel's view—while at the same time offering Syria an opportunity to negotiate with Israel a return of the Golan. The logic of this position seemed to elude Assad, who was studiedly noncommittal. My hopes for securing his agreement on the letter before I left for Amman went aglimmer. We agreed to convene again in two days, just before I returned to Washington.

During my visit to Jordan on September 19 to meet with King Hussein again, I'd pressed for a meeting with the Palestinians in Amman to symbolize dramatically that movement toward forming a joint delegation was now occurring. I'd asked Mubarak to lean on the PLO not to block the meeting, and Shamir to facilitate Hanan Ashrawi's travel from Ramallah through the West Bank to Amman. Until Jordanian Foreign Minister Taher al-Masri woke me up at 3:00 A.M., I'd assumed there would be no meeting. I knew the Israelis didn't like Ashrawi because of her ties to Fatah. But their interest in producing a Jordanian-Palestinian delegation overrode their qualms about her militancy.

Tough, proud, courageous, and occasionally militant, she was nonetheless extraordinarily articulate and determined in arguing her brief. Instinctively, I liked her. When she wasn't chain-smoking cigarettes, she spoke excellent English. Initially she was Faisal Husseini's translator, but as time went by, she came to assume a more dominant role in the delegation, and ultimately became an eloquent public spokesman for the Palestinians. As a Palestinian Christian, Ashrawi seemed particularly outraged that the Israelis would claim that the territories were the biblical land of Israel. Her ancestors had inhabited those lands for centuries, she argued, and they were followers of Christ.

I gave Ashrawi a draft letter of assurances and reminded her that Palestinian paralysis was the greatest threat to the failure of the process. If the Palestinians stayed out, they risked being left on the sidelines. She predicted the Arabs would never go to a conference without the Palestinians. I knew she was wrong. "Partial solutions are not our preference," I said, "but we will take whatever we can get. Some progress is preferable to *no* progress." It was time for her to convey the message that the time to decide was at hand. "I've always admired your tenacity and single-mindedness on an issue which has defeated so many others," she remarked. I appreciated the compliment and wondered whether the entrenched ideology of her people would defeat my efforts as well. I gently reminded her in conclusion that if the contents of the letter now in her possession leaked to the press, the process was dead and I could go fishing. "Perhaps that would be the best outcome for you, Mr. Secretary," she said with a chuckle, demonstrating not for the first time her droll sense of humor.

Another Syrian Roadblock

On September 20, I arrived back in Damascus at 11:20 A.M. On the ride in from the airport, Shara surfaced new trouble. Assad, he said, was disappointed in the letter of assurances. I wasn't pleased to hear this news. The bad vibes continued in what stretched into another painstaking meeting of nearly five hours.

I said I was disturbed to have heard that Shara had been spreading the notion that the United States had worked out the Syrian letter of assurances with the Israelis. "I said that we had *not* shown any party's letter to any other party," I said. "I'm in the habit of telling the truth. It's very important that my word be seen as truthful." Assad defended Shara and tried to mollify me. "The Minister didn't mean that you and the Israelis had gotten together to write it," he claimed. "He means that the Israelis had a role. Precisely what role, I don't know."

Plainly, Assad wanted to thrust me onto the defensive from the outset. He claimed to have stayed up until past midnight parsing news accounts about the Israeli letter of assurances. The more he read, the less he liked. In his erroneous judgment, the letter destroyed the terms of reference to the conference—something I'd assured him wouldn't be allowed to happen.

"This means we are back to square one and have wasted our time," Assad said. "The assurances given to Israel destroy the progress we think we've made and destroy all our previous contacts with the United States."

"I'm sorry you feel that way," I said. Turning his attention to the draft letter of invitation I'd shown him, Assad then demonstrated that no detail was too minuscule for his attention. A phrase describing negotiations as "direct, face-to-face" was deemed objectionable. "They are direct," he said. "Isn't that enough?"

"Face-to-face is better than back-to-back," I quipped. "All that's missing," he complained, "is to say 'and smiling.' "

"Okay, I'll buy that," I offered. He wasn't amused. "No, I don't want smiling," he said, taking me literally. I agreed to his omission.

Out of the blue, Assad flung down a new procedural roadblock. "I was really surprised," he said, "that there are to be multilateral committees to work to discuss regional issues while our lands are still occupied." I told him I was frankly shocked that he was prepared to hold the work of these committees hostage to an issue that might take decades to resolve.

"How can we discuss economic cooperation where a state of war still exists?" Assad replied. "This has never happened since the beginning of history. If anyone wants to discuss economic cooperation with Israel, let him go ahead and do so. The masses will hold any such person accountable."

I reminded Assad that he and I had spoken many times about this subject. As we debated the merits over the next hour, however, it was apparent we had a fundamental difference on this point. I believed multilateral talks on water rights, refugees, and economic development would complement the peace process by improving the atmosphere and establishing common ground among all these ancient enemies. Assad, however, wanted the invitation to stipulate that multilaterals would begin only after bilateral talks were "successfully completed"—a formulation I knew would require years. I told Assad he was free to spurn the multilaterals, and agreed to consider compromise language to the effect that they would begin only after "substantial progress" in the bilaterals. In return, I asked to shorten the time for the start of the bilaterals to two days after the opening ceremonies instead of five to seven. We agreed to consider these amendments and meet again in a few weeks. As we concluded, I wanted Assad to recognize that an implicit statute of limitations applied to his haggling. "Remember that in the end, this is *our* invitation," I said. "At some point, we will issue it"—regardless of Syrian objections.

I concluded that Assad's position, while consistent with his long-standing views, was more ploy than principle. He was probing to see what more he might get from me. But he was also signaling his desire to hold all other considerations hostage to the status of his negotiations with Israel. Never-theless, I predicted in a cable to the President that Assad would attend the conference. "Indeed, I believe that our ultimate lever on all the parties right now is the invitation . . . that's the one thing that will force decisions and put everyone in a position where they have to say yes or no—and no one wants to be seen as saying no." But time was slipping away for an October conference. Like Mubarak, I worried that the process would begin to un-ravel with any delay. Reluctantly, I knew another trip to the region couldn't be avoided.

The Endgame Cometh

Late on the evening of Saturday, October 12, I left Washington for the Mid-dle East, my fourth visit in as many months. The President had decided that invitations to the conference should be issued the following Friday, when by prearrangement I would meet Boris Pankin, the new Soviet Foreign Minister, in Israel. I'd long since begun to believe that each time I resolved two items of dispute, five more would surface. Increasingly, I was being nickel-and-dimed at every turn. Only the stark reality of a public invitation would silence those still maneuvering to delay or abort the process. I had six days to bring my shuttle diplomacy to closure through stops in Cairo, Amman, Damascus, and Jerusalem. I now was convinced we were in the endgame. But three months after Assad's letter of acceptance, his participa-tion in the conference remained uncertain. And the Gordian knot of Pales-tinian representation still cast an uncertain pall over the prospects for an historic breakthrough.

This trip was preceded by three weeks of intensive diplomacy designed to narrow the differences with the parties over the letters of assurances. The most significant of these efforts was my meeting with Shara in my suite at the Waldorf-Astoria Hotel in New York during the U.N. General Assembly session. It promptly degenerated into a particularly unpleasant meeting when he handed me a Syrian draft that bore faint resemblance to the U.S. version I'd left in Damascus on September 20. Still worse, the letter laid out several understandings that represented significant changes in American policy on several critical issues. One by one, I rejected Shara's language as inconsistent with the purpose of the assurances. "Frankly, Farouk, I worry about your good faith," I said. "You're changing the ground rules."

"These requests are all consistent with your policy," Shara claimed. By now he'd exhausted my tolerance for politeness. "Don't tell *me* what *our* policy is," I erupted, pounding my fist on the table. "*I'll* tell *you* what our policy is. Our policy is *not* self-determination for the Palestinians. I went through this with you before. I told you we're not going to change our policy for the Israelis on 242, and we're not going to change our policy for *you* on 242."

As I continued to pummel the table, Shara's appetite for additional dialogue suddenly vanished. "You're making me ill," he protested. "I don't mean to make you ill," I replied. "But when you try to put words in our mouth, it makes me goddamn *mad.*"

On Saturday, October 12, I began my eighth trip to the Mideast in little more than a year by going to Cairo and Amman. My messages to Mubarak and King Hussein were identical. I asked their help in putting together a Palestinian delegation by the time I saw Shamir. I needed a list of names— "and names that won't give me a problem." I also needed the Palestinians to know that if the PLO announced the names, the process was finished. And Assad should be told that he must come to the conference even if he eschewed the multilaterals. I asked one additional favor from the King. It was critical, I urged him in a private meeting, to convey through his own means the list of names, so Shamir would be reassured of no embarrassments. "You're the only one who can do this," I stressed. "He'll trust you more than us on this one. There's nothing I need you to do more. This is the key to the whole process." He agreed to help—and was relieved to learn I was actively pursuing his urgent request to purchase an advanced version of an antimissile defense system for his personal aircraft.

Both leaders had assured me that, despite outward appearances, both Assad and the Palestinians had already made a basic decision to participate. While I didn't share the confidence of Mubarak and Hussein, I did think we were very well positioned and I knew that the Palestinians not only wanted the process, but were scared to death of being blamed for its failure. That night, I wrote the President: "So I'm going to press ahead and I'm going to make it clear that I'm near the end of the road, and either we're going to make this thing work now or I'm going to walk away from it and I'm going to point the finger at who's responsible."

One Last Try at Hooking Assad

At 12:45 P.M. on October 15, I visited Assad again, in hopes of bridging our remaining differences. The meeting began amiably enough with a dissertation by Assad on his allergies and a colloquy about the confirmation process for U.S. senior government officials. I offhandedly observed that the potential for difficulty in these matters was usually linked to the importance of the position. "The higher the monkey climbs," I replied, "the more you see of his behind." Assad smiled. "True," he said.

Tedium quickly set in as Assad laid out fourteen changes he wanted in the letter of assurances. The most important of these involved the multilaterals. I offered him new language designed to finesse our disagreement. The reformulation called for the participants to meet to organize multilaterals within two weeks, not actually begin them. When we continued our discussion that evening after a five-hour break, Assad rejected this idea. He wanted language saying the multilaterals wouldn't start until the bilateral committees "successfully complete their work." This, I knew, was a prescription for indefinite delay. I tried another compromise: we would also stipulate the Syrians weren't obliged to participate by changing the language from "the parties" to "those parties who will attend the multilateral negotiations . . ."

"I do not want to enter such a minefield—one in which minesweepers would not work," Assad said. "We in Syria cannot agree to something like this unless we have something tangible to bring to our people. We cannot move even one step in this direction."

"I'm not asking you to do anything," I said.

"I cannot even move with words. I cannot even say I agree. If I did, I would be responsible before my people." I sensed the situation was deteriorating, and Assad confirmed my suspicion by terminating the dialogue. "Now we are back to square one," he said. "We cannot move in accordance with these conditions. In any event, we are making you sleepy." By now I was not only wide awake, but furious.

"I've learned something about the Arab mentality in dealing with the peace process," I said in conclusion. "Unlike we Westerners, you Arabs will never start down a road unless you know where that road ends. But if we don't *start* down this road, we'll never get to its end—or for that matter, anywhere."

I returned to my suite, exchanged my suit for a white terry-cloth bathrobe, and assembled my staff at 1:30 A.M. around the dining room table of my suite in the Sheraton. "It's like pulling teeth with that guy," I complained. "Nothing is easy. You think it's a done deal and then there's always something else that needs fixing."

We suspected the Syrians had bugged the suite, so I lowered my voice. "I'll give on this one if I have to." I motioned with my hands as though I were practicing my fly-fishing technique. "We've got to hook Assad into this process if we're going to succeed. And that's what we're going to do." If necessary, I told them, I would capitulate on the multilaterals. Israel would balk, but I felt Shamir would never opt out of the process over the multilaterals if Syria had agreed to meet face-to-face with Israel.

In my cable to the President, I noted that Assad had failed to understand that the multilaterals could encourage tangible concessions from Israel by demonstrating the Arabs were willing to treat them as regional partners. "Assad is unswayed by some of these realities," I wrote. "Put simply, he wants to keep Israel isolated and make clear there are no regional rewards until the Israelis withdraw from the Golan. His weakness, not strength, drives him to oppose any multilaterals, particularly as he fears the other Arabs will get into them, start forging agreements, and reduce Israel's need and incentives in responding to him.

"As you can see, I've just had another day on the Middle East roller coaster. I don't intend to ride it for much longer."

I concluded this cable with a personal afterthought: For years the President had lightheartedly joked with me about the necessary but occasionally tedious aspects of politics, using as his example Young Republican conventions. I wanted my friend to know just how harrowing these eight hours of arm wrestling with Assad had been. "This is almost as much fun as a Y.R. convention!" I scribbled in longhand. That was *one* diplomatic note I knew wouldn't need expert translation.

By the next morning, my staff had labored furiously to complete language on another draft of the letter of assurances and the letter of invitation, which we hoped could satisfy Assad on the multilaterals. Their efforts to talk me out of sacrificing the multilaterals had failed. "We have to be willing to bend," I said, shortly before I met again with Assad. After a considerable amount of sparring over language I considered extraneous, Assad was beginning to wear me down.

"I'll give you something on that issue in the Palestinian letter," I said, with considerable exasperation. Suddenly, unexpectedly, something snapped within me, the result of Assad's brinkmanship and a bone-wearying fatigue that had brought on several dizzy spells during my shuttling. For once, I wasn't being angry merely for effect. "It's a good letter," I snapped. "If you don't like what we're doing, and you think you can get the Golan back (without sitting down with Israel), then go ahead and get it back."

Assad was unfazed by my outburst. "You are not doing this for us in the first instance," he replied. "You also have interests."

"Yes, but it is in the interest of the peoples of this region. All we can do is be a catalyst. We can't impose it. There are some things we can do and some things we cannot."

We took a short break so Assad could read the letter of invitation. In the interim, Shara pressed me to add a clause in the letter of assurances that "Jerusalem is part of the occupied territories." He knew full well this was long-standing American policy. He also knew such language was so inflammatory that Israel might well refuse to attend the conference over its insertion.

"You're asking me more than the Palestinians asked," I protested. "I don't think that's appropriate. You're pushing us too far. Maybe you don't want a process. I don't want to give Israel any reason not to come. Maybe you do."

Upon Assad's return, I restated my point. This was the best I could do, I said. Assad persisted, raising some new quibble which brought me to the edge of a second eruption.

Mahmud Qaddur, Syria's Minister of Public Affairs, leaned over to Assad. "Take care," he cautioned in Arabic. "He's really angry." Assad seemed puzzled. "Why is he angry?" he asked. "We're negotiating." Then he and I made eye contact. He seemed to sense that he'd reached a certain unhealthy threshold.

Suddenly, Assad uttered the words I needed to hear: "We agree on the letter of assurances. I guess these are all of the issues." Dennis Ross scribbled a note to me. "Take the money and run. Let's get out of here!" Inexplicably, Assad hadn't even raised the subject of multilaterals.

Closing Down the Palestinian Souk

I flew from Damascus to Tel Aviv, and met with the Palestinians shortly after 8:00 P.M. in Jerusalem. At long last, progress had been made. They had seen King Hussein in Amman and were picking names for the delegation. A list of twenty candidates had appeared in the Jordanian press. The Palestinians assured me they were working hard on a list of acceptable names. Then, unexpectedly, they reopened the subject of Jerusalem, asking for another impossible concession. Months of frustration coupled by fatigue caused a reaction which was pure emotion rather than tactical calculation.

"How many times have we done this?" I exploded. "I am sick and tired of this. With you people, the souk never closes. I've had it. Have a nice life." I got up and walked out of the room into a guest room at the rear of the residence.

I have a tendency to pace in two circumstances: when I have unexpected free time, and when I'm really angry—both of which were now the case. Dennis Ross recalls that I was pacing furiously and muttering, "These people, these people," when he caught up with me five minutes later. The Palestinians had asked him to retrieve me. Ross told them I'd never come back unless they dropped their new demand. They agreed on the spot. When he told me this, I calmed down. "Let's wait a few minutes before we go back," I suggested. I wanted to let their anxiety build up, so I delayed another fifteen minutes.

When I returned, they'd gotten the message. "I believe we can have names for you by tomorrow night or Friday morning," Husseini ventured. I said that if it would help produce the list, I would see them for the first time in East Jerusalem, in a bow to their courage.

"I think our prospects are looking up," I reported to the President. I still needed names from the Palestinians, "and I've learned one is never going to grow rich betting on them. Still, I think we made enough headway today to get very close."

By contrast, my meeting with Shamir the next morning was a model of clarity and cordiality. Like Assad, however, the Israelis were still working the margins, probing for whatever else they might squeeze from me. In previous discussions, Israeli negotiators had asked for forty-five changes in the letter of assurances and the letter of invitation. We'd already accommodated thirty-two of them. Some of the remaining thirteen were almost frivolous—like asking us to ensure that all opening statements at the conference would be moderate in tone. Others, like a blanket commitment to all existing bilateral agreements, understandings and assurances—even those by previous administrations—were more brazen. I pointed out to Shamir that I'd already rejected Assad's demand that I publicly endorse a 1974 verbal promise given by President Nixon that the United States would tell Israel to return the Golan Heights. "I won't go down this road with any party," I said.

Shamir said surprisingly little during this meeting, which told me these discussions were essentially semantic. With Assad's participation now assured, Shamir's alternatives were effectively closed off. Unless the Palestinians gave him an eleventh-hour reprieve, Shamir could not say no. Now it was either yes or my dead cat.

At 7:55 A.M. the next morning, October 18, I met with ten Palestinians at the U.S. Consulate in East Jerusalem. Instead of the required fourteen names, they gave me seven, assuring me the rest would be in hand shortly. For all their vacillation, they had persevered in the face of death threats and the PLO's opprobrium. I wanted to salute their courage and determination. At the end, I asked them to gather around me. "I know how difficult this has been for you," I told them. "But this is your last chance—and no one can say you haven't seized it."

It was a momentous and emotional moment, the beginning of the end of an arduous journey for them. In the end, it wasn't so much my persuasive skills or my dead cat that had carried the day, but their fear of abandonment. I think they finally understood that if they passed up *this* opportunity, they might drift forever in the wilderness.

All that remained was to finalize plans for issuing the invitations with Boris Pankin. I drove from East Jerusalem to the King David Hotel, where I met Pankin in a third-floor suite. We had tentatively decided to make a joint announcement in the late afternoon. During this meeting, however, I learned the Palestinians had publicly denied giving names to me, and that they were engaged in what was described to me as a food fight at the Palace Hotel, arguing over the seven additional names. My more cautionary tendencies overcame my desire to have the process sealed. I told Pankin that I'd changed my mind. Perhaps the invitations should wait for a day or two. He was agreeable; the Soviets were so pleased to be co-sponsors that I essentially had their proxy for any arrangements. Dennis Ross slipped out of the suite and passed word to the party traveling with me that the joint press conference was being postponed.

A few minutes later, Ross returned and said his team needed to meet with me urgently to appeal this decision. I was annoyed for the interruption, but Pankin graciously retired to an adjoining room. For the next twenty minutes, I debated the merits of delay with Tutwiler, Ross, Dan Kurtzer, Bill Burns, Aaron Miller, and Ambassador Bill Brown. They were all adamant in urging me to reconsider. The parties were as close as they would ever be, they argued. No amount of further negotiation could bring them closer. Unless I imposed the reality of an invitation on them, the Palestinians would never produce seven more names. "Delay here will lead to erosion," said Kurtzer, who was the most fervent supporter of moving without delay. "This is the moment. We've got to go now and take the risks, because the risks are in our favor." In the end, I was persuaded. Resuming my meeting with Pankin, I said I'd changed my mind. We'd go forward as planned. At 4:25 P.M., we issued the invitations at a joint press conference, giving all the invitees five days to respond.

That night, I watched CNN over a dinner of smoked salmon, salad, and dried fruits in my suite with Ross, Tutwiler, and Brown. We were all utterly drained. We still didn't have formal acceptances from the parties, but for all intents and purposes, it was finally over. I indulged myself in a couple of celebratory martinis as we toasted the possibility of ending perhaps the greatest taboo in the Arab-Israeli dispute—the unwillingness of the parties to even meet and talk with each other.

En route to Madrid the next morning to thank the Spaniards for agreeing to host the conference at the last moment, I received a message that the Palestinians had produced the other seven names, all of which were acceptable to the Israelis. The Palestinians had one request. They wanted us to announce they'd been the first to respond to the invitation. I had to chuckle at that request. As the Scriptures remind us, the last will be first and the first will be last.

If It's Tuesday, It Must Be Madrid

By mid-August, the prospects for actually convening a peace conference in late October had been sufficiently promising that the selection of a suitable venue could no longer be avoided. I began discussions with Ross, Tutwiler, and Karen Groomes, my chief trip planner. We quietly began searching for a location able to accommodate the substantial political and logistical requirements of the conference. But reaching consensus on a suitable site proved just as arduous as everything else associated with the peace process. In the end, the choice of Madrid was an eleventh-hour compromise with virtually no advance notice.

For obvious reasons, our first choice had been Washington, which was quickly endorsed by Israel. As co-sponsors, however, the Soviets were predictably less enthused by this idea than we. They preferred Prague, and supported Cairo as an alternate. But even though Egypt was at peace with Israel, Shamir objected to staging the conference in an Arab capital. Moreover, he didn't want to reward what he correctly considered Mubarak's personal coolness toward him. Switzerland was an obvious candidate and, like several countries, wanted the role, but we knew the heavy United Nations permanent presence in Geneva would fuel Israeli sensitivity about U.N. participation. Moreover, the failure of the 1973 Geneva peace conference, which the Syrians and Palestinians had boycotted, might prompt unfavorable historical comparisons.

As a consensus developed in favor of a European capital, we settled on The Hague. By every yardstick, it seemed an ideal locale. The Netherlands enjoyed good relations with the Israelis, but the Dutch were serving as president of the European Community at the time, a coincidence we thought would appeal to Assad's preference for a larger European role. Moreover, since Assad had suggested the term "peace conference," we thought he'd appreciate the symbolism of the tentative meeting site—the Peace Palace, home of the International Court of Justice. The Hague also had enough hotel rooms and meeting facilities to absorb not only eleven delegations and seven hundred delegates, but also a horde of reporters estimated at between 6,000 and 7,000. And Shamir had included The Hague on his "acceptable" list.

In late September, I dispatched a small group of experts headed by Groomes to The Hague to begin secretly planning the conference with Dutch protocol officials. Groomes's team included former White House, State, and Treasury officials experienced in all aspects of advancing major events. These meetings were so secret that even the American embassy wasn't informed of the mission. After three weeks of intensive delibera-

tions, a detailed logistics plan was in place. All that remained was the delicate task of selling the site to the participants themselves.

I broached the idea with Assad in the first of our two meetings on October 15. He wasn't enthusiastic, citing the lack of a Syrian embassy and a
"political problem" Syria had with the Netherlands. (Assad wouldn't spec-
ify what the "political problem" was, so I had Karen Groomes call Hans Van
Den Broek who said that Assad's problem likely stemmed from an economic sanction the Netherlands had voted for.) He preferred Switzerland,
where he and President Carter had met in 1978. "A neutral country is better for us all," he suggested. At the end of the session, I resurrected The
Hague again. Once more he resisted, also rejecting my alternative suggestions of Copenhagen ("we have no embassy") and Prague ("it is not suitable").

Around midnight that night, I asked Margaret Tutwiler to provide a
detailed briefing on the impressive facilities and arrangements at The
Hague. Although Tutwiler made a strong presentation, showing Assad floor
plans and a book on The Hague, our efforts failed to sway him. (An irritated
Tutwiler was overheard observing that having torpedoed her handiwork,
the Syrians would surely be the first to complain if anything didn't work
perfectly at the conference.) "What city would be acceptable?" I asked
Assad. "Rome, Bonn, Paris, Geneva, London, Lausanne, Vienna—any Italian city is acceptable," he replied. "Monte Carlo—this is the biggest gamble
in history!" I quipped. "But the negotiators will go gambling," Assad said,
laughing.

"How about Madrid or Lisbon?" I finally asked. Syria had no embassy
in Portugal. "Madrid is better than Lisbon," Assad said. I knew we finally
had a compromise—if the Spaniards could do it on such short notice—because Madrid was on the list of acceptable venues given to us by the Israelis.

In the early-morning hours of October 17, I called Spanish Foreign
Minister Paco Ordonez from my room in Jerusalem's King David Hotel. I
asked him to inquire of Prime Minister Felipe Gonzalez whether Spain was
able and willing to host a conference, and that we needed an answer in
thirty minutes. Ordonez soon called back. "The hour is late," he said, "but
we'll just have to do the best we can." In two days, after obtaining the
approval of Pankin and Shamir, I was on my way to Madrid. The staffers
who had done such painstaking work secretly organizing for a conference
at The Hague were told to dismantle everything and get to Spain. We had
eleven days to make it work.

Organizing this first-ever multilateral Arab-Israeli peace conference
proved to be an enormous logistical challenge. In addition to arrangements
ensuring proper security and accommodations for both the delegates and

the press, we had to determine nearly every aspect of the actual meeting—such details as the length and order of speeches, the design of the table (which we had specially built) where representatives would be seated (which was the subject of extensive squabbling among the parties), and the amount of office space allotted to each delegation. The organizational team—Tutwiler, Groomes, Dan Kurtzer, Lynn Dent, Gary Foster, and Bill Gaskill—deserve a special share of the credit for Madrid's success. What they put together with less than two weeks of lead time was truly an impressive accomplishment.

Crawling Before We Walk

Except for a vivid painting of Charles V slaughtering the Moors, hurriedly warehoused for obvious reasons, Madrid's Royal Palace proved a splendid setting for the peace conference. Beneath eight stunning chandeliers in the ornate Hall of Columns, representatives of Israel, Syria, Egypt, Jordan, Lebanon, and the Palestinians warily convened around a T-shaped table on the morning of October 30, 1991. The opening ceremonies were hosted by Presidents Bush and Gorbachev, whose eloquent remarks contributed to the sense of high drama and spectacle.

The scene exuded all the warmth of an arranged courtship, which in fact it was. Delegates appraised one another furtively, shunning direct eye contact and taking pains to avoid even a perfunctory handshake. Except for the co-sponsors, national flags were banned from the ceremonies in deference to Israel's refusal to sit with a Palestinian delegation under the multicolored banner of the PLO. I cannot remember any meeting so devoid of diplomatic trappings.

Yet by every reasonable barometer, Madrid was a resounding triumph. Its enduring legacy was simply that it happened at all. After forty-three years of bloody conflict, the ancient taboo against Arabs talking with Israelis had in the space of one carefully choreographed hour been dramatically consigned to the back benches of history. Like the walls of Jericho, the psychological barriers of a half century came tumbling down with resounding finality that clear fall morning.

None of us swept up in the satisfaction of the moment harbored any illusions about the travails ahead. As I told reporters afterward, "We have to crawl before we walk, and we have to walk before we run, and today I think we all began to crawl." As I write these words over three years later, the peace process has matured to the point where these ancient adversaries are walking and may even learn to run. I'm hopeful that in my lifetime we'll see a splendid sprint toward a lasting peace. And I hope it doesn't sound arrogant to say that I'm proud to have contributed to a process which has begun to replace hatred with hope, and fear with friendship.

Some of my advisers said later they'd never seen me so serene. After eight months of grueling and oftentimes exasperating diplomacy, I suspect they simply confused serenity with sheer exhaustion. But in truth, I knew the President and I had accomplished something significant in the search for peace, and I hope to be forgiven some measure of self-satisfaction in that regard.

During a break in the opening session, I spotted Eytan Bentsur in the last row of the Israeli delegation. A career Foreign Service officer, Bentsur was a senior aide to David Levy, who, like his boss, was one of the few members of Shamir's government who I felt wholeheartedly supported the peace process. As early as September of 1990, in fact, in a meeting with Dennis Ross at a New York delicatessen, he'd proposed the two-track formula that later became the centerpiece of the U.S. initiative. I grasped his hand warmly, then he enveloped me in a giant bear hug. "We did it, Mr. Secretary, we did it," he said, with quiet emotion so infectious that it overpowered my usual reserve. "You're right, Eytan," I said. "We did it."

CHAPTER 28

THE EMPIRE SHAKEN

If you feed the people with revolutionary slogans, they will listen today, they will listen tomorrow, they will listen the day after tomorrow, but on the fourth day, they will say, "To hell with you."
                                                                        —*Nikita Khrushchev*

While I'm a Texan through and through, one other state has competed for my affection since I was a teenager: Wyoming. Ever since I first glimpsed the grandeurs of the Thorofare wilderness in 1944, during my first elk-hunting expedition with my dad, I've loved Wyoming as much as a born-and-bred Texan can love another state.

I've spent at least part of every August there since 1988, relaxing as much as a type A personality can, and generally wishing away the rest of the world and its complications. This was particularly true during my tenure as Secretary of State, because while there were lots of times when I wanted to leave the job behind, most of the time the job would find me. But at least at my ranch on the western slope of the Wind River Mountains, it was more difficult. I relished those few August days when I could just hike around the property and the surrounding wilderness, tracking moose, deer, and elk or going down to the stream to fish for the native trout basking in the summer sun. When I'm there, I try to live with the land as much as I can, rising with the dawn to see the wild game feeding, and settling down for the night as the sun sets behind the craggy peaks.

That's how I found myself the evening of Sunday, August 18, 1991, fast asleep at 10:21 P.M., Mountain Daylight Time, when the phone rang. It was the State Department Operations Center, and the watch officer wanted to brief me on the disturbing day that was then unfolding in Moscow. According to a Radio Moscow announcement at 6:00 A.M. and the Soviet news agency, TASS, Vice President Gennady Yanayev had taken over as President of the USSR "due to Gorbachev's inability to perform his duties for health reasons." A "State Emergency Committee" had been formed. Composed of Yanayev, Defense Minister Dmitri Yazov, KGB Chairman Vladimir Kryuchkov, Interior Minister Boris Pugo, Prime Minister Valentin Pavlov, and three others, the "Gang of Eight," as they would come to be known, had imposed a state of emergency, albeit a "temporary" one.* The committee had taken its actions "with the aim of overcoming the profound and comprehensive crisis; political, ethnic, and civil strife; chaos; and anarchy that threaten the lives and security of the Soviet Union's citizens and its sovereignty, territorial integrity, freedom, and independence." The Gang of Eight said it wanted to "prevent society from sliding into national catastrophe and ensure law and order."

Beyond these statements, we had very little to go on at the time. I knew that Gorbachev had gone to the Crimea on vacation, but was due to join republic leaders in Moscow for Tuesday's signing of the Union Treaty, which would essentially devolve power away from central Soviet structures. I also knew that Alexander Yakovlev, Gorbachev's key aide and the intellectual father of perestroika, had resigned from the Communist Party the previous Friday, warning of a coup. He now seemed only too prescient. And as I lay there in bed, unable to sleep, my mind flashed back to the warnings we had given Gorbachev and Bessmertnykh about a possible coup two months earlier.

I called the President. He was vacationing in Kennebunkport and had just talked to Brent Scowcroft, who was staying at an inn there and who had seen the first reports on CNN. There was no real information beyond what we had already learned, but we both immediately appreciated the potential gravity of the situation. The President suggested that we swear in Bob Strauss, our Ambassador-designate to the USSR, and consider sending him to Moscow right away. Jim Collins, our chargé d'affaires, was one of the most capable diplomats in the foreign service, but Strauss had political cachet that derived from his friendship with the President and me (notwithstanding that he had been a partisan Democrat), and what he said and did could send some very strong signals. I agreed that that was a good idea, but we decided to wait a few hours to see how events developed in Moscow.

"What's going on?" Susan asked once I had hung up.

"It looks like we might have a coup in Moscow," I replied.

---

*The others were Oleg Baklanov, a leading advocate of the military-industrial complex, Vasili Starodubtsev, chair of the reactionary peasant's union, and Alexander Tizyakov, president of the State Enterprise Association.

"There goes another vacation," she said. The August before, of course, the Gulf crisis had begun.

"Don't worry, honey, I'll be back here in no time," I said reassuringly. "It won't be like last year," I added, more out of hope and bravado than anything else. I felt that it would be hard for reactionary forces in the Soviet Union to put the freedom genie back in the bottle now. Reform had gone too far. But, emotionally, I must admit I was nervous. I was especially worried about Eduard Shevardnadze. He may have resigned from Gorbachev's government, but he was still a living, breathing symbol of perestroika, both in the USSR and the West. He almost certainly would be arrested, I felt, and God only knew what would happen to him after that. This, after all, was the Soviet Union, and the Gang of Eight threatened "decisive measures." I worried about a 1991 version of the Bolshevik Revolution under the guise of an "Emergency Committee."

The Coup: Day One

At 1:54 A.M. on Monday, August 19, I called the Ops Center back for what would become the first of several oral briefings I would receive that day. Radio Moscow and Soviet TV were broadcasting classical music, a telltale sign of political upheaval, and armored personnel carriers and tanks were reported on some Moscow streets. In Lithuania, the television station had been occupied by Soviet troops. While these activities were worrisome, the coup seemed to be unfolding a little too haphazardly. I thought to myself: They should have arrested Yeltsin and other democrats by now. They should have cut off links with the outside world. But the watch officer reassured me that we could still call through to Moscow, and CNN was still broadcasting. It was very puzzling.

I told Kim I wanted harder information and asked that any intelligence be sent as soon as it was available. Meanwhile, sleep was impossible. Shortly after 5:00 A.M., when I'd normally be getting up to go watch the animals, several intelligence items came in, which I read carefully before calling the Watch at 5:47 A.M. to get an update. It was now afternoon in Moscow. Tanks had taken up positions around various key buildings, and it appeared that a broader military operation was under way in the Baltics. In his own news conference, Boris Yeltsin had described the coup as "madness" and "an illegal act," and had stood on a tank and called for the people to strike and defy the State Emergency Committee.

I had the Ops Center patch me through to Bob Strauss, who was vacationing in California prior to taking up his new duties, and I warned him to pack his bags and get ready to return to Washington. Things were heating up.

At 6:14 A.M., the Ops Center put me through to Scowcroft, who briefed me on the early-morning press conference the President had just concluded. (It was quarter after eight in Maine.) Unsure of exactly what was happening in Moscow, the President and Scowcroft had decided to respond in a low-key way for the moment, though the President had pointed out, "I think it's also important to know that coups can fail, they can take over at first and then they run up against the will of the people." The President was going to return to Washington immediately, and I told Brent that Strauss and I would, too. After I hung up, Larry Eagleburger, who was acting Secretary in my absence, called, for the first of five conversations we would have that day as we coordinated our response with the White House and foreign governments.

A few minutes later, Hans Van Den Broek called from the Netherlands. He wanted to convene a meeting of NATO foreign ministers, and I agreed, though I suggested we wait a few days to give us some time to determine the extent of any changes in Moscow. "I hope the coup can be reversed," I said. "The allies must pursue any chance of reversing it."

"Would you view a CSCE meeting as an illusion under present circumstances?" he asked. I told him, to the contrary, "the reformers have placed great faith in CSCE. A CSCE meeting might be an appropriate way to force the current Soviet regime to take a stand on Helsinki principles and the Charter of Paris. It could separate the wheat from the chaff."

Three minutes after Van Den Broek and I finished, Dennis Ross, who was vacationing in New Hampshire, called. Ross felt the Soviet military was key; first, he told me, the Soviet military was unlikely to use violence against Soviet citizens, and, second, we were beginning to see fissures on the ground in Moscow—some of the troops were going over to Yeltsin—and that could cause the coup to unravel. "These guys may try to rally support by pointing to an external threat, and we need to take that away from them," Dennis stressed.

I made those same points with Hans-Dietrich Genscher, who called at 7:40 A.M., thirty minutes later. I also stressed that we wanted to keep the focus on Moscow, and not allow the Gang of Eight to attempt to transform the crisis into an East-West conflict. That was one of the reasons I preferred to avoid a NATO meeting for a few days. I asked Genscher if he had any information on Alexander Bessmertnykh, who had been on vacation but had planned to return to Moscow that day. The German Foreign Minister said he didn't know where Bessmertnykh was.

Following my talk with Genscher, I spoke again to Eagleburger, then Strauss, then Ross, and finally Margaret Tutwiler and her deputy, Richard Boucher, to pin down the line we would take in the noon press briefing.

Bob Zoellick, who was on vacation in Scotland, called ninety minutes later to emphasize one theme with me. "We don't have a lot of leverage in this situation, but one lever we have is legitimacy. We need to deny any political legitimacy to the Gang of Eight," he stressed, and the way to do that was through our statements. He, too, suggested that we appeal to the military, and gave me a useful line: "No army of the people can fire on its people."

At 11:30 A.M., Eagleburger called to tell me that the Soviet Ambassador, Viktor Komplektov, had requested a meeting, which Larry had agreed to in order to deliver a stern dressing-down. The Ambassador had begun by saying, "Gorbachev is ill, and this is why all this is happening." He'd handed over a letter from Yanayev to the President. Warning of "a situation of uncontrollability with too many centers of power" and "a real threat of the country's disintegration," Yanayev wrote. "Under these circumstances we have no other choice but to take resolute measures in order to stop the slide into catastrophe." Nonetheless, in an effort to dampen our response, Yanayev had pledged that treaties and agreements would remain in force and that the new leadership was determined "to expand mutually beneficial cooperation with our foreign partners." The letter ended with a ham-handed attempt at reassurance: "For your information, Mikhail Sergeyevich is in complete safety, and nothing is threatening him." I thought, That's easy for you to say.

In return, Larry had handed Komplektov a tough position paper that outlined our view. Stating that "this misguided and illegitimate effort to by-pass both Soviet law and the will of the Soviet peoples is in no one's interest," the position paper noted that we were "deeply disturbed" by events and "condemn the unconstitutional resort to force."*

Douglas Hurd was next in my phone queue. Hurd had been coordinating with his EC colleagues, and they wanted me to join them in Brussels on Wednesday for a North Atlantic Council meeting. I agreed and told him, "While we need to firmly condemn the coup, we need to stake out our positions with some care, as no outsider has enough influence within the USSR to reverse the course of events on their own." Her Majesty's government took the same basic position, he said, and had not looked with favor on the call by some in the West for the people of Moscow to take to the streets. Western incitement could backfire and result in civil war or chaos. But we had to make the point that coups could fail—and we did. He said Europeans were considering an EC summit, and I told him that I was concerned "such a meeting could degenerate into unprofitable hand-wringing

---

*The first draft of the paper had been started at 6:00 A.M. that day in the State Department by Larry Napper, head of the Soviet desk, and Andrew Carpendale on the Policy Planning Staff.

without a definite agenda." Instead, I said, Prime Minister Major might consider visiting the President when he returned to Kennebunkport.

Four minutes later, I called the President, who was now in Washington. He'd flown back that morning through Hurricane Bob, which was battering the East Coast—and Air Force One, as it bobbed and weaved its way southeast. I told him about my conversation with Hurd. The President had talked to thirteen heads of state and now felt a NATO meeting made sense. Indeed, he was growing somewhat confident that the coup would fail. In the sixteen hours since the Radio Moscow announcement, we still hadn't seen any signs of a classic coup d'état. The intelligence community had determined that troops were surrounding Gorbachev's vacation dacha on the Black Sea, and an unusual number of warships were located offshore, but the plotters still hadn't shut down the media, the military effort lacked coherence, and no one had been arrested. In a press conference, the State Emergency Committee had talked tough, but Yanayev's hands shook as he talked and at least one of his colleagues looked drunk. At 5:30 P.M. Moscow time, Yanayev had imposed martial law, but people were still moving freely about the city. It was a most curious affair.

On the other hand, Yeltsin's strength seemed to grow as the pressure on him increased. Yeltsin was masterful at playing to the crowd, calling the coup a "putsch" and demanding the restoration of Gorbachev. He seemed to have emboldened the people of Moscow, including Yakovlev and Shevardnadze. While I was relieved that both were free and speaking out, I was also puzzled: Why hadn't they been arrested? Hell, I thought to myself, I would certainly have arrested them if I were leading a coup.

The President and I both felt momentum was growing *against* the coup. We agreed that a stronger presidential statement would be useful, especially because Yeltsin had asked for just that. (Collins had received the request from Andrei Kozyrev, the Russian Foreign Minister.)

Then more news: On the military front, elements of the elite Tamansky Regiment, including ten tanks, had apparently defected and were now setting up to defend the Russian Federation (RSFSR) Parliament Building—the Russian White House, as it was known. Could the tide be turning?

The rest of my afternoon was occupied with more phone calls to Eagleburger, another call from Hurd, and a call from my Canadian counterpart, Barbara McDougall, who wanted a meeting of the G-7, in addition to NATO, which would thereby make the Western response more political and less military.

Meanwhile, after a large interagency meeting to discuss options and assess intelligence, the President decided to take a tougher public line, and issued the position paper that Eagleburger had given Komplektov, just in time to make that evening's news.

At quarter to five in the evening, I boarded an Air Force jet in Pinedale, Wyoming, to return to Washington. I had several traveling companions, including Bob Strauss, White House spokesman Marlin Fitzwater, and Pentagon spokesman, Pete Williams, who had been hiking in the back country when a Wyoming Army National Guard helicopter had landed nearby, and he'd been told there was a coup in the Soviet Union. He was still wearing his trail gear as our jet headed east and, after a short refueling stop at Wright-Patterson Air Force Base in Ohio, landed at Andrews Air Force Base at 11:30 P.M. Meanwhile, the sun had risen in Moscow. As the President said, "What is it about August?"

The Putsch That Fizzled

I began Tuesday morning by talking to Jim Collins in Moscow, who saw a stalemate developing. I felt that was a good sign; the coup needed momentum to succeed, and Yeltsin's defiant stance was preventing the Gang of Eight from consolidating their hold on the country. At 10:00 A.M., I joined the President as Bob Strauss was sworn in during a private ceremony in the Oval Office. The President had begun his day by calling Boris Yeltsin, to bolster the Russian leader and undermine the coup leaders. The President stepped into the Rose Garden for a press conference at 10:30 A.M. and stated unequivocally, "The unconstitutional seizure of power is an affront to the goals and aspirations that the Soviet peoples have been nurturing over the past years. This action also puts the Soviet Union at odds with the world community." Then he announced, as one columnist put it, "the electrifying news" that he had just spoken to Boris Yeltsin and had "assured Mr. Yeltsin of continued U.S. support for his goal of the restoration of Mr. Gorbachev as the constitutionally chosen leader." The President had used the fastest source available for getting a message to Moscow: CNN.

Following the Rose Garden event, the President chaired an Oval Office session to discuss contingencies. There were unsubstantiated reports that Pavlov had fallen ill and that Yazov had resigned from the Committee. Outside of Russia, the Kazakh leader, Nursultan Nazarbayev, had come out strongly against the coup, as had leaders in Ukraine and Moldavia. We all hoped that the Gang of Eight would splinter, but couldn't count on it. The State Emergency Committee's imposition of martial law the previous evening was worrisome, but once again, the committee was weak on implementation. Force had been used in the Baltics, but not elsewhere in the Soviet Union. Beyond that, there was the danger of civil war, especially if we continued to see divisions within the military, and it was quite likely that republics would break off if any stalemate continued.

The President decided to expand our support for Yeltsin, in part by using the Voice of America to spread Yeltsin's message throughout the Soviet Union. He also wanted to continue to deny the plotters any legitimacy and to implement the freeze on economic support. But he decided to hold off taking any other actions, such as economic sanctions or the cancellation of scheduled meetings, until we saw how the day played out in Moscow. Strauss would go to Moscow, but he would not meet with or present his credentials to the new regime.

The President had been trying to reach Gorbachev since Monday, with a singular lack of success. I had been trying to do the same with Sasha Bessmertnykh, with equally poor results. At quarter to twelve, while I was still at the White House, Komplektov called. "Do you have a Foreign Minister?" I asked him. "It's a curious thing that for three years I've been able to pick up the phone and talk to the Soviet Foreign Minister, and now I can't."

Komplektov told me that Bessmertnykh had been vacationing in Minsk and had come back on Sunday to Moscow. The Soviet Foreign Minister had a "high fever" and was "not diplomatically ill. He is all right politically." I was worried about Sasha. He had been a stalwart supporter of U.S.-Soviet cooperation and had been instrumental in finishing START and in advancing the Middle East peace process, but this was no time to get ill—not when people were taking to the barricades.

I spent the rest of Tuesday preparing for Wednesday's NATO meeting and held one bilateral with Jiři Dienstbier, the Czech Foreign Minister. He told me that the coup was extremely unsettling. Dienstbier pointed out that his country could be overwhelmed by refugees if the coup resulted in civil war or chaos. Already, the Czechs had beefed up the number of border guards on the fifty-five-mile frontier they shared with the Soviet Union.

At 5:35 P.M. my nerves were jangled by reports of automatic-weapons fire near the U.S. embassy and the RSFSR building a few hundred yards away, and then again when, a short while later, additional reports predicted an attack on the Russian White House before dawn, which was just hours away in Moscow.

I finally left the State Department a bit after six o'clock in order to get ready for the overnight flight to Brussels a few hours later. I've seldom felt so powerless in my life, as I hurtled across the Atlantic in the middle of the night. I kept waiting for the other shoe to drop, for the Ops Center or Sit Room to call with news that KGB and Interior Ministry troops had attacked and overrun the barricades, killing Yeltsin in the process.

But the other shoe never dropped. As I arrived in Brussels, I received the best news I could have asked for: there hadn't been an all-out attack. There had been some military movements, and three courageous defenders had been crushed when a line of APCs had maneuvered within a few blocks of the White House. But Yeltsin was alive, and the barricades were intact.

The NATO session was dominated by breaking developments in Moscow. After meeting with Secretary-General Woerner and then Douglas Hurd, I sat down for a working lunch with my counterparts before a formal meeting of the North Atlantic Council. Throughout the lunch and ministerial, we received a mixture of reports, from which it was hard to discern any pattern: the commander of the Volga military district had come out for Yeltsin. Kiev and Yerevan were calm. The KGB was moving against foreign joint ventures. Tanks were seen leaving Moscow.

At one point, Woerner was called out of the ministerial to take a phone call from Yeltsin. Finally, we started getting some hard news. Things seemed to be happening fast now: The Russian Prime Minister, Ivan Silayev, and the RSFSR Vice President, Alexander Rutskoi, were personally flying to the Crimea to pick up Gorbachev and return him to Moscow. (They had asked several Western embassies to provide representatives, and Collins had tried to join their entourage, but the military units leaving Moscow had snarled traffic, which prevented him from making the flight.) TASS confirmed that the Ministry of Defense had ordered all troops to leave Moscow. Embassy officers reported that the tanks that had deployed in defense of the Russian White House were departing.

Following the session, I held a press conference, met briefly with Hurd and Dumas, and then called the President. The coup seemed to be collapsing, but we were wary of saying anything definitive until we were absolutely certain. Meanwhile, I met with Kozyrev, who publicly asked the "democratic countries to be on guard. This is no time for euphoria." Until all members of the Gang of Eight were in jail and Gorbachev was back in Moscow, he felt we couldn't be sure the democrats had succeeded.

Just after my meeting with Kozyrev, Genscher came up to me and said that Alexander Yakovlev was on the phone and wanted to talk to me. I took the call in the American staff room at NATO. "All the troops and tanks have left Moscow," Yakovlev told me. "Gorbachev will be arriving in fifteen or twenty minutes. We've arrested several members of the junta for crimes against the constitution." I called the President to give him this good news, in effect "from the horse's mouth" in Moscow.

But my elation slipped back into caution just five minutes later, when Sasha Bessmertnykh phoned. "Be careful about the media reports, especially CNN, because the situation is not normal yet," he cautioned. "Stick to your original reaction of calling for the restoration of the legitimate Soviet government." I told him we would, and after a brief conversation about the

Middle East peace process, I asked him about his personal situation. "I understand from your ambassador in Washington that your illness was not diplomatic," I said. "It wasn't a virus, but was much graver," he replied.*

Finally, at 2:15 A.M., an Aeroflot jet taxied to a stop in Moscow. Mikhail Gorbachev, looking grim and somewhat shaken, walked down the jetway. The coup was over. But the chain reaction had just begun.

Still Soviet, But Is It a Union?

I returned to Washington Wednesday night, then flew to Kennebunkport Thursday morning to discuss next steps with the President. We concluded that with the victory of Center (Gorbachev) and Republic leaders (Yeltsin) who were committed to reform, and the diminished influence of the security services and the military, we should expect the political leadership to move aggressively on reform now. A host of considerations and needs crowded our discussions: (1) a radical economic reform package; (2) prompt implementation of START, CFE, and follow-up on arms control talks; (3) civilian control of the military and security services; (4) reduced military spending; (5) continuity in foreign policy; (6) serious negotiations on de facto Baltic independence; (7) expanded technical economic cooperation; and (8) adherence to international human rights norms.

Gorbachev, however, seemed to misread completely how much the world had already changed. From the Bush family residence on Walker's Point, the President and I watched on television as Gorbachev announced the need to "renew" the Communist Party. We were absolutely shocked. The people obviously wanted the end of the Party, not its renewal, and were making their intentions clear by toppling monuments to Lenin throughout the USSR. The Soviet Union was unraveling fast, and with it Gorbachev's position. By Saturday, Gorbachev was pressured to resign as head of the Party, the Central Committee was disbanded, and all Party property was turned over to the Soviet parliament. Outside Russia, the Ukrainian parliament voted overwhelmingly for independence, followed the next day by Belorussia, and two days later by Moldavia.

I returned to the ranch, intent on getting some rest before some other part of the world blew up. I spent the following week getting what little rest I could while thinking a lot about these startling events as I trekked across the ridges that tower over my ranch. The questions we faced seemed infi-

*Two days later, I learned how grave it had been when Bessmertnykh called me to tell me that he had been forced to resign. He had been too passive during the coup, and it would be impossible for him to continue as Foreign Minister. What he didn't tell me until well into our conversation was that his conversation with me was being filmed at his end by Ted Koppel of "Nightline."

nite: Could Yeltsin and Gorbachev cooperate? How would we deal with what was essentially a coalition government? Would the Soviet Union even stay together? I shook my head at the magnitude of these questions.

I found a few answers in two memos drafted by Policy Planning Staff Sovietologists Andrew Carpendale and John Hannah. The first, entitled "What Has to Be Done," a play on Lenin's 1902 book, argued that the Russian people had routed the last vestiges of Stalinism, and that now the possibilities for radical economic and political reform were wide open. "The Center and its institutions continue to exist for the time being," the memo stated, "but largely at the indulgence of the republics. To survive, the Center must transform itself into the vanguard of radical reform. If it fails to do so, it becomes part of the problem rather than part of the solution. Under those circumstances, the republics will try to sweep the Center aside and find a new vehicle through which to work out their relations." In sum, Gorbachev's days were numbered unless he could become more of a democrat than Yeltsin, a prospect I found unlikely.

I began to consider a series of discrete initiatives raised in the memo (e.g., convening a donors' conference for humanitarian aid, a large ramping up of U.S. technical assistance, creation of enterprise funds, Peace Corps programs for the republics, a "Plowshares Fund" for Soviet defense conversion) as well as several new policy departures—for example, tying assistance to elections, shifting START II discussions to cover dangers of accidental war, and banning land-based MIRVed ICBMs (which we had proposed, and Moscow had rejected, in the spring of 1990).

Until we had a better sense of how the Gorbachev-Yeltsin and Center-Republic relationships were going to play out, I was wary of writing Gorbachev off completely. I also thought it premature to take a host of new initiatives to the President before I had a chance to go back and take stock directly of how events in Moscow, and elsewhere in the Soviet Union, were evolving.

In any case, the President's initial priority was the Baltics. Following the failure of the putsch, they had moved aggressively to gain independence, and Yeltsin had created an opening by recognizing Estonia and Latvia on August 24. (Russia had already recognized Lithuania on July 29.) Several Scandinavian countries had moved quickly to recognize them, too, and there was growing pressure for us to follow suit. Since we had never formally recognized incorporation of the Baltics into the USSR, the President simply announced on September 2 that we would establish diplomatic relations with Estonia, Latvia, and Lithuania, and would work to make independence a reality.

The bigger political question revolved around the other republics. I was looking for a diplomatic tool to help shape their behavior. I found a useful idea in the second memo. It began by noting that "as the Soviet external empire collapsed in 1989, the Soviet *internal* empire seems to be collapsing now." While most of the independence rhetoric seemed connected to a conscious effort by each republic to increase its leverage in any negotiation, the memo warned "there is the real possibility that these current declarations of independence will now lead to territorial, economic, and military disputes between republics." That very week, Yeltsin had warned that Russian-dominated sections of Ukraine and Kazakhstan would not be allowed to secede. The memo continued: "While events will be determined on the ground, our *words* will—as they clearly did during the coup—have a great impact on how leaders act." By articulating "five principles," we could "set the philosophical and practical framework within which the process of Soviet dissolution can occur peacefully and orderly."

The principles themselves were straightforward: first, peaceful self-determination consistent with democratic values and principles; second, respect for existing borders, with any changes occurring peacefully and consensually; third, respect for democracy and the rule of law, especially elections and referenda; fourth, human rights, particularly minority rights; and fifth, respect for international law and obligations. But their simplicity was their strength; like the President's "four principles" that had guided our approach to German unification, the "five principles" could create a political structure to help us through what I saw as an increasingly turbulent transition period.

Nevertheless, I saw some real opportunities in the days ahead. The people had shown their desire for freedom, and I felt it was unlikely those aspirations would be bottled up again. Democracy had a window of opportunity because communism was a spent force, although many apparatchiks were masquerading as democrats merely to maintain power. The greatest risks lay in the possibility that fragmentation and disintegration would lead to interrepublic or interethnic violence, a situation all the more worrisome in a country with thousands of nuclear weapons.

My inclination to go ahead with the principles was reinforced by a meeting about this time between Jim Collins and Sergei Tarasenko in Moscow. Speaking on behalf of Shevardnadze, Tarasenko warned Collins that Yeltsin's appeal to Russian nationalism was very dangerous. "There is no serious counterweight to nationalist emotions and forces pushing fragmentation," Tarasenko believed. "The President is weak, and central government structures are nearly incapable of independent action." Shevardnadze felt that a statement by us that emphasized Helsinki principles and the need to resolve disputes peacefully could do much to dampen the potential for conflict.

After discussing the five principles with Scowcroft, who agreed with the approach, I announced them in a White House press briefing on September 4. The same day I sat down with the President to discuss Soviet economic priorities. There were three. The first was to urge the new Soviet Economic Commission that had been created in the coup's aftermath to develop a comprehensive market-reform plan, in collaboration with the International Monetary Fund and the World Bank: Until that was done, large-scale assistance would continue to be virtually useless. Our second priority was humanitarian aid, in an effort to get the Soviets through what had the potential to be a very tough winter. The third was technical assistance, and we hoped to target food distribution, energy, and defense conversion.

Far more important than either politics or economics to the President, however, was the question of nuclear weapons. During the coup, U.S. intelligence had picked up several anomalous indicators involving the Strategic Rocket Forces (SRF), the nuclear arm of the Soviet military. While there had been no indications that the threat of a nuclear accident had increased, these anomalies quite naturally concerned him, and he asked me to pay particular attention to nuclear command-and-control questions when I talked to Gorbachev, Yeltsin, and the military leadership.* That would be soon, for we had decided that there was only one way to determine what was truly going on in the Soviet Union—and that was for me to go there myself.

Moscow on the Verge . . . of What?

Every time I landed in Moscow, I seemed to encounter a new city, and on September 10, it was no different. Indeed, my first day in Moscow was surreal. I went from the Osobnyak, which was eerily deserted, to the Kremlin, which seemed impervious to the chaos of the last weeks, to the Russian White House, around which could be seen the remnants of barricades. In fact, the barricades stood almost equidistant between our embassy and the White House, and at the corner you could see the flowers and wreaths that had been laid in commemoration of the three youths who had given their lives fighting the putsch.

I spent most of the day with Gorbachev and Yeltsin, and gave each of them one of the American flags that had flown over the U.S. Capitol on August 21. After my meeting with Yeltsin, I went to the CSCE conference, where I witnessed the Lithuanian Foreign Minister giving his speech to

---

*The President also instructed Dick Cheney and Colin Powell that he wanted new and serious ideas to reduce the danger of nuclear war. After considerable discussion and debate among his advisers, he announced on September 27 a series of radical steps, including unilaterally eliminating or consolidating tactical nuclear weapons, canceling mobile ICBMs and short-range attack missiles (SRAMs), and proposing the elimination of MIRVed ICBMs.

those assembled. "If two months ago," I wrote the President that night, "someone had told us an independent Lithuanian Foreign Minister would be making a very positive speech to a CSCE meeting *in Moscow* in September, we would have asked what he was smoking. That typifies the enormous changes that have taken place here."

Both Gorbachev and Yeltsin were supremely confident. The shaken Gorbachev of late August was gone, replaced by his former self—the Soviet reformer with little if any self-doubt. Yeltsin, too, beamed with power, those moments on the tank and hours in the besieged White House having transformed him from a maverick upstart to a true world figure in his own right.

I said to Gorbachev, "The time for talk is past. We need action. You now have greater opportunity for action, because constraints have been removed. It is now critical to act decisively." (I made a similar case to Yeltsin.) I stressed that they needed a credible program, worked out with the IMF and the World Bank, for moving to a market-based economy. Both agreed, but each also stressed the need for foreign assistance, particularly to meet humanitarian requirements, which were likely to grow as the Russian winter set in.

Gorbachev praised President Bush privately and publicly for his personal role during the coup, and he pulled me aside with some emotion to thank the President. "You know, after the coup, everyone is being so nice to me. Now, we see only too clearly, both inside the Soviet Union and outside, who was with me and who was not. Those words of President Bush were important in mobilizing others." At our press conference, Gorbachev asked me to give the President one of the four videotapes he had prepared in the Crimea during his darkest hour. Yeltsin, likewise, was highly appreciative, particularly of the President's phone call on the second day of the coup.

These weren't their only points of common agreement—far from it, at least for the moment. Quite frankly, I was surprised by the extent of their coordination and agreement, which ran across the spectrum of issues. I asked both of them, "Who will have control of nuclear weapons? We have said publicly that we want to see one central command authority. We do not want to see more nuclear states." Both agreed that the Center must retain control of all nuclear weapons, strategic and tactical, and Gorbachev indicated that the chain of command ran through him.

They agreed that there should be only one currency in a new economic union. And they agreed that an economic union—properly forged through an "economic treaty," which Grigori Yavlinsky was drafting with the republics—was critical for governing what they called the "emerging common economic space."

Their need for each other was unmistakable—at least in the short term. In fact, each made a strong and very conscious pitch to me that they were cooperating with the other. Gorbachev emphasized Yeltsin's courage, Yeltsin spoke of Gorbachev as a "changed man" and said that the two of them were on the phone all the time with each other. Yeltsin's stand against the coup gave him a legitimacy with average Soviet citizens that Gorbachev undoubtedly craved; Yeltsin resonated with them as a *vozhd*—a czarlike boss who could provide the stability they undoubtedly desired after the chaos of the perestroika era. That legitimacy was something Gorbachev now lacked and, just as important, needed, if he was going to resurrect himself as *the* leader of the country. But Yeltsin, despite his finger-pointing and lecturing of Gorbachev after the coup, also needed Gorbachev. For the moment, Yeltsin needed Gorbachev's experience at running a government. He also wanted help, it seemed, with the other republics, who feared the Russians in general, and Yeltsin in particular.

At heart, however, their areas of agreement fundamentally reflected a negative agenda: they needed to deter another coup attempt, to prevent complete disintegration and anarchy, and to avoid a famine. "There were," Gorbachev said, "forces sympathetic to the coup which did not speak up. We cut off the head, but need to move rapidly to prevent a recurrence."

Accelerated cooperation with the West, particularly the United States, was also a nexus. Given the highly uncertain Soviet future, we were in even more of a hurry to "lock in" gains then and there. Moreover, to unlock Western aid, Moscow had to resolve several foreign policy problems. "It's important for us to be able to point to some concrete results from this visit, especially on foreign policy," I said. "Let's close out some of the things we couldn't close before. Let's take some actions that we could use to make it absolutely clear that there's a new day here." They jumped at my offer, and indeed were almost competitive in trying to be cooperative. I pushed both of them hard on several issues from our old agenda, in particular military supplies to Afghanistan and financial subsidies for Cuba, and the Soviet military presence on the island. I said that the West would be far more willing to support them and to help them with their debt if it was clear they were no longer subsidizing Communist regimes around the world. "Yes, we spent eighty-two billion dollars on ideology," said Gorbachev, making an ironic joke of the Soviet debt.

Yeltsin was so action oriented that when I proposed cutting off arms supplies to promote an Afghan settlement, he interjected, "I will tell Gorbachev to do it." After the meeting, he did call Gorbachev, and then called to assure me that the Soviet Union would agree to a January 1, 1992, deadline for an arms cutoff to Kabul. I was stunned by how swiftly we could make progress. Gorbachev agreed in my meeting with him to begin withdrawing

ABOVE: Colleagues and friends who made it all possible . . . On the right, Dick Cheney, with me and President Bush. *(White House/Bush Library.)*
BELOW: Brent Scowcroft. *(White House/Bush Library.)*

LEFT: Colin Powell, with me at the Alfalfa Club annual dinner in 1993. *(Mark Thiessen.)*
BELOW: Larry Eagleburger, the best deputy I could have had. *(White House/Bush Library.)*

RIGHT: Margaret Tutwiler.
(Washington Times.)
BELOW: With John Kelly,
Ed Ney, and Bob Kimmitt.

RIGHT: NSC meeting
with Reg Bartholomew
and Dick Cheney.
*(White House/Bush
Library.)*
BELOW: On the plane:
with Caron Jackson
and Bob Zoellick.
(Caron Jackson.)

ABOVE: Caron Jackson and Karen Groomes on U.S.S.R. *Maxim Gorky* during the Malta Summit. *(Caron Jackson)*
BELOW: Janet Mullins. At left, Curt Kammen.

ABOVE: Some of our traveling staff hard at work. *(Caron Jackson.)*
RIGHT: Backgrounding the press on the airplane. *(Caron Jackson.)*

ABOVE: With Bernard Aronson at OAS foreign ministers' meeting. At left, with glasses on forehead, is U.S. Ambassador to OAS, Luigi Einaudi. *(Roberto Ribeiro.)*
BELOW: At the "Two-plus-Four" Ministerial, with, left to right, Bob Zoellick, Dennis Ross, Margaret Tutwiler, Ray Seitz, and Bob Blackwill.

The Madrid Peace Conference. Listening to Egyptian Foreign Minister Amre Moussa are, left to right, Margaret Tutwiler, Dennis Ross, John Kelly, Dan Kurtzer, Ed Djerejian, Bob Pearson, Bill Burns, me, and Wes Egan. *(AP/Wide World.)*

the Soviet brigade in Cuba. Without expecting him to say yes, I asked as we were walking to our press conference in St. George's Hall if he could mention this. He said he could, and did. This announcement dominated the press coverage of our meeting and created considerable angst and hard feelings in Cuba, which learned about it for the first time from those press accounts. Later, Yeltsin told me that all military and economic assistance to Cuba would be cut off by January 1, 1992, and that all Soviet military personnel in Cuba would be out of Cuba by the same date. It was clear to me that a key motivation behind this step, which wouldn't go over all that well even in Moscow, despite the defeat of the coup, was to clear the way for stronger U.S. support. My meetings with the new Soviet Foreign Minister, Boris Pankin, and with Andrei Kozyrev, the Foreign Minister of the Russian Republic, mirrored my sessions with their bosses. Both pledged their complete cooperation.*

Above all, Gorbachev and Yeltsin had in common the short-term political task of dissuading anyone else from challenging their authority. But over the long term, which would require development of a positive agenda for action, I was less sure. "I don't know how long it [their cooperation] will last," I wrote the President that night, "but they clearly each see that it is in their interest now."

But as I looked at what was good and hopeful in the political situation, the dangers were equally plain. The economy was wrecked and humanitarian needs were huge. Gorbachev continued to show little understanding of the basic steps needed to transform a command economy to a market economy, and more than ever, chaos seemed to dominate economic relations. (At one point, Gorbachev said they needed tight control of any stabilization fund because, "Things disappear around here. We got a lot of money for German unification, and when I called our people, I was told they didn't know where it was. Yakovlev told me to call around, and the answer is no one knows." Yakovlev later told me, "It's just gone.")

The talks my staff and embassy personnel had with Soviet citizens on the street revealed a sense that all they heard was talk, and meanwhile food and other basic goods were becoming harder and harder to get—much more so than just a year or two before. One acquaintance of Margaret Tutwiler's from prior trips said that the first person who put vodka on the shelves would walk away with the prize. There seemed to be lots of latent support, too, for anyone who could promise order. Some were explicit: Eight are gone, they said, but thousands more are still out there. The feeling

---

*Kozyrev began our meeting by pointing to stains on the wall. "As you can see, our walls are pretty barren. This used to be Communist Party headquarters, and we've taken down the old pictures, but we haven't decided what to put up instead."

seemed to be that if the reactionaries had another chance, the next round wouldn't be an amateur act.

All these impressions were reinforced by my next two days of talks. I began Thursday, September 12, by meeting with Ivan Silayev, head of the new economic commission and an articulate man brimming with energy. His group included both Pankin and Kozyrev, along with Yavlinsky, who now was less interested in grand bargains and more interested in a plan that would meet IMF and World Bank approval. (The evening before at dinner, Yavlinsky had told Bob Zoellick that he had been part of the group that had gone to arrest Interior Minister Pugo. While they were entering Pugo's apartment, Pugo and his wife had committed suicide with handguns.)

Silayev began by ironically thanking the leaders of the coup who, he said, had planned the putsch in the very room in which we were meeting. Their actions had accelerated a confrontation between conservatives and reformers, and now the reformers were on top. Nonetheless, he was realistic, even pessimistic, about the prospects for turning the economy around. "The situation is very grave," Silayev said. "The roots of the defunct structures are still here. So are those who advocated the old methods. There might be some hotheads who try to take advantage." The task of his "caretaker administration," he felt, was to avoid further economic deterioration and stave off famine. We touched on Center-Republic relations, but I had the sense there was still much to be worked out. While Silayev noted that they had managed to put economic issues ahead of political issues, I wasn't sure how far they could go without resolving the underlying political relationships.

That point was underscored by my next interlocutor, Mayor Popov. "Each republic finds itself in a different situation. Some can live on their own, others cannot. This will come out looking like a layer cake," he said. In his view, there was no "meaningful government. There is nervousness and uncertainty. Russia may have to take on the role of being the Center. Others would join, but not if Russia is a decisive part." The West needed to channel assistance to the Center, but in a way that prevented the Center from being re-formed—not altogether an easy task.

Far more so than the national leaders, the mayor was concerned about real problems, such as feeding his people. "Moscow cannot support itself through this winter," he said. "We need fifteen thousand tons of eggs, two hundred thousand tons of milk, ten thousand tons of mashed potato mix. Some of this material is stored by your army, which throws it out after three years. But a three-year shelf life is all right for us." It was a sobering admission of the problems faced by a country whose leader once talked about "burying" the West.

My meeting with Shevardnadze was the most emotional moment of all.

Almost nine months to the day, he had warned of a coup, resigned in principle, and later courageously joined Yeltsin in defeating that coup. I felt, Here was a man of integrity. I was honored to call him my friend. He said that there was a "vacuum" of authority and legitimacy, and tremendous social tensions across the country. He warned us not to judge the country by what was happening in Moscow and St. Petersburg; elsewhere, the democrats were not nearly as strong. He, too, was worried about the winter. "The people could come out on the street, and that threat really exists," he said. "I think Gorbachev has finally decided to move radically. My friend has a lot on his conscience. Simple analysis will tell you that the threat was real. He took off for vacation after a dress rehearsal for this coup, and didn't see it."*

Real power in the economy had devolved to the republics, Shevardnadze said. Once again, I stressed the need for some form of arrangement so the outside world could know where power resided economically. This was also a must for implementation of a credible economic program.

In the political sphere, Shevardnadze, as always, was looking well into the future. The five principles would work during the transition period, he noted, but the longer term was a different question. In Central Asia, he predicted, fundamentalism would be a problem by the turn of the century. "You will find yourself in a brand-new world. You must tell them that there must be a new union or there will be chaos," he implored me.

That evening, when I hosted republic leaders for dinner—a mixed group of presidents, prime ministers, and foreign ministers—I saw around the table and in the conversation a microcosm of the post-coup Soviet Union's potential—and its problems. Whatever euphoria that they felt with their post-putsch independence declarations had given way to a marked degree of realism. "Independence sounds nice, but we have to live, and we have to be practical," observed the Prime Minister of Moldova, Valeriu Muravsky.† That was the persistent theme that I heard from every one of the republic leaders, with the sole exception of the Georgian Prime Minister, Vissarion Gugushvili, though even he spoke of the need for economic cooperation once Georgian independence was recognized internationally.

All noted the significance of the five principles, and when I emphasized that relations with the United States and support from us would depend upon living up to those standards, I found marked approval. The five principles, I wrote the President that night, could "become a very useful tool for

---

*Gorbachev had told me, "The fact is that the coup had been foreseen for eighteen months."

†Moldavia had become Moldova—an example of the nationalization of culture that was sweeping the Soviet Union. More changes occurred in two other republics: Belorussia became Belarus, and Kirghizia became Kyrgyzstan.

affecting the behavior of republic leaders." The leaders also recognized that they all lived in what they described as a "single economic space," and understood that cooperation and coordination on assistance was essential. I explained the difficulties the West would have in funneling humanitarian and other economic assistance in the absence of arrangements that defined where the authority for economic decision-making would be located.

Yet it was equally obvious that nationalist passions were not far below the surface. In a typical example, I ended up as the go-between at the end of the evening between Silayev and the Ukrainian Prime Minister, Vitold Fokin. The Ukrainian leader told me that Ukraine would sign the economic union treaty, provided it received assurances that distribution of aid from the outside world would be equitably distributed—as clearly had not been the case with the moneys associated with German unification. Silayev agreed to such a commitment, but the mutual suspicion was obvious. Nationalistic pressures in the new competitive politics of each of the republics seemed almost certain to exert themselves. Whatever rational economic reasons there were for coming together were more than balanced by passionate political reasons for pulling apart.

I started Friday with Yakovlev, Shevardnadze's owlish comrade-in-arms. "It's difficult to understand that this was a real revolution, particularly in the minds of the people," he began. I was struck by a singular contrast: Shevardnadze and Yakovlev were unfailingly gentle and civil, yet their role in defeating the coup had been amazingly powerful. "Both my children went to the barricades at the White House. I had not imagined this possible! Now power is in the democrats' hands. Many really do not know what democracy means. They just opposed the Party."

He warned there would be mistakes. "We are appointing some people to jobs who are total civilians, like the new KGB chief—he is two hundred percent civilian. I've heard the new Moscow police chief knows nothing about being a policeman. But we have to protect this democracy with civilians." He felt Marshal Akhromeyev's suicide—three days after the coup—was a real tragedy. As for Bessmertnykh, "He is a good man, a democrat in his heart. But he had not courage."

I met with the new Minister of Defense, Yevgeny Shaposhnikov, in a large conference room, adorned with three huge murals of military battles, on the fifth floor of the ministry—a building which we had driven past many times, but one in which the United States Secretary of State had never been welcomed before. Shaposhnikov began his presentation by noting, "This was not a military coup. We did not use any weapons against our people. A small group of plotters did this, and they were unaware of what was going on in our nation. They should have looked out their windows. They should have taken a walk. The people, the army, and the times we are living in—that's what stopped the coup. Democracy is a broad stream, not a narrow one, like they thought. My country has moved on the path of democracy.''

I told him I understood and that we noted his personal courage during the coup, and asked how he saw the Soviet army fitting into this new democracy.

He said he had met with all the republic leaders. The Baltics were a special case. They wanted Soviet troops out immediately. "If houses are built here in Russia, I will move the people out faster," he said. He told the Baltic leaders it would take time, but he felt they understood the problems he faced.

For Shaposhnikov, economic transformation was the number one challenge, though on politics he cautioned me, "Please do not be in a hurry to recognize all these new republics." Then, somewhat innocently, he turned to Margaret and said, "Please, Miss Tutwiler, do not say what I have just said on television." I assured him we would not be quoting him to our press, but it was a reminder of how truly new—and even naive—the new leaders were. He, like Gorbachev and Yeltsin, was adamant about maintaining central control of nuclear weapons, though he wanted to abolish tactical nuclear weapons. In addition, both Shaposhnikov and General Oleg Lobov—the new Chief of the General Staff, with whom I met for thirty minutes—were clearly in the process of reassessing the size and shape of the military, as well as its force structure. Both were eager to meet with Dick Cheney and Colin Powell, and I was convinced this could have not only long-term implications for Moscow's behavior externally, but could also contribute to making the military more of a bulwark in defense of reform internally.

As with all my other meetings, Center-Republic relations were at the forefront of my discussions. Shaposhnikov wanted to implement reforms that would fundamentally change the nature of the Soviet military to reflect the changing balance between the Center and the republics. Shaposhnikov spoke of the military, in effect, having a treaty relationship with each republic. The military's presence in a republic, he outlined, would be worked out according to a certain code that requires the military to protect the borders of the republic, while obligating it never to intervene in its internal affairs. He spoke of the local commander being in the chain of command of the general staff, but working in concert with a local council of ten to fifteen leaders of each republic. He asked to see a generic Status of Forces Agreement (SOFA)—the legal instruments we use to base American forces overseas—clearly with an eye toward shaping the relationship between the military and each of the republics.

Though he was a marshal of the air force, Shaposhnikov wanted to transform the defense ministry into a civilian-based institution. He was also interested in transforming the Soviet military's image in society by borrowing from us a different juridical code for prosecution of crimes committed by military personnel. He felt that would make the military more professional, as well as less threatening, in the eyes of the public.

Later that afternoon, I arrived at Dzerzhinsky Square, site of the Lubyanka, KGB headquarters, to find the new head of the KGB, Vadim Bakatin, waiting at the curb to greet me. In front of our press, he said, "I'm a little nervous," which I found a disarmingly frank admission. If it was remarkable for an American Secretary of State to meet in the Soviet Defense Ministry, it was nothing short of incredible for that to happen in the bowels of the KGB itself. I went through a variety of issues with him on which we needed their help, notably POWs and MIAs in Vietnam. "We will open our archives," he said. "Maybe there is something on POWs and MIAs, but to be honest, this organization was not known for keeping very extensive records. They also have destroyed so much, I don't know if we will ever find it." He said he was going to revamp the structure of the KGB. "The KGB was blown out of all proportion. The organization got too fat. We will be reducing it." The previous week, Bakatin had hosted a meeting of all twelve republic KGB heads, and they agreed to work "for, not over, the republics." His job would be to coordinate efforts, and he talked of transforming the KGB into an organization much like the CIA. Bakatin emphasized that its primary role would be one of foreign intelligence, not internal political suppression and intimidation. He felt there must be a legal basis for the KGB, and had been studying how U.S. legislation underpinned our intelligence community and its prerogatives. He made a point of asking whether we would be open to extensive exchanges between the KGB and the CIA— something he saw as beneficial, at least in part for the effect it would have on transforming the KGB into the kind of professional institution he wanted it to become. I thought to myself, This is one helluva country; a month ago the head of the KGB is arresting President Gorbachev, and now the head of the KGB is studying American legislation in order to model his organization after the Central Intelligence Agency!

He was cool, but sincere and open, and only came close to being emotional when discussing Center-Republic relations. "The republic leaders are acting irresponsibly. Independence is okay, but act responsibly," Bakatin argued. "I am not speaking of the Baltics, but of the others. They think that separation will help them, and that the West will save them. We can live only together—not like in the past, but together, especially in the Ukraine."

I told him that I felt the republics would cooperate economically.

Bakatin agreed, but emphasized, "We need political stability or we will slide into the abyss. Russia, Kazakhstan, and the Ukraine cannot exist without the Union. We need a loose union for people to feel safe."

That evening, we flew to St. Petersburg (which had reverted back to that name after sixty-seven years as Leningrad) for a working dinner with Anatoly Sobchak, the city's mayor, who had been as courageous as Yeltsin in defying the coup. (He had been helped by Col. Gen. Viktor Samsonov, commander of the Leningrad Military District, who had refused to deploy his troops during the putsch. Samsonov sat next to Sobchak during our dinner.) I was impressed by Sobchak's charisma and felt he was headed for national leadership. Besides his personal charm, he was clearly intrigued by new ideas, which were in almost as great a demand as milk, eggs, and other humanitarian assistance. As I listened to Sobchak, I was inspired by his enthusiasm and his values. But all the reformers lacked practical knowledge of how to build a civic society, and their views on a market economy were incredibly naive; communism had not only destroyed freedom, but, for most, even practical ideas for how to achieve it. I realized Sobchak and the others would need to find their own way to democracy and free markets, and while we could help with this staggering task, we could never replace their efforts. As I looked around me, I thought how ironic it was to be in St. Petersburg, the birthplace of the Bolshevik revolution, and to be listening to one of the handful of men responsible for undoing Lenin's legacy. I wondered how history would judge men like Sobchak and Yeltsin—and hoped history would be kind.

In a note to the President, I summed up the challenge we faced: "The simple fact is we have a tremendous stake in the success of the democrats here. Their success will change the world in a way that reflects both our values and our hopes. What may be at stake is the equivalent of the postwar recovery of Germany and Japan as democratic allies, only this time after a long Cold War rather than a short, hot one. The democrats' failure would produce a world that is far more threatening and dangerous, and I have little doubt that if they are unable to begin to deliver the goods, they will be supplanted by an authoritarian leader of the xenophobic right wing. . . . Given the long odds, I think we need to be realistic in recognizing that success might amount to simply holding off a counterreaction and giving the democrats the space and time to stay with what will be a long journey. But that in itself would be an historic legacy.

"At this point, the onus is still on them to step up to the plate and prove that they are prepared to carry out an economic revolution that matches their political revolution. But if they do that—indeed, if they really do work with the IMF and the World Bank to shape a very credible program for moving to a market economy, the onus will be on us, especially if we hang back. Notwithstanding everything they're up against, I don't think we should assume that they are going to shy away from the task of carrying out an economic revolution. We should begin to position ourselves to deal with that possibility."

The Independent Baltics—At Last

I spent the next day, Saturday, September 12, hopscotching around the Baltics, starting in Tallinn, Estonia, then making the short hop to Riga, Latvia, and ending up in Vilnius, before returning to St. Petersburg. Each stop was a marked change from Moscow and St. Petersburg, though not in reminders of the coup. (At each site I visited, I saw either barricades, sand-bags, or huge boulders that had been placed in front of the government buildings to protect them.) The difference was in part a function of size; Moscow and St. Petersburg are like New York and Los Angeles—over-whelming and sprawling. But the Baltics just felt different. I had a real sense that underneath the Communist facade, ancient historical and national roots were ready to flourish.

In all three states, there was an understandable preoccupation with the need for economic renewal and for accelerating the "divorce with the So-viet Union," as Estonian Prime Minister Edgar Savissar put it. The Estonians seemed the most advanced on economic reform, primarily because of their close association for some time with Finland. Latvia's leaders were very impressive, especially Prime Minister Godmanis, and were guiding their people clearly in the most sensible direction in terms of economic reform. In Lithuania, Landsbergis and Gedimanas Vagnorius, his Prime Minister, "talked the talk" on privatization and economic reform. It remained to be seen if they were fully prepared to "walk the walk."

The Baltic leaders were very interested in the package of assistance that President Bush had approved and which I announced at each stop, but they also saw the arrival of the U.S. Secretary of State as politically very impor-tant; Lithuanian Foreign Minister Algirdas Saudargas told one of my col-leagues, with considerable hyperbole, "When the Secretary stepped off his airplane, I noted the time on my watch. It's an important step, almost as important as when Neil Armstrong stepped on the moon." Our offer of Peace Corps delegations was the biggest hit; President Arnold Ruutel of Es-tonia said, "Please send three battalions."

But removing Soviet troops was the main item on their agenda. The Estonians wanted to elevate the issue to the international level as a way of pressuring the Soviets to act. The Latvians were prepared to take in the issue in stages. First, they wanted the troops to withdraw from all civilian areas and remain only on military bases. Second, they wanted to develop a process for complete withdrawal. All three states faced one major difficulty with regard to the military: a singular lack of information from Moscow regarding the status of forces, equipment, and installations in their republics. "We want to be a nuclear-free zone," President Anatolijs Gorbunovs told me, "and according to the Soviets there are no nuclear weapons on our territory, but we don't know if the information is accurate." The Lithuanians were very dogmatic, insisting on things that would never happen in the short term: the immediate and total withdrawal of Soviet troops, the demilitarization of Belorussia, and restrictions on any movement of military goods to Kaliningrad—the slice of Soviet land that abuts Poland and which was now isolated by Lithuania's independence. All of them wanted the United States to take the lead in pushing their agenda items with Moscow.

I listened to what each of the leaders had to say and told them we hoped the Soviet withdrawal would take place as quickly as possible, and would make that view known to the Soviets, but that they would have to negotiate the specifics with the Soviets. I also conveyed the points Shaposhnikov had made with me: The Soviets understood and recognized the independence of the Baltics and were under no illusions that their forces could stay. Moreover, citizens of the Baltic states would be released from the Soviet armed forces. Because of the housing shortage, Moscow would need until January 1, 1994—a date clearly tied to the completion of German unification—to finish withdrawals. But troops that had been associated with provocative acts—notably, the black berets—would be withdrawn soon.

The Lithuanians dismissed all of this, the Estonians seemed intrigued, and the Latvians were clearly interested. I wrote the President, "Perhaps we were hearing some deliberate posturing and the Lithuanian position will be more reasonable when dealing directly with the Soviet military. The one thing I feel strongly about is that we should not get in the middle of this." To do otherwise, I felt, would have resulted in the responsibility landing on us when we needed to be on the sidelines prodding each party to an agreement.

Besides the troops, each of these new states also had to contend with the problem of the Russians and others who had moved in during the Soviet occupation and now called the Baltics home. In my meetings, I emphasized the Helsinki principles of respect for human rights and equal treatment to minorities. Once again, the Latvians seemed most reasonable. The Estonians seemed less so, as they were talking about having all Russians who were in the defense, internal security, or military-industrial sectors leave Estonia—no matter how long they had been retired from these positions and no matter how long they had lived in Estonia. The Lithuanians seemed to be the least tolerant of Russians. While explaining that they were not exonerating all those imprisoned by the Soviets for war crimes in World War II, I got the distinct feeling that in Lithuanian eyes, some citizens were more equal than others. It was another reminder that communism had frozen long-standing ethnic antagonisms in place, and now with the ice of the Cold War melting, the axis of conflict was more likely going to lie along ethnic lines than interstate rivalries.

Alma-Ata: Is This Still the Soviet Union?

I spent most of Sunday flying close to six hours east and south to Alma-Ata, the capital of Kazakhstan. The "place of apples," Alma-Ata sits high in the mountains that separated the Soviet Union from Mongolia, China, India, Iran, and other lands to the south. As I looked out over the rugged peaks and stark land below, I felt for a moment that I had returned to Wyoming. I would soon learn that President Nursultan Nazarbayev definitely wanted me to feel at home.

That night, Susan and I joined Nazarbayev and his wife and their daughter for a private dinner, joined on our side only by Bob Strauss, Dennis Ross, and Peter Afanasenko. Nazarbayev's daughter played the piano for us, and we drank many toasts to what the Kazakh leader called a "U.S.-Kazakh strategic alliance." Once his wife and daughter, Sara, left, following the dinner, he explained why his country needed such an alliance. "If you traveled around my country, you'd see Russian kids beating up Kazakh kids," he noted. "That's how it was for me. It's not easy to live with them." Nazarbayev was extremely intelligent and capable and had been a close ally and strong supporter of Gorbachev. He was particularly concerned about Yeltsin and the people around him, the "Sverdlovsk mafia" from Yeltsin's hometown behind the Urals. In an almost carbon copy of the message Tarasenko had conveyed to Collins, Nazarbayev warned of their "dangerous nationalism." The Kazakhs, surrounded virtually on every side by a great power, wanted to reach out to the United States, the one power in the world that could ensure their peace and stability.

Dennis walked him through the five principles. It was obvious that Nazarbayev understood how the principles could help him protect his country against extreme Russian nationalists. However, he seemed less interested in the democratic elements in them. We stressed that adherence to the principles would be critical, not just for Western political support but also for Western assistance.

After our meeting, Nazarbayev asked if I'd ever had an "eastern style" sauna. When I said no, he said simply, "Let's go." We had covered a lot of substantive ground and he had been very gracious. It seemed the least we could do. So soon enough, our interpreter, Peter Afanasenko, Bob Strauss, and I had stripped down and were sitting with Nazarbayev and our vodka in the presidential *banya*—a Russian sauna that was large and comfortable, even by Western standards. Ron Mazer and the rest of my security detail posted itself outside, along with Dennis Ross, who had begged off, citing a cold. Nazarbayev told us about Kazakh customs and history, Peter tried to interpret through the steam, and Strauss and I relaxed, leaving geostrategic worries far behind. After about twenty minutes, Nazarbayev picked up a large bundle of eucalyptus branches and beat me on the back and legs in order to open the pores and increase the therapeutic value of the heat. Upon seeing this, Strauss said he'd had enough and stepped out.

"Damn!" he jokingly told my security detail outside. "Get me the President of the United States on the phone. His Secretary of State is buck naked, and he's being beaten by the President of Kazakhstan!"

We ended up wishing Nazarbayev good night well after midnight to return to our presidential guest house, only to find most of my staff wide awake, concerned that I had launched a major new initiative!

"How did it go?" they asked.

"Great," I said, leaving them none the wiser.

The next day as our jet climbed into the sky to hop over the mountains for another Middle East shuttle, I was truly thankful that the coup had failed, and that a potential disaster had been averted. But it was quite clear that we were not out of the woods as far as momentous change in the Soviet Union was concerned—and, therefore, clear as well that difficult challenges lay ahead.

CHAPTER 29

SETTLEMENTS, LOAN GUARANTEES, AND THE POLITICS OF PEACE

For the sake of 3.9 million Israeli Jews and a million Israeli Arabs who should not have to mortgage their future because of the 100,000 settlers in the territories, I intend to persevere.

—Yitzhak Rabin to Secretary Baker, Jerusalem, July 20, 1992

Much has been made and written of the often tempestuous relationship between the United States and Israel during the Bush administration, and I wouldn't deny the obvious. Despite America's abiding commitment to Israel's security from the moment of her creation—a commitment which we reaffirmed early and often during the Bush administration—our bilateral relations were in fact periodically strained during my tenure as Secretary of State. After all, during one particularly contentious eight-month period in 1991, we seriously considered declaring the Israeli Ambassador to the United States persona non grata, and Israel's Prime Minister accused the President of the United States of attacking "the deepest foundations of Jewish and Zionist consciousness"—an allegation totally without merit.

It's important, however, not to lose sight of the fact that, in spite of these tensions over fundamental policy disagreements, between 1989 and 1992 the United States made five significant contributions to Israel's well-being and security above and beyond what our predecessors had accomplished.

During this period, our diplomacy and our Treasury enabled Israel to absorb hundreds of thousands of Russian, Syrian, and Ethiopian Jews. We were instrumental in helping Israel establish diplomatic relations with forty-four countries, including the Soviet Union. We were decisive in bringing about the repeal of the abhorrent 1975 United Nations resolution equating Zionism with racism. American military might in Operation Desert Storm not only expelled Iraq from Kuwait, it also effectively disposed of the strategic threat from Israel's most dangerous Arab antagonist. And finally, history will record, I believe, that the most important single act of our country on Israel's behalf was when we brought her Arab neighbors to the peace table for direct negotiations, something Israel had sought for more than forty years, and an accomplishment that has now resulted in peace between Israel and Jordan and an historic Declaration of Principles between Israel and the PLO.

This rejuvenation of the Middle East peace process, which took root at the October 1991 Madrid conference and continues to this day, required the Bush administration to make some very tough and politically unpopular choices. Arguably, the hardest of these—particularly with respect to our bilateral relations—were our decisions in late 1991 and the spring of 1992, first to postpone, and later to put conditions on, Israel's request for $10 billion in loan guarantees to absorb Soviet Jewish emigrants. These decisions earned us credibility in many quarters and opprobrium in others, especially among more hard-line elements of the Israeli government and many of its staunchest allies in the United States. To some degree, they also contributed to the defeat of the Shamir government in June of 1992, and its replacement by a more moderate Labor government headed by Yitzhak Rabin. The contretemps over loan guarantees, while painful and momentarily disruptive to the historic links between Washington and Jerusalem, was nevertheless crucial to the quest for peace and thus to Israel's strategic interests. But it was also a difficult and divisive episode, made even more so by its intersection with the most explosive issue of all: Israel's ever-expanding settlements in the occupied territories.

Our Historic Commitment to Absorption

Like all of our predecessors, the Bush administration understood that the absorption of Jews from throughout the world was a bedrock of Israel's fulfillment as a state. Since 1948, millions of Diaspora Jews from four continents have emigrated to Israel (during my tenure alone, Israel took in 500,000 immigrants). In the last decade, the overwhelming majority of these immigrants came from the Soviet Union, nearly one million since 1987 alone. It should also be remembered that aggressive diplomacy by the Reagan and Bush administrations was vital in convincing the Soviets to grant exit visas for Jewish emigration, that as Vice President, George Bush was personally responsible for securing the emigration of Falasha Jews from Ethiopia, and that I was able to persuade Hafez al-Assad to allow some Syrian Jews to travel.

Historically, the United States has strongly supported the cause of Jewish emigration, and a considerable portion of our financial assistance to Israel each year has been used to fund absorption programs. Under both Democratic and Republican administrations, however, American policy has always made a clear distinction between the absorption of Jews into Israel itself, and the settling of them in the occupied territories. Early in the administration, we'd concluded that such settlements constituted a serious obstacle to peace in the Middle East, and as a matter of principle, we believed that we should not in good conscience allow U.S. tax dollars to fund activities contrary to American policy and peace. In all meetings with our Israeli counterparts at every level, we expressed our reservations about the Shamir government's settlements policy. Nevertheless, as Soviet Jewish emigration exploded overnight from 13,000 in 1989 to 185,000 the next year, Israeli settlement activity escalated, and many of these new settlements were in the West Bank and Gaza Strip. As it became clear that Shamir was unwilling or unable to meet the President's concerns about settlements, a crisis was inevitable. It arrived in the form of a 1989 Israeli request for $400 million in U.S. housing loan guarantees.

Such guarantees were one of several forms of U.S. foreign aid to Israel. Typically, Israel sought loans in world financial markets to raise funds for immigrant absorption, and a U.S. pledge to guarantee these loans in the event of default enabled Israel to secure more favorable interest rates. The full faith and credit of the United States was, in effect, the collateral. (It's not well known, but by federal law, the annual amount of U.S. economic assistance to Israel must be *more* than the annual amount due on Israel's outstanding loans guaranteed by the U.S. Treasury.)

On May 25, 1990, Congress approved $400 million in loan guarantees "for the purpose of providing housing and infrastructure in Israel for Soviet refugees" for the fiscal year beginning October 1. The legislation expressed a sense of the Congress that the guarantees should not be used for settlements outside of Israel's pre-1967 boundaries—the so-called Green Line. Over the next several months, we repeatedly made clear to Israel, both in public statements and private conversations, that the resettling of Soviet Jews in the occupied territories and the building of new settlements were jeopardizing the peace process. Since U.S. money could not be provided for such purposes, the Agency for International Development withheld approval for the guarantees pending receipt of assurances.

On March 1, I had told the House Appropriations Subcommittee on Foreign Operations that support for the $400 million in loan guarantees was contingent upon "satisfactory assurances" from Israel that none of the money would be used in the territories. At a minimum, the administration would insist on advance notice of plans for new settlements, and a strict accounting of how the $400 million would be disbursed.

I made the same point later that day in a phone call with Shamir, who accused the United States of conditioning our support of Israel for the first time ever.* "We're not conditioning the three billion dollars in aid we're already giving you," I responded. "But for us to support an additional amount, it's reasonable for us to ask for assurances." At that point, Shamir seemed to concede. "It's reasonable that you should want to know how your money would be used," he said. The fact of the matter is that we knew that some of the other three billion dollars we had been giving to Israel annually had been used to support her settlements policy, but we didn't want to see what in effect were additional U.S. taxpayer dollars used to facilitate the aggressive expansion of a policy that a succession of Presidents of both parties had consistently opposed.

Meanwhile, new settlements continued to spring up, including one in the Christian quarter of East Jerusalem. After a State Department spokesman called this "an insensitive and provocative action," the Israeli Foreign Ministry declared, "It is the right of Jews to live everywhere . . . and especially in Jerusalem."

On September 5, I met with Foreign Minister David Levy in Washington in hopes of defusing a looming crisis. Iraq's occupation of Kuwait had entered its second month, and Israel's goodwill and restraint in the event of a Gulf war would be essential. "I want to resolve this issue," I told him, "and I want to resolve it with you." He told me that Israel was prepared to agree to some prior notification of new settlement activity. I gave him a draft letter detailing the assurances *we* would need to approve U.S. loan guarantees. Three weeks later, in a follow-up meeting in New York, Levy and I worked out some particulars. I told him I wanted the assurances in writing and on October 2, Levy gave me a letter pledging that Israel would keep the United States informed of new settlement activity and would undertake "best efforts" to itemize budgetary expenditures for settlements in the territories. (Most important, he pledged that immigrants would not be settled beyond the Green Line.) Based on those assurances, the President agreed that the $400 million in loan guarantees could be released once an interagency review process was completed.

Unfortunately, these pledges were disregarded. Despite Levy's assurances, the information I'd been promised was never forthcoming. On Octo-

---

*Shamir's allegation was dead wrong. In fact, many U.S. aid programs to Israel carry substantial conditions—particularly those involving military assistance.

ber 18, Levy sent me a letter retracting his commitment not to resettle Soviet émigrés in East Jerusalem. I felt Levy's heart was in the right place, but I wasn't pleased with what appeared to be bad faith on the part of the government generally. Moreover, reports soon reached the American embassy in Tel Aviv that immigrants were being taken on tours of settlements in the territories to encourage them to settle there. When we reminded the Israelis of their promises to provide us information, we were repeatedly assured that the check was in the mail. It never arrived, and as a result, we refused to release the loan guarantees.

The $10 Billion Question

On January 22, 1991, six days after coalition forces launched the air campaign against Saddam Hussein's forces in Kuwait and Iraq, Israeli Finance Minister Yitzhak Modai announced that his government would shortly ask for $13 billion in additional aid from the United States—$10 billion in loan guarantees for settling Soviet Jews, and $3 billion in compensation for the damage inflicted on Israeli cities from Scud attacks. The first U.S. government official to learn of this was Larry Eagleburger, who was in Israel trying to persuade Shamir to refrain from retaliating against Iraq. Within minutes of learning about the request from Modai personally, Eagleburger heard the news on Israeli radio. He sent a message to Shamir, saying the timing of such a request was terrible and that it should be withdrawn immediately.

Shamir was embarrassed by this disclosure and upbraided his Finance Minister, but the psychological damage had been done. Certainly, some recompense was warranted. There was great appreciation within the administration, and the country as a whole, for Israel's admirable restraint—the first time in her history that she hadn't acted with swift vengeance against an attack. But now, with no consultation, she was publicly demanding a payoff in the form of the largest single foreign-aid package in American history. At the very least, it was an audacious gambit—particularly since no attempt had been made to justify the request with empirical data. It was as though Shamir's government had simply picked a comfortably large number out of the air. It's an understatement to say that the way it was handled wasn't well received. Publicly, we said the United States would "fully consider" the request. But we had no intention of doing so until a more appropriate moment. With America at war in an effort to defeat Iraq, the greatest threat to Israel's security, it was the wrong time to distract from that overriding effort with a congressional fight over the proper size of a supplemental package of aid to Israel.

In the end, however, while we weren't prepared to act then on the $10 billion request, a compromise agreement with Israeli Ambassador Zalman Shoval released the disputed $400 million in loan guarantees, and gave an additional $650 million in direct aid as compensation for Israel's wartime losses. This latter sum was quite generous, since an interagency review had estimated that the actual cost to compensate Israel for the damage caused by Iraqi Scuds was less than $200 million. In exchange, Israel agreed to defer its request for the $10 billion until Congress returned from its summer recess in September. By then, the war would be over, and the issue of additional loan guarantees would be delayed until the next fiscal year.

Muzzling a Loose Cannon

As if there weren't enough trouble already, this dispute was complicated by an ill-timed outburst from Ambassador Shoval. A wealthy banker without close ties to either Shamir or Levy, he owed his appointment to coalition politics. Shoval was a leading member of a part of Likud's coalition not represented in Shamir's cabinet, and had developed a reputation as a bit of a loose cannon. Not long before our first meeting, he had publicly described Israel as a "poor cousin" that the United States wanted to keep in a back room.

His penchant for "shoot-from-the-lip" diplomacy crossed the line on February 14, when Shoval was quoted by the *Washington Post* as telling Reuters news agency that "we sometimes feel we are being given the runaround" by the United States. He also complained that Israel had yet to receive "one cent of aid" to compensate for huge losses, including a loss of tourism, as a result of the Gulf War. It was quite a Valentine's Day present from a close ally.

In my view, Shoval had demonstrated remarkably bad faith in going public with his criticism—particularly since he'd been alerted only the day before that we would shortly release the $400 million in loan guarantees. I was sufficiently steamed that I asked my staff to research the legal requirements for declaring Shoval persona non grata and expelling him from the United States for what was really an intolerable breach of diplomatic etiquette. I talked to the President, who was also quite unhappy with what had happened.

Ultimately, I concluded that asking for Shoval's recall would only exacerbate relations at a particularly delicate moment. But at 5:00 P.M. that day, I summoned him to my office for a formal dressing-down. I was in no mood for diplomatic pleasantries. "We have a problem, Zalman," I began, "and it's not a small one—it's a large one.

"You said some things that simply aren't true. You said we haven't given you a cent. Well, what are the Patriots? What are the U.S. crews that we're paying for? What about the missiles that are being expended at a million dollars a pop? What about the U.S. lives that are at risk in the Gulf dealing with the foremost strategic threat to the State of Israel?"

Going to the press to try to drive American policy, I cautioned him, was an extremely counterproductive strategy. "I'm sorry to have to say this to you," I said, "but the fact is that you don't have that kind of license. If you have a problem, you come and tell the Secretary of State and you *don't* call in the press and issue threats and criticism. You don't have *anyone* in this administration who's going to go out and get you the money if I don't. I simply don't remember an incident in which an ambassador even from a *hostile* country was saying such things like this toward us." If the American ambassador had behaved in such fashion, I suggested, "You'd send him home."

"Oh, I don't think we'd do anything so rash, I don't think so," Shoval contended. "Instead, I think we'd sit down like you're doing." Shoval apologized and promised that "I'll always try to be honest and straight with you."

"But you didn't. Instead, you went public. You could have told us, but you chose not to. And I've got to tell you, we are outraged," I repeated. "I'm sorry to have to conclude the meeting on this note, but that's it." I made no effort to see him out.

I believe Shoval was genuinely chastened by my outburst. "So, all the best, there'll be better days, I hope," he said. "We'll see," I replied.

To make sure that Shoval clearly understood, the President sent an oral message to Shamir through our Ambassador, and I followed up with this letter:

Yesterday, your ambassador made a series of statements about Israeli-U.S. relations which I found not only inaccurate or misleading, but deeply offensive. I must tell you in all frankness that it will be difficult to continue to conduct our diplomatic business through him, given the obvious prejudice in his attitudes.

Were the times not so tense and critical as they are now, I would not accept that he continue as your representative in Washington. As it is, Mr. Prime Minister, I will suppress my feelings in recognition of the importance of the fact and the appearance of maintaining close and continuous contact between our two countries in this complex period. However, should there be a repetition of the ambassador's performance of yesterday, I would have no choice but to ask him to leave.

I regret having to burden our relationship with yet another problem, but behavior such as he exhibited simply cannot be tolerated. I trust you will so advise him.

In short order, Shamir sent me back a letter, saying that he would make sure nothing of the sort occurred in the future. And it didn't. Subsequently, I developed a good relationship with Shoval, who was instrumental in helping persuade his government to participate in the Madrid peace talks. When I left the State Department, he hosted a farewell dinner for me at his embassy and was quite complimentary of my accomplishments on Israel's behalf. We've made it a point to see each other several times since we both left government—in Israel as well as in Washington.

Six days after my session with Shoval, I telephoned Levy to say that the President was releasing the $400 million in loan guarantees. For the next six months, the issue of guarantees lay dormant, as the administration concentrated on winning the war, securing a more stable peace, dealing with the Iraqi refugee problem, and restarting the Middle East peace process.

But tensions over Israel's settlements policy escalated during this period, as Ariel Sharon, Shamir's belligerent Housing Minister, aggressively pushed settlements expansion. During my first visit to Israel in March, I warned Levy that the President's decision on the $10 billion guarantee request would be dictated by the course of settlement activity over the next few months.

On my second trip a month later, Shamir flatly rejected my suggestion that Israel curtail the expansion of settlements as a goodwill gesture for peace. Five days later, on April 16, settlers moved into a new settlement at Revava in the West Bank. After U.S. Ambassador Bill Brown filed an official protest, the Israeli Housing Ministry disclosed that plans were under way for 24,000 new units in the territories to house 88,000 settlers. To compensate for the absence of American loan guarantees, Israel pressed other nations, notably France and Germany, for loan guarantees and outright grants to help finance immigrant absorption through additional settlement activity.

In the midst of all this, the Israeli government announced that Sharon would be visiting Washington in early May. Before his arrival, an old friend, attorney Leonard Garment, called me and said Sharon had asked to meet with me. I told Garment that I couldn't think of *anyone* I'd less like to meet. "But he may be the next Prime Minister," Garment protested. I replied that Sharon's settlements policy had damaged the hopes for peace as well as our relations with Israel. I not only refused to see him, I intervened with the President to block a meeting between Sharon and Secretary of Housing and Urban Development Jack Kemp at Kemp's office. The meeting, which was ill advised under any circumstance, was held at the Israeli embassy to avoid any appearance that the United States government was lending credibility to Sharon and his unhelpful policies. Like his settlements policy, Ariel Sharon was an obstacle to peace.

Despite a growing tension in our relations, the United States continued to champion the cause of Jewish emigration. In May, Israel began an airlift of 16,000 Ethiopian Jews. Their emigration was the direct result of an appeal from President Bush to acting Ethiopian President Lt. Gen. Tesfaye Gebre-Kidan. And in each of my meetings with President Assad during the year, I pressed him repeatedly to allow Syrian Jews to travel.

Playing for Time—and Peace

If the truth be told, we all hoped the loan guarantee issue would somehow quietly disappear. Instead, it resurfaced at the worst possible moment. Ironically, as the prospects for Mideast peace brightened in the summer of 1991, the specter of a confrontation over settlements and loan guarantees hovered over the peace process like Banquo's Ghost, threatening to derail the considerable progress achieved since the end of the war. It was crucial that some way be found to keep the issue dormant until the end of the year.

The most potent political argument for delay had the added virtue of being literally true—the peace process would go right down the drain otherwise. During my visits to the Middle East in the spring and summer, every Arab leader had repeatedly expressed his unhappiness over the prospects of loan guarantees in the absence of some sort of restraint on settlements. The Palestinians were particularly outraged by this prospect. The objections I heard from President Mubarak and King Fahd were more practical than ideological, however. They argued that the guarantees had essentially become a litmus test for American evenhandedness with respect to the peace process.

"My friend, your credibility as an honest broker is the most important card you can play," King Fahd told me during our meeting in July. "I understand your country's commitment to Israel's survival. But this is mechanical, not survival, and you must be credible." I knew he was correct. Without a comprehensive settlements freeze, which was literally impossible, a loan-guarantee program of the magnitude Israel was seeking would inevitably be seen in the Arab world as American financial endorsement of Likud's territorial agenda, and they feared it would appear that they were acquiescing in it.

Conversely, a public dispute over settlements could well persuade Shamir that he should refuse to participate in the peace process and call new elections.

In short, addressing the guarantees controversy frontally was a no-win proposition. There was no way to avoid losing either the Israelis or the Arabs. In any case, the peace process would be dead.

By midsummer, congressional allies alerted us that Israel and AIPAC were preparing the ground for a massive offensive to win congressional approval for the $10 billion in loan guarantees, with or without administration support. Dennis Ross and Janet Mullins began meeting with Tom Dine and other senior AIPAC officials in an effort to persuade them that their timing was terrible, and that deferral was preferable to a fight that would be a lose-lose situation for all. These meetings failed to persuade AIPAC. Even when Dine and his colleagues were told the President would fight if necessary, they didn't believe it. They told Shamir, in fact, that the President didn't have the political will to take on AIPAC and, in any event, would quickly succumb to the legislative juggernaut.

By August, AIPAC was circulating draft legislation to its friends in Congress and had stepped up its lobbying of congressional leaders. Their strategy, we learned, was to convince Senate Majority Leader George Mitchell and House Speaker Tom Foley to endorse the guarantees, and so present the President with a fait accompli. We had no choice but to launch a preemptive strategy of our own.

On August 27, Mullins laid out the congressional strategy in a one-page memorandum. "The first step is to make sure the leadership understands that proceeding now on loan guarantees will doom the peace process," she wrote. "Further, we would emphasize that the responsibility for that would fall directly on the Congress." Under those circumstances, "I believe there is a chance we can persuade the leadership that proceeding now is simply too risky for them politically. However, we must do that convincing before they have . . . signaled their public support."

From my ranch in Wyoming, I telephoned Mitchell and Foley in late August with a simple message: give peace a chance. I told them that when I met with Shamir in two weeks, I wanted to be able to say that in the interests of advancing peace, Congress had joined with the President in deferring the issue. With a target date for the peace conference in late October, that would allow sufficient time to get the process irrevocably under way first, before surfacing the irritant of settlements and guarantees. Anything less, I made clear, would doom the peace process. If we went ahead with the guarantees, we would lose the Arabs. If we rejected guarantees, we'd lose Israel.

"This is the single most important step you could take at this point to get these historic peace negotiations launched," I told them both. They were noncommittal, but said they'd consider my request. I had the feeling that Foley would be helpful, but I was worried about Mitchell, who was being pressed hard by AIPAC.

At 12:45 P.M. Rocky Mountain time on September 1, I spoke with Shamir by telephone from my Wyoming cabin. I told him that when we agreed to take up loan guarantees again in September, I had no idea we'd be so close to direct negotiations with the Arabs. Now there was a genuine likelihood of a regional peace conference in October featuring direct negotiations with Israel's Arab neighbors, something Israel had always wanted.

"We need a little bit more time from you," I said. "If we come forward now, we threaten the possibility of direct talks. I want to avoid any debate in Congress that highlights the difference between us on settlements. That will only help those who don't want the peace process to go forward." I asked Shamir to defer a formal request for the $10 billion for 120 days, or until the first of the year.

Shamir replied that he was very tired from a long day of battles over his budget and didn't fully understand everything I was saying. He said he wanted to think about these matters more carefully, confer with his associates, and then talk again on a telephone line with a better connection. But I distinctly remember him telling me that, at first blush, he thought my deferral request was not unreasonable under the circumstances. We agreed to talk again in forty-eight hours, and did so on the afternoon of September 3, after I'd returned to Washington.

I reiterated to Shamir in this conversation that the President and I were "absolutely committed" to the successful absorption of Soviet Jews in Israel. But I expressed my "deep concern" that raising the issue of loan guarantees and settlements on the eve of a peace conference would "become a lightning rod for rejectionists."

"If the issue is forced now," I argued, "there won't be any way to avoid a public fight over settlements, and I'm afraid an historic opportunity for direct negotiations could be lost. It's as simple as that." At a very minimum, I asked him to defer a formal request for the guarantees until after our meeting in Jerusalem two weeks hence.

Shamir's tone was conspicuously different from our previous exchange. He said that upon reflection he could not agree to any delay. It was a matter both of fiscal urgency—"this will burden the budget," he said of a deferral—and principle. "We cannot accept a linkage of this issue to the peace process," he informed me. "We've waited long enough. We have to go."

I told him that I was disappointed in his decision, and would reluctantly recommend that the President seek a delay of 120 days despite Israel's position. We didn't seek a fight with Israel, I said, but the risk to the peace process was too great to ignore.

His abrupt change of tone from amenable to adamant was puzzling, until I later learned that he and his advisers had consulted with their friends in the United States and had been assured that Congress would approve the guarantees handily.

The day after this conversation with Shamir, I had lunch in my office with Senator Patrick J. Leahy of Vermont and his subcommittee chief of staff, Eric Newsom. I'd dealt with Leahy, who was a good friend of one of my Princeton roommates, in my previous incarnations at the White House and Treasury. In December of 1988, Leahy asked to see me in my transition office at the State Department. He told me that he'd be taking over the Appropriations Subcommittee on Foreign Operations. "It's a thankless job," he admitted. "But I just want you to know that I want to help you in every way I can to make progress in the peace process."

Although he'd been critical of their settlements policy from time to time, Leahy was considered a very reliable friend of Israel. In effect, he was telling me that if the President and I could demonstrate genuine progress toward peace, he was willing to stand up in Congress and support us, even if it might be an issue Israel opposed. It was a principled and frankly courageous position from a member of the opposition who could often be just as partisan as the next senator. I told him I appreciated his candor and suspected I'd need to take him up on his offer in due course. Now, nearly three years later, that time had come.

Leahy and Newsom were properly nervous because they understood the political realities of taking on AIPAC. I reiterated that the last thing the President wanted was a fight. "But if you don't defer," I said, "there'll be one. You'll leave us no choice. And have no illusions what the fight will be like." I left no doubt that the dead cat I'd been carrying in my baggage throughout the Middle East was now available for domestic use if the Congress insisted on moving forward at this very sensitive time, notwithstanding our warnings about the adverse effect on the peace process.

The three of us then drove to the White House. As President Reagan's Chief of Staff, I'd observed on many occasions how even the most virulent critics frequently melted beneath the magisterial aura of the Oval Office. President Bush was quite eloquent in stating the case for deferral on the merits, but he also said, in a polite but unmistakably firm tone, "We'll point out who bears responsibility."

There was no longer any room for half measures. AIPAC had let it be known that this was a defining issue for them. Any member who voted for deferral, they vowed, would be branded a foe of Israel. In a full-fledged fight, the risks to the administration would be substantial. As my friend the late Lee Atwater liked to observe, in such high-stakes circumstances, at the end of the day "you're either a champ or a chump." But Lee never shied away from a challenge, and this one could not and should not be avoided. Mideast peace was riding on the outcome.

On September 12, before making a public appeal for delay, the President had met as a courtesy with Jewish leaders at the White House. One of his guests had pointedly warned him that he should think twice about pushing this issue, since Israel's friends would embarrass him if he insisted on a vote. George Bush is not prone to folding his tent without a fight in such situations. This challenge was the antecedent of the President's subsequent remarks that he was "one lonely guy" fighting "powerful political forces" amounting to "something like a thousand lobbyists."

These remarks were misinterpreted by critics as having suggested that friends of Israel shouldn't have the right to lobby Congress for redress of grievances, and that the President was raising the specter of dual loyalty. That wasn't his intent, and everyone who knows him well knew it, but by saying this he'd inadvertently given AIPAC an opening to charge that he was hostile to Israel. However, it was a wholly spurious allegation that didn't carry the day. Indeed, by the end of the debate, even many of Israel's supporters in Congress were privately conceding that AIPAC was guilty of an arrogance which seemed to say that if asking for loan guarantees now rather than waiting four months scuttled chances for peace, so be it. This tactical error, coupled with the fact that the President was still riding high after the Gulf war, helped our cause considerably. But most important, most members of Congress recognized that a simple request for delay was eminently reasonable under the circumstances.

As battle lines hardened on Capitol Hill, I returned to the Middle East. My first stop was Jerusalem, where I met with Shamir on September 16 and 17, after my trip to the Soviet Union. The primary focus of our two sessions was working out the modalities of a peace conference. While some progress was made in this regard, I made no headway whatever on the guarantees issue.

I outlined for Shamir the President's six-point proposal for deferring the matter until January, pledging there would be no subsequent delays, and that any financial loss to Israel as a result of the delay would be compensated. "My suggestion to you is to call off the dogs and strike the subject off the agenda for the next 120 days," I said. I rejected a proposal by Arens that we agree to $2 billion in guarantees and defer discussion of the balance until January. I pulled from my briefcase a *New York Times* editorial headlined "The President Is Right on Israel," which was greeted with silence.

"We're on an historic threshold," I told Shamir. "Peace is too important to jeopardize with a fight over this." His aide, Ely Rubenstein, responded that Israel was fully prepared for a fight. "We have this historical duty," he said, "and our friends in America and in Congress tell us it's winnable." It was—but by us, not them. By then, I knew we had the votes in the Senate to win this argument. Leahy was now publicly supporting a postponement, and an intensive lobbying campaign led by Mullins had revealed that most members weren't willing to risk the collapse of the peace process by opposing a modest postponement. It was apparent to me that the government of Israel had received some conspicuously bad information from its friends in Washington and was underestimating President Bush's determination as a result.

At first, Shamir said Israel had no choice but to go forward and that Israel opposed our linking the settlements to the guarantees. "If you want U.S. guarantees," I responded, "you will have to accept our position on settlements. We can't just sign off unconditionally on ten billion dollars." Finally, Shamir seemed to signal that, despite the reservations of Arens and several other advisers, his government could reluctantly accept a delay. "This is an American decision," he told me. "We'd like it to be otherwise, but we'll live with this decision."

On October 2, 1991, the Senate agreed to postpone consideration of the loan guarantees for 120 days. Some said it was only the second time that AIPAC had ever been defeated on a legislative initiative—the first being the 1981 Senate vote on AWACS radar planes for Saudi Arabia at the start of the Reagan administration. A month later, Israel opened another settlement—this one on the Golan Heights.

Once More into the Breach

As the 120-day interregnum came to an end in early 1992, the administration reappraised the guarantees/settlements landscape. We concluded in fairly short order that the President's position had been strengthened in the intervening four months. Likud's aggressive settlements expansion policy had continued, but at a price. One poll showed that 76 percent of the Israeli people seemed willing to accept the policy of settlements conditionality laid down by the administration as reasonable. Sentiment within the American Jewish community had also begun to shift against Likud's hard line.

Nevertheless, Shamir's budget for 1992 projected 5,500 new housing units in the occupied territories. Moreover, his budget estimates assumed he'd be receiving $2 billion in U.S. loan guarantees to help pay for these settlements, the first installment of the $10 billion in dispute. Clearly, he seemed to believe he could have it both ways. It was important that he understand he couldn't.

"The key to our strategy," Dennis Ross wrote succinctly in a memorandum dated January 10, 1992, "must be to focus on the need for the Shamir government to make a basic choice between meeting the historic challenge of absorbing Soviet Jews, or continuing unchanged settlement building in the occupied territories."

I concurred in this judgment, but preferred trying to find a middle ground. A credible alternative had been advanced by Pat Leahy at a Christmas Eve meeting in my office the previous month. Leahy proposed that

loan guarantees be conditioned on a ban on any new settlements and reduced by the amount spent by Israel to finish construction of settlements
already under way. I thought this was a creative way to split the difference
with Israel and to deal with the problem of the fungibility of money. By
reducing the amount of loan guarantees dollar for dollar, Israel would be
unable to divert funds from elsewhere and then claim our loan guarantees
weren't being used for new settlements or the expansion of existing ones.

On January 26, Shamir flatly rejected a proposal along these lines that
I'd given to Ambassador Shoval two days previously. Shoval and I continued to discuss possible compromises. On February 21, he said Israel was
prepared to accept $2 billion in loan guarantees for one year, but would not
under any circumstances agree to a freeze on new settlements. I rejected
this counterproposal.

On February 24—the same day that a new round of peace talks
resumed in Washington between Israel and her Arab neighbors—I unveiled
the President's position in testimony before a House subcommittee chaired
by David Obey of Wisconsin. Obey was Leahy's counterpart on the House
side and a firm opponent of settlements. He'd privately assured me that he
would support us on this issue. I told the committee that the President
would grant the full $10 billion in guarantees over five years only if Israel
froze all settlement activity in the territories. If that were unacceptable, I
explained, we would approve a much lesser amount on a year-to-year
basis. The cost of finishing settlements already under construction would be
deducted from the amount of any U.S. guarantees—the so-called Leahy
deduction. In either event, Israel would have to halt all *new* settlements in
the territories.

Israel's friends continued to press for more favorable terms. On March
17, the President met with Leahy and Senator Robert Kasten of Wisconsin,
Leahy's ranking Republican and a staunch champion of Israel's interests.
They submitted a compromise which would have given Israel $2 billion in
immediate guarantees, to be reduced by $200 million, which Israel ex-
pected to spend on settlements in 1992. The fine print, however, was rid-
dled with exclusions, exemptions, and loopholes. The net effect was that
Israel would be free to use $1 billion in new loan guarantees to keep build-
ing settlements at an expanded rate for at least another year. I was sure
such an eventuality would drive the Arabs from the peace table. In addition, it flew directly in the face of our opposition to settlements activity.
President Bush rejected this compromise as unacceptable, and vowed to
veto any loan guarantees legislation which did not include a freeze on all
new settlements.

The President's ultimatum effectively settled the issue. Congressional opposition collapsed under the veto threat, and the foreign-aid bill that passed in April did not contain any loan guarantees for Israel.

The merits of the President's position were the most important consideration in the way this matter turned out. But seldom is life or politics so idyllic that results flow solely from the merits. Aside from the Shamir government's intransigence, which helped turn American public opinion against Israel's position on this particular issue, our cause was helped considerably by the generic unpopularity of foreign aid—particularly in an election year.

Without any doubt, however, AIPAC's previous failure to block our request for a 120-day delay was a powerful psychological weapon in our behalf. Having lost in September, AIPAC was now simply no longer perceived as politically invincible on Capitol Hill. As a result, the merits of the President's position were easier to sustain.

Visiting "A New Israel"

On June 23, 1992, Israeli voters delivered a stunning rebuff to Likud, sweeping Shamir's party from power by a sizable margin. The new Labor government would be headed by Yitzhak Rabin, a voice of moderation whose views on the issues of settlements and peace were markedly different from Shamir's.

In hindsight, it's obvious that the controversy over loan guarantees clearly contributed to Likud's defeat. At the time, however, we didn't really appreciate the significance it would have in the Israeli election. In fact, I believed that Likud would win, emboldening Shamir in his hard-line policies. Instead, Likud's failure to secure the loan guarantees from Israel's closest ally undercut it. The chill in relations with the United States as a result of an intransigent settlements policy cost Likud dearly, because proper management of the U.S. relationship is a must for any Israeli government to succeed. In retrospect, I believe the Shamir government could have been sufficiently flexible to obtain the loan guarantees without compromising its principles.

A few critics have insinuated that the Bush administration's hard line on loan guarantees was deliberately pursued as a means of greasing the skids for Likud. This is simply not true. What *is* true is that most of my Middle East specialists believed that the peace process would always be in some peril so long as the Shamir government remained in power. I can remember being told by an aide on the plane returning from Madrid that while Shamir's participation had been essential to arranging a peace conference, dramatic progress would be impossible until the Shamir government was replaced by one committed to exchanging territory for peace. I concurred in this assessment. But it was not a conscious policy on our part to exploit the issue of guarantees/settlements in order to influence Israeli elections. Shamir himself had told me on many occasions that the United States must act as an honest broker in the peace process. We could not have done so without conditioning loan guarantees to restrictions on settlements activity. Failing to do so would have meant the end of the peace process.*

When we were accused of trying to dictate to Israel on a domestic policy matter (settlements), our position simply was that we weren't saying Israelis weren't free to live anywhere they chose, or that the government wasn't free to build settlements in the territories—but simply that we weren't going to furnish U.S. tax dollars to pursue a course that ran counter to American policy under all previous administrations, Republican and Democratic.

With Rabin's victory, the ingredients were in place to reach a compromise on settlements and guarantees. On July 13, I telephoned Rabin, and suggested that during my upcoming trip to the region we should lay the groundwork for an agreement that would sever the Gordian knot over this issue once and for all. He told me that I'd be pleased to learn that his government planned to make significant reductions in settlements activity.

Six days later, I met with the new Prime Minister in Jerusalem. This time, my arrival in Israel wasn't greeted by the opening of a new settlement. To the contrary, Rabin had already frozen contracts to build 7,000 new units in the territories. He told me that, notwithstanding legal problems, he intended to cancel those contracts. He was also moving to eliminate various incentives and subsidies that Shamir's government had used to entice Israelis to move into the territories. The settlers' movement was up in arms, Rabin said, but he would not be deterred. "For the sake of 3.9 million Israeli Jews and a million Israeli Arabs who should not have to mortgage their future because of the 100,000 settlers in the territories," he said, "I intend to persevere." In a moment of great poignancy, Rabin also assured me, "We will do what we say and we will not lie to you." The atmospheric change was positively seismic.

Rabin had determined, however, that the political and financial costs of canceling 11,000 units already under construction were prohibitive, and hoped that U.S. loan guarantees could be arranged. I told him that while

---

*Interestingly, three days after the election, Shamir was quoted in the Israeli newspaper *Maariv* as saying that he'd privately intended to drag out peace talks for ten years, during which time he would have continued an aggressive policy of settling the occupied territories. Shamir denied the report through a spokesman, but it nonetheless tended to confirm my strong suspicion that he was extremely reluctant to go to Madrid or negotiate seriously on the basis of territory for peace.

several questions remained to be resolved, I believed there was every reason to expect an agreement could be reached when Rabin visited the United States.

"I have just visited a different Israel," I wrote the President on July 21. "The mood is different and the atmosphere is one of hope. Rabin was open, direct, and very clear about his objectives. He is reordering Israel's priorities away from the territories and to revitalizing Israel's economy."

On August 10, President Bush hosted Rabin for talks at his summer home in Kennebunkport. As it turned out, the negotiations were more difficult than I'd anticipated, lasting until 4:00 A.M. before an agreement was reached. The main issue in contention involved so-called strategic settlements the Israelis had established on the Golan Heights and in the Jordan Valley. Rabin made a clear distinction between these settlements and "political" settlements, and would not agree explicitly to refrain from "thickening" strategic settlements if necessary. But he assured us that the settlement population in strategic areas was declining and that his government expected to maintain those trends. "We do not plan any new settlements in these areas," he told the President, "but I can't give you a blanket commitment."

But more significantly, Rabin *did* commit to a fundamentally different policy on settlements. "We're reordering our priorities," he noted emphatically. The government of Israel would not create or sanction any new settlements and would prevent settlements by private individuals. Arab lands in the territories would no longer be expropriated for settlements. Moreover, Israel agreed to our insistence that any money spent to complete construction already under way in the territories would be deducted against any loan guarantees.

Based on these and other assurances from Israel's Prime Minister, the President announced that he would ask Congress to approve the $10 billion in loan guarantees promptly. On October 5, Congress approved the guarantees. After months of unremitting friction over this issue, the relationship between the United States and Israel was no longer subject to this tension.

CHAPTER 30

INTO THE DUSTBIN— WITH A WHIMPER, NOT A BANG

The Soviet Union as we know it no longer exists. What matters now is how the breakup of the Soviet Union proceeds from this point onward. Our aim should be to make the crash as peaceful as possible.

—*State Department policy memorandum, October 25, 1991*

For over forty years, the United States led the West in the struggle against communism and the threat it posed to our most precious values. This struggle shaped the lives of all Americans. It forced all nations to live under the specter of nuclear destruction. That confrontation is now over.

—*President Bush, December 25, 1991*

Wa hile I was spending most of September and October 1991 putting the Madrid Middle East Peace Conference together, we were warily watching as the Soviet Union was tearing itself apart. The revolutionary fervor of late August and early September had somewhat faded, but Gorbachev's efforts to renegotiate the ill-fated Union Treaty had foundered nonetheless. The republics continued to assert their independence, a trend that was catapulted forward in mid-October, when Ukraine announced that it would not join the new economic treaty. Two weeks later, on Monday, October 28, saying that the time had come for decisive action, Boris Yeltsin proposed economic shock therapy for the Russian Republic, which included the lifting of price controls by year's end, the acceleration of privatization, and the ceasing of financial support for Soviet ministries. In his speech, Yeltsin asked the other republics to join his program, but he stated bluntly that Russia would not tolerate any further delay, and would go it alone if necessary.

The next day, I joined President Bush in Madrid, on the eve of the Peace Conference, for what would turn out to be his last meeting with Mikhail Gorbachev as Soviet leader. Gorbachev was as unfocused as I had ever seen him. It wasn't his mind; that was as sharp as ever. Rather, it was the overwhelming complexity of the multiple challenges beating down on him. Gorbachev would begin discussing the Middle East, but then would quite naturally become distracted by his own internal problems and veer off to talk about them. He railed against the republic leaders for the "disastrous course" they were following, and told the President that further dissolution of the USSR would destabilize the globe. He seemed like a drowning man, looking for a life preserver. It was hard not to feel sorry for him.

Early in the morning of the last day of the conference, long after the two presidents had left, Soviet Foreign Minister Pankin and I had a twenty-minute session. He, too, was more interested in Center-Republic relations than in the Arab-Israeli dispute. "If I may," he said, "I'd like to suggest a response your President might give to Yeltsin's speech." I decided to hear him out, though I knew George Bush was not going to give Boris Yeltsin advice on Russian politics. First, Pankin said, the President should tell Yeltsin that his economic program was solid—but it really needed to be implemented now. Second, Pankin felt the President should tell Yeltsin, "When you attack central government structures, you may be damaging your own interests. These central government structures have been reformed and changed. They are needed to get and to administer assistance from the rest of the world. The point is that the foreign policy of the USSR is positive; many good things have been accomplished. Destruction of the Ministry of Foreign Affairs will tarnish your image as a political leader who thinks and works in a global way." I told him I'd pass his comments along, but I saw his statement as another indicator of how far the Center had crumbled; here was the Soviet Foreign Minister imploring me to ask President Bush to make the case to the Russian Republic President to keep his ministry intact.

As things turned out, Pankin could have used some help to keep his own job intact. On November 13, while I was in Seoul for an APEC meeting, Dennis Ross sent me a message that Frank Elbe, Genscher's aide, had just talked to Sergei Tarasenko, who said that Shevardnadze would be reappointed as Foreign Minister. "But his appointment," Dennis warned, "probably reflects a desire on Gorbachev's part (with Shevardnadze's agreement) to get us to play a more active role in preserving the Union." We ought to be wary of that, I thought, because our objective should be to advance our interests (for example, preventing the proliferation of weapons of mass destruction), not to support the Center or a union per se.

Recognizing Ukraine

The competitive politics of nationalism that had concerned me in September were intensifying, and it was becoming obvious that the first of December was shaping up as an important date for our Soviet policy. On that date, Ukrainians would go to the polls to vote on a referendum confirming independence. Throughout the last two weeks of November, we held several discussions about whether we should then recognize that independence.* The Defense Department was the most forward leaning, starting at the top with Dick Cheney. Dick wanted to see the Soviet Union dismantled, felt Ukraine was key, and, moreover, believed that by getting in "on the ground floor" with recognition, the Ukrainian leadership would be more inclined to a positive relationship with us. I took a slightly different tack. I wanted to be sure the Soviet Union was dismantled *peacefully,* and that meant, above all, preventing a Russian-Ukrainian clash. In the triangular political game among the Center, Russia, and Kiev, I didn't want to see us move precipitously and provoke or exacerbate a dispute that could be avoided. Moreover, while I believed that the "five principles" I had announced on September 4 had helped to channel republic political aspirations in a positive direction, recognition was a more powerful card. It was political leverage, and I wanted to play this card only when we had received specific assurances from each republic on issues such as nuclear command and control.

Unfortunately, before we could even discuss our views with the President, Jeff Smith of the *Washington Post* laid out the debate in an article on Monday, November 25, headlined, "U.S. Officials Split Over Response to an Independent Ukraine." I was furious and felt sandbagged, not by Cheney, but by the DOD bureaucracy that clearly had been the initial source of the story. It was the only time I can remember during the Bush administration when a real policy dispute in which I was involved was aired in the press before we could resolve it among the principals.

At 8:37 A.M. Tuesday morning, Shevardnadze—fully back in charge of Soviet foreign policy—called to discuss the Middle East. I took the occasion, however, to ask him about Ukraine. He felt the vote would be for independence, but that it would not necessarily lead to secession from the Union. "If Ukraine does secede," he predicted, "this will give rise to highly unpredictable consequences: the problem of relations between Russia and Ukraine, the status of Crimea, and the Donbass region [a coal-mining and metal-producing region that is a state on its own merits, populated mostly

---

*It was a foregone conclusion that the vote would be overwhelmingly in favor of it.

by Russians]. The eastern Ukraine would also be an issue." His hope was that the leadership would make "significant adjustments" regarding relations with the Center and the Union as a whole.

"What will your position be regarding recognition if republics declare independence but remain part of a confederated state or loose association of sovereign states?" I asked.

He felt that wouldn't be a problem. The latest draft of the Union Treaty would allow for it, he implied, although "the Center will have solid state structures with impressive levers of power, but its members will have the right to establish relations with others." That approach seemed illogical to me, but I didn't want to press him any further.

Two hours later, I went over to the White House for an NSC meeting on Ukraine. In the options paper, written by Ed Hewett, who had replaced Condi Rice as the President's Special Assistant for Soviet Affairs, most of the State-DOD differences had been resolved. After a short discussion, the President chose the State option of "delayed recognition," though we all agreed that meant weeks, not months. The President also decided to send a special emissary to Kiev after December 1, to issue a strong statement of support for the wishes of the Ukrainian people, and to have Bob Zoellick go to Brussels to work for a consensus within NATO and with the EC. In addition, we agreed that I would go to Ukraine and other parts of the Soviet Union later in December. In less than an hour, we had put to rest a potentially explosive issue—or so I thought.

By Thursday morning, we had a firestorm on our hands. The President, meeting privately with a small group of Ukrainian-Americans, had outlined our position, and they had promptly leaked everything he had told them— putting a very forward-leaning spin on it in the process. The nuances of our position were lost in the press coverage. Keeping the allies on board with our approach was going to be much more difficult, and in Moscow, Gorbachev was reportedly furious.

Nonetheless, Gorbachev kept his anger in check when the President called him on Saturday to brief him on our position. Gorbachev told Bush the vote wouldn't necessarily be a break from the Union—which was wishful thinking at best. The President also called Yeltsin, and I sent a message to Shevardnadze via Ambassador Strauss. Bob Strauss's return message was extremely pessimistic. Shevardnadze was devastated by press reports of our position, he said—and Strauss emphasized that he had not seen Shevardnadze this upset even during the coup.

On December 1, as expected, over ninety percent of the Ukrainian people voted for independence, and Leonid Kravchuk was elected president. The next day, Marlin Fitzwater stated, "The United States looks forward to the kind of normal relationship with Ukraine that one would expect it to have with a democratizing country." In the eyes of the international community, the Soviet Union had at least one foot in its grave.

Back to Princeton

That week, I discussed with Margaret Tutwiler, Bob Zoellick, and Dennis Ross the policy line I thought we should follow in the aftermath of the Ukrainian referendum. I also made tentative plans to articulate that policy approach in a speech on December 12 at Princeton. Returning to my alma mater in this way would be a nice homecoming for me, but it would also allow us to reinforce our main theme: the collapse of the Soviet Union. George Kennan, the principal author of the doctrine of containment, was at the Institute for Advanced Study in Princeton, and I knew he would come to the speech if he could.

The approach I had in mind was not only a decisive departure from containment (which we had already been moving away from for two years), but also from our theretofore correct emphasis on Gorbachev. I felt Gorbachev was a true historic figure, perhaps responsible for transforming the world as we'd known it. He'd ended the Cold War and ended the Soviet empire peacefully, and for that we should be grateful and respectful, but now it was obvious that a new era was beginning.

On Sunday, December 8, when Bob Schieffer asked me on CBS's "Face the Nation" whether I thought Gorbachev could hold the Soviet Union together, I stated what I thought was the obvious: "I think the Soviet Union, as we've known it, no longer exists. I think that there will continue to be efforts to maintain some sort of a center. Who's to say what the powers of that will be?" I went on to make the case that while there were great opportunities, there were also great dangers, and if things did not unfold peacefully, we could run the risk of seeing a "Yugoslavia with nukes."

Meanwhile, on the other side of the globe, Boris Yeltsin was in the process of ensuring that the Soviet Union would no longer exist. Meeting with Leonid Kravchuk and the Belarussian President, Stanislav Shushkevich, at a hunting lodge near Brest, close to the Polish border, in Belarus, the Russian President agreed with his colleagues to announce the formal dissolution of the Soviet Union. In its place, they had agreed to establish a Commonwealth of Independent States (CIS), whose capital would be Minsk. The Brest Declaration spoke of a "unified command of common military-strategic space" along with coordination of foreign policy and a customs and economic union. Given their weight—in terms of population, industrial output, and the armed forces—the Commonwealth could not be seen as anything less than a complete repudiation of Gorbachev's efforts to renegotiate a Union Treaty. It was a fait accompli that Gorbachev would have severe difficulty overcoming.

Yeltsin added insult to injury by calling President Bush Sunday afternoon to debrief him on the Brest accord—before he called Gorbachev. This Commonwealth agreement was, in part, deliberately designed to win our support; the communiqué included the five principles I had enunciated, besides taking all the right positions on nuclear weapons. But Yeltsin's call was intended as much for a domestic audience. The mere fact that he called President Bush created the impression that the United States approved of the Commonwealth.

By Monday, Gorbachev was fighting back. Calling the Commonwealth "illegitimate and dangerous," he said, "it can only intensify chaos and anarchy." On Tuesday, he went to the Soviet Defense Ministry in a conspicuous effort to woo the military.* Yeltsin held his own two-hour meeting with the Soviet high command on Wednesday. These moves were the stuff of a geopolitical nightmare: Two Kremlin heavyweights jockeying for political power, calling on the army to follow them, and raising the specter of civil war—with nuclear weapons thrown into the mix.

In this crisis atmosphere, my speech on Thursday, December 12, took on added importance. (Indeed, the day of the speech I woke at 4:30 A.M., concerned about a line in the speech, and called Margaret Tutwiler to make sure the speech hadn't been released to the press. It hadn't.)

I began by paying homage to Kennan (who was sitting in the first row). Containment had worked, I argued. "The state that Lenin founded and Stalin built held within itself the seeds of its demise." Now, "as a consequence of Soviet collapse," I continued, "we live in a new world. We must take advantage of this new Russian Revolution, set in motion with the defeat of the August coup, to cultivate relationships—relationships that can benefit not only America but the entire world."† While I praised Gorbachev for making these transformations possible, I made it clear that we believed

---

*In Washington that day, Bob Gates, wearing his new hat as Director of Central Intelligence, in testimony before a subcommittee of the House Armed Services Committee, correctly warned: "Severe economic conditions, including substantial shortages of food and fuel in some areas, the disintegration of the armed forces and ongoing ethnic conflict will combine this winter to produce the most significant disorder in the former USSR since the Bolsheviks consolidated power."

†Originally, I had planned to refer to U.S. relations with "Russia, Ukraine, and the other republics," but the creation of the Commonwealth and the ongoing negotiations over it required me to back off slightly from this sole focus on the republics. I used the painful phrase, "Russia, Ukraine, the other republics, and any common entities" (referring, for example, to the Commonwealth) to cope with any interrepublic institutions that might be created after the republics had finished their negotiations.

his time had passed, stating, "His place in history is secure, for he helped end the Cold War peacefully. And, for that, the world is grateful and respectful."

I laid out a conceptual framework for managing the rapid change associated with the Soviet collapse. I also argued that "as we organized an alliance against Stalinism during the Cold War, today America must mobilize a coalition in support of freedom." To catalyze this new coalition, I proposed a "Coordinating Conference" to accelerate our efforts to provide humanitarian aid to the Soviet peoples. The Conference was intended not only as a device to get international efforts moving, but also as a way to overcome bureaucratic inertia in the U.S. government. The speech went on to outline a series of initiatives designed to manage risks associated with nuclear weapons, support democracy and independence in the republics, and assist with the ongoing humanitarian disaster and promote free markets. These initiatives—twenty-one, all told—included such concrete steps as sending technical experts to help the republics establish export controls on dangerous military technology, expanding our exchanges to teach local and republic leaders democratic forms of administration, expanding Peace Corps missions into the republics, and naming Larry Eagleburger "czar" of our assistance program (which required overcoming much bureaucratic resistance).

The speech concluded with a telling metaphorical shift. "If during the Cold War we faced each other as two scorpions in a bottle, now the Western nations and the former Soviet republics stand as awkward climbers on a steep mountain. Held together by a common rope, a fall toward fascism or total chaos in the former Soviet Union will pull the West down, too. Yet equally as important, a strong and steady pull by us now can help the Russians, Ukrainians, and their neighbors to gain their footing, so that they, too, can climb above to enduring democracy and freedom. Surely we must strengthen the rope, not sever it."

As I headed for Moscow just over forty-eight hours later, I wondered whether it would be possible to find any solid footing in a country dissolving into chaos.

Back in the USSR—For the Last Time?

When I arrived in Moscow on Sunday afternoon, December 15, I was fortunate to be met by a motorcade that could actually go somewhere. More than ninety airports in the Soviet Union had closed because of a jet fuel shortage, most of Aeroflot was grounded, and our embassy was having problems finding gasoline for its cars—all this in a country with the largest proven oil reserves in the world! Kozyrev had assured me on the phone that the fuel crisis "was not that bad," but as usual, Lynn Dent and the Air Force crew that ferried us to the farthest points on the globe had done a brilliant job in overcoming any and all logistical problems.

While we were getting a few hours' rest at the Penta Hotel, Strobe Talbott from *Time* magazine came by and gave Dennis the transcript of an interview he had conducted with Gorbachev, and a message from "someone" on Gorbachev's staff who had been assured of anonymity. In the interview, Gorbachev criticized me for being "overly hasty in saying, 'The Soviet Union no longer exists.' Things are in flux here. While we're trying to figure things out, the U.S. seems to know everything already! I don't think that's loyalty."* Gorbachev was apparently considering resigning, but for now was keeping his options open and might consider a role in the CIS, provided he was not humiliated. But, the staffer's note continued, there was at least a fifty percent chance that Gorbachev would be a "private figure" within a few weeks, and some were trying to engineer criminal proceedings against the Soviet President. Yeltsin ought not be involved in such proceedings, the note cautioned. The message combined a willingness to serve in the Commonwealth under appropriate conditions with a legitimate fear of a politicized show trial. The message was a concrete indicator of the anxiety and instability sweeping Moscow—a feeling reinforced a few minutes later when Bob Pearson, my executive secretary, told me that Gavril Popov had resigned as mayor of Moscow.

A short while later, I sat down for a meeting with Andrei Kozyrev in the old Communist headquarters building in Moscow's Staraya Square. Kozyrev noted that this was probably the last time we would meet there, indicating that he planned to take over the Soviet Foreign Ministry buildings soon. After calling my Princeton speech "splendid," Kozyrev got right to the point. "This is a time of hope and challenge. A major new effort by the United States is needed as part of its effort to support democracy in the world."

I explained that my speech had been intended both to give hope to reformers in the Soviet Union and to build a consensus in America behind our engagement. "We see both significant opportunities and dangers in developments here," I said. "But we do not intend to inject ourselves into these internal processes"—a point President Bush had underscored with me in our conversations that week. I went on to outline the objectives of my trip, which included understanding Soviet political developments, particularly the Brest Declaration, clarifying nuclear command and control issues, and initiating a broader humanitarian effort.

"As the former state disintegrated, it became more and more danger-

*The "as we've known it" qualifier had been omitted by Talbott.

ous," Kozyrev said, brushing aside the Soviet Union even before it was completely gone. "Remnants of the Center were causing chaos in the country and were impeding the reasonable desire of the republics for self-determination. With the Commonwealth, we tried to put this process into a political and legal framework. While everything is far from settled, our view is to try to strengthen this process."

Kozyrev explained that he feared possible disintegration if the Center attempted to reassert itself in some new form. "If the old Center tries to create a new Center, and if we lose this momentum toward the Commonwealth," he warned, "we will lose the Russian Republic, the Ukraine, and there will be further uncontrolled fragmentation. There is a fear, an allergy to any Center, especially as long as vestiges of the old Center remain. The other republics will be less prepared to cooperate, even with Russia, until all the elements of the old Center are gone." He then argued that in order to have a "meaningful" Commonwealth, the United States should recognize Russia, Ukraine, and Belarus.

In response, I explained that serious issues needed to be sorted out before the United States would grant recognition. "There are several different interpretations of the Commonwealth, and these need to be resolved," I explained. "Will you have a common foreign policy? Are you asking for recognition of the Commonwealth as a single entity? Do you speak for other Commonwealth republics? Will there be a common defense policy? What states make up the Commonwealth?"

Kozyrev answered that the Commonwealth was "like an umbrella. Each state is an independent state, and the Commonwealth is like a friendly agreement among these states. Some claim that this agreement is only a declaration of intent. It is more, and it reflects the basic situation. Of course, it would be an exaggeration to say that everything is settled." The only "center" of any kind would be in the military sphere.

His explanation did little to clear up our confusion. "You say there will be a central military command," I asked, "but who will control the individual forces in the territories?" Kozyrev pointed out that some forces would be under the control of republic authorities and others would be under the control of Marshal Shaposhnikov.

"But who will he take orders from?" I asked. "How will you conduct foreign policy?"

Other members of my delegation joined in. Ambassador Strauss asked whether Russia intended to recognize the other members of the Commonwealth, and exchange ambassadors. Dennis Ross asked about the Middle East peace process. Reggie Bartholomew asked what would happen with conventional arms transfers. Ed Hewett asked about shipping fees on grain shipments, and Tom Niles, the new Assistant Secretary of State for European Affairs, asked about what was happening to hard-currency revenues from oil and gas.

Kozyrev had few, if any, answers.

"Do we have to have ten sets of discussions?" I asked.

More than anything else, our discussion confirmed what I had expected: in the middle of this revolution, there were going to be far more questions than answers. Kozyrev had little concrete to offer me, which may have been one reason he focused on recognition. But there were two other considerations driving him. On the one hand, he felt recognition would give a boost to the Commonwealth, because Ukraine in particular would adhere to a coordinating mechanism only if its psychological need for an independent international standing and legitimacy was fully recognized. Once this psychological need was satisfied, he assumed, the Ukrainians would have the confidence and the political basis to go along with coordinating arrangements on nuclear, military, economic, and border issues. If the Ukrainian need for identity was not recognized, Kozyrev was convinced, Kiev would pull away and oppose any of the elements that would make the Commonwealth meaningful.

On the other hand, he seemed to feel that immediate recognition of Russia was necessary in order to overcome the confusion of authority between Russia and the Center that made it difficult for anyone to be held accountable. Kozyrev's argument for immediate recognition of Russia was driven largely by his concern that there were no decision-making rules. The Yeltsin government needed to assume the responsibilities of a real state. In the meantime, the existence of two presidents in Moscow—one for the Soviet Union and one for Russia—had created confusion, ambiguity, and competition over authority and power.

But Kozyrev's inability to provide specifics, particularly on questions about who could help us work out the logistics, distribution, and monitoring of food assistance, revealed that the Russians had yet to address basic questions of governing. "Recognition alone isn't going to solve this problem," I cabled the President that night. "If the Russians want us to help them, they're going to have to make it possible for us to do so."

I bounced some of these thoughts and concerns off my by-now old friend and colleague Eduard Shevardnadze over dinner that evening. Once again, we were hosted by his friend Zurab Tseretelli, the Georgian artist. As I entered Tseretelli's apartment from the street, I was struck by the presence of a single Soviet cameraman. In the past, a meeting with Shevardnadze would have been the first on the trip and would have generated enough press to overflow into the street and clog traffic. We both shared the sense that the end was nearing for the Soviet Union. Shevardnadze's role would end, too, and it was almost as if Shevardnadze had come back as Foreign

Minister to be there at perestroika's end, much as he had been there at the beginning.

In a room walled by boldly colored abstract paintings, we met around a white plastic table with multicolored patio furniture. Shevardnadze began our conversation by stressing the importance of U.S. support for the Soviet transformation. "It is very important that you have come," he said. "The United States cannot afford to stand on the sidelines; you cannot be an outside observer. You cannot let go and let things get out of control."

Concerning the Commonwealth, Shevardnadze agreed that it was the only reasonable way to sort out political relations and ensure peaceful change. Yet he felt that the Commonwealth had been hastily put together, and that Yeltsin and the other leaders hadn't thought through all the details. I told him that, based on my conversation with Kozyrev that afternoon, I agreed with his assessment. "I, like you, worry that the parties to this new Commonwealth don't know exactly where they are going," I said. He emphasized that America should use its unique leverage to push the members of the Commonwealth to the necessary understandings on the critical issues of nuclear command and control.

Shevardnadze was most concerned by the potential for military fragmentation and mob rule. "The armed forces are in tough shape," he said. "Their emotional state of mind is very bad right now. The Defense Minister doesn't know what to do or who to follow. He respects Gorbachev, but sees that the real power is with Yeltsin." To move the parties in the right direction, Shevardnadze suggested we withhold recognition—our "big card"—until the republics sorted things out. He warned that if the military command and control issue was not solved, the Commonwealth would likely fail, and we'd see disintegration in Russia and the other republics.

While he was worried about the potential for chaos and disorder with the Soviet Union's demise, he was able to step back and look at the whirlwind around him philosophically. "We started all of this in Wyoming and Malta. The old way, the enemy was the United States," he noted. "Now we are rid of all that. Everything that has taken place seems natural and appropriate. When Gorbachev and I started, we understood that the state as we knew it couldn't stay. But we didn't have timelines or schedules."

"There was no way to foresee the multiple effects of letting the freedom genie out of the bottle," I responded. "You and Gorbachev will go down as enlightened leaders with unparalleled personal and political courage. That will be the judgment of history. The other way would have been a violent explosion, and you still could have civil war," I warned.

"At least, we made reform a controllable process and prevented a Romanian, violent version, but we should have done more in the economic field," he said, somewhat dejectedly.

"But look at what you did," I said, feeling sorry for him. "Germany is united peacefully. Central and Eastern Europe are peaceful. This may not end in conflict."

"It's a little late to talk about history," Shevardnadze interjected. "Let the historians do that. We could have come out for a market economy. Our mistake was not getting the stages and timing right. Second, we didn't understand our people very well—the ethnic and nationality loyalties. We underestimated nationalism.

"I made mistakes. Gorbachev made mistakes. The coup plotters are the ones who really ripped this apart. They should be on Gorbachev's conscience. I warned Gorbachev; we all did. How can you excuse yourself and go on a vacation? Gorbachev dragged these men in from nowhere and made them what they are."

Nonetheless, Shevardnadze told me, "You need to support Gorbachev in a kind way. He is in a tough spot." (Sergei Tarasenko told us that Shevardnadze would leave his apartment at night and go spend long hours with Gorbachev, just to talk.) He blamed Strobe Talbott and *Time* for giving Gorbachev a bad translation of my "Face the Nation" remark by omitting the "as we have known it" qualifier, and suggested Gorbachev wouldn't have said I had been overly hasty if the full text of what I actually had said had been given to him.

We adjourned to a room downstairs and relaxed as we began our dinner. Trading stories and jokes over a wonderful meal that included boar's head, interspersed with toasts of green Tarkhuna vodka, I felt at home with Shevardnadze—in part because he felt so comfortable with himself. There he was in the twilight of his power, but rather than being embittered or jealous, he was secure with the past and ready, if anxious, for the future.

The Peaceful Coup

The next day I saw firsthand the Soviet Union's past and Russia's future. In nearly ten hours of meetings with Yeltsin, Gorbachev, Shaposhnikov, and Shevardnadze, I watched the transfer of power occur before my own eyes. It began with my meeting with Yeltsin in St. Catherine's Hall in the Kremlin. That room, comparable to the Cabinet Room in the White House, was *the* seat of Soviet power, and Gorbachev had always received me there during my previous visits to Moscow, just as he had other foreign ministers and heads of government. But this time, Yeltsin had insisted that he meet me there, symbolically brushing Gorbachev and the Soviet Union aside. Yeltsin reinforced this unmistakable political statement by seating the Soviet Union's Defense Minister, Yevgeny Shaposhnikov, right next to him, even though I was scheduled to see Shaposhnikov later that day.

"Welcome to this Russian building on Russian soil," Yeltsin greeted us. He was obviously feeling his oats and ready to show who was boss.

I told Yeltsin that, given the lack of specifics in my meeting with Kozyrev the previous afternoon, "this is an important time to have a detailed discussion. Our only interest is to help you where we can."

"Surely," Yeltsin wryly interjected, "that's not the only U.S. interest."

"That's true," I said. "The transformations sweeping this area are obviously of concern to the United States. Though I must note that it is our intention to keep out of Russia's internal affairs." I then asked him to explain the events leading up to the December 8 agreement in Brest and its implications.

"The first version of the Union Treaty perished in the coup," he said, and in the ensuing months, Russia and the other republics had negotiated with Gorbachev. But that had resulted only in a "basic difference over the shape of the future union. Gorbachev insists on a unified state with a single, powerful Center." That didn't stand a chance with the Russian Supreme Soviet. "In the end, however," Yeltsin said, "the decisive factor in the death of the Union Treaty was the Ukrainian referendum, since no union without Ukraine made any sense. In these circumstances, Russia could not stand aside," Yeltsin emphasized. Gorbachev had tried to convince Kiev, but Yeltsin felt obliged to organize the Brest meeting. "Otherwise," he said, "Russia and Ukraine would have ended up on opposite sides of the barricades with independent armies and separate currencies." The CIS agreement would have certain "unified areas," including unified nuclear forces with one command, but Yeltsin categorically rejected press reports that Gorbachev might be made commander in chief of the Commonwealth.

Yeltsin explained that the leaders of the five Central Asian states had met and agreed to join the Commonwealth. Yeltsin, Kravchuk, and Shushkevich were planning on meeting the Central Asians in Alma-Ata on December 21 for a signing ceremony. Armenia and Moldova would also sign, he added with satisfaction, bringing the total number of signatories to ten. "It was natural," he concluded, "that the three republics, founders of the Union in 1922, have declared its abolition. Most of the USSR ministries and other organs will be disbanded. Those that survive will be taken over by Russia." Russia would take over all embassies and foreign trade missions. He said it would assume the Soviet Union's seat on the U.N. Security Council, would absorb the Soviet Foreign Ministry, Interior Ministry, and at least part of the KGB. It would respect all international agreements and treaties of the former USSR, with the sole exception of foreign assistance to Communist regimes, which, he said, "is being phased out rapidly."

It was hard not to be a bit taken aback after this stunning presentation. It had been one thing for me to say that the Soviet Union as we had known it no longer existed, but quite another to have this fact outlined in detail by the President of Russia in the very room that was the principal site of Soviet power. I told Yeltsin I now had a pretty good understanding of the political situation, and added, "I also understand the degree to which we might be helpful in other capitals by promoting steps needed to resolve the remaining questions." Now that it was my turn to speak, I wanted Yeltsin's commitment to make several public assurances on issues vital to us; by asking him (and all the other republic leaders I met) to make *public* pronouncements, I wanted to establish a standard to which we could hold them in the future. Four of the assurances involved security questions, in which I sought Yeltsin's agreement to work with the other republics on command, control, and storage of nuclear weapons; to take part in efforts for safely disabling nuclear weapons; to curb nuclear proliferation; and to cooperate with us to assure the speedy ratification of the START and CFE treaties.

Yeltsin was reassuring on command and control questions (and was reinforced by Shaposhnikov, who nodded in agreement), making it clear that there would be a single, highly unified command and control structure in the new Commonwealth. Joint management of the "button" would not be possible, Yeltsin continued, and Russia would end up being the only nuclear power in the CIS after nuclear force reductions were implemented. He also agreed to enter discussions with us on dismantling and disabling warheads, on safe storage of weapons, on joint planning for contingencies involving nuclear accidents, and on follow-up to the President's de-MIRVing initiative that had been announced on September 27.

The final assurance I sought concerned our interest in mobilizing humanitarian assistance. My meeting with Kozyrev had done little to allay my concerns that there were no structures in place to assure the distribution of aid once it had been delivered. I told Yeltsin that we needed names of city and oblast officials who could serve as our points of contact. Yeltsin promised that we would get a list of names, and also assented to my idea that U.S. military personnel work in conjunction with the Soviet military to deliver the aid. He welcomed our efforts to broaden the circle of donors and criticized the German assistance program in 1990 as being too Moscow-centric.

Yeltsin then made several points of his own. Besides recognition, he wanted Russia to be the successor state to the Soviet Union, hoped to have Russia, Belarus, and Ukraine admitted to CSCE, and requested that all three be admitted to the North Atlantic Cooperation Council Ministerial on December 20.* In a clear sign of his distrust of Gorbachev, he pointedly de-

---

*The NACC was a NATO initiative that I had launched with Hans-Dietrich Genscher to reach out to the former Warsaw Pact states. It was part of our effort to transform NATO for the post–Cold War world and to expand its political influence.

manded that if Shevardnadze attended that meeting for the USSR, he wanted it understood that Shevardnadze could not "in any way" represent Russia.

I told him all these issues revolved around the issue of recognition, and we would not be able to resolve that until we had a better understanding of the substantive content of our relations.

Over the longer term, he said, he wanted the military organization of the CIS to "merge" with NATO. "It would be an important part of Russia's security to associate with the only military alliance in Europe," he concluded.

Before our session concluded, Yeltsin and I were left alone so we could discuss the specifics of nuclear command and control. With lingering questions about who exactly controlled the USSR's nuclear forces, Yeltsin provided me with an unprecedented outline of how the current launch system operated and how he envisioned the CIS system would operate. He told me that they had put in place a nuclear "hot line," which he shared with Gorbachev and Shaposhnikov. That system enabled the three participants to coordinate a nuclear launch—each had a briefcase with the launch codes, and all had to agree in order to push the button. The CIS system, he explained, would work similarly, but only he and Shaposhnikov would have briefcases. The other "nuclear" leaders would be included in the nuclear "hot line," but would not have the ability to order a launch.

"The leaders of Ukraine, Kazakhstan, and Byelorussia do not understand how these things work, that's why I'm telling only you," he said. "They'll be satisfied with having telephones." With five parties on the nuclear "hot line" but only two controlling the briefcases, Yeltsin said that the most accurate way to describe the CIS command and control system was one of "consultation, not coordination."

I raised one last issue: the rumors of a possible prosecution of Gorbachev. I told Yeltsin that we had heard the rumors of possible criminal proceedings against Gorbachev. That would be a mistake that would not be understood by the international community, I said. We hoped the transfer of power could be done in a dignified way—as in the West. Humiliating Gorbachev would serve no purpose. Despite a clear personal antipathy for Gorbachev, Yeltsin took the point and indicated his agreement.

With only a half hour until I was scheduled to meet Gorbachev, I hurried (as much as I could—my motorcade was reduced to a crawl due to a heavy afternoon snow) to the U.S. embassy for a quick tuna sandwich. After a twenty-minute lunch in Jim Collins's embassy office, I returned to the Kremlin for my three o'clock meeting. When my delegation arrived at the door, the Chief of Protocol of the Kremlin, who had watched us leave less than an hour before, complimented our quick turnaround with a knowing smile.

I met Gorbachev in the same room I had left thirty minutes before, but the heavy winter snow had darkened an already overcast day, and it was almost pitch dark outside as the meeting began.

Where Yeltsin had swaggered, Gorbachev was subdued. He was surrounded by his two original partners, Shevardnadze and Yakovlev. They had helped him launch perestroika, glasnost, and new thinking, but they had also criticized him at different times and had been estranged from him to the point where each had resigned. Nevertheless, now they had returned and were at his side as his role was coming to an end. It was an interesting reminder that these were men of character and conviction, and could be counted on to stand by their beliefs (and their friends) even when times were tough.

Gorbachev began solemnly, "It is truly important that developments here proceed under our constitution, and that they not fall into chaos. I remain committed to reform this multinational state. This process is not at an impasse," he argued unconvincingly. "On November twenty-fifth, we decided to send a draft treaty to the republics. We all signed this draft treaty. I personally spoke with six republic leaders."

My throat grew dry and so I reached for a Velamint—which I always carried, especially for my long meetings with Assad—and when Gorbachev noticed it, I gave one to him and to Shevardnadze. "Yes," Gorbachev said, tasting it and seemingly wanting to remember a more pleasant time, "that's the same thing you gave me at Camp David."

Gorbachev then continued by saying that Yeltsin argued that without Ukraine the Union Treaty would not work—which Gorbachev said he fully understood. "I really don't want to give you an analysis of what happened, but this is our concern and for us to sort out. Maybe there have been some mistakes, some grave blunders on my part and some on yours," he noted, apparently referring to the press reports of the President's meeting with Ukrainian-Americans and my "Face the Nation" interview. "What we have to discuss, however, is the future and the realities as they exist today. I see my role to use all my potential, so that the process under way proceeds in such a way that we don't see greater disintegration."

He went on to criticize the Brest agreement, but then he shifted tack, giving in to reality. "I want myself and my longtime colleagues to help establish the future of the Commonwealth and continuity of succession. I now really want them to succeed, but I don't believe they will. If they don't succeed, all that we have worked so hard for over these years will be jeopardized."

Then, in a haunting question, he seemed to recognize the reality of the situation: "Given the fact that you have talked to Yeltsin and to two foreign ministers, what do you plan to discuss with me today?" he asked.

I told him we did not want to get involved in their internal affairs and had taken great care in that regard. I told him that I shared his concerns about the generality of the Commonwealth agreement, and said that I had just spent four hours drawing specifics from the Russian President. "At best this agreement is a shell," I said. "But if this process does not succeed, I agree, there will be greater disintegration."

Gorbachev confirmed that he and Yeltsin had agreed to a transition time frame "on how this process should evolve," presumably including when Gorbachev would step down as leader of the USSR. But then he became defiant again: "They met in the woods of Brest, and they closed down the Soviet Union. This is a kind of coup. I was only told about this agreement after President Bush was told. So I said: I remain committed to my position. Let the people decide. Act like democrats, not highway robbers!"

He expressed dismay that Yeltsin seemed to be accelerating the terms of their agreement by "making decisions about the USSR's ministries behind my back. Of course they took the liberty of saying the Soviet Union is no more. If that is so, then there are no laws, no role in the U.N. . . . If the Soviet Union is no more and the Commonwealth doesn't yet exist, then what is there?"

He urged us not to recognize the new states immediately. We could help best, he believed, by using recognition as a goal to be achieved.

We had no interest in prolonging the Soviet Union, but my meetings had already convinced me that no one was going to resuscitate the Communist corpse collapsing in front of us. We did have a clear interest in shaping the outlook and behavior of its successor states. Recognition was the largest "carrot" we had available, and I wanted to maximize our leverage by holding it back until we had reached certain understandings with the Russian Republic, Ukraine, and the other republics.

After some additional back-and-forth, Gorbachev ended the meeting with some nobility. "We bear responsibility for the people, for this country. We will help this process. I hope this difficult mission has given you greater understanding. Please give President Bush my best."

As we walked out, I asked Yakovlev if he had passed us the message through Talbott. He hadn't.* But he then took the occasion to say, "I will continue to support Gorbachev to see this thing through. I hate to see him demeaned."

"I do, too," I replied, realizing that this would almost certainly be Gor-

---

*I learned later it had been Pavel Palazchenko.

bachev's last meeting with a high-ranking Western official. He had shown incredible courage in undertaking perestroika, glasnost, and new thinking in the first place, and had transformed the Soviet Union and East-West relations as a result. History, I felt, would be kind to him, but I hoped, too, that he soon realized that his role had played out, and would step aside gracefully.

We went back out into the snow to the Soviet Defense Ministry for my second meeting in three months with Defense Minister Shaposhnikov. Although Yeltsin had provided me his vision of how the CIS military questions would be solved, there were some details missing, and I wanted to hear them directly from the military. Moreover, as the "Commander of Strategic Forces" and one of the two individuals with the power to launch a nuclear strike, Shaposhnikov personally was a major factor in assuring the safety of the vast Soviet nuclear arsenal. As such, I wanted to make sure we saw things eye to eye.

The Defense Minister was quite relaxed and seemingly confident that he had complete control and would be able to work out the details of the military transformation ahead. "Life is rushing ahead," he started, "and there is no slowing down in the face of change."

He reviewed the command and control arrangements modified for the CIS, and confirmed what Yeltsin had explained to me earlier. "Who gives you orders today?" I asked.

"Gorbachev," he replied.

"Will that change on December twenty-first?" I followed, referring to the upcoming Alma-Ata meeting.

"It doesn't depend upon me," Shaposhnikov replied, in a transparent attempt to keep the military out of Kremlin intrigues—even though the meetings Gorbachev and Yeltsin had held with the high command the previous week and Shaposhnikov's presence at my meeting with Yeltsin indicated otherwise.

I asked him about tactical nuclear weapons, the class of weaponry slated to be completely eliminated by President Bush's September 27 proposal. "All the republics have the good sense to fulfill the understanding between Presidents Bush and Gorbachev regarding their elimination," Shaposhnikov assured me. "We are in the process of withdrawing all tactical nuclear systems from the other republics to Russia," and pledged that the withdrawal would be complete by early 1992. This was a critical assurance; after command and control, we were most concerned with the danger of "loose nukes," tactical weapons small enough to be smuggled out of the country and to places like Baghdad and Tripoli.

Kravchuk's decision to take over Soviet forces on Ukrainian territory had caused a "problem," Shaposhnikov noted, but in several conversations

with the Ukrainian President, he had found workable solutions. More important, Shaposhnikov stated, "Kravchuk has confirmed that he has no
claims on nuclear forces and that he is not seeking a nuclear button." Belarus had expressed a similar position.*

Shaposhnikov then explained to me the arrangements for military decision making in the CIS. Noting Yeltsin's statement earlier that day that
there would be no "Center" in the CIS, he said that "as a general proposition, this is true, but of course the military field is different and we cannot
do without a Center. Many issues bring us together, such as the need for a
single operational and strategic space." He envisioned a "defensive alliance" where "aggression against one is aggression against all." He then
described a set of decision-making and logistical arrangements that seemed
very familiar. "If this sounds like NATO," he said ironically, "don't be surprised. I've studied your alliance very carefully." Shaposhnikov's description was certainly plausible (indeed, it had served NATO well), but it would
of course require the full cooperation of the other republic leaders. He said
that discussions were ongoing, and that he would attend the upcoming
meetings in Alma-Ata to clarify these arrangements.

I then raised the issue of U.S. support for dismantlement of Soviet nuclear forces. Agreements such as START were scheduled to be implemented, and I felt that there was an urgency to move forward, in large part
to reassure people everywhere. Both Yeltsin and Shaposhnikov had assured me that the CIS would adhere to all treaties previously agreed to by
the USSR, but we wanted to confirm that these commitments would be
translated into facts on the ground. Moreover, I told Shaposhnikov that
"Congress has appropriated substantial funds for this purpose. It is up to
you to decide whether you want us to help you, and if so, where." Shaposhnikov said that while the arms race had been expensive, "the effort to
disarm will be costly as well." He was not yet ready to get into details of how
we might help, but he said that he welcomed our expertise, "especially if
you are ready to pay part of the cost."

For my final meeting of the day, I went to the Osobnyak for another
dinner meeting with Shevardnadze. We went directly to the small room in
which we had met for the first time in May 1989. I was reminded of the
many meetings we had held there and of the accomplishments that had
emerged from these meetings. As on the night before, I found Shevardnadze matter-of-fact about his future. His concerns were much less for himself and much more for what he saw coming.

---

*When I asked him about Ukraine's plan for a 400,000-man army—which had so alarmed us
that we had criticized it publicly—Shaposhnikov said that "would make all of Europe worry"
and that Kravchuk had agreed with him to end talk of such a large force.

"We have to try to preserve all the things we have accomplished over these years," he said. He was worried that the combination of price liberalization, massive unemployment, and the potential exhaustion of currency reserves might bring an "explosion" in February. "The people will be anxious," he said, "and there are grounds for apprehension that extremists may come to power—that's why your continued contacts with reform leaders are so important." He explained that the population was extremely concerned about shortages, saying, "My wife even hoards. My apartment is full of things that we do not need." He elaborated that the only way to head off extremists and to give people a reason to believe in the democrats was to begin to get enough goods and food available, and that meant free-market reform, including price liberalization and privatization.

Shevardnadze then told me that he would not attend the NACC in Brussels, but instead would send a deputy representative of the Foreign Ministry. "What's the point of my going?" he said, explaining that the "Soviet Union" would have six seats at the meeting, which would enable foreign ministers of the key republics to attend.

"I told Tarasenko I should not have returned to the Foreign Ministry," he said, trying to sum up his feelings. "We felt something bad would happen, but I have no regrets. We made friends again with Gorbachev. In these, the last days of the Soviet Union, we are still here together."

"You always did the right thing in the eyes of the international community. I do not think you know how much you are respected," I replied.

Following a brief press conference, my security agents unexpectedly whisked me out a back entrance in order to avoid some protesters chanting in the lobby. That left me without a chance to thank my friend for all he had done for East-West relations, and to say good-bye. As soon as I got back to my suite at Penta Hotel, I called Shevardnadze to explain what had happened.

"I deeply regret not having a chance to say good-bye to you in person," I said. He fully understood. "I want to thank you for everything we have done together, and tell you that I am proud to call you my friend," I continued. In my meetings throughout that day, I had been struck by the fact that, as much as anything else, the force of friendship based on trust was the reason Shevardnadze and I had been able to accomplish what we did. "I fully expect to see you again soon either in Washington or Moscow."

In my report to the President that night, I said that my day had been "filled with contrast" between Yeltsin's energy and confidence and Gorbachev's anxiety and concern. I worried that Yeltsin and the republic reformers were focusing too much on broad political arrangements and, as Shevardnadze had pointed out, not doing enough to deal with the real problems experienced by common people—food shortages and unemployment, for example. "The critical question," I told the President, "is can Yeltsin translate his revolutionary enthusiasm into changed behaviors and real improvements on the ground? The odds are very long and . . . things are almost certain to get worse before they get better. In addition, I continue to worry that there remains too much of a tendency to focus on broad political arrangements and to continue to ignore the importance of dealing with the real problems that people are experiencing." The next day, my words would echo back to me.

A Central Asian Angle

I left Moscow on Tuesday, December 15, and flew south into the heart of Central Asia, headed for Bishkek, Kyrgyzstan. In the flux surrounding the formation of the Commonwealth, Kyrgyzstan's President, Askar Akayev, was an appealing figure. In a region more prone to warlords than Jeffersonian democrats, Akayev was an anomaly who genuinely believed in democracy and free markets. I felt my visit there would be an important symbol for Akayev and the Muslims in this region that the United States was ready to support their reforms—a point Shevardnadze had made with me, too. I knew that it would be important to show Muslims in the region the same encouragement we showed the Slavs in Russia, Ukraine, and Belarus.

Upon our arrival in snowy Bishkek, we were greeted by President Akayev and his entire cabinet. As I descended the plane's steps, Akayev had his hands clasped in fists above his head as though he had just won the welterweight boxing title. After a traditional "bread and salt" welcoming ceremony, we drove through the very rural Kyrgyz countryside to the presidential residence.

I found Akayev very committed to the Commonwealth. As he put it, it was very important for Kyrgyzstan's security to maintain close relations with Russia. He said there were two central reasons that relations with Russia were important: the need to contain radical Islamic fundamentalism and to counter potential problems with China. His only reservation about the Commonwealth, he explained, was that the Central Asian nations had to be formally accorded equal status. He promised to raise this issue in Alma-Ata as a possible amendment to the Commonwealth treaty.

Following our private session, we joined our staffs downstairs for an unexpected traditional Kyrgyz dinner.

"Your visit has brought us a sign of good luck—the first snow of the season, which means well for the next harvest," he said in the opening toast. "Your visit in peace is historic. Please, keep coming!"

During our private meeting and throughout the meal, Akayev was clearly more relaxed about the details of the Commonwealth than his colleagues in Moscow. Undoubtably a main reason was the fact that Kyrgyzstan had no strategic nuclear forces and "does not wish to acquire them." All Kyrgyzstan wanted, Akayev said, was "a national guard amounting to about one thousand people—we do not need a military." Instead, he explained that Kyrgyzstan would rather be "armed" with our five principles. This statement captured what I felt was the central lesson of this quick visit: that with our enormous moral authority with many of these republics and their leaders, the United States had a unique responsibility to support reform efforts. We had to do this both with symbols (such as my visit here) and substance (humanitarian and technical assistance).

After dinner, I left Bishkek for the forty-five-minute flight to Alma-Ata, Kazakhstan, and a meeting with President Nazarbayev. Nazarbayev had been a pivotal player in the efforts to reshape the Soviet Union, and he recognized the importance of better clarifying the Commonwealth agreement. Although one of four leaders with strategic nuclear weapons, Nazarbayev had not been in Brest. In four days, he would host the Commonwealth meeting, so I felt it was crucial to outline some of our concerns and, most important, hear some of his.

Nazarbayev began with a lengthy but fascinating monologue that laid out surprising background to the birth of the Commonwealth. "Gorbachev invited Shushkevich, Yeltsin, Kravchuk, and me to see him on the afternoon of Monday, December 9. On Sunday, December 8, I went up to Moscow. While I was in the airport after arriving, I received a message that Yeltsin was looking for me. He was calling me from Brest. Brest is way out in the woods. He said, 'We're sitting here, and we're deciding on the Commonwealth.' I said, 'You didn't tell me about this earlier.' I had talked to him on the sixth and he told me he was going to Minsk—and remember, this was the sixth—to work out a bilateral agreement with Shushkevich. He said he was asking Kravchuk to come to tell the two of them about the future.

"Yeltsin told me he wanted to look Kravchuk in the eye and ask him what he wanted to do about the Monday meeting that Gorbachev had called. Instead, what happened, he goes to Minsk and he cuts a deal. Why was he in such a hurry to cut this deal? I mean, if nothing else, it's like an off-the-top-of-the-head deal. It's an off-the-cuff deal. It's totally unprepared."

Nazarbayev was angry but not agitated. He had asked Yeltsin, "Is this the last deal like this? Is this the last deal that's going to be cut?" Shushkevich had told the Kazakh President he was sorry how things had been done. Nazarbayev said to him, "We're not talking about personal ambition here, but we're dealing with a very big set of issues."

Still in Moscow, Nazarbayev had called Gorbachev on December 9 to tell him that he was not going to come, and the others weren't coming, either. "He said, 'Why don't you come by here for ten minutes?' So I did," Nazarbayev told me. "But Yeltsin was there. He didn't know that I was going to be there, and I certainly didn't know that he was going to be there. Gorbachev asked Yeltsin a number of simple questions about citizenship, borders, the army, and Yeltsin couldn't answer any of them.

"Now the fact is the three of them held a meeting and the three of them signed a deal. Why should you have three nuclear powers meet and leave out the fourth? There was never any reason given to me why I was excluded."

The Slavic troika had clearly wounded Nazarbayev's pride and, more important, scrambled his geopolitical calculations, but he was not one to dwell on the past. Having walked me through the short history of the Commonwealth, he then proceeded to lay out his strategic thinking. Nazarbayev said that, given Kazakhstan's limited options—join the Commonwealth, establish a Central Asian federation, or go it alone—he would work to help make the Commonwealth succeed. Gorbachev's preferred option—another reworked Union Treaty—was "not possible. We're finished with that," the Kazakh President said dismissively. Instead, he said, "I want to do all I possibly can to produce a normal accord here in Alma-Ata." As a first step, he said he would insist that three amendments would have to be added to the accord.* He had estimated his leverage very precisely: He had the weight of the other four Central Asian republics with him. He also had nuclear weapons. And, he said, "They have one hundred electrical power stations in Russia and Ukraine that can only run on our coal, the coal out of Kazakhstan. I'm amazed how they don't think through what it is they've done." Now, he told me, "They've all apologized, and it's over. Once again, I'm going to have to get into being a firefighter, I'm going to have to get them all together."

With his soliloquy finished, I began by repeating what I had told everyone in Moscow: "I've made it very clear that it is not our place to involve ourselves in this process. It's a process that has to be worked out by the participants here, not by us."

Nazarbayev indicated that Yeltsin had used his phone call with Presi-

---

*The first amendment was to make all members of the Commonwealth "founding" members in order to avoid a split between Slavic and Asian republics (which was almost exactly what Akayev had told me earlier). "This is the way one has to do business. You can't do business the way they have done it," Nazarbayev said. The second was to have the four nuclear republics sign a treaty that specified nuclear command and control mechanisms. "They have written their draft in a 'loosey goosey' way," Nazarbayev put it. The third amendment was to re-sign the agreement in Alma-Ata, suitably modified.

dent Bush to argue that he had U.S. support. I told him that the President had not taken a position, privately or publicly, and had made it clear this was something for the republics and the Center to work out. Nazarbayev accepted my explanation, but his initial misunderstanding did shed some light on some apparent confusion in Moscow over our position on the Commonwealth. I suspected that Yeltsin must have also told Gorbachev that he and the Commonwealth had received the President's blessings, which likely explained Gorbachev's overreaction to my comments that the Soviet Union, as we had known it, no longer existed.

I then raised with Nazarbayev two other crucial issues: Kazakhstan's accession to the Nuclear Nonproliferation Treaty (NPT) and the possibility of U.S. humanitarian and technical assistance. "If the international community recognizes and accepts Kazakhstan," Nazarbayev said, "we will declare ourselves a non-nuclear state. This is the best way that our territorial integrity will be assured. That's what we require." It was a reassuring answer, although I'd learn in the spring of 1992 that Nazarbayev could, not surprisingly, string out negotiations for any and every advantage he could find.

On relief aid, Nazarbayev welcomed anything we could provide. He was eager to receive Western expertise to help transform Kazakhstan's economy and arrange projects to attract Western investment. "Send me advisers and investors—not money," he exclaimed. I told him that in addition to raising these issues with our Western allies and the IMF, I would send Bob Fauver, who had moved from the East Asian Bureau to become Deputy Under Secretary for Economic Affairs, to help accelerate reform.

When I got to my room that night at 3:00 A.M., I felt that my three hours with Nazarbayev were among the best I had had thus far. He was a very impressive leader, one that could not be underestimated. His near future would undoubtably be rough—he had a full plate of enormously complex issues to iron out in the days ahead and the Commonwealth meeting in three days would be pivotal. But Nazarbayev had both a vision of what was needed, as well as an acute sense of how to get things accomplished on the ground.

The Two Other Nuclear Republics: Belarus and Ukraine

I spent Wednesday, December 18, with Belarus President Stanislav Shushkevich in Minsk and Ukraine President Leonid Kravchuk in Kiev reviewing the same basic issues: nuclear safety, dismantlement, and command and control; adherence to existing arms control treaties; commitment to economic and political liberalization; and the promise of points of contact at the local level to help coordinate and distribute humanitarian assistance.

In my first meeting in Minsk with Shushkevich, I found him confident and generally agreeable. A former physicist, Shushkevich had assumed office only in September. As the press left the meeting room following the obligatory pre-meeting photo op, Shushkevich told me that he found responding to journalists on camera "an awkward experience—I'm not used to that part of the job."

"Welcome to democracy," I said.

Shushkevich was at pains to emphasize that Belarus would accept anything we wanted on nuclear weapons. Having lived through the trauma of Chernobyl, Shushkevich felt it was essential to get all nuclear weapons off Belarus territory. He eagerly sought U.S. expertise for disabling and dismantling purposes, and I pledged that we would supply such.

He was also quick to explain how Belarus was moving on political and economic reform. He claimed that Belarus led the way in all republics on privatization, and that the parliament was currently discussing the elements of a new democratic constitution. He said that he wanted to put the effects of the Cold War behind Belarus, and that "we wish in no way to repeat the experience of the last forty years. We wish to become a healthy, normal state."

On the CIS, Shushkevich said that he hoped for success at Alma-Ata, and was prepared to work toward it. Although we did not discuss Nazarbayev's proposed amendments specifically, I felt that neither Yeltsin nor Shushkevich would have any problem with them. We wanted the Alma-Ata meeting to succeed, I said, in part because we saw the danger of radical Islamic fundamentalism sweeping into what had been Soviet Central Asia. "By an association of the Central Asian republics with the Slavic republics," I continued, "the Central Asians could serve as a bridge between West and East and a secure buffer against the spread of radical Islamic fundamentalism."

"In general," Shushkevich replied, "we are in full agreement with your position."

That evening in Kiev, Kravchuk was similarly cooperative. This was reassuring, because, going into the meeting, I had been concerned about Kravchuk. While in Kazakhstan, I had received reports that Kravchuk was likely not to attend the Alma-Ata meeting. Since it was second in geostrategic weight only to Russia, I feared that Ukraine's non-participation might cause the Commonwealth to implode, and possibly cause the region to fall into chaos.

Surprisingly, Kravchuk opened our discussion by going out of his way to pour praise on the Commonwealth. He had apparently consulted with Nazarbayev and Yeltsin before seeing me, and his posture on the Alma-Ata meeting had changed—he was quick to tell me that he was going and that Ukraine was ready to participate.

I asked him what would happen in Russia if the CIS failed to hold. What would happen regarding the various ethnic groups, such as the Chechen and Ingush people?

"Under those circumstances, Russia will face enormous difficulty with pressures toward independence by various regions. Russia faces serious ideological problems because it is a conglomerate of Christianity and Islam." He said that even though the CIS was a Ukrainian idea, the Russians were the most interested in it and had embraced it "most fervently." He also warned, "There are also Russian desires for a 'superstate.' This is unacceptable."

Ukraine was prepared to join the NPT and had already asked the International Atomic Energy Agency (IAEA) to send its representatives to Kiev to get compliance started. He said that Ukraine would abide by all existing nuclear agreements, and would welcome U.S. expertise to assist in the safe storage, transfer, and destruction of its nuclear forces. Like Nazarbayev, the Ukrainian President favored a single control over strategic forces, and emphasized that until all logistics were worked out, nuclear forces on Ukrainian soil would be "inactivated."

Following my evening in Kiev, I was more confident than I had been earlier in the week that political disputes could be contained. I was convinced that the Commonwealth would take shape in some form at the Alma-Ata meeting. My gut feeling was that it would not have a long life, but at a minimum the Commonwealth could serve as a mechanism for mediating disputes between republics as they asserted and developed their independence.

In all my meetings that week, one theme had been uniform: the intense desire to satisfy the United States. Nazarbayev had told me he kept the five principles in his desk, and Kravchuk asked us to send experts to assure the Ukrainians' implementation of the principles. Our moral authority, I cabled the President, "creates an extraordinary opportunity; it also requires a responsibility. Because of our standing and their desire to be accepted—indeed, almost 'approved' by us—they look to us to help them. Our willingness to do so can be used to shape what they do, and can also be used by them to build their authority." I argued that "recognition can't be put off for long—and it shouldn't be," but I felt we should wait until after the Alma-Ata meeting.

The End

I spent Thursday, December 19, at a North Atlantic Council meeting in Brussels and Friday at the first session of the NACC. The Soviet Union seemed to crumble by the hour; as we arrived, we heard that Yeltsin had issued a decree taking over the Kremlin, the Foreign Ministry, and the Interior Ministry. With my alliance colleagues, I proposed that NATO help provide logistic support for food and medicine shipments into the republics. The alliance not only had the capability, but it would also be an important symbolic shift from an organization geared to deterring aggression to one helping build a new peace. (The initiative was also symbolic of the smooth way State and Defense cooperated during the Bush administration. We developed the idea on the trip and finalized it in Kiev with calls to Colin Powell and Dick Cheney. The only downside was lack of sleep; both Steve Hadley, Cheney's able arms control and security specialist, and Gen. John Shalikashvili, then Powell's assistant, had to pull all-nighters.)

I also spent some time calming down the Europeans about the Coordinating Conference, which many of them saw as an assault on their turf. I told the Italian Foreign Minister Gianni De Michelis that our mistake was in not including the EC in the invitation. "No," replied Gianni, "our [the EC] mistake was not to have thought of it first. We need to have this Coordinating Conference of yours as soon as possible." I found similar sentiments among most of our alliance partners, though with the French I took a different tack, since President Mitterrand had called it a "pretty superfluous" initiative. "On the Coordinating Conference," I told Roland Dumas, "don't worry about it. You don't have to come if you don't want to. We'll put you down as a 'no.' " It worked. The French came and participated in a meaningful way.

The NACC meeting marked a political watershed. In the room where many an East-West crisis had been managed, I could look around and see foreign ministers from all the former Warsaw Pact states. It was quite a sight. But the meeting also marked NATO's initial effort to leave the Cold War behind and to plant the seeds of post–Cold War institutions by reaching out to the East and to expand the community of democratic nations.

In between ministerial and bilateral meetings, I tried to call Nazarbayev several times, only to be told at one point by AT&T that there were only two international telephone lines into Kazakhstan. I wanted to talk to Nazarbayev before the Commonwealth meeting began, to fill him in on the positive feedback from my meetings in Minsk and Kiev. I finally got hold of him the evening of the twentieth, just as he was greeting the delegates arriving to the historic conference.

"I wanted to let you know as you go into these meetings that I wish you luck," I began. "I've given my NATO colleagues a full report on my visit with you, and with respect to your assurances on nuclear safety, they are very pleased."

Nazarbayev sounded optimistic that the concerns he had outlined to me three days before would be resolved. His worries about Ukraine remained, but were subdued. And it appeared that he had received favorable responses on his proposed amendments to the Commonwealth treaty. "I have assurances from everyone here that we will be successful in creating this Commonwealth," he said. "I will not let anyone leave here without a deal."

"If anyone can move this forward, you can," I said. "I look forward to hearing about the results and ultimately seeing Kazakhstan as a member state of the international community."

The next day, while returning to Washington, Nazarbayev called me on my airplane to give me the results of the meeting. He gave me extraordinarily good news. "The Alma-Ata meeting is over," he began. "Eleven republics participated in the meeting. In addition to the eight that you knew about,* Armenia, Moldova, and Azerbaijan also participated. We have formulated a Commonwealth of Independent States."

The details of the agreement were definitely a positive step forward. "We are determined," he said, "that there will only be four nuclear republics, but that control of nuclear weapons will be handed over to Russia. Ukraine and Belarus will transfer their nuclear weapons by 1998 to Russia, where destruction of all tactical nuclear weapons will take place. Strategic nuclear weapons will remain in Russia and Kazakhstan; however, Kazakhstan will declare itself a non-nuclear zone when it is admitted to the United Nations."

He also said that "we also decided that Gorbachev should be absolutely safe and he should be provided for. We've reported President Yeltsin's request [which, I later learned, he had made publicly in the press conference following the Alma-Ata meeting] that President Gorbachev be taken care of in his work and his way of life."

"First," I responded, "let me tell you how grateful I am for your call and your very full report. It is consistent with everything that you and I discussed with the Republic leaders."

"Thanks, but it wasn't easy," he said.

"You've done remarkably well," I added. "I want you to know that

---

*The three Slavic republics (Russia, Belarus, and Ukraine) and the five Central Asian states (Kazakhstan, Kyrgyzstan, Tajikistan, Turkmenistan, Uzbekistan).

we're going to move expeditiously on the question of recognition of most of the members of the Commonwealth, and that certainly includes Kazakhstan."

With a chuckle, he said, "Mr. Secretary, I hope Kazakhstan will be one of the first ones."

"You can count on that for sure. We'll be in touch soon."

Four days later, on Christmas Day, Mikhail Gorbachev resigned. The red flag with the hammer and sickle that had flown over the Kremlin for seventy-four years came down for the last time. It was replaced by the Russian tricolor. The Union of Soviet Socialist Republics was dead. The experiment begun by Karl Marx and Vladimir Lenin, and carried on by Joseph Stalin and others, had failed.

CHAPTER 31

ENTERING A NEW ERA

I remember Secretary Dean Rusk saying ruefully that . . . at any moment in the day at least two-thirds of the people around the world are awake and some of them are making mischief.   —*Former Secretary of State Cyrus Vance, 1983*

A s one of only six men privileged to have held both positions, I'm occasionally asked to describe the difference between being Secretary of State and Secretary of the Treasury. Obviously, both are challenging and extraordinarily interesting portfolios. At Treasury, however, there's far more flexibility to choose the issues on which you concentrate. The Secretary of the Treasury is relatively free to allocate his time and shape his priorities in the pursuit of the President's policy agenda, and for the most part, while demanding, the universe of issues requiring attention is fairly predictable.

The Secretary of State, however, is more hostage to his environment than is any other member of the Cabinet. Any number of times, I would arrive at my seventh-floor office at 7:00 A.M. with the day ahead meticulously organized, only to scrap my schedule entirely to deal with one or more unexpected developments in remote corners of the globe. Trouble, I learned at State, has an uncanny knack for finding you.

Some of these events, such as Iraq's invasion of Kuwait, explode into full-fledged crises commanding the attention of the entire world. Others never even make the newspapers, much less the front pages. The vast majority fall somewhere in between. But all are critical to the successful conduct of foreign policy and deserving of considerable time and attention.

At any given moment, public and media scrutiny are understandably reserved for the most critical foreign policy issues of the day. In the Bush administration, these were the Gulf War, the unification of Germany, Soviet-American relations, and the Middle East peace process, and these are mostly what I've written about so far. None of these matters of overriding strategic interest was pursued in a vacuum, however. Indeed, as the President and his principal foreign policy advisers grappled with these issues, we simultaneously dealt with an overlapping array of others. Some were the result of our own initiatives, others were thrust upon us by events. But all of them required effective, ongoing supervision to ensure that our country's interests were protected and advanced. What follows is by no means a complete compendium of some of those other issues whose day-to-day management was just as important to the successful conduct of American foreign policy as issues requiring more high-profile management.

China: Saving a Troubled Marriage

By 1990, given the overwhelmingly hostile climate toward China in the aftermath of the Tiananmen Square massacre, any significant overtures to thaw the Sino-American relationship were neither justified nor possible. We were not willing simply to write China off, however. As a result, the emphasis in our policy shifted toward multilateral opportunities, where we could deal with the Chinese in a larger and less controversial context on issues of mutual interest.

The most notable undertaking in this regard was our successful effort to dissuade the Chinese from casting a veto in the United Nations Security Council that could have crippled U.S. efforts to force Saddam Hussein out of Kuwait. Our diplomatic persistence was also helpful in the Chinese decision to join U.N. efforts to reach a negotiated settlement to the war in Cambodia—an initiative that culminated in the 1991 Paris Peace Agreement, which restored a measure of stability to that troubled land.* We also worked to engineer the admission of China, Taiwan and Hong Kong into the APEC regional economic process in 1991. This last was a powerful message to the Chinese that, while we were seriously concerned with their domestic repression, the President was committed to remaining strategically engaged where possible.

By mid-1991, the case for bilateral engagement had become more persuasive. Despite their cooperation in the Gulf, we had grown increasingly concerned about Chinese complicity in weapons proliferation. Our intelli-

---

*This initiative was launched in 1989, after international peace talks on Cambodia had broken down, when the United States proposed that efforts be made to reach a solution under the auspices of the U.N. Perm Five.

gence confirmed that Beijing was selling surface-to-surface missiles to Pakistan, Syria, and Iran, and antiaircraft weapons to Libya, which was using them to protect its chemical weapons facility. More ominous, for some time the Chinese had been assisting the nuclear programs of Iran and Pakistan both of which were suspected of trying to produce nuclear weapons. It was crucial to engage the Chinese on these matters regardless of the domestic political climate. The simple truth was that China was too important to our global interests to try to isolate. Indeed, by the end of the Gulf War, many of our most vociferous congressional critics were privately acknowledging the necessity of dealing with the Chinese.

Nevertheless, we repeatedly pushed the Chinese to ease their repression of pro-democracy forces. They were more interested, predictably, in demanding that U.S. sanctions be lifted and in having a high-profile symbol such as a visit by the American Secretary of State to Beijing. Unhappy with the lower-level contacts the President had authorized in order to keep the dialogue alive, they repeatedly pressed me to schedule a trip. In two meetings with Qian Qichen in November 1990, which focused on the Persian Gulf crisis, I emphasized that any future visit to China by a senior U.S. official was contingent on greater progress on human rights. "We cannot improve relations unilaterally," I told Qian on November 30. "Without clear progress on your part, I cannot visit your country, and we have no chance to convince Congress and the American people of the importance of moving forward." As a goodwill gesture, Bob Kimmitt was dispatched to China in December and authorized to talk about a visit by me—but only so long as tangible progress on human rights was made.

By the fall of 1991, Beijing's response to our frequent démarches had been mixed. In the area of missile proliferation, they'd rebuffed our requests to embrace publicly the guidelines of the Missile Technology Control Regime (MTCR), an international agreement designed to stem the flow of medium-range ballistic missiles. They *had* agreed in principle, however, to accept the terms of the Nuclear Nonproliferation Treaty (NPT), and at our behest had pressed their North Korean clients to do likewise. Moreover, they had privately assured us they would cancel the sale of M-9 missiles to Syria.

On human rights, China had refused to release or reduce the sentences of most dissidents, rebuffed U.S. efforts to obtain a list of the dead and imprisoned, and rejected pleas from several nations to allow the International Committee of the Red Cross (ICRC) to inspect their prisons. On the other hand, they had allowed Fang Lizhi and his family to leave China, as well as spouses of dissidents living in the United States; released about nine hundred people detained after the Tiananmen Square massacre; accredited a correspondent from the Voice of America (VOA) to replace the VOA reporter expelled at the time of Tiananmen; and resumed Fulbright Scholarship and Peace Corps programs, which they'd cut off after the massacre.

These gestures were clearly inadequate to allay the opposition in Congress to lifting sanctions. But when combined with their willingness during the Gulf War not to veto Security Council resolutions that they really did not support, the President and I believed that sufficient grounds now existed to allow me to travel to China, in hopes of impressing upon their leadership the real risks that their repressive policies posed.

We still weren't convinced the Chinese understood just how devastating the massacre had been for Sino-American relations, so I scheduled another meeting with Qian on September 27, 1991, during the U.N. General Assembly meeting in New York. Before committing to a visit, we wanted to warn the Chinese that this was their last, best chance. If my trip were viewed as unsuccessful back home, there was no doubt in our minds Congress would take over U.S.-China policy from the President, with predictably poor results.

"I want to come to China," I told Qian, "but I have to know that my visit will enhance our relations and not make it more difficult to move forward. What I need to know is what I can accomplish by a visit." Qian was inscrutably vague.

"I want to leave China with something on human rights and proliferation," I pressed. "Congress is waiting to override the President on MFN. Can we talk specifics? Eyeball to eyeball, I need to know whether there will be something the President and I can point to."

Any issues can be discussed, and I am sure there will be some successes, he soothed. I told Qian that wasn't enough. Once again he politely evaded my inquiry, but I felt he'd absorbed the message.

On November 9, six days after the Middle East Peace Conference concluded in Madrid, I left Europe, where I'd attended a NATO Summit with the President, for Japan, Korea, and China. I arrived in Beijing at 2:25 P.M. on November 15, and began three days of talks with a meeting with Qian at the Diaoyutai guest house. He began with a laundry list of concessions he wanted from me, the most prominent being a lifting of all sanctions. In response, I ran through the entire range of bilateral and multilateral issues, reserving my bluntest language for human rights.

"Now it's time for you to be practical," I said, in concluding a forty-five-minute presentation. "I'm not expecting miracles. But I *do* expect you to recognize your own self-interest. I need concrete results—not promises, not meetings, not delays. When I get on my airplane, judgments will be formed immediately about the success or failure of this visit. If I am seen as having failed, the Congress will take China policy away from the President."

It had no effect on Qian, who summarily dismissed my requests that China grant amnesty to anyone convicted of nonviolent protest during the June 1989 uprisings and allow the ICRC to inspect substandard conditions in Chinese prisons.

In all my subsequent meetings, I tried to hammer home the point that our relationship was at a crossroads. I sensed from my meeting with Qian that the Chinese leadership simply could not fathom that the Tiananmen massacre had destroyed bipartisan support for restoring ties between our countries. At the end of the day, I saw no reason for much optimism.

The next morning, my first of six meetings was with Premier Li Peng. He was a technocrat by temperament and experience, a hard-liner who made absolutely no apologies for his role in crushing the pro-democracy movement. I'd been warned that he would be difficult, but I didn't expect him to be totally unreconstructed. He turned a deaf ear to virtually everything I said, particularly on human rights, where, as he put it, "because we have different values and different ideology we can only make a commitment to discussion."

His main agenda item was immediate and unconditional Chinese entry into the GATT trading system. He was especially adamant that China be allowed into GATT before Taiwan. China deserved to be treated like other world powers, he insisted. I told Li Peng that the PRC must liberalize its trading practices to conform to international standards before the United States would endorse GATT membership. I also told him the United States would support PRC and Taiwan for GATT entry but would not promise that the PRC could enter first. He was irritated with my position and reiterated his demand several times.

When I steered the dialogue back to human rights, he was utterly unyielding. When he quarreled with my description of the events of June 1989 as a tragedy, I knew the prospects for significant movement were bleak. "The actions in Tiananmen Square were a good thing," he contended. "We do not regard them as a tragedy. Look at Central and Eastern Europe and the Soviet Union today." If other nations had dealt with dissent as forthrightly as China had, he asserted, they would be suffering from fewer problems. "Our people support what we did during that time," he insisted.

To put it mildly, I was appalled—especially since it was quite clear he believed it. "I'll be frank," I replied. "If what you have just told me is all you have to offer, President Bush and I will not be able to sustain this relationship."

Li Peng was unfazed. "You should be happy that I am even seeing you," he admonished. "You're getting all these meetings with high government officials." For good measure, he even complained that the Chinese had been insulted by being excluded from the Middle East Peace Conference in Madrid.

From start to finish, it was a surreal performance—so much so that the thought fleetingly crossed my mind that perhaps I should simply walk out of the meeting. I knew that would be unwise and continued in rather dispirited fashion until the rest of our agenda items had been raised.

I thought this meeting was a disaster—a view shared by some members of our delegation, who later told me that they had privately concluded that the visit was doomed and, if asked, would have recommended that I drive directly to the airport and leave China immediately.

But matters quickly degenerated even further. At my next meeting, President Yang Shangkun, a genial figurehead, told me that "your biggest achievement had been to hear firsthand the views of Chinese leaders who had been misinterpreted by others."

"Mr. President," I replied, "this is not the sort of achievement I consider to be money in the bank."

The only interlocutor who seemed the slightest bit reasonable was Jiang Zemin, the party chairman. Like Li Peng, he didn't think the slaughter at Tiananmen was a tragedy. "But I would not say it was a blessing, either," he allowed. But Jiang was more interested in telling stories and, like his counterparts, filibustered me when I raised human-rights concerns.

Two days of exceedingly tough, difficult talks had yielded absolutely nothing on human rights, the political gold standard for gauging the success or failure of my mission. The Chinese typically employ a scorched-earth strategy in negotiations. They hector and argue and give no quarter until the last instant, and sometimes not even then. They'd been true to form in these talks, only more so. I wanted to believe that my recalcitrant hosts would relent at the end, but in fact I had real premonitions that these talks were about to crash and burn, and that relations would degenerate even further as a result of Chinese intransigence, compounded by the effort and risk we were taking by my visit.

My third and final day in China was consumed by a marathon meeting with Qian and several other officials. I began by reading a letter to Deng Xiaoping from President Bush. I'd asked to deliver the letter to Deng personally, only to be rebuffed. The President had hoped Deng might be swayed by a personal appeal from an old friend, but the government's rejection told me the letter was a futile gesture. I insisted, however, on reading it aloud, in the hope that someone in the meeting would convey its contents to Deng.

I then cut to the chase. "I've heard nothing on human rights," I told Qian, "which is the area on which the success of my visit will be judged. I hope you have something this morning in this area."

THE POLITICS OF DIPLOMACY

Then, having waited until we were near the end of the meeting in the usual Chinese fashion, Qian began to list what his side was willing to do to be responsive. He said China would support a nuclear-free Korean peninsula and would ask the party congress to ratify the NPT by the end of the year. China was also prepared, he added, to observe MTCR guidelines if the United States lifted certain sanctions against Chinese companies. In addition, we were able to achieve two good trade agreements dealing with access to the Chinese market and protection of intellectual property rights.

At the very last, he turned to human rights. China would allow dissidents who had served their sentences to travel abroad. Two prominent critics of the regime would soon be released. He offered an accounting of the status of 733 protesters whose names I had given him in our first meeting. It was patently incomplete; 340 people we had strong reason to believe had been taken into custody could not be found, Qian insisted. He promised to address concerns about reported use of prison labor to manufacture exports, and accepted my request to allow American diplomats to visit prisons.

It wasn't an impressive haul, but at least it was progress. I told Qian I wanted to consult with my staff. I declined his offer of a nearby conference room, assuming it was bugged. Instead, I adjourned with my senior aides to the steps of the guest house, where we sat in the sun and pondered our options.

It was obvious to all of us that while good progress might be made on proliferation issues, depending on the language we could negotiate, no major breakthrough on human rights had been achieved. Some of my staff thought we should end the meeting at this point and leave China two hours early to evidence our displeasure. I concluded that we should stay and press the Chinese, even though the odds of squeezing more from Qian were long. "I've made a decision we will say we're disappointed in the human rights area," I said. "It's not enough." There was no argument. We also decided to reject the Chinese demand to lift sanctions in exchange for an MTCR agreement.

When we resumed, I proposed to Qian that we adjourn into working groups to draft language on the major issues of contention. I also told him that I wanted to be able to say publicly that our dialogue on human rights would continue beyond this meeting. He was predictably noncommittal.

Two hours later, we reconvened. I read Qian word-for-word the language our working groups had hammered out so there could be no misunderstanding. The language on MTCR provoked a spirited debate. I suspected why: the Chinese had signed lucrative contracts to deliver missiles to Pakistan. In all probability, several senior government and party officials or their families stood to gain from the performance of those contracts. Moreover, a strong Pakistan was a counterweight to India, which shared a border with China.

The Chinese side kept trying to arrange loopholes. They insisted on striking specific references to Syria, Pakistan, and Iran, and also objected to language saying China "will observe" the MTCR guidelines, demanding that it be changed to "intends to observe." By arguing so forcefully for a less categorical pledge, it seemed as though Qian were tacitly acknowledging the possibility that some entity in China's defense community might cheat on this commitment. (In 1993, the Clinton administration imposed sanctions on the Chinese for selling missiles to Pakistan in violation of the MTCR.)

Five hours after we'd begun, it was over. Eighteen hours of grueling negotiation over three days had finally yielded just enough to keep the trip from being characterized as a failure. In my press conference, I made a point of noting that the Chinese had agreed that Dick Schifter, the Assistant Secretary for Human Rights, would continue a dialogue with his Chinese counterpart. It was a small but important victory, the first time the Chinese had agreed to talk about these matters they considered their internal business on a continuing basis.

The results of the trip proved sufficient to keep the bilateral relationship alive, and ward off subsequent congressional attempts to remove most-favored-nations status for China. In a larger sense, our policy was also successful in establishing the reality that, no matter the gulf between our two systems, China is not Cuba. Overriding strategic interests of the United States require engagement, not isolation. Happily, that is a lesson our successors finally seem to have learned, but only after a policy flip-flop that seriously damaged U.S. credibility.

North Korea: Engaged and Persistent Diplomacy

The Democratic People's Republic of Korea, an oxymoron of the first order, is arguably the most ominous rogue regime left on earth. Always a formidable conventional military power in Asia, their determination to build a clandestine nuclear-weapons program has made them even more dangerous. Ironically, as the threat of wholesale conflict dissipated with the end of the Cold War, the specter of nuclear proliferation subsequently intensified in one of the most unstable areas of the globe—the Korean peninsula.

Even as they signed the Nuclear Nonproliferation Treaty (NPT), the North Koreans secretly escalated their nuclear-weapons development program. Their duplicity in this regard has now been convincingly documented by international inspectors. While the North Korean nuclear threat is far from being resolved, Pyongyang no longer enjoys the luxury of pursuing their nuclear ambitions unchallenged. That in large measure is the direct result of little-noticed but intensive diplomacy by the Bush administration to force the North Koreans, after years of evasion, to live up to their international commitments by signing a safeguards agreement with the International Atomic Energy Agency (IAEA).

When North Korea joined the NPT in December 1985, it was obligated to sign this agreement and allow inspection of its nuclear facilities at Yongbyon within eighteen months. Three years later, as the Bush administration took office, they had yet to sign the agreement. Accordingly, in early 1989 we set in motion a two-track strategy to deal with the problem. The President ordered an increase in our intelligence activities to determine exactly what the North Koreans were up to at Yongbyon. At the same time, our diplomatic strategy was designed to build international pressure against North Korea to force them to live up to their agreement to sign a safeguards agreement permitting inspections.

The United States, of course, had zero influence with the totalitarian regime of Kim Il-Sung. Consequently, we enlisted the help of North Korea's superpower patrons—the Soviet Union and China—to pressure their client state. I raised this issue in my third meeting with Eduard Shevardnadze in Paris on July 29, 1989. I told Shevardnadze that the U.S. government believed the North was "probably" building the infrastructure for a nuclear-weapons program that might be operational by the 1990s. I asked for "a very active Soviet effort" to press the Koreans to stop reprocessing plutonium and to agree to IAEA safeguards. "We are already working on this issue," Shevardnadze replied. "They deny they are developing nuclear weapons." But he agreed to launch new high-level consultations to clarify the matter.

Two months later, during our September ministerial in Wyoming, Shevardnadze was less responsive. "We have heard your complaints before," he said when I pressed him again. "We refuse to stop sending (conventional) arms to North Korea when there is such a massive presence of U.S. military forces in the South." However, he agreed that stability on the Korean peninsula was a matter of serious concern and agreed to continue pressing the North about a safeguards agreement.

Throughout 1990, I raised this topic with Shevardnadze at almost every meeting, and pressed the Chinese likewise. During my Washington meeting with Foreign Minister Qian Qichen to discuss the Gulf crisis on November 30, Qian told me his government had "repeatedly" raised the matter with Pyongyang, which steadfastly denied any malevolent intentions.*

---

*The Chinese were always more defensive about North Korean intentions than the Soviets. During my November 1991 meeting with Premier Li Peng in Beijing, he brushed off my con-

Slowly, the cumulative effect of our diplomacy to isolate the North began to bear fruit with the Soviets. In June 1990, in a stinging symbolic rebuke to their longtime client in the North, Mikhail Gorbachev met with South Korean President Roh Tae Woo in San Francisco. Three months later, the Soviets established diplomatic relations with the South. Pyongyang was being squeezed, and when the Chinese subsequently declined to veto the entry of both Koreas into the United Nations, it was obvious that North Korea's contempt for proliferation standards was leading it on a course toward international isolation.

By 1991, American diplomacy also had the benefit of a powerful new psychological weapon—our stunning victory in the Gulf War. The awesome display of American military power during Desert Storm surely gave Pyongyang pause. They saw in dramatic fashion precisely what American technology had done—and could do to them, if it came to that. North Korea is a regime built and sustained by strength and force. They understand little else. This reality now worked to our advantage. If they continued to behave as an outlaw regime, they now feared that at some point they might have to confront the United States. Suddenly, we enjoyed significant credibility with a country with whom we had no diplomatic relations.

At the same time, the Gulf experience lent new impetus to our diplomatic offensive. After the war, it was apparent that Iraq's nuclear, chemical, and biological programs were far more advanced than Western intelligence had previously imagined. As a result, we intensified U.S. surveillance of the Yongbyon nuclear complex to try and determine more precisely what was occurring. And while the situation never reached the point of our actively considering a military strike against North Korea's nuclear facilities, the Pentagon nonetheless refined existing contingency plans for such an attack using cruise missiles, whose performance had been so impressive in the Gulf.

By design, U.S. diplomatic strategy toward the North Koreans during this period was a mirror image of what we'd done during Desert Shield. As we had in the Gulf, we were once again beginning to build an international coalition to press for a peaceful resolution, while raising the specter of United Nations sanctions if diplomacy proved fruitless—and when all else failed, allowing our use of force in the Gulf to speak for itself with Pyongyang.

At the same time, our policy offered the North some important carrots along with the sticks. In September 1991, President Bush unveiled his pro-

cerns. "I'm a nuclear engineer," he said. "They don't have the capacity to do this." Nevertheless, at my final meeting of that visit, Qian Qichen pledged that his government would continue to press the North Koreans to comply with IAEA safeguards.

posal to ban all tactical nuclear weapons worldwide. In concert with that decision, we announced on October 23 that all U.S. nuclear weapons would be removed from South Korea by April 1992. A month later, the first of those weapons was withdrawn. Suddenly, Pyongyang's ultimate rationale for developing its own nuclear arsenal—to provide a nuclear deterrent against an attack from the South—had evaporated.

This development in effect forced North Korea to begin discussions with Seoul—which at the time appeared to be the first step toward normalization. In December 1991, North and South Korea signed agreements pledging peaceful coexistence and confirming that the Korean peninsula should be free of nuclear weapons. On December 26, 1991, North Korea also agreed to sign the NPT safeguards agreement and allow IAEA inspectors into Yongbyon. Thus was American diplomacy directly responsible for an end to six years of intransigence by the North. In January 1992, senior U.S. and North Korean officials met for the first time in forty years at the United Nations. The U.S. delegation was led by Arnold Kanter, the new Under Secretary for Political Affairs. Kanter pointedly made clear that Pyongyang had a choice: live up to the international agreements it had just signed or face further isolation and the economic deprivation that went along with it.

Subsequent events, of course, suggested another factor in Pyongyang's decision-making process. Clearly, they believed they could camouflage the true extent of their program and dupe the international community into believing their intentions were wholly innocent. This proved to be a major miscalculation.

As part of the IAEA regime, North Korea was obliged to provide a written record of its nuclear program. This report gave technical experts important new information to compare with previous intelligence analyses. This triangulation quickly revealed that the North was concealing the true extent of their weapons program. IAEA inspectors promptly came to the same conclusion; an examination of materials turned over to them revealed that the North Koreans had reprocessed more plutonium than they were admitting.

In this same period, U.S. satellites discovered the existence of two suspicious facilities not listed in the documents provided to inspectors by the North. One of these sites was a building the North Koreans had hastily buried under tons of dirt and dotted with freshly planted trees. American intelligence easily detected the existence of this "hill."

In January 1993, one of the final acts of the Bush administration was to provide satellite photographs to the IAEA of this facility, which we had strong reason to believe had been used to conceal nuclear waste. That same month, the IAEA announced that plutonium samples suggested that weapons-grade fuel had been secretly diverted when North Korea shut down its reactor in 1989. After four years, and as a direct result of American efforts, North Korea's duplicity had been exposed.*

Angola: Ending the Cold War in Africa

At the start of the Bush administration, the Soviet-American proxy war in Angola was finally beginning to show signs of fatigue. Since 1975, Jonas Savimbi and his National Union for the Total Independence of Angola (UNITA), backed by the Reagan administration and many members of Congress on the political right, had waged a guerrilla war against the Marxist government of Angola, led by Jose Eduardo dos Santos and his Popular Movement for the Liberation of Angola (MPLA). Dos Santos's government was propped up by massive Soviet aid, more than 1,000 military advisers, and approximately 50,000 Cuban troops stationed in the former Portuguese colony. Savimbi was similarly sustained by millions of dollars in covert U.S. aid, and by assistance and support from South Africa.

Angola was a conflict that for the better part of two decades had been elevated by geostrategists into a pillar of Cold War rivalry. Like Central America, however, I saw Angola more as an issue of regional underbrush to

---

*The situation remained in an uneasy deadlock while the international community negotiated with North Korea to permit inspections of the two disputed sites. Then, in the face of North Korean threats to withdraw from the NPT, the Clinton administration struck its 1994 agreement with North Korea.

Our policy of carrots and sticks gave way overnight to one of carrots only—fuel oil to help run North Korea's beleaguered economy, two new nuclear reactors, and diplomatic ties. Moreover, Pyongyang has been given another five years to do what they agreed to do in 1991—allow a full inspection of their nuclear facilities. This agreement was an abrupt policy flip-flop, and in the end, in my view, will prove to have been a mistake that will make stability on the Korean peninsula less, not more, likely.

I hope I'm proven wrong in this view, and those who criticize have an obligation to suggest an alternative approach. Instead of caving in to Pyongyang's belligerent threats of war, I think the United States should have gone to the U.N. Security Council and obtained political and economic sanctions against the North for breach of its solemn international obligations, much as we did against Iraq (in my view, based on my conversations with them, the Chinese would not at that time have vetoed U.N. sanctions because they oppose a nuclear capability on the Korean peninsula), beefed up our forces in South Korea to whatever extent necessary, and quietly made clear to the North Koreans that for over forty years the U.S. nuclear deterrent kept the peace in Europe against an overwhelming Soviet conventional superiority, and that we were quite prepared to do the same on the Korean peninsula to meet our security obligations to South Korea and Japan.

Given their track record, there's substantial reason to question whether the North Koreans will keep their side of the current agreement. The worst part of it is that a dangerous message has been sent to other would-be proliferators in capitals such as Tehran, Tripoli, and Baghdad: sometimes crime pays.

be cleared away in the process of forging a cooperative strategic relationship with the Soviets. While this confrontation was understandable in an earlier time, by 1989 neither of the superpowers had overriding reasons for being embroiled in this conflict. It was time to move on to more critical issues—and the Angolan civil war seemed ripe for resolution.

In December 1988, a U.S.-brokered peace agreement guaranteeing the independence of Namibia was signed in New York. Under its terms, Cuba agreed to withdraw its troops from Angola while South Africa pledged to pull its forces out of Namibia. As a result, I believed there might be a way to bring peace to Angola that was acceptable to Savimbi. In every meeting with Eduard Shevardnadze in 1989 and 1990, I urged him to join with me in supporting peace negotiations that could lead to a reasonable settlement in Angola. He never gave me a formal commitment, but his remarkable candor about the deteriorating state of the Soviet economy persuaded me that Mikhail Gorbachev might be looking for a way out of regional entanglements such as Angola. My view was reinforced by intelligence reports that Soviet aid to Angola, while still substantial, had been reduced by approximately one-half in 1989.

Unfortunately, the Soviets and their MPLA proxies appeared to believe that with the departure of South African troops from Angola pursuant to the Namibian accords, they had one last chance to win a military victory. In December 1989, the MPLA launched a major offensive to crush UNITA once and for all. An emergency infusion of U.S. military aid, including lethal shoulder-fired Stinger antiaircraft missiles, helped Savimbi's forces repel an MPLA assault at Mavinga. After this it was apparent that neither side could win a military victory. During my March 1990 meetings with dos Santos in Namibia and Savimbi in Zaire, I urged them to recognize the inevitability of stalemate, and enter into peace negotiations.

During my December 1990 ministerial meetings with Shevardnadze in Houston, Angola was a prime topic of discussion. A pessimistic progress report by Hank Cohen, the Assistant Secretary for African Affairs, made it apparent that neither MPLA nor UNITA seemed willing to make any concessions for peace. When I asked him if he had any ideas about how to proceed, Shevardnadze surprised me with his answer.

"These guys can't make it on their own in negotiations," he said. "We need to give them a push." He proposed that Cohen and his Soviet counterpart adjourn for a few hours and craft the outlines of a conceptual framework for a peace agreement. "Then we need to bring in all the parties and sell it to them," Shevardnadze said.

I was initially somewhat dubious that we could broker an agreement in which the principal combatants were secondary parties to the deliberations. As we talked, however, Shevardnadze persuaded me that the Soviets were willing to use their leverage on the MPLA to force them to the bargaining table. I knew that we could do the same with UNITA.

The document hammered out by Cohen and the Soviets included among its provisions a cease-fire, guarantees to protect UNITA's political rights, and a timetable for free elections. The key to the document, however, was what came to be known as the triple-zero formula. As part of a peace agreement, the United States would stop military aid to Savimbi, and the Soviets would do likewise with MPLA. In addition, we would both publicly support a ban on arms shipments to either side by outside parties—a veiled reference to South Africa. Without lethal aid, it was a given that neither side could win a military victory, and both would quickly recognize that reality.

After agreeing on the terms of this framework agreement on December 11, we hurriedly arranged a meeting in Washington two days later between American, Soviet, Portuguese, MPLA, and UNITA representatives. To signal our determination to exert our respective leadership in unmistakable terms, Shevardnadze met with Savimbi, and I met with Angolan Foreign Minister Pedro Castro van Dunem. Our messages were identical and clear: in the interests of bringing peace to Angola, the United States and the Soviets were fully prepared to suspend arms shipments to their longtime surrogates.

The superpower intervention had the predictable effect. On May 1, 1991, following several weeks of negotiations in Portugal, MPLA and UNITA reached agreement on peace accords. A de facto cease-fire began two weeks later, followed by the departure of the last Cuban troops on May 25. Six days later, I was delighted to attend ceremonies in Lisbon, where the peace agreement was signed by Savimbi and dos Santos.

Before the ceremony, I met privately with Savimbi to reassure him that the United States was firmly committed to continuing non-lethal aid to UNITA and would only recognize an Angolan government that emerged from the elections scheduled for September 1992.

Those elections were held on schedule, and by most accounts were fairly conducted. Four days later, however, Savimbi claimed election fraud. On October 11, much to my disappointment, fighting resumed in Angola. The United Nations negotiated a cease-fire in November that held for only four weeks. In December 1992 UNITA agreed to respect the cease-fire, and an uneasy peace settled over that war-torn country. But not for long. The pain and suffering unfortunately was not over.* However, at least the An-

---

*After yet another cease-fire, a new peace accord was signed in November 1994. With the help of several thousand U.N. advisers, that cease-fire has held, and a government of national reconciliation has been agreed to.

golan conflict was no longer a proxy war. The Cold War had ended in Africa.

Haiti: Taking What Democracy Gives You

George Bush often spoke about our hopes to build in the Americas "the world's first completely democratic hemisphere." But tiny, tragic Haiti was a glaring exception. When Haitians went to polling places in the 1987 presidential elections, more than forty were massacred in political violence.

When Lt. Gen. Prosper Avril, Haiti's dictator, balked at moving forward with new elections in 1989, we took advantage of an attempted coup against him from within the military to press for his departure. We provided strong support and resources to move the electoral process forward and urged the Organization of American States, United Nations, and the National Endowment for Democracy to flood Haiti with international observers. The December 1990 elections were the freest and most peaceful in Haitian history. The winner, Jean-Bertrand Aristide, was reputed to be "anti-American." Still, the United States was the first government to recognize him, and our administration provided more economic assistance to Haiti after his election than all other governments in the world combined.

When Aristide was overthrown by a military coup on September 30, 1991, the President immediately suspended all U.S. assistance. Two days later, I addressed an emergency meeting of the OAS in Washington. I told my fellow foreign ministers: "We do not and we will not recognize this outlaw regime. Until President Aristide's government is restored, this junta will be treated as a pariah throughout this hemisphere—without assistance, without friends, and without a future." At U.S. urging, the OAS adopted unanimously the first hemispheric trade embargo levied against a coup d'état.

Some within the administration believed it would have been more prudent to support the return of democracy in Haiti while distancing our policy from Aristide himself, a leader with a mixed reputation and record. We all had concerns about his erratic behavior and human rights record. Our experience in dealing with him during his eight months in office, and following the coup, left most of us feeling he was a bit of a weak reed.

At the same time, there was never substantial debate about separating U.S. policy from Aristide. My position was simple: if you support democracy, you support what democracy brings you, so long as the process is free and fair, and the victors are not clearly bent on using the electoral process simply to gain power and then in effect destroy democracy by establishing authoritarian rule. By his resounding 67 percent margin of victory, for better or worse Aristide embodied the democratic concept—even if it could be argued that he himself was something less than the perfect embodiment of that concept.

Moreover, I believed a larger issue was at stake. It was the hemisphere, not simply Haiti. Democracy was on the march throughout the Americas, but it was a fragile and reversible process. If the coup in Haiti were allowed to succeed, a chain reaction could easily ensue throughout the region. Haiti had to be the object lesson of our policy—the singular example that the United States government was not prepared to allow other coups to succeed. An unequivocal and unambiguous response was absolutely critical. In June 1991—just three months before the coup—every nation in the OAS had voted to adopt a proposal, authored by our administration, that committed the nations of the hemisphere to respond collectively through the OAS to any threat to any member's democracy. The "Santiago Declaration," as it was known, was a revolutionary political change in our hemisphere. Latin America and the Caribbean, chastened by the OAS failure in Panama, rejected the doctrine of noninterventionism, and committed our hemisphere's democracies to the collective defense of freedom.

Haiti was the first test case of that commitment. Would-be coup makers were watching our response. Had the U.S. and the OAS failed to enact tough sanctions, that commitment would have degenerated into an empty and meaningless threat, and others in the hemisphere would have been undoubtedly moved to overthrow democratic governments. Instead, under the Santiago Declaration, the OAS pressured President Alberto Fujimori to call for new elections in Peru following his dismissal of the Peruvian congress in April 1991, and successfully rolled back similar action by President Jorge Elias Serrano of Guatemala in May 1993.

The Bush administration believed that there was a national interest in seeing democracy restored to Haiti, but it was not sufficiently vital (when the security of our country or the safety of our citizens was not at risk) to require using military force. Therefore, no serious consideration was given to the use of such force to restore Aristide to power in Haiti. In our view, the national interests of the United States clearly did not require risking American lives and expending billions of dollars in a full-scale military invasion and occupation. And history had taught us that it could not have been done *without* an extended occupation—something our successors now know.

El Salvador: Making Peace

Although the initial focus of our Central American policy was to promote democratic elections in Nicaragua, we believed we also had an opportunity to end the war in El Salvador. Indeed, we thought that the democratization of Nicaragua would further the prospects of peace in El Salvador.

From the beginning, we looked for opportunities to signal our support for a negotiated settlement, particularly one related to elections and democracy. When the FMLN antigovernment Marxist guerrillas floated a proposal in February 1989 to delay the upcoming presidential elections for six months as part of a peace settlement, I commented publicly that the proposal "merited serious consideration." Although this proposal was not adopted, the newly elected President Alfredo Cristiani surprised observers when he said in his inaugural address that his top priority was to bring the war to an end through a negotiated settlement.

The massive FMLN offensive into San Salvador in November 1989, though a military defeat for the guerrillas, was in many ways a catalyst for negotiations. On the one hand, it ended any illusions among the guerrillas that the civilian population was ready to follow their call for an armed uprising against the government. But it also shattered the military's hopes that the guerrillas were a spent force and that the war would soon end through attrition. Finally, the brutal murder of Jesuit priests by elements of the armed forces in the final days of the offensive galvanized the U.S. Congress as never before to threaten the Salvadoran government with a cutoff of military aid.

Navigating through these currents was difficult. On the one hand, we had to signal to the Salvadoran military that they must support a negotiated peace—and a purge of human-rights violators—or risk losing U.S. support. On the other, we had to convince hard-line factions among the guerrillas that if they continued the war, the United States would not abandon El Salvador. To send varied messages, we worked closely with Mexico, Venezuela, Spain, and Colombia—the nations designated by U.N. Secretary-General Boutros-Boutros Ghali to be "friends" of the peace process. We also began a dialogue with the FMLN factions whom we were convinced were most committed to negotiations. As in Nicaragua, the Soviet Union joined the United States in strong support of the negotiations.

We worked closely behind the scenes with all of the actors in El Salvador to promote concrete agreements between the government and the guerrillas. The trust and goodwill engendered by the Bipartisan Accord on Central America and the successful elections in Nicaragua made an important difference. At crucial moments in the peace process, we urged key congressional Democrats to give us the running room we needed to keep the negotiating process moving forward, and they responded constructively.

There were many twists and turns in the process, but slowly, steadily the momentum for peace prevailed. One of my most satisfying moments as Secretary of State was to participate in the January 1992 signing ceremony in Mexico City of the peace accords between President Cristiani and the leaders of the FMLN. The Salvadoran peace was a victory for all sides; the guerrillas agreed to lay down their arms and join the democratic process, but far-reaching reforms of the armed forces, judiciary, and political and land systems were also enacted. Most heartening to me was witnessing the start of genuine national reconciliation between Salvadorans who had fought for more than a decade in one of Latin America's bloodiest civil conflicts.

The Economics of Diplomacy:
Laying a New Foundation

When George Bush asked me to be his Secretary of State, I understood that international economic affairs would be an important part of my portfolio. It was certainly a part for which I felt well qualified. As Secretary of the Treasury, I had spent nearly four years on matters as varied as helping to hammer out a free-trade agreement with Canada or working with our leading trading partners to bring some order to the chaotic world of exchange rates. I took special pride in proposing that the Group of Five Industrialized Nations (G-5) be expanded to a group of seven (G-7) by adding Italy and Canada, and then in fostering an active cooperative spirit among the G-7. When it came to international economics, I knew the issues and the players.

My years at Treasury had convinced me that the political, diplomatic, and military strength of the United States were all indelibly linked in a delicate balance to economic vitality. To put it another way, our country's strength derives in large part from its economic power. The importance of this principle has not always been recognized by American policy makers. Throughout my prior public service, I'd watched time and again as U.S. economic chits were traded away for foreign-policy gain. In my first speech to State Department employees in April 1989, I called attention to this practice and suggested that it be eliminated. Shortly thereafter, our posts abroad were notified to that effect. I was determined that henceforth, the economics of diplomacy would no longer receive such short shrift.*

The 1990s were shaping up to be an era of economic opportunity and risk. Interdependence was inexorably binding our domestic economy to the outside world. Economic rivalry between the United States and its traditional allies in Western Europe and Japan was on the rise, a trend that grew stronger as the common Soviet threat receded. South Korea, Taiwan,

---

*I also made clear in that session that while I thought State had an important role in international economic policy, the lead agency in this area should be Treasury, as it had been when I was Secretary.

Singapore, and Hong Kong—the "tigers" of East Asia—were growing with lightning speed. The People's Republic of China was becoming an economic giant in her own right. Even Latin America, sunk for decades in debilitating debt and self-destructive policies, was showing signs of economic life. Free-market ideas were sweeping the world. Finance ministers and central bankers everywhere were putting away their Karl Marx and dusting off their Adam Smith.

In short, the geostrategic revolution of my years at State would be matched by an economic one. Our stakes in its outcome were vast. All bets, it seemed, were off, but where and how should we place our new ones?

"Where" was more obvious than "how." Western Europe and East Asia were clearly critical: we and the major economies of these two regions generated three-quarters of world output. Latin America was also a clear priority: it was geographically close, boasted a population of 450 million, and thanks to the political and economic reforms taking hold throughout the continent, represented an increasingly attractive market for American goods, services, and investment.

But how? Clearly one-on-one efforts with our trading partners would be an important part of our strategy. Indeed, during my time at State, the United States would negotiate scores of bilateral agreements liberalizing two-way trade and investment. But it was also vital that we complete the negotiations begun in the second Reagan term for a new multilateral trade agreement under GATT. Further liberalization would clearly benefit the United States, the world's greatest exporting nation. But there was another compelling reason to push for a GATT accord: the risk that the world might fracture into regional trading blocs, with the European Community (EC) leading the way. Only GATT could ensure that regional groups would not exclude outsiders, including the United States.

I was also convinced that we could advance our economic interests through innovative *regional* strategies. Regional agreements could deliver greater results, in terms of opening markets to American goods and service, than one-on-one negotiations. They could complement other American interests in a region by extending our presence and enhancing our influence. And they could help lay the institutional groundwork for ongoing economic cooperation. Issues come and go. But institutions abide.

The great generation of American leaders who set the course of American postwar policy during the late 1940s knew as much. Men like Truman and Acheson were above all, though we sometimes forget it, *institution builders*. They created NATO and the other security organizations that eventually won the Cold War. They fostered the economic institutions—GATT itself, the World Bank, and the International Monetary Fund—that brought unparalleled prosperity to the nations of the free world during the decades following World War II. At a time of similar opportunity and risk, I believed we should take a leaf from their book.

Ronald Reagan had dreamed of a North American Common Market that would unite the United States, Canada, and Mexico. With the 1988 U.S.-Canadian Free Trade Agreement, half of that dream had become a reality. But the time had simply not been ripe for a similar agreement with Mexico. Under President de la Madrid in 1986, Mexico started to make the turn away from economic autarky and toward free markets. I had worked with many of these new thinkers on Mexico's debt problem in the 1980s. But we knew that much more liberalization of the Mexican economy was required. Just as important, given Mexico's political sensitivity about the U.S., we knew a major free-trade initiative had to come from the Mexicans. We could prepare the way, but Mexico had to take the first step.

From the beginning of the Bush administration, improving our ties with Mexico was part of a broader regional strategy. This included progress toward a peaceful resolution of the conflict in Central America, progress on Latin debt issues, and reform of the Latin American economies themselves.

The administration moved quickly on the economic front. During the transition and early in 1989, Brent Scowcroft and I worked with Federal Reserve Chairman Alan Greenspan and Treasury Secretary Nick Brady to craft a plan to reduce the burden of debt in the Third World, especially in Latin America. Brady's plan, announced in March, differed in detail from the strategy we pursued under the Reagan administration—the so-called Baker Plan—which had extended the maturities of existing loans and offered additional ones. The new plan emphasized debt forgiveness. Both, however, shared a fundamental tenet: relief was linked to reform. By August, Mexico had negotiated important debt relief under the Brady Plan. Other Latin American nations were to follow.

By 1990, economic liberalization, however uneven, was taking hold from the Rio Grande to Tierra del Fuego. This represented a double opportunity for the United States. By supporting economic reform we could promote our political goals of stability and democracy in a region not traditionally known for either. At the same time, we could open up new and growing markets for American exports and investment.

The Enterprise for the Americas Initiative (EAI), developed by Treasury with input from State and announced by President Bush on June 27, 1990, represented the administration's response to the new economic reality in Latin America. It included additional debt relief, the creation of a multilateral investment fund for Latin America, and a formal administration offer to negotiate free-trade and investment agreements with Latin American nations. The last was the most significant. President Bush believed correctly that "trade, not aid" would best serve the cause of hemispheric prosperity.

A major step toward achieving that goal had occurred two weeks earlier, when the President and Mexican President Carlos Salinas de Gortari had announced their intent to negotiate a free-trade agreement. The process that would eventually lead to the North American Free Trade Agreement (NAFTA) had begun.

From the beginning, we all knew that NAFTA would be no cakewalk. Indeed, some of the President's advisers were initially less than enthusiastic about proceeding. Negotiators would eventually produce a text that ran to five volumes. It would cover trade, investment, the environment, regulation, standards, and mechanisms to resolve disputes. The talks would be complicated by the addition of Canada, which formally sought participation shortly after the Bush-Salinas announcement.

We would also have to sell the agreement politically in the United States. Free-trade agreements always produce losers in some sectors of the economy. But overall, they always generate greater economic activity, which produces far more winners than losers. NAFTA would be a boon to the American economy, create hundreds of thousands of jobs, and generate tens of billions in additional output. It would also be the cornerstone of a new relationship with Mexico and enhance close ties on the whole set of issues that don't respect borders: narcotics, the environment, and immigration. And it would help advance other U.S. objectives in Mexico, including the democratization of its political system. But opposition would still be strong. Important elements of organized labor and the environmental movement would oppose it, as would their allies in the Democratic-controlled Congress.

The political problems confronting President Salinas would be even greater. A free-trade agreement would demand accelerated but painful reform of the Mexican economy. Powerful industrial and agricultural interests would fight tooth and nail against opening their markets. Finally, Salinas would have to overcome a hundred-and-fifty-year tradition of anti-American sentiment: he would be accused of selling out to the *yanquis* every step of the way.

Salinas's personal commitment proved critical to negotiating NAFTA. Just weeks after George Bush's election, I had accompanied him to Houston for the traditional get-together between the American President-elect and his Mexican counterpart. This time the meeting was especially opportune: Salinas himself had just been elected. Between them, the two presidents-elect created the "Spirit of Houston": a new partnership that looked forward to common opportunity, not back to an often-troubled past. The subject of a free-trade agreement was not raised. Indeed, at the time Salinas was still publicly opposed to the idea. But the Spirit of Houston provided the personal foundation for the revolution in bilateral relations that occurred during the next four years.

For my part, I took the lead in raising the profile of the U.S.-Mexico Binational Commission, a meeting of cabinet members from both nations that had last convened in 1987. I brought nearly half the Bush cabinet with me to the Mexico City meeting of the commission in August 1989. The American side developed strong working relationships with key Mexican players. These relationships proved decisive when the two sides, joined by Canada, got down to the difficult business of negotiating NAFTA.

As with GATT, other agencies took the lead in the actual negotiation of NAFTA. But I retained a strong personal interest in the course of the talks. My focus was not on the technical details of the agreement, but rather the domestic politics that could ultimately make or break it. In particular, I worried about two deadlines.

The first was the expiration of congressional fast-track authority in early 1991. This authority limited Congress to an up or down vote on trade agreements negotiated by the President. Without it, individual members could literally amend an agreement to death. Opponents of NAFTA saw the fast-track vote as a chance to derail negotiations almost before they had begun. Even with concessions on labor and environmental concerns, it took a full-court press to win congressional renewal of fast-track authority in May 1991.

The second deadline that worried me was the 1992 election. Like the President, I wanted NAFTA completed during his first term. The earlier in 1992 we could submit an agreement to the Congress, the better. Any slippage into the campaign season proper would further politicize an already contentious issue. Time was of the essence. At State and later the White House, and together with Brent Scowcroft, I always stressed the need for sustained progress, not only to the Mexicans and Canadians, but also to those in our administration who didn't seem to give NAFTA the priority it deserved. Bob Zoellick, my right-hand man on NAFTA, set up an informal channel of communications with José Cordoba de Montoya, Salinas's chief of staff. Through it, the two sides could identify problems and prod our respective bureaucracies.

Negotiations went forward with stunning speed, considering the complexities involved. U.S.-Mexican talks began in the summer of 1990. Canada joined in mid-1991. As late as July 1992, serious differences still divided us. But on August 12, 1992, President Bush was able to announce that a draft text was complete. On December 17, President Bush, President Salinas, and Canadian Prime Minister Brian Mulroney signed the agreement in Mexico City.

By then, of course, a new Democratic President and Congress had been elected. Final approval of NAFTA had to wait. But its ultimate form was all but identical to the one negotiated under President Bush. And I think today it is, as we always believed it would be, one of George Bush's enduring legacies. Not only has the agreement created a free-trade zone 375 million inhabitants strong, but it represents a truly historic breakthrough in our relations with Mexico and the rest of Latin America. By the end of the Bush administration, Chile was already formally seeking to join NAFTA. Other Latin American countries were close behind. President Bush's vision of a hemispheric system of free trade—larger even than Ronald Reagan's dream of a North American Common Market—had captured the imagination of a continent.

At the beginning of this century, one of my predecessors, John Hay, declared that "the Mediterranean is the ocean of the past, the Atlantic the ocean of the present, and the Pacific the ocean of the future." By the time I became Secretary of State, Hay's prophecy was rapidly becoming a fact: the year 2000 would herald the beginning of the "Pacific Century." My job was to make sure the United States would be a major part of it.

Above all, I was determined that any move toward economic integration in East Asia include the United States. At State, I would try to check any move by the East Asians to exclude us—gently if I could, not so gently if I must. But I wanted also to use broadened economic cooperation in more positive ways. Closer links to the economies of East Asia would help open up dynamic markets to American exports and investment. In addition, they would complement our existing political and strategic ties to a region that we had considered vital since the time of Teddy Roosevelt.

While I was at Treasury, Bob Zoellick and Bob Fauver, an able career public servant, had brainstormed about a U.S.-East Asian consultative group along the lines of the G-7. I even suggested the possibility of such an organization in a speech. The 1988 campaign intervened and the idea remained embryonic. But when both joined me at State, we kept our eyes trained east for an opportunity. It arrived the month of George Bush's inauguration—from Australia.

That January, Prime Minister Bob Hawke publicly proposed the idea of an East Asian group to promote free trade in the region. His proposal did not include the United States, but we had no difficulty persuading Hawke, a good friend of the United States and George Bush, to extend us an invitation to a November 1989 meeting of the forum for Asia-Pacific Economic Cooperation (APEC) in Canberra. Twelve nations were to be APEC's charter members: Australia, the United States, Japan, Canada, South Korea, New Zealand, and the members of the Association of Southeast Asian Nations (ASEAN)—Indonesia, Malaysia, the Philippines, Singapore, Thailand,

and Brunei. Together, APEC members generated half the world's output and over a third of global trade. Even though APEC involved international economic matters, I felt it was such an important concept that I made a point of leading the American delegations to APEC ministerial meetings.

APEC members reflected widely divergent states of economic development. Beneath a diplomatic veneer, mistrust was rampant, especially of the Japanese. APEC might possess limitless long-term potential. But in the short-term, it would have to choose its issues carefully. Anything too far ranging—for instance, a move to transform it rapidly into a free-trade zone—could divide APEC's members and doom it in its infancy. In the beginning at least, our focus would be less on issues than on institutionalization. We needed first to regularize meetings, formalize consultation, and build trust. To assist in this regard, we agreed that an ASEAN nation would host every other annual meeting. Before APEC could run, it would have to walk.

We achieved two key objectives at the Canberra meeting. Singapore and South Korea agreed to host the next two annual ministerials. And expert working groups were commissioned to study ways in which APEC could encourage cooperation on a broad range of economic, educational, and environmental issues. With the 1990 Singapore ministerial, APEC gained some sense of permanence, though my personal participation was hampered by a bad case of intestinal flu—the worst bout of illness that I endured while Secretary of State.

The third ministerial, at Seoul in 1991, found both APEC and me in good health. China, Taiwan, and Hong Kong were now full members—a critical step forward that had required much negotiation before a final compromise on representation could be reached. The expert working groups were producing reports on subjects as varied as the promotion of tourism, the development of trade and investment databases, and pilot projects to combat marine pollution. A Group of Eminent Persons had been appointed to make recommendations on the organization's future development. Only two years old, APEC was a going and growing concern.

Despite this progress, agitation for an exclusively East Asian trading bloc refused to go away. Malaysian Prime Minister Mahathir bin Mohamad, in particular, continued to hawk his idea of an East Asian Economic Group (EAEG) along the lines of the EC. Mahathir was not seen as particularly pro-American and was considered likely to cause mischief if crossed, so I took a moderate line on his idea in public. In private, I did my best to kill it. Some East Asian APEC members were inclined to go along with it merely to placate the insistent Mahathir. At the APEC meeting in Seoul, Korean Foreign Minister Lee Sang Ok suggested his country might support Mahathir's proposal out of Asian solidarity. I reminded Lee that it was Americans, not Malaysians, who had shed their blood for Korea forty years before. My message was simple: All countries are *not* equal. The South Koreans got it, and did not press for an EAEG.

Without strong Japanese backing, the EAEG represented less of a threat to our economic interests in East Asia. Here, as in so much else in the Pacific region, the U.S.-Japanese partnership was key. If the partnership held, then freer trade and investment through APEC was not only possible but likely. If it fractured, an East Asian trading bloc was a virtual certainty. And U.S.-Japanese relations were troubled. The reason, as always, was trade.

I was glad enough to leave the task of trade negotiations with the Japanese to Carla Hills, the capable and tenacious U.S. special trade representative (USTR). However, because our security relationship with Japan was so important, having been the source of stability in East Asia and the Pacific for over forty years, I always kept a watching brief on U.S.-Japanese economic relations. I was no apologist for Tokyo: Japan's restrictive trade practices were an international scandal. But I knew from my own experience at Treasury that only patient, determined, *private* negotiation would work with the Japanese. At State, I did not hesitate to intervene in U.S.-Japanese trade relations when I felt the risk of an absolute rupture had grown too high.

A case in point was the Structural Impediments Initiative (SII). Launched by President Bush and Japanese Prime Minister Sousuke Uno at the 1989 Paris economic summit, the SII represented a high-level effort to avoid American trade sanctions against Japan and a possible trade war. The U.S.-Japanese talks under SII, which were very capably headed by Dick McCormack, the Under Secretary of State for Economic Affairs, were easily the broadest ever undertaken between the two countries. For the first time, Japan agreed to consider addressing some of the microeconomic fundamentals that drove its trade surplus with the United States. These included land-use policies, business organization, and pricing.

On February 23, 1990, however, the talks collapsed. Prime Minister Toshiki Kaifu and President Bush met at Palm Springs in early March to reaffirm their commitment to the SII process. But time was short. Under intense pressure from Congress, USTR would probably have to announce another round of trade sanctions as early as April 30. I knew that former Prime Minister Noboru Takeshita would be visiting Washington in mid-March. I had worked closely with Takeshita both when he was Prime Minister and, even earlier, when he was Finance Minister. He was still a major power within Japan's ruling Liberal Democratic Party.

It was a good time, I felt, for a game of golf with an old friend—and a little behind-the-scenes negotiation. We played eighteen holes. We explored options. Takeshita was prepared to offer, on behalf of the Japanese government, a number of concessions, chief among them a massive increase in public investment aimed at stimulating domestic demand. Our informal discussions provided the framework for an eventual compromise. Talks resumed. And the interim assessment issued by the two sides at the end of the month was positive enough (barely) to avoid the imposition of sanctions. U.S.-Japanese relations continued to exhibit occasional strains, and I weighed in from time to time. But a major crisis had been reached and passed.

I've long believed that the U.S. has no bilateral relationship in the world today that is any more important than its relationship with Japan. As Secretary of the Treasury, I worked with several Japanese governments to coordinate our underlying economic policies in the interests of promoting exchange rate stability. In 1989, I called for a "global partnership" between the U.S. and Japan and believe that that idea has merit even today. Japan has been a model of economic development for the rest of the world. And yet for powerful historical reasons, Japan has yet to exert political influence commensurate with its economic might. Over the last decade, however, Japan has slowly but steadily begun to assume greater international leadership—a development I welcome and have long encouraged. Japan's strategic engagement is an essential counterbalance to ensuring that China and North Korea do not yield to the temptation of regional adventurism. Moreover, a greater Japanese role through the United Nations—including, eventually, the possibility of some sort of status on the Security Council—can help assure that Japan's power is a force for stability around the world as well as in the Pacific. Despite our differences over trade, when the Bush administration left office, this critical partnership was still sound.

On November 23, 1993, the Congress approved the North American Free Trade Agreement. It went into effect on January 1, 1994. In November of that year, the leaders of APEC countries meeting in Indonesia committed themselves to a free-trade zone reaching from New York to Bangkok by the year 2020. And on December 1, 1994, Congress approved a final GATT agreement, marking an end to a process that had begun eight years before at Punta del Este, Uruguay.

Of course, these events occurred after the Bush administration was over. But none would have been possible without the sustained efforts of our administration. As I followed the press coverage, I confess to feeling a slight pang of regret. After all, in the world of might-have-beens, it should have been another President celebrating these triumphs. But I also felt profound pride in what President Bush and his administration had accomplished. With NAFTA, GATT, and APEC, we had in fact laid the groundwork for a new and liberalized international trading system, firmly rooted in free-market principles, that would promote prosperity in the United States and around the world for decades to come.

CHAPTER 32

SUPPORTING FREEDOM IN THE NEW INDEPENDENT STATES

Are we still adversaries or not?
—*Boris Yeltsin to George Bush, Camp David, February 1, 1992*

C old. Bitter cold. That's the only way I can describe the world outside my frosted car window on February 14, 1992, as we hurtled down what passed for a highway deep in the heart of Russia. In a scene straight from *Dr. Zhivago*, the steppe was buried in snow, the wind whistled over frozen lakes, and the pockets of birch and evergreen trees that dotted the landscape seemed like oases in a desert. At one point, I saw a horse and sleigh cutting across a field, crossing the snow-covered expanse that seemed to go on forever. From Yekaterinburg, several hundred miles east of Moscow on the Siberian side of the Urals, I was headed two hours south for Chelyabinsk-70, a city that most of the world had not even known existed a few months before.

One of the Soviet Union's two nuclear-design facilities, Chelyabinsk-70 was analogous to our Los Alamos or Lawrence Livermore labs, with one major difference: its mere existence, let alone the work being done there, was a state secret. It had never appeared on Soviet maps, and few people in Yekaterinburg, the closest major city, even knew about Chelyabinsk-70 until shortly before our arrival. In the Soviet Union, Chelyabinsk was a black hole, but in the month-old Russia of February 1992, it was a potent symbol of U.S.-Russian cooperation and, in perhaps a fitting coincidence, Americans were visiting it for the first time on Valentine's Day.

After a long journey off the main highway, and passage through a series of checkpoints, we crossed several perimeter fences of barbed wire to arrive at a rather run-down, eight-story research building. In almost every window, I could see the scientists, technicians, and clerical assistants pressed against the glass, waving enthusiastically and cheering, their voices just perceptible through the storm windows reinforced to keep out the harsh Russian winter. I felt a bit as though I had landed from Mars, an alien curiosity that these men and women just had to see with their own eyes. Set aside the cold and multiply the size of the crowd geometrically, and I could have been back in Tirana, Albania, in June 1991: the outpouring of emotion for America felt the same.

We were escorted to a cramped lecture hall to meet with twenty-five of the center's senior scientists. The room reminded me of my undergraduate days at Princeton but surely would be unrecognizable to today's undergraduates. It was a throwback to the 1950s, but I knew that the men who sat before me were some of the most modern, sophisticated minds in the world. As we sat down, I thought, Here are the men that designed the weapons that defined the Cold War, and we're about to discuss how we in the West can help them secure their future. History is indeed ironic.

Our meeting began with a detailed description of the former Soviet nuclear research program and the work in which the scientists were now engaged, under the direction of the newly independent Russian Republic. "There is no shortage of ideas, but the main difficulty lies in economics," one of the scientists told me and my staff. Indeed, they raised a number of ideas with me: from manufacturing synthetic diamonds to developing fiber optics, to improving nuclear magnetic resonance imaging. Clearly, these men were thirsting to turn the knowledge they had gained designing warheads to peaceful, cooperative uses.

But they faced a severe problem, one told me. "In recent years, the financial situation of the institute has been trying," and it was obvious that unless a way could be found to pay them, the Iranians, North Koreans, and other rogue regimes would try to buy their nuclear know-how on the cheap—what we had come to call the "brain-drain" problem.

"That is exactly what we're here to address," I answered. "Rather than thinking of this as a 'brain-drain' problem, we should think of it as a 'brain gain,' in which the international community works with Russia and the other independent states to help you turn your talents to interesting and useful civilian projects."

I described our proposal for a joint scientific center, which would act as a clearinghouse to match nuclear-weapons scientists with interesting and intellectually challenging research projects. They reacted enthusiastically. They then explained that what they needed immediately were facilities for safe storage of disarmed nuclear weapons, and help in finding ways to use these destroyed materials beneficially.

After the meeting, we took a group photo at a statue of Igor V. Kurchatov, the father of the Soviet nuclear program. Since no cameras or tape recorders had ever been allowed in the facility, it took some effort on my part to persuade the institute's management to allow the picture. As I argued the point back and forth with the chief scientist, Yevgeni Avrorin, and the Deputy Minister for Atomic Energy, Viktor Mikhailov, several of the scientists whispered, "Let him do it. Let him do it." Finally, Avrorin and Mikhailov relented. "See, it is a new day," I said to the beaming scientists, who clearly wanted the world to know and see more about their work.

I then went with a handful of aides to the materials-testing laboratory, where lithium, plutonium, and uranium were handled experimentally. Since we would be in areas that might contain radioactivity, my aides and I donned white robes and white hats—I felt as if I were at a bakers' convention—and then put on clear plastic boots over our shoes. We were also given a personal Geiger counter. We looked like the cast from "Lost in Space." The labs seemed decades out of date. It was another reminder of how the Soviets had had to compete with the West; facing chronic technological inferiority, the Kremlin had solved military-strategic problems by devoting massive resources to them, and eventually managed to find solutions only after much expenditure of effort. But in the process, Moscow had bankrupted the state and society, impoverishing all but the most elite apparatchiks.

By the time we finished our lab tour—and checked to be certain we weren't glowing—darkness had fallen heavily, and we loaded into our motorcade for the ride back to Yekaterinburg. We had to circle around the compound to leave, and as we did, we traveled past a well-lit machine shop. In it stood a solitary man, working away on what looked to be a lathe. As we drove by, he stopped his work, looked up, and slowly lifted his arm into the air, pointing his thumb skyward as if to say: Thank God the Cold War is over. Let us now be friends.

In the weeks and months that followed, as I traveled across the newly independent states of the former Soviet Union and worked with President Yeltsin and other Russian reformers, I would often think of the man in the machine shop and his humane and touching gesture. Whenever my energy would flag, his image would remind me of our unique opportunity to help build democracy and freedom, and it would revitalize my hope, my faith, and my efforts.

The Coordinating Conference

Following a few days in Houston for the Christmas holidays, I returned to Washington on January 5 for what I knew would be a hectic month. Besides traveling to Mexico City for the signing of the El Salvador peace accords, and to Managua, Nicaragua, I would host the Coordinating Conference, travel to Moscow for a follow-on meeting to the Madrid Middle East Peace Conference, attend meetings at the United Nations, and join President Bush and President Yeltsin at Camp David.

Looking ahead, I knew that we were approaching a critical stage in our relationship with Russia and the newly independent states. With the Soviet Union's collapse in December, each republic was trying to establish positive relations with the West, especially the United States, and our ability to affect their behavior would never be greater. At Princeton, I had outlined three major areas—politics, economics, and security—in which we hoped to move forward. On the security front, I knew we needed to act decisively to secure the safety of Soviet weaponry, particularly weapons of mass destruction. While the states of the former Soviet Union were now formally independent, most were also members of the Commonwealth of Independent States, and questions lingered about nuclear command and control, implementation of existing treaties, and nonproliferation policy. To that end, I sent Reg Bartholomew and a team of interagency experts to Moscow in mid-January to meet with their counterparts, to discuss how the United States could provide assistance for both safe storage and elimination of Soviet nuclear weapons, particularly tactical warheads. "I want you to know," I wrote Andrei Kozyrev on January 14, "how critically important it is that we can show some real progress on identifying ways to support accelerated, safe disablement, consolidation, and elimination of Soviet nuclear weapons."

In terms of Western support for economic and political reform, I wanted to use the Coordinating Conference, scheduled for January 22–23, to jump-start assistance efforts in three ways. First, I wanted to send a very clear signal of support to the Russians, Ukrainians, and others that the entire world wanted their experiments with democracy, free markets, and independence to succeed. That goal would be partially fulfilled by the makeup of the conference itself, which included seven international organizations and forty-seven states, ranging from Argentina and Australia to Thailand and the United Arab Emirates, hardly your typical Eurocentric conference.*

But I also wanted to add a touch of drama that would break through the

---

*With less than a month to prepare what would be the largest conference ever held at the State Department, it was worst nightmare for Karen Groomes, Lynn Dent, and Bill Davis, who supervised the historic eighth-floor rooms of the State Department. They solved it with their usual grace and creativity, which included ferrying fifty-four foreign ministers and heads of organizations to lunch at Blair House by two school buses, a solution that gave security services headaches.

typical media coverage of such a diplomatic event. I wanted to create a story line that might be transmitted by CNN and other international media to help instill hope in those in need in the former Soviet Union, while also galvanizing a public consensus (and private efforts) in the United States. Margaret Tutwiler came up with the perfect vehicle: an airlift of medicine and food to every one of the new emerging democracies. Much as the Berlin Airlift created an image of support, a humanitarian airlift to the former Soviet Union—using U.S. Air Force planes—would be a clear signal that we had entered a new era. At my request, Rich Armitage, who had taken command of our assistance efforts to the former Soviet Union, put together what we called "Operation Provide Hope"—a plan to fly fifty-four sorties of food and medicine in one week to all of the new independent states, including an initial twelve sorties of giant C-5 transport aircraft out of Rhein-Main Air Base in Frankfurt. All in all, Operation Provide Hope would deliver over 38 million pounds of medicine and food.*

My second main goal was to expand the number of states involved in providing humanitarian assistance to Russia and its neighbors, and also to foster cooperation among the donor governments. For the most part, aid programs had been conducted bilaterally—and almost all of that had come from either the United States or Europe. We wanted to see a truly global, coordinated effort.

The Europeans were still upset that we hadn't proposed that the EC cosponsor the Coordinating Conference—with the French and the EC Commission in particular showing their pique. In my meetings on the margins of the conference, I tried to explain to the Europeans that our effort was intended to expand the sources of assistance to the former Soviet Union and that it would help lift the load off them. I felt the more thoughtful of my interlocutors—Douglas Hurd, Hans-Dietrich Genscher, Hans Van Den Broek, for example—understood me, but I wasn't sure about the rest.

My point, however, was underscored by what resulted from the conference, which had been organized around working groups in four key sectors: energy, food, medicine, and shelter. In each, we managed to have the international participants develop an action plan that would be imple-

---

*Since we had only days to put the plan together, the airlift required the extensive cooperation and support of both the Department of Defense and the Joint Chiefs of Staff. Dick Cheney and Colin Powell spared no effort both in the planning stage—in which JCS military planners and Eric Edelman, Cheney's chief Sovietologist, came over to State and helped identify "targets" for sorties—and in the actual execution of the airlift. They gave Armitage everything he needed, including on-the-ground support in the former Soviet Union through the On-Site Inspection Agency (OSIA). Five years before, the targeters would have been identifying sites to be hit by ICBMs, and the OSIA staff would have been chasing Soviet missiles. It was yet another indicator that the Cold War had been turned on its head.

mented as we moved into spring. Manfred Woerner also offered NATO support in logistics and planning. Jean-Claude Paye, Secretary General of the
Organization for Economic Cooperation and Development (OECD), suggested it should serve as a clearinghouse for technical-assistance programs.
Getting fifty-four nations and multilateral institutions to coordinate in this
fashion was a monumental task, one ably directed by Ken Juster, Larry
Eagleburger's deputy and my point man for organizing the conference.

In addition, governments outside of Europe and North America also
made large unilateral offers of assistance, showcasing the global nature of
the effort. For example, the Philippines provided training programs in rural
banking, mid-level management, and small business; Thailand approved
$450 million in commodity credits; Argentina offered to house 100,000 ref-
ugees; Korea announced over $1 billion in export-import and commodity
loans; Saudi Arabia released $1.25 billion in assistance; and Oman pledged
$200 million to help Azerbaijan develop its oil production and export ca-
pacity.

My third objective was to use the Coordinating Conference as a deadline to get our own bureaucracy moving. In early January, I went to my
colleague, Dick Darman, the Director of the Office of Management and
Budget, and basically shook him down for $645 million, which the Presi-
dent announced in opening the conference. In addition, however, I wanted
to show there were non-cash sources of assistance that could be equally
valuable. In a mad rush, Larry Eagleburger, Dennis Ross, Margaret Tutwiler, and Bob Zoellick, supported by two maniacal staffers, Sheila Heslin
and Lonnie Keene (whom Margaret came to call the "kids" for their enthusiasm), found, cajoled, borrowed, and begged a wide variety of assistance
from other government programs. These included such diverse things as
five C-5 aircraft-loads of medical supplies, $8.7 million of oral antibiotics
left over from Desert Storm, funding for a Farmer-to-Farmer program,
money for the creation of a Eurasia Foundation, 400 tons of dried milk for
St. Petersburg, and 10,600 tons of butter, butter oil, and bulgur wheat to
Armenia.

Yeltsin the Leader Emerges

Four days after the end of the Coordinating Conference, I arrived in Moscow. Although co-hosting the first session of the Middle East Peace Process
Multilateral Talks was the principal reason for my trip, I saw my time in
Russia as a key opportunity to engage Yeltsin, Kozyrev, and the rest of the
new Russian leadership.

Shortly after my arrival on January 27, I met with Kozyrev in the Bo-
gayevsky Room of the Osobnyak—he was the fourth Foreign Minister I had

met there in three years. After a quick discussion on the next day's Middle East talks, Kozyrev steered the discussion to the situation in Russia. "I appreciate your efforts during last week's conference," Kozyrev said. "President Yeltsin is very enthusiastic about the airlift and has given orders to local Russian officials to assure that the supplies get delivered." We also touched on nuclear issues—since both President Bush and President Yeltsin were about to launch major new initiatives—but we left the real substance for my meeting with Yeltsin.

I raised our concerns over possible Russian arms sales to countries such as Iran. "I know Russia has a pressing need for the hard currency earned from these sales," I began. "But these will threaten regional security and create real problems in U.S. public opinion," which was essential if we were to provide Russia with any more aid. Kozyrev said that while he understood our views, "arms are one of the few commodities Russia can sell, and our government is under great pressure from the military to proceed with these sales." We agreed that the two presidents would discuss this issue further at Camp David.

After a day of Middle East talks, which were marred by the Palestinians' refusal to attend, I sat down with Boris Yeltsin on the morning of January 29. Two days before, Yeltsin had suddenly left Moscow for an "undisclosed location," prompting rumors in the Western press about his health and stability.

After five minutes, however, it was clear that if Yeltsin had disappeared for any reason, it was not to recuperate, but to put the final polish on his brief. He was impressive. I saw a different Yeltsin from the man I'd seen before. Whereas in the past, he had often seemed vague and rather glib, now he spoke at great length, with no notes, about highly technical issues. He focused almost exclusively on security questions—on the arcana of the strategic nuclear-reduction proposals President Bush and he had initiated, on the dismantling and destruction of nuclear weapons (strategic and tactical), on his vision of joint U.S.-Russian strategic defenses, on the "brain-drain" problem, and on the need to establish understandings on conventional arms transfers.

Yeltsin praised the "new tradition" in U.S.-Russian relations, exemplified by the fact that Washington and Moscow had previewed their nuclear proposals privately instead of announcing them through the press. He felt our positions were "so close."

"This is much better than the old habit of one-upmanship," I responded. "Three years of experience has convinced me that without sufficient will at the top, the opportunities our nations have will not be realized."

"I couldn't agree more," Yeltsin said. "The militaries won't do it by themselves."

Yeltsin wasn't eager to discuss the economic situation, but had several ambitious ideas on security issues. Among them were joint U.S.-Russian efforts to create a global defense system and, in order to help stem the "brain drain," funding of projects to keep former Soviet scientists busy. With remarkable candor, Yeltsin told me that in the past we had been deceived on the existence of a Soviet biological weapons program. "It will be dismantled within a month," Yeltsin promised, after which international inspectors would be allowed full access to the site. On nuclear command and control, he said that he had final control over all strategic missiles in the former Soviet Union. A phone link was going to be established between the four nuclear states, and if all agreed, "then God forbid, I would have responsibility to push the button." He then added, "In any case, in a few days, they won't be aimed at the United States."

Although Yeltsin had alluded to retargeting Russian missiles in a recent interview on ABC, the gravity of this comment nearly jolted me out of my chair. "Could you clarify that last point about targeting?" I asked.

"If President Bush and I could agree," he responded, "none of the Russian missiles would be targeted on the U.S., since the two countries would effectively be allies." In order to assure that weapons not under Russia's direct control could not be retargeted, Yeltsin said, "we are considering whether during routine maintenance of missiles in the other three republics, a minor component could be switched to disable the systems."

In going over the upcoming Camp David agenda, Yeltsin asked me what I thought about putting together a joint statement to follow his talks with the President. "Such a statement would have worldwide significance," he said, and I nodded in agreement. "We have to overcome forty years of bad feelings in our country," I said. "Such a statement would help."*

That night, I wrote the President that Yeltsin was coming to America "as a leader determined to exude confidence, and determined as well to show that he is every bit the player on the international stage that his predecessor was." Yeltsin's two-hour performance that day, and his focus

---

*I also weighed in with the President. "Frankly," I cabled him, "I think such a statement happens to be very much in our interest, as well. It would bolster Yeltsin and his own stake in his approach to us. I think it would also fortify a basic premise he now seems to be operating on: namely, we're no longer adversaries; we're no longer estranged countries; instead, we should be friends, and even allies. As such, he doesn't just seek cooperation, he seeks real partnership." As had been the case with the Vnukovo and Helsinki joint statements during the Gulf crisis, I had my staff work up a pithy draft statement.

on security issues in particular, showed that he wanted to be taken seriously. He was moving symbolically (namely, his nuclear-targeting initiative because they could, in any event, be quickly and easily retargeted), but also substantively in ways that could genuinely transform the nature of the U.S.-Russian relationship.* I knew that if he were to continue such a course, it would be important that we give Yeltsin all the support we could. From this perspective, I told the President, "it will be very important to him to show at Camp David that he has established the same kind of close personal relationship with you that Gorbachev had."

Before leaving Moscow, I met with Defense Minister Shaposhnikov, who as the senior defense official of the Commonwealth of Independent States, had the unenviable task of controlling, organizing, and dismantling the vast Soviet military. For an officer raised in the Soviet school, Shaposhnikov displayed extraordinary respect for the democratic process and for the expansion of relations with the United States.

"We should talk more and more," he said in his welcoming remarks. "It helps us avoid mistakes." In describing a recent meeting of 5,000 military officers in Moscow, he added that "some hotheads among us say that we should give ultimatums to the Presidents. They can't understand that the Presidents are elected by the people."

On the Iranian arms issue, Shaposhnikov assured me that Russia had "no buyers" in Tehran, but criticized our sales to allies like Turkey. Like Kozyrev, he said that the Presidents should discuss this at Camp David. "We need to agree, not just talk," he observed.

Although some differences remained, I thought that, like Yeltsin and Kozyrev, Shaposhnikov was doing a remarkable job in an extraordinarily difficult situation. "Before I leave," I told him, "I want you to know that we appreciate your efforts and wish you well with your difficult task."

"I don't mind having to deal with these problems," he said. "But I must admit that at times I envy my predecessors and the relatively easier times they enjoyed, when the enemy was clear and the issues seemed simple."

As we left Moscow, in one of the fiercest snowstorms we had ever encountered in all my travels as Secretary of State, I was optimistic about the meetings ahead. In a little over a month since independence, Russia, although still clearly a state in transition, appeared stable. The nuclear issues were being addressed. And every leader with whom I had sat down—Yelt-

---

*However, I added an important caveat in my night note to the President: "We need to remember that for all his desire to develop and affirm a relationship of friendship with us, Yeltsin is a genuine Russian nationalist. He will be sensitive to charges that he is making unilateral concessions and is being exploited by us."

sin, Kozyrev, and Shaposhnikov—was serious, responsible, and anxious to cooperate with us.

The Spirit of Camp David

After the first meeting at the United Nations of the leaders of the five permanent members of the Security Council, I headed to Camp David on February 1 for President Bush's meeting with Yeltsin. Since this was a "working" visit of the Russian President (rather than a full-dress "state" visit), President Bush felt that it would be better to meet informally in the rustic confines of Camp David. As had been the case in Wyoming in 1989 with Eduard Shevardnadze, and at Camp David in 1990 with Mikhail Gorbachev, the President hoped that getting outside the Washington Beltway would promote a more relaxed and informal discussion.

Indeed, Yeltsin was relaxed, but in the way a championship tennis player is relaxed right before a match: on the top of his game, fully prepared, and ready to go at it. Speaking once again without notes, the Russian President opened with a discussion of economic reform. (This was a welcome topic, since the issue had been virtually absent during my talks with him in Moscow.) "We are five years late in starting," he said, because genuine reform "only really became possible after the collapse of the empire and Communist ideology." He argued that Russia had "a clear program" that it had initiated with the freeing of prices on January 2. Yeltsin admitted the shortcomings of Moscow's approach, noting that they had not been following a "classical plan" because they did not have time to adopt reforms in banking, taxation, and other areas before allowing prices to rise.

While there had been "hard times" since the price rise, he was more concerned about February, March, and April, which he said would be "critical. We hope the people can stand it. If reform fails, the current forces in power will be replaced by conservative forces, hawks, who will reject these reforms. We will have a police state, repression, and the arms race will recommence. It will be a waste of billions of dollars for the U.S. and involve the whole world."*

He stressed that food was his main concern. "I am thankful for the major airlift," he said, but understandably pointed out, "one cannot feed Russia with that." Noting that it would take the efforts of "dozens of states" and "mass transportation" from all over the world, he thanked the Presi-

---

*He noted that his team, led by Yegor Gaydar, was young but talented. "The President," he said, "must protect this team from criticism in the Supreme Soviet and elsewhere. Gaydar would have been eaten by wolves without the protection of the President."

dent for the Coordinating Conference, indicating that it was a positive step in the right direction.

Switching to politics, Yeltsin said, "So far, our cooperative relationship has moved slowly—I am talking about the last seven months now. This was a period when you didn't know who to deal with between Gorbachev and Russia." He indicated that he understood our ambivalence, but "today, the situation is crystal clear. You must send aid to Russia and the other Commonwealth states." He felt the move to the Commonwealth was "correct and inevitable. When the Union collapsed, states would have moved in all different directions had there not been a Commonwealth. There would have been four nuclear states and the army would have divided into bits."

While the Commonwealth was young—he had told me in Moscow that it was a "fragile infant"—it had been effective in reducing disputes among the republics. "We won't allow conflicts between us and Ukraine," he pledged. "We seek to be flexible and not push Ukraine around."* As he said that, Marshal Shaposhnikov nodded. "Russia has no imperial designs and has no wish to dominate others. We want all in the Commonwealth to be equal. Each meeting of heads of state emphasizes that. But we cannot idealize the situation. The baby," Yeltsin concluded, "is only two months old, and we must take care of it and be careful not to drop it."

Yeltsin then moved on to nuclear-weapons issues, a subject he had obviously spent the bulk of his time preparing for. "The launch button is in my control and is second with Marshal Shaposhnikov," he began. "The four heads of state have instantaneous communications. If, God forbid, anything happened, we could talk right away. It is incumbent on me to act, and on Marshal Shaposhnikov. It is technically not feasible for the others to control the nuclear weapons. It is impossible."

Although nothing in his background suggested that he had a special aptitude for interest in arms control, Yeltsin got into every detail imaginable, almost as if to show off his knowledge—and, more important, his seriousness. At one point, after describing to us how you could transform plutonium 239 and uranium 235 into "cakes" usable for civilian atomic power stations, he playfully remarked, "Do I sound like an expert?"

His greatest concern was proliferation, and the most acute threats were from the south. "Saddam Hussein is not in a position to steal a nuclear warhead from the top of a missile," he pointed out, "but plutonium and uranium could be taken from a storage facility. This could blackmail the

---

*Yeltsin later noted that there were 11 million ethnic Russians in Ukraine and said, "I don't think Ukraine will take any sharp turns due to this fact." He also said that Ukraine was the "main destabilizing factor," but stressed his good personal relations with Kravchuk. "I talk constantly with him by phone."

world." The Russians were also "hurrying to remove tactical nuclear weapons from the other independent states, first from Kazakhstan, to prevent them from falling into Islamic hands."

On the "brain drain," I previewed the science center idea. Yeltsin agreed that this was "a fundamental issue that had to be tackled" and that we should work together on this idea. "We have two thousand nuclear experts," he said. "If we launch a joint program, we can provide employment for many of them."

When it was time to break for lunch, Yeltsin interjected, "One last matter. Are we still adversaries or not?"

"No, we are not," the President said. He gave Yeltsin the final draft of the joint declaration I had discussed with the Russian President in Moscow. "This moves us away from the old era." The statement proclaimed a new era of U.S. and Russian "friendship and partnership" and declared a formal end to more than seventy years of rivalry. Yeltsin was eager to add to the statement that the relationship had moved to one of allies, but the President was reluctant to go that far. "We are using this transitional language because we don't want to act like all our problems are solved," he said.

In the press conference following lunch, the two presidents released the joint statement and announced that they would exchange formal visits before the end of the year. Both leaders were effusive in their praise toward one another. "Russia and the United States are charting a new relationship, and it's based on trust," the President said. Yeltsin followed: "From now on, we do not consider ourselves to be potential enemies."

As we headed back to Washington that night, I thought back on the presidential meetings I'd attended during my government career and realized how truly special and historic this intense session with Yeltsin had been. For the first time, the elected leader of a democratic and independent Russia had sat down with an American President. Together, the two had begun to chart a course of cooperation. I thought to myself, Talk about "beyond containment"!

To the Kishinev Station!

Just over a week after Yeltsin left the United States, I left Washington for a ten-day journey that would take me across the former Soviet Union, from Moldova, on the border with Romania, through the Caucasus and Central Asia to Siberia. The collapse of the Soviet Union had liberated Russia, but it had also created eleven other new states (fourteen, if you counted the Baltics) which were all searching for an international identity and an appropriate model for political and economic development. For the first time in decades, even centuries, these nations were finally free from Kremlin control. As the first high-ranking U.S. official to visit most of these countries, I wanted to reinforce their sovereignty and independence (as a hedge against any Russian revanchism and, in Central Asia, to counter Iranian influence) and to influence their governments toward democracy and free markets. I had few illusions. I knew many of these governments were run by apparatchiks-turned-democrats and that their political cultures had deeper roots in traditional authoritarianism than democracy. But having defeated Soviet communism, our prestige was at its zenith, and I hoped to influence events on the margin.

It was perhaps the most fascinating journey I took as Secretary of State. Most of the places we visited had been closeted from the West for decades, and several of the cultures were virtually unknown outside the region. The majority of the stops were so radically different from Moscow and from Russia that I often felt I was in the Middle East or South Asia. Several times, I found myself thinking, We shouldn't be asking ourselves why the Soviet Union fell apart. With so many different peoples spread so far apart, we should be asking how it managed to stay together so long.

The trip itself was a logistical nightmare, as some of the new independent states were ready to put up only the hardiest of visitors. Indeed, it wasn't even clear at first that we would be able to make the trip at all; most airports in the former Soviet Union had been closed by a fuel shortage, and Lynn Dent had to carry thousands of dollars in cash to pay for fuel to get us from stop to stop. They didn't sell on credit, even to the U.S. government, in places like Dushanbe and Bishkek. For most of the trip, we had to carry our own water—three hundred bottles of it; throughout the cabin of our plane, there were quarts of mineral water tucked everywhere, so much so that my staff joked that they were more likely to drown in the event of a plane crash than burn to death. We also carried much of our own food. Heat and hot water were also going to be hard to find. While I found all of this exciting and even enjoyable, I'm not sure all of the staff enjoyed it with the gusto I did.

Before heading into the CIS, my first stop, on the morning of February 10, was Rhein-Main Air Force Base in Frankfurt, Germany, for the ceremonial opening of Operation Provide Hope. True to his reputation, Rich Armitage had delivered. In fact, he had overdelivered, and managed to get several other states to join in the airlift.

That evening, we were off to our first stop—Kishinev, Moldova—a mere slice of a state wedged between Romania and Ukraine. There I met with Moldovan President Mircea Snegur, whose biggest challenge was trying to contain the efforts of ethnic Russian separatists in the Dniester region (which unfortunately erupted into violence that summer). I told Snegur that I planned to support full U.S. recognition of Moldova soon, provided the government could abide by certain assurances.*

Snegur's comments to me reflected what I found to be a recurring theme throughout the trip. "This transition has led to a breakdown of many of the links which bound the former Soviet Union together, leaving many problems to be resolved," he said frankly. "We in Moldova know that we must change the system. We want to open up to the outside world, and the U.S. has a position of particular importance in this process."

"It's not always easy to move toward democracy and free markets, especially when you've been going in the opposite direction for a long time," I responded. "But we will continue to support you as long as you support the principles you've just outlined." We also discussed economic reform, and as at every other stop, I had Ed Hewett pass along several "model" agreements (for example, a tax treaty and bilateral investment agreement) that were the customary basis for commercial relations. (By the time we finished the trip in Central Asia, we were calling Ed the "Father of Central Asian Capitalism.")

The Cauldron in the Caucasus

That afternoon, we flew southeast across the Black Sea and over the Caucasus Mountains, their snow-capped peaks cutting through the clouds to bask in the bright sunlight. From the plane we saw Mount Ararat, believed to be the site of the remains of Noah's Ark. Landing in Yerevan, Armenia, we quickly saw the distress resulting from a massive earthquake and the continuing brutal war over Nagorno-Karabakh. This war had resulted in an energy embargo of Armenia by Azerbaijan. Despite the region's beauty, politics in the Caucasus were among the most strife ridden in the world, so dangerous in fact that we skipped Georgia because of the civil war raging there.

I had never found a city in the former Soviet Union to be well lit, but in Yerevan there was little if any light at all, and even less heat in the buildings. In contrast to the cheeriness of Kishinev, Yerevan seemed eerily

*While the United States had recognized the independence of all the former Soviet republics, establishing diplomatic relations depended upon receiving certain assurances, which I pressed with each leader that I met. Among these were commitments to CSCE principles; our "five principles"; open, democratic elections; human rights, including minority rights; free emigration; accession to the Nuclear Nonproliferation Treaty; accession to international conventions relating to weapons of mass destruction; strict export controls; a defensive military; and a free-market economy, with an agreement to pay a fair share of the financial commitments of the former Soviet Union.

empty, even spooky, with little life on its dark, quiet streets. After a moment's rest at our massive guest quarters—some of my staff must have been a good three hundred yards away and we were all in one building—I departed for the presidential residence for a working dinner with President Levon Ter-Petrosyan. (His Foreign Minister, Raffi Hovanissian, was an American citizen from Los Angeles, and such a dapper dresser that my security detail came to refer to him as "Valley Dude.")

The bulk of our discussion that night concerned the situation in Nagorno-Karabakh, an ethnic Armenian enclave in Azerbaijan which was fighting for independence. Similar to the situation in Moldova's Dniester region, the Armenia-Azerbaijan struggle over Nagorno-Karabakh symbolized the real dangers of virulent, ethnic nationalism in the post-Soviet states.

"We are delighted to be in a free, democratic, and independent Armenia," I opened. "The United States has a special affinity for Armenia, but the situation in Nagorno-Karabakh must be dealt with through peaceful means."

"I realize that the only guarantee of Armenia's independence is to live in peace," President Ter-Petrosyan said. "We are seeking a peaceful resolution to the Karabakh issue—and are participating in negotiations toward that end." Ter-Petrosyan had an easygoing, folksy style that cut right to the point. "This is a question, above all, of self-determination," he continued. "Yesterday I spoke with the Azeri President, and he agreed that a peaceful solution is the only way."

I knew that while these assurances did not guarantee an end to the conflict, they were certainly a step in the right direction. "I want you to know that if the U.S. can help, you should tell us. We will be quick to say no if we cannot. Both you and Azerbaijan have a large task before you to build independence—that alone is a big enough job. It is important that resources, time, and attention not be diverted."

"As much as we in Armenia have done to overcome our tragic past, Nagorno-Karabakh may cause a return to that," Ter-Petrosyan closed. "Your presence alone will serve as a stabilizing factor in the region."

The next day, we took the short hour hop to Baku, Azerbaijan, where we saw the other side of this struggle. The first thing I noticed in Baku were the large number of oil derricks jammed right up against one another, and the pipelines, most of which were aboveground. The whole town smelled of crude oil, and for a moment, I was reminded of my youth, when I would often drive through the Goose Creek–Baytown area adjacent to Houston and experience the same sights and smells. The second thing I noticed was complete chaos; the Azeri Foreign Minister dived into our staff van, and President Ayaz Mutalibov made me late for my next stop, as a "bite to eat" turned into a multicourse lunch. But the third thing I realized was that everyone had a viewpoint 180 degrees at odds with what I had heard in Armenia the evening before. For a moment, I thought some unfair god had delivered me back into the middle of another peace process.

When I met with President Mutalibov, he predictably laid all the blame for the crisis on Armenian expansionism and a concomitant effort to destroy his government. His account was noticeably more bitter and pessimistic than Ter-Petrosyan's.

"The former Soviet Union under Gorbachev, and Russia under Yeltsin, are biased against Azerbaijan," he exhorted. "The international media has been influenced by the Armenian diaspora."

I told him firmly that, while I was not an expert on every aspect of Nagorno-Karabakh, both Armenia and Azerbaijan had enough problems "and do not need the added burden of this crisis." I reiterated that the United States was willing to do what it could to help the parties find a negotiated solution, but that we supported the mediation efforts of Russia, Kazakhstan, and CSCE.

Before I left Baku, I cabled messages describing my talks on Nagorno-Karabakh to Andrei Kozyrev and Nursultan Nazarbayev, who were leading the efforts to mediate the conflict. While both Ter-Petrosyan and Mutalibov struck me as pragmatic leaders with a healthy appreciation of their conflict's complexities, "you have got your work cut out for you," I wrote the two leaders.

I also cabled the President my view that we should avoid direct involvement in mediating this unrelenting crisis. "After hearing both sides of the story," I wrote, "I am more convinced than ever that this is a crisis in which we should support the efforts of the Russians and the CSCE to broker a solution."

A New "Great Game" in Central Asia?

After visiting briefly with U.S. Army personnel who had just arrived in Baku with an Operation Provide Hope shipment, we headed across the Caspian Sea to Central Asia and Ashkhabad, Turkmenistan.* Having seen Kazakhstan and Kyrgyzstan, I was eager to see more of Central Asia and the lands where the British and other European powers had played the "Great Game" of high-stakes diplomacy in the nineteenth century. We, of course, were concerned about Iran, and supportive of Turkey's efforts to bring Central Asia more into its sphere of influence.

---

*Armitage, ever one to impress our traveling press corps, had made sure that there was a U.S. Air Force C-5, C-141, or C-130 loaded with medicine or food at each of our stops.

Moreover, while Moldova, Armenia, and Azerbaijan were all unique, the states of Central Asia were truly exotic—a fact that was clear to me as we landed low over the Kara Kum Desert into Ashkhabad and could see Iran only twenty miles away. As soon as I stepped onto the runway, I was greeted by a group of men in native costume with big sheepskin hats. And as we drove to the presidential palace, the streets were lined with people waving, no doubt having been given the day off for that purpose. (Some practices died hard in the former Soviet Union.)

I met with Turkmen President Saparmurad Niyazov in a traditional thatched-roof wooden yurt on the grounds of his dacha. When we entered the yurt, Niyazov gave me a huge robe lined with caribou pelt, and, bypassing the standard diplomatic accommodations, we sat on the floor.

I opened the meeting by reviewing with Niyazov the assurances needed to establish U.S. diplomatic recognition, and he affirmed his commitment to each. When I came to the assurance concerning nuclear nonproliferation, he told me that Turkmenistan had three sets of tactical nuclear weapons from the former Soviet army. Nonetheless, he was committed to nuclear nonproliferation. (Since we knew about the existence of the tactical nuclear weapons, I had checked with the Agency and DOD and learned that Moscow had disarmed and deactivated the weapons—but hadn't told the Turkmens.)

On economic reform, Niyazov said simply, "We need help. We support the idea of marketization, but we need your businessmen." Turkmenistan's economy was among the most primitive of the former Soviet republics, and I promised him that we and others would be prepared to help. When he asked that we send "forty to fifty businessmen who would be prepared to invest at least one million dollars in a new enterprise," I explained that "while our economy doesn't work that way, we would be pleased to negotiate with you a legal framework within which U.S. companies would feel confident in investing here."

We then went next door, where our aides were beginning the sixth course of a fifteen-course traditional Turkmen meal, including stuffed birds and delicious mutton in all shapes and sizes. Feeling that it would be rude to have the President and me join halfway, our Turkmen hosts insisted that the meal start over from the first course. I've always prided myself on my eclectic appetite, but this was too much. "I can't eat another thing," I whispered to Tom Niles and Margaret Tutwiler. "You wouldn't believe how much food we had back there in that yurt."

All in all, it was a fantastic (if almost overwhelming) dinner, complete with music, dancing, and singing. After a marathon of toasting, President Niyazov stood to signal the end, and we finally left for a bit of rest—and digestion.

After starting the next day visiting a museum and rug factory, we left the desert of Turkmenistan for the mountains of Dushanbe, Tajikistan. While one of the most underdeveloped of the former Soviet republics, Tajikistan is one of the richest in terms of natural scenery. Wedged between Pakistan and Afghanistan high in the middle of the Pamir Mountain range (the "roof of the world," we were told), Tajikistan holds the two highest peaks in the former Soviet Union, and more than fifty percent of the country lies above 10,000 feet.

While the Tajiks have rich mining resources, they have little arable land. Unlike other Central Asians, the Tajiks are Persian, most of them speak a language similar to Farsi, and thus they have more ties and contacts with Tehran. Given that, Iran was a primary topic of our discussion.

My two hours with Tajik President Rakhman Nabiyev was similar to all of my meetings during the past few days: he was effusive in his praise for the United States and agreed to work to fulfill all of the assurances I outlined. He stressed his desire to move toward a market economy, and explained that mining might be the road to Tajik prosperity. "This is not a large country," he said, "but it is rich with natural resources. When God distributed the wealth, Tajikistan got the mountains." (He also told me, "We have the highest birth rate in the world—and we won't give this away.")

Nabiyev ominously noted that the Iranians "are showing a lot of interest in Tajikistan." I explained that, while the United States understood why Tajikistan would want to have good relations with its larger neighbors, "Iran creates problems for many countries, not just the U.S." I cautioned Nabiyev that as the Iranian regime seeks to export its revolution, "one doesn't need a crystal ball" to see why Iran might be interested in Tajikistan. "If asked for my advice on dealing with Iran," I said bluntly, "I'd respond with two words: be careful." Nabiyev nodded in agreement.

Following our meeting, I put on some casual clothes and visited a village named Ramit in the middle of the Pamir Mountains, about an hour's drive outside of Dushanbe. There I met with the village leader and his eight children in his home. The villagers all wore colorful native dress, and many of the men had long white beards. After witnessing the presentation of a village "tea and salt" ceremony, we went deeper into the mountains to see a beautiful game preserve. My guides told me that Afghanistan lay on the other side of the ridge that loomed above us, and when, months later, Tajikistan dissolved into civil war, partially abetted by Afghan guerrillas, I didn't find it surprising.

The next morning, we left the Tajik mountains for Yekaterinburg, formerly Sverdlovsk, the hometown of Boris Yeltsin, and one of Russia's leading industrial cities. While most of one whole day was spent on my visit to

Chelyabinsk, I also had the opportunity to view the execution site of Czar
Nicholas II and examine what were believed to be his remains and those of
most of his family. The opportunity came completely by chance. During
dinner with the region's governor, he told me that the Czar's remains were
nearby, and asked if I would like to see them. I, of course, said I would, so
the next day Governor Rossel gave me a tour of the site.

Since the Bolshevik Revolution, the Soviet government had denied the
very existence of the killings and had protected the location of the site very
closely. Indeed, the chief scientist who had discovered the bones told me
that he had known of their existence ten years before, but had been too
scared to let anyone know. He showed us a black-and-white photograph of
a soldier standing on the site of the buried bones. The soldier had died, and
his family had given the photograph to the scientist, and that's how they
had found where the Czar was buried.

First, we visited the actual spot of the assassination, marked merely by
red carnations in the snow and an Orthodox Russian cross.

We then went to view the skeletons—and the stench of formaldehyde
told you right away you were in a morgue. Downstairs, in a small, dimly lit
room, the skeletons were lined up on tables with white linen tablecloths. I
could see places where bullets had shattered bones after first snuffing out
the lives of their victims. The Czar's skull had half a row of gold-crowned
teeth, and the Czarina still had many of her teeth. The chief scientist told
me that they still had not been able to locate the skeletons of the son Alexis
and one of the daughters.

The Russians wanted independent confirmation that these bones were
genuine, and so I agreed to make forensics experts from the FBI and our
armed services available to them.

I left Russia for our final Central Asian stop, Uzbekistan, on Saturday,
February 15. Uzbeks have historically dominated the region, in part because they comprise nearly forty percent of Central Asia's population, and it
was obvious to me that President Islam Karimov felt that that dominance
had been justified. He told me we had concentrated too much on Kazakhstan by going there first.

More authoritarian than democrat, Karimov spent three hours delivering a long monologue detailing the litany of abuses Uzbekistan had suffered
at the hands of the old Soviet regime. He nevertheless expressed his appreciation and commitment to the five principles I had outlined in September
1991. (When he did so, he showed me that he carried around a copy of the
principles in a notebook in his coat pocket.) Although I was pleased to hear
Karimov's verbal commitment to these principles, his track record in following them had been less than stellar. "I'm glad you support our principles
but we are primarily interested in performance," I told him. When I pressed

him about his government's refusal to register opposition political parties, he initially defended his position by claiming that the parties he acted against were linked to Libya or the KGB. When I pushed him further, he finally agreed to "relax" party registration requirements. Indeed, Karimov's near-filibuster had made me late for my meeting with the opposition, the leaders of Erk and Birlik, whose courage in the face of Karimov's decidedly undemocratic practices reminded me of the opposition groups with whom I had met in Bulgaria and Romania in 1989.

Uzbekistan, as was the case with every other Central Asian stop, would not have been complete without a banquet. After the standard double-digit-course meal, the entertainment arrived—first some traditional singers, followed by dancers.

The next day, we flew with President Karimov on his plane to his hometown, the ancient city of Samarkand. One of the hubs of the Great Silk Trail that linked Asia and Europe, Samarkand was fascinating. From the Ulug-Bek Observatory to the Guri-Emir Mausoleum, virtually every sight and sound reminded us of the vibrancy and endurance of Central Asian culture.

Yet as we walked around the city, which some archaeological investigations suggested was thirty-eight centuries old, I knew that underneath its calm exterior lay deep-rooted ethnic animosities. In the past, the Tajiks had laid claim to Samarkand and another Uzbek city, Bukhara. Indeed, much of the former Soviet Union was a patchwork quilt of different linguistic and national groupings.

Tragically, communism had doubly burdened all the new states. First, central planning had left their economies crippled or, at the very least, severely distorted. Second, the imposition of Marxism-Leninism, an alien ideology and organizing principle, had frozen in time deep-seated ethnic antagonisms. Indeed, the Communists, especially Stalin, had deliberately shifted populations and borders to pit one nationality against another to maintain Moscow's rule. The combination had created a witches' brew of interethnic conflict, fueled by competitive nationalism. This danger was quickly overtaking fears of nuclear war as the emerging security challenge of the post–Cold War world—and not just in Eurasia, but in the heart of Europe as well.

CHAPTER 33

"HUMANITARIAN NIGHTMARE" IN BOSNIA

These are real people who are dying. We are not talking politics anymore.
> —*Bosnian Foreign Minister Haris Silajdzic to Secretary Baker, April 14, 1992*

Once in, where does it end?
> —*British Prime Minister Major to Secretary Baker, May 22, 1992*

While I was in Yugoslavia on June 21, 1991, warning against its descent into conflict and chaos, Janja Loncar, the wife of the Foreign Minister, was introducing Susan to the people and places of Belgrade, a city eerily calm for a nation teetering on the precipice of war. The centerpiece of the tour was a luncheon, held in her honor. Attending were women from the capital's political, legal, artistic, and professional circles, and they represented a variety of Yugoslavia's elite. But this was not a normal social affair, for at the lunch, as elsewhere in the city that day, the talk of the table was war and its inevitability.

"No one wants a war, but we are going to have one, nonetheless," Susan was told repeatedly. It was all the more puzzling, she told me later that day, because the women represented the full range of Yugoslavia's nationalities, and none wanted violence but all expected it.

"What about the religious leaders? Can't they do anything?" she asked, only to be told that they had been coopted during Tito's time and had no real influence.

"But I don't understand," she questioned more than one of her tablemates, "why you're going to have a war if no one wants it."

"Two bull-headed mountain men wouldn't have it any other way," several of the ladies told Susan, in a clear reference to Serbian leader Slobodan Miloševic and his Croatian counterpart, Franjo Tudjman.

This pessimistic outlook paralleled the concerns of Brent Scowcroft and Larry Eagleburger, both of whom had spent years in Yugoslavia (Brent as a military attaché, Larry as Ambassador). My day in Belgrade left me equally gloomy. As I wrote the President on my way home from the Balkans that June, my visit to Yugoslavia had been "downright depressing. Frankly, I think it's easier to deal with Shamir and Assad than it is to try to affect Miloševic and Tudjman.

"What I found in Yugoslavia was an air of unreality among the key players, and I am afraid it will be very difficult to head off a violent collision. . . . To make matters worse, those locked in their positions have a false sense of security, basically believing the worst can't or won't happen. (Tudjman told me the fears of civil war are greatly exaggerated. This from a man who is rapidly arming a civil guard in Croatia.)"

As the conflict in the Balkans expanded that summer and fall, and exploded in Bosnia-Herzegovina the following spring, I often recalled what Susan had been told. It symbolized for me the true tragedy of what became of Yugoslavia: It was a war only extremist nationalists such as Slobodan Miloševic and Franjo Tudjman could want, and in the face of such "bullheaded" nationalists, it became a conflict others could not prevent, short of the massive use of military force, including ground forces, that would have cost many, many lives for those seeking to deter the war. Once unleashed, conflict in the former Yugoslavia acquired a perverse logic of its own. And as its horrifying course acquired momentum, the war became impossible to stop by the outside world, least of all by a divided international community in the midst of trying to develop new institutions and adapt old ones for the post–Cold War world.

The Serbo-Croatian War

Four days after my visit to Belgrade, the Croatian and Slovenian parliaments voted for independence. The war in Yugoslavia began in earnest the next day, with the Slovenes battling the Yugoslav National Army (JNA) for control of Slovenia's thirty-seven border crossings. We issued statements criticizing Ljubljana and Zagreb for their unilateral declarations of independence, which foreclosed any possibilities for a peacefully negotiated breakup, as well as for their forceful seizure of border ports—all in violation of the Helsinki Accords. We also criticized all parties for the violence. But the critical question facing us was what role we should take in trying to initiate a peace process. There was never any thought at that time of using U.S. ground troops in Yugoslavia—the American people would never have supported it. After all, the United States had fought three wars in this century in Europe—two hot ones and one cold one. And three was quite enough, particularly having just fought another major war—this one in the Gulf.

In the Persian Gulf crisis the previous August, the President had realized immediately that American vital interests were at stake and had moved quickly to assert U.S. leadership over the international community's efforts. Following the successful completion of Desert Storm in February 1991, he had sent me to the Middle East to jump-start the peace process. This turn of events had left many European leaders and diplomats feeling the need to be more assertive and involved in developments affecting the international community. After all, "EC92" was less than a year away, the Soviet Union was in decline, and the talk in Brussels, Paris, Bonn, Rome, and other European capitals was of an emerging European superpower. By this line of reasoning, if Europe was going to assume its place as a great power, then the Europeans, not the Americans, should take the lead in managing the Yugoslav crisis, which after all was occurring on Europe's doorstep. The Europeans wanted the lead and welcomed the chance to deal with the problem through the EC.

The Bush administration felt comfortable with the EC's taking responsibility for handling the crisis in the Balkans. The conflict seemed to be one the EC could manage. More critically, Yugoslavia was in the heart of Europe, and European interests were directly threatened. And the Europeans had a long, if less than successful, history of dealing with the Balkans, given the complex history and convoluted web of nationalities in the region.

Most important, unlike in the Persian Gulf, our vital national interests were not at stake. The Yugoslav conflict had the potential to be intractable, but it was nonetheless a regional dispute. Milošević had Saddam's appetite, but Serbia didn't have Iraq's capabilities or ability to affect America's vital interests, such as access to energy supplies. The greater threat to American interests at the time lay in the increasingly dicey situation in Moscow, and we preferred to maintain our focus on that challenge, which had global ramifications for us, particularly with regard to nuclear weapons. Moreover, in the summer of 1991, we were already consumed by the Middle East peace process and close to getting the parties to the table.

There was another reason why we felt comfortable letting the EC handle the conflict. We had been engaged in a political battle in Brussels over the relationship of the Western European Union (WEU)—the EC's defense arm—and NATO. At its heart, this rather theological battle revolved around different conceptions of America's role in Europe. Some Europeans—certain that political and monetary union was coming and would create a

European superpower—were headstrong about asserting a European defense identity in which America's role on the Continent was minimized. We had been fighting this for some time, and trying to get them to recognize that, even with a diminished Soviet threat, they still needed an engaged America. But our protestations were overlooked in an emotional rush for a unified Europe. The result was an undercurrent in Washington, often felt but seldom spoken, that it was time to make the Europeans step up to the plate and show that they could act as a unified power. Yugoslavia was as good a first test as any.

Consequently, throughout the summer, we played a supporting role, as the EC, led by its special envoy, Lord Carrington, attempted to mediate the conflict. Unfortunately, the EC's efforts led to only intermittent success throughout July and August of 1991. The Yugoslav parties would talk at EC-sponsored negotiations, but they would also continue fighting on the ground. As the summer drew to a close, the EC's efforts were again flagging.

Meanwhile, our concerns about the USSR expanded with the attempted coup against Mikhail Gorbachev on August 19. While the crisis itself lasted only three days, it was obvious that political developments in the Soviet Union had been radically accelerated. Clearly, our central focus for months to come would be on managing the peaceful dissolution of the USSR. Personally, the President was most worried by a series of disturbing incidents regarding this nuclear command and control during the coup attempt, and spent much of September managing this nuclear initiative, which he announced on September 27.

During the fall, I had several discussions with Hans Van Den Broek concerning the fighting between the Serbs and Croats. On September 18, I told him that we would continue to support the EC in its efforts to resolve the crisis. As the chair of the rotating EC presidency, he was at that time most concerned about keeping the EC together; long-held historical tendencies, nationalist passions, and expatriates who had settled in nearby European states were being aroused. The Germans and Italians had a real affinity for the Croatians and Slovenians, while the British and French tended to be the strongest supporters of Serbia, having had close relations with them during World War II. Van Den Broek was also concerned that the conflict was slipping away from the Community, and that the EC would have to involve the United Nations Security Council. He was concerned both about the impression this would leave regarding Europe's ability to manage a conflict in its own backyard and the possibility that some in the Security Council might not want to take on Yugoslavia as a U.N. operation. He believed that the Chinese might veto any involvement in what Beijing considered a Yugoslav "internal affair."

Our greatest problem with involving the United Nations was that it would broaden the number of actors involved. The EC was having its own problems maintaining a coherent policy; adding the United Nations to the mix would only complicate matters. We also felt that U.N. involvement might increase the pressure to recognize independence-minded republics before a comprehensive peace settlement could be implemented. We were under no illusions, and understood that Yugoslavia as a common political entity had disappeared forever. But we had few instruments we could use to moderate the behavior of the various parties, and I was personally convinced by a note Dennis Ross had sent me on July 5 that "U.S. interests will not be served by uncoordinated, ad hoc declarations and recognitions—or rejections. They will be best served if we can help develop the philosophical and practical framework within which this and future independence moves in the East, and around the world are decided." Each of the republics craved legitimacy in the West, and withholding recognition (or conferring it) was the most powerful diplomatic tool available. "Earned recognition" was one of our key points of leverage over the combatants.*

Access to arms was another. As the Serbs besieged the Croatian town of Vukovar and fighting erupted on the Dalmatian coast in September, we joined the EC in U.N. Security Council Resolution 713, which imposed an arms embargo on all factions.† Six weeks later, at a summit with the EC at The Hague, we joined the EC in economic sanctions and efforts to strengthen the arms embargo.

In November, the Serbs and Croats agreed to the demilitarization of Dubrovnik. Both also accepted the deployment of U.N. peacekeepers. On November 27, the Security Council approved a special envoy to Croatia and Serbia, and former Secretary of State Cyrus Vance was named to fill the position. While I remained somewhat concerned about involving the United Nations in what had been an exclusive EC negotiating process, I had a good relationship with Vance (who was very close to Larry Eagleburger), so I felt we would be able to work well with what was emerging as an EC-U.N. negotiating process. (Moreover, Javier Pérez de Cuéllar had consulted me prior to the announcement, because he was selecting a former American Secretary of State as special envoy, and I encouraged his doing so.) Unfortunately, one of the keys held by Vance and Carrington in their

*While the Europeans joined us in holding the line on recognition, throughout the summer and fall of 1991, we continually picked up disturbing reports that some European governments were "back-channeling" to various Yugoslav factions, urging them to "go for it." Indeed, on the margins of the NATO Summit in Rome in November, we strongly pressed the Germans not to break the non-recognition consensus.

†Many months later, some would criticize this embargo because it prevented the Bosnian government from arming itself. But at the time, the embargo was aimed at Serbia and Croatia, and there was no fighting in Bosnia.

negotiations—a unified Western position on recognition of the individual Yugoslav republics—would soon be gone.

The Dilemma of Recognition

The dam burst when the Germans, caving in to domestic pressures, unilaterally recognized Croatia and Slovenia on December 23. That undercut efforts by Van Den Broek and Carrington to keep the rest of the EC in line—efforts which we tried to bolster by sending in our ambassadors to EC member governments to argue that recognition of Croatia and Slovenia would only make a bad situation worse. But these attempts were for naught, as the Community followed the Germans in recognizing the two breakaway republics on January 15, 1992.

After the EC decision, I had Larry Eagleburger talk to Cy Vance. He told us to wait at least two weeks, and preferably a month, before moving ahead with recognition. That would allow time to begin the deployment of a U.N. peacekeeping force. Vance felt that our decision to withhold recognition had had an important restraining effect on the Serbs and had discouraged Miloševic and Tudjman from carving up Bosnia. This put us in a difficult position domestically with the Croatian-American lobby, but I told the President at lunch on January 24, "We can and should take the public and congressional heat. We should do all we can to support Vance's efforts, because our best hope for resolving the crisis is maintenance of the cease-fire and introduction of U.N. peacekeepers." The President agreed, and so we waited.

The issue was joined with the Bosnian referendum, scheduled for March 1. On the one hand, we were almost certain that the Muslims and Croats in Bosnia would vote for independence. But we were wary that the hard-line Bosnian Serbs would use the vote as a pretext for instigating violence and calling for help from their fellow Serbs in Belgrade.

On February 27, Tom Niles, then the Assistant Secretary of State for European Affairs, sent me a paper outlining five options on recognition. At the time, forty-five states had recognized Slovenia and Croatia, while only Bulgaria and Turkey had recognized Macedonia and Bosnia. All the options included recognition of Slovenia and Croatia. The real question marks were Bosnia and Macedonia, and whether we should act independently or in conjunction with the EC.

Niles neatly summarized our dilemma. "There is a real possibility that intercommunal violence could erupt at any time in Bosnia-Herzegovina," he wrote. "Recognition is seen as a way to reinforce stability, especially if the outcome of the Bosnian referendum clearly favors independence." Moreover, failing to recognize Bosnia (and Macedonia) "leaves them vulnerable to political pressures and activities of radicals. Macedonian President Gligorov and Bosnian President Izetbegovic—the two most reasonable actors in the Yugoslav crisis—have warned us they would be destabilized if the U.S. recognizes other republics but not theirs." Conversely, "There is also no guarantee that our recognition would prevent breakdown in Bosnia."

These arguments were also made by Warren Zimmermann in Belgrade. He held the pragmatic hope that recognizing Bosnia-Herzegovina might be one way to internationalize the problem and deter the Serbs from meddling.

In short, coordinated Western recognition of Bosnia might deter Serbian and Croatian violence, but in the Balkans, no one was willing to bet the farm on it. After laying out the pros and cons, Niles came down in favor of recognizing Slovenia, Croatia, and Bosnia, while indicating our intention to work with the EC on the question of Macedonia. (The notion that Bosnia was more volatile than Macedonia and that recognizing Macedonia might cause Prime Minister Mitsotakis's government to fall in Athens was implicit in the recommendation.)*

In a cover note to Niles's memo, Larry Eagleburger cut through the chaff, as usual. "My concern all along has been that a halfway policy on recognition," he wrote, "would invite Serbian and Croatian adventurism in Bosnia-Herzegovina and in Macedonia. That is still my concern.

"Additionally, on the issue of principle, both Macedonia and Bosnia-Herzegovina will have met every criterion regarding recognition. They have used a democratic process to establish the groundwork for their declaration of independence; they have both moved very reluctantly toward independence recognizing that the situation in Yugoslavia has left them with no alternative as a simple matter of self-preservation; their governments are, at least by standards of the region, representative and committed to the principles of democracy." In short, Larry's bottom line was this: How could we recognize Croatia and Slovenia, which had pursued independence unilaterally and in violation of Helsinki principles, and not recognize Skopje and Sarajevo, which had done so in a peaceful and democratic manner? Moreover, not recognizing Bosnia and Macedonia, he noted, "could create real instability, which less than mature players in Serbia and Greece might decide to exploit."

I found Eagleburger's argument convincing, and in a March 2 meeting

---

*For a variety of deep-rooted historical and political reasons, the Greeks were vehemently opposed to the use of the name *Macedonia* by the Yugoslav republic. Indeed, hundreds of thousands of people marched in the streets of Athens arguing against any give in the government's hard-line position.

with Tom Niles, Reggie Bartholomew, Bob Pearson, Margaret Tutwiler, and Larry, I decided to go ahead and test the waters before we committed ourselves. I did that through a letter on March 5 to the Europeans, Lord Carrington, and Cyrus Vance. I suggested a U.S.-EC meeting the next week to discuss recognition, and proposed that the United States would move ahead with recognizing Slovenia and Croatia while the EC would join us in recognizing Bosnia and Macedonia shortly thereafter. "As I am sure is true for you," I wrote, "we have wrestled with the question of whether recognition of Bosnia-Herzegovina's independence would contribute to stability in that delicately balanced republic or encourage efforts by the large Serbian minority to destabilize the situation. We have concluded that while there obviously is no external influence that can guarantee the stability and territorial integrity of Bosnia-Herzegovina, we can best contribute to that objective by a collective recognition of that republic's independence, and warning against efforts from within or without to undermine its integrity." Serbia, I noted, was already trying "to destabilize the situation, and we have sent a strong warning to President Miloševic to cease these activities or run the risk of adverse consequences to Serbia's future relationship with the United States."* I made a similar case on Macedonia, stressing that failure to move rapidly on recognition would encourage "adventurism which could rapidly escalate to open conflict."

While the EC members were defensive about the box the Greeks had erected for the Community regarding Macedonia, they were nonetheless reluctant to push Athens, which predictably disliked our proposal. Foreign Minister Samaras said, "Let's have a meeting, but don't rock the boat," while Mitsotakis expressed "strong concern." On Bosnia, we found more support, particularly from the Germans and British, though all the EC members didn't want to complicate the ongoing EC-sponsored intra-Bosnian talks.

Carrington reportedly felt out-of-touch with the EC's attitude on Macedonia and believed that recognition could cut either way on Bosnia, though on the whole he thought it would be helpful. Cy Vance expressed some concern to Larry Eagleburger that we were moving too quickly and that recognition might hinder efforts to get U.N. peacekeepers installed. But he understood our reasoning and was, in Larry's words, "relaxed" about it overall. Because of Vance's concerns, I spoke directly to Lord Carrington the afternoon of March 9, the day before my meeting with the EC. Carring-

---

*On March 3, I had instructed Zimmermann to deliver a message to Miloševic that we saw a "clear pattern of Serbian tactics aimed at annulling the results of the referendum." Moreover, we regarded Serbia's complicity in Bosnian Serb leader Radovan Karadzic's destabilization efforts with "the utmost gravity."

ton told me that he and Vance agreed that recognition of Bosnia before the arrival of U.N. peacekeepers, scheduled for two weeks later, would be a mistake. Carrington wanted us to move in concert with the EC, and he said the EC would recognize Bosnia when it met on April 6.

I told him that we would move jointly with the EC and would agree to a timetable that was also acceptable to Cy Vance and the United Nations. I also said it was unfortunate that Bosnia and Macedonia had received little reward despite having gone the right way in fulfilling the conditions for recognition. He agreed.

The next day in Brussels, I went to the Charlemagne Building for my ministerial with the EC. Within a few speakers, it became obvious that the EC was by no means unified. Roland Dumas, in fact, suggested that we take another look at the modest sanctions then in force against Serbia, saying, "We do not want to penalize a major player." Since it was clear that the Greeks would continue to veto any EC move on Macedonia, I backed off and devoted my energies to Bosnia. The most useful intervention came from Douglas Hurd, who mirrored Eagleburger's reasoning when he said, "We can't leave these republics in limbo because we have created the present situation [by recognizing Slovenia and Croatia]." We ended the meeting with a private understanding that the EC would recognize Bosnia at its next meeting on April 6 and that we would follow shortly thereafter with recognition of the three. Macedonia, I was learning, was going to take much more time. Publicly, we issued a rather bland statement that "positive consideration" would be given to recognition of Bosnia-Herzegovina and Macedonia (though Greek sensitivities prevented even the inclusion of the word *Macedonia* in the statement).

I reviewed the U.S.-EC meeting the next day with the Bosnian Foreign Minister, Haris Silajdzic. "Bosnia," he said, "can be a successful model of a pluralistic state if external forces stop meddling in its affairs." Stability, he argued, could best be promoted by Western recognition. I asked him about the JNA, and he said it "was behaving" and "out of politics." I found that surprising, but Silajdzic said that the Bosnian government had assured the army that if it stayed out of politics and cut its levels, the government would support it as much as it could.

Three weeks later, on Monday, April 6, the EC recognized Bosnia, and we followed suit the next day while the Security Council approved deployment of peacekeepers for Bosnia. We also recognized Slovenia and Croatia. Meanwhile, the Bosnian Serbs declared their own independent Bosnian republic, and JNA jets launched rocket attacks around Sarajevo. That Friday, I instructed Ambassador Zimmermann in Belgrade to warn Miloševic that we were concerned by Serbian force and intimidation, and that if Belgrade wanted any kind of relationship with us, it would have to respect the independence and territorial integrity of its neighbors. Miloševic, typically, denied any complicity.

While the particulars would change, Miloševic usually responded to our démarches by cocking an eyebrow and asking Zimmermann, "Why are you coming to see me? This is a Bosnian issue. No Serbs from Serbia are involved. Serbs aren't even threatened in Bosnia," he'd conclude with sad irony. Ever disciplined in his deviousness, he'd absolve himself from responsibility, taking a "hidden hand" approach to events in Bosnia.

We followed the message to Miloševic with one to our European partners, recommending that they, too, instruct their ambassadors to deliver a démarche in Belgrade. We also tried to build support for expelling Serbia and Montenegro as "Yugoslavia" from international organizations, which would delegitimatize the regime. Over the weekend, following two days of EC-sponsored talks, the Bosnian factions agreed to a cease-fire, but by Monday fighting had flared up again.

This became a pattern throughout the spring and summer: We would raise our concerns with Belgrade; Miloševic would deny any responsibility, but the fighting would ebb; then, a few days later, the Serbs would initiate another offensive. Miloševic may be a tough, but he is a sophisticated tough who understands Western politics. He was a master at undercutting the international community's resolve by backing off and taking conciliatory steps when he needed to.

On Tuesday, April 14, Silajdzic visited me in Washington. I told him that we had sent an extraordinarily strong message to Miloševic and that we were concerned about what was happening to Bosnia. I told him we would work to energize the EC and the international community, though I didn't want to mislead him that U.N. peacekeepers could become peace makers.

"Please, tell me about your situation," I began.

"As we speak, sir," he responded, "people are dying. They are killing civilians as if they were animals. These are real people who are dying. We are not talking politics anymore." His soft-spoken manner made his plea all the more compelling, and his plain language revealed the pain his countrymen were going through in a way a diplomatic démarche never could. It was without doubt one of the most emotional meetings I had as Secretary of State. Much like my time with the Kurds on the mountain, my meeting with Silajdzic cut through the diplomatic miasma and pushed me to action.

After the meeting, I had Larry Eagleburger take Silajdzic to see the EC troika political directors (who happened to be visiting the Department) and asked Margaret Tutwiler to talk to the Foreign Minister about the importance of using Western mass media to build support in Europe and North America for the Bosnian cause. I also had her talk to her contacts at the four television networks, the *Washington Post,* and the *New York Times* to try to get more attention focused on the story.

Meanwhile, I started calling European ministers. I reached Douglas Hurd first. "Bosnia has pursued independence in the right way and deserves our support," I told him. "We need to muster support to ostracize Miloševic and Serbia. I question whether Belgrade should be allowed to remain a member of CSCE." Hurd told me he agreed and would convey my concerns to Lord Carrington, whom he would be seeing the next morning. But he was concerned about trying to introduce U.N. forces into Bosnia until the situation had stabilized.

The next morning Genscher called me from Greece, where he had been trying to resolve the Macedonian issue. "We need to coordinate steps to deal with this tragic situation," I said, and stressed that the United States and Europe could not deal with Bosnia on a "business-as-usual basis." Genscher told me the EC had just agreed "on a very soft line" on Bosnia, but that he would try to have the position strengthened. A few minutes later, Hurd called me back. Having spoken to Carrington, Hurd agreed that the only real leverage against Miloševic was derecognition of the rump Yugoslav state, but he felt it was also important to address the activities of Croatian irregulars stirred up by Tudjman. He also reiterated his concerns about peacekeeping forces and made it clear that the WEU had neither the will nor the ability to undertake such an operation.

In the afternoon, I reached Portugese Foreign Minister João de Deus Pinheiro, who had assumed the EC presidency, succeeding Van Den Broek. "While we are fully behind the current EC and U.N. efforts in Bosnia and do not want to get out in front of you," I began somewhat deferentially, "we cannot stand by and see people being slaughtered. The Bosnian situation is different from the Croatian." Whereas Tudjman had acted unilaterally, had been indifferent to minority rights, and had allegedly exhibited an interest in carving up Bosnia, the Bosnian leaders had scrupulously followed Helsinki norms and democratic principles. "Miloševic is worried about retaining Yugoslav legitimacy," I continued, "and he needs to be told that the U.S. and Europe will hold him responsible." Deus Pinheiro said he was concerned that the JNA was no longer operating under unified control. He said he agreed with my approach, but that Paris would create difficulties.

My phone calls were another reminder of two conflicting tendencies that were emerging in the European Community's approach to the breakup of the former Yugoslavia. The first was its rigid adherence to acting only when every EC member state was in agreement. This unanimity-only approach caused both delays (as all the members had to be polled for even the smallest decision) and lowest-common-denominator policies. The Europeans' second tendency was to become prisoners of their own history, falling back on alliances that had been developed decades or even centuries before. For example, initially the British and French often sided with the Serbs, while the Germans consistently gave the Croats the benefit of doubt. This further undermined the negotiations, as the parties in the region quickly learned to play the Europeans off against one another, effectively neutralizing the EC.

Lisbon

As April gave way to May, the violence in Bosnia escalated, and the Serbs laid siege to Sarajevo. On May 12, we finally managed to get Yugoslavia suspended from CSCE—the first time CSCE had ever taken a formal decision without consensus, as the delegation from Belgrade had objected. The next day, we announced we would recall Warren Zimmermann, once he had finished making arrangements to facilitate humanitarian assistance to the Bosnians. And on May 16, I instructed Zimmermann to seek assurances from Belgrade that the Serbs would open the Sarajevo airport and allow the free passage of humanitarian aid. The Serbs responded by attacking a Red Cross relief convoy and killing a member of the International Committee of the Red Cross. They also took hostage a convoy of women and children who were fleeing Sarajevo. We immediately cut off the authority of the Yugoslav Airlines (JAT) to fly to and from the United States, and I tasked the Building to come up with additional political and diplomatic steps that we could take to punish Belgrade.

That Friday, May 22, on my way to Portugal for an aid conference for the former Soviet Union, I met with Prime Minister Major at 10 Downing Street. "We're seeing mounting public concern and criticism over impotent Western inaction in the face of a true humanitarian nightmare," I began. "A terrible precedent is being set by Milošević's so-far successful use of force to achieve his aims." I asked Major to get the EC to move more aggressively against Serbia. "We've got to do something about the atrocities there. And we have to get humanitarian aid through—and that's going to require strong EC support," I told him. Both Major and Hurd agreed with my assessment and supported the steps we were prepared to take. "Can the United Kingdom join in immediately?" I asked. "In theory, yes," Major replied, "in practice, no," citing the need to confer within the EC. He went on to warn that the situation could go on for years—"like the situation we have here with Northern Ireland. Once in," he asked, "where does it end?" In European eyes, Sarajevo was becoming Saigon, and that didn't bode well for decisive action, or as Douglas Hurd trenchantly concluded the discussion, "Blood will be flowing under the door of the CSCE Summit," scheduled for July.

Following my meeting with Major, I used a press availability to turn up the rhetoric. Stating publicly for the first time that the situation in Bosnia was "a humanitarian nightmare" and "is unconscionable," I announced the unilateral political and diplomatic measures the United States would take: refusal to recognize Belgrade as the continuation of the Yugoslav state until all its forces were withdrawn from neighboring states and minority rights respected; the permanent withdrawal of Zimmermann from Belgrade; the closing of two Yugoslav consulates; the breaking of contacts with the JNA by pulling our military attachés (except for the air attaché, who would stay to coordinate humanitarian relief efforts); and the drawing down of our embassy personnel in Belgrade.

I wanted to put pressure on the EC to also take at least political and diplomatic action, and with foreign ministers from dozens of countries converging on Lisbon, the timing seemed right to get the Europeans to move. My statement had the effect I intended: it was the lead story the next day in American and, more important, European newspapers.

Upon arriving in Lisbon, I met first with the new German Foreign Minister, Klaus Kinkel. "We need all twelve members of the EC to go along with what I announced in London," I began. "We have tried to support the EC and the U.N. peace effort and have been consistent in our policy—though we disagreed with you on recognition. But now there is a humanitarian nightmare in the heart of Europe. This is an outrage. We cannot sit back and do nothing. We are going to do what is right." As I continued, I got more and more worked up. "What you have in the twelve is a lowest-common-denominator operation. If some of the EC twelve can't come along, so be it. But I hope that Germany can join us. We want you to look at Chapter VII sanctions in the U.N. We need support of the major European countries. We are willing to look at an oil embargo on Serbia."

Kinkel told me, "We are in agreement. We were for this from the beginning. We were stopped by others. We agree with what you mentioned last night in London."

"This is just a bunch of talk," I interjected. "It's mumbo-jumbo. That's all we have been hearing. While we are talking, people are dying." I *was* worked up—but I also knew that I needed the Germans to move the French, so I was going overboard in being emotional with Kinkel.

"As I said," Kinkel replied diplomatically, "we welcomed the proposals you made in London. I'm new here and will try to do what I can, even looking at the military. We are aware that words are not enough. But at the EC lunch I just came from, France and Greece continue to be very difficult."

"The only lever we have is to isolate Milošević," I said, "and I just cannot understand how Europe can stand by and let this happen."

From my meeting with Kinkel, I went to the Bellem Cultural Center for the conference itself. In all my meetings, I raised the dangers of continued escalation and the need to isolate Serbia further, including Chapter VII sanctions like those we had used initially in the Iraq crisis. In the plenary session and the side meetings of the conference on aid to the former Soviet Union, almost everyone else was discussing Bosnia, too. Indeed, given the conflicting web of nationalities that made up the former Soviet Union, many of the emerging democracies were acutely concerned that Bosnia might become their future, so they were as interested as anyone in calling for Western action to prevent further "ethnic cleansing." In my own intervention, I said, "No longer should the international community tolerate this barbarity, this affront to our collective conscience."

I used the conference's concluding press conference the next day to put the spotlight on European indifference, even inaction. Armed with statistics Margaret Tutwiler had gathered for me, I laid out the realities of the horror: 35,000 diabetics without insulin; 6,000 women and infants without milk, medicine, or baby formula; twelve U.N. aid trucks hijacked. "Clearly, none of us should try to find reasons for not forcefully and specifically condemning what has happened," I implored my European colleagues. "And none of us should try to find reasons for not taking some sort of action to try and end what truly is a humanitarian nightmare in the heart of Europe." In an effort to send a clear signal to Belgrade about where we could be headed unless the siege of Sarajevo was ended, I even refused to rule out the use of force (except by the United States unilaterally), and made references to the Gulf War coalition. By the time I finished, the Europeans were squirming.*

"What we are seeing once again," I informed the President from Lisbon, "is that the Europeans want to be active but need a push from us to do so—even when it's on an issue where they want to be in the lead and should be in the lead. Collective engagement works, and multilateral responses can be real but tend not to get energized unless we serve as the catalyst." Clearly, the EC wanted to play a major political role, but its internal contradictions would stymie it—unless it were prodded into action by our private and, more important, public diplomacy.

Following Lisbon, the Europeans finally overcame their internal differences and began to act. Four days later, the EC imposed additional eco-

---

*My remarks also had an effect in Belgrade. While I was in Lisbon, the Serbs passed word that they wanted to send a special envoy to meet with Larry Eagleburger in Bucharest—a request we rejected. We wanted to keep Milošević isolated until the Sarajevo airport was open and humanitarian convoys were receiving safe passage. Belgrade also wrote the U.N. Secretary-General in an effort to prevent the imposition of sanctions.

nomic sanctions on Serbia. Within a week of my remarks in Lisbon, by a 13–0 vote (with China and Zimbabwe abstaining), the Security Council passed Resolution 757, which enacted a complete economic embargo on Serbia. At least the rump Yugoslav state was now effectively isolated.

The Politics of Not Using Force

But Belgrade's political and economic isolation didn't prevent the continuing military assault in Bosnia-Herzegovina. On the evening of Monday, June 8, I called the President on the secure line and told him how radically the situation was deteriorating. I had just seen Andrei Kozyrev, who had been very optimistic at Lisbon about the prospects for peace. Following the conference, he was going to the Balkans and felt the Serbs would listen to advice from a fellow Slav. But now Kozyrev's trip to the region had changed his position 180 degrees; he was as pessimistic as anyone.

By Wednesday, the President had approved the use of U.S. transport aircraft to bring humanitarian aid into Sarajevo once a cease-fire was in place. The real question that concerned us, however, was whether we would ever get a sustainable cease-fire in the first place.

Two weeks later, there was still no cease-fire, and Sarajevo remained isolated. As a result, in Senate testimony on Tuesday, June 23, I upped the ante with the Serbs by announcing that we'd be shutting their last consulate, expelling their ambassador, and working with others to suspend the rump Yugoslav state from international organizations. That exhausted virtually all possible political and diplomatic measures, yet I was under no illusion that these steps would be enough to change fundamentally the behavior of the Bosnian Serbs and Belgrade. So that afternoon, I went over to the White House to discuss with Scowcroft the possibility of using the one instrument—Western military force—that might change the course of the war. Scowcroft had become as disheartened by the situation in Sarajevo as I was, but we both knew the President didn't want to, and shouldn't, get involved in an open-ended military commitment in the former Yugoslavia. We both knew as well that the Pentagon was deeply opposed to any military involvement in Bosnia, for reasons we both appreciated. Nevertheless, we agreed that something further had to be done and that I would come up with a proposal that would permit the use of force for the sole purpose of delivering humanitarian assistance.

Overnight, Andrew Carpendale, Arnie Kanter, Dennis Ross, and Margaret Tutwiler put together a two-page memo for me, entitled "Game Plan: Next Steps on Bosnia." The plan's objective was "to do whatever is necessary" to deliver humanitarian relief to Sarajevo. It outlined four major actions: first, to move an aircraft carrier immediately into the Adriatic;

second, to impose a multilateral naval blockade of ports for sanctions enforcement (notably the Montenegrin port of Bar); third, to make a high-profile increase in sanctions enforcement by cutting the oil pipeline that ran into Serbia from Romania; and fourth, to "demonstrate willingness to conduct multilateral air strikes (e.g., against artillery in hills) as necessary to create conditions for delivery of humanitarian relief."

The game plan did not envision the unilateral use of American military power, nor was force envisioned as a means to resolve the underlying conflict. We were motivated, however, not just by humanitarian concerns but by our recognition that the use of U.S. military force in any manner or for any purpose would have substantial political and diplomatic ramifications. All actions would be taken multilaterally under U.N. authority with explicit congressional support, and there would be "no U.S. combat troops on ground." The plan included a tight timetable for enacting these steps, beginning with presidential phone calls almost immediately, and with a trip by me to the major European capitals as well as Moscow. The model we had in mind was the Gulf War coalition-building effort, and we planned to pass a U.N. resolution authorizing "all necessary means" within ten days.

After talking about the proposal with the President and Scowcroft, the President set a principals meeting for Friday morning. I knew both Powell and Cheney would be vehemently opposed to this initiative, fearing that it would put us on a slippery slópe leading to greater military involvement down the line. Their model for using force was, understandably, the Gulf War—and Bosnia had more characteristics of Vietnam than Iraq. On the other hand, if the authority for the use of force strictly and properly was limited only to the delivery of humanitarian relief, and not expanded to resolution of the underlying political conflict, I thought the "slippery slope" concern was substantially diminished, if not eliminated. And so I took a step that I had occasionally used before during the Bush administration: I went directly to George Bush to try to work around the interagency process and pre-cook the result. On Wednesday afternoon, I went over to the White House for a private discussion with the President. I briefed him on the game-plan proposal and argued that it was the least we could do in light of the nightmare now occurring on Western Europe's doorstep. He told me that he felt what I had outlined would work. His initial inclination to stay completely away from the Yugoslav imbroglio militarily had been altered by the continuing horrors in Bosnia and by his disappointment with the Europeans' inability to get their act together. He indicated that on Friday he would probably suggest that the Pentagon put the plan into action.

The Friday-morning principals' meeting was one of the most spirited I had ever attended as Secretary of State. Cheney and Powell went through the dangers associated with using any military force, even just for delivery of humanitarian relief. Brent and I stressed that we had already exhausted all diplomatic, political, and economic means, and that the implications of the suffering extended far beyond Bosnia. After substantial discussion, the President squarely backed the game plan I had outlined, although Cheney and Powell convinced him that if he were going to do this he should move a Marine Amphibious Ready Group (MARG) into the Adriatic instead of an aircraft carrier.

I returned to the Department and instructed Dennis Ross and Arnie Kanter to put State's part of the game plan into action. Ross called Bandar and told him we were going to press Bucharest to cut the oil pipeline, and that it would be helpful if the Saudis could offset some of the costs the Romanians would endure as a result. He said he would try to help. (We felt there would be a solid chance for getting Saudi support, since King Fahd had written the President of his concerns about Western inaction on Bosnia.)

Over the weekend, events began to move in our direction. The United Nations issued a forty-eight-hour ultimatum to the Serbs, and the European Council followed suit with a strong statement Saturday calling for all necessary measures to open the Sarajevo airport. The President previewed our approach with key allies, including Boris Yeltsin, and found that they all favored an "all necessary means" resolution, similar to the one the Security Council had passed in authorizing the Gulf War. My own phone calls— with Canadian Foreign Minister Barbara McDougall, Turkish Foreign Minister Hikmet Cetin, and Klaus Kinkel—revealed a surprising level of support, too. In fact, we found so much support that we decided over the weekend to put off my trip. There seemed to be little reason, since we were almost certain we could get a U.N. resolution anyway.*

Indeed, by Monday, the U.N. flag flew over Sarajevo airport. The Serbs, for the moment, had backed down. Four days later, the United States started relief flights into Sarajevo. And on July 7, the G-7 leaders meeting in Munich strongly condemned the use of violence in Bosnia and announced their support for other measures, "not excluding military means," to achieve humanitarian objectives.

There my involvement with the former Yugoslavia ceased. The following week, while vacationing at my ranch in Pinedale, Wyoming, the President asked me to come back to the White House as Chief of Staff to coordinate the reelection effort. My focus turned to domestic politics and away from foreign policy.

---

*Putting off the trip may have been a mistake, as it would have created an action-forcing event and would have allowed me to overcome both the bureaucratic and diplomatic impediments that eventually strangled our initiative.

And now as this is written, almost three years later, the "humanitarian nightmare" in the heart of Europe continues. I do not believe it could have been prevented by any combination of political, diplomatic, and economic measures. In my opinion, the only way that it might have been prevented or reversed would have been through the application of substantial military force early on, with all of the costs, particularly in lives, that that would have entailed—and, by everyone's reckoning, in that environment the casualties would have been staggering. President Bush's decision that our national interests did not require the United States of America to fight its fourth war in Europe in this century, with the loss of America's sons and daughters that would have ensued, was absolutely the right one. We cannot be, and should not be expected to be, the world's policeman, and the necessary support by the American people for the degree of force that would have been required in Bosnia could never have been built or maintained.

CHAPTER 34

FROM COLD WAR TO
DEMOCRATIC PEACE

For many years our two nations were the two poles, the two opposites. . . . That affected the destinies of the world in a most tragic way. The world was shaken by storms of confrontation. It was close to exploding, close to perishing beyond salvation. —*Boris Yeltsin, June 17, 1992*

A s I left the State Department and headed east on Constitution Avenue toward the Capitol on a sunny June day in 1992, it was hard not to recall the first time I had made the journey to the House Chamber to listen to an address to a joint session of Congress. On January 26, 1982, as White House Chief of Staff, I had sat in the audience for President Reagan's first State of the Union, an electrifying speech in which the President had stated his views in his customary way: with passion and vision, and with the conviction that comes from knowing you are on the right side of history.

That day Ronald Reagan had been particularly eloquent in describing the challenge posed by the Soviet Union. "Our foreign policy must be rooted in realism, not naïveté or self-delusion," he had said. "A recognition of what the Soviet empire is about is the starting point. Winston Churchill, in negotiating with the Soviets, observed that they respect only strength and resolve in their dealings with other nations. That's why we've moved to reconstruct our national defenses. We intend to keep the peace—we will also keep our freedom."

Now, a decade later, as I took my place in the chamber, the spectacular success of President Reagan's policy of "peace through strength" hit home. For the members of both houses of Congress were filing in to hear the first freely elected President of Russia, Boris Yeltsin, who had come to Washing-

652

ton for a summit with President Bush, and the order of the day was "partnership and friendship," not competition and rivalry. In 1982, no one would have predicted that ten years later, the Soviet Union would be in history's dustbin, replaced by an independent Russia working to develop democracy and free markets, and by fourteen other newly independent states.

But there Yeltsin stood, and he, too, was eloquent in making his case. "Reason," he said, was beginning to "triumph over madness. We have left behind the period when America and Russia looked at each other through gunsights, ready to pull the trigger at any time.

"The world can sigh in relief," he continued. "The idol of communism which spread social strife, animosity, and unparalleled brutality everywhere, which instilled fear in humanity, has collapsed. It has collapsed, never to rise again. I am here to assure you: We shall not let it rise again in our land."

But he was most impassioned when he discussed American concerns about Vietnam-era prisoners of war. On the eve of his departure from Moscow, Yeltsin had told NBC News that some archival records indicated that in the 1960s and 1970s, the Soviet regime, working with the Communist government in Hanoi, had transferred American POWs to the USSR for interrogation. "We can only surmise that some of them may still be alive," he said speculatively. Naturally, this had created a controversy in both the Senate and the House and threatened to mar the visit.

Departing from his text, he thundered, "I promise you that each and every document in each and every archive will be examined in order to investigate the fate of every American unaccounted for. As President of Russia, I assure you that even if one American has been detained in my country, and can still be found, *I* will find him. I will get him back to his family." The chamber erupted into a standing ovation as members shouted, "Bor-is, Bor-is, Bor-is."

It was a political masterstroke that instantly won over a reluctant Congress and paved the way for the Freedom Support Act, the administration's omnibus assistance legislation for the former Soviet Union. To most people, it was a welcome surprise. But I knew differently.

The previous day, in a large meeting devoted mainly to nuclear arms control, the President had passed me a handwritten note. It read, "Yeltsin needs to tell Congress: I do not know if one single American POW/MIA is alive in Russia or anywhere in the former Soviet Union. But I will tell you this, we will go through every record of every archive in order to shed light on the fate of Americans unaccounted for. I can assure you if any American has been held and can be found, I will find him. I will bring him to his family." George Bush's instincts were exactly right, and pursuing the President's suggestion, we passed his precise words to the Russian delegation.

Reflecting back on this small incident, I believe it illustrates the strides we made in the first half of 1992 in building U.S.-Russian cooperation across the entire spectrum of our relationship. With the collapse of the Soviet Union, we entered uncharted geostrategic territory, and those first six months of our relations with Russia and its neighbors reveal the complex mixture of political idealism and realism that guided our policy.

On the one hand, we believed that the defeat of communism and the rise of the democrats created an unprecedented opportunity. We hoped to build our relations with Russia, Ukraine, and the other new independent states on the basis of democracy and free markets: what we came to call a "democratic peace," the type of peace we enjoyed with Germany and Japan. This peace would be based on shared democratic values, not just converging interests. While the democratic impulse in Russia and in most of the new independent states of the Commonwealth was genuine, these nations had little in the way of democratic traditions, and we were far from certain that democracy would take root. But we did not want to create a self-fulfilling prophecy by pursuing a pure balance-of-power policy that assumed from the outset that these states would eventually return to authoritarianism.

Nonetheless, our policy included a heavy dose of political realism as a hedge against any reversals in reform. So while we worked with democrats in Russia, Ukraine, and the other independent states to bolster democracy and institutionalize free markets, I also spent much of that spring managing issues of realpolitik—namely ensuring there was no proliferation of nuclear weapons states on the territory of the former Soviet Union, ensuring that all tactical nuclear weapons were transferred to Russia, and slashing the strategic arsenal of Russia through the START II agreement, so that it would no longer pose a first-strike threat.

Stabilizing Russia's Economy: The Freedom Support Act

At the end of my "Confusistan" trip in February 1992, I saw Boris Yeltsin in Moscow. Unlike my visit in January and his Camp David meeting with President Bush on February 1, when the Russian President had been primarily interested in discussing security and political issues, economic assistance was now Yeltsin's first priority.

The Russian government, Yeltsin said, was committed to tightening credit, cutting the deficit, restricting the money supply, and privatizing state enterprises. He even said he felt that some headway was being made on strengthening the ruble against the dollar.

Nevertheless, Russia was going to need outside help—and he was looking to the United States to lead the international community. Grain was a particular problem. Even though Moscow had received supplementary credits from the British, French, and Canadians, Russia would still need more—something on the order of $600 million in credit guarantees from us, Yeltsin said.

But Russia's needs were not limited to grain. Yeltsin felt that a stabilization fund would be necessary for the ruble. Such a fund, used successfully in Poland, would basically serve as an insurance policy for the ruble, backing the currency as Russia moved through economic "shock therapy."

During the Gorbachev regime, the topic of a stabilization fund had been raised repeatedly. Yet despite our efforts to educate the Soviets (for example, through our bilateral talks and by proposing special associate status in the IMF in December 1990), Gorbachev had not shown a sufficient commitment to a free market (or its key elements) in any of the various economic plans the Soviets had pursued for a stabilization fund to have worked.

The Yeltsin government, however, was radically different. The plan, engineered by then–Deputy Prime Minister Yegor Gaidar, was serious and credible in terms of its financial and economic components. Just as critically, Yeltsin himself had staked his own personal prestige behind it, which gave it political credibility, both within Russia and abroad.

I told Yeltsin that he needed to reduce the level of government spending, cut the growth of the money supply drastically, and remain current on foreign debt. Beyond these specifics, I urged him to continue working with the IMF and World Bank, as they would be the best source of significant funds and their approval was a political precondition to receiving large-scale funds from the G-7. He asked for our technical expertise in helping his government provide answers to questions posed by the Fund and the Bank. I readily agreed, understanding full well that it was another indicator of how much he was looking to Washington for assistance.

"I personally will push for a stabilization fund," I assured Yeltsin. I didn't want to leave it to the "green eyeshades," my term for officials who looked at questions like these in technical and accounting terms, without factoring in the broader geostrategic and political context that mattered most of all. I told Yeltsin we would try to rally the international community to put together a stabilization fund.

Of course, that was going to take quite a bit of work. Forty-seven countries and seven international organizations had come to the Coordinating Conference in January, but that had been for humanitarian aid, which would cost far less than a full support package. Moreover, in Germany, the costs of paying for unification were skyrocketing, and the Germans, having paid the Soviets billions already, were in no mood to ante up once again. In

Japan, the government was intent on retrieving the northern territories, and was holding back on economic assistance until Moscow moved on that issue.

Meanwhile, in Washington, the Treasury Department had not liked the idea of a stabilization fund at all, though Treasury had begun to shift its position in February, when, instead of coming to Camp David with Yeltsin, Gaidar stayed in Washington and discussed the reform program with leading officials. But even if we could get a government-wide consensus, we would still need support in Congress, and in the midst of a slow economy, few members of Congress were interested in voting for more foreign aid.

Nonetheless, I felt that if we pursued a threefold strategy, we could get the necessary support. First, the Russians needed to maintain the economic momentum Yeltsin had generated, by freeing prices at the beginning of the year and following through with a credible reform plan. The longer Moscow showed its commitment to real reform, the more the international financial institutions could be counted on to endorse a stabilization plan—and the greater the pressure would build on the G-7 to agree to such a fund.

Second, we'd need to push the G-7 along, through the deputy finance ministers who were coordinating this issue. Because of Treasury's recalcitrance, I had several conversations with the President and Brent Scowcroft, and Brent and I had lunch with Nick Brady to lay out our concerns. Bob Zoellick and the NSC's Ed Hewett also did quite a bit of heavy lifting to get the financial side of the government moving. (Hewett died tragically of cancer in early 1993. He was one of the unsung heroes of our Soviet policy, a man who checked his ego at the door and got the job done with efficiency and humor. I'll never forget his loping stride, wide grin, and world-class intellect.) Third, I wanted to create a vehicle around which we could coalesce public support—and votes on the Hill. In the late fall, Steve Berry, Janet Mullins's principal deputy in Congressional Affairs, had developed the concept of a single piece of legislation that would eliminate Cold War restrictions and provide assistance to the former Soviet Union. I had included this initiative in my Princeton speech in December. Now, with Mullins and Berry coordinating the effort and drawing on the full range of the Department's experts, we put it on a fast track and by mid-March came up with the Freedom Support Act.*

On March 25, I saw the President and explained where things stood. The IMF, World Bank, and G-7 finance deputies were making good prog-

---

*These experts included Todd Buchwald from the Legal Adviser's Office, Dan Speckhard from Larry Eagleburger's shop, and Gardner Peckham and Scott Cleland from Janet Mullins's office.

ress; indeed, they were on the verge of approving a program for Russia. But that, I argued, would not be enough. The Russians would look to us to lead—and without our leadership, the package might crumble.

"We have a chance now, but it will be fleeting, to seize the high ground on helping the former Soviet Union make it," I told the President. "The best way to help, and ensure that we won't bear responsibility for having 'lost Russia,' is to do everything we can to help reform succeed, and that means going forward with this omnibus, stand-alone legislation," I continued.

Domestically, the draft legislation represented an ambitious agenda for U.S.-Russian cooperation, and I wanted the Congress to respond to us, not vice versa. Bureaucratically, I didn't want the legislation watered down in interagency wrangling. "If I have to negotiate this internally," I argued, "we won't get it out. We'll lose the moment. That will simply fortify the view that we're doing nothing, we're hanging back on the single greatest issue affecting the security of the next generation of Americans." The President had always agreed what was at stake geopolitically, but now electoral considerations had to be taken into account. Notwithstanding those considerations, however, he was ready to move.

I outlined the window we had to work with in order to introduce the legislation. We didn't want to do it before March 31, the deadline for a continuing resolution in the Congress regarding foreign assistance. If we moved before that date, the Freedom Support Act would be held hostage to other assistance issues; moreover, the act would be labeled as "just more foreign aid," which would put it in a hole politically. Hence, we needed to move *after* March 31, but *before* April 6, the date for the opening of the Congress of People's Deputies in Russia. Conservatives were mobilizing against Yeltsin, and he needed to be able to point to the stabilization fund and the Freedom Support Act to show that the West truly was supporting the democrats in Russia. Consequently, we were left with two days— Wednesday, April 1, or Thursday, April 2—to announce the initiative. (As a rule, we wouldn't make such a major announcement on a Friday, Saturday, or Sunday, which effectively ruled out April 3–5.)

With the G-7 deputies finalizing the multilateral package in Paris on March 27 and the IMF formally endorsing the Russian reform program on March 31, the way was paved for dual announcements on April 1—by the President in Washington and Helmut Kohl in Bonn, since the Germans were hosting the G-7 Summit that year. The multilateral package consisted of $18 billion in loans, debt deferrals, and other financial assistance from the IMF and the World Bank, as well as a $6 billion stabilization fund for the ruble. The U.S. share came to roughly 20 percent.

In addition, the President announced the Freedom Support Act, which not only authorized most of our contribution to the multilateral effort but also became the foundation for mobilizing U.S. support to Russia and the other new independent states. Its specific provisions included the repeal of Cold War legislation that impeded economic cooperation with Russia, encouragement of the American private sector to develop business ties with Russia, and the expansion of our technical assistance and exchange programs. But any one of these was less important than the fact that the act provided a focus for our efforts during an election year in which the President was being criticized by some for being too much of an internationalist. At the time, I argued that the Freedom Support Act was defense by other means—that is, by helping to build democracy and free markets, we were creating the political foundations for a lasting peace. I still believe that, and even if we can't remake other societies in our image as perfect democracies, the more democratic we can help them become, the better.

Of course, the announcement on April 1 was just the beginning of a long campaign to win support for the act, which included major speeches by the President and me and an intensive lobbying effort by Bob Strauss, whose intervention with congressional Democrats was critical in ensuring the act's passage that summer.

From Four Nuclear Powers to One: The START Protocol

On the security side of the equation, I spent most of the spring of 1992 managing two different yet interrelated nuclear issues. The START agreement, which the President had signed with Mikhail Gorbachev in July 1991, had been a treaty between the United States and the Soviet Union. When the USSR had collapsed, Russia had become its successor state in legal terms, but in practice, strategic nuclear weapons remained on the soil of three other republics: Ukraine, Kazakhstan, and Belarus. We had a vital interest in ensuring that only one nuclear power emerged from the breakup of the former Soviet Union. We had begun this revolution with one nuclear power on that strategic space and did not wish to see a proliferation of nuclear countries when the dust settled. Moreover, despite the Commonwealth, the political disputes between Russia, Ukraine, and Kazakhstan were real, and we definitely did not want to see states with these kinds of conflicts end up in uneasy nuclear standoffs with one another.

In addition, the President was committed to go beyond the START agreement and push through another round of deep cuts in nuclear forces. The President complemented his September 27, 1991, initiative on tactical nuclear weapons with a strategic nuclear proposal, which he unveiled in his State of the Union speech on January 28, 1992. He announced that the

United States would take several unilateral steps (such as ceasing production and deployment of the Midgetman missile, and shifting a substantial
portion of the bomber force to conventional roles), but the most important
aspect of the speech concerned force levels. While START would reduce
U.S. nuclear warheads from roughly 13,000 to 9,500, the President proposed in his State of the Union a START II agreement to reduce warheads to
roughly 4,700—a fifty percent reduction below START levels (and equivalent to the United States' levels in 1971, before the first strategic arms control agreement had been signed). The forces in the former Soviet Union
would drop to equally low levels. But most important, the President resurrected his de-MIRVing initiative, which I had floated with Shevardnadze in
Windhoek, Namibia, in the spring of 1990. If the President's proposal were
accepted, MIRVed ICBMs would be eliminated, thus leading to a far more
stable nuclear balance.

At roughly the same time, President Yeltsin was coming forward with
his own arms control initiative that also included a series of unilateral steps.
(As a small sign of the new era we had entered, the presidents previewed
their proposals with each other beforehand; during the Soviet era, both
initiatives almost certainly would have been released publicly first.) Yeltsin
proposed even deeper cuts, to a level of 2,000 to 2,500 warheads. He argued
that all MIRVs were "the root of evil—from the point of view of threats to
stability," as he put it in a letter to President Bush on January 27, 1992. He
managed to get to such levels by a proposal to eliminate all MIRVed missiles, both land-based (ICBMs) and sea-based (SLBMs). Unfortunately,
since we relied heavily on SLBMs, Yeltsin's proposal would have had the
effect of radically changing the U.S. force structure, and shifting us away
from the stabilizing triad of bombers, ICBMs, and SLBMs, that had been the
hallmark of the U.S. nuclear deterrent for decades.

While I discussed ways to bridge the gaps between the two proposals on
my visits to Moscow in January and February, my sense was that we were
not going to make much progress on START II until we first resolved the
proliferation problem with Ukraine, Kazakhstan, and Belarus. While the
members of the Commonwealth had signed an agreement on strategic
forces on December 30, 1991, it was becoming clear by March that political
disagreements among Russia, Ukraine, and Kazakhstan were quickly making that agreement irrelevant. The Russians and Ukrainians had been sparring over the disposition of the Black Sea fleet. President Kravchuk had
required an oath of loyalty from all military personnel based in Ukraine,
and then on March 12, Kravchuk suspended the transfer of tactical nuclear
weapons from Ukraine to Russia.

On March 18, two days before a Commonwealth Summit, I held my
first meeting with the new Russian Ambassador, Vladimir Lukin. He told

me that the deputy foreign ministers from the four states had met and had come to an agreement that would allow us to implement the START agreement's provisions, "although you can never know with our Ukrainian brothers," warned Lukin. On START II, he told me, "Some way needs to be found to avoid negative effects here and in Russia. Yeltsin cannot give the impression that he is dismantling everything."

But whatever agreement had been reached at the deputy minister level clearly didn't find its way to the heads of state. The Commonwealth Summit dissolved in acrimony, without the sides even addressing the nuclear issues. It became clear to me that we would have to solve the problem for the four or risk losing the START Treaty. The Un-Group—the senior interagency arms-control body in the government below the level of principals—had already begun developing options.* The most elegant solution was to have the four sign a protocol to the START Treaty, which would have the legal effect of making Russia the successor state to the Soviet Union, while Ukraine, Kazakhstan, and Belarus became non–nuclear weapons states consistent with the NPT.

On April 7, I called Andrei Kozyrev and broached this idea with him. "From our perspective," I began, "substance is more important than form. We have a small window for START ratification by our Congress, and if the four of you can't find a solution among yourselves, then I'd like to invite you to Washington to settle this."

"I'm not sure that will be necessary," Kozyrev replied. "I've spoken with Anatoly Zlenko [Ukraine's Foreign Minister]. He now wants to settle the issue and will come to Moscow."

But a week later, Kozyrev called and stated bluntly, "I don't have very good news." We were still dead in the water, as the April 11 meeting among Kozyrev, Zlenko, and their Kazakh and Belarussian counterparts had resulted in no resolution of the issue.

Moreover, this technical arms-control issue was becoming increasingly politicized. On a previously scheduled visit to show our support for Ukraine, Dennis Ross, Ed Hewett, and Paul Wolfowitz, the Under Secretary of Defense for Policy, found the Ukrainians increasingly wary of the Russians. "The Russians see themselves as the Center," and "the Russians still have the mentality of empire" were the kinds of statements they heard from the Ukrainian leadership. Kiev was also fixated on the symbols of

*The group (named the Un-Group because no one was supposed to know of its existence) included Reggie Bartholomew and Jim Timbie from State; first Arnie Kanter and later John Gordon from the NSC; Doug MacEachin from the CIA; Vic Alessi from the Energy Department; Steve Hadley from DOD; and from the JCS, the Chairman's assistant, first Howard Graves, then John Shalikashvili, and finally Barry McCaffrey.

independence, and that meant that Ukraine wanted to be a party to the START Treaty.

Without American intervention, we were going to remain stalled, so I sent a message to Kozyrev and we talked on April 16. Kozyrev agreed with our proposed protocol in which the three would adhere to the NPT as non–nuclear weapons states, and would commit to the removal of all strategic nuclear weapons from their territories within seven years (the START time frame).

Later that day, I called President Kravchuk to discuss the proposed protocol. I outlined the concept over the phone and told Kravchuk that I would have our chargé in Kiev, Jon Gunderson, deliver a draft so the Ukrainian President could review it. Kravchuk called my initiative "very realistic" and said he'd call back the next day, which he did. "Your approach is very constructive," he said. "It shows the U.S. government is ready to take into consideration the positions of all countries involved. Ukraine supports the form and content of the protocol. I have a few comments on it, but these are not matters of principle."

With one down (or so I thought), I turned to Belarus and Kazakhstan. On April 19, I spoke by telephone to Stanislav Shushkevich of Belarus, who foresaw no problems with the protocol. The Chernobyl disaster had quite understandably led the Belarussians to acquire a severe aversion to anything nuclear.

I also spoke that day with President Nazarbayev of Kazakhstan. In a letter to President Bush a few days earlier, Nazarbayev had tried to find a "third way" with regard to the NPT. He wanted Kazakhstan to become a "temporary" nuclear power for purposes of the nonproliferation pact. He had linked the length of time it would take Kazakhstan to join the NPT as a full non-nuclear state to security guarantees from nuclear weapons states, notably the United States. I told him that security guarantees had been addressed in the original NPT negotiations and that the United States had formally declared its intent in 1968 to seek U.N. Security Council assistance if any non-nuclear state were threatened by a nuclear power. I told Nazarbayev that we stood by this commitment, and would reiterate it in terms of Kazakhstan.

Nazarbayev was rather cagey, thanking me and noting that he hoped our "special relationship" would continue—but he also elliptically said that he felt certain I recognized Kazakhstan's special geopolitical role. He ended by urging me to use American diplomacy to influence the Russian leadership. "If Russian chauvinism is not checked, blood may be shed, civil war might erupt, all the reforms could go up in smoke, and Kazakhstan might get involved," he concluded.

I decided that we weren't going to make much progress with either the Ukrainians or the Kazakhs until their political needs were met. We were fortunate that we had scheduled Kravchuk and then Nazarbayev for meetings with the President in Washington in May. Yeltsin would come in June for a full-fledged summit. The political symbolism of being received at the White House would certainly help the Ukrainians' psychological need to demonstrate their independence as well as Nazarbayev's desire to exhibit our "special relationship." To reinforce both, we drafted "joint statements" for the Ukrainians and Kazakhs, to illustrate the close ties they had to America.

I felt that if we could get the Ukrainians pinned down on the START Protocol, that would give us the leverage we needed to get the Kazakhs to agree as well. By obtaining a commitment to non-nuclear status by Ukraine, Belarus, and Kazakhstan, we would, in turn, address one of the most serious security challenges in the region, as well as meet our objective that only one nuclear power survive the breakup of the Soviet Union. Furthermore, it would strengthen the domestic position of Yeltsin and the democrats against rabid nationalists, and provide further impetus for Russian reform and the expansion of U.S.-Russian cooperation during the summit. Moreover, Moscow clearly was not going to act to reach agreement on START II until this aspect of START itself was solved.

As a consequence, from April 28 through May 4, I spoke to Zlenko eight times, as we haggled over the protocol and the side letter of assurances that would go along with it. Initially, the Ukrainians had two sets of problems. The first related to the Ukrainian Rada, its parliament; Kravchuk was unwilling to make a legally binding commitment or agree to a date certain for eliminating nuclear weapons, because he felt that these were decisions for the Rada. Second, Ukraine wanted security guarantees and wanted the elimination of nuclear weapons on the territory of the former Soviet Union to be under international control.

While Zlenko and I worked through the draft protocol and side letter, I came to feel a high degree of uncertainty about whether any issue we had supposedly resolved had truly been put to bed. There was a certain amount of "play" in the Ukrainian formulations, and I was nervous that we might never close the negotiation. On May 1, for example, Zlenko added the phrase "territorial integrity" to the side letter, a clear reference to the dispute then under way with Russia over the Black Sea fleet and the Crimea. I eliminated that, but we still didn't have complete agreement.

To ensure I didn't lose the Russians, I called Kozyrev on May 1 and again on May 2. I explained to him that we were now working to obtain a protocol and legally binding side letters, and that because of the need for parliaments to ratify the NPT, Belarus, Kazakhstan, and Ukraine would agree to accede to the NPT at the "earliest possible time," instead of a date certain. Kozyrev was concerned about the ambiguities inherent in some of our proposed language, but felt our approach would work nonetheless if everyone could be convinced to sign on. I told him that even though Kravchuk was due in Washington in three days, I was far from certain of obtaining Ukrainian agreement. "Additional pressure on the Ukrainians might lead to the signing of the protocol," Kozyrev observed, "though Kiev is playing a very dangerous, if typically Soviet, psychological game," a clear reference to the Communist Party backgrounds of Kravchuk and Zlenko.

On May 4, I called Zlenko to try to complete the side letter. His draft text included the language on international supervision of the elimination of nuclear weapons, an approach we couldn't accept because it would make the international community, not Ukraine, responsible for removing or destroying nuclear weapons on Ukrainian soil. When I tried to point out that we had already decided that that approach would not work, Zlenko told me that the idea of international supervision had been proposed by the Ukrainian President and the Rada. "Moreover, the letter is already signed. President Kravchuk is out of his office and will be unavailable to sign a new letter prior to departing for Washington. In any event, he would be irritated by any changes."

"The START Treaty does not provide for international control or supervision," I responded, "and the U.S. government is not willing to have this as a condition of Ukraine following through on its obligations." I told him that, if need be, we could amend Kravchuk's letter in ink, but if agreement couldn't be reached prior to the Ukrainian President's arrival, then President Bush would have to take up the issue directly with him.

"I want you to know," I continued, "how deeply I regret that this matter is still unresolved." I then read him an editorial in that day's *New York Times,* entitled "Nuclear Backsliding in Ukraine." It suggested that political and economic support be withheld from Ukraine until it made a commitment to eliminate nuclear weapons. "That's why I've been working at this for three weeks, so it won't mar President Kravchuk's visit," I said.

Finally Zlenko got the message. He said he "personally" saw no problem with eliminating the disputed phrase, but would have to try to reach Kravchuk. An hour later, he called me back, a little more frantic than before, and said he hadn't been able to talk to Kravchuk. I told him we'd just have to talk when they arrived in Washington.

Upon Kravchuk's arrival, I rode with him to Blair House, where he would be staying during the visit. "Mr. President," I began, "this visit is very important for both our countries. For the first time, the leader of a democratic and independent Ukraine is visiting the United States." I went on to explain how much we wanted his visit to succeed, but that required closing on the protocol and the side letter. I told him, "We understand why you want some form of control over weapons once they leave Ukraine." But we couldn't accept that in START. He only needed to add the words "the position of Ukraine" to the offending sentence and we would be done. He agreed, and the visit ended up as a major success for U.S.-Ukrainian relations.

Just as important, it isolated Nazarbayev, who had given an interview on May 5—the day of the Bush-Kravchuk meeting—with the *Washington Post*, in which he said he was seeking security guarantees from Russia, China, and the United States before Kazakhstan would give up its nuclear weapons. But with the Ukrainians on board, Nazarbayev had nowhere to go, so I felt fairly confident when I wrote him on May 13, outlining our suggested approach to START and reiterating our 1968 NPT commitment. He called me back on May 16, two days before he was due to arrive in Washington to see President Bush. He told me that Kazakhstan had received a collective security guarantee from Russia and, combined with our NPT commitment, he felt secure in signing the START Protocol and joining the NPT as a non–nuclear weapons state. I noted that we also needed a side letter, and he said he would send one through our Ambassador, Bill Courtney. But in Moscow, on the way to the United States, Nazarbayev remarked, "The question of giving Kazakh territory for our common defense and for deployment of nuclear missiles will be decided on mutually advantageous grounds," a signal that he might be trying to cut a deal with the Russians to keep part of his nuclear arsenal.

Once the Kazakh President arrived in Washington at midafternoon on Monday, May 18, I spent an hour with him at Blair House, and then we breakfasted for an hour the next day in an effort to finish off the agreement, which we did in time for President Bush and Nazarbayev to announce it Tuesday afternoon. The START Protocol was done, and we would sign it that weekend in Lisbon, where all the states involved were meeting for the conference on assistance to the former Soviet Union. I breathed a sigh of relief. Three months of negotiating were over—or so I thought.

Unfortunately, even as I was headed to Lisbon, we were still haggling. In London for a stopover, I found out that the Ukrainians were balking, and so I called Zlenko from my suite at the Churchill Hotel. Within a minute of the conversation, it became clear he was backing away from minor issues we had already resolved. That infuriated me; there's nothing worse in a negotiation than to have an interlocutor who you begin to feel can't be trusted. Finally, I had enough and slammed down the receiver. "This guy's a liar," I blurted to no one in particular. "He is nothing more than a Communist. I'm sick of this issue."

Dennis Ross, who had been listening in on the conversation as my note taker, came into the room with a huge smile on his face. "What are you smiling at?" I asked.

"Zlenko didn't realize you weren't on the line anymore. He kept talking and talking and when he didn't get any response, he said, 'Mr. Secretary? Mr. Secretary? Mr. Secretary! Oh, no, he hung up.' "

In Lisbon, it was just as bad. At 4:30 P.M. on Saturday, May 23—the day we were scheduled to sign the protocol—I had Zlenko and Kozyrev come to my holding room. Without any staff or note takers, I asked them to sit down. "Gentlemen," I said, "you need to work this out, and I'm not going to let you leave here until you do. So you better get to work." After looking at each other warily like two boxers in a prizefight, Zlenko and Kozyrev finally started talking and resolved their differences. After Zlenko left, Kozyrev exclaimed, "This is worse than dealing with a Bulgarian Communist!"*

Frankly, by that point, I didn't care. I just wanted the protocol completed. Finally, at 8:10 P.M., I filed into the Winter Garden Room of the Ritz Hotel with representatives from Belarus, Kazakhstan, Russia, and Ukraine. In an austere, wordless ceremony—we didn't want a shouting match—the protocol was signed, the letters were exchanged, and six minutes later, we had reached our goal: there would only be one nuclear power on the territory of the former Soviet Union.†

A Visit to a Friend

From Lisbon, I left on a six-hour flight to the former Soviet Union, not to negotiate over nuclear arms but to visit Georgia, the former Soviet republic now led by my friend Eduard Shevardnadze. Georgia was the only republic I had not visited since the August coup. It had been racked with turmoil in the past months, as its democratically elected leader turned despot, Zviad Gamsakhurdia, had been violently ousted in January after a year of oppressive rule. Armed thugs still roamed Tbilisi's streets at night, and with the perpetual threat of unrest looming, the government implemented an 11:00 P.M. curfew.‡

Shevardnadze had returned that spring as Georgia's interim President,

---

*In my report to the President that night, I wrote, "Suffice it to say, the wrangling brought back some pretty vivid memories of eight trips to the Middle East and what it took to nail down the invitation for the Madrid Conference."

†However, the Clinton administration had to deal with some delay and backsliding by Ukraine in taking the actions agreed to in the protocol.

‡The curfew was better at protecting innocents than deterring criminals. Indeed, during the night, gunfire could be heard outside the guest house where I was staying.

and he aptly described his homeland as "a small country with big problems." Although it was a long detour (3,000 miles) for a visit that would last less than twenty-four hours, I wanted to go to Georgia because I felt to do so would help give their fragile society an important boost for democracy and, hopefully, provide Shevardnadze and his allies a psychological lift as they headed toward the general elections scheduled for October 11.

We arrived at the airport that evening to find Shevardnadze, with his familiar shock of white hair, waiting on the tarmac, with Sergei Tarasenko and Tyamuraz Stepanov, his other loyal aide, at his side. While he was concerned about Georgia's plight, he was obviously quite pleased and proud to have me visit his home as he had visited mine in December 1990. From the airport we went to a government guest house for dinner and meetings. The huge wooden guest house was in the hills outside of Tbilisi, and had been formerly occupied by Lavrenti Beria, the dreaded head of Stalin's NKVD, the predecessor to the KGB. I found it almost unbelievable to be staying in a house once used for vacationing by Beria, one of Stalin's most notorious and murderous henchmen, and someone about whom I used to read in American publications.

We met in the cozy sitting room on the cottage's second floor. I began by asking Shevardnadze to "let us know of any specific needs you have. We will work overnight to see what we can do. We have a number of programs, and some are easier to tap than others." Earlier, I had asked my staff to contact Rich Armitage in Washington to see what we could do to get new supplies of food and medicine delivered immediately to Georgia.

Shevardnadze thanked me for my offer, and said that he was grateful that we had acted to recognize Georgia. "It is awkward for you because you had a legitimate President [Gamsakhurdia] that was overthrown. It was not a simple matter for you, I recognize that." He said that other key nations, like Russia, had not yet taken such action.

He continued by outlining the challenge ahead of building democracy. "There is no tradition of democracy in this country," he explained. "People here still think Stalin's method was the best way to run this country. Many colleagues have urged me to take all the power. While I seem to have the trust of the people, I know that I have to move on elections. We need to elect a normal parliament. We've got to solve the tremendous economic problems we have. We have good, young, interesting people who are starting to trust democracy."

While he was saying this, I couldn't help but think back to the many meetings we had had together. I remembered how I had felt when I was first exposed to the strong Georgian outlook of his wife, Nanuli, over dinner in his Moscow apartment in May 1989. But, in particular, I was reminded of something Shevardnadze had said during our meeting in Namibia more than two years earlier. At the time, I was pushing him very hard on Soviet repression in the Baltics, and trying to convince him that the Soviets would be better off to let them go. His response had been simple: "Jim, if we do that, where will it end? How will we be able to defend not letting others go? Some of the others will want to go." That was exactly what had happened, and now he was back in his Georgian homeland, trying to piece together the puzzle of democracy.

Shevardnadze assured me that in the Wild West atmosphere of Tbilisi, his security was all right, being "a minor question, really, in light of what we are facing as a country." He did admit, however, that things may get "worse closer to the election. These people needed me to come back for their own political reasons right now. I will be less needed the closer we get to the election." On the election, Shevardnadze predicted that "it will come off, but we need further stability here. Twelve to fifteen percent of the population still supports Gamsakhurdia, and in the western part of the state, there are a lot of fanatics."

The next morning, we began our day with Shevardnadze taking me to a fantastic eleventh-century monastery that sat in the ring of mountains surrounding Tbilisi. The cathedral reflected this small nation's rich religious heritage and had been the burial place of rulers during the period of the Georgian monarchy. Downtown Tbilisi is one of the few places in the Caucasus where one could find sites representing nearly every major religion: a Muslim mosque, a Jewish synagogue, and Armenian and Georgian Christian Orthodox churches. Inside the mountain monastery, the monks performed a beautiful ceremony and we were given candles to light.

I then met with the Georgian State Council, the governing body of the government, where I reaffirmed our support of Georgia's efforts to build democracy and a free-market system. Among my delegation was Lt. Gen. John Shalikashvili, who had led Operation Provide Comfort and was now Colin Powell's representative on the trip. Shalikashvili's father had fled Georgia from the Soviets in 1921, and his ancestry there had been prominent. As such, Shalikashvili took on a sort of celebrity status during our visit, as he was met with a media deluge from the moment we hit the ground.

On the way to the airport, we drove through the areas of downtown Tbilisi destroyed in the civil unrest earlier that year. The parliament building looked like something from World War II newsreels. At the end of this boulevard of destruction, there was an enormous square filled with people celebrating Georgia's "National Day," a holiday commemorating that date in 1918 when Georgia had declared independence. This day obviously had special significance this year, and the crowd was particularly large and boisterous.

When we neared the square, Shevardnadze wanted to get out of our car to mingle with the crowd. We did, and this spontaneous move did not please my security agents. We had been told earlier that nearly everyone in Georgia had a gun, and that at night this square was basically a war zone. The happiness on the faces I saw took away any sense of danger that I might have felt, and Shevardnadze and I both spoke to the crowd from a stage in the square. Indeed, the enthusiasm and appreciation of the crowd of thousands were reminiscent of my visit to Albania the year before.

A Nuclear Breakthrough: START II

Throughout the negotiations over the START Protocol, I had remained in constant contact with Andrei Kozyrev, with an eye not only toward finishing START but also to making progress on START II. We made some gains on minor issues—clearing away the underbrush, as it were—but could not bridge the gap on the major differences in our positions.

With completion of the START Protocol—and with Yeltsin's summit with the President less than a month away—the Russian position began to shift. In Lisbon, Kozyrev presented a proposal that called for a phased approach. In the first phase, both sides would reduce to 4,500 to 4,700 warheads during the seven-year period enshrined in START. In the second phase, the sides would drop to 2,500 warheads by the year 2005 and eliminate all MIRVed ICBMS.

This marked a significant shift toward President Bush's State of the Union initiative. The aggregate force levels in the first phase were the same as those President Bush had proposed. And the commitment to de-MIRVing included only ICBMs, not SLBMs. The downside to Kozyrev's proposal was the 2,500-warhead limit—which was far lower than our Defense Department was willing to go.

I told Kozyrev we wouldn't be able to accept the 2,500-warhead limit, and if the phased approach were predicated on that, then we wouldn't be able to accept it. However, I suggested that if we could record in writing a commitment simply to pursue further reductions in the second phase, we could go along with the phased approach. He said he thought they could agree to phase one on that basis. This was critical to us, because in order to get down to the 4,700-warhead level of phase one, the Russians would have to de-MIRV eighty percent of their ICBMs. I felt we were closing on the deal, but we needed to study the details and ensure there were no bureaucratic problems in Washington, so I told Kozyrev we'd get back to him soon.

On June 2 and 3, I called Kozyrev to explore his proposal further, but it was readily apparent that he had no more room in which to maneuver. I asked if a letter or phone call from President Bush to President Yeltsin would be useful, and he said that the timing wasn't right. On Thursday, June 4, I met with Scowcroft, Cheney, and Powell to discuss where we should go next. "De-MIRVing will be a major substantive and political triumph for the President, something he needs," I argued. "This is his issue. This is not old-style arms control, in form or substance," I continued. "We're not in Geneva negotiating a four-hundred-page text. We are looking for an agreement at the summit between the presidents that will decide all the major issues."

I bluntly stated my bottom line: "They have offered us what we want, and what no one else has ever come close to: zero MIRVed ICBMs, and without eliminating MIRVed SLBMs. We can't let this slip through our fingers because we think we need a *higher* total number. That is not sustainable with the public or the Congress."

We agreed to invite Kozyrev to come to Washington and determine whether he had any give in his position. I spent most of Monday, June 8, and Tuesday morning, going through various ways our proposals might be amended to reach agreement. We quickly agreed on a 4,700-warhead limit. But we could not agree on the sublimits on ICBMs, SLBMs, and bombers under the overall 4,700-warhead ceiling, and our time frames for destroying weapons were also different. I told Kozyrev I was willing to go to Moscow to eliminate any differences. "That just won't work," he replied. "We're accepting twenty-four billion dollars in aid, and the U.S. Secretary of State comes to Moscow to get what he wants." Kozyrev also warned me that the reformers' room for maneuver was limited. He said we needed to pay attention to Yeltsin's Security Council. "I've been outvoted seven to two on many issues," he noted. "We have some hard-line thinkers who say moderate things to Westerners, but in private, there is no change."

After further interagency talks and a political blast from Yeltsin, who told a meeting of senior army officers that the United States was seeking unilateral advantage, I flew to London on Thursday, June 11, for another round with the Russian Foreign Minister. On the flight to London, we took aircraft number 27000. (That's the tail number of the aircraft and the way we identified the various Air Force planes we flew.) I remembered the first time I had been on that plane—with Gerald Ford in 1976, when it had been Air Force One—and marveled at how much the world had changed since then.

In London, Kozyrev told me that Yeltsin had called him at 1:00 A.M. the night before. "Do you think the U.S. will take our latest initiative?" Yeltsin asked. Kozyrev had told him that we probably would not. Yeltsin then ordered Kozyrev to meet him at the Kremlin at 9:00 A.M. When Kozyrev had arrived, all of Yeltsin's top national security advisers, including the military brass, were already seated. "Explain to us why the U.S. will not take our proposal and why it will not cost money to do what the U.S. proposal suggests," Yeltsin had instructed him. Kozyrev had gone through an explanation, the generals had been forced to agree it wouldn't cost extra, and Yeltsin had given Kozyrev more room in which to manuever in the negotiation.

In London, Kozyrev came with more flexibility, and we managed to narrow our differences even more. After outlining where things stood, I asked our Un-Group experts bluntly, "What questions do you need answered?" They could identify only three concrete questions I should put to Kozyrev. I could feel a compromise emerging, but we were still not there yet.

On Monday, June 15, Yeltsin, Kozyrev, and the rest of the Russian delegation arrived in Washington, and Kozyrev came directly to the State Department to continue our talks. From just before 7:00 P.M. until 11:30 P.M., I was either negotiating with the Russians or negotiating with elements of our own government. For once, our Department of Defense seemed to be a bigger problem than Moscow's. However, we did settle two critical technical questions: the rules for counting bombers, and the limitations on downloading missiles (i.e., altering a missile from a MIRV to a single-warhead ICBM).

I reconvened the next day with the arms controllers at 8:20 A.M., then met with Kozyrev for almost forty-five minutes. I was beginning to lose patience with our side. The Russians had moved as far as they were going to, and the arms control theologians at the Pentagon seemed to prefer no agreement than one that got us "only" ninety percent of what we wanted.

I went over to the White House for the official arrival ceremony and then joined the President for his first bilateral session with Yeltsin.

Much as he had been in Camp David, the Russian President was on top of his brief. The Russian side, he said, wanted to complete the START II agreement. He proposed a unique approach. Instead of agreeing to a one-number "ceiling," why didn't we agree to a "range" instead? In phase one, he proposed that each side lower its number of warheads to between 3,800 and 4,250 total warheads; in phase two, the range would drop to between 3,000 and 3,500 warheads. The benefits of this approach were immediately apparent. It would allow the Russians to go to lower limits (which they wanted to for economic reasons) and it would allow us to have slightly higher numbers (which were consistent with our force structure). Above all, Yeltsin's approach recognized that in the realm of nuclear weapons, a few-hundred-warhead advantage, when both sides had over three thousand warheads, was not all that important. The President told Yeltsin we would consider his proposal.

I returned to the State Department, and just before going upstairs for a working luncheon in honor of President Yeltsin, I called the President. "I hope you're going to accept Yeltsin's proposal," I said. "I think this will be a significant achievement for your presidency, but you're going to have to tell the arms-control theologians you want it to happen. I've done all I can trying to roll this rock uphill."

"I hear you," he responded.

That afternoon, we reconvened in the Cabinet Room for another session. The President told Yeltsin we were ready to agree to his proposal, and the two leaders decided to make their announcement at 3:00 P.M. that afternoon. "With this agreement," announced President Bush, "the nuclear nightmare recedes more and more for ourselves, for our children, and for our grandchildren."

With the final agreement, the two sides would lower their total warheads to between 3,800 and 4,250 warheads by the year 2000, and to between 3,000 and 3,500 warheads by the year 2003. The accord would reduce the number of strategic weapons held by both sides to the lowest levels since 1969 and, more important, fundamentally reverse the arms race by eliminating land-based MIRVs. These weapons, which required each side to adopt a hair-trigger posture of "use 'em or lose 'em," would disappear—much as the Cold War, the Soviet empire, and the Soviet Union itself had also disappeared.

Four weeks later, I traveled with President Bush to my ranch in Pinedale for a couple of days of fishing with our sons Jamie Baker and Jeb Bush. His campaign for reelection was not going as well as he had hoped, and it was there that the President asked me to return to the White House as Chief of Staff and Senior Counselor. I couldn't help but think of other times and other requests: of 1976, when President Ford had asked me to resign as Under Secretary of Commerce and assist his election effort; of 1984, when President Reagan had asked me as White House Chief of Staff to coordinate his campaign for reelection; and of 1988, when Vice President Bush had asked me to resign as Secretary of the Treasury to manage his campaign.

I did not want to leave the State Department. We had accomplished so much—but so much more remained to be done. But I had never said no before, and I certainly wasn't going to do so now.

Thus it was, on August 13, 1992, that I stepped to the podium in the Dean Acheson Auditorium at the State Department to announce that I was going to resign as Secretary of State ten days later. As I began my remarks and looked out over the familiar faces, I told the gathered employees— foreign-service officers, career civil servants, and political appointees alike: "I wanted to have this talk with you, here at the State Department, because over the last three and one half years, we have together run through a whirlwind of history. We have set the pace and marked a course through an era of revolutionary change. And we've made some history in the process. I want to thank you for that."

I ended, struggling unsuccessfully to maintain my composure, by saying simply: "It's been an honor to serve with you. I thank you and I salute you."

As I reflect back now on my time as Secretary of State, I'm struck by my good fortune in occupying that office during a time of revolution, war, and peace: a revolution of freedom that swept away communism, a war of liberation that reversed a dictator's aggression, and progress toward peace, that established a foothold of reason in a region of enmity and conflict.

That fortune is most clear when I look back over the world my predecessors were forced to navigate. From 1945 through 1989, eleven Secretaries of State steered America's way across a geopolitical map shaped by World War II and the Cold War. In three and one half years, those borders and boundaries were permanently redrawn. Indeed, the very nature of the international system as we had known it was transformed.

In this transformation, diplomats can—and should—take only modest credit. For the true responsibility for the changes in the world we inhabit lies in the ordinary men and women who sought freedom, who struggled against the darkness of totalitarianism, and who rose up to seize liberty for themselves. It may have taken a leap of faith, but faith was something these peoples had in ample supply. And from Alma-Ata to Vilnius, and Albania to Mongolia, the people took destiny into their own hands and showed once and for all that freedom *does* work.

To some, looking back today with the hindsight that comes from a distance, there is a certain nostalgia for the Cold War. Given the intractability of some of the regional conflicts across the globe today, these rosy-eyed pessimists wish for the clarity of the East-West confrontation. While I would agree that the world is a dangerous place and the imperative of American leadership is as great as ever, I certainly do not harken back to that prior time, and it is for one simple reason: The world today is infinitely freer and safer than it has been during any other time in my life—and for that, I am grateful.

INDEX

Abdel-Meguid, Esmat, 124
Abrams, Elliott, 51
Abu Abbas, 129
Abu Hassan, 319
Abu Nidal, 262
Acheson, Dean, 29, 605
Afanasenko, Peter, 9, 211, 538, 539
Afghanistan, 74, 528
Africa: politics, 218–19; safari, 217–18
Agha, Zakariah Al-, 465
Aharon, Yossi Ben, 466, 499
AIPAC (American-Israel Public Affairs
    Committee), 121–22, 548–49, 551–53,
    555
Air Force, U.S., 284; Forth-eighth Tactical
    Fighter Wing, 366–69
Airlift to former Soviet states, 618, 623–24,
    626
Akayev, Askar, 578–79
Ake, Simeon, 315–16
Akhromeyev, Sergei, 169n, 206, 236, 242,
    253, 254, 401; suicide of, 532
Albania, 484–86
Alessi, Vic, 660n
Alexander, Michael, 95
Algeria, 497
Ali, Abidine Ben, 497
Allenby Bridge, 465
Alma-Ata, Kazakhstan, 538, 579, 582–83,
    585
Ambassadors, 29, 35, 165n; to U.N., 305
ANC, 224; Mandela and, 225–26
Andriessen, Hans, 90
Angola, 218, 225, 228, 598–601
Apartheid, 218–19, 221–22, 224, 227
APEC (Asia-Pacific Economic Cooperation),
    3, 44–45, 588, 609–13

Aptemocin, Ahmet, 433
Aquino, Corazon, 158
Arab Cooperation Council (ACC), 290
Arab peacekeeping force, 413
Arab world, 420; and Iraq, 262–63, 270,
    372–78, 385; and Israel, 117, 416; and
    Kuwait invasion, 7, 15, 277, 279; and
    Middle East peace process, 126–27,
    416–17, 428; and Saddam, 274, 280,
    291–92, 295
Arafat, Yasir, 118, 130, 423, 464, 491
Arens, Moshe, 118–19, 122, 124, 125, 127,
    128, 130, 386–88, 444, 499, 552
Argentina, aid to former Soviets, 619
Arias Sanchez, Oscar, 51
Armenia, 570, 585, 627–28
Armitage, Rich, 618, 626, 629n, 666
Arms control, 145, 151, 212–13, 413, 526,
    588–89, 668–69; CFE treaty, 473–75, 571,
    624–25; negotiations, 70–72, 74, 77,
    82–85, 90, 204, 236–37, 242, 247–48,
    252n, 470
Arms embargo, Serbo-Croatian war, 638
Army, Soviet, 533, 568
Aronson, Bernard, 51–53, 59, 187, 327; and
    Panama, 182, 183, 189, 190, 191
ASEAN (Association of Southeast Asian
    Nations), 494; and APEC, 609–10
Ashkhabad, Turkmenistan, 629–31
Ashrawi, Hanan, 423, 465, 491–93, 496–97,
    500–501
Aspin, Les, 335, 344
Assad, Hafez al-, President of Syria, 117,
    288, 295–98, 349, 464, 465, 490, 493–94;
    and Middle East peace process, 417, 420,
    425–28, 447–49, 454–57, 459–63, 468–69;

and peace conference, 487–89, 500–507, 511; and war with Iraq, 373–74, 376–77, 389
Atlee, Clement, 174
Atomic bomb, 196
Atwater, Lee, 551
Australia, 377–78, 609–13
Avril, Prosper, 601
Avrorin, Yevgeni, 616
AWACS radar planes, 118
Azerbaijan, 203, 585, 619, 628–29
Aziz, Tariq, 264–66, 271, 320–21, 340, 345–46, 354–65, 403–4, 405, 442

Bahrain, 306; Emir of, 420
Bakatin, Vadim, 534–35
Baker, Doug, 35
Baker, Howard, 48, 92, 132
Baker, James, xiii, 133–34, 217–18, 275–76, 368–69, 671–72; and Bush, 17–21, 406; China visits, 98–99, 590–94; and Congress, 54–58, 333–34, 339–40; death of mother, 458
Baker, Jamie, 97, 671
Baker, Mary Bonner (daughter), 18, 98
Baker, Mary Stuart (wife), xiii, 18, 260–61; death of, 37
Baker, Susan, 49, 77, 98, 217, 421, 423, 458, 515–16; in Yugoslavia, 634–35
Baker Plan, 606
Baklanov, Oleg, 515n
Baku, Azerbaijan, 628
Baltic states, 146–48, 203, 238–41, 257, 378–81, 524, 533, 534, 536–38, 635
Banca Nazionale del Lavoro (BNL), and Iraq, 265, 266
Bandar, Prince (Saudi Ambassador), 289, 307, 354, 372, 386, 417, 420, 438, 453, 459–60, 490, 499–500, 650
Barkley, Richard, 173
Barnes, Joe, 356
Bartholomew, Reggie, 213, 566, 617, 641, 660n
Baz, Osama el-, 126, 452
Begin, Menachem, 118, 119, 445
Begleiter, Ralph, 104, 384
Belarus (Belorussia), 523, 531n, 571, 572, 576, 581–82, 585, 658, 659, 661–65
Belgrade, Yugoslavia, 478–83, 634–35
Bentsen, B. A., 314
Bentsen, Lloyd, 42, 92, 155, 314
Bentsur, Eytan, 513
Beria, Lavrenti, 666
Berisha, Sali, 470, 485–86
Berlin, Four Powers meeting, 171–73
Berlin Wall, 158–59; fall of, 163
Berry, Steve, 656
Bessmertnykh, Alexander, 19, 169n, 254, 379, 380–82, 391–95, 463, 470, 487, 532; and coup against Gorbachev, 471, 517,

521, 522–23; and Middle East peace process, 428, 494; and war with Iraq, 384, 403–4, 406–8
Bevan, Aneurin, 39, 91
Bevin, Ernest, 39, 91, 174
Biden, Joe, 49
Bierbauer, Charles, 104
Bilateral agreements, 605
Binational Commission, U.S.-Mexico, 608
Biological weapons program, 621
Bipartisanship, 31, 41–42, 47–60, 219
Blackwell, Bob, 234, 475
Blackwill, Bob, 215, 478
Bladder diplomacy, 454–57
BNL (Banca Nazionale del Lavoro), 265, 266
Boidevaix (French Ambassador), 171
Bolton, John, 433
Bondarenko, Aleksandr, 242
Bonn, Germany, Two-plus-Four meeting, 235–36, 244, 247
Border guarantees, Mideast, 455–57
Borders, international, German unification and, 210, 212, 233
Boren, David, 244
Bosnia-Herzegovina, 478–79, 634–51
Bosnian Serbs, 642, 648
Botha, P. W., 221, 222, 224
Botha, R. F. "Pik," 221–22, 223, 227
Botswana, safari in, 217–18
Boucher, Richard, 36, 517
Bouez, Faris, 464
Boutros-Ghali, Boutros, 603
Bradley, Bill, 92
Brady, Nick, 606, 656
Brady Plan, 606
"Brain-drain" problem, 615, 621, 625
Breslauer, George, 69
Brest Declaration, 562–63, 565–66, 570, 573–74, 579–80
Brezhnev Doctrine, repudiation of, 76
Brill, Ken, 36
Britain, 44, 86–87, 94, 279, 378, 518, 645; and German unification, 167, 172, 198, 209–10, 232, 234; and war with Iraq, 11, 280–81, 313–14, 369–70, 377
Brooks, Jack, 263
Brown, Bill, 123, 509, 547
Brunei, 609
Bruntland, Gro, 88
Brzezinski, Zbigniew, 139
Buchanan, Patrick, 51
Bucharest, Romania, 207–8
Buchwald, Todd, 656n
"The Building," State Department, 27–28, 36
Bukhara, Uzbekistan, 633
Bulgaria, 206–7
Bureaucracy, 30, 75; NATO, 258; Soviet, 138; State Department, 28–30, 32, 68
Burney, Derek, 86

Burns, Bill, 36, 117, 509
Burns, Nick, 36
Burt, Rick, 88, 172
Bush, Barbara, 99
Bush, Bucky, 169n
Bush, George, xiii, 17–21, 25, 27, 37–38, 50, 58, 67, 68, 70–71, 144–45, 158, 168, 175–76, 228, 230, 262–63, 267, 317, 333, 346, 406, 411, 450–51, 494, 524, 601, 611, 639, 671; and arms control, 93–96, 596–97, 658–59, 670–71; and bipartisanship, 47, 57; and Bosnia, 648–51; and China, 98–101, 109–10, 323; and CIS, 565, 581; and coup against Gorbachev, 471, 515, 517, 519–21, 522; and dissolution of Soviet Union, 525–26, 558; and German unification, 159–60, 197, 213–16, 230, 252–53; and Gorbachev, 65, 168–71, 248, 291–94, 407–8, 527, 559; and Israel, 118, 120, 122–23, 128, 131–32, 541–42, 551–55, 557; joint statement with Russia, 9, 394; and Kurdish refugees, 433–34; and Lithuania, 239, 244, 379; and Mexico, 607–8; and Middle East peace process, 415, 417, 459, 468, 489, 500, 512, 557; Mubarak and, 420; Mulroney and, 42; and NAFTA, 608–9; and NATO, 44, 92; and Noriega, 178, 179–80, 183, 185–86, 188, 189–90; and Persian Gulf war, 2–4, 8–11, 276–77, 282–83, 303–4, 321, 329–31, 338–39, 347–49, 351, 353–54, 382–84, 399–400, 404–6, 435–37; and Salinas, 43; and Shamir, 123, 125; and Shoval, 545, 546; and South Africa, 219, 220, 223–24; Soviet Union and, 63, 477; and Syria, 296; and Tiananmen Square massacre, 104–5, 107, 108; and Yeltsin, 563, 623–25, 653
Bush, Jeb, 671
Bush administration, xiii, 30–31, 35, 85, 159, 180, 333, 602, 606–7, 613, 636; and Israel, 541–44, 555–56; and North Korea, 595–97; and South Africa, 219–20, 221; Soviets and, 59, 70–71
Bushnell, John, 31, 190–91
Byrd, Robert, 92

CAAA (Comprehensive Anti-Apartheid Act), 219, 227
Cabinet members, and politics, 39
Callaway, Bo, 33
Cambodia, war in, 588
Camp David, meetings at, 232–34, 623–25
Camp David Accord, 445
Canada, 42–43, 86, 604, 608, 609; and war with Iraq, 336, 377
Cape Town, South Africa, 226
Career bureaucrats, 28–31
Carpendale, Andrew, 11, 518n, 524, 648

Carrington, Lord (EC envoy), 637, 639, 641–42, 644
Carter, Jimmy, 24, 60, 183, 262, 334, 445
Carter administration, 122, 179, 290
Casaroli, Agostino, Cardinal, 192
Casey, William, 48, 50
Castro, Fidel, and Noriega, 184
Castro van Dunem, Pedro, 600
Caucasus, politics in, 627–29
CEMA (COMECON), 149
Center, Soviet, 524, 530, 533–35, 560–61, 566, 567; dissolution of, 559
Central America, 42, 46, 47–58, 602–4; Soviet Union and, 59, 76–77, 81
Central Asian states, 570, 629–33
Cetin, Hikmet, 650
CFE. See Conventional Forces in Europe
Chamorro, Violeta, 60
Charles, Sandy, 363
Charter of Paris, 473
Chebrikov, Victor, 144
Checkpoint Charlie, 255
Chelyabinsk-70 nuclear facility, 614–16
Chemical weapons, 151, 359, 408; Iraq and, 264, 268, 269; Libya and, 589
Cheney, Dick, 22–25, 26, 70, 258, 261, 302, 560, 584, 618n, 649–50; and arms control, 526n, 669; and CFE, 92, 93–94; and Panama, 189, 191, 193; and Persian Gulf war, 282–83, 303, 304, 311, 338, 355, 382, 386, 409, 434, 435; Soviets and, 75, 533
Chernyayev, Anatoliy, 471
Chetverikov, Sergei, 171, 197, 379–80, 404
Chief of Staff, Reagan administration, 19–20, 50
Chile, and NAFTA, 609
China, 23, 44, 97–114, 588–96, 605, 610, 637; and Persian Gulf war, 9, 280–81, 308–9, 316, 321–24, 326
Chinoy, Mike, 104
Churchill, Winston, 174, 196
CIA (Central Intelligence Agency), 4–5, 20; KGB and, 534
Cicconi, Jim, 38
CIS. See Commonwealth of Independent States
Cisneros, Marc, 192
Citizens' Democracy Corps, 202
Civil war: Georgia, 665; Iraq, U.S. and, 440–41; Tajikistan, 631; Yugoslavia, 479–83
Clark, Bill, 30, 38
Clark, Joe, 86, 95, 208, 213, 216; and Persian Gulf war, 315, 335–36
Clarke, Dick, 8
Clausewitz, Karl von, 260, 436
Cleland, Scott, 656n
Clientitis, 29; of Woerner, 184
Clinton, Bill, and China policy, 113

Clinton administration, 594, 598n, 665n
CNN, 10, 104, 163, 191, 349, 361, 509, 618;
  and coup against Gorbachev, 515, 516,
  520, 522; and war with Iraq, 284, 367,
  384. *See also* Television
Coalitions, xv, 91–92; international, against
  Iraq, 11, 15, 278–99, 301, 303, 304, 333,
  350–52, 369–78, 383–95, 441
Cohen, Hank, 221, 222–23, 599–600
Cold War, 24, 92, 155, 196; end of, 2–3, 16,
  41–46, 112–13, 163, 277, 672
Cold War legislation, repeal of, 658
Collective action, OAS and, 194
Collins, Jim, 515, 519, 520, 522, 525, 572
Colombia, 194, 318–19, 325
Colonialism in Africa, end of, 225
Commodity Credit Corporation (CCC), and
  Iraq, 263, 265, 266–67, 270
Common sense, politics and, 39–40
Commonwealth of Independent States
  (CIS), 562–63, 565–86, 617, 624, 626–33;
  and arms control, 658, 659–60
Communications, Mongolia, 9
Communism, 45–46, 60, 61, 535, 538, 633,
  653; collapse of, 232, 484–86
Communist Party, Soviet, 136, 202–3, 205,
  259, 523; Shevardnadze and, 77, 208–9;
  Yeltsin and, 472
Comprehensive Anti-Apartheid Act (CAAA),
  219, 227
Conable, Barber, 284–85
Congress, U.S., 31, 35, 42, 49–50, 54–58,
  219, 240, 333, 603, 611, 653, 656–58; and
  China, 105, 108, 110, 113, 590, 594; and
  Iraq, 273, 352; and Lithuania, 244n, 379,
  380; and loan guarantees to Israel,
  549–55, 557; and NAFTA, 607, 608, 612;
  and Nicaragua, 48–58; and Panama, 186,
  193; and war with Iraq, 278, 303, 330–33,
  335, 337–44
Congress of People's Deputies, 76, 657
Consensus, domestic, 31, 41–42, 346–47,
  350
Constitution, U.S., and Presidential powers,
  334
Containment policy, 41, 48, 562, 563
Contras, 53; aid to, 52, 56–57
Conventional Forces in Europe (CFE);
  negotiations, 63, 91, 92, 94, 96; Soviet
  Union and, 82, 212–13, 246; treaty, 317,
  473–74, 475, 477, 571
Coordinating Conference, 564, 584, 617–19,
  624, 655
Cordoba de Montoya, José, 608
Coups, 602; against Gorbachev, 470–72,
  515–23, 532–33, 535, 637; against
  Noriega, 185–87
Courtney, Bill, 664
Covey, Jock, 31
Creagan, Jim, 192

Crisis management, 186; Kimmitt and, 35
Cristiani, Alfredo, 603
Croatia, 478–82, 483n, 635, 639, 641, 642
Crocker, Chester, 221, 225
Crowe, William, 26n, 92, 93–94, 343, 352
Crowley, John, 153
Crown Prince of Kuwait, 306–7, 374–75,
  419–20
CSCE (Conference on Security and
  Cooperation in Europe), 172, 173, 202,
  254–55, 257, 258, 473, 479, 517, 526–27,
  571, 645; German unification and, 196,
  231–32, 253, 254; Soviet Union and, 235,
  246
Cuba, 305; and Angola, 598–99, 600; and
  Persian Gulf war, 278, 321–22, 327;
  Soviet Union and, 59, 528–29
Cultural Revolution, China, 103–4
Czechoslovakia, 160, 200–202, 521; Prague
  demonstrations, 63, 171

Dancy, John, 485
Darman, Richard, 32, 619
Davis, Arthur, 180–81, 183
Davis, Bill, 617n
DC. *See* Deputies' Committee
Deaver, Mike, 27
Defense Department, 560, 618n, 670
Defense Ministry, Soviet, 563
Defense policy, 154–55
Defense Secretary, 70
de Klerk, F. W., 220–24, 226–28
Delors, Jacques, 90
Delvalle, Eric Arturo, 179
de Michelis, Gianni, 195, 216, 372, 584
Democracy, 6, 194, 202, 601–2, 666–67;
  Soviet people and, 532–33, 535–36; Soviet
  Union and, 45–46, 72, 73, 138, 203, 525
Democratic party, U.S., 31, 55–58, 112–13
Democratic peace, 654
Democratic People's Republic of Korea. *See*
  North Korea
Deng Xiaoping, 98, 107, 109, 592
Dent, Lynn, 512, 565, 617n, 626
Department of Agriculture, and Iraq, 263,
  267, 270–71
Deputies, 34
Deputies' Committee (DC), 35, 186; and
  Iraq, 4, 8, 269–70, 271, 304–5
Desert Shield; Desert Storm. *See* Persian Gulf
  war
Deus Pinheiro, João de, 466
Deuvan, Linda, 34
Development bank, Middle East, 413
Devroy, Ann, 96
Dialogues, political, 153–55, 416
Diaspora Jews, 541–44
Diaspora Palestinians, 491, 492
Dictators, economic chaos and, 476
Dienstbier, Jiri, 521

Dine, Tom, 122, 549
Diplomacy, xiii, xv, 10, 32, 134, 273, 293, 604–13; coercive, against Saddam, 277; television and, 361, 365
Diplomats, Soviet, lifestyle, 7
Djerejian, Ed, 297, 426, 454, 456, 459, 460, 469, 487–88
Dobrynin, Anatoly, 62–23
Dodd, Christopher, 49, 56, 57, 92, 341
Dole, Robert, 55, 92, 126, 269, 337
dos Santos, Jose Eduardo, 225, 598–600
Downing, Wayne, 192–93
Drew, Elizabeth, 161
Drug traffic, Noriega and, 177, 180
Dubcek, Alexander, 63, 201
Dubinin, Yuri, 62, 145, 197, 202
Dulles, John Foster, 29, 174
Dumas, Roland, 13, 90, 110, 259, 324, 347–48, 370, 378, 522, 584, 642; and German unification, 200, 209–11, 215
Dushanbe, Tajikistan, 631

EAEG (East Asian Economic Group), 610–11
Eagleburger, Lawrence, 26, 34, 35, 94, 143, 190, 564, 619, 635, 638, 643; China trips, 109–10, 113; and coup against Gorbachev, 470–71, 517–20; and former Yugoslav states, 639, 640–41; and Israel, 385, 388–90, 415, 544
EAI (Enterprise for the Americas Initiative), 606
EAP (East Asia and Pacific Bureau), 44
East Asia, 605; U.S. and, 609–13
East Asian Economic Group (EAEG), 610–11
Eastern Europe, 40, 45, 91, 148–49, 170–71; reforms in, 63–64, 67; Shevardnadze and, 75–76, 140–41
East Germany, 149–50, 158, 162–66, 171–75, 232–34, 237; refugees, 160–61. *See also* German unification; Germany
East Jerusalem, negotiations, 458
EBRD (European Bank for Reconstruction and Development), 249
EC. *See* European Community
Economic aid: to Haiti, 601; to Iraq, 263–67, 270, 271; to Israel, 542, 544–45; to Russia, 654–55
Economic reform, 150–51; China, 101–2; former Soviet states, 533, 536, 558–59, 581, 582, 617, 623, 627, 654–58; Mexico, 607; Soviet, 77–78, 82, 138–39, 203, 400, 477–78, 523–24, 526, 527, 529, 531, 535–36, 577
Economics of diplomacy, 604–13
Economic union, Soviet, 527, 532
Economy: Russia, 654–58; Soviet Union, 63, 476, 529, 616; Turkmenistan, 630; U.S., Persian Gulf crisis and, 336–37; Yugoslavia, 480
Edelman, Eric, 618n

Egypt, 116, 118, 124, 270, 280, 288, 416, 420–21; and Persian Gulf war, 15, 308, 375–76
Einstein, Albert, 64
Elbe, Frank, 199, 559
Election campaigns, 20–21, 24, 671
Elections, 46; Angola, 600; El Salvador, 603; Georgia, 666–67; Haiti, 601; Mongolia, 6; Nicaragua, 51–53, 55, 58, 59–60, 76–77; Palestinian, 120–21, 124; Panama, 182–83; U.S., and NAFTA, 608
Elephants, protection of, 218n
Elias Serrano, Jorge, 602
Elizabeth, Queen of England, 377
Ellis, Helen, 33
El Salvador, 42, 184, 602–4
Embody, Kathie, 434
Emigrants, Jewish, 540, 541–44, 548
Emir of Kuwait, 271, 289–90, 306, 366, 419
Endara, Guillermo, 183, 189, 190
Enterprise for the Americas Initiative (EAI), 606
Environmentalists, and NAFTA, 607
Espionage cases, Moscow meeting, 74
Esquipulas, Guatemala, accord, 52–54
Estonia, 524, 536–37
Ethiopia, 244, 315, 326
Ethiopian Jews, emigration of, 548
Ethnic conflict, 139, 144, 537–38, 633
Eurasia Foundation, 619
European Community (EC), 44, 172, 173, 284, 446, 518, 584, 605, 618; and Yugoslavia, 480, 482, 636–48
Evans, Gareth, 377–78
Evans, Rowland, 83
Eyskens, Mark, 315

Fahd, King of Saudi Arabia, 3, 270, 282, 289, 300, 548; and Persian Gulf war, 307–8, 373, 374; and Middle East peace process, 417–19, 420, 444, 452–53, 459–60, 490
Fang Lizhi, 106–7, 589
Farmer-to-Farmer program, 619
Fascell, Dante, 339, 342, 344
Fauver, Bob, 44, 581, 609
Financial support for Gulf War costs, 288–91, 298–99, 308, 371–75
First Cavalry Division, U.S. Army, 306
Fitzwater, Marlin, 189, 406, 520, 561–62
Five principles for diplomatic relations, 525–26, 531–32, 560, 563, 627n; former Soviet states and, 538, 579, 583, 632–33
Fokin, Vitold, 532
Foley, Tom, 92, 344, 549
Ford, Gerald, 20, 22, 23, 26, 424, 500
Ford, Guillermo, 183
Foreign affairs committees, 339–44, 412–14
Foreign aid, unpopularity of, 555

Foreign policy, 29–30, 36, 38–39, 41–46, 61,
  65, 70, 109, 143–44, 154, 334, 378,
  566–67, 587–88, 604; bipartisan, 47, 219;
  changes in, 30, 273; and defense policy,
  154–55; strategic review, 68–70
Foreign Service, 28–31, 34
Former Soviet states, 614–33
Forty-eighth Tactical Fighter Wing, USAF,
  366–69
Foster, Gary, 512
Four Powers meeting, 171–72, 197
France, 378, 547, 646; and Coordinating
  Conference, 584, 618; and German
  unification, 167, 172, 198, 209–10, 232,
  233n, 234; and NATO, 258, 259; and
  Persian Gulf war, 11, 14, 280–81, 314–15,
  321, 370
Freedom, 672
Freedom Support Act, 653, 656–58
Freeman, Chas, 289, 373
Free-trade agreements, 607; U.S.-Canada,
  42–43, 86, 606; NAFTA, 607–9, 612
Freij, Elias, 496n
Friedman, Tom, 131, 154
Friendships, 21; Bush, 18–19; Genscher, 88;
  Shevardnadze, 77, 135, 474–75, 577
FSOs (Foreign Service officers), 28–29, 31, 35
Fuel shortage, Soviet Union, 564–65, 626
Fujimori, Alberto, 602
Fukuyama, Frank, 168

Gaidar, Yegor, 655, 656
Gamsakhurdia, Zviad, 665
Gang of Eight, Soviet, 515, 517–18, 520
Garment, Leonard, 547
Gaskill, Bill, 484, 512
Gates, Bob, 94, 156–58, 385, 563n
GATT, 591, 605, 612
Gaviria Trujillo, Cesar, 318–19
Gaydar, Yegor, 623n
GDR. See East Germany
Gebre-Kidan, Tesfaye, 549
Genscher, Hans-Dietrich, 87–88, 95, 160–61,
  164, 195, 225, 233–34, 255, 378, 571n,
  618, 644; and coup against Gorbachev,
  517, 522; and German unification, 198,
  199–200, 209, 211, 213–15, 247
Georgia, 71, 78, 147, 531, 627, 665–68
Gephardt, Dick, 44
Gerasimov, Gennadi, 163, 166
German unification, 158–60, 165–68,
  172–76, 195–216, 230–32, 237–38, 244,
  294; costs of, 655; Soviet Union and,
  241–42, 245–47, 250–54, 259
Germany, 44, 45–46, 87, 149, 159, 280, 288,
  298–99, 378, 547, 639, 646; and NATO,
  90–91, 94, 164. See also East Germany;
  German unification
G-5 (Group of Five Industrialized Nations),
  604

Gibson, Charlie, 350
Gilbert, Clairo, 34
Gilmore, Harry, 173
Gingrich, Newt, 92
Giroldi, Moises, 185–86
Glasnost, 46
Glaspie, April, 266, 268, 269, 272, 274, 355
Glienicke Bridge, 173
Gligorov, Vladimir, 480–81, 640
Global aid program, 618–19
Global defense system, 621
Gnehm, Skip, 268
Godmanis, Ivars, Prime Minister of Latvia,
  536
Golan Heights, 421, 422, 424–25, 427,
  455–57, 461–62, 493–94, 557
Gonzalez, Felipe, 511
Gorbachev, Mikhail, 13, 15, 45–46, 48–49,
  62, 63, 65, 67–68, 79, 87, 92, 96, 136,
  144, 155, 168–69, 202, 232, 248–54, 400,
  474–75, 526–27, 561–65, 568, 579–80,
  585, 596, 599; and arms control, 85, 145,
  212–13, 236, 572; coup against, 470–72,
  497, 515–23, 532–33, 535, 637; and
  dissolution of Soviet Union, 559, 573–75;
  domestic problems, 257, 259, 294–95,
  401–2, 475–77; and East Germany,
  161–63, 165; and economic reform, 203,
  477–78, 655–58; and German unification,
  166–67, 198, 205–6, 211–12, 230–32,
  234–35, 257, 259; and Lithuania, 240–45,
  378–81; meetings with, 70–83, 168–71,
  494; and Middle East peace process, 428,
  495, 512; and Persian Gulf war, 12, 13,
  283, 286–87, 291–94, 310–13, 316–17,
  321, 384, 391, 394–400, 402–8; relations
  with, 135, 142–43, 472–73; resignation of,
  523, 586; Shevardnadze and, 77, 398,
  569; strategies of, 69–70, 89, 93; Yeltsin
  and, 528–29, 563, 569–72
Gorbunovs, Anatolijs, 537
Gordon, John, 660n
Gore, Al, 344
Goshko, John, 122
Grain, Russia's need for, 655
Graves, Howard, 8, 11, 310–11, 355–56,
  361, 374, 660n
Gray, Boyden, 58
Greece, 88, 640n, 641–42, 646
Greenberger, Bob, 154
Greenspan, Alan, 606
Grenada, invasion of, 334–35
Groomes, Karen, 34, 85–86, 150, 173, 209,
  356, 358, 510–12, 617n
G-7 (Group of Seven Industrialized Nations),
  519, 604, 650, 656, 657; summit
  meetings, 259, 488–89
Guatemala, OAS and, 602
Guerrilla warfare: Angola, 598; El Salvador,
  603–4

Gugushvili, Vissarion, 531
Gulf Cooperation Council, 420, 459–60
Gunderson, Jon, 661

Haass, Richard, 292, 329–30
Hadley, Steve, 584, 660n
Hague, The and peace conference, 510–11
Haig, Alexander, 30
Haile Selassie, 326
Haiti, 601–2
Hamdoon, Nizar, 264
Hamilton, Lee, 49, 349
Hannah, John, 524
Hannibalsson, John Baldwin, 86
Han Xu, 106–7
Hauslohner, Peter, 7, 16
Havel, Václav, 200–201
Hawke, Bob, 44–45, 109, 609
Hay, John, 609
Helal, Gemal, 357, 456
Helicopters, Iraqi, 439–40
Helms, Jesse, 55, 56, 108, 193, 186
Helsinki Final Act, 233, 251–52, 480
Herrera, Omar Torrijos, 179
Heslin, Sheila, 619
Hewett, Ed, 561, 566, 627, 656, 660
Hills, Carla, 611
Hoffman, David, 154
Hoggard, Kim, 34, 88–89, 215, 356
Hoghaug, Eric, 158
Holliman, John, 384
Honecker, Erich, 160–63
Hong Kong, 44, 588, 605, 610
Hormats, Bob, 23
Horn (Hungarian Foreign Minister), 160
Hostage crisis, Iran, 261–62
House Foreign Affairs Committee, 342–44, 414
Houston Economic Summit, 472
Hovanissian, Raffi, 628
Howe, Geoffrey, 86, 87, 95
Hoxa, Enver, 484
Humanitarian aid: to contras, 50, 52, 53, 57, 58; to former Soviet states, 571, 581, 584, 618, 623–24, 626, 645, 648–50; to Kurdish refugees, 433–35; to Soviet Union, 526, 530
Human rights issues: China and, 100–106, 589–94; El Salvador and, 603; Soviet Union and, 72; in Yugoslavia, 480
Hungary, 63–64, 160, 161
Hunter, Duncan, 58
Hunting, Baker and, 217–18
Hurd, Douglas, 165, 255, 258, 314, 323, 347–48, 378, 618, 642; and Bosnia, 644, 645–46; and coup against Gorbachev, 518–19, 522; and German unification, 167, 199, 209–10, 211, 215; and Persian Gulf war, 320, 369–70
Hussein, King of Jordan, 3, 10, 260, 274,
290–91, 386, 450–51, 497, 500; and peace process, 451–52, 464–65, 468, 490–91, 504; Shamir and, 423, 425
Hussein, Saddam, 2–7, 129, 261–62, 267–69, 271–72, 276, 284, 285, 287, 290–92, 300–301, 314–15, 321, 331–32, 347, 364–65, 374, 375, 396–97, 407, 410, 423, 431, 450–51, 499–500; Assad and, 295, 297–98; Saudi Arabia and, 307–8, 373, 417; and Soviet Union, 286–87, 403; survival in power, 414, 435, 436–42; and U.S., 264, 272–74, 349–50, 353–55, 367, 381
Husseini, Faisal, 423, 465, 491–92, 496–97, 500, 508
Hyde, Henry, 51, 186

IAEA (International Atomic Energy Agency), 583, 595, 597–98
ICBMs (intercontinental ballistic missiles), 236
Idealism in American foreign policy, 654
Ideas, power of, xv
Iliescu (Romanian President), 207
IMF (International Monetary Fund), 259, 605, 655, 657
Incirlik, Turkey, air base, 284
Independence: Namibia, 225, 236; Soviet republics and, 524, 531–32, 534, 558
Indonesia, 44, 609
Indyk, Martin, 127
INF (Intermediate Nuclear Forces) Treaty, 82, 84
Initiatives, 196, 258, 524, 564, 658–59; in Soviet-U.S. relations, 45, 67–70, 86, 87, 93, 170, 236–37
"Inner circle," State Department, 32–35
Institutions, 45, 46, 609; economic, 605
Integrity, Baker and, 134
Intellectual property rights, 593
Intelligence community publications, 154
Interdependence, economic, 604
International conference on Middle East, 291–93, 371
International economic affairs, 604–13
International leadership, Japan and, 612
International system, change of, 672
Intifada uprising, 117
Iran, 43, 66, 78, 280, 589, 629–30, 631; and Iraq, 261–62, 385, 439
Iran-contra scandal, 27, 48
Iraq, 43, 261–62, 300–301, 385–90, 435–42, 596; and Kuwait, 1–16, 271–73, 276, 383–95, 406–12, 473; Soviet Union and, 396–408; U.S. and, 263–67, 269–71, 273–74, 349–63. See also Persian Gulf war
Irkutsk, Siberia, meeting in, 3–4
Iryani, Abdul Kareem, 375
Islamic fundamentalism, CIS and, 582

Israel, 43, 116, 268–69, 274, 415, 421, 444, 540–57; economic aid to, 127, 542; and peace process, 415–17, 421–25, 444–47, 449–50, 466–67, 494–96, 498, 499; and Persian Gulf war, 15, 306–8, 344, 383, 385–90, 408; Soviet Union and, 428, 495

Italy, 89, 298, 372, 604

Ivory, ban on importation, 218n

Ivory Coast, 315–16, 317

Izetbegovic, Alija, 480–81, 482, 640

Jackson, Caron, 35, 86, 131, 174, 487

Jackson, Don, 497n

Jackson, Jesse, 225

Jackson Hole, Wyoming, meeting at, 3, 137, 144–52, 155

Japan, 44, 280, 604, 609–12, 656

Jensen, Uffe Ellmann, 88

Jesuit priests, murder of, 603

Jewish community, U.S., 116, 122, 128

Jews, Soviet, program against, 244

Jiang Zemin, 592

Jitkoff, Andrew, 61–62

JNA (Yugoslav National Army), 635; in Bosnia, 642, 644

Jobs, Persian Gulf crisis and, 336–37

Johansen (Czech foreign minister), 160

Johnson, Ardis, 34

Johnson, Lyndon B., 331

Joint Chiefs of Staff, and airlift to former Soviets, 618n

Joint military exercise, 271–72

Joint scientific center, 615

Joint statement, U.S.-Russian, 621, 625; on Persian Gulf war, 7–16, 291–94, 392–95

Jordan, 280, 491; and Israel, 386, 425; and peace process, 451–52, 464–65

Journalists, 154

Juster, Ken, 619

Kaifu, Toshiki, 128, 611

Kaliningrad, 537

Kammen, Curt, 74

Kanter, Arnold, 597, 648, 650, 660n

Karadzic, Radovan, 641n

Kara Kum Desert, 630

Karimov, Islam, 632–33

Kasten, Robert, 270, 554

Kazakhstan, 525, 535, 538, 579, 586, 661; and nuclear weapons, 572, 585, 658, 659, 661–65

Keene, Lonnie, 619

Kelly, John, 117, 266, 292, 325, 327; and Saddam, 267, 268

Kemp, Jack, 547

Kempster, Norm, 154

Kennan, George, 41, 562, 563

Kennedy, John F., 64

Kennedy, Pat, 85–86, 173, 207

Kerensky, Alexander, 62n

Kernz, Egon, 171

Kerr, Dick, and Kuwait invasion, 4

Kerrey, Bob, 349

Kerry, John, 49, 193

KGB, and Soviet reforms, 534

Khaddam, Abdul Halim, 461

Khalifa, Isa bin Sulman al-, 306

Khomeini, Ayatollah, 66, 261

Khrushchev, Nikita, 64, 514

Kimmitt, Robert, 34, 35, 38, 190, 191, 266, 280, 309, 324, 327, 434, 589; and Persian Gulf war, 4, 6, 8, 268–70, 279, 302, 305, 329–30, 352, 375

King, Coretta Scott, 225

Kinkel, Klaus, 646, 650

Kipling, Rudyard, 115

Kirghizia (Kyrgyzstan), 531n

Kirkpatrick, Jeane, 30, 50

Kishinev, Moldova, 626–27

Kissinger, Henry, 22–24, 29, 40, 129, 165, 457, 469

Kohl, Helmut, 87, 90, 92–93, 149, 199, 206, 298–99, 371–72, 378, 657; and German unification, 160, 166, 172, 175, 198, 213–15, 230–34

Kollek, Teddy, 421

Kolt, George, 475

Komplektov, Viktor, 518, 521

Koppel, Ted, 523n

Korea. See North Korea; South Korea

Korean War, Baker and, 368–69

Kostmayer, Peter, 342–43

Kovalev, Anatoly, 235n

Kozak, Michael, 178, 180–82, 187–88, 192

Kozyrev, Andrei, 519, 522, 529, 530, 564–67, 617, 619–20, 629, 648, 665; and nuclear weapons, 660–63, 668–70

Kravchuk, Leonid, 561, 562, 570, 575–76, 581–83, 659, 661–64

Krenz, Egon, 163, 166

Kryuchkov, Vladimir, 471, 515

Kucan, Milan, 481, 482

Kurchatov, Igor V., 616

Kurdish rebellion in Iraq, 439; refugees, 431–35, 442

Kurtzer, Dan, 36, 117, 509, 512

Kuwait, 261, 306–7, 314, 332, 352, 372–73, 419–20; Iraq and, 1–16, 271–73, 276, 301; war damage, 411–12, 419–20

Kuwait City, after war, 419–20

Kyrgyzstan (Kirghizia), 531n, 578–79

Laboa, Sebastian, Monsignor, 192–93

Labor government, Israel, 541, 555

Lake, Joe, 8

Lake Baikal, Siberia, 3–4

Lance missiles, 84–85

Landsbergis, Vytautas, 240, 241, 245, 536

Latin America, 605, 606, 609

Latvia, 524, 536–37

Law, 427; Baker and, 18–19, 37–38, 40, 133–34; rule of, communists and, 72
Leadership, xv, 92, 103, 275–77, 612
League of Nations, 326
Leahy, Patrick J., 551–54
Lebanon, and peace process, 464
Lee Sang Ok, 610–11
Lehman, Ron, 213
Leningrad (St. Petersburg), 535
Letters of assurances, 498, 501–3, 508
Levine, Mel, 131
Levy, David, 130, 385, 421–22, 444, 513, 543–44, 547
"Liberty Wing," 366–69
Libya, 184, 589
Liebengood, Chris, 206
Lieberman, Joe, 344
Lifestyle, Soviet, 7
Ligachev, Yegor, 144, 208, 234
Likud party, defeat of, 555–56
Lilley, James, 100, 103, 107, 109
Lincoln, Abraham, 329
Lineberry, Liz, 35
Li Peng, 102, 591–92, 595–96n
Lithuania, 203, 231, 524, 536–38; Soviet Union and, 238–45, 249–50, 257, 378–81, 402
Loan guarantees for Israel, 541–43, 545, 547–57
Lobov, Oleg, 533
Loncar, Janja, 634
London: G-7 summit, 488–89; NATO Summit, 258–59, 472
Longfellow, Henry Wadsworth, 84
Lord, Bette Bao, 101
Lord, Winston, 101
Lott, Trent, 24, 92
Loyalty, of Bush, 21
Lugar, Richard, 243, 337
Lukin, Vladimir, 477n, 659–60
Lukyanov, Anatoliy, 471
Lyman, Princeton, 433

McCaffrey, Barry, 660n
McCain, John, 57, 184
McClure, James, 269
McCormack, Dick, 266, 611
McDonald's, Moscow, 247
McDougall, Barbara, 519, 650
MacEachin, Doug, 660n
Macedonia, 479, 639–42
McManus, Doyle, 154
McWethy, John, 384
Madigan, Peter, 57
Madrid conference, 488, 510–13, 541
Mahathir bin Mohamad, 610–11
Major, John, 377, 519, 645
Malaysia, 44, 316, 318–20, 325, 609–11
Mallaby (British Ambassador), 171
Malmierca, Isidoro, 321, 327

Malta Summit, 167, 168–71
Management policies of Baker, 31–32
Mandela, Nelson, 217, 221–22, 224–26, 228
Mandela, Winnie, 225
Marine Corps, Baker in, 368–69
Market economy, Gorbachev and, 529
Markovic, Ante, 479, 480, 482–83
Marshall, George, 367
Martin, Lynn, 405
Masri, Taher al-, 449, 500
Materials-testing laboratory, Russia, 616
Matlock, Jack, 145, 235n, 470–71, 474
Maxwell, Robert, 132
Mazer, Ron, 358, 539
Mazowiecki, Tadeusz, 232, 233n, 247
Mead, Jim, 368
Media, 618; and foreign policy, 587–88. See also CNN; Television
Meguid, Esmat Abdel, 447–48
Menger Hotel, San Antonio, 24–25
Meridor, Dan, 445
Mesic, Stipe, 480, 482
Metzenbaum, Howard, 269
Mexico, 42, 43, 606–9
Meyer, Steve, 69
Michel, Bob, 48, 49, 55, 92
Middle East, 77; policy goals, 43
Middle East Development Bank, 413
Middle East peace process, 115–32, 263–65, 294, 371, 443–69, 477, 487–513, 541, 547–53, 555–56, 636; Persian Gulf war and, 412, 414–15, 441; Syria and, 296, 298
Mikhailov, Viktor, 616
Military action, 15, 154–55, 271–73, 287, 334–35, 602; in Bosnia, 648–50, 651; in Panama, 177–78, 181–85, 189–94. See also Persian Gulf war
Military control, CIS and, 566, 568, 575–76
Miller, Aaron, 117, 130, 509
Milosevic, Slobodan, 481, 635, 636; U.S. and, 641, 642–44, 647
MIRVed ICBMs, ban of, 236–37, 659, 668–69
Missile Technology Control Regime (MTCR), China and, 589, 593–94
Mitchell, George, 58, 92, 143, 338, 549
Mitchell, John, 20
Mitsotakis (Prime Minister of Greece), 640, 641
Mitterand, François, 96, 173, 175–76, 314–15, 370–71, 378, 584; and German unification, 167, 233n, 234
Mobutu Sese Seko, 228
Modai, Yitzhak, 544
Modrow, Hans, 167, 174–75, 199, 201
Moe, Grace, 34
Moldova, 523, 531, 570, 585, 626–27
Momper, Walter, 165, 172
Monetary stabilization, Russia, 655–56

Mongolia, 6, 8–9, 11, 494
Montenegro, 478–79, 482
Moriatis, Peter, 88
Morocco, 497
Morton, Rogers, 19, 22
Mosbacher, Bob, 107
Moscow, 2, 71–83, 202, 247, 494, 526
Mossad (Israeli intelligence), 274
Mossberg, Walt, 154
Most-favored-nation status, for China, 106,
  113, 594
Moynihan, Pat, 92
MPLA (Popular Movement for the
  Liberation of Angola), 598–600
Mubarak, Hosni, 10, 15, 225, 260, 265, 290,
  308, 499; and Middle East peace process,
  120, 124, 125, 420–21, 444, 447, 452,
  453, 463–64, 489–90; and Saddam, 3,
  274, 290–91, 365, 366, 375, 442
Mulholland, Doug, 154
Mullins, Janet, 34, 35, 57, 190, 330–31, 333,
  337, 656; and Israel, 549, 552
Mulroney, Brian, 42, 86, 208, 377, 608
Multilateral working groups, peace
  conference, 459–60, 467, 502, 505–6
Muravsky, Valeriu, 531
Murkowski, Frank, 269, 341
Murray, Bob, 71
Mushabshwa, Katanya, 315
Muskie, Ed, and Foreign Service, 29
Mutalibov, Ayaz, 628–29
Mutual Balanced Force Reduction (MBFR),
  63

Nabiyev, Rakhman, 631
Nadam (Mongol sports event), 8
NAFTA (North American Free Trade
  Agreement), 607–9, 612
Nagorno-Karabakh war, 627, 628–29
Namibia, 218, 224–25, 236, 599
Napper, Larry, 518n
Nastase, Adrian, 316
National Advisory Council on International
  and Financial Policies (NAC), 267
National Endowment for Democracy, 60, 601
Nationalism in Soviet republics, 479–83,
  525, 532, 538, 560, 628–29, 633, 635
Nationalities problems, Soviet Union, 77–78,
  139, 144–48, 203, 239–45, 248
National Security Council, 21–22, 25–27,
  100, 109, 117, 179, 258, 561; and German
  unification, 198, 215; and Persian Gulf
  war, 9, 269, 270–72, 277
National Security Directive 26 (NSD-26),
  263–64, 266
NATO, 43–45, 84–91, 164, 284, 370, 584,
  605, 636–37; changes in, 253, 255,
  257–59; CIS and, 572, 576; and coup
  against Gorbachev, 517, 519, 522; and
  German unification, 159, 173, 230–38,

246, 251–55, 259; Soviets and, 92,
  148–49, 235, 253; Summit meetings,
  92–96, 258–59, 472
Natural resources, Tajikistan, 631
Nazarbayev, Nursultan, 520, 538–39,
  579–81, 584–86, 629, 661–62, 664
Nazarbayev, Sara, 538
Negotiations, Baker and, 134–35
Nemeth, Miklos, Hungarian Prime Minister,
  160
Netanyahu, Benjamin, 129
Netherlands, The, 89–90, 234, 510–11
Newman, Marilyn, 35
Newsom, Eric, 551
"New thinking," Soviet, 71, 72, 76, 78
New York Times, 40, 58, 83, 259, 552, 663
New York Times Magazine, 19
New Zealand, 609
Nicaragua, 42, 48–58; elections, 76–77, 602;
  Soviets and, 59, 81, 151
Nicholas II, Czar of Russia, 632
Nikonov, Viktor, 144
Niles, Tom, 566–67, 630, 639–41
Nine assurances, 250–51, 252, 257
Nixon, Richard, 29, 33, 34, 48–49, 116,
  169–70
Niyazov, Saparmurad, 630
Noriega, Manuel Antonio, 177–83, 185–87
  191–94, 437
North Atlantic Cooperation Council
  (NACC), 571, 584
North Korea, 589, 594–98, 619
Norway, and German unification, 234
Novak, Robert, 83
Novo-Ogarevo, dacha at, 311–12
Nuclear arms control, 204, 624–25; CIS and,
  568, 572, 581–82, 621
Nuclear Nonproliferation Treaty (NPT), 581,
  583, 661–63, 664; China and, 589, 593;
  North Korea and, 594–95, 597
Nuclear research, Soviet, 615–16
Nuclear testing agreement, 151
Nuclear weapons, 258; China and, 589, 593;
  former Soviet states and, 571, 575–76,
  579, 582, 583, 585, 621–22, 630, 654;
  North Korea and, 594–98; Soviet, 82–83,
  527, 533, 617; Soviet collapse and, 526,
  658
Nunn, Sam, 92, 335, 352, 364

Oberdorfer, Don, 96, 154
Obey, David, 57, 92, 554
Occupied territories, settlements in, 117,
  120, 122–23, 126–28, 130, 444–46,
  489–90; U.S. and, 541–44, 547, 548,
  553–57
Oil prices, 336–37, 364
Olechkowski, Tadeusz, 64
Oman, aid to former Soviets, 619
O'Neill, Judy, 34

O'Neill, Tip, 334
One-on-one meetings, 67, 80–81, 298; with Shevardnadze, 73, 74, 146
On-Site Inspection Agency (OSIA), 618n
Operation Blue Spoon, 190–93
Operation Just Cause, 193–94
Operation Provide Comfort, 434
Operation Provide Hope, 618, 626, 629
Opposition parties, Soviet Union, 472–73
Ordonez, Felipe, 370
Ordonez, Paco, 511
Organization of American States (OAS), 183, 194, 601, 602
Organized labor, and NAFTA, 607
Ortega, Daniel, 52–53, 60
OSIA (On-Site Inspection Agency), 618n
Osobnyak Guest House, Moscow, 73
Ottowa Conference, 208–16
Ozal, Turgut, 283–85, 309, 377, 428, 431–32

Packwood, Bob, 92
Pakistan, China and, 589, 593–94
Palach, Jan, 201
Palazchenko, Pavel, 79, 211, 212, 574n
Palestinian Liberation Front, 129
Palestinians, 280, 423, 445, 451, 490–91; and Israel, 117, 415–16, 419, 425; and peace process, 428, 445, 446, 452, 465–66, 488, 491–93, 495–501, 504, 507–9. See also PLO
Pamyat, 244
Panama, 177–78; U.S. and, 179–94, 437
Pankin, Boris, 503, 509, 529, 530, 559
Papandreou, Andreas, 88
Parallel reciprocity, 416, 418–20, 422, 427–28
Paris: meetings, 135–41, 473; agreement on Cambodia, 588
Patriot missiles, 388, 389–90, 500
Pavlov, Valentin, 471, 478, 515, 520
Paye, Jean-Claude, 619
PDF (Panama Defense Forces), 179, 184, 185, 187, 191
Peace conference, Middle East, 294, 448, 452–55, 466–67, 487–513; invitations to, 503, 509; Palestinian delegation, 495–98, 504, 507–9
Peace Corps, Baltic states and, 536
Peace initiative, Soviet, 396–408
Peacekeepers, UN, in Bosnia, 638, 642, 644
Pearson, Bob, 470, 565, 641
Peckham, Gardner, 656n
Pelletreau, Robert, 118, 130
Pelosi, Nancy, 108
Pentagon, 33; and Iraq, 409, 439; and Panama, 177, 178, 189
People's Republic of China. See China
Peres, Shimon, 128, 449
Perestroika, 63–64, 67, 69, 80, 81, 170, 203, 401, 476; Shevardnadze and, 65, 77, 78,

138–39, 147, 241, 568; U.S. and, 65, 70–71, 73, 75, 155–56
Peresypkin, Aleksandr, 242
Pérez de Cuéllar, Javier, 324–25, 347, 638
Perkins, Ed, 221
Permanent Five ministers, 324, 347–48
Persian Gulf, U.S. policy, 263–64
Persian Gulf war, 1–16, 261, 278, 280, 331, 336–37, 412, 435–36, 473, 596, 636; China and, 114, 588; financial support for, 288–91, 298–99, 308; international coalition for, 301–28; Israel and, 383, 541, 544; last-chance meeting, 349–63
Peru, elections, 602
Petrocelli, Gustavo, 43
Philippines, 609, 619
Pickering, Tom, 325
PLO (Palestine Liberation Organization), 116–18, 120, 125, 129–30, 317, 423, 425, 451, 499; and peace process, 444, 446, 464, 491, 498, 500, 504
Pohl, Karl Otto, 159
Poland, 64, 136, 148, 161; and German unification, 210, 212, 232–33, 247
Policy, 33; politics and, xiv-xv
Policy Planning Staff, 198
Politburo, purge by Gorbachev, 144
Political reform: China and, 100–102; Eastern Europe, 63–64, 76; in former Soviet states, 582, 617; Soviet, 46, 77–78, 203, 530, 531, 533, 534–35
Politics, xiv-xv, 134, 153–55, 168, 263; Baker and, xiii, 19, 37–39; and diplomacy, 31, 32; Secretary of State and, 38–39, 143–44
Poos, Jacques, 370
Popov, Gavril, 470, 472, 530, 565
Portugal, 89
Post–Cold War world, policy goals, 46
Post-Vietnam syndrome, 331, 333, 438
Potsdam, 173–75, 195–96
Powell, Charles, 95
Powell, Colin, 26, 185, 258, 359, 383, 440, 533, 584, 618n, 649–50; and arms control, 526n, 669; and Panama, 189–91; and Persian Gulf war, 282–83, 301–3, 311, 355, 410, 435
Powers, Francis Gary, 173
Prague Spring, Czechoslovakia, 63
Presidential elections, 20–21, 24
Presidential visit, China and, 589, 590
Press, 33–34, 89, 96, 154; Gorbachev and, 80, 81, 83; leaks, 498, 561
Primakov, Yevgeny, 206, 350, 396–400, 402–6, 478
Princeton, speech at, 562–64, 565
Prisoners of war, Vietnam-era, 653
Problem management, 34
Protocol, 34; Baker and, 36
Prunskiene, Kazimiera, 248, 250

Public opinion, and Gulf war, 329–44
Public relations, Gorbachev and, 82–83, 89
Pugo, Boris, 515, 530
Pull-aside meetings, 210, 211, 227

Qaddur, Mahmud, 507
Qian Qichen, 97, 99, 105, 110–12, 308–9, 316, 321–24, 326, 347–48, 590–95
Quadripartite Agreement, 171

Rabin, Yitzhak, 117, 121, 126–27, 424–26, 540, 541, 555, 556–57
Rafsanjani, Hashemi, 300n, 439
Ramit, Tajikistan, 631
Reagan, Ronald, 1, 27, 30, 46, 48, 79, 86, 87, 92, 99, 122–23, 134, 159, 179–80, 200, 220n, 334, 606, 652
Reagan administration, 48, 50, 70, 80, 177, 219, 261–62, 598; foreign policy, 26–27, 31; and Nicaragua, 52, 54
Recognition, diplomatic, 524, 560–62, 566–67, 572, 574, 583, 586, 627n; of former Yugoslav states, 638–45; of Israel, 540–41
Red Cross, 589, 591, 645
Reed, Joseph, 34
Refugees: East German, 160–61; Kurdish, 431–35, 442
Regional trade agreements, 605
Religion, 667; Shevardnadze and, 248
Revolution, 40, 64, 138
Rice, Condi, 235, 292, 561
Ridgway, Roz, 40
Rogers, John F. W., 34
Rogers, William, 174
Roh Tae Woo, Gorbachev and, 596
Roman (Romanian Prime Minister), 207
Romania, 206, 207–8, 316
Roosevelt, Franklin D., 276
Roosevelt, Theodore, and Panama, 179
Rose, Charlie, 263
Ross, Dennis, 32, 33, 40, 67, 86, 95, 117, 145, 156, 202, 212, 223, 254, 292, 293, 295, 312–13, 365, 398, 412, 421, 513, 538, 539, 565, 566, 619, 660, 664–65; and German unification, 198–99, 256; and Israel, 549, 553; and Lithuania, 241, 243; and Middle East peace process, 126, 127, 131, 132, 458, 459, 463, 494, 507, 509, 510; and Persian Gulf war, 6–7, 9–10, 268–69, 352–54; and Soviets, 11–13, 16, 69, 142–43, 517, 559, 562; and Yugoslav conflict, 638, 648, 650
Rossel (Russian Governor), 632
Rostenkowski, Dan, 92
Roy, Stapleton, 158, 164
Rubenstein, Ely, 132, 499, 552
Rubino, Frank, 187
Ruble, stabilization of, 655–56
Rule of law, communists and, 72

Rumsfeld, Donald, 22
Rushdie, Salman, 66
Rusk, Dean, 587
Russia, 530, 535, 558–59, 567, 570–72, 578, 583, 614–17, 620–25, 653–54, 660–61; and nuclear weapons, 585, 668
Russians, in Baltic states, 537–38
Rutskoi, Alexander, 522
Ruutel, Arnold, 536
Ryerson, William, 486n
Ryzhkov, Nikolai, 136

Sadat, Anwar, 445
Saint Petersburg (Leningrad), 535
Saleh, Ali Abdullah, 10, 318
Salinas de Gortari, Carlos, 43, 607–8
Salisbury, Lord, 37
Samaras (Greek Foreign Minister), 641
Samarkand, Uzbekistan, 633
Samsonov, Viktor, 535
Sanctions: China, 105–8; Haiti, 601, 602; Iraq, 10, 277–79, 283, 291, 297, 299, 300–301, 308–10, 319–20, 333, 337–38, 341–42, 441; Panama, 179; Serbia, 638, 648–49; South Africa, 219, 227, 228
Sandinistas, 47–50, 52–53, 55, 59, 184, 194
Santiago declaration, 194, 602
Sarajevo, 645, 648, 650
Sarbanes, Paul, 341
Saud, Prince (Saudi Foreign Minister), 289, 307, 372–73, 375, 417, 452, 490
Saudargas, Algirdas, 536
Saudi Arabia, 118, 271–72, 294–95, 327, 387, 417–20, 422, 450–53, 459–60, 619, 650; and Persian Gulf war, 7–8, 270, 278, 282, 288–89, 300, 307, 317, 352, 354, 372
Savimbi, Jonas, 228, 316, 598, 599, 600
Savissar, Edgar, 536
Schabowski, Günter, 158, 163, 165
Scheduling, 34, 85–86
Schieffer, Bob, 562
Schifter, Dick, 74, 594
Schultz, George, and INF Treaty, 84n
Schwarzkopf, Norman, 261, 303, 374, 387, 388, 410, 417, 438–40
Scowcroft, Brent, 22, 24–26, 70, 92–94, 142, 157, 165, 168, 254, 258, 292, 515, 517, 525–26, 606, 608, 635, 656, 669; and Bosnia, 648–50; China trips, 109–10, 113; and German unification, 162, 213–14; and joint statement with Soviets, 11, 393–94; and Middle East peace process, 122, 415, 468; and Panama, 182, 188, 189; and Persian Gulf war, 7, 268, 281–83, 303, 304, 330, 338, 346, 350–51, 385, 409
Scud missiles, 311, 383, 385–90, 544–45
Secession law, Soviet, 239
Secretary of State, 70, 143–44, 587; Baker as, 17–19, 21, 26–28, 31–36, 38–46, 153–54

Security guarantee, Middle East, 414, 455–57, 461–62
Security issues, U.S.-Russian, 74, 621
Seitz, Ray, 199, 210, 235
Selin, Ivan, 34
Senate Foreign Relations Committee, 270, 298–99, 340–42, 413
Serbia, 478–82, 636, 641, 648
Sestanovich, Steve, 68–69
Shalikashvili, John, 434, 584, 660n, 667
Shamir, Yitzhak, 116, 119, 122, 123, 125, 130, 132, 371, 382, 385–90, 415–16, 424, 441, 541; Mubarak and, 421, 447, 452; and peace process, 117, 120–21, 124–29, 417, 422, 444–47, 449–50, 457, 466–67, 469, 487, 488, 493–96, 498, 499, 508, 546–47, 549–56; and U.S. financial aid, 543, 544
Shapiro, Norman, 133
Shaposhnikov, Yevgeny, 532–34, 566, 569, 571, 572, 575–76, 622, 624
Shara, Farouk al-, 389, 420, 460, 463, 468–69, 501, 503–4, 506–7
Sharon, Ariel, 119, 123, 444, 446, 547
Shatalin, Stanislav, 477
Shaw, Bernard, 384
Shcharansky, Anatoly, 173
Shcherbitsky, Vladimir, 144
Shevardnadze, Eduard, 40, 59, 67–68, 79–80, 135–37, 141–42, 146, 151–52, 169n, 197, 230, 236–37, 247–48, 257, 279, 347–48, 364, 401, 472–75, 516, 519, 525, 530–32, 559–61, 567–68, 595, 599–600; and German unification, 166, 204–5, 208–12, 231–32, 234–35, 237–38, 247, 251–57, 259; and Lithuania, 238–44, 378; meetings with, 3–4, 64–67, 73–78, 150–52, 225, 244–47; and Persian Gulf war, 1–2, 5–6, 9–16, 269, 274, 277, 278, 281–83, 285–87, 291–92, 310–13, 316–17, 320–21, 350; as President of Georgia, 665–68; and Primakov, 397, 398; and Soviet dissolution, 568–69, 573, 576–77; and Soviet reforms, 136–41, 144–46, 202–3; and Yeltsin, 476, 572
Shevardnadze, Nanuli, 77, 78, 474, 666
Shia rebels, Iraq, 438–39
Shmelyev, Nikolai, 150–51
Shoval, Zalman, 408, 545–47, 554
Shultz, George, 21, 28, 30, 50, 64, 86, 117–18, 157, 225, 296
Shushkevich, Stanislav, 562, 570, 579, 581–82, 661
Shuttle diplomacy, 443–69, 488–513
Sicherman, Harvey, 414
Sigler, John F., 169
SII (Structural Impediments Initiative), 611
Silajdzic, Haris, 634, 642, 643
Silayev, Ivan, 522, 530, 532
Silva, Cavaco, 89

Simon, Paul, 43, 341
Simons, Tom, 40
Simpson, Alan, 92, 269
Singapore, 44, 605, 609, 610
Sisulu, Albertina, 220–21, 222
Sisulu, Walter, 224
Skubiszewski, Krzysztof, 210, 247
Slovenia, 478–79, 481, 482, 483n, 635, 639; U.S. and, 641, 642
Smith, Jeff, 560
Smith, Matthew, 150
Snegur, Mircea, 626–27
SNF (short-range nuclear forces), 82–88, 90, 94–96
Sobchak, Anatoliy, 472, 535
Social disorder, Soviet, 529–30
Sofaer, Abraham, 266
Solarz, Stephen, 108, 344
Solomon, Dick, 9
Somalia, evacuation from, 378
South Africa, 43, 218–29, 598–99
Southcom, 183–88
South Korea, 44, 99, 596, 597, 604–5, 609, 610
Soviet Economic Commission, 526
Soviet troops, Baltic states and, 536–37
Soviet Union, 1, 40, 45–46, 59, 71, 91, 135–37, 236–37, 244, 255, 294–95, 533–34, 541–44, 595, 599–600, 603, 614–16, 652, 653; and Central America, 48–49, 59; changes in, 202–3, 279; collapse of, 273–74, 525, 558–86, 617, 625–26, 637; coup against Gorbachev, 497, 515–23, 532–33, 535; and German unification, 161, 165–67, 198, 204, 209, 230–32, 234–38, 245–47, 254–57; and Lithuania, 239–45, 249–50, 378–81; and Middle East peace process, 417, 428, 444, 493, 494, 509, 510; and NATO, 43–44, 251, 253; and Persian Gulf war, 1–2, 6–16, 277, 278, 280–83, 285–87, 291–92, 309–13, 317, 320–21, 350, 365, 383, 384, 391–400, 402–7, 436; and reform, 63–64, 138–41, 523–24; relations with, 41–42, 61, 80–81, 155–56, 245, 248–49, 294, 400–406, 472–78, 528–29, 652–53
Spain, 89, 187–88, 370, 509–13
Speckhard, Dan, 656n
Stalin, Joseph, Potsdam Conference, 196
Stalingrad, World War II, 161
Starodubtsev, Vasili, 515n
START Protocol, 661–64, 668
START Treaty, 470, 477, 487, 494, 571, 576, 659–64; negotiations, 77, 82, 151, 236–37, 252n
START II agreement, 654, 659, 668, 670–71
State Department, 27–36, 41–46, 100, 272–73, 604, 617n
State Emergency Committee, 516, 519, 520
Status of Forces Agreement (SOFA), 533

Stepanov, Tyamuraz, 666
Stimson, Henry, 195
Stoltenberg, Gerhard, 159, 162
Strategic nuclear proposal, 658–59
Strategic review, 68–70, 73–74
Strategic Rocket Forces (SRF), 526
Strauss, Bob, 19, 49, 131, 515, 516, 520, 538, 539, 561, 566, 658
Strauss, Helen, 49
Strauss, Ted, 19
Strikes, Soviet Union, 136, 137, 138
Sullivan, Mike, 150
Summit meetings, 81, 252–54, 291–94, 472, 473, 488–89, 494, 653
Sununu, John, 128, 292–93, 338, 394
Superpower, U.S. as, 414–15
Sverdlovsk (Yekaterinburg), Russia, 631–32
Sweden, and German unification, 234
Swing, Bill, 227
Syria, 117, 280, 417, 420, 422, 425–28, 447–49, 468–69, 487–88, 589; and Persian Gulf war, 15, 295–98, 373–74, 376–77, 389

Tacit Rainbow, 252n
Taiwan, 44, 588, 591, 604–5, 610
Tajikistan, 631
Takeshita, Noboru, 611–12
Takriti, Barzan al-, 357
Talbott, Strobe, 565, 569
Tarasenko, Sergei, 5, 6, 7, 10, 11–13, 67, 145, 241, 256, 292, 293, 398, 474, 525, 559, 569, 577, 666
Tbilisi, Georgia, 71, 667
Technical assistance, 526, 581
Television, 103, 104, 353, 384; and diplomacy, 361, 364; Soviet, and coup against Gorbachev, 516. See also CNN
Teltschik, Horst, 213
Ter-Petrosyan, Levon, 628, 629
Terrorism: Syria and, 426; Palestinian, in Israel, 129–30, 421
Tesfaye, Dinka, 315
Textiles, Chinese, importation of, 23
Thailand, 44, 609, 619
Thatcher, Margaret, 7, 86–87, 242, 304, 307; and German unification, 167, 172, 199, 234; and NATO, 94–96, 258; and Persian Gulf war, 278–79, 313–14
Third World debt, 606
Thomas, Lowell, 98, 99
Threats against Baker, 479
Thucydides, The Peloponnesian War, 345, 365
Thurman, Maxwell, 184, 185, 187
Tiananmen Square massacre, 44, 97–98, 102–7, 110–11, 138, 590–92
Tibet, visit to, 98–99
Timbie, Jim, 94, 660n
Time magazine, 29–30, 475, 569
"Tin cup trip," 288–91

Tirana, Albania, 484–86
Tizyakov, Alexander, 515n
Tomasek, Cardinal, 201
Tower, John, 24–25
Trade agreements, 254, 593, 605, 606–9. See also Free-trade agreements
Trade embargos, 283, 288, 301, 601. See also Sanctions
Trade relations: with China, 101; with Japan, 611–12
TransAfrica, 224–25
Treasury Department, and Russian stabilization fund, 656
Treasury Secretary, 587, 604
Triple-zero formula, Angola, 600
Troop reduction, Gorbachev and, 212–13
Truman, Harry S., 196, 605
Truth, trial law and, 133–34
Tseretelli, Zurab, 397, 567–68
Tudjman, Franjo, 481–82, 635, 644
Tunisia, 497
Turkey, 88, 278, 280, 283–85, 288, 309, 372, 375, 377, 428, 431, 629
Turkmenistan, 629–31
Turnberry, Scotland, NATO meeting, 255
Tutu, Desmond, 220n
Tutwiler, Margaret, 9–12, 32–34, 126, 137, 190, 202, 296, 312–13, 317, 365, 384, 393, 421, 465, 509–12, 517, 529, 533, 562, 563, 618, 619, 630, 641; and Bosnia, 643–44, 647, 648; and Kurdish refugees, 431, 434; and Persian Gulf war, 5, 268, 352
Two-plus-Four, 195–216, 230, 235–37, 244–47, 250

Ukraine, 523, 525, 532, 535, 558, 560, 567, 570–72, 582–83, 585, 617, 624, 658–65
Ulan Bator, American embassy, 8
Under secretaries, State Department, 35
Un-Group, 660, 670
Union Treaty, Soviet, 476, 515, 561, 563, 570, 580; failure of, 558, 573
UNITA (National Union for the Total Independence of Angola), 598–600
United Arab Emirates, 271–72, 290
United Democratic Front, South Africa, 220
United Nations, 45, 317, 434, 600, 601, 603, 612, 638, 650; and Israel, 118, 448, 495, 541; and Middle East peace process, 117, 419, 448, 455, 458, 460; and Persian Gulf war, 10, 277, 278–81, 285–87, 299, 304–28, 332
United Nations Security Council, 570, 588; and Kuwait invasion, 9, 278–81, 283, 286, 304–28, 332; and Yugoslav conflict, 637–38, 642, 644, 648
United States, 63–64, 85, 100, 103, 170, 275–77, 324–25, 370, 414, 420, 438, 604, 636–37; and Angola, 598–601; and APEC,

609–13; and Baltic states, 238–39, 536–37; and Bosnia, 644–51; and China, 588–94; and Colombia, 318–19; and El Salvador, 602–4; and former Soviet states, 482–83, 538, 560–62, 565–86, 609–33, 636, 664, 666–68; and German unification, 167–68, 172–73, 175–76; and Haiti, 601–2; and Iraq, 7–16, 261–62, 269–71, 272–74, 349–63, 366–69, 383–95, 408–10, 439–41; and Israel, 127, 540–57; and Japan, 611–12; and Lithuania, 243–44, 378; and Mexico, 607–9; and Middle East peace process, 117–19, 124, 415–29; Middle East policy, 262–64; military presence in Turkey, 284; and North Korea, 594–98; and Panama, 179–94; and Russia, 614–17, 620–25, 652–54; and South Africa, 218–29; and Soviet Union, 40–42, 59, 155–56, 245, 248–49, 400–406, 472–78, 525–26, 528–29, 637
Uno, Sousuke, 611
U.S. Army, First Cavalry Division, 306
U.S.S. Independence, 8
Uzbekistan, 632–33

Vagnorius, Gedimanas, 536
Vance, Cyrus, 587, 638–39, 641–42
Vandenberg, Arthur, 47, 60
Van Den Broek, Hans, 89–90, 95, 216, 511, 517, 618, 637, 639
Varkonyi, Peter, 61, 63–64
Vatican, and Noriega, 192
Venezuela, 183
Vietnam syndrome, 331, 333
Voice of America (VOA), 521, 589–90
Vyacheslav (Soviet GDR Ambassador), 171

Walters, Vernon, 165, 171, 173
Wan Li, 102
War, 154–55, 345–46. *See also* Persian Gulf war
War powers, questions of, 334–35, 339
Warsaw Pact, 84, 148–49, 235, 252–53, 255
Washington, D.C., Summit meeting, 252–54
Washington Post, 545, 664
Weapons-inspection program, Iraq, 441
Weapons proliferation, China and, 588–89
Weinberger, Cap, 50
Welch, David, 36
Western Europe, 85–96, 171, 604
Western European Union (WEU), 636–37, 644
West Germany. *See* German unification; Germany
White House Chiefs of Staff, 31–32
Williams, Pete, 520

Williamson, Molly, 36
Woerner, Frederick, 184
Woerner, Manfred, 90, 370, 522, 619
Wolfowitz, Paul, 385, 660
Woolsey, Jim, 213
World Affairs Council, speech to, 335
World Bank, 284–85, 605, 655
World War I and II, 275
Wright, Betty, 49
Wright, Jim, 47, 49–50, 52, 57, 92
Wyoming, 217, 514; summit meeting, 137

Yakovlev, Alexander, 515, 532, 573, 574; and coup against Gorbachev, 519, 522
Yanayev, Gennady, 515, 518, 519
Yang Shangkun, 592
Yao Yilin, 162
Yates, Nell, 22–23
Yavlinsky, Grigori, 478, 527, 530
Yazov, Dmitri, 471, 515, 520
Yekaterinburg (Sverdlovsk), Russia, 631–32
Yeltsin, Boris, 71, 142, 379, 401, 472, 475–78, 524, 526–27, 538, 561–63, 565, 569–70, 577–81, 584, 614, 620–25, 650, 652, 653; and arms control, 659, 669–71; and coup against Gorbachev, 471, 516, 519–23; and economic reform, 558–59, 654–55; Gorbachev and, 528–29, 574, 575, 585
Yemen, 280, 304, 305; and Persian Gulf war, 278, 317–18, 325, 326–27, 375
Yerevan, Armenia, 627–28
Yeutter, Clayton, 266–67
Yoden, Mary Ann, 34
Yom Kippur War, 402
Yugoslavia, 478–83, 634–51
Yugoslav National Army. *See* JNA

Zagorsk, Russia, 248
Zaire, 228, 315
Zarechnak, Dmitri, 79
Zayed, Sheikh, and war with Iraq, 374
Zelikow, Phil, 213
Zero option, INF Treaty provision, 84n
Zhao Ziyang, 102, 107
Zhivkov, Todor, 164
Zimmerman, Warren, 479, 640, 641n, 642–43, 645, 646
Zionism as racism, U.N. resolution, 495, 541
Zlenko, Anatoly, 660, 662–65
Zoellick, Bob, 6–7, 13, 32, 33, 42, 44, 51, 94–95, 143, 223, 478, 530, 561, 562, 608, 609, 619, 656; and Germany, 159, 172, 198–99, 210, 211, 215, 235, 256; and Gorbachev, 69, 89, 517–18
Zohar, Gadi, 465